RESEARCH GUIDE TO BIOGRAPHY AND CRITICISM

Volume II
LANG-Z
Index

Edited By
Walton Beacham

Research Publishing

Library of Congress
    Cataloging in Publication Data

Research guide to biography and criticism: literature/ edited by Walton
    Beacham— Washington, D.C.: Research Publishing, 1985.
        2 v.; 24 cm.

    Bibliography.
    Includes index in v. 2.

    Description and evaluation of the most important biographical, autobio-
graphical, and critical sources for 335 British, American, and Canadian writers.

    1. English literature—History and criticism—Bibliography. 2. English
literature—Bio-bibliography. 3. Authors, English—Biography—Bibliography.
4. American literature—History and criticism—Bibliography. 5. American
literature—Bio-bibliography. 6. Authors, American—Biography—
Bibliography.
    I. Beacham, Walton, 1943-

Z2011.R47   1985   016.82'09   85-2188
(PR85)

Library of Congress Catalog Card Number: 85-2188

Complete Set   ISBN: 0-933833-00-8
Volume 1   ISBN: 0-933833-01-6
Volume 2   ISBN: 0-933833-02-4

Printed in the United States of America
First Printing, July 1985
Second Printing, November 1985
Third Printing, January 1986

PREFACE

With so many biographical and critical works available in most libraries, it is often difficult for students to know which sources relate to their specific needs, or for general readers to know which biographies interest them the most.

The *Research Guide to Biography and Criticism* has been designed to assist students in narrowing and researching topics for term papers and essay exams, and to provide librarians with a tool which will help them lead students to valuable, accessible resources. The guide is especially useful for libraries which might have limited holdings on a particular author. With clear content description and exact bibliographical information for every book reviewed, it is much easier to locate the needed resources in other libraries.

With these expressed goals, the Research Guide has limited its scope to those authors who are most often studied. The contents in no way reflect any editorial opinion as to a writer's historical importance, or to the quality of his work. The contents were compiled with the assistance and advice of some three hundred university professors and librarians.

The second criterion for including an author is the amount and availability of biographies, autobiographies, and critical materials about him. Most contemporary writers have not been included because there is yet no full biographical or critical treatments of their lives. Most dramatists and world authors are not included because Research Publishing has scheduled their inclusion in a separate, parallel set in 1985. These two volumes contain British and American poets, novelists, and prose writers.

The third criterion is that the sources discussed are generally available in United States libraries. Books which are out-of-print or difficult to locate are clearly distinguished from the resources which a librarian could reasonably expect to find.

Finally, an auxilliary Contents has been prepared which groups authors generally by their literary periods. This is intended only as an aid for researching specific periods, not to organize writers into schools. The index contains the writers included, as well as all the principal books and articles which have been *explained.* There are many more resources contained in the articles. Book and article titles which are not self-explanatory contain in parentheses the author whom the book discusses. Where there are two or more biographies with the same title, the biographers' names are placed in parentheses.

Research Publishing is continually interested in producing books which are devoted to improving the research capabilities of students. We welcome any suggestions for revising this title or ideas for other types of books. Write to: Research Publishing, 2113 "S" Street, NW, Washington, D.C. 20008.

Walton Beacham

CONTRIBUTORS

David L. Ackiss

Timothy Dow Adams

Consuelo M. Aherne, S.S.J.

Barbara Taylor Allen

David G. Allen

Andrew J. Angyal

Stanley Archer

Robert A. Armour

Edwin T. Arnold

Marilyn Arnold

Stephen C. B. Atkinson

Dennis Baeyen

Margaret Ann Baker

Jane L. Ball

Melissa E. Barth

Richard H. Beckham

Sue Bridwell Beckham

Thomas Becknell

James P. Bednarz

Kirk H. Beetz

Anthony Bernardo

Winifred Farrant Bevilacqua

Robert G. Blake

Leslie Rebecca Bloom

Harold Branam

Jeanie R. Brink

Carl W. Brucker

Larry Brunner

Mitzi M. Brunsdale

Hallman B. Bryant

Elizabeth Buckmaster

Paul Budra

Marilyn S. Butler

Marilyn D. Button

Richard J. Calhoun

Susan L. Carlson

Thomas Carmichael

John Carpenter

Michael Case

S. Catharine Christi, S.S.J.

John R. Clark

Pamela J. Clements

Samuel Coale

William Condon

John J. Conlon

Fred D. Crawford

Gloria L. Cronin

Richard H. Dammers

Frank Day

Dennis R. Dean

Phyllis T. Dircks

Richard J. Dircks

Robert DiYanni

Henry J. Donaghy

David C. Dougherty

William R. Drennan

Gweneth A. Dunleavy

John J. Dunn

Margaret M. Dunn

Phyllis Fahrie Edelson

Bruce L. Edwards, Jr.

Richard A. Eichwald

Robert P. Ellis

Ann W. Engar

Bernard F. Engel

Robert C. Evans

Patricia A. Farrant

Richard Fine

Benjamin Franklin Fisher, IV

James Flynn

Anne-Marie Foley

John Miles Foley

Howard L. Ford

Robert J. Forman

Thomas C. Foster

Warren French

Robert A. Gates

Edward V. Geist

Scott Giantvalley

Richard B. Gidez

James R. Giles

C. Herbert Gilliland

Joe Glaser

Alan Golding

Liela H. Goldman

Dennis M. Goldsberry

Sidney Gottlieb

Kenneth B. Grant

Glenn A. Grever

Edward Guereschi

Lyman B. Hagen

Jay L. Halio

David Mike Hamilton

Gertrude K. Hamilton

Katherine Hanley, C.S.J.

Maryhelen C. Harmon

John P. Harrington

Henry Hart

Joseph M. Hassett

William J. Heim

Terry Heller

Michael Hennessy

John T. Hiers

Maria Hinkle

Barbara Horwitz

Kenneth A. Howe

Dolan Hubbard

Mary Anne Hutchinson

James M. Hutchisson

John L. Idol, Jr.

S. E. Jackson

Philip K. Jason

Ed Jewinski

Irma M. Kashuba, S.S.J.

Steven G. Kellman

Rebecca Kelly

James M. Kempf

Barbara A. King

Lawrence F. Laban

Mary Lago

Thomas M. Leitch

Joan M. Lescinski, C.S.J.

Michael M. Levy

Leon Lewis

Henry J. Lindborg

James C. MacDonald

R. D. Madison

James Maloney

Stella Maloney

Joseph Marotta

Kathleen Massey

Charles E. May

Laurence W. Mazzeno

George E. McCelvey

Kathleen McCormick-Leighty

Linda E. McDaniel

Carmela Pinto McIntire

Thomas F. Merrill

Richard E. Meyer

Jim Wayne Miller

Ray Miller, Jr.

Joseph R. Millichap

Sally Mitchell

Gene M. Moore

Robert A. Morace

Ann R. Morris

Robert E. Morsberger

Claire Clements Morton

Gerald William Morton

Michael Mott

Kevin Mulcahy

John Mulryan

Lisa A. Murray

Marilyn K. Nellis

Robert D. Nixon

George O'Brien

James M. O'Neil

Robert Otten

Cóilín Owens

Richard J. Panofsky

Sandra Manoogian Pearce

Nancy W. Prothro

Steven Reece

James A. W. Rembert

Jack Wright Rhodes

Thomas Jackson Rice

Marinelle Ringer

Samuel J. Rogal

Mary Rohrberger

Lucy E. W. Rollin

Robert L. Ross

David Sadkin

Dale Salwak

Joachim Scholz

Margaret K. Schramm

Lisa M. Schwerdt

Wanda LaFaye Seay

Barbara Kitt Seidman

Steven Serafin

Lynne P. Shackelford

Eric Paul Shaffer

Allen Shepherd

William David Sherman

John C. Shields

Jack Shreve

R. Baird Shuman

Charles L. P. Silet

Dale W. Simpson

Thomas J. Slater

Marjorie Smelstor

Charlotte Spivack

Marlene Springer

L. Robert Stevens

William B. Stone

H. R. Stoneback

Michael L. Storey

Edmund M. Taft, IV

Daniel Taylor

Joseph R. Taylor

Welford Dunaway Taylor

Michael S. Tkach

Thomas J. Travisano

E. F. J. Tucker

A. Gordon Van Ness

Nancy Walker

Robbie Jean Walker

Ronald G. Walker

Gary F. Waller

Tomasz Warchol

John Chapman Ward

Mark A. Weinstein

Judith A. Weise

Charmaine Wellington

Craig Werner

Faye Pauli Whitaker

Edward P. Willey

Donald E. Winters

Stephen F. Wolfe

Chester L. Wolford

John A. Wood

Dorena Allen Wright

Eugene P. Wright

Linda Yoder

Bruce W. Young

Eugene Zasadinski

CONTENTS BY LITERARY PERIODS
BRITISH

Koestler, Arthur
Lawrence, D. H.
Lewis, C. S.
Lewis, Wyndham
MacNeice, Louis
Mansfield, Katherine
Maugham, Somerset
O'Connor, Frank
Orwell, George
Owen, Wilfred
Rhys, Jean

Richardson, Dorothy
Saki
Sayers, Dorothy
Snow, C. P.
Stead, Christina
Thomas, Dylan
Tolkien, J. R. R.
Waugh, Evelyn
Wells, H. G.
Woolf, Virginia
Yeats, William Butler

CONTENTS BY LITERARY PERIODS
AMERICAN, CONTEMPORARY BRITISH/AMERICAN, CANADIAN

Colonial American

Bradstreet, Anne
Brown, Charles Brockden
Byrd, William
Franklin, Benjamin
Freneau, Philip
Rowson, Susanna
Taylor, Edward
Wheatley, Phyllis

American Romanticism

Benét, Stephen Vincent
Bierce, Ambrose
Cable, George Washington
Chesnutt, Charles
Cooper, James Fenimore
Dickinson, Emily
Emerson, Ralph Waldo
Harris, Joel Chandler
Hawthorne, Nathaniel

Irving, Washington
Jewett, Sarah
Lanier, Sidney
Longfellow, Henry W.
Lowell, Amy
Melville, Herman
Poe, Edgar Allan
Simms, William Gilmore
Stowe, Harriet Beecher
Thoreau, Henry David
Twain, Mark
Whitman, Walt

American Realism/Naturalism

Chopin, Kate
Crane, Hart
Crane, Stephen
Dreiser, Theodore
Freeman, Mary Wilkins
Garland, Hamlin

Modern American

WILLIAM LANGLAND
1330(?)–1390(?)

Author's Chronology

Born probably in the 1330's in the West Midlands region of England; *1350's* and *1360's* is educated, becomes a clerk in minor orders, marries, and settles in London; mid-*1360's* composes the A version of *Piers Plowman* (and perhaps also an earlier Z version); around *1377* composes the B text of *Piers Plowman;* *1380's* or *1390's* composes the C text, the final version of the poem, and dies.

Author's Bibliography

Piers Plowman, the Z text, 1360's; *Piers Plowman,* the A text, 1360's, but after the Z text; *Piers Plowman,* the B text, around 1377; *Piers Plowman,* the C text, 1380's or 1390's.

Overview of Biographical Sources

Since virtually nothing is known for certain about the life of the author of *Piers Plowman,* biographical accounts are necessarily quite hypothetical. While most scholars agree that the single author of all of the poem's versions must be reflected in Will, the poem's narrator, this is by no means a necessary assumption, and there are scholars who maintain that all three (or, now, perhaps four) versions of the poem could not possibly have been composed by the same person. In *Piers the Plowman: Literary Relations of the A and B Texts* (Seattle: University of Washington Press, 1961), David C. Fowler argues that different poets wrote the different versions and suggests that B may have been composed by John of Trevisa, the Middle English translator of Fitzralph's attacks on the friars. George Kane's *Piers Plowman: The Evidence for Authorship* (1965) is the most convincing elaboration of the theory that a single poet wrote all of the poem's versions.

Those who do accept the theory of single authorship point to a note in an early fifteenth-century C-text manuscript attributing the authorship of the poem to "William de Langlond," the son of Stacy de Rokayle. Since the de Rokayle family was quite prominent and Will mentions his own poverty, there has been some speculation that Langland was de Rokayle's illegitimate son. Allan H. Bright's *New Light on 'Piers Plowman'* (London: Oxford University Press, 1928) goes into great, albeit completely speculative, detail about Langland's illegitimacy. A less fanciful consideration of Langland's possible biography can be found in E. Talbot Donaldson's *Piers Plowman: The C-Text and Its Poet* (New Haven: Yale University Press, 1949). Elaborating on Will's autobiographical remarks, Donaldson explains the duties of a clerk in minor orders and concludes that Langland probably earned his living by praying for the souls of the living and the dead in return for patronage.

Evaluation of Selected Biographies

Kane, George, *Piers Plowman: The Evidence for Authorship*. London: Athlone Press, 1965. Kane argues very persuasively that there is no evidence, either extrinsic or intrinsic to the poem, to disprove the assumption that a single author named William Langland composed all of the versions of *Piers Plowman*. There can be no charge that the different versions were written in different dialects, for instance, because the original dialects of each version are not completely determinable. Perhaps Kane's most persuasive point is his assertion that a wholly fictitious poetic persona is alien to fourteenth-century literature. Medieval writers customarily equated themselves, to at least some extent, with the narrators of their works. Since there is only one narrator of *Piers Plowman*, Kane suggests, there must have been only one poet.

Autobiographical Sources

Since Langland left no autobiography, scholars have to rely on those autobiographical remarks that Will the narrator makes in *Piers Plowman*. Corroboration for the poet's name can be found in the narrator's remark, "I haue lyued in londe . . . my name is longe wille" (B.XV.153), for "Long Will of the Land" sounds remarkably like "William Langland." The narrator also mentions living in the Cornhill district of London with his wife "Kytte" and his daughter "Calote." He describes himself as being somewhat resentful of the wealthy and the powerful in society, and he indicates that he is quite uneasy about spending so much of the time he could spend in prayer on the composition of his poem.

Overview of Critical Sources

Although *Piers Plowman* is a notoriously difficult poem, recent scholarship has made strides in at least clarifying the nature of its difficulties. Perhaps the most important breakthroughs have been in the establishment of standard texts. While controversial, the editions of the A and B versions published by the Athlone press seem to have caused a significant improvement in scholars' understandings of what Langland really wrote, rather than what he *and the various scribes who copied the manuscripts* wrote. A. G. Rigg and Charlotte Brewer have recently argued in their *Piers Plowman: The Z Version* (Toronto: Pontifical Institute of Medieval Studies, 1983) that a heretofore puzzling manuscript of what seemed to be the A version is, in fact, an earlier draft of the poem. If Rigg and Brewer's contention is accepted, it could lead to a significant increase in the understanding of Langland's compositional method.

While the most dramatic breakthroughs have been in textual criticism, a number of critical studies of both the poem's medieval background and its structure and content have added to an understanding of the poem.

Evaluation of Selected Criticism

Bloomfield, Morton W. *Piers Plowman as a Fourteenth-Century Apocalypse*. New Brunswick, NJ: Rutgers University Press, 1962. This very informative book shows how *Piers Plowman* reflects the medieval belief in the imminence of Christ's second coming. Bloomfield presents the monastic background of Langland's ideas and explains the significance to Langland of Joachim of Flora's apocalyptic thought.

Carruthers, Mary, *The Search for St. Truth: A Study of Meaning in Piers Plowman.* Evanston: Northwestern University Press, 1973. This complex and very important book considers the nature of Langland's allegorical composition and argues that the poem shifts from the personification allegory it is known for. Carruthers maintains that Will comes to recognize chaos in the world and a lack of conformity between men's words and deeds. Gradually Will realizes that, instead of searching for the personifications "Do Well," "Do Better," and "Do Best," he would do better to embody their attributes in all of his actions. Will's struggle to achieve personal coherence is reflected in the growth of the poet.

Kane, George and E. Talbot Donaldson, eds. *Piers Plowman: The B Version.* London: Athlone Press, 1975. Editors Kane and Donaldson's intention is to present the original, authorial text of *Piers Plowman* B—a text that is not wholly present in any of the existing manuscripts of the poem and one that, they demonstrate in a long and extremely technical discussion, probably was not even present in the manuscript that was the source of today's extant manuscripts! Their argument that no manuscript has complete authority over the others leads them to reconstruct the original text by comparing the various manuscript readings and those from A and C manuscripts and by then evaluating the variants, not only according to editorial understandings about scribal errors but also according to the customary patterns of the alliterative lines and the contexts and meanings of the variants. They present all of the variant manuscript readings and they clearly mark their emendations. Although this edition contains neither a glossary nor notes on the poem's meaning, it is the most important edition of the poem in this century.

Robertson, D. W., Jr. and Bernard F. Huppé, *Piers Plowman and Scriptural Tradition.* Princeton: Princeton University Press, 1951. Robertson and Huppé shed light on the poem's opacities by tracing many of the frequent scriptural allusions back to their biblical sources, and by then examining how medieval and patristic exegetes understood those biblical passages. Some exegetical contexts fail to illuminate some of the poem's passages, and the authors' applications of other contexts can sometimes seem forced. But their demonstration of Langland's deep knowledge of patristic literature is very convincing, and their method—sometimes called "Robertsonianism"—has proven fruitful in the works of other scholars. Perhaps the book's greatest drawback is that the many Latin quotations are left untranslated.

Other Sources

Hussey, S. S. ed. *Piers Plowman: Critical Approaches.* London: Methuen, 1969. Contains many important essays.

Kirk, Elizabeth, *The Dream Thought of Piers Plowman.* New Haven: Yale University Press, 1972. Particularly insightful on the poet's progression from A to B texts.

Salter, Elizabeth, *Piers Plowman: An Introduction.* Cambridge: Harvard University Press, 1962. The best introduction to the poem.

Skeat, Walter W. ed. *The Vision of William Concerning Piers the Plowman, in three parallel texts.* London: Oxford University Press, 1886. A two volume edition containing A, B, and C that is still very valuable for its glossary and notes.

Selected Dictionaries and Encyclopedias

British Writers, Vol 1., Charles Scribner's Sons, 1979, pp. 1-18. Merrill Coghill offers a useful summary of many of the poems.

David G. Allen
The Citadel

SIDNEY LANIER
1842–1881

Author's Chronology

Born February 3, 1842, Macon, Georgia; *1857* enters Sophomore Class, Oglethorpe College, near Milledgeville, Georgia; *1858* writes earliest known poems; *1860* graduates from Oglethorpe with highest honors; becomes a tutor; *1861* enlists in Macon Volunteers, Georgia Infantry, C.S.A., stationed near Norfolk, Virginia; *1863* begins only novel *Tiger-Lilies,* based on war experiences; *1864* captured and imprisoned at Point Lookout, Maryland; *1865* released, returns in poor health to Macon; *1867* becomes principal of Academy at Prattville, Alabama; *Tiger-Lilies* published; marries Mary Day; *1868* suffers first hemorrhage; Academy closed for health and financial reasons; *1869* admitted to Georgia bar; begins work on long, unfinished, chivalric poem "The Jacquerie"; *1873* moves to Baltimore, named first flutist for Peabody Orchestra, Peabody Institute; *1875* "Corn" and "The Symphony" published; beginning of national reputation; *1877* publishes *Poems; 1878* publishes "The Marshes of Glynn"; begins lectures on Shakespeare at Peabody Institute; *1879* lectures at Johns Hopkins University on "English Verse, especially Shakspere's;" *1880* recurrence of tuberculosis; *1881* lectures at Johns Hopkins University on "The English Novel;" dies of tuberculosis on September 7 at Lynn, North Carolina.

Author's Bibliography (selected)

Tiger-Lilies, 1867 (novel); *Florida,* 1876 (travel book); *Poems,* 1877; *The Boy's Froissart,* 1879 (juvenile); *The Science of English Verse,* 1880 (criticism), *The Boy's King Arthur,* 1880; *The Boy's Mabinogion,* 1881 (juvenile); *The Boy's Percy,* 1882 (juvenile); *The English Novel and the Principles of Its Development,* 1883 (criticism); *Poems,* 1884; *Music and Poetry,* 1898 (criticism); *Shakspere and His Forerunners,* 1902 (criticism). The section on Lanier in Jacob Blanck, *Bibliography of American Literature* (New Haven: Yale University Press, 1970), V, 280–298, thoroughly describes all published editions of Lanier's works. Furthermore, almost all of Lanier's writings were published in Charles R. Anderson's, *The Centennial Edition of the Works of Sidney Lanier.* This standard-setting scholarly work presents the definitive texts of Lanier's writings.

Overview of Biographical Sources

After his early death in 1881, Sidney Lanier became a romantic figure, the soldier-poet who struggled courageously against a debilitating disease and passed away even as he was realizing a new and powerful stage of creativity. Thus, most of the early biographical material, especially from the Southern viewpoint, is highly sympathetic. Of these, the most balanced is William

Malone Baskervill's biographical essay in *Southern Writers* (New York: Gordian Press, 1897), I, 137–298. There have been three full-length biographies of Lanier written in the 20th century: Edwin Mims, *Sidney Lanier* (1905); Aubrey Starke, *Sidney Lanier: A Biographical and Critical Study* (1933); and Lincoln Lorenz, *Sidney Lanier* (New York: Coward and McCann, 1935). Mims' biography is very respectful; Starke's is the most scholarly; while Lorenz's can be dismissed as a popular work which adds nothing to the other two. A reassessment of Lanier's work and life can be found in Charles Anderson's General Introduction to *The Centennial Edition of the Works of Sidney Lanier* and in the individual introductions to volumes I–VII.

Evaluation of Selected Biographies

Anderson, Charles R. ed. *The Centennial Edition of the Works of Sidney Lanier.* 10 vols. Baltimore: The Johns Hopkins Press, 1945. The introductions to these volumes are models of scholarship and carefully relate the works to the life. Of especial interest are the chronologies found at the beginning of volumes VII–X, which contain the *Letters.*

Mims, Edwin, *Sidney Lanier.* Boston: Houghton Mifflin, 1905; rpt. Port Washington, New York: Kennicat Press, 1968. Mims, a noted Southern scholar and teacher, had the co-operation of Lanier's widow and children in writing the first full-length biography, which is enriched by his use of family letters and unpublished manuscripts. It is not a critical study of the work. Mims concentrates on the life, especially the early part, and concludes that while Lanier's work was uneven, his life was "one of the most heroic recorded in the annals of men" (p. 4).

Starke, Aubrey H. *Sidney Lanier: A Biographical and Critical Study.* Chapel Hill: University of North Carolina Press, 1933; rpt. New York: Russell and Russell, 1964. Starke's work is less a biography than a critical study of the entire body of Lanier's work, published and unpublished. Like Mims, he sees Lanier as an heroic figure, but whereas Mims stressed Lanier's role as a Southerner, Starke emphasizes his importance as a national figure. He also argues that Lanier was a forerunner of the Fugitive-Agrarian writers, a conclusion to which a number of these writers took angry exception.

Autobiographical Sources

Lanier gave a fictional account of his pre-war and war experiences in his only completed novel *Tiger-Lilies,* a very romantic work written when Lanier was a young man. Still, his accounts of the chaos of battle and the horror of prison are remarkable, and it remains a flawed but fascinating book. Lanier's correspondence, found in volumes VII–X of *The Centennial Edition of the Works of Sidney Lanier,* are also extremely informative.

Overview of Critical Sources

Critical interest in Lanier has lessened considerably since the publication of *The Centennial Edition* in 1945. Lanier is today generally regarded as a minor literary figure and an interesting critic of his time, although some scholars, most importantly Jack De Bellis, have made strong arguments for his accomplishments as a poet and a Southern man of letters.

Evaluation of Selected Criticism

Allen, Gay Wilson, *American Prosody*. New York: American Book Company, 1935, pp. 277–301, 305–306. Allen presents an early, thoughtful discussion of Lanier's poetic complexities. He anticipates a number of the arguments which would later be made in defense of Lanier as a poet and gives a thorough discussion of *The Science of English Verse*.

De Bellis, Jack, *Sidney Lanier*. New York: Twayne, 1972. De Bellis offers the most comprehensive and convincing study of Lanier's "unique talents" as a poet and of his role as a leader of the Southern Renaissance. De Bellis's work is essential to a full appreciation of Lanier.

Parks, Edd Winfield, *Sidney Lanier: The Man, the Poet, the Critic*. Athens: University of Georgia Press, 1968. In this three-part study (based on lectures), Parks approaches Lanier as a man, an artist, and a thinker. In "The Man," he gives a straight biography. In "The Poet," he argues that Lanier did not achieve greatness because of his early death and tendency to moralize. In "The Critic," he finds Lanier to be inconsistent and didactic.

Pearce, Roy Harvey, *The Continuity of American Poetry*. Princeton: Princeton University Press, 1961, pp. 236–246. In what De Bellis calls the "best single essay on Lanier's work," Pearce discusses the poetry in terms of its social and philosophical significance. He feels that Lanier's experimentation took him beyond Southern traditionalism and toward a kind of impressionism in his later poems.

Other Sources

De Bellis, Jack, *Sidney Lanier, Henry Timrod, and Paul Hamilton Hayne: A Reference Guide*. Boston: G. K. Hall, 1978, pp. 3–105. Annotated entries on all books, articles, and reviews on Lanier from 1868 to 1976.

Graham, Philip and Joseph Jones, *A Concordance to the Poems of Sidney Lanier*. Austin: University of Texas Press, 1939; rpt. New York: Johnson Reprint Corporation, 1969.

Hubbell, Jay B. *The South in American Literature: 1607–1900*. Durham: Duke University Press, 1954, pp. 758–777. A fine overview of Lanier's life and accomplishments which places him in the larger Southern context.

Lenhart, Charmenz S. *Musical Influences on American Poetry.* Athens: University of Georgia Press, 1956, pp. 210–288, 309–313. Study of the ways in which Lanier's knowledge of music affected his verse; argues that his best poems were musical impressions.

Rubin, Louis D., Jr. "The Passion of Sidney Lanier," in *William Elliott Shoots a Bear: Essays on the Southern Literary Imagination.* Baton Rouge: Louisiana State University Press, 1975, pp. 107–144. A rethinking of Lanier's strengths and weaknesses as a writer and thinker.

Warren, Robert Penn, "The Blind Poet: Sidney Lanier," *American Review,* II (November 1933), 27–45. Attack on Starke's biography; Warren argues that Lanier never really "saw" the world.

Wilson, Edmund, *Patriotic Gore.* New York: Oxford University Press, 1962, pp. 450–466, 519–528. Surprisingly sympathetic discussion of Lanier as a Southern writer.

Selected Dictionaries and Encyclopedias
American Writers: Supplement I, Part 1, Charles Scribner's Sons, 1979. Excellent discussion of Lanier's career.

Dictionary of American Biography, Charles Scribner's Sons, 1933, Vol. X. Written by Mims, this is a summary of his main points in the biography.

Edwin T. Arnold
Appalachian State University

RING LARDNER
1885–1933

Author's Chronology

Born Ringgold Wilmer Lardner March 6, 1885, Niles, Michigan; *1905* begins work as a newspaperman for the South Bend *Times; 1908* follows White Sox for Chicago *Examiner* and Cubs for Chicago *Tribune; 1911* marries Ellis Abbott; works briefly as editor for *Sporting News,* then returns to the *Examiner; 1913* begins "In the Wake of the News" (column for Chicago *Tribune*); *1914* begins "Busher's Letters" (*The Saturday Evening Post*); *1915* publishes *Bib Ballads* (poems); *1916* publishes *You Know Me Al; 1917* makes first trip to France; *1919* moves to Greenwich, New York; begins writing for the Bell Syndicate; *1921* moves to Great Neck, Long Island; befriends F. Scott Fitzgerald; *1924* publishes *How to Write Short Stories;* makes second trip to France; *1929* publishes *Round Up; 1930* publishes *June Moon* (play); writes for Ziegfeld; *1931* enters Tucson sanitorium for tuberculosis; *1932* health failing, attempts new "Busher" series for *The Saturday Evening Post;* September 25, 1933 dies of a heart attack.

Author's Bibliography (selected)

Bib Ballads, 1915 (poems); *You Know Me Al,* 1916 (collected "Busher's Letters"); *How to Write Short Stories,* 1924; *The Story of a Wonder Man,* 1927 (mock-autobiography); *Round Up,* 1929 (collected short stories); *June Moon,* 1930 (play).

Overview of Biographical Sources

Because of the many occupations and interests of his youth, the important social and professional contacts of his productive period, and the extremely painful physical and emotional collapse of his last years, the whole of Ring Lardner's life is rarely treated with equanimity. The two most complete accounts remain Donald Elder's *Ring Lardner: A Biography* (1956) and Jonathan Yardley's *Ring: A Biography of Ring Lardner* (1977). For additional information concerning Ellis Abbott Lardner and their four sons, see Ring Lardner, Jr.'s *The Lardners: My Family Remembered* (New York: Harper and Row, 1976).

Evaluation of Selected Biographies

Elder, Donald, *Ring Lardner: A Biography.* Garden City, NY: Doubleday, 1956. Elder discusses Lardner's childhood and youth in considerable detail. His treatment of Lardner's later years—despite numerous excerpts from the columns, stories, and correspondence—is not as well-developed.

Yardley, Jonathan, *Ring: A Biography of Ring Lardner.* New York: Random House, 1977. Yardley covers the courtship by correspondence Lardner conducted to obtain the hand of Ellis Abbott (1907–1911), using many of the letters in their entirety. He is also reasonably successful in his attempt to account for Lardner's melancholy resignation during the final years. An annotated bibliography makes this volume especially useful.

Autobiographical Sources

Lardner was not given to self-revelation. His mock-autobiography, *The Story of a Wonder Man,* has little bearing on the actual events in Lardner's life, and, perhaps even more unfortunately, does not reflect his characteristic wit. Nevertheless, Matthew J. Bruccoli and Richard Layman have compiled certain autobiographical articles originally printed in *The Saturday Evening Post*—as well as some of Lardner's darker, more revealing stories—in *Some Champions* (New York: Charles Scribner's Sons, 1976).

Overview of Critical Sources

Opinions concerning Lardner's contribution to literature vary considerably. Some critics are still inclined to see him largely as an American humorist and sports writer. The most recent trend, however, involves the recognition of Lardner as a major satirist and innovator—even an American "Dadaist." The current body of criticism about Lardner's work is neither impressive nor extensive.

Evaluation of Selected Criticism

Frakes, James R. *Ring Lardner: A Critical Survey.* Unpublished dissertation, University of Pennsylvania, 1953. After over thirty years, Frakes' study remains one of the few serious critical accounts.

Friedrich, Otto, *Ring Lardner.* Minneapolis: University of Minnesota Press, 1965. This volume in the series of "University of Minnesota Pamphlets on American Writers" combines brief biographical material with critical commentary; however, the criticism tends toward simple plot summary.

Other Sources

Bruccoli, Matthew J. and Richard Layman, *Ring Lardner: A Descriptive Bibliography.* Pittsburgh: University of Pittsburgh Press, 1976. An indispensable tool for the Lardner student, this volume even cites his dust-jacket blurbs; a glance at the eight sources listed as "Principal Works About Ring W. Lardner" readily reveals the need for more attention to Lardner and his work.

Caruthers, Clifford, ed. *Ring Around Max: The Correspondence of Ring Lardner and Maxwell Perkins.* Dekalb, IL: Northern Illinois University Press, 1973. Reflects Lardner's friendship and professional association with Maxwell Perkins, then editor of Charles Scribner's Sons.

Fitzgerald, F. Scott, *The Crack-Up,* ed. Edmund Wilson. New York: New Directions, 1945. Includes Scott Fitzgerald's "Ring" in its entirety.

Patrick, Walton R. *Ring Lardner.* New York: Twayne, 1963. Although the quality of the volumes in the Twayne author series is inconsistent, this piece on Lardner's work is excellent.

Woolf, Virginia, *The Moment and Other Essays.* New York: Harcourt Brace, 1948. Woolf's essay "American Fiction" provides an early and significant estimate of Lardner's contribution.

Selected Dictionaries and Encyclopedias

The Baseball Encyclopedia, Macmillan, 1969. One of many sports encyclopedias that treat of Lardner's early involvement with baseball's major figures.

Dictionary of American Biography, Charles Scribner's Sons, 1946. A concise account of major events in Lardner's life which also provides brief synopses of many of his works.

Marinelle Ringer
Oklahoma State University

PHILIP LARKIN
1922

Author's Chronology

Born August 9, 1922, Coventry, Warwickshire; *1930–1940* attends King Henry VIII School, Coventry; *1940* enters St. John's College, Oxford; *1943* B.A. with first-class honors in English, appointed librarian at the public library in Wellington, Shropshire; *1945* publishes first volume of poetry, *The North Ship; 1946* appointed assistant librarian at University College, Leicester; *1950* appointed sublibrarian at Queen's University, Belfast; *1955* appointed librarian at the Brynmor Jones Library, University of Hull; *1961* begins reviewing jazz and jazz recordings for the *Daily Telegraph; 1965* awarded the Queen's Medal for Poetry; *1969* awarded honorary D. Lit., Queen's University, Belfast; *1970* Visiting Fellow, All Souls College, Oxford, and D. Lit., University of Leicester; *1973* Honorary Fellow, St. John's College, and D. Lit., University of Warwick; *1983* Whitbread Award for *Required Writing*.

Author's Bibliography (selected)

The North Ship, 1945 (poems); *Jill,* 1946 (novel); *A Girl in Winter,* 1947 (novel); *The Less Deceived,* 1955 (poems); *The Whitsun Weddings,* 1964 (poems); *All What Jazz: A Record Diary 1961–68,* 1970 (criticism); *High Windows,* 1974 (poems); *The Oxford Book of Twentieth Century English Verse,* 1980 (editor); *Required Writing,* 1983 (criticism).

Overview of Biographical Sources

Philip Larkin has always tried to make his life seem at best unremarkable and at worst dull. One time he said that his biography could begin when he was twenty-one and omit nothing of importance; at another he described his childhood as a "forgotten boredom"; and he has persistently stressed the absence of the spectacular in his adult experiences. Nevertheless, critics continue to show interest in Larkin's life, particularly as it relates to the development of his extraordinary gifts as a poet. Four bio-critical studies offer a comprehensive blend of biographical information about Larkin and critical assessments of his writings. All of them focus chiefly on Larkin's childhood, on the Oxford period, and on the recurrence of certain themes and images in the verse and later prose. None of them offers sweeping generalizations or large psychological speculations in the assessment.

Evaluation of Selected Biographies

Martin, Bruce K. *Philip Larkin.* Boston: Twayne, 1978. In this general introduction to Larkin's life and works, Martin considers those biographical elements that contributed to his pessimistic outlook. Included is a helpful, straightforward account of Larkin's childhood, work as a librarian, writing, and continuing interest in jazz.

Motion, Andrew, *Philip Larkin.* London and New York: Methuen, 1982. Motion's qualification for writing this book is that he himself is an award-winning poet and editor of *Poetry Review.* His evaluation of Larkin's private and public lives reflects the latest in scholarship and thinking. A concise, readable study.

Thwaite, Anthony, ed. *Larkin at Sixty.* London: Faber & Faber, 1982. Seven of the twenty essays in this collection—all written by Larkin's friends and colleagues—offer perceptive biographical commentaries. The essays cover fascinating episodes in Larkin's private life as a student (at King Henry VIII and Oxford) and librarian.

Timms, David. *Philip Larkin.* New York: Barnes and Noble, 1973. Important as the first book-length study of the poet's life and work, Timms examines the poet's career largely from a social and biographical base, with much less of the concentrated and extended analysis the others offer.

Autobiographical Sources
Certainly the most helpful autobiographical materials have been collected in Larkin's *Required Writing* (London: Faber & Faber, 1983; New York: Farrar, Straus, and Giroux, 1984). Part I of the book offers incisive, often humorous accounts of his experiences at Oxford and Leicester University, as well as the circumstances that lead to the publication of *The North Ship.* Reprints of interviews from the *Observer* and *Paris Review* are important for what they reveal of Larkin's attitudes toward his life, his work, and his contemporaries. Additional information about his childhood and early adult years may be found in interviews by the *Times Literary Supplement* (July 13, 1956, p. 933), by John Horder in the *Manchester Guardian* (May 20, 1965, p. 9), by Philip Oakes in the London *Sunday Times Magazine* (March 27, 1966, pp. 63–65), by Anthony Thwaite in *Contemporary Poets of the English Language* (Chicago and London: St. James Press, 1970), by Francis Hill in the *Times Educational Supplement* (May 19, 1972, p. 19) and by John Haffenden in *Viewpoints: Poets in Conversation* (London: Faber, 1981). For exclusive information covering Larkin's long friendship with novelist Barbara Pym, scholars should consult *A Very Private Eye* edited by Hilary Pym and Hazel Holt (London: Macmillan; New York: E. P. Dutton, 1984) as well as the collection of his letters to her on hold at the Bodleian.

Overview of Critical Sources
Throughout Larkin's career there has been a wide divergence of opinion about the man and his work—ranging from derision to praise. The majority of

the criticism—and there are over twenty-five books and a thousand academic essays on him—centers on his poetic technique, subject matter, and attitudes. To some writers, Larkin is refined and witty; to others, he is confining and dull. Few readers on either side of the Atlantic have reacted with indifference, which is one reason why reading his critics can be so interesting. All of this is brought together between the covers of B. C. Bloomfield's definitive work: *Philip Larkin: A Bibliography* (London: Faber & Faber, 1980).

Evaluation of Selected Criticism

Brownjohn, Alan, *Philip Larkin.* Essex: Longman Group, Ltd., 1975. The author concentrates on major themes in Larkin's works, with brief biographical details. A helpful book to the newcomer to Larkin, but slight in its treatment.

Martin, Bruce, *Philip Larkin.* Boston: Twayne, 1978. Important as a brief but concise survey of all of Larkin's poetry and fiction. Examines both background and foreground. Especially helpful for what he says about Larkin's "poetic theory."

Morrison, Blake, *The Movement: English Poetry and Fiction of the 1950s.* New York and Oxford: Oxford University Press, 1980. A thorough study of the milieu in which Larkin began to write. Expands on what Timms reveals in his study.

Motion, Andrew, *Philip Larkin.* New York and London: Methuen, 1982. Important for his analysis of Larkin's literary relationship with Hardy and Yeats and the later Movement poets. His analysis of Larkin's two novels goes beyond anything else that has been written. His study is especially valuable because he refers to uncollected reviews and articles as well as to unpublished manuscripts. Unlike most critics who have emphasized the empirical and melancholy aspects of Larkin's writing, Motion focuses on the Symbolist and transcendent elements in his work as well as its range and variety.

Petch, Simon, *The Art of Philip Larkin.* Sydney: University of Sydney Press, 1981. An introduction useful to new readers of Larkin as well as those already familiar with his work, Petch explores the genius of Larkin's ability to penetrate central aspects of human life in ways that are comprehensible and accessible to the common reader.

Timms, David, *Philip Larkin.* New York: Barnes and Noble, 1973. This is the first brief study of Larkin's poetry and fiction published in book form. Its strength is what it reveals about Larkin's early reputation. It is especially helpful for seeing Larkin's poems in their biographical and British contexts.

Other Sources

Chambers, Harry, ed. *Phoenix: Philip Larkin Issue.* 11/12 (Autumn and Winter 1973/4). This issue brings together some of the best writing that has appeared on the work of Larkin.

Selected Dictionaries and Encyclopedias

Contemporary Poets, St. Martin's Press, 1980. Brief overview of Larkin's career with commentary on representative poems and biographical sketch.

Critical Survey of Poetry, Salem Press, 1983. Brief biography, evaluation of his literary reputation, and analysis of best-known poems.

Dictionary of Literary Biography, Gale Research, 1983. Helpful listing of major episodes in Larkin's life together with summary of his poetic themes.

Dale Salwak
Citrus College

MARGARET LAURENCE
1926

Author's Chronology

Born Jean Margaret Laurence, July 18, 1926 in Neepawa, Manitoba, to Robert and Verna (Simpson) Wemyss; *1930* mother dies suddenly; *1935* father dies; *1944–1947* studies English at United College of the University of Manitoba, Winnipeg; *1947* receives degree; marries Jack Laurence, a civil engineering student; becomes a reporter for *The Winnipeg Citizen; 1950–1952* the Laurences live in the British Protectorate of Somalia; 1952 daughter Jocelyn is born; *1952–1957* the Laurences live in Ghana where son David is born in 1954; *1957–1962* Laurence writes her Africa stories in Vancouver; *1962* separates from husband and lives in England with her children; *1968 A Jest of God* is filmed as *Rachel, Rachel; 1969* the Laurences divorce; *1969–1970* Writer-in-Residence at University of Toronto; receives a number of academic honors in the early 1970's; August *1973* moves from England back to Canada; *1975* receives the Governor General's Award for Fiction; *1980–1983* Chancellor of Trent University; *1985* lives at Lakefield, Ontario, and serves on the Honorary Board of Governors of Trent University.

Author's Bibliography (selected)

A Tree for Poverty, 1954 (anthology of Somali folk literature); *This Side Jordan,* 1960 (novel); *The Prophet's Camel Bell,* 1963, reprinted as *New Wind in a Dry Land,* 1964 (essays); *The Tomorrow-Tamer: Stories,* 1963; *The Stone Angel,* 1964 (novel); *A Jest of God,* 1966 (novel); *Long Drums and Cannons: Nigerian Dramatists and Novelists, 1952–66,* 1968 (criticism); *The Fire-Dwellers,* 1969 (novel); *A Bird in the House,* 1970 (short stories); *The Diviners,* 1974 (novel); *Heart of a Stranger* (collected essays), 1976.

Overview of Biographical Sources

Clara Thomas is Laurence's chief biographer. Her first treatment, a 64–page biography (1969), traces Laurence's development and provides an early assessment of her work. Thomas's full biography, *The Manawaka World of Margaret Laurence* (1975) gives the real-world matrix of Laurence's writing. In a long chapter of her *Three Voices* (Toronto: Clarke Irwin, 1975) Joan Hind-Smith provides biographical information, including interview material and publishing history.

Evaluation of Selected Biographies

Morley, Patricia, *Margaret Laurence.* Boston: Twayne, 1981. Morley uses the journey metaphor to treat both the life and the writings of Laurence. Thus she devotes much of the book to explaining the African sojourn and what Laurence learned from it. About half of the book discusses the Manawaka cycle of novels, skillfully summarizing and at the same time enlarging and explaining the novels. Brief bibliography.

Thomas, Clara, *The Manawaka World of Margaret Laurence.* Toronto: Mc-Clelland and Stewart, 1975. Noting Laurence's concern with the past, both personal and cultural, and with a sense of place, Thomas pays special attention to Laurence's background. This she integrates with a discussion of the works, so that this biography is also a useful critical resource.

Autobiographical Sources

The Prophet's Camel Bell is a travel memoir of Laurence's two years in the Somali desert, but since it was written nearly ten years later from diary sources, it is written with an awareness of ten years' development. Another autobiographical source is the collection of essays published as *Heart of a Stranger* in 1976. Laurence has been generous in granting interviews with magazines and newspapers, so these provide a rich, although scattered, source of autobiographical material.

Evaluation of Selected Criticism

New, William H. ed. *Margaret Laurence: The Writer and Her Critics.* Toronto: McGraw-Hill Ryerson, 1977. This collection of reviews, critical essays, and several essays by Laurence herself was chosen to reveal a wide range of perspectives on the works. Essays deal with themes, techniques, her fictional world, and her development as an artist.

Overview of Critical Sources

The *Journal of Canadian Studies* devoted a special issue to Laurence studies (13, No. 3, Fall 1978). Critics deal with the idea of the Canadian hero, everyday life as political life, the sense of place and voice in Laurence's fiction, her African writings and how their vision produced her later fiction, and Laurence's use of Old Testament symbolism and poetry. Although the reader is wisely warned in the introduction to be aware of the "pervasive pressures of Canadian nationalism" to which Laurence criticism is subjected, several essays in this collection deserve separate mention. Patricia Morley's "Margaret Laurence's Early Writing: 'a world in which Others have to be respected' " deals with Laurence's discovery of the complexities of the imperialistic relationship, and of how she deals with these—both in their comic and their tragic possibilities—in fiction. Kenneth James Hughes' "Politics and *A Jest of God*" gives a pervasively political reading to that novel, a reading which he sees lying beneath an "apparently unpolitical surface." Sherrill Grace's "A Portrait of the Artist as Laurence Hero" analyzes the character of the Laurence heroine as a type of the Canadian hero, a figure with an amazing consistency. Sherrill shows how the heroines of the five Manawaka novels both embody the character of this Canadian hero, and show a development in consciousness. David Blewett in "The Unity of the Manawaka Cycle" sees in the novels a vision not completely rendered until the cycle is completed. He explores the various ways in which this unity is worked out—the meaning of place, the use of paired persons and images, and an elaborate parallel with Eliot's symbolism of the four elements in *The Waste Land.*

Other Sources

A comprehensive Laurence bibliography is found in Volume I of *The Annotated Bibliography of Canada's Major Authors,* Downsview, Ontario, ECW Press, 1979.

Selected Dictionaries and Encyclopedias

Contemporary Novelists, St. Martin's Press, second edition, 1976. Brief descriptions of the principal works.

Critical Survey of Long Fiction, Salem Press, 1983. Summarizes major works and identifies recurring themes and concerns.

Linda Yoder
West Virginia University

MARY LAVIN
1912

Author's Chronology

Born June 11, 1912, East Walpole, Massachusetts of Irish parents; *1921* leaves America with mother to stay with mother's family in Athenry, County Galway, Ireland; *1922* settles with mother and father in Dublin and enters Loreto convent school; *1930* enters University College, Dublin; *1934* graduates with honors in English; *1936* completes M.A. thesis on Jane Austen and then begins Ph.D. studies (never completed) while teaching French at Loreto convent school; *1939* publishes first short story, "Miss Holland," in *Dublin Magazine; 1942* marries William Walsh; *1943* wins James Tait Black Memorial Book Prize for *Tales from Bective Bridge* (published *1942*); in same year gives birth to first daughter, Valentine; *1945* gives birth to second daughter, Elizabeth; *1953* gives birth to third daughter, Caroline; *1954* becomes widow; *1959* wins Guggenheim award, which is renewed in *1960; 1961* wins Katherine Mansfield Prize for "The Great Wave"; *1967* holds writer-in-residence position at University of Connecticut, Storrs (again in *1971*); *1968* awarded Honorary Doctor of Literature by University College, Dublin; *1969* marries Michael Scott, a friend from college days and a laicized Jesuit; *1971–1975* serves two terms as president of Irish Academy of Writers; *1972* receives Ella Lynam Cabot Award; *1974* receives Eire Society Gold Medal; *1975* awarded Gregory Medal; *1979* awarded American Irish Foundation Literature Prize; *1982* receives Aos Dana Award; *1985* continues to reside alternately in Dublin and on her farm in Bective, county Meath.

Author's Bibliography (selected)

Tales from Bective Bridge, 1942; *The Long Ago and Other Stories*, 1944; *The House in Clewe Street*, 1945 (novel); *The Becker Wives and Other Stories*, 1946; *At Sallygap and Other Stories*, 1947, *Mary O'Grady*, 1950 (novel); *A Single Lady and Other Stories*, 1951; *The Patriot Son and Other Stories*, 1956; *A Likely Story*, 1957 (children's book); *The Great Wave and Other Stories*, 1961; *In the Middle of the Fields and Other Stories*, 1967; *Happiness and Other Stories*, 1969; *Collected Stories*, 1971; *A Memory and Other Stories*, 1972; *The Second-Best Children in the World*, 1972 (children's book); *The Shrine and Other Stories*, 1977.

Overview of Biographical Sources

There is no standard biography of Lavin to date. There are only short biographical accounts in the critical literature. Of these, the most extensive is by Richard F. Peterson, who devotes the opening chapter of *Mary Lavin* (Boston: Twayne, 1978) to Lavin's life. Zack Bowen, in *Mary Lavin* (Lewisburg:

Bucknell University Press, 1975), also offers a valuable sketch of Lavin's life. Both Peterson and Bowen interviewed Lavin and Michael Scott, her second husband, before completing their books, and both use biographical materials in a limited way to elucidate Lavin's stories.

Evaluation of Selected Biographical Source

Peterson, Richard F. *Mary Lavin.* Boston: Twayne, 1978. Peterson stresses those aspects of Lavin's life that have been most influential in her fiction: her parents' courtship and marriage; her relationship with her father, Tom Lavin; her early life at Athenry and Bective; and, after the death of her first husband, the struggle to deal with her tragic loss, raise her three children, and regain confidence in her writing talent. Peterson's account enables the reader to gain a greater understanding of both the genesis and meaning of Lavin's fiction.

Autobiographical Sources

Lavin has not written an autobiography, nor is there a published collection of her correspondence. Some of her correspondence, however, is available, along with manuscripts of her work, in three places: the Mugar Memorial Library of Boston University; the Morris Library of Southern Illinois University; and State University of New York at Binghamton, which houses The Lavin Collection. There have been a number of interviews with Lavin published in newspapers and journals. Some of her ideas about the nature of fiction are in the preface that she wrote for *Selected Stories* (1959). Many of her stories, especially the later ones, have strong autobiographical elements. Vera Traske emerges in the later stories as a Mary Lavin figure. The reader should be aware, of course, that the autobiographical elements have been blended with purely fictional elements.

Overview of Critical Sources

Lord Dunsany and Frank O'Connor were early admirers of Lavin's fiction, but extended serious commentary did not begin until twenty years after publication of Lavin's first book of short stories. Augustine Martin, in "A Skeleton Key to the Stories of Mary Lavin" (*Studies,* 52, Winter 1963, 393–406), was the first to give extended consideration to Lavin's aesthetic approach, creative techniques, and recurrent themes. Since then there has been a small but steady procession of articles about Lavin and her fiction. In the last decade three books have appeared that have given valuable appraisals of her work, both its technical characteristics and its thematic patterns. Given the quality and amount of fiction that Lavin has written, it is certain that many more critical studies will appear in the future.

Evaluation of Selected Critical Sources

Bowen, Zack, *Mary Lavin.* Lewisburg: Bucknell University Press, 1975. One of the *Irish Writers Series,* this monograph is a solid introduction to Lavin's fiction. Bowen examines many of the short stories and both novels, finding that freedom and its domestic, social, and religious restrictions is Lavin's recurrent theme. Bowen's third chapter, on the techniques and style of the short stories, is particularly valuable. In it, he discusses such stylistic elements as Lavin's humor and her use of symbol to epitomize a character's situation. He is in general agreement with other critics that the novels, though commendable in some respects, are artistically flawed, but he finds that overall Lavin has achieved a level of literary quality in her works that places her in the first rank of Irish writers.

Kelly, A. A. *Mary Lavin, Quiet Rebel: A Study of her Short Stories.* New York: Barnes and Noble, 1980. Kelly's thesis is that Lavin, while choosing to express her vision of society within the narrow confines of the short story, has quietly rebelled against certain stifling aspects of society. Three chapters are devoted to these aspects: the social hierarchy, the family and intimate relationships, and religious conventions. Kelly shows how Lavin relies on irony, nuance, and implication to carry out her quiet rebellion. The fourth chapter considers the ways in which Lavin uses such elements as narrative tones, states of feeling, and description to achieve her artistic intentions, and the fifth chapter discusses the significance of Lavin's later revisions of early stories. Although this book travels over some terrain already well mapped by Bowen and Peterson, readers will find some new insights about Lavin's fiction.

Peterson, Richard F. *Mary Lavin.* Boston: Twayne, 1978. Peterson's very fine book is the most extensive study of Lavin's canon. He examines the stories and novels in chronological order, thus showing the development of Lavin's fictional techniques and her continual treatment of the theme of loneliness and suffering in the lives of ordinary people. Peterson shows how Lavin began by writing stories that capture the emotional ordeals of their characters, but then switched in mid-career, at the urging of friends and critics, to stories with heavily patterned plots, often having surprise endings. He maintains that because these patterned stories impose, rather than capture, a truth, Lavin found them unsatisfactory and returned gradually in the 1960's and 1970's to the earlier type of story, but this time with much more autobiographical material, especially her experiences as a widow. In analyzing Lavin's two novels, Peterson shows how they were shaped in part by Lavin's understanding of and appreciation for Jane Austin's novels. Presenting a balanced assessment, he praises Lavin for having achieved in the novels some of Austin's techniques but also points out such flaws as melodrama, sentimentality, and lack of character credibility. In the last chapter, Peterson traces the influence of other writers, especially Sarah Orne Jewett, on Lavin and ascertains Lavin's place in Irish and world literature.

Other Sources

Dunsany, Lord, "A Preface," *Tales from Bective Bridge.* Boston: Little, Brown, 1942. The earliest published praise of Lavin's fiction by an established writer.

Irish University Review: A Journal of Irish Studies, 9 (Autumn 1979). A special issue devoted to Mary Lavin, including an interview with Lavin, a bibliography, and articles on her stories, short novels, and novels.

Selected Dictionaries and Encyclopedias

Contemporary Novelists, 3rd ed., St. Martin's Press, 1982. Brief biography, bibliography, and concise analysis of Lavin's literary qualities.

Critical Survey of Short Fiction, Salem Press, 1981. Brief biography and valuable commentary on selected stories by Lavin.

Dictionary of Irish Literature, Greenwood Press, 1979. Brief biography and concise analysis of Lavin's literary characteristics.

Dictionary of Literary Biography, Gale Research, 1983. Concise overview of Lavin's life and fictional works, including the novels.

Michael L. Storey
College of Notre Dame
of Maryland

DAVID HERBERT LAWRENCE
1885–1930

Author's Chronology

Born September 11, 1885, Eastwood, Nottinghamshire, England, to a school-teacher and a miner; *1898* enters Nottingham High School on a county scholarship; *1906* enters Nottingham University College; *1908* begins teaching at Croydon; *1909* publishes first poems in *The English Review; 1911* publishes first novel, *The White Peacock;* May *1912,* leaves for the Continent with Frieda von Richthofen Weekley, wife of Lawrence's former language professor; *1913* publishes *Sons and Lovers; 1914* marries Frieda and publishes first volume of short fiction, *The Prussian Officer; 1915* completes *The Rainbow,* officially proscribed in England; *1916* completes *Women in Love; 1917* expelled from Cornwall as suspected spy; *1919* leaves England permanently; *1920* completes *Studies in Classic American Literature; 1922–1925* travels and writes about Ceylon, Australia, Mexico and New Mexico; *1925* suffers near-fatal collapse; *1928* publishes third and last version of *Lady Chatterley's Lover* and *The Collected Poems; 1929* writes *Last Poems* (published *1932*) and last novella, *The Man Who Died,* while beset by British censorship; dies March 2, 1930, Vence, France.

Author's Bibliography (selected)

Sons and Lovers, 1913 (novel); *The Rainbow,* 1915 (novel); *Women in Love,* 1920 (novel); *Lady Chatterley's Lover,* 1928 (novel); *Phoenix: The Posthumous Papers of D. H. Lawrence,* 1936 (essays); *The Complete Short Stories,* 1955; *The Complete Poems of D. H. Lawrence,* 1964; *The Cambridge Edition of the Complete Works of D. H. Lawrence,* 1979, edition-in-progress; *The Letters of D. H. Lawrence,* 1979, edition-in-progress.

Overview of Biographical Sources

Lawrence's short but turbulent life and his contradictory personality inspire a broad range of biographical treatments. Early volumes of adulation, often inadvertently ludicrous, are offset by denunciations by Lawrence's former friends. Few personal accounts achieve the equilibrium of Richard Aldington's *D. H. Lawrence: Portrait of a Genius, But* . . . (New York: Duell, Sloan, and Pearce, 1950). Fortunately, Edward Nehls' three-volume *D. H. Lawrence: A Composite Biography* (1957–1959) offers an indispensible multidimensional portrait through the words of Lawrence himself and those who knew him. The post-1960 upsurge in Lawrence studies has produced many biographies, but none definitive, though one may follow the *Cambridge Edition of the Complete Works of D. H. Lawrence* and *The Letters of D. H. Lawrence,* both in progress. The increasing availability of biographical materials has outdated Harry T. Moore's *The Priest of Love: A Life of D. H. Lawrence* (1974), a revision of *The*

Intelligent Heart: The Story of D. H. Lawrence (New York: Farrar, Straus and Young, 1954). Specialized biographies of Lawrence abound, but many advance outdated individual biases. Valuable information also appears in biographies of Lawrence's associates, notably Robert Lucas' *Frieda Lawrence: The Story of Frieda von Richthofen and D. H. Lawrence* (New York: Viking, 1973).

Evaluation of Selected Biographies

Delany, Paul, *D. H. Lawrence's Nightmare: The Writer and His Circle in the Years of the Great War.* New York: Basic Books, 1978. Delany sympathetically traces Lawrence's "quest for a salvationist philosophy" from 1914 to 1918. The conclusion that Lawrence's desire for intense personal relationships resulted from his effort to break away from a smothering homeland is well supported and scrupulously documented.

Moore, Harry T. *The Priest of Love: A Life of D. H. Lawrence.* New York: Farrar, Straus and Giroux, 1974. The basis for the 1981 feature film, this biography provides neither critical discussion nor documentation of the many citations from Lawrence's works and correspondence, matters left to Moore's *D. H. Lawrence: His Life and Works* (2nd edition. New York: Twayne, 1964), which relies heavily on the restatement of biographical material. In *The Priest of Love* Moore contends that Lawrence's "prophetic" aspect is tripartite, involving a dubious mysticism, a common-sense condemnation of machine-age pollution, and, most authentic, according to Moore, a celebration of "blood-knowledge" to "bring about that balance which life needs."

Nehls, Edward, *D. H. Lawrence: A Composite Biography.* 3 vols. Madison: University of Wisconsin Press, 1957–1959. Nehl's work fulfills his intention of creating "both autobiography and biography, a blend of Lawrence's life as he himself and others saw it," without editorial commentary. The 1500 pages of text include autobiography, essays, letters, memoirs, and interviews, many either produced especially for the work or available earlier solely in out-of-print editions, and in only a few cases was Nehls forced to cite passages from Lawrence's fiction as autobiography. Nehls' biographical glossary of "The Lawrence Circle" and his table of major first editions have not been superseded materially by subsequent research. The portrait of Lawrence that emerges from this complex mosaic of memoirs is suited precisely to the idiosyncracies of its subject, reflecting a multifaceted man and artist and standing alone as the most complete biography of Lawrence to date.

Sagar, Keith, *The Life of D. H. Lawrence: An Illustrated Biography.* New York: Pantheon, 1980. One of the shortest of Lawrence's biographies, this nonetheless is useful to both specialists and general readers. This is an album sifted from Lawrence's copious correspondence and cemented with knowledgable narrative, comfortably conversational in tone. Many of the 165 photographs and documents are reproduced here for the first time. Based solidly on the comprehensive research that makes Sagar's previous volume, *D. H. Lawrence: A Calendar of His Works* (Austin: University of Texas Press, 1979) a gold mine for scholars, *The Life of D. H. Lawrence* reveals Lawrence's considerable human warmth, too often hidden beneath his strident jeremiads against the evils of modern civilization and the alleged pornography of his fiction, poetry, and paintings. While consistently allowing the well-known contradictions of Lawrence's personality to appear, Sagar, like Nehls, achieves a paradoxical unity of impression, the man in the blood of the artist, the artist at the heart of the man.

Autobiographical Sources

Shortly before his death, Lawrence made several unsuccessful attempts at what Edward McDonald, editor of *Phoenix: The Posthumous Papers of D. H. Lawrence* (New York: Viking, 1936), calls "a straightforward and extended account of his life." The nineteen-page untitled "autobiographical fragment" which closes *Phoenix* seems the first draft of what might have been a healing self-revelatory work, had Lawrence lived to finish it. This literary return to his youth thirty years before affords Lawrence a springboard for reflections on the death he was then awaiting as his ultimate adventure. Combining the mysticism of his *Last Poems* and *The Man Who Died* with the earthiness of the once-sensual miner he by now had accepted as his spiritual as well as physical father, this fragment stands as Lawrence's largest effort at autobiography, although his vital experience is inseparable from everything that he wrote.

Phoenix also contains other autobiographical essays. "Adolf" and "Rex," pet sketches, yield a far more sympathetic view of Lawrence's father than does *Sons and Lovers.* "Nottingham and the Mining Countryside" recalls his revulsion at the industrial devastation of what he called "the country of my heart." Like his four travel books, Lawrence's posthumous travel sketches often reveal his emotional and physical responses to the "spirits of place" he keenly sensed. "New Mexico" demonstrates Lawrence's recognition of "the oldest religion" he encountered there and sustained as his hope for regenerate man.

Phoenix II: Uncollected, Unpublished and Other Prose Works by D. H. Lawrence (New York: Viking, 1968) contains "Return to Bestwood," a thinly-disguised autobiographical sketch lacking the mystical element of the *Phoenix* fragment; "On Coming Home," an account of Lawrence's bitter return visit to the England that had spurned him; and two brief untitled autobiographical sketches, one for his agency, Curtis Brown, and the other published in 1929. Still other essays record his experiences as a young teacher in Croydon and the early days of his relationship with Frieda. All typify the intensity which Lawrence brought to experience and contribute essential figures to the tapestry of his artistic works. However, while his novels, stories, plays and poems also incontrovertibly spring directly from his life, they ought never to be accepted as literal recreations of it. To do so would be to deny Lawrence the literary genius he called his "demon," realizing the potential for pain and glory with which it would grace him throughout his life and art.

Overview of Critical Sources

Initially accused of promulgating obscenity in his works, Lawrence has become widely known for what T. S. Eliot called "fitful and profound insights" into human behavior. After the censorship trials of *Lady Chatterley's Lover*, Lawrence's literary reputation fell to its nadir during the 1940's, but subsequently critics have begun to observe his strongly religious, though hardly traditionally Christian orientation, and the estimate of his artistry mounts steadily. While worldwide a burgeoning body of scholarship accepts Lawrence as one of the major literary figures of the century, critical approaches to his *oeuvre* differ sharply. Most agree, however, that Lawrence's passionately subjective vision affords a unique and powerful affirmation of life.

Evaluation of Selected Criticism

Hough, Graham, *The Dark Sun: A Study of D. H. Lawrence.* New York: Macmillan, 1957. Still one of the most valuable studies of Lawrence as an artist, this assesses nine novels as manifestations of his prophetic aspect, and closes with an unsurpassed resumé of his philosophical doctrine.

Jarrett-Kerr, Martin [Father William Tiverton], *D. H. Lawrence and Human Existence.* rev. ed. London: Rockliff, 1961. Jarrett-Kerr approaches Lawrence's artistic growth "specifically from a Christian angle" and traces the development of a religious impulse unconventionally but perceptibly akin to Christianity.

Leavis, F. R. *D. H. Lawrence: Novelist.* New York: Alfred A. Knopf, 1956. This may be the most controversial study of Lawrence's works. Leavis, in the 1930's one of the first and most outspoken of Lawrence's proponents, later tempered his estimates of certain pieces, but consistently intended "to win clear recognition for the nature of Lawrence's greatness" and largely succeeded, influencing a generation of Lawrence scholars through his insistence on Lawrence's basically religious approach to modern social issues.

Sagar, Keith, *The Art of D. H. Lawrence.* Cambridge: Cambridge University Press, 1966. Sagar's "spiritual-artistic biography" chronologically develops the symbiosis of Lawrence's life and his art. The work includes comprehensive bibliographies and thorough documentation. Unlike too many of Lawrence's critics, Sagar escapes the temptation of accepting his works *in toto* as autobiography.

Sanders, Scott, *D. H. Lawrence: The World of Five Major Novels.* New York: Viking, 1974. Sanders perceptively explores the clash of "nature and culture" which he believes underlies Lawrence's social, political, religious, and aesthetic thought. The concluding essay probes the impact of the tensions between "literary consciousness and social reality" on Lawrence's evolving concept of the novel.

Other Sources

Carswell, Catherine, *The Savage Pilgrimage: A Narrative of D. H. Lawrence.* New York: Harcourt, 1932. A sympathetic memoir whose title has become a metaphor for Lawrence's life.

Ravagli, Frieda Lawrence, *"Not I, But the Wind . . ."* New York: Viking, 1934. Frieda's account of her life with Lawrence.

Rice, Thomas Jackson, *D. H. Lawrence: A Guide to Research.* New York: Garland, 1983. Useful annotated primary and secondary bibliographies.

Sagar, Keith, *A D. H. Lawrence Handbook.* New York: Barnes and Noble, 1982. Invaluable collection of biographical references, including Rose Marie Burwell's revised catalog of Lawrence's known reading, Sagar's Lawrence travel calendar, and chronologies.

Schorer, Mark, "The Life of D. H. Lawrence," in *D. H. Lawrence.* New York: Dell, 1968. Succinct location of major works in biographical context.

Selected Dictionaries and Encyclopedias

Cambridge Guide to English Literature, Cambridge University Press, 1983. Biographical sketch, overview of works, and evaluation of literary achievement.

Critical Survey of Long Fiction, Salem Press, 1983. Brief biography and concise analysis of several novels.

Critical Survey of Poetry, Salem Press, 1984. Brief biography and a discussion of Lawrence's poetry.

Critical Survey of Short Fiction, Salem Press, 1981. Brief biography and analysis of Lawrence's best-known short fiction.

Mitzi M. Brunsdale
Mayville State College

LAYAMON
fl. 1200

Author's Chronology

Born sometime in the 12th century, precise date unknown, the son of Leovenath; serves as a priest in the parish church at Areley Regis located near the Severn River in Worchestershire; c. *1189–1205* writes the *Brut;* date of death unknown.

Author's Bibliography

Layamon's Brut, ed. Sir Frederic Madden, 1847; *Arthurian Chronicles: Wace and Layamon,* tr. Eugene Mason, 1912; *Layamon: Brut,* ed. G. L. Brook and R. F. Leslie, 1963, 1978.

Overview of Biographical Sources

Scholars know little about Layamon's life other than what he reveals in the opening lines of the *Brut,* his Arthurian verse chronicle. Indeed, the absence of historical documentation combined with the limited autobiographical information makes an extended biography of Layamon virtually impossible. No book-length life of Layamon exists, and there is little likelihood that one will ever be written. J. S. P. Tatlock in *The Legendary History of Britain* (Berkeley: University of California Press, 1950) does suggest that perhaps Layamon was born in Ireland and returned with his family to Worchestershire, thereby explaining the poet's surprising knowledge of Irish matters. Although skillfully constructed, Tatlock's theory has not won wide critical acceptance. The author of the *Brut* continues to remain a problem for biographers.

Autobiographical Sources

In the beginning of the *Brut* Layamon reveals his name—in one manuscript Layamon and in the other Lawman, its cognate; his father's name, Leovenath; his occupation, priest; his parish, Areley Regis; his pleasure, reading books. These introductory comments along with a few other personal admissions comprise Layamon's autobiographical efforts. From this sparse store of information, researchers have been able to construct a pair of theories establishing dates of composition between 1189 and 1205.

Yet even what Layamon chooses to tell us must be approached with caution. His list of sources employed in the *Brut* is faulty, and he apparently confuses the authors of the texts he cites. With no other documentary evidence to assist them, scholars have combed through the *Brut* for signs of the man behind the poem. They have found evidence of the author's likes, dislikes, and interests. These personal revelations—most uncharacteristic for a medieval author—

illustrate Layamon's unusual stock of nautical knowledge, his familiarity with Ireland, his love of nature, and his primitive, bloodthirsty streak.

Overview of Critical Sources

Although scholars praise his artistry, Layamon continues to be neglected by the reading public. This unpopularity may be due in part to the difficulty of understanding the language in which Layamon wrote as well as the misapprehension that his *Brut* is a slavish translation of Wace's *Roman de Brut* rather than a creative expansion. In addition, the lack of a complete, modern edition has made the study of the poem more difficult. Madden's definitive edition of the *Brut* was published in 1847, and the final volume of Brook and Leslie's new edition (over twenty years in progress) is still patiently awaited. Critical studies have branched into three areas: general poetic evaluations, metrical studies, and source studies. In addition, there is some interest in Layamon by scholars writing on the tale of King Lear, whose story is first recorded in English in the *Brut*. Efforts to encourage study of Layamon's art have occurred sporadically, and though he has been acknowledged by Wyld as the greatest English poet between the Anglo-Saxon period and Chaucer, critical attention remains scanty.

Evaluation of Selected Criticism

Gillespy, Frances Lytle, *Layamon's Brut, a Comparative Study of Narrative Art*. Berkeley: University of California, 1916. This early comparative study of Layamon and Wace continues to be of value. Gillespy analyzes Layamon and Wace independently in order to focus attention on Layamon's superior narrative power.

Ringbom, Hakan, *Studies in the Narrative Technique of Beowulf and Lawman's Brut*. Abo, Finland: Acta Academiae Aboensis Humaniora Series A, 1968. Ringbom's monograph notes that Layamon employs "loosely structured recurrent phrases," rather than the traditional Anglo-Saxon poetic formula. His careful analysis also covers themes and narrative devices found in the *Brut*.

Tatlock, J. S. P. *The Legendary History of Britain*. Berkeley: University of California Press, 1950. Tatlock's chapter devoted to Layamon presents the clearest summary of critical attitudes on the poet. In addition to suggesting a possible birth in Ireland for Layamon, Tatlock advances 1189–1199 as the period of composition for the *Brut* rather than 1205. Tatlock contributes a number of interesting theories on the poet's knowledge of nautical matters and the Welch tradition.

Other Sources

Friedlander, Carolynn VanDyke, "The First English Story of King Lear: Layamon's *Brut*, Lines 1488–1877," in *Allegorica 3* (1978), 42–76. Useful introduction and analysis precede this translation of the Lear story from the *Brut*.

Loomis, Roger Sherman, "Layamon's *Brut*," in *Arthurian Literature in the Middle Ages* Oxford: Clarendon Press, 1959. A concise overview of Layamon's life and work.

Tatlock, J. S. P. "Layamon's Poetic Style and its Relations," in *The Manly Anniversary Studies.* Chicago: University of Chicago Press, 1923. A readable study identifying the *Brut's* poetic style as popular, rather than classical Anglo-Saxon in nature.

Wyld, Henry C. "Layamon as an English Poet," in *Review of English Studies,* 6 (1930), 1–30. An enthusiastic summary of Layamon's poetic achievements.

Selected Dictionaries and Encyclopedias
Critical Survey of Poetry, Vol. 4, Salem Press, 1982. A short biography coupled with a general evaluation and analysis makes this introduction to Layamon's life and work quite useful.

Dictionary of National Biography, Vol. 11, Oxford University Press, 1885–1900. A brief introduction to Layamon and the *Brut.*

Kenneth B. Grant
University of Wisconsin Center
Baraboo/Sauk County

SHERIDAN LE FANU
1814–1873

Author's Chronology

Born August 28, 1814, Dublin, Ireland to a Huguenot family; *1826* family moves to Abington, county Limerick; tutored by his father, Philip, a noted clergyman; *1837* graduates with honors in classics from Trinity College, Dublin; *1839* called to the Irish bar but never practices law; *1841* becomes owner and editor of *The Warder; 1844* marries Susan Bennett, a union that produces two sons and two daughters; *1851* returns to Dublin; *1858* wife dies, begins a life of seclusion; *1861* becomes proprietor and editor of the *Dublin University magazine;* February 7, 1873, dies of heart disease in his home at Merrion Square, Dublin.

Author's Bibliography (selected)

The Cock and Anchor, 1845 (novel); *The Fortunes of Colonel Torlogh O'Brien,* 1847 (novel); *Ghost Stories and Tales of Mystery,* 1851 (stories); *The House by the Churchyard,* 1863 (novel); *Wylder's Hand,* 1864 (novel); *Uncle Silas,* 1864 (novel); *Guy Deverell,* 1865 (novel); *All in the Dark,* 1866 (novel); *The Tenants of Malory,* 1867 (novel); *A Lost Name,* 1868 (novel); *The Wyvern Mystery,* 1869 (novel); *Checkmate,* 1871 (novel); *The Rose and the Key,* 1871 (novel); *Chronicles of Golden Friars,* 1871 (stories); *In a Glass Darkly,* 1872 (stories); *Morley Court,* 1873 (novel); *Willing to Die,* 1873 (novel); *The Purcell Papers,* 1880 (stories); *The Poems of Sheridan LeFanu,* 1896.

Overview of Biographical Sources

Among the most prolific of Victorian authors, Sheridan LeFanu is known to most modern readers only as the author of "Carmilla," a vampire tale second in reputation to Dracula and certainly one of the most frequently anthologized ghost stories in English. A recluse by choice during the most productive years of his literary career, this author of one famous work and volumes that deserve greater fame has attracted little biographical interest. Of course, brief essays including summaries of the life are commonly included as introductions to the several available story collections. Devendra P. Varma's introduction to *The Collected Works of Joseph Sheridan LeFanu* (New York: Arno Press, 1977), the only complete edition of LeFanu's published works, is one of the more thorough such studies. While LeFanu's fiction is largely unknown to modern readers, it is the fiction rather than the life that has received the greater scholarly attention. There are biographical-critical studies, but the emphasis is so overwhelming on the critical that those works are treated later under the appropriate heading. Certainly the major biography is W. J. McCormack's *Sheridan LeFanu and Victorian Ireland* (1980). McCormack draws from the major manuscript collections in Great Britain and the United States to present the most detailed account of the life yet to appear.

Evaluation of Selected Biographies

McCormack, W. J. *Sheridan LeFanu and Victorian Ireland.* Oxford: Oxford University Press, 1980. Unlike the several introductions and chapters that relate the facts of LeFanu's life, McCormack's biography examines the author and his works in the context of nineteenth-century Anglo-Irish society. McCormack's LeFanu is a man at conflict with himself. As a member of an upper-middle class, protestant family, he was loyal to the values of his class, values which included the rightness of the union and British rule. Still, on a personal level, he was keenly aware of the ultimate isolation of his order in an Ireland defined by nationalism and social change. The susceptibility to corruption of individuals isolated in their own narrow understanding of what is important and real is the major theme of LeFanu's finest fiction. McCormack's discussions of the works can certainly stand on their own as insightful introductions to particular works, but the unique contribution of this biography is its tightly unified presentation of a body of literature as the product of a life which is itself a product of a time and place.

Overview of Critical Sources

Considering the growth of interest in supernatural or occult literature, it is not surprising that more attention has been paid to the works of the creator of such classics as "Carmilla" and "Green Tea" than to the efforts of forgotten Victorians who chose less popular genres. Several anthologies are introduced with critical commentary. Especially helpful is E. F. Bleiler's introduction to *Best Ghost Stories of J. S. LeFanu* (1964). Nelson Browne's *Sheridan LeFanu* (London: Arthur Barker, Ltd., 1951) is a book-length study that includes a brief biography but concentrates on summaries and discussions of the major works; general, it is still a fine overview and a good starting point for students. *Joseph Sheridan LeFanu* by Michael H. Begnal (Lewisburg: Bucknell University Press, 1971) presents three essays which examine the author in relation to the gothic tradition and then focus on his achievement in particular novels. LeFanu's contribution to the horror genre is treated with considerable insight by Jack Sullivan in *Elegant Nightmares: The English Ghost Story from LeFanu to Blackwood* (1978).

Evaluation of Selected Criticism

Bleiler, E. F. ed. *Best Ghost Stories of J. S. LeFanu.* New York: Dover, 1964. Bleiler's introduction to this readily available collection of LeFanu's finest stories presents a brief but perceptive evaluation that focuses on the author as psychologist. Bleiler argues that for LeFanu, supernatural manifestations were more than mere catalysts for adventure. The mind of the victim is as central to the fiction as the apparition itself, and the conflict of the two allows the author to explore facets of the human personality.

Sullivan, Jack, *Elegant Nightmares: The English Ghost Story from LeFanu to Blackwood.* Athens: Ohio University Press, 1978. Sullivan shows LeFanu to be a most careful craftsman in the evocation of horror. His stage is the readers' world of assumed realities, and his characters' lives are neatly ordered to extract from that reality whatever comfort is available. Then somthing intrudes that replaces the old assumptions with doubt, and as the evidence of chaos become undeniable, order and comfort collapse into insanity and horror.

Other Sources

Summers, Montagne, *The Vampire, His Kith and Kin.* New Hyde Park: University Books, 1960. Summers' discussion of literary vampires cites "Carmilla" as the best vampire tale in English.

Selected Dictionaries and Encyclopedias

Critical Survey of Long Fiction, Salem Press, 1983. Analysis of the major novels and a brief account of the life.

Great Writers of the English Language: Novelists and Prose Writers, St. Martin's Press, 1979. A list of LeFanu's works and a brief but insightful critical statement.

William J. Heim
University of South Florida

C. S. LEWIS
1898-1963

Author's Chronology

Born Clive Staples Lewis November 29, 1898, Belfast, Northern Ireland of Irish parents; *1908* mother dies; *1910-1913* Lewis and brother sent to schools in Malvern, England; *1916* wins scholarship to University College, Oxford; *1917-1918* serves in army as Second Lieutenant in light infantry; *1919* publishes book of poetry, *Spirits in Bondage* under pseudonym Clive Hamilton; *1919-1924* resumes residence at Oxford; *1925* elected to fellowship in English Language and Literature at Magdalen College, Oxford; *1926* publishes *Dymer;* *1929* conversion to Christianity; *1936* publishes *Allegory of Love,* winning Gollancz Award and establishing himself as medieval scholar; *1941* presents "Broadcast Talks on Christianity," later published as *Mere Christianity; 1942* publishes *The Screwtape Letters; 1950* publishes *The Lion, the Witch and the Wardrobe; 1955* accepts Professorship of Medieval and Renaissance Literature at Magdalene College, Cambridge; publishes *Surprised by Joy; 1956* marries Joy Davidman; *1960* Joy Davidman dies; *1963* dies November 22.

Author's Bibliography (selected)

Spirits in Bondage, 1919 (poem); *The Pilgrim's Regress,* 1933 (autobiographical allegory); *The Allegory of Love,* 1936 (criticism); *Out of the Silent Planet,* 1938 (science-fiction novel); *The Screwtape Letters,* 1942 (theology); *The Lion, the Witch and the Wardrobe,* 1950 (children's fiction); *Mere Christianity,* 1952 (theology); *Surprised by Joy,* 1955 (autobiography); *Till We Have Faces,* 1956 (novel); *A Grief Observed,* 1961 (pseudonymous autobiography); *Letters to Malcolm,* 1962 (theology).

Overview of Biographical Sources

There remains to be written a substantial, definitive biography of Lewis. The first and only major attempt at a biography of Lewis is Roger Lancelyn Green and Walter Hooper's *C. S. Lewis: A Biography* (1974). This biography was co-written by two associates of Lewis, Green, a long-time friend and fellow writer, and Hooper, personal secretary to Lewis for a brief period at the end of Lewis's life. Notebooks, manuscripts, photographs, holograph letters, the eleven unpublished volumes of the *Lewis Papers: Memoirs of the Lewis Family 1850-1930,* and the unexpurgated diary of Warren Lewis (brother of C. S.), await a future biographer at the Marion C. Wade Collection at Wheaton College. A few collections of letters and reminiscences which provide valuable biographical information have been published. *The Letters of C. S. Lewis* (New York: Harcourt, Brace and World, 1966), edited and selected by his brother Warren and *They Stand Together: The Letters of C. S. Lewis to Arthur Greeves*

(New York: Macmillan, 1979), edited by Walter Hooper, provide candid glimpses of the younger Lewis as well as the prolific, older Lewis who carried on an enormous load of correspondence with his readers. *C. S. Lewis at the Breakfast Table* (New York: Macmillan, 1979), edited by James Como, is an informative collection of reminiscences by people who knew Lewis well.

Evaluation of Selected Biographies

Carpenter, Humphrey, *The Inklings*. Boston: Houghton Mifflin, 1979. Carpenter's work is a rich tapestry which explores the relationships of the "Inklings": Lewis, J. R. R. Tolkien, Charles Williams and their circle of literary associates at Oxford during the 1930's and 1940's. While the work deals with each of these men and their achievements, Lewis emerges as the focal point of the work. Based on a number of unpublished sources, this volume is particularly valuable for its evocation of the conversation and atmosphere of the Inklings in their weekly meetings during the war years. This is the most personal look at Lewis the man.

Green, Roger Lancelyn and Walter Hooper, *C. S. Lewis: A Biography*. New York: Harcourt, Brace, Jovanovich, 1974. This biography, written by a long-time Lewis protégé and Lewis's personal secretary, is an uneven compilation of facts, dates and personal sketches which fails to capture the breadth and depth of Lewis's life and literary career. The book presents information accurately and chronologically, but is oddly dispassionate and matter-of-fact when discussing areas of Lewis's life about which there is great public interest and enthusiasm. This volume captures none of the vitality or exuberance which Lewis's own works evince.

Lindskoog, Kathryn, *C. S. Lewis: Mere Christian*. Downers Grove: Inter-Varsity Press, 1981. This modest but compelling work gives the reader an accurate and succinct overview of Lewis's life and work, covering both the essentials of his biography and the main patterns of his thought on literature, science, religion and education.

Autobiographical Sources

Lewis recounted his conversion from atheism to Christianity in a whimsical allegory published in 1933, *The Pilgrim's Regress*. Parodying the Bunyan classic, *The Pilgrim's Progress*, Lewis takes his hero through a series of adventures which parallels his own flight from skepticism to committed Christian faith. The work is, however, fairly inaccessible to those who are not already familiar with the broad outline of Lewis's life and is useful only as a commentary for the initiated.

A more accessible document is Lewis's *Surprised by Joy*, a vivid and candid account of his early years which takes the reader through Lewis's childhood to his conversion to Christianity. It is primarily a spiritual autobiography and focuses little on Lewis's relationships with family and friends. It is the recounting of one individual's journey from religious skepticism to vibrant religious faith. Another autobiographical volume, *A Grief Observed,* originally published by Lewis under the pseudonym, N. W. Clerk, is a poignant account of Lewis's devastation at the death of his wife, Joy, and provides insights into the mature Lewis's understanding of faith and doubt.

In addition to these sources, Lewis's critical works often reveal his personal disposition toward the modern world which unfavorably compares the technologized 20th century to the less jaded medieval and renaissance civilizations. Lewis never hid his distaste for most of what may be called "modern," lashing out against what he called the "chronological snobbery" of his times.

Overview of Critical Sources

The last two decades have seen an explosion of interest in Lewis, both for his fiction and for his theological writings. Lewis has become particularly and spectacularly well-known as a writer of children's fiction through his Narnian stories and much critical attention has been turned as well toward his mythopoeic works such as *Till We Have Faces* and *Perelandra* (1944). While there is a growing body of criticism assessing individual works of Lewis and a large number of volumes devoted to an analysis of his Christian apologetics, there is still no single book length critical study that provides scholars with a systematic treatment of the entire *ouevre.*

Evaluation of Selected Criticism

Carnell. Corbin Scott, *Bright Shadow of Reality: C. S. Lewis and the Feeling Intellect.* Grand Rapids: Eerdmans, 1974. Carnell's study is an exegesis of the concept of *sehnsucht,* or "joy," in Lewis's fiction and apologetics. This work contains one of the most helpful treatments of the relationship between Lewis's religious faith and his fiction and criticism.

Hannay, Margaret P. *C. S. Lewis.* New York: Frederick Ungar, 1981. Hannay presents a general bio-critical introduction to Lewis's life and works, discussing in equal depth Lewis's science-fiction, Narnian Chronicles, apologetics, criticism and poetry. Hannay provides basic plot summaries of each of his prose works and her evaluation of Lewis's criticism and literature is admirably balanced and fair.

Howard, Thomas, *The Achievement of C. S. Lewis.* Wheaton: Harold Shaw, 1980. Howard's work deals exclusively with Lewis's seven Narnian tales, his three science-fiction novels, and his work of myth, *Till We Have Faces,* in an evocative, enlightening critical reading of each work. This should be the first work consulted by anyone seeking to understand the impulse behind and broad themes of Lewis's fiction.

Kreeft, Peter, *C. S. Lewis: A Critical Essay.* Grand Rapids: Eerdmans, 1969. An early pamphlet about Lewis which nevertheless contains more insights per page than most book-length studies. Kreeft discusses Lewis's fiction and apologetics works primarily.

Lindskoog, Kathryn, *The Lion of Judah in Never-Never Land.* Grand Rapids: Eerdmans, 1973. This full-length study of Lewis's seven Narnian tales explains the theology and Biblical allusions which form the underlying structure of these children's novels.

Schakel, Peter, *Reason and Imagination in C. S. Lewis: A Study of Till We Have Faces.* Grand Rapids: Eerdmans, 1984. Schakel's work is the most thoroughgoing treatment of reason and imagination in the work of Lewis, two concepts always in tension in his work. It consists of two parts. The first part, "the work itself," presents a masterful exegesis of Lewis's most difficult work, *Till We Have Faces;* the second part, "the work in context," offers an extended analysis of Lewis's critical theory and practice chronologically ordered.

Other Sources

Gibb, Jocelyn, *Light on C. S. Lewis.* New York: Harcourt, Brace and World, 1965. An anthology of essays by Lewis's contemporaries which examine him as a teacher, theologian, novelist and poet.

Holmer, Paul L. *C. S. Lewis: The Shape of His Faith and Thought.* New York: Harper and Row, 1976. Holmer, a Yale philosopher, analyzes the philosophical and theological underpinnings of Lewis's fiction, criticism and apologetics.

Schakel, Peter, *Reading with the Heart: The Way into Narnia.* Grand Rapids: Eerdmans, 1979. A helpful introduction to the Narnian tales.

Smith, Robert H. *Patches of Godlight: The Pattern of Thought of C. S. Lewis.* Athens: University of Georgia Press, 1981. Survey of Lewis's theological thinking as it informs his writing.

Selected Dictionaries and Encyclopedias

Critical Survey of Long Fiction, Salem Press, 1984, Vol. 4. Analysis of *Out of the Silent Planet, Perelandra, That Hideous Strength, Till We Have Faces,* and the Narnian fables.

Bruce L. Edwards, Jr.
Bowling Green State University

MATTHEW GREGORY "MONK" LEWIS
1775–1818

Author's Chronology

Born July 9, 1775, London, England; *1780* enters preparatory school, Marlebone Seminary; *1781* parents separate; *1790* enters Christ Church, Oxford; *1792* travels to Weimar to study German; *1793* returns to Oxford; *1794* takes bachelor's degree; joins the staff of the British embassy, The Hague; *1796* publishes *The Monk* anonymously; enters Parliament; *1812* father dies; inherits considerable fortune and property; *1815* visits his estates in Jamaica; *1816* returns to England; *1817* visits Lord Byron and Percy Bysshe Shelley in Italy; returns to Jamaica; May 16, 1818, dies on board ship of yellow fever; buried at sea.

Author's Bibliography (selected)

The Monk: A Romance, 1796 (novel); *The Castle Spectre,* 1798 (drama); *Alfonso, King of Castile,* 1801 (drama); *The Bravo of Venice: A Romance,* 1805 (novel); *Feudal Tyrants: or, The Counts of Carlsheim and Sargans: A Romance,* 1806 (novel); *Poems,* 1812; *Journal of a West India Proprietor, Kept During a Residence in the Island of Jamaica,* 1834 (autobiography).

Overview of Biographical Sources

Much more attention has been paid to the character of Matthew Gregory Lewis than to his life. Critics have reasoned that the author of so shocking a work as *The Monk* must himself be a devil, or the author of so enlightened a work as the *Journal of a West India Proprietor, Kept During a Residence in the Island of Jamaica* must be a saint. For more than a century, the standard biographical source was Mrs. Cornwell Baron-Wilson's *The Life and Correspondence of M. G. Lewis* (London: Henry Colburn, 1839). A loyal member of the saint school of Lewis biographers, Mrs. Baron-Wilson conveyed her enthusiastic appreciation better than she reported accurate facts. Still, her inclusion of significant amounts of unpublished autobiographical materials makes this an important contribution to the knowledge of Lewis's life. The definitive biography is Louis F. Peck's *A Life of Matthew G. Lewis* (1961). Peck, too, includes a great number of previously unpublished letters, but unlike Mrs. Baron-Wilson's, his text reflects a scholar's concern for accuracy.

Evaluation of Selected Biographies

Irwin, Joseph James, *M. G. "Monk" Lewis.* Boston: Twayne, 1976. Irwin's bio-critical study is a well-organized and clearly written account of Lewis and his works. The works, despite the tremendous influence of *The Monk,* fall short of greatness. Lewis borrowed the conventions of the Gothic tale, added a few new ones that later writers would borrow, and expressed it all in the stilted language expected in the fiction of his day. If the works are good but not great, the author, as Irwin presents him, was anything but conventional, and in his efforts to improve the lot of his Jamaican slaves achieved a genuine human greatness. Irwin's chapter on the Jamaican journal is longer than his chapter on *The Monk*, which may be appropriate for a biography, for it is the former that reveals what Samuel Taylor Coleridge called "a not inconsiderable man."

Peck, Louis F. *A Life of Matthew G. Lewis*. Cambridge: Harvard University Press, 1961. In this, the standard biography, Peck corrects the inaccuracies of Lewis's early biographer, Mrs. Cornwell Baron-Wilson. Peck's objective, but very readable, presentation of the facts strips away the misconceptions created on the one hand by Mrs. Baron-Wilson's enthusiasm, and on the other by generations of hostile critics. Peck writes with no motive to make his subject more or less than he was. Ninety pages of Lewis' own letters added to an informative text provide readers ample material from which to draw their own conclusions.

Autobiographical Sources

Unpublished until after his death, Lewis's *Journal of a West India Proprietor, Kept During a Residence in the Island of Jamaica* has been viewed by several critics as the outstanding achievement of his career. The vivid descriptions of life on a slave plantation enlivened with dialogue and song lyrics make this a work of genuine literary merit. Sincerely concerned for the well-being and advancement of the people who had become his possessions, Lewis can be seen as representative of the ideals of freedom and individual human dignity that are commonly associated with the Romantic movement. This significant auto-biography has been reprinted in an edited text with an introduction by Mona Wilson (New York: Houghton Mifflin, 1929).

Overview of Critical Sources

As one of the most famous Gothic novels in English, *The Monk* is of course discussed, however briefly, in virtually every book about horror, terror, and the supernatural in literature. Among the best of these short treatments is found in Devendra P. Varma's *The Gothic Flame* (New York: Russell and Russell, 1957). Varma points out Lewis's fondness for graphic horror rather than subtle terror, an observation also treated by Edith Birkhead in *The Tale of Terror* (New York: Russell and Russell, 1963). Book-length studies of a clearly critical rather than bio-critical thrust are few. Lewis's efforts to leave so little to the readers' imaginations seem to have left little for the critics to note that is not obvious to all.

Evaluation of Selected Criticism

Conger, Syndy, *Matthew G. Lewis, Charles Robert Maturin and the Germans: An Interpretative Study of the Influence of German Literature on Two Gothic*

Novels. Salzburg: Institut für Englische Sprache und Literatur, 1977. In this carefully researched and scholarly study, Conger examines the influence of the German Storm and Stress authors on English Gothic fiction. The early English criticism of *The Monk* lamented the corrupting influence of the continent; Conger considers this question of influence objectively and identifies what is sometimes valid and sometimes misunderstood in these old critical assumptions.

Parreaux, André, *The Publication of The Monk: A Literary Event 1796–1798.* Paris: Librairie Marcel Didier, 1960. The publication of perhaps no other English novel created such controversy as the appearance of *The Monk.* Quoting extensively from contemporary sources, Parreaux presents and analyzes the many attacks, viewing them in the context of late eighteenth-century political, religious, and social concerns. This interesting study is a valuable source for students of Lewis and the history of criticism as well.

Other Sources

Evans, Bertrand, *Gothic Drama from Walpole to Shelley.* Los Angeles: University of California Press, 1947. An examination of Lewis's plays.

Summers, Montagne, *The Gothic Quest: A History of the Gothic Novel.* London: Fortune Press, 1938. The chapter on Lewis in this classic study is still an excellent introduction to the author and his works.

Wolf, Leonard, *A Dream of Dracula: In Search of the Living Dead.* Boston: Little, Brown, 1972. A brief discussion presenting *The Monk* as an attempt of the adolescent mind to give order to the dark dream fragments thrown into the consciousness by the yet undeveloped and misunderstood sexual urge.

Selected Dictionaries and Encyclopedias

Critical Survey of Long Fiction, Salem Press, 1983. A brief biographical summary and a critical overview of Lewis's achievement.

Great Writers of the English Language: Novelists and Prose Writers, St. Martin's Press, 1979. An author's biography and a brief critical note.

William J. Heim
University of South Florida

SINCLAIR LEWIS
1885-1957

Author's Chronology

Born Harry Sinclair Lewis, on February 7, 1885 in Sauk Centre, Minnesota, the third son of Dr. Edwin J. and Emma Kermott Lewis; *1891* mother dies; *1892* father marries Isabel Warner; attends public schools in Sauk Centre, reading voraciously but indiscriminantly; *1898* runs away from home to enlist in Spanish American War as drummer boy, but father locates him in nearby town and brings him home; *1901* writes local news stories and does odd jobs on Sauk Centre newspapers *Herald* and *Avalanche; 1902* enters Oberlin Academy in Ohio to prepare for entrance into Yale University; *1903* enrolls at Yale; *1906* leaves Yale to spend several months at Upton Sinclair's Utopian Colony in Englewood, New Jersey; later spends time in New York City working as a free lance writer and editor; *1907* returns to Yale and receives a degree in June, 1908; *1908-1910* roams United States, holding various odd jobs and selling short story plots to Jack London; *1910-1915* holds a number of positions in New York City connected with publishing, editing and writing; *1912* publishes first novel; *1914* marries Grace Hegger in New York City; *1915* quits work to become full time writer; *1917* a son, Wells Lewis is born; *1921* after publication of *Main Street,* lectures to sizeable audiences with considerable publicity; *1923* collects material for *Arrowsmith,* writing novel in France and revising it in London; *1924* returns to United States and spends summer with brother, Claude; *1926* refuses Pulitzer prize for *Arrowsmith;* father dies; *1928* divorces Grace Hegger Lewis and marries Dorothy Thompson in England; buys farm at Barnard, Vermont; *1930* receives Nobel Prize for Literature, the first American to be so honored; second son, Michael, born; spends some years working in collaboration with various people on several plays including *Jayhawker, Dodsworth,* and *It Can't Happen Here; 1936* awarded Honorary Degree by Yale; makes frequent lectures during this period and is active as actor, playwright, producer, and director; *1940* teaches writing at the University of Wisconsin; *1942* divorces Dorothy Thompson and becomes special lecturer in English at the University of Minnesota; *1942-1946* makes extended trips to New York and elsewhere while living intermittently in Minnesota; *1944* first son is killed in action; *1945* buys a house in Duluth, Minnesota; *1946* moves to Storvale farm in Massachusetts near Williamstown; *1949* sails for Italy, health failing; *1951* dies January 10 in Rome of heart disease; ashes buried in Sauk Centre.

Author's Bibliography

Hike and the Aeroplane, 1912 (written under the pseudonym Tom Graham); *Our Mr. Wrenn,* 1914 (novel); *The Trail of the Hawk,* 1915 (novel); *The Job,* 1917 (novel); *The Innocents,* 1917 (novel); *Free Air,* 1919 (novel); *Main Street,*

1920 (novel); *Babbitt,* 1922 (novel); *Arrowsmith,* 1925 (novel); *ManTrap,* 1926 (novel); *Elmer Gantry,* 1927 (novel); *The Man Who Knew Coolidge,* 1928 (novel); *Dodsworth,* 1929 (novel); *Ann Vickers,* 1933 (novel); *Work of Art,* 1934 (novel); *It Can't Happen Here,* 1935 (novel); *Jayhawker,* 1935 (play); *The Prodigal Parents,* 1938 (novel); *It Can't Happen Here,* 1938 (play adaptation); *Angela Is Twenty-Two,* (unpublished manuscript of play written around 1938); *Bethel Merriday,* 1940 (novel); Gideon Planish, 1943 (novel); *Cass Timberlane,* 1945 (novel); *Kingsblood Royal,* 1947 (novel); *The God-Seeker,* 1949 (novel); *World So Wide,* 1951 (novel); *From Main Street to Stockholm: Letters of Sinclair Lewis, 1919–1930,* 1952; *The Man from Main Street:* A *Sinclair Lewis Reader,* 1953; *I'm a Stranger Here Myself and Other Stories,* selected with an introduction by Mark Schorer, 1962.

Overview of Biographical Sources

The earliest biographical works on Lewis were commissioned by Lewis' publishers. One of these, *Sinclair Lewis: A Biographical Sketch,* by Carl Van Doren (Garden City, NY: Doubleday, Doran, 1933) was for many years a major source of information. In 1951, Lewis's first wife, Grace Hegger Lewis, published a perceptive account of their life together, *With Love from Gracie: Sinclair Lewis: 1912 to 1925* (1951). The "official" biography of Lewis was written by Mark Schorer, *Sinclair Lewis: An American Life* (1961). This major work running to more than 800 pages took Schorer some ten years to write. He had the cooperation of the executors of the Sinclair Lewis estate, including the right to all literary properties belonging to the estate. In addition, he had the complete cooperation of Grace Hegger Lewis, Dorothy Thompson, and Marcella Powers, a young woman with whom Lewis formed a relationship lasting from 1938 to 1947. Another biography chronicling the life of Sinclair Lewis and Dorothy Thompson is Vincent Sheean's, *Dorothy and Red* (1963). In his book, Sheean, a friend of both Sinclair Lewis and Dorothy Thompson Lewis, is able to draw not only upon his own reminiscences, but also upon correspondence and diaries. Since Lewis' novels and stories seem more closely tied to his personal life than to an esthetic frame, most of the critical sources also make use of biographical details or provide short biographical accounts.

Evaluation of Selected Biographies

Lewis, Grace Hegger, *With Love from Gracie: Sinclair Lewis—1912–1925.* New York: Harcourt, Brace, and Company, 1951. Grace Hegger Lewis presents a perceptive account of her life with Lewis in which she confesses that she believes neither of them really knew each other and that they remained for the twelve years of their marriage heroic or mythological figures—he the courageous writer and incorruptible public figure, she a mannekin out of the medieval tradition of courtly love. The biography seems an honest attempt by a woman to understand not only the man she married but also what he became during the years of their marriage. Since her narration focuses on Lewis' early and most productive years the work has a particular poignancy and interest.

Schorer, Mark, *Sinclair Lewis: An American Life.* New York: McGraw-Hill, 1961. All in all, Mark Schorer is perhaps the most well known American critic to focus on the life and works of Sinclair Lewis in both books and articles. Schorer's biography is notable not only for its inclusiveness, but also for it's readability and its portrayal of Lewis' life and times. Although another complete biography may be written, it is doubtful that another could be so well informed, since Schorer had access not only to documents but to live people—hundreds of Lewis' contemporaries.

Sheean, Vincent, *Dorothy And Red.* Boston: Houghton Mifflin, 1963. A writer and frequent guest in the home of Sinclair Lewis and Dorothy Thompson Lewis, Sheean is able to draw from his own personal knowledge events related to his subject. Sheean makes many of the points noted earlier by Grace Hegger Lewis and by Mark Schorer: Lewis was not introspective, was incapable of subjective analysis, seemed unable to handle the decline in his powers, indulged in erratic behavior, drank too much, and never really understood either the reasons for his success or for his decline.

Autobiographical Sources

Lewis wrote no autobiography, though he reveals much about himself in his *From Main Street to Stockholm: Letters of Sinclair Lewis* (New York: Harcourt, Brace, 1952) in the essays and articles that he published throughout his life, and in various other letters collected by scholars. His letters reveal, for example, that the money and success he earned at the start of the 1920's after the success of *Main Street* were troublesome to him. He could not understand why, in spite of his achievements, he had not earned the respect from other writers that he thought he deserved. He found himself in the position of being a successful author living with the suspicion that if his books were popular, they must be aesthetically defective.

Overview of Critical Sources

All of the scholars familiar to students of early twentieth-century literature, including such giants as, B. L. Parrington, *Main Currents In American Thought* (New York: Harcourt, Brace, 1930), Malcolm Cowley, *After the Genteel Tradition* (New York: Harcourt, Brace, 1937), Herbert J. Muller, (*Modern Fiction: A Study of Values* (New York: Funk and Wagnalls, 1937), Frederick Lewis Pattee (*The New American Literature—1819–1930:* New York: Century, 1932), T. K. Whipple (*Spokesmen* New York: Appleton, 1928) commented briefly upon Lewis but in startlingly different ways. He has been seen as an American Diogines, as an emancipator of American fiction, as a rebel against older traditions, as in the American comic tradition, as superficial, as lacking in passion and thought and indulging in meretricious writing.

Evaluation of Selected Criticism

Dooley, D. J. *The Art of Sinclair Lewis.* Lincoln: University of Nebraska Press, 1967. Dooley attempts a balanced explication of Lewis and his achievements. He notes the instances of failure in artistic control and the reasons to doubt whether Lewis can handle the subjective realm of the spirit and the intellect.

Grabstein, Sheldon Norman, *Sinclair Lewis.* New York: Twayne, 1962. Although beginning with a free admission of Lewis' literary flaws, Grabstein, nevertheless, insists that Lewis is more important than we now admit. In trying to prove his thesis, Grabstein points to the apparent split in Lewis' sensibility: half of him is satirist and realist and half romancer and yea-sayer. Grabstein insists that it is this very ambivalence which makes Lewis' novels interesting both as sociological documents and as literary works of art.

Lundquist, James, *Sinclair Lewis.* New York: Frederick Ungar, 1973. Lundquist believes that there is no doubt that Lewis will have his share of enduring fame. His reputation, Lundquist states, has rested and will continue to rest on his polemics. Lewis' appeal, Lundquist believes, was wider than that of any other American writer. Lundquist says that had Lewis' novels been written any other way, had they been as tightly structured as James', for example, they would not have had the lasting effect that they have had.

Other Sources

The American Short Story—1900–1945: A Critical History. Boston: G. K. Hall, 1984. Makes the point that with Lewis a distinction must be made between what is said and how it is said. The "what" catches the imagination and has held it for half a century; the "how" embarrasses most critics, who are a small part of the reading public.

The Modern American Novel. New York: Oxford University Press, 1983. Devotes two pages to Lewis's contribution to the novel.

Mary Rohrberger
Oklahoma State University

WYNDHAM LEWIS
1882–1957

Author's Chronology

Born November 18, 1882 on yacht off Nova Scotia of English mother and American father; *1888* family moves from America to England; attends Rugby School *1897–1898* and Slade School of Art *1898–1901;* lives as artist in Paris and travels European continent *1902–1908; 1909* first stories published in *English Review; 1911–1915* involvement in English art avant-garde, culminating in leadership of Vorticist movement; *1916–1919* serves in the army during World War I; *1919–1925* resides in London, painting, reading, and writing; *1926–1930* great period of creativity as writer of fiction, philosophy, social comment, and art and literary criticism; *1930* secretly marries Gladys Anne Hoskyns; early and mid-*1930s* increasingly poor health, alienating controversies, poverty, and initial sympathy for German fascism; *1938* Royal Academy rejects his portrait of T. S. Eliot; *1939* renounces earlier support of Hitler, sails to Canada where spends most of World War II in poverty; *1945* returns to England; *1953* becomes totally blind but continues to write until his death; *1956* is awarded a retrospective exhibition of Vorticism at Tate Gallery; dies March 7, 1957.

Author's Bibliography (selected)

Blast (I and II), 1914–1915 (avant-garde art journal); *Tarr,* 1918, revised 1928 (novel); *The Art of Being Ruled,* 1926 (political and social analysis); *The Lion and the Fox,* 1927 (literary criticism); *Time and Western Man,* 1927 (philosophy and cultural analysis); *The Wild Body,* 1927 (short stories); *The Childermass,* 1928 (novel); *The Apes of God,* 1930 (novel); *Hitler,* 1931 (social criticism); *Enemy of the Stars,* 1932 (play); *One-Way Song,* 1933 (poetry); *Men Without Art,* 1934 (literary criticism); *Self Condemned,* 1954 (novel); *The Demon of Progress in the Arts,* 1954 (art criticism).

Overview of Biographical Sources

Lewis made a special point while alive to limit and control information about his life, to the extent that many of his acquaintances did not realize for many years that he was married. The earliest attempt to give an overview of Lewis's life is the opening chapter of Geoffrey Wagner's *Wyndham Lewis: A Portrait of the Artist as the Enemy* (1957), published in the year of Lewis's death. Another short overview is offered in William Pritchard's *Wyndham Lewis* (1968). The long wait for a more complete biographical treatment of Lewis ended with the publication of Jeffrey Meyers' *The Enemy: A Biography of Wyndham Lewis* (1980), the only full-length treatment of Lewis's life.

Evaluation of Selected Biographies

Meyers, Jeffrey, *The Enemy: A Biography of Wyndham Lewis.* London: Routledge & Kegan Paul, 1980. This is the only full-length biography and clearly the place to go to find the facts of Lewis's life. It is somewhat disappointing in that it does not go very far beyond the facts. It is written in an uninviting, pedestrian manner, giving too much about Lewis's activities, and too little about the shaping forces in his life, the nature of his genius, and a penetrating assessment of his work and its relation to the larger artistic and intellectual world. The biography does succeed in the difficult task of presenting a balanced yet sympathetic view of a very contentious genius whose work and conduct created both strong admirers and devoted enemies.

Pritchard, William H. *Wyndham Lewis.* New York: Twayne, 1968. Pritchard devotes ten pages and a chronology to Lewis's life. He makes factual errors (the dates of Lewis's marriage and death, for instance), but this is a good place to go for a very quick biographical summary.

Wagner, Geoffrey, *Wyndham Lewis: A Portrait of the Artist as the Enemy.* New Haven: Yale University Press, 1957. While primarily a critical book, this work begins with a cursory summary of Lewis's career. It does not give much biographical information beyond the 1920's however. The facts of Lewis's life are found in much more detail in later works, but Wagner's evaluations of Lewis's life are still worth reading.

Autobiographical Sources

Lewis wrote two autobiographical works, both good sources of information about his views and impressions, but neither particularly revealing of the private person. *Blasting and Bombardiering* (1937) is Lewis's account of his activities just before and during World War I. He gives his account of the Vorticist movement which he led, and of the other artists and writers with whom he was involved. Lewis provides some details about his own experiences in the war, on which he blames the premature end of what had been a promising time in the arts.

After the Second World War, Lewis once again tried his hand at autobiography in *Rude Assignment: A Narrative of My Career Up-to-Date* (1950). Lewis reviews his career and offers his characteristic uncompromising defense of his intellectual and artistic principles. He acknowledges his frequent battles with others but blames it on "the times" rather than on any love of controversy on his part. He readily admits to being an elitest and makes no apology for his low view of the common person (educated and otherwise) and of popular culture.

The Letters of Wyndham Lewis (1963), edited by W. K. Rose, is similar to the autobiographies as a helpful source for Lewis's characteristic values and outlooks, and give insight into some of the many struggles, artistic and otherwise, that characterized his life. Even the letters, however, are not intimate or greatly self-revealing in the usual sense.

Overview of Critical Sources

The single best introduction to Lewis remains one of the first, Hugh Kenner's *Wyndham Lewis* (1954). Another early work that is still valuable is Wagner's *Wyndham Lewis: A Portrait of the Artist as the Enemy* (1957) mentioned in the biographical section. Also mentioned there is William Pritchard's *Wyndham Lewis,* one of the earlier full-length books devoted to Lewis. Three other books, while not exclusively about Lewis, are about Vorticism, a movement in which Lewis was the most important figure and which is perhaps the single most important period in his career. These books—*Vorticism and the English Avant-Garde* (1972) by William Wees, *Vorticism and Abstract Art in the First Machine Age* (1976) by Richard Cork, and *Vortex: Pound, Eliot, and Lewis* (1979) by Timothy Materer—are important sources of information and critical insight about Lewis.

Evaluation of Selected Criticism

Cork, Richard, *Vorticism and Abstract Art in the First Machine Age.* Berkeley: University of California Press, 1976. The definitive work on Vorticism, it exhaustively explores the art aspects of the movement, setting it in the wider artistic context of the time.

Kenner, Hugh, *Wyndham Lewis.* Norfolk, CT: New Directions, 1954. Kenner sets the terms for most later Lewis criticism by focusing on his powerful sensibility and its expression in a unique style. He establishes Lewis as a major modernist figure in a study that Lewis himself thought excellent.

Materer, Timothy, *Vortex: Pound, Eliot, and Lewis.* Ithaca, NY: Cornell University Press, 1979. This work focuses more on the literary end of Vorticism than the previous two books, placing Lewis in relation to two other great modernists, Ezra Pound and T. S. Eliot.

Pritchard, William H. *Wyndham Lewis.* New York: Twayne, 1968. For the person totally unfamiliar with Lewis, Pritchard's account is the best place to begin not because it matches the originality or insight of the other critical works, but because it is the most systematic and condensed introduction to all the major aspects of his writing. One should not be content with this book, however, for anything other than an initial overview.

Wagner, Geoffrey, *Wyndham Lewis: A Portrait of the Artist as the Enemy.* New Haven: Yale University Press, 1957. Longer than Kenner's study, this early work is not clearly focused but is still full of valuable insights into specific works and into Lewis's temperament and worldview.

Wees, William, *Vorticism and the English Avant-Garde.* Toronto: University of Toronto Press, 1972. The first thorough investigation of Vorticism, it is narrowly focused but a helpful historical explanation of the movement.

Other Sources
Agenda, 7–8 (Autumn-Winter 1969–1970). A special issue devoted entirely to Lewis.

Bridson, D. G. *The Filibuster: A Study of the Political Ideas of Wyndham Lewis.* London: Cassell, 1972. Book title indicates its focus.

Chapman, Robert, *Wyndham Lewis: Fictions and Satires.* London: Vision Press, 1973. Focuses on Lewis's use of satire.

Holloway, John, *The Chartered Mirror.* London: Routledge and Kegan Paul, 1960. Contains very good chapter on Lewis.

Kenner, Hugh, *The Pound Era.* Berkeley: University of California Press, 1971. This important work places Lewis in context with other modernists.

Materer, Timothy, *Wyndham Lewis The Novelist.* Detroit, Wayne State University Press, 1976. Study of Lewis's fiction.

Michel, Walter, *Wyndham Lewis: Paintings and Drawings.* Berkeley: University of California Press, 1971. The best source for Lewis's art.

Morrow, Bradford and Bernard Lafourcade, *A Bibliography of the Writings of Wyndham Lewis* Santa Barbara; CA. Black Sparrow Press, 1978. The definitive bibliography of Lewis's writings and secondary works on Lewis. Indispensable for in-depth work on Lewis.

Shenandoah, 4 (Summer-Autumn 1953). Special issue devoted entirely to Lewis.

Selected Dictionaries and Encyclopedia
British Writers, Vol. 7, Charles Scribner's Sons, 1984, pp. 71–85. Discusses Lewis in terms of his quarrels with prevailing modern artistic and intellectual notions, deciding in Lewis's favor.

Dictionary of Literary Biography, Vol. 15, Gale Research, pp. 306–22. A very good overview of Lewis's life and major accomplishments. Written by Lewis's biographer, Jeffrey Meyers.

Daniel Taylor
Bethel College, St. Paul

VACHEL LINDSAY
1879–1931

Author's Chronology

Born November 10, 1879, Springfield, Illinois to parents Dr. Vachel Thomas Lindsay, a general practitioner whose financial stability sustained Lindsay in his slowly developing career as a poet, and Esther Catharine Frazee Lindsay, a college math teacher and instructor of painting, whose moral support was essential to Linday's self-confidence; *1900* left Hiram College without a degree after three years of studying, writing for the college's literary publications and developing oratorical skills; studied at the Art Institute at Chicago with hopes of becoming an illustrator and painter; *1906–1912* took walking tours of the United States from Florida to Kentucky, New York to Ohio, and Illinois to New Mexico, exchanging poetry and prose for bread, collecting experience for writing; *1912* after many attempts to be published, had "General William Booth Enters into Heaven" accepted by *Poetry* editor Harriet Monroe and began public career; *1913* published the volume *General William Booth Enters into Heaven and Other Poems* and began a series of public readings, his major source of income from *1913* to his death in *1931;* read to hundreds of thousands, most often performing the rousing "Congo;" *1914* wins the Levinson prize for "The Chinese Nightingale" and published, most by Macmillan, six volumes of verse and one novel in the next ten years, the most important being *Collected Poems of Vachel Lindsay* in *1923; 1923–1924* teaches poetry at Gulfport Junior College for Girls in Gulfport, Mississippi after canceling most of a grueling tour of recitals; *1925* having courted many women through his twenties and thirties, including poet Sara Teasdale, marries Elizabeth Conner in May; *1924–1929* moves to Spokane, Washington; lives in a hotel, and then several rented residences; diagnosed in *1924* by the Mayo Clinic for a serious ailment whose nature, because the diagnosis is still confidential, is unknown; suffering from financial, physical and emotional discomfort, commits suicide on December 5, 1931 in Springfield, Illinois.

Author's Bibliography (selected)

General William Booth Enters into Heaven and Other Poems, 1913; *The Congo and Other Poems,* 1914; *Adventures while Preaching the Gospel of Beauty,* 1914 (prose); *The Chinese Nightingale and Other Poems,* 1917; *The Golden Book of Springfield,* 1920 (novel); *The Daniel Jazz and Other Poems* (published in England), 1920; *Collected Poems of Vachel Lindsay,* 1923; *Selected Poems of Vachel Lindsay* (Hazelton Spencer, editor), 1931; *Selected Poems of Vachel Lindsay* (Mark Harris, editor), 1963; *The Poetry of Vachel Lindsay* (Dennis Camp, editor), 1984.

Overview of Biographical Sources
   Lindsay's late development as a poet, his sudden rise to national fame, his spectacular readings, and his suicide, all stimulated interest in his life. In his own lifetime there was a sensible, brief biography: Albert Edward Trombley, *Vachel Lindsay, Adventurer* (Columbia, MO: Lucas Brothers, 1929); shortly after his death his fellow-poet Edgar Lee Masters produced *Vachel Lindsay, a Poet in America* (1935). The most comprehensive and carefully researched biography to date is Eleanor Ruggles's work, *The West-Going Heart: A Life of Vachel Lindsay* (1959). A most useful source is Marc Chénetier's *Letters of Vachel Lindsay* (New York: Burt Franklin Press, 1979); here are 199 letters, to public figures and friends, from all stages of Lindsay's life. Ruggles and Chénetier together provide a good basis for a consideration of Lindsay's life although neither helps the reader to address the questions of Lindsay's literary significance or the value of particular works. On the other hand, almost no literary critical approach to Lindsay, in essay or book form, ignores the extent to which knowledge of his experience helps one interpret his poetry. Consequently, there are comments on his biography sprinkled liberally throughout all critical considerations of Lindsay.

Evaluation of Selected Biographies
   Masters, Edgar Lee, *Vachel Lindsay, a Poet in America.* New York: Charles Scribner's Sons, 1935. Masters' biography is impressionistic, idiosyncratic, occasionally long-winded; he speculates on the reasons for Lindsay's difficulties at length. This volume remains highly regarded because of Masters' reputation as a poet. Masters had access to the same materials, among them private family archives, as Ruggles, but sometimes used those sources carelessly. Fellow-midwestern poet though he was, Masters seemed to have little sympathy or understanding for Lindsay's successes and failures.

   Ruggles, Eleanor, *The West-Going Heart: A Life of Vachel Lindsay.* New York: W. W. Norton, 1959. Ruggles' work is precise, accessible and compassionate. It is a dependable, well-written record of the events of Lindsay's career; her use of diaries, journals and private correspondence, researched meticulously, is both economical and effective. She does not choose to comment on the poems individually and avoids psychological and sociological speculations; the facts are all here and readers are invited to reach their own conclusions.

Autobiographical Sources
   Lindsay wrote accounts of his walking tours, explaining his Christian-democratic vision and chronicling the events of those excursions: *Adventures While Preaching the Gospel of Beauty* (published in 1914 about his 1912 tramp) and *A Handy Guide for Beggars* (published in 1916 about his walks in 1906 and 1908).

These works introduce many of the themes and ideals of his poetic career, from the perspective of the then undiscovered poet.

Overview of Critical Sources

Critics of Lindsay's work are inclined to consider the question of his significance to American literature each time they write; there is no consensus that he deserves to be among the major poets of the twentieth century. Most scholars argue explicitly for or against his inclusion in the *canon*. Even his most ardent supporters generally agree that his best work in the *Collected Poems of Vachel Lindsay* is heavily outnumbered by poems of questionable value. Thus critical debate centers on a handful of poems, those best known in his recitals, with the result that most of Lindsay's poetry, great and not so great, remains unknown. Finally, it is clear that even the once familiar selections, "General William Booth Enters into Heaven," "The Congo," "The Chinese Nightingale," "Abraham Lincoln Walks at Midnight," and a few others, are no longer included in the anthologies of American poetry where they once were printed. The reading public may have difficulty finding Lindsay's work in the future.

Evaluation of Selected Criticism

Massa, Ann, *Vachel Lindsay, Fieldworker for the American Dream.* Bloomington: Indiana University Press, 1970. This is the only full-length study of Lindsay's work, and is organized by the major topics or themes which preoccupied Lindsay. Massa, a professor of American literature at Leeds University in England, brings a fresh and objective perspective to her subject, and discusses the way Lindsay tried to affect his culture as well as the ways in which it shaped his career. This book is an exercise in American Studies—broadly speaking—and not primarily concerned with poetic ability.

Flanagan, John T. ed. *Profile of Vachel Lindsay.* Columbus, OH: Charles E. Merrill, 1970. One of a series of Merrill profiles of American authors, Flanagan collects essays on Lindsay, the most recent of which, except for his own retrospective appraisal, is dated 1951. For the most part these essays were written to evaluate Lindsay's work in his lifetime or to summarize his career shortly after his death. Most insightful among them is Austin Warren's contribution, "The Case of Vachel Lindsay," but together they express the dismissive, critical attitude of the academic community towards Lindsay's work. The exception is the essay credited by Flanagan to William Rose Benét, but which, in fact, was written by Lindsay's sister and submitted on her behalf by Benét to the *Saturday Review* in 1945.

Other Sources

Harris Mark, *City of Discontent: An Interpretative Biography of Vachel Lindsay, Being Also the Story of Springfield, Illinois, USA, and the Love of the Poet for That City, That State, and That Nation.* Indianapolis: Bobbs-Merrill, 1952. A novelistic rendering of Lindsay's life, largely plausible except for Harris' emphasis on Lindsay's relations with women; Harris imagines that Lindsay was sexually experienced whereas it is clear that he was a rather sheltered and idealistic lover.

Harris, Mark, "Introduction," *Selected Poems of Vachel Lindsay.* New York: Macmillan, 1963, vii–xxii. A fine general introduction to Lindsay's life and work.

Wesling, Donald, "What the Canon Excludes: Lindsay and American Bardic," in *Michigan Quarterly Review,* XXI, #3 (Summer 1982), 479–484. An insightful explanation of Lindsay's dilemma, his ambiguous position in American letters today.

White, William, "Lindsay/Masters/Sandburg: Criticism from 1950–1975," in *The Vision of This Land.* ed. Hallwas and Reader. Macomb: Western Illinois University, 1976. White's research makes hard-to-find critical material accessible.

Selected Dictionaries and Encyclopedias

Critical Survey of Poetry, Salem Press, 1982. Brief biography and analysis of "General William Booth Enters into Heaven," "The Gospel of Beauty," "The Chinese Nightingale," and "The Flower-fed Buffaloes."

Twentieth Century Authors: A Biographical Dictionary of Modern Literature, H. W. Wilson, 1942. A brief but sensible entry, marking Lindsay's reputation a decade after his death.

John Chapman Ward
Kenyon College

THOMAS LODGE
1558–1625

Author's Chronology

Born 1558, the second son to Sir Thomas Lodge, Lord Mayor of London; *1564?* page to the Stanleys, earls of Derby; *1571* enters the Merchant Taylors' School; *1573?* matriculates at Trinity College, Oxford; *1577* receives B.A. from Oxford; *1578* is admitted to Lincoln's Inn, but abandons study of law soon after; *1579* answers Stephen Gosson's *School of Abuse* and engages in a literary quarrel; *1587* travels with Captain Clarke to the Canaries and the Azores; *1591* sails with Thomas Cavendish for South America, visiting the Straits of Magellan and Brazil; *1593* returns to England; *1595* in "To the Reader" of *A Fig for Momus* complains that he has been "unjustly taxed" for plagiarism; *1596* moves from London to Low Leyton, Essex; *1597* enters the University of Avignon to study medicine; *1598* awarded the degree of Doctor of Medicine from Avignon; *1602* incorporated M.D. at Oxford; *1606?* suspected of being a Roman Catholic; flees the country; *1610?* returns to England, and is admitted to Licentiate of the College of Physicians in London; *1614* translates works of Seneca; *1619* sued by the actor Alleyn for debt and imprisoned; *1625* dies in Old Fish Street, London, of the plague.

Author's Bibliography (selected)

Reply to Gosson, 1579 (pamphlet); *The Wounds of Civil War,* 1586? (play); *Scillaes Metamorphosis,* 1578 (epyllion); *Rosalynde: Euphues Golden Legacie,* 1590 (prose); *Euphues Shadow, the Battaile of the Sences,* 1592 (prose); *Phillis,* 1593 (poetry); *A Fig For Momus,* 1595 (satiric poetry); *A Margarite of America,* 1596 (prose).

Overview of Biographical Sources

Information concerning Lodge's biography has been greatly expanded so that errors incorporated in earlier books were corrected by extremely competent works written in the 1930's. These provided a much more thorough examination of documentary evidence, and they remain the basic studies of Lodge's life. Nathaniel Paradise's *Thomas Lodge: The History of an Elizabethan* (1931), challenged a number of false assumptions in Sidney Lee's article in *The Dictionary of National Biography* (London: Smith, Elder, and Company, 1893). Charles Sisson's *Thomas Lodge and Other Elizabethans,* (1933) incorporated evidence culled from the records of the Perogative Courts of Law, and drew an even clearer picture of Lodge's family life and the relation between the writer's experience and his work. Alice Walker's "Life of Thomas Lodge," *Review of English Studies* IX (1933), 410–432; X (1934), 46–54, covered much of the same territory but in shorter form, treating the sources of Lodge's books and some new biographical data. These books have cleared up details, corrected errors, and have drawn an intriguing sketch of an extremely adventurous life.

Evaluation of Selected Biographies

Paradise, Nathaniel, *Thomas Lodge*. New Haven: Yale University Press, 1931. This is an accurate, easy-to-read treatment of Lodge as a literary figure. The first chapters contain an account of his life, and later ones cover his literary career as "A Man of Letters" and "The Dramatist." Appendices contain wills he made, sources for his literary borrowings, and chronological list of his writings. This book is excellent for anyone interested in either Lodge or Elizabethan times.

Rae, Wesley, *Thomas Lodge*. New York: Twayne, 1967. Rae combines Lodge's endeavors in both exploration and literature, and concludes with a bibliography. While it lacks the vividness of Paradise or Tenny, it is readily accessible.

Ryan, Thomas, *Thomas Lodge, Gentleman*. Hamden, CT: The Shoe String Press, 1958. Printed on the fourth centenary of Lodge's birth, this volume supplies a rather simple and uncluttered story of Lodge's fascinating life.

Sisson, Charles, *Thomas Lodge*. Cambridge: Harvard University Press, 1933. This detailed biography would ordinarily only suit the needs of graduate students and specialists, but it is so rich in its scope and in its recreation of the Elizabethan milieu that it also serves as stimulating reading for all those who have any interest in social and cultural dynamics of England in the sixteenth century. Sisson is a superb historian who creates a compelling narrative of the Lodge family undergoing the extremes of success and failure. He also convincingly traces the impact of Lodge's personality on his writing.

Tenny, Edward, *Thomas Lodge,* Ithaca, NY: Cornell University Press, 1935. The author has set for himself the task of combing all the recent findings on Lodge's life and varied careers as a dramatist, prose writer, poet, and doctor. He has produced a very reliable text. Tenney fills out the story of Lodge's participation in Cavendish's second, tragic attempt to circumnavigate the globe. This chapter is derived largely from pertinent travel literature of the period.

Autobiographical Sources

Although Lodge never wrote an autobiography, his literary works are colored by self-reference in a fictionalized form. His pamphlet *An Alarum Against Usurers* (1584) springs from his own experience, and his most important work, *Rosalynde,* parallels his own troubled family situation. The difficulties between the older brother Saladyne and his younger brother Rosader in that work mirrors the constant litigation that engaged Thomas, the younger son, and his older brother, William, whom he accused of having beaten him and his servant. But although these associations are clear, readers should remember that Lodge has idealized his own persona far out of proportion with reality. Where in fact he was quite a profligate and had spent large sums of money he had inherited, Lodge's Rosader is wholly abused by his malignant brother. In prefatory material, Lodge explicitly refers to his own condition. There are few prominent examples. His commendatory poem to Barnaby Rich's *Don Simonides* (1581) speaks of his "long distress" and the "breaking" of his "pleasant vein" after his debate with Gosson and financial troubles. In verses of *Scillaes Metamorphosis,* he tells of his desire to "write no more" for the theatre.

Overview of Critical Sources

The criticism about Lodge generally focuses on his four important contributions to English literature. First, he is recognized as having had a lasting impact on English drama, since *Rosalynde* became the principal source for Shakespeare's *As You Like It* (1599). Second, he published the first erotic epyllion, *Scillaes Metamorphosis,* written in a genre perfected by Marlowe and Shakespeare. His third contribution to literature was *A Fig for Momus,* the first satire published in English based on classical models, particularly the works of Juvenal and Horace. He was one of the initial poets who inaugurated this vogue that would transform the dominant tone of Elizabethan poetry from panegyric to invective, reaching its climax in Donne's lyrics. Fourth, Lodge was a staunch advocate of the drama, defending it against detractors in the *Reply to Gosson.* He therefore holds a prominent place in the history of the theatre.

Evaluation of Selected Criticism

Baker, Ernest, *A History of the English Novel.* Vol. 2. New York: Barnes and Noble, 1929. This is an informative account of Lodge's place in the development of prose fiction championed by Sidney and Lyly. Baker argues convincingly that *Rosalynde* fuses motifs from *Arcadia* and *Euphues,* and views the author in a derivative tradition that includes Greene, Munday, and Warner.

Bush, Douglas, *Mythology and the Renaissance Tradition.* New York: Pageant Book Company, 1957. Bush gives *Scillaes Metamorphosis* a prominent position in this study of the florescence of Ovidian mythological narrative poetry in the Elizabethan period. He catalogues the manner in which Lodge transformed his material by utilizing Petrarchan conceits and rhetorical adornment.

Davis, Walter, *Idea and Act in Elizabethan Fiction.* Princeton: Princeton University Press, 1969. Chapter 3, "Pastoral Romance: Sidney and Lodge," contends that accepted ideals of man's possible ennoblement by love, contemplation, and humility are submitted to the test of experience in the *Arcadia* and *Rosalynde.* This is certainly one of the best studies of Lodge's prose fiction, and it contains excellent philosophical insights into the author's sophisticated questioning of the pastoral conventions he manipulated.

Grubb, Marion, "Lodge's Borrowings from Ronsard," *Modern Language Notes,* XLV (1930), 357–360. This article documents echoes of the French poet in the lyrics, especially in *Phillis.*

Helgerson, Richard, *The Elizabethan Prodigals.* Berkeley: University of California Press, 1976. According to this critic, Elizabethan writers often depicted themselves as self-indulgent and created characters of excess that need to find restraint. A chapter in this book on Lodge illustrates the theme of the prodigal son in his prose works.

Jusserand, J. J. *The English Novel in the Time of Shakespeare.* trans. Elizabeth Lee. London: T. F. Unwin, 1908. An early authoritative treatment of the sources of prose fiction in the Elizabethan period, this volume places Lodge's *Rosalynde* in the encyclopedic context of realistic and Arcadian traditions of narrative.

Lewis, C. S. *English Literature in the Sixteenth Century Excluding Drama.* Vol. 3 of *The Oxford History of English Literature.* Oxford: Clarendon Press, 1954. This is the most comprehensive overview of Lodge's career now available in print. Lewis includes extensive and varied comments on Lodge throughout this study, covering the pamphlets as well as narrative and poetry. The judicious evaluation of Lodge's metrical experiments is unsurpassed.

Ringler, William, *Stephen Gosson.* Princeton: Princeton University Press, 1942. This book furnishes a definitive commentary on the quarrel between Gosson and Lodge on the nature of drama. Careful, fully researched, this study considers the debate on the ethics of dramaturgy that absorbed the interest of early Elizabethans, including Sidney, whose *Apology for Poetry* was another "reply" to Gosson.

Ward, A. W. and A. R. Waller, eds. *The Cambridge History of English Literature.* Vol. 3. Cambridge: Cambridge University Press, 1909. Chapter 16, on Lodge, provides a competent summary of Lodge's life and extensive analysis of the sources for *Rosalynde,* his experiments in the sonnet form, and the topical issues treated in the pamphlets.

Other Sources
Chambers, E. K. *The Elizabethan Stage.* Vol. 3. Oxford: Clarendon Press, 1923. In the chapter on "Plays and Playwrights," Chambers summarizes Lodge's literary career, lists collections of his works, and includes a summary of those that are of doubtful authorship.

Johnson, Robert, *Elizabethan Bibliographies, Supplements.* Vol. 5. London: Nether Press, 1968. This volume notes scholarship on Lodge from 1939–1965.

Selected Dictionaries and Encyclopedias

Chamber's Cyclopedia of English Literature, Gale Research, 1978. Lodge is discussed as a good craftsman who could at times produce tedious, artificial writing. Several long excerpts from the prose and poetry are supplied as evidence.

Critical Survey of Poetry, Vol. 4, Salem Press, 1982. Although the article on Lodge contains a biography and considers other literary forms, it concentrates on the metrical and rhetorical features of his epyllion, satire, and lyrics.

Crowell's Handbook of Elizabethan and Stuart Literature, Thomas Crowell, 1975. A short outline of Lodge's career is followed by a set of suggestions on his connection with Shakespeare's work, particularly *As You Like It* and *Venus and Adonis.*

The Library of Literary Criticism of English and American Authors, Vol. 1. Peter Smith, 1959. Here a short biography is followed by selected excerpts of criticism on *Rosalynde* and the lyrics, from a variety of perspectives, although treatment of his style is emphasized.

James P. Bednarz
Long Island University

JACK LONDON
1876–1916

Author's Chronology

Born January 12, 1876, in San Francisco, to Flora Wellman and William Henry Chaney; mother marries John London same year; *1893* sails aboard *Sophia Sutherland* to Japan and writes first published story, "Typhoon Off the Coast of Japan"; *1897–1898* prospects for gold in Canadian Yukon; publishes first magazine story in *Owl; 1900–1901* marries Bessie May Maddern, and first child (Joan) born; *1902* settles in Piedmont, California; second child (Becky) born; later travels to London where he writes *The People of the Abyss; 1903–1904* separates from Bessie, and sails to Korea to cover the Russo-Japanese War; *1905* divorces Bessie, marries Clara Charmian Kittredge, then moves to Glen Ellen, California; *1906–1909* builds yacht *Snark* and begins voyage around the world, abruptly aborting trip in Australia, when he becomes seriously ill; *1910* begins developing Beauty Ranch in Glen Ellen; *1913* Wolf House destroyed by fire under mysterious circumstances; sails around Cape Horn on *Dirigo; 1914* covers Mexican dispute for *Colliers; 1916* dies 22 November.

Author's Bibliography (selected)

The Son of the Wolf, 1900 (stories); *The God of His Fathers,* 1901 (stories); *The Children of the Frost,* 1902 (stories); *The Call of the Wild,* 1903 (novella); *The Faith of Men,* 1904 (stories); *The Sea-Wolf,* 1904 (novel); *White Fang,* 1906 (novel); *Love of Life and Other Stories,* 1907; *The Iron Heel,* 1908 (novel); *Martin Eden,* 1909 (novel); *Lost Face,* 1910 (stories); *When God Laughs,* 1910 (stories); *South Sea Tales,* 1911; *A Son of the Sun,* 1912 (stories); *The House of Pride,* 1912 (stories); *John Barleycorn,* 1913 (novel); *The Valley of the Moon,* 1913 (novel); *The Strength of the Strong,* 1914 (stories); *The Star Rover,* 1915 (stories); *The Red One,* 1918 (stories).

Overview of Biographical Sources

London's myth-making proclivities and penchant for the dramatic have inspired many biographies. Most are seriously flawed, however, by their writers' inability to separate London's fictional story-telling about himself from actual fact. This task was made even more difficult by the tight control exercised over access to London's archives. The result has been a dearth of biographical material written about London by writers drawing material in great part from London's published writings and newspaper accounts, such as Henry Mulford Tichenor's *Life of Jack London* (Girard, Kansas: Haldeman-Julius, 1923), Rose Wilder Lane's *He Was a Man* (New York: Harper, 1925), Robert Barltrop's *Jack London: the Man, the Writer, the Rebel* (London: Pluto, 1976), or John

Perry's *Jack London: An American Myth* (Chicago: Nelson Hall, 1981). Georgia Loring Bamford's *The Mystery of Jack London* (Oakland: Privately printed, 1931), Joseph Noel's *Footloose in Arcadia* (New York: Carrick & Evans, 1940), and William McDevitt's *Jack London as Poet and As Platform Man* (San Francisco: Recorder-Sunset, 1947), while largely inaccurate, at least draw from personal knowledge of London and his friends, family, and acquaintances.

Until recently, the accepted standard biography of London was Irving Stone's *Sailor on Horseback* (1938). A better book is Richard O'Connor's *Jack London: A Biography* (Boston: Houghton Mifflin, 1964), which presents a much more credible view of Jack London as a writer. Joan London's *Jack London and His Times* (1939) emphasizes London's socialism, socialist writings, and the turbulent politics of his era. Charmian London's *The Book of Jack London,* (1921) on the other hand, tends to emphasize the personal life London led, in a sometimes sentimental, yet none-the-less mostly credible study of London's life.

More recently written have been a number of biographies and studies of London utilizing the author's archive, beginning with Franklin Walker's masterful *Jack London and the Klondike* (1966), the fact-filled *A Pictorial Life of Jack London* (New York: Crown, 1979) by Russ Kingman, and two psychobiographical treatments of London: Andrew Sinclair's *Jack* (1977), and Joan Hedrick's *Jack London: Solitary Comrade* (Chapel Hill: University of North Carolina Press, 1983).

Evaluation of Selected Biographies

London, Chairmain, *The Book of Jack London.* New York: The Century Company, 1921. Perhaps the most credible of the early biographies, this two-volume work presents an often candid portrait of London, especially the often-neglected 1910–1916 period. It suffers, however, from an oftentimes sentimental style, wordiness, and an occasional, deliberate alteration of fact.

London, Joan, *Jack London and His Times.* New York: Doubleday, 1939. While this book by his daughter lacks adequate scholarly apparatus, it does present an excellent picture of the culture and background of early twentieth century California life, and gives adequate space to London's writings as well. Although the emphasis on London's socialist writings over his now classic short stories does not allow for a balanced view of London's life, the book must remain one of the few credible biographies of Jack London.

Sinclair, Andrew, *Jack.* New York: Harper & Row, 1977. Sinclair is the first biographer since Irving Stone to write a biography that draws freely from the London archives. The psychobiography has been criticized for factual error and the dark, one-dimensional picture it presents of London as a quasi-psychopath on a never-ending downward path toward destruction.

Stone, Irving, *Sailor on Horseback*. Boston: Houghton Mifflin, 1938. Stone's lack of documentation and his tendency to dramatize have caused serious doubt over the scholarship of this work. (The book was later subtitled "A Biographical Novel.") Nevertheless, Stone was the first—and one of the few—to gain access not only to London's archives and papers, but to his friends and family as well. Although cited by many early London scholars, Stone's wholly undocumented biography draws freely from London's own text, and his dramatic treatment and sometimes careless handling of fact, has created a deadly masterpiece.

Walker, Franklin, *Jack London and the Klondike*. San Marino: Henry E. Huntington Library, 1966. After two years of research, Walker abandoned his attempt to write a full-scale biography of London, instead settling for this fine scholarly examination of London's formative Klondike years.

Autobiographical Sources
London's intended autobiography, "Sailor on Horseback," was never written. His *Martin Eden, The Road, Tales of the Fish Patrol,* and *John Barleycorn* contain much autobiographical data, but separation of fact from fiction in these works is difficult, even for the professional biographer. Two collections of his letters have been published. The first, *Letters from Jack London* (London: MacGibbon & Kee, 1966), edited by King Hendricks and Irving Shepard, very lightly documented and footnoted, is now out of print. The second, *Jack London's Letters* (Stanford: Stanford University Press, 1985), edited by Robert Leitz, Earle Labor, and Milo Shepard, is a three-volume, well-documented, major work.

Overview of Critical Sources
Until recently, critics often viewed London as little more than a popular writer of adventure stories for boys, and thus unworthy of critical attention. The popular and sometimes sensational biographical work written about London tended to substantiate this critical assessment, and discourage scholarly effort. Furthermore, the little critical work that had been done utilized Stone's biography. Most of the significant critical work on London has appeared since 1960, beginning with King Hendrick's work early in the decade, and aided enormously by the work of Earle Labor in the 1970's and, later, Richard Etulain, James McClintock, Robert Leitz, Charles Watson, and others.

Evaluation of Selected Criticism
Hendricks, King, *Jack London: Master Craftsman of the Short Story*. Logan: Utah State University, 1966. One of the first literary studies of London's literary craftsmanship, Hendrick's short pamphlet identifies London's masterpieces

as "To Build a Fire," "The Law of Life," "The Chinago," and "Love of Life," presenting plot and thematic analysis of each story.

Labor, Earle, *Jack London.* New York: Twayne, 1974. Labor's book is, to date, the finest critical study of both London's life and writings. Labor focuses on what he calls London's primordial vision.

McClintock, James I. *White Logic: Jack London's Short Stories.* Cedar Springs: Wolf House Books, 1975. This first, full-length book devoted specifically to London's short stories studies London's evolution as a short story writer, and discusses his formula, technique, and style, noting the influence of Kipling on the early Alaskan stories, and, later, the writer's study of Freud and Jung.

Watson, Charles, *The Novels of Jack London.* New York: Syracuse University Press, 1984. Although London's novels were generally slighted, this scholarly study of London's craft reappraises London's skill as a novelist, and his shortcomings as a romanticist.

Other Sources

Noel, Joseph, *Footloose in Arcadia.* New York: Carrick & Evans, 1940. Noel's book, about George Sterling, Jack London, and Ambrose Bierce, is a "sour grapes" account of a friendship gone awry because of unfortunate business dealings. Accordingly, Noel's rather one-dimensional view of London as a carouser and drunkard is highly suspect.

Starr, Kevin, *Americans and the California Dream.* New York: Oxford University Press, 1973. A study of wish fulfillment, overly emphasizing London's neuroses.

Walker, Dale L. *The Alien Worlds of Jack London.* Grand Rapids: Wolf House Books, 1973. A study of London's fantasy fiction.

Selected Dictionaries and Encyclopedias

Critical Survey of Long Fiction, Salem Press, 1983. Brief biography, and short analysis of some of London's important novels.

Critical Survey of Short Fiction, Salem Press, 1981. Brief biography, and discussion of "To Build A Fire" and other of London's short-story masterpieces.

Encyclopaedia Britannica, Vol. 14, pp. 263, 1973. The short, well-researched London biography was written by Franklin Walker.

David Mike Hamilton
Palo Alto, California

HENRY WADSWORTH LONGFELLOW
1807–1882

Author's Chronology

Born February 27, 1807, Portland, Maine to Stephen and Zilpah Longfellow; *1822* enters Bowdoin College; *1825–1828* studies languages in France, Germany, Spain, and Italy; *1829* appointed to chair of modern languages at Bowdoin College; *1831* marries Mary Storer Potter; *1835* publishes first substantial literary effort, *Outre-Mer; A Pilgrimage Across the Sea;* first wife dies in Rotterdam, the Netherlands, of complications following miscarriage; *1836* begins work as Smith Professor of Modern Languages at Harvard; *1843* marries Francis Appleton, daughter of a wealthy Boston merchant; *1854* resigns from Harvard in order to have more time for writing; *1861* second wife dies of burns; *1868* makes a triumphal tour of Europe where he is celebrated by royalty, famous writers, and awarded honorary degrees at Oxford and Cambridge; *1882* dies in Cambridge, Massachusetts on March 24.

Author's Bibliography (selected)

Voices of the Night, 1839 (poems); *Ballads and Other Poems,* 1842 (poems); *The Belfry of Bruges and Other Poems,* 1846 (poems); *Evangeline, A Tale of Acadie,* 1847 (dramatic verse); *The Seaside and the Fireside,* 1850 (poems); *The Song of Hiawatha,* 1855 (epic poem); *The Courtship of Miles Standish and Other Poems,* 1858; *Tales of a Wayside Inn,* 1863 (poems).

Overview of Biographical Sources

Probably no poet has ever achieved the degrees of both popularity and rejection as Henry Wadsworth Longfellow. Dearly beloved during his own time and lauded by all levels of society in both America and Europe, Longfellow has been judged out of place in the twentieth century. His rhythmic and uplifting elucidations of a balanced universe and epic American history have not found favor in an era of radical change and fragmented lifestyles. Nevertheless, recent scholars have found that his poetry still contains literary qualities and philosophic moods that maintains its value. To say the least, much of it is pleasant and enjoyable. These drastic shifts in the consideration of Longfellow characterize the changing nature of the biographical studies of him. Thomas Wentworth Higginson's *Henry Wadsworth Longfellow* (Boston: Houghton, Mifflin, 1902) is an appreciative work that defines Longfellow as a great writer concerned throughout his life with creating a national poetry. Following the trauma of World War I, Herbert S. Gorman produced *A Victorian American: Henry Wadsworth Longfellow* (New York: Doran, 1926). In tune with the literary spirit of the times, Gorman was intent upon debunking Longfellow as a romantic.

Thirty years later, Edward Wagenknecht produced the seminal revisionary study of the poet's life and works: *Longfellow: A Full-Length Portrait* (1955). Though sometimes ponderous, Wagenknecht must be praised for recognizing and revealing Longfellow's value in terms of both his poetic skills and personal philosophy. Each of these authors employed an increasingly broad and detailed study of original materials. Since Wagenknecht, other biographers have taken on the process of distilling the available information into works of narrower focus. Some books have concentrated on Longfellow's time in Europe and others on his youth. The most valuable of the post-Wagenknecht studies is Newton Arvin's *Longfellow: His Life and Work* (1963). Arvin still considers Longfellow's entire life, but he concentrates on the psychological aspects as they relate to the poet's works. Though Longfellow will never be considered a major poet, his biographers have rendered a valuable service in documenting a man, an era, and a body of work that still holds the value of pleasant and refreshing reflection.

Evaluation of Selected Biographies

Arvin, Newton, *Longfellow: His Life and Work.* Boston: Little Brown, 1963. Concentrating on the poet's best works and the most important aspects of his life, Arvin presents a concise scholarly defense of Longfellow. By integrating his literary analysis with his biography, Arvin reveals the relationship of Longfellow's work to his mental traumas and the artistic and thematic strengths and weaknesses of the poet. Arvin also discusses Longfellow's verse technique and lyric style. Arvin's own style is intelligent, but not ponderous.

Wagenknecht, Edward Charles, *Longfellow: A Full-Length Portrait.* London: Longmans, Green, 1955. Wagenknecht's work is the major revisionary study of Longfellow. The author took a more thorough look at more original documents, including notebooks, letters, and manuscripts, in order to provide a significant reappraisal of Longfellow's works, major and minor. Wagenknecht burdens the reader with unimportant detailed scholarly debates, but produces a lively account of Longfellow's second marriage and social life. His first appendix, "Longfellow's Unwritten Works," reveals the true breadth of the poet's imagination.

Autobiographical Sources

Longfellow's first wife died in Rotterdam, the Netherlands in 1835. Shortly afterwards, Longfellow began courting Francis Appleton. The process of winning her took seven long years and caused him much suffering. This period of his life formed the basis for *Hyperion: A Romance* (New York: Samuel Colman, 1839) in which the hero wanders across Europe suffering from the loss of a "friend," finds a new love that he is unable to win, and eventually resolves to stop his mourning for the past and his hopeless romance and live only for the future. Longfellow's second wife died in 1861 from burns suffered when she accidentally caught fire while melting wax to seal some envelopes. Longfellow later wrote of his suffering and constant memory of her in "The Cross of Snow," published in *The Masque of Pandora and Other Poems* (Boston: James R. Osgood, 1875). Charles Eliot Norton includes thirty autobiographical poems in his *Henry Wadsworth Longfellow: A Sketch of His Life Together With Longfellow's Chief Autobiographical Poems* (Boston: Houghton Mifflin, 1928). These works include "A Psalm of Life," "The Wreck of the Hesperus," "The Bridge," and "Morituri Salutamus." *Life of Henry Wadsworth Longfellow*, 2 vols. (Boston: Ticknor, 1886) by the poet's brother Samuel Longfellow purports to be a biography but is actually a chronological blending of letters and journal entries accompanied by a few superficial notes by the author. Finally, *The Letters of Henry Wadsworth Longfellow*, 6 vols. (Cambridge Harvard University Press, 1967–1974), ed. Andrew Hilen, contains all (1,200) of the existing letters Longfellow wrote. The collection begins with a letter written by the poet at the age of seven and reveals his personal and professional struggles and his comfortable New England childhood. Hilen provides copious annotations to lend further insight into the man and his times.

Overview of Critical Sources

While much of the analysis of Longfellow focuses on his function in integrating European and Scandinavian influences into American culture, much of it is also simply concerned with how seriously Longfellow should be considered as a poet. His role in American literature is not dependent upon the value of his poetry, which has been fairly well agreed upon, but on the philosophical bent of the times. With the increasing fragmentation of twentieth-century life, Longfellow may either be rejected for his simplicity or accepted for the very same reason. His work is not necessarily of little value because it is simple and clear, and Longfellow is therefore capable of becoming the basis for a cultural movement. Those thoughts can be gathered from essays and chapters about Longfellow from respected literary men who recognize his value but leave a deeper examination of his work for someone else. Wagenknecht's and Arvin's biographies provide the most complete appreciations of Longfellow, but other volumes present valuable considerations of particular aspects of his life and work.

Evaluation of Selected Criticism

Hatfield, James T. *New Light on Longfellow.* Boston: Houghton Mifflin, 1933. Hatfield details Longfellow's fascination with the German language and literature, particularly the poems of Heinrich Heine. Longfellow's experiences in Germany stimulated his natural Puritanism. He was influenced by German family life, folklore, and social customs in his writing and teaching. Hatfield draws extensively on Longfellow's carefully kept diaries and detailed letters.

Hilen, Andrew R. *Longfellow and Scandinavia: A Study of the Poet's Relationship With the Northern Languages and Literatures.* New Haven: Yale University Press, 1947. Hilen provides not only a detailed account of Longfellow's ability to master the languages and literature of Scandinavia, but also a full documentation of the region's influence on the poet and on American literature through him. Included in this volume are transcriptions of Longfellow's Scandinavian journals and letters and a list of Scandinavian books and publications about the region that formed a part of the poet's library.

Other Sources

Longfellow, Fanny (Appleton), *Mrs. Longfellow: Selected Letters and Journals.* ed. Edward Wagenknecht. London: Longmans, Green, 1956. This volume provides a compelling portrait of an intelligent, active, and strong woman and her era from the time of her childhood to that of her accidental death.

Selected Dictionaries and Encyclopedias

American Writers: A Collection of Literary Biographies, Charles Scribner's Sons, 1974. A twenty-page biography commenting on social changes during Longfellow's lifetime and providing some concise analysis of his work.

Dictionary of Literary Biography, Gale Research, 1983. Brief biography, focusing on Longfellow's career, accompanied by a short analysis.

Thomas J. Slater
Oklahoma State University

RICHARD LOVELACE
1618–1658(?)

Author's Chronology

Born 1618 in either Woolwich, Kent, or in Holland, eldest son of Sir William Lovelace, a landowner and soldier who was killed during a military expedition to Holland in *1627; 1629* nominated by King Charles I for foundation support (i.e., as a scholarship student) to attend Charterhouse School, London; *1634* enters Gloucester Hall (now Worcester College), Oxford; writes a comedy, *The Scholars,* now lost; *1636* granted an M.A. degree during a visit of Charles I to Oxford; *1637* enrolls at Cambridge; leaves to attend the King at court; *1639–1640* takes part in military expeditions against Scotland; writes a tragedy entitled *The Soldier,* now lost; *1640* returns to Kent and takes possession of his estates; April, *1642* delivers a pro-Royalist document, the Kentish Petition, to the House of Commons; sent to the Gatehouse Prison in Westminster for two months; leaves England for Holland and France; *1642–1646* serves as a soldier in English and French military ventures; *1646* wounded at the siege of Dunkirk; *1648* sent to Peterhouse Prison; prepares his poetry for publication; April, *1649* released from prison; May, *1649* publishes *Lucasta: Epodes, Odes, Sonnets, Songs & c., to Which is Added Amarantha, A Pastorall;* lives remainder of his life in obscurity and, perhaps, poverty; *1657* or *1658* dies in London and is buried in St. Bride's Church; *1659* publication of *Lucasta: Posthume Poems.*

Author's Bibliography (selected)

Lucasta: Epodes, Odes, Sonnets, Songs, & c., to Which Is Added Amarantha, A Pastorall, 1649; *Lucasta: Posthume Poems,* 1659. The definitive edition of Lovelace's collected works is *The Poems of Richard Lovelace,* ed. by C. H. Wilkinson, 1930.

Overview of Biographical Sources

There is no definitive biography of Lovelace. In the introduction to *The Poems of Richard Lovelace* (1930), C. H. Wilkinson provides a concise yet complete account of what is known about Lovelace's life and reproduces relevant excerpts from contemporary records and early biographical sources. C. H. Hartmann's *The Cavalier Spirit and Its Influence on the Life and Work of Richard Lovelace* (1925) examines Lovelace in the context of social upheavals and cultural movements of the seventeenth century. The first chapter of Manfred Weidhorn's *Richard Lovelace* (1970) is a biographical survey based primarily on Wilkinson and Hartmann.

Evaluation of Selected Biographies

Hartmann, C. H. *The Cavalier Spirit and Its Influence on the Life and Work of Richard Lovelace.* London: George Routledge & Sons, 1925. Hartmann adds little, if any, new information to Lovelace's biography. Presenting Lovelace as the embodiment of the Cavalier spirit, Hartmann offers a mixture of seventeenth-century English history with an account of Lovelace's life, which he unhesitatingly augments with conjectures when the biographical sources are sparse.

Weidhorn, Manfred, *Richard Lovelace.* New York: Twayne, 1970. The first chapter of Weidhorn's book is a biographical survey, based on standard published sources. Weidhorn provides a good, brief summary of what is known about Lovelace's life, to which is added a concise definition of "Cavalier" and a discussion of the identity of Lucasta and the convention of pseudonyms in love lyrics.

Wilkinson, C. H. *The Poems of Richard Lovelace.* Oxford: Oxford University Press, 1930. Wilkinson's introduction remains the most authoritative biographical source. He gathers all available information and reproduces excerpts from relevant contemporary records. His essay is judicious, factual, and readable. Wilkinson, for the most part, avoids interpreting the facts, but he does argue against the prevailing view that Lovelace spent the last years of his life in utter poverty.

Overview of Critical Sources

There are few substantial critical studies of Lovelace's poetry. Only two books have been devoted exclusively to Lovelace. For the most part critics have been content to view him as an uneven minor poet, chiefly of interest for what his work shows about Cavalier poetic practice and sensibility. Attempts to bring critical attention to Lovelace's poetry in its own right have taken three main directions: close readings or explications of individual poems; textual studies; and analyses of complex meanings in some of the poems, often through demonstrating Lovelace's subtle handling of conventional emblems or themes.

Evaluation of Selected Criticism

Allen, D. C. "Richard Lovelace: 'The Grasse-Hopper,' " in *Image and Meaning: Metaphoric Traditions in Renaissance Poetry.* Baltimore: The Johns Hopkins Press, 1968; reprinted in *Ben Jonson and the Cavalier Poets.* New York: Norton, 1974. Allen examines the poem in light of classical symbolism of the grasshopper and the plight of defeated Cavaliers, and argues that the poem, far from being a simple Cavalier lyric, is about the imaginative creation of revivifying spiritual idealism. Allen's important article has influenced the critical approach to Lovelace's poetry by demonstrating that a poem by Lovelace can repay close critical attention informed by an understanding of the conventions of Renaissance emblems.

Hartmann, C. H. *The Cavalier Spirit and Its Influence on the Life and Work of Richard Lovelace.* London: George Routledge & Sons, 1925. Hartmann adds little to a critical understanding of Lovelace's poetry. Generally, he is interested in using the poems to establish details about Lovelace's life instead of the other way around. He provides only a broad, superficial assessment of Lovelace's poetry, finding it fully representative of the Cavalier Spirit.

Miner, Earl, *The Cavalier Mode from Jonson to Cotton.* Princeton: Princeton University Press, 1971. An excellent book delineating main features of Cavalier poetry and sensibility. Lovelace is discussed throughout, and several of his poems are analyzed in light of classical tradition, conventional emblems, and social context.

Weidhorn, Manfred, *Richard Lovelace.* New York: Twayne, 1970. Weidhorn's book is a far from definitive treatment of Lovelace's *oeure.* Perhaps because the book follows the somewhat formulaic organization of the Twayne English Authors Series, of which it is part, it fails to develop a clear, focused view of Lovelace's poetry. The consideration of poems according to various topics, such as subject matter, imagery, and poetic form, tends to fragment the discussion. The book serves to bring together previously published critical commentary and provides some insights about individual poems. The level of critical treatment seems appropriate for college undergraduates, although the sometimes confusing topical organization makes it less valuable as a ready source of information about individual poems.

Other Sources

Anselmont, Raymond A. " 'Griefe Triumphant' and 'Victorious Sorrow': A Reading of Richard Lovelace's 'The Falcon,' " in *Journal of English and Germanic Philology* 70 (1971), 404–417. Argues, by appealing to emblem tradition, that the falcon represents "ennobling heroism," and that the poem is an "idealistic vision" of the Cavalier defeat.

Brooks, Cleanth, "Literary Criticism: Poet, Poem, and Reader," in *Perspectives in Contemporary Criticism: A Collection of Recent Essays by American, English, and European Literary Critics.* ed. Sheldon Grebstein. New York: Harper's, 1968, pp. 96–107. A subtle, readable analysis and appreciation of "The Grasse-Hopper" by a masterful critic.

Evans, Willa McClung, "Richard Lovelace's 'Mock-Song,' " *Philological Quarterly* 24 (1945), 317–328. Evans has produced a series of fine articles comparing manuscripts of musicial settings of some of Lovelace's poems with published versons to show evidence of their effective revision.

Holland, Norman, "Literary Value: A Psychoanalytic Approach," in *Literature and Psychology* 14 (1964), 43–55, 116–127. Suggestive psychoanalyses of "The Scrutiny" and "To Lucasta, Going to the Wars."

Jones, G. F. " 'Lov'd I Not Honour More': the Durability of a Literary Motif," in *Comparative Literature* 11 (1959), 131–143. Survey of the literary tradition of the topic of "honour" to illuminate "To Lucasta, Going to the Wars."

King, Bruce, "Green Ice and a Breast of Proof," in *College English* 26 (1965), 511–515. A provocative article that offers an interpretation of "The *Grasshopper*" as an example of the defeated Cavalier building "defenses against demoralization."

Palmer, Pauline, "Lovelace's Treatment of Some Marinesque Motifs," in *Comparative Literature* 29 (1977), 300–312. Compares some of Lovelace's poems to similar ones by the Italian poet Marino.

Pearson, Norman H. "Lovelace's 'To Lucasta, Going to the *Warres*,' " in *Explicator* 7 (June, 1949), item 58. Fine detailed analysis of the "integrated structure" of the poem.

Van Doren, Mark, *Introduction to Poetry*. New York: Holt, Rinehart and Winston, 1951. Contains an insightful, close reading of "To Lucasta, Going to the Wars."

Wadsworth, Randolph L., Jr. "On 'The Snayle' by Richard Lovelace," in *Modern Language Review* 65 (1970), 750–760. Traces the emblematic tradition of the snail image in Renaissance England and applies findings to Lovelace's poem.

Walton, Geoffrey, "The Cavalier Poets," *From Donne to Marvell.* Baltimore: Penguin, 1956. General impressionistic descriptions and evaluation of Lovelace's poetry.

Selected Dictionaries and Encyclopedias

British Writers, II, Charles Scribner's Sons, 1979. Brief critical assessment of Lovelace's poetry.

Critical Survey of Poetry, Vol. 4, Salem Press, 1982. Concise overview of Lovelace's life, and a discussion of Lovelace's poems.

James Flynn
Western Kentucky University

AMY LOWELL
1874–1925

Author's Chronology

Born February 9, 1874, Brookline Massachusetts to a distinguished fifth-generation New England family; travels to Europe at age eight and suffers first nervous disorder; begins private school age nine; *1895* becomes hostess of Sevenels; *1898* travels in Europe until second nervous illness strikes; *1902* discovers vocation as poet watching the Duse perform; *1907* begins her famous entertaining at Sevenels; *1913–1914* visits Ezra Pound and the Imagists in England; *1912–1921* publishes twelve volumes of verse and prose and seventy-two essays; also becomes famous for lectures and readings; *1917* begins serious Oriental studies; *1919* publishes first mature work, *Pictures of the Floating World; 1920* declining health; *1920–1925* writes her best poems; *1922* publishes *A Critical Fable; 1924* completes massive two volume work on Keats; dies May 12, 1925; final three volumes of poetry published posthumously; *What's O'Clock* wins Pulitzer Prize *1925.*

Author's Bibliography

A Dome of Many Colored Glass, 1912 (poems); *Tendencies in Modern American Poetry,* 1917 (criticism); *Pictures of a Floating World,* 1919 (poems); *A Critical Fable,* 1922 (poem); *John Keats,* 2 vols, 1924 (biography); *What's O'Clock,* 1925 (poems); *Selected Poems of Amy Lowell,* 1928; *Complete Poetical Works of Amy Lowell,* 1955; *A Shard of Silence: Selected Poems of Amy Lowell,* 1957.

Overview of Biographical Sources

There are four full-length biographies of Amy Lowell, most of which reflect the ambivalence early scholars felt toward her. Most biographers have become caught up in the unusual and exotic details of her personal habits, and many took exception to her outspoken and manipulative presence both on the public scene and in the field of publishing. Clement Wood's *Amy Lowell* (1926) is stiff, pedantic and generally disapproving. Wood disliked both Lowell and her poetry. S. Foster Damon's *Amy Lowell: A Chronical With Extracts From Her Correspondence* (1935) is the definitive biography. Scholarly and free from bias, this book did much to restore Lowell's reputation. Foster detailed as objectively as possible the important and minute events of her life, thus restoring a measure of perspective and balance to the biographical portrait of Lowell. However, Horace Gregory's *Amy Lowell* (1958) is full of disdain for both the poetry and poetic theory. Neither does he have much respect for Lowell's methods of getting her poetry published and her dominance of the public scene during her last years as visiting lecturer and poet. Jean Gould's *Amy: The World of Amy Lowell and the Imagist Movement* (New York: Dodd, Mead,

1975) dispels the earlier emphasis on Lowell's invalidism and neuroses, presenting instead a vital, strong woman whose entrepreneurship of her own poetry, and that of the modern movement, is presented as a feminist *tour de force* to be applauded, rather than as something shocking or irritating. Gould's primary contribution to the understanding of Lowell is her depiction of the importance of Lowell's life-long companionship with Ada Russell. Many of the love poems are identified for the first time as having been written to Ada Russell. Three useful short accounts include: Elizabeth Sergeant's *Fire Under the Andes* (New York: Alfred A. Knopf, 1927) pp. 11–31, in which she talks of Lowell's personality and homelife from the perspective of a life-long personal friend, and Donald Heiney's chapter in *Recent American Literature,* (New York: Barrons, 1958). The third account is Margaret Widdener's "The Legend of Amy Lowell" published in *Golden Friends I Had* (New York: Doubleday, 1962) pp. 107–122, in which she provides a lively firsthand account of Amy's personality as hostess and mistress of Sevenels. This account also attempts to dispel the "legend" and reveal the poet in her true personal relations with community, fellow poets and close friends.

Evaluation of Selected Biographies

Damon, S. Foster, *Amy Lowell: A Chronicle With Extracts From Her Correspondence.* Boston: Houghton Mifflin, 1935. Damon, who enjoyed a long personal friendship with Lowell, has written the definitive biography which is monumental in its detail. It is also heavily laced with Lowell's letters, the inclusion of which allows the poet to speak for herself. A much warmer and more real woman than Clement Woods' emerges from Damon's treatment. Clearly and carefully written, this book presents a distanced and unbiased account of her life, and makes no attempt at critical evaluation of the poetry itself. Damon did much to pave the way for the major reassessment of Lowell which took place in the late 1960's and 1970's.

Gregory, Horace, *Amy Lowell.* New York: Thomas Allgreen, 1958. Gregory, like Wood, is negative about the lasting influence of Lowell's poetry. He presents her as a rather arrogant Boston Brahmin too used to getting her own way. Gregory fails to see beneath the surface of his subject and makes much mileage out of reviving the Lowell "myth."

Wood, Clement, *Amy Lowell.* New York: Vinal, 1926. Wood's account of Lowell, though valuable for its depiction of the literary scene in America during Amy Lowell's heyday, now appears dated and opinionated. Wood was an Anglo-phile who took an unnecessarily patronizing attitude to experimental poetry in American poetry and Lowell's in particular. Her "bohemian" ways and aristocratic hauteur offended his New England sense of a woman's proper place in society. He presents her as a forceful, organizing personality and major influence of dubious proportions. He shows no sympathetic interest in her poetry or the private woman. Content to revive the "legendary" Amy Lowell who was formidable to deal with and seemed not to know her proper place, Wood takes delight in detailing the negative effects she had on people she encountered.

Overview of Critical Sources

Because of Wood and Gregory's unflattering assessments of Lowell's poetry, there has been more interest in her life and influence than in her poetry. All of Lowell's biographers but one have been men, and two of these demonstrated very early a "Bostonian" disapproval of Lowell's oddity and refusal to honor Victorian social proprieties. Partly as a consequence of this there are very few serious full-length studies and relatively few periodical articles of any depth. Only Ruihley's book deals with Lowell's capacity for feeling, quality of thought, religious intuitions and social values. All agree that Lowell published too much inferior material. However, with the advent of a small trickle of articles and three books during the late 1960's and 1970's, a period of reassessment began which has done much to reveal her determination to bring new idioms, cadences, verse forms and startling images to American poetry. Finally the picture of an extremely hard-working and disciplined poet has emerged to counteract the image of the bluestocking eccentric. These later biographers acknowledge more readily the debt American poetry and many of its practitioners owe to Lowell's sponsorship of the Imagist movement and modern poetry.

Evaluation of Selected Criticism

Flint, F. Cudworth, *Amy Lowell*. Minnesota: University of Minnesota Pamphlets on American Writers, 1969. This useful, brief study provides a good synopsis of previous critical opinion and highlights from Lowell's life. It also deals informatively and intelligently with the poet's literary theory, influence, and selected poetry and prose.

Gould, Jean, *Amy: the World of Amy Lowell and the Imagist Movement*. New York: Dodd, Mead, 1975. Gould's biography fills a needed gap in Lowell biography because it details, for the first time, the centrality of Lowell's relationship with Ada Russell. It also identifies many of the love poems quite positively as having been written for Mrs Russell. Gould makes much of Lowell's eccentricities by presenting them positively as a reaction against a restrictive masculine world. She de-emphasizes Lowell's invalidism and neuroses, and portrays her as a dynamic promoter of the cause of modern poetry. Gould does not make much critical commentary on the actual poetry.

Ruihley, Glenn Richard, *The Thorn of a Rose: Amy Lowell Reconsidered*. Hamden, CT: Archon Books, 1975. Ruihley's is the most sensitive, thorough and important full-length study. Beginning with the assertion that the unevenness of her work has caused her to be underestimated, he demonstrates that the content of the poetry is not mere physical description but impressions of nature and man which are spiritual or transcendental. Ruihley also claims that the Imagist attitude and technique was based chiefly on Zen Buddhist and French Impressionist principles, thus ruling out Pound as the originator of the idea. He adds an important new dimension to the study of Imagism and Lowell's poetry by establishing the origins and depth of Lowell's knowledge of things Oriental. Ruihley is also the first critic to perceive and comment on the deeply religious strain in Lowell's poetry, its nature and origins.

Other Sources

Carlson, E. W. "The Range of Symbolism in Poetry," *South Atlantic Quarterly* 48 (1949), 442–451.

Kenner, Hugh, "Mao or Presumption," *Shenandoah* 21 (1970), 84–93.

Overmeyer, Janet, "Which Broken Pattern?: A Note on Amy Lowell's 'Patterns,'" *Notes on Contemporary Literature* 1. 4 (1971), 14–15.

Gloria L. Cronin
Brigham Young University

ROBERT LOWELL
1917–1977

Author's Chronology
Born March 1, 1917, Boston, the only child of Robert T. S. and Charlotte Winslow Lowell; *1930* enters St. Mark's School and gets to know the poet Richard Eberhart who teaches there; *1935–1937* attends Harvard; *1937–1940* transfers to Kenyon College where he majors in Classics and studies under John Crowe Ransom; *1940* converts to Catholicism and marries Jean Stafford; *1943* because of opposition to Allied practice of saturation bombing refuses to report for draft induction and is sentenced to jail for one year and a day; *1946* awarded Pulitzer Prize for *Lord Weary's Castle; 1948* divorces Jean Stafford and in *1949* marries Elizabeth Hardwick; *1960* wins National Book Award for *Life Studies; 1965* achieves public notoriety by rejecting an invitation to a White House Arts Festival because of President Johnson's involvement in Vietnam; *1972* divorces Elizabeth Hardwick, marries Caroline Blackwood and decides to live in England; September 12, 1977, dies in a taxi in New York on returning from England.

Author's Bibliography (selected)
Lord Weary's Castle, 1946 (poems); *The Mills of the Kavanaughs,* 1951 (poems); *Life Studies,* 1959 (poems); *Imitations,* 1961 (free translations); *For the Union Dead,* 1964 (poems); *Near the Ocean,* 1967 (poems); *Notebook 1967–68,* 1969 (poems); *History, For Lizzie and Harriet, The Dolphin,* 1973 (poems); *Selected Poems,* 1976; *Day by Day,* 1977 (poems).

Overview of Biographical Sources
Besides a handful of sketches by friends and acquaintances such as Robert Fitzgerald, Frank Bidart, Louis Simpson and Seamus Heaney the only "authoritative" biography is Ian Hamilton's *Robert Lowell.* Most critical books about Robert Lowell (e.g., Steven Gould Axelrod's *Robert Lowell: Life and Art,* 1978) provide biographical details that elucidate his poetry, but none provide a complete portrait.

Evaluation of Selected Biographies
Hamilton, Ian, *Robert Lowell.* London: Faber and Faber, 1983. Hamilton, a poet of good standing himself, is eminently equipped to offer insights into Lowell's difficult personality and poetry. He begins by tracing the poet's New England origins in the two patrician families of Lowell and Winslow, and accounts for some of the poet's youthful hostility towards them. He explores Lowell's early infatuation with Catholicism and poetic formalism and tells how,

as he grew older, he struggled to throw off some of these religious and literary restraints.

The book presents a compelling psychological and literary portrait of Lowell, and without an obfuscating mass of technical terms. Although Hamilton is perhaps too harsh in his evaluations of Lowell's early poems, such as the ones collected in *Lord Weary's Castle,* he is especially good when he comes to *Life Studies* and *For the Union Dead.* This is a well-documented account of a major poet, his suffering from what he called his "enthusiasms" and which led to manic-depressive breakdowns, and his determined efforts to rise above his ailments and write great poetry.

Autobiographical Sources

Lowell, as he grew older, tried to strip away his masks of "impersonality" and "symbolism" perfected under the tutelage of the New Critics, and to reveal his intense personal life with excruciating candor. With the appearance of *Life Studies* his poetry became more and more autobiographical or, as one critic put it, "confessional". The second part of *Life Studies* is a thirty-five page autobiographical reminiscence, which candidly describes growing up in Boston, his difficult relations with his parents, and his attitudes towards his relatives and ancestors. The book's poems also reveal intimate details of the poet's private life, his breakdowns and hospitalizations.

Later volumes such as *Notebook 1967–68* and *The Dolphin* again provide much autobiographical information. *Notebook 1967–68,* for example, chronicles the period when the poet participated in a widely-publicized peace demonstration in Washington D.C. *The Dolphin* goes so far as to incorporate actual love letters between the poet and his second wife, Elizabeth Hardwick, which indicate the collapse of their marriage. While Lowell's poems are steeped in autobiography, they give a dramatic impression of the life rather than an exact rendition. Philip Cooper, in *The Autobiographical Myth of Robert Lowell* (1970), has shown how Lowell translates personal materials into his poems so that fact and fiction intertwine.

Overview of Critical Sources

Critical debate usually divides itself between those who favor Lowell's early 'formalist' poetry, which is dense with historical and religious allusion, and those who favor his middle period, which is more relaxed and accessible. The final books, from *Notebook 1967–68* to *Day by Day,* are generally thought to be inferior to the preceding ones, although these too have their advocates. While much of the shorter criticism is of a polemical nature, either canonizing or damning Lowell, much of the longer work seeks to explain the poet's dramatic stylistic shift away from Allen Tate and John Crowe Ransom and towards Elizabeth Bishop and William Carlos Williams. Several of the longer critical studies concentrate on the poet's religious attitudes, historical sense, neurosis, and commitment to social and political issues.

Evaluation of Selected Criticism

Axelrod, Steven Gould, *Robert Lowell: Life and Art.* Princeton: Princeton University Press, 1978. While focusing on Lowell's life and how he transmogrified it into art, this book also maps the stylistic changes that characterized his career. It describes the different reactions to *Life Studies,* especially those of his old mentor, Allen Tate, who thought the private material should be withheld from publication, and those of his new mentor, Williams, who thought the poems constituted some of his best work.

Fein, Richard J. *Robert Lowell.* Boston: Twayne Publishers, a Division of G. K. Hall, 1979 (2nd ed.). Fein provides a good introduction to Lowell's career. He begins by telling about his own first encounter with Lowell's poetry and ends with another kind of personal anecdote in "Looking for Robert Lowell in Boston," about a tour he took to many of the sites behind the poems. The bulk of the book offers lucid commentaries on Lowell's important poems, plays, and translations.

London, Michael and Robert Boyers, eds. *Robert Lowell, A Portrait of the Artist in His Time.* New York: David Lewis, 1970. This is a good collection of important essays written about Lowell. Many prominent critics and poets are represented, from Tate, R. P. Blackmur, Randall Jarrell, and Williams to M. L. Rosenthal, Geoffrey Hartman and Irvin Ehrenpreis. Also included is the famous passage from Norman Mailer's *The Armies of the Night* about Lowell's participation in the Vietnam demonstration. The book ends with an interview and extensive bibliography.

Staples, Hugh, *Robert Lowell: The First Twenty Years.* New York: Farrar, Straus & Cudahy, 1962. One of the most intelligent books about Lowell, this was also the first. It should be the first consulted in any study of Lowell's technique and themes. It concentrates on Lowell's religious and historical concerns, as well as the stylistic improvement between *Land of Unlikeness,* Lowell's first book, and *Lord Weary's Castle,* its successor which won the Pulitzer Prize. Its Appendix provides many of the sources of Lowell's more difficult poems and is especially useful.

Other Sources

Cosgrave, Patrick, *The Public Poetry of Robert Lowell.* New York: Taplinger Publishing, 1972. A stern appraisal of Lowell's work, influenced by the moral, rationalist strictures of Yvor Winters.

Mazzaro, Jerome, *The Poetic Themes of Robert Lowell.* Ann Arbor: University of Michigan Press, 1965. Explains some of the Catholic influences on

Lowell's early writing and how, when he became more secular, he also became more "confessional."

Parkinson, Thomas, ed. *Robert Lowell: A Collection of Critical Essays.* Englewood Cliffs: Prentice-Hall, 1968. Offers different critical appraisals of Lowell's poetry, early and late.

Williamson, Alan, *Pity the Monsters.* New Haven: Yale University Press, 1974. Delves into the psychological and political observations of Lowell and makes use of Freudian and post-Freudian modes of interpretation.

Yenser, Stephen, *Circle to Circle.* Berkeley: University of California Press, 1976. Concentrates on the unifying symbolic patterns in Lowell's work.

Selected Dictionaries and Encyclopedias

The Concise Encyclopedia of English and American Poets and Poetry, Hutchinson, 1970. Brief biography and introduction to most of Lowell's work.

Crowell's Handbook of Contemporary American Poetry, Thomas Crowell, 1973. Contains a good summary of Lowell's career, excluding the last few years.

The Oxford Companion to American Literature, Oxford University Press, 1983. Good introduction to Lowell's most important books of poems, plays and translations.

Henry Hart
The Citadel

MALCOLM LOWRY
1909-1957

Author's Chronology

Born July 28, 1909, in Liscard, Cheshire, England; *1923* enters public school, The Leys; *1927* ships out for Far East; *1929* begins literary apprenticeship under Conrad Aiken; enters St. Catherine's College, Cambridge; *1930* visits novelist Nordahl Grieg in Norway; *1933* publishes *Ultramarine,* his first novel; travels in Spain with Aiken; *1934* marries Jan Gabrial in Paris; *1935* spends ten days in psychiatric wing of Bellevue Hospital, New York; *1936* sails with Jan Gabrial from Los Angeles to Mexico, settling in Cuernavaca; begins writing *Under the Volcano; 1937* Jan Gabrial leaves him for good; *1939-1940* relocates in British Columbia; marries Margerie Bonner and moves into a squatter's shack at Dollarton Beach; *1944* completes fourth and last draft of *Under the Volcano; 1945-1946* returns with Margerie to Mexico; deported after six months; *1947* publishes *Under the Volcano;* travels to Europe via the Panama Canal; *1948-1949* visits Paris, Italy, and Brittany; back in Canada, works on *Dark as the Grave Wherein My Friend Is Laid,* and *La Mordida,* and several short stories; *1950-1954* works on *October Ferry to Gabriola; 1955* stays in London; hospitalized for psychiatric treatment; settles in Ripe, Sussex; *1957* dies "by misadventure" on June 27, in Ripe.

Author's Bibliography (selected)

Ultramarine, 1933 (novel); *Under the Volcano,* 1947 (novel); *Hear Us O Lord from Heaven Thy Dwelling Place,* 1961 (short fiction); *Selected Poems,* 1962; *Lunar Caustic,* 1963 (novella); *Selected Letters,* 1965; *Dark as the Grave Wherein My Friend Is Laid,* 1968 (novel); *October Ferry to Gabriola,* 1970 (novel).

Overview of Biographical Sources

The brief, tragic life of Malcolm Lowry is inevitably the stuff of legend—a sort of case history of the pathology of creative genius—and so it is unsurprising that the man has attracted as much attention as his works. Indeed, it has proved nearly impossible to write of the works without reference to the man, and difficult to write of the man apart from the legend. Lowry himself was responsible for much of this legend, which has been perpetuated and embellished by nearly all who knew him, as well as by many scholars who did not. Notable biographical accounts include the celebrated life by Douglas Day, chapters in critical studies by M. C. Bradbrook and Tony Kilgallin, and more than a dozen colorful essay-length memoirs by various of Lowry's friends. A good selection of the memoirs appears in *Malcolm Lowry: Psalms and Songs,* edited by Margerie Lowry (New York: New American Library, 1975). To these should be added the vivid reminiscences of Lowry by his literary mentor, Conrad Aiken, in *Ushant: An Essay* (New York: Duell, Sloan, & Pearce, 1952).

Evaluation of Selected Biographical Sources

Bradbrook, M. C. *Malcolm Lowry: His Art and Early Life, A Study in Transformation.* Cambridge: Cambridge University Press, 1974. Born in the same town as Lowry and his contemporary at Cambridge, Bradbrook is uniquely situated to assess Lowry's English origins. If her findings about Lowry's childhood in Leasowe are somewhat sketchy, her chapter on Cambridge life in 1929–1933 is helpful. Bradbrook's emphasis is on how Lowry both drew on and transformed his childhood and school experiences in his art.

Day, Douglas, *Malcolm Lowry: A Biography.* New York: Oxford University Press, 1973. Day's approach is decidedly Freudian, and while he presents much new information, the dominant image is that of the doom-haunted Lowry of the last years which, trenchantly recounted at the outset, controls the tone of the whole inquiry. This framework resembles that of *Under the Volcano*, but Day's emphasis, unlike Lowry's, is basically etiological. The explanations of Lowry's sexual phobias, alcoholism, and pathological "fear of his own art" are plausible and extremely vivid. Day's presentation of comparatively sanguine periods, such as Lowry's childhood and his early years in British Columbia, is less satisfactory because the biographer seems to find them less engaging. One is left wondering how this compulsively self-destructive, terrified man could have written such a masterful novel as *Under the Volcano*, save by kind of glorious fluke. Still, Day's biography is unquestionably forceful and will likely remain definitive.

Kilgallin, Tony, *Lowry.* Erin, Ontario: Press Porcepic, 1973. Kilgallin devotes a long chapter to Lowry's life, with emphasis on the Canadian years. Much of this information is derived from Kilgallin's interviews with various friends of the Lowrys in British Columbia. Some of the anecdotes seem legend-inspired rather than factually based, but Kilgallin is disinclined to view them critically.

Autobiographical Sources

The Selected Letters of Malcolm Lowry, edited by Harvey Breit and Margerie Lowry (New York: Lippincott, 1965). Written with endearing candor, wit, and sensitivity, Lowry's letters record his struggles with poverty, alcohol, neglect, self-doubt, and his creative "daemon." They are indispensable sources of insight into his character and his work.

Overview of Critical Sources

Since 1969, twenty books and monographs on Lowry have been published in English; half of these have appeared since 1978, and most are still in print.

Despite these signs of growing critical acceptance, Lowry's standing as a major modern writer is less than certain. While few can still doubt that *Under the Volcano* is one of the greatest novels of this century, the remainder of the Lowry canon, mostly consisting of heavily edited, fragmentary works published posthumously, is on the whole so much less accomplished that many critics have treated them less as literature, however incomplete, than as evidence of Lowry's psychological and alchoholic difficulties. At its worst this view can lead to a devaluation of *Under the Volcano* itself. Therefore one welcomes the attempts of recent critics to illuminate the entire *oeuvre* and to situate *Under the Volcano* firmly within it. However, until the lesser works are published in more complete and authoritative editions than are currently available, it will remain difficult to resolve all doubts about their potential artistic value.

Evaluation of Selected Criticism

Cross, Richard, *Malcolm Lowry: A Preface to His Fiction.* Chicago: University of Chicago Press, 1980. Of the several brief introductions to Lowry's works for the general reader, this one is probably the best. Reacting against the exclusively symbolist readings of *Under the Volcano,* Cross views the novel within the tradition of high modernism, which synthesized symbolism with mimetic representation of the mind and of the sensory world. Cross believes that the post-*Under the Volcano* works, except for one story, "The Forest Path to the Spring," fail because in them the synthesis collapses and realism is sacrificed to introspective symbolism.

Day, Douglas, *Malcolm Lowry: A Biography.* New York: Oxford University Press, 1973. Day's account of the writing and revision of *Under the Volcano* is informative and insightful. His analysis of the novel has become a touchstone for all subsequent critics. Finding it "the greatest religious novel of this century," Day decries the rarified attention critics have afforded isolated aspects of the work and calls for a holistic or "Gestalt" approach. He identifies five interrelated levels of meaning: the human, the political, the *chthonic,* the magical, and the religious. Since Day views Lowry as basically a one-book writer, his comments on most of the other fiction amount to summary dismissals.

Grace, Sherrill, *The Voyage That Never Ends: Malcolm Lowry's Fiction.* Vancouver: University of British Columbia Press, 1982. Grace vigorously argues that Lowry's *oeuvre,* though far from fully realized, is best seen as unified by the master-plan he devised in 1951. This was a monumentally ambitious scheme for gathering all his longer fiction, past and future, into a single interconnecting prose epic of multiple narrative and metafictional perspectives, and embodying the theme of life as an ongoing journey involving cycles of withdrawal and return, death and rebirth. Grace maintains that even *Under the Volcano* gains in significance from being seen in this hypothetical epic context. Larger claims may never be made for viewing Lowry's canon as an integral whole. The intentional fallacy notwithstanding, Grace does show how beneficial this "holistic" approach can be. Her interpretation of *October Ferry to Gabriola,* for instance, should go far toward salvaging that novel's standing.

Markson, David, *Malcolm Lowry's* Volcano: *Myth, Symbol, Meaning.* New York: Times Books, 1978. Markson, a friend and novelist-disciple of Lowry, aims to " 'retell' *Under the Volcano* in terms of those Joycean utilizations of myth and symbol that comprise its texture, dictate much of its interior form, and evince most of its meaning." Markson argues that the essential form is "spatial" rather than linear and temporal, and that suggestive juxtapositions of wide-ranging allusions, enriched by Lowry's shifting narrative context, build toward a massive, cumulative revelation of human worth tragically destroyed. This is an ambitious study, and its execution is sometimes difficult to follow. Yet if the overall interpretation is elusive, the piecemeal insights into the subtleties of the novel are often valuable.

Other Sources

Ackerley, Chris and Lawrence J. Clipper, *A Companion to Under the Volcano.* Vancouver: University of British Columbia Press, 1984. Exhaustively detailed notes and commentary on the novel's multifarious references to history, literature, topography, foreign terms, cabbalistic mysticism, and events in Lowry's life.

Binns, Ronald, *Malcolm Lowry.* London and New York: Methuen, 1984. Useful and well informed discussion of the Lowry myth, *Under the Volcano* as a modernist masterpiece, and the later works as experiments in metafiction.

Costa, Richard Hauer, *Malcolm Lowry.* New York: Twayne, 1972. A perceptive and cogent survey of the Lowry canon from a Jungian perspective; helpful annotated bibliography.

Edmonds, Dale, *"Under the Volcano:* A Reading of the 'Immediate Level,' " *Tulane Studies in English,* XVI (1968), 63–105. Pioneering study of the novel's realistic surface, its story, characters and setting.

New, William, H. *Malcolm Lowry: A Reference Guide.* Boston: G. K. Hall, 1978. A comprehensive, well-annotated bibliography of writings about Lowry through 1976.

Ronald G. Walker
University of Houston-Victoria

JOHN LYDGATE
c. 1370–1449

Author's Chronology

Born about 1370 in small village of Lydgate in Suffolk, England; about *1382* recruited as novice to great abbey of St. Edmund's at Bury; *1389* admitted to minor orders; *1397* ordained priest; c. *1397–1408* studies at Benedictine school in Oxford where he probably makes acquaintance of Prince of Wales, later Henry V; c. *1400–1410* composes early court poems and love-allegories, his first significant achievements; *1412* commissioned by Prince Henry to write story of Troy; *1423–1434* serves as prior at Hatfield Broadoak, Sussex (in residence only *1423–1426*); *1426–1428* probably in France; works on translation *Pilgrimage of the Life of Man* for Earl of Salisbury; *1429* returns from France, celebrates coronation of Henry VI in a number of occasional poems; *1431* commissioned by Humphrey of Gloucester, brother of Henry V and patron of new humanistic learning, to write the *Fall of Princes,* based on Boccaccio's *De Casibus Virorum Illustrium; 1434* writes *Life of St. Edmund* at request of Henry VI; *1449* dies, is buried in the abbey at Bury St. Edmunds.

Author's Bibliography (selected)

"Complaint of the Black Knight," "Flower of Courtesy," *Temple of Glass, Reason and Sensuality,* before 1410 (courtly love complaints and allegorical dream visions); *Troy Book,* 1412–1420 (epic); *Siege of Thebes,* 1420–1422 (chivalric romance); *Pilgrimage of the Life of Man,* 1426–1428 (religious allegory); *Fall of Princes,* 1431–1438/9 (encyclopedic collection of historical and legendary tales); *Life of St. Edmund,* 1433 (saint's legend); poems difficult to date but which reflect Lydgate's best work in a range of literary genres: "Churl and the Bird" (moral fable); *Life of Our Lady* (devotional legend); "As a Mydsomer Rose" (didactic lyric); *Ballade at the Reverence of Our Lady* (religious lyric).

Overview of Biographical Sources

A literary biography of Lydgate is near impossible for there is little sense of self-expression or inner development in his poems which are written more in adherence to conventional literary models than in response to particular events in his life. Moreover, the sheer bulk of his output coupled with uncertainty about the dates in much of the Lydgate canon has presented a daunting challenge to biographers. The one book that can be regarded as definitive is Walter F. Schirmer's *John Lydgate: A Study in the Culture of the XVth Century,* translated from German by Ann E. Keep. The result of over twenty years of research on the poet, Schirmer's thorough-going discussion of the monastic and courtly influences upon Lydgate's work is highly rewarding, but even his study, as the subtitle suggests, is more a detailed picture of an age than a life of the poet.

Evaluation of Selected Biographies

Schirmer, Walter F. *John Lydgate: A Study in the Culture of the XVth Century.* Berkeley: University of California Press, 1961; original in German 1952. Written by the foremost of Lydgatian scholars, Schirmer's book is the first attempt to give a full-length account of the life and writings of the poet. Schirmer does not, however, discuss any of Lydgate's works in great detail and his critical judgments are sometimes questionable. The great value of this study lies in the scholarly assessment of biographical information and in the substantial discussion of the social and cultural milieau of the fifteenth century. Though all scholars do not share Schirmer's belief that Lydgate and the fifteenth century are important for signaling a new direction in English literary traditions, his exhaustive study must be regarded as a starting point for all Lydgate readers. Erudite and learned, Schirmer's work has nonetheless been translated into a pleasant, readable style.

Autobiographical Sources

Scattered autobiographical comments can be found throughout Lydgate's work, but much of this material must be approached with caution. For example, one poem that purports to be "autobiographical" is his *Testament,* nearly 900 lines long, probably written in old age. The modern reader may be attracted by the lively, realistic details describing the poet's childhood follies, but even these "personal passages" are largely conventional and serve more formal literary and religious purposes in the poem. Only in a very loose sense can these and similar passages be considered "autobiographical."

Overview of Critical Sources

Textual scholars, linguists, literary historians, and students of the history of ideas have all been long attracted to the vast body of Lydgate's poetry, but his work until recently has suffered from a lack of modern critical studies. Consequently, many biographical dictionaries and standard histories of English literature still commonly regard Lydgate as an incompetent, prolix, and dull imitator of Chaucer. Along with Schirmer's biography, two other recent books by eminent medievalists have done much to define more accurately Lydgate's literary skills and historical importance. Alain Renoir's *The Poetry of John Lydgate* (1967) argues Lydgate's role as a transitional figure and precursor of the Renaissance in England. Derek Pearsall, *John Lydgate* (1970) challenges Renoir's views by seeing Lydgate as fundamentally representative of the Middle Ages and its intellectual, religious, and literary traditions. While the scholarly debate sparked by these studies continues, the greater number of critics has tended to side with Pearsall's position.

Evaluation of Selected Criticism

Pearsall, Derek, *John Lydgate.* Charlottesville: The University Press of Virginia, 1970. Pearsall's book presents the most accurate critical discussion and evaluation of Lydgate's poetry to have yet appeared. In place of the negative modern image of the poet, Pearsall establishes a picture of a highly professional and skillful craftsman in a wide range of poetic genres. This he does by reading the poetry neither as a forerunner of Renaissance attitudes nor according to modern esthetic theories but rather as perfectly representative of its age. By re-assessing Lydgate's work in light of its conventional, rhetorical poetic, Pearsall makes a valuable contribution to Lydgate studies. Written in a clear, brisk, often witty style, Pearsall's book is essential reading for anyone interested not only in Lydgate but also in late medieval culture and the rhetorical nature of its poetry.

Renoir, Alain, *The Poetry of John Lydgate*. Cambridge: Harvard University Press, 1967, Renoir's is the first major literary study to re-assess Lydgate's critical reputation and place in English literary history. Renoir finds in Lydgate a poet not so typical of the Middle Ages, not so Chaucerian as literary historians have assumed but one whose work anticipates Renaissance themes and attitudes. He centers his argument upon three major poems, the *Troy-Book, Fall of Princes,* and the *Siege of Thebes,* and shows how they all reflect a more distinct political consciousness and a humanistic attitude toward classical antiquity and man's intrinsic dignity. While Renoir's thesis has been seriously challenged by Pearsall's more balanced discussion, this study is nevertheless significant for the new light it throws on Lydgate's literary competence and the cultural climate in which he wrote.

Other Sources

Ayers, Robert W. "Medieval History, Moral Purpose, and the Structure of Lydgate's *Siege of Thebes,*" in *Publications of the Modern Language Association,* LXXII (1958), 463–474. Important, much-cited analysis of how Lydgate structures the poem by moralizing history to create a "mirror for princes."

Benson, C. David, *The History of Troy in Middle English Literature.* Haverhill, Suffolk: St. Edmundsbury Press, 1980, pp. 97–129. Best recent account of Lydgate's narrative strategies and poetic craftsmanship in the *Troy Book.*

Hammond, Eleanor P. ed. *English Verse between Chaucer and Surrey.* Durham, NC: Duke University Press, 1927, pp. 77–187. Despite the early date, still an excellent critical introduction to Lydgate's poetry; extensive selections from the poems and scholarly commentary.

Norton-Smith, John, ed. *John Lydgate: Poems.* Oxford: Clarendon Press, 1966. Brief biographical outline but full, learned notes on poems illustrating Lydgate's wide range of competence in different genres and styles.

Pearsall, Derek, "The English Chaucerians," in *Chaucer and Chaucerians.* ed. D. S. Brewer. University of Alabama: University Press, 1966, pp. 201–239.

Though not exclusively on Lydgate, this essay has an illuminating, succinct discussion of the rhetorical basis of his poetry which will be of interest to the advanced student and specialist.

————, "John Lydgate," in *British Writers,* Vol. I. ed. Ian Scott-Kilvert. New York: Charles Scribner's Sons, 1979; originally 1969, #211 British Council series *Writers and Their Work.* Discriminating overview and the best short introduction to Lydgate's poetry and significance for students and general readers.

Selected Dictionaries and Encyclopedias

Critical Survey of Poetry, Salem Press, 1982. Brief biography and a discussion of several of Lydgate's important works.

The Critical Temper: A Survey of Modern Criticism, Frederick Ungar, 1969. Collection of excerpts that record the shifts in modern critical taste concerning Lydgate's achievement.

Joseph Marotta
St. John's University

ARCHIBALD MACLEISH
1892-1982

Author's Chronology

Born May 7, 1892, Glencoe, Illinois; *1907* attends Hotchkiss School; *1915* graduates Yale; *1916* marries Ada Hitchcock; *1917* World War I: Ambulance Corps and Army; *1919* law degree from Harvard; *1923* moves to France with wife and two children; during Paris period, *1923-1928* writes *Happy Marriage,* 1924, *Nobodaddy,* 1926, *Streets in the Moon,* 1926; makes a five-month trip to Persia; *1928* returns to farm at Conway, Massachusetts; *1930* joins *Fortune* magazine; *1939* appointed Librarian of Congress; *1940-1945* appointed Assistant Secretary of State; helped plan UNESCO; *1949-1962* Boyleston professor at Harvard; *1962-1967* teaches at Amherst College; *1932* receives Pulitzer Prize for *Conquistador; 1959* Pulitzer Prize for *J. B.: Play in Verse; 1966* Academy Award for best screen play, *Eleanor Roosevelt Story;* dies April 20, 1982, in Boston, Massachusetts.

Author's Bibliography (selected)

Tower of Ivory, 1917 (poems); *The Happy Marriage and Other Poems,* 1924; *The Pot of Earth,* 1925 (poem); *The Hamlet of A. MacLeish,* 1928 (poem); *New Found Land,* 1930 (poem); *Conquistador,* 1932 (epic poem); *Frescoes for Mr. Rockefeller's City,* 1933 (poems); *Poems 1924-1933* (first anthology); *A Time to Speak: The Selected Prose of Archibald MacLeish,* 1941 (essays); *A Time to Act: Selected Addresses,* 1942 (essays); *The American Story,* 1944 (play); *Collected Poems: 1917-1952,* 1958; *J. B.: A Play in Verse,* 1958; *The Dialogues of Archibald MacLeish and Mark Van Doren,* 1964; *The Eleanor Roosevelt Story,* 1966 (screen play); *The Human Season: New and Selected Poems, 1926-1972,* 1972; *New and Collected Poems,* 1976; *Riders on the Earth,* 1978 (essays and recollections).

Overview of Biographical Sources

Although MacLeish is a celebrated writer, there is not any extensive study of his life or works. Materials published and available since his death, especially his *Letters: 1907-1982* may lead to an eventual and complete biography. Biographical sketches are available in encyclopedias, the *Annual Obituaries* (1982), and in the *Contemporary Authors* Series, a bio-bibliographical guide to current authors and their works. The most complete autobiographical material is in Signi Falk, *Archibald MacLeish* (New York: Twayne, 1965). This book gives a chronological approach to his life and works. It is not an in-depth study, but is interestingly written and readily available.

Autobiographical Sources

The work that presents the most autobiographical detail is *The Dialogues of Archibald MacLeish and Mark Van Doren,* edited by Warren Bush (New York:

E.P. Dutton, 1964). Originally produced as a television experiment and broadcast in 1962, it gives excellent insight into both these authors. Not autobiographical in the traditional sense of the word, it records their spontaneous ruminations on poetry and drama, on social and political events of the Kennedy era, on teaching and writing. It is an expression of each author's values, his perception of God and man. One can see, especially in MacLeish, a fundamental belief in the destiny of America and in love and friendship.

MacLeish's last book, *Riders on the Earth* (Boston: Houghton Mifflin, 1978), contains essays and recollections. A section entitled "Autobiographical Information" speaks mainly of his Paris experience and literary acquaintances, especially of Ernest Hemingway, his recollections as a football player at Yale, and his reactions to winning the Pulitzer Prizes. Some of MacLeish's poems are admittedly autobiographical, especially those entitled so by himself in the first part of *The Human Season* (1972). In 1983 his *Letters: 1907–1982* (Boston: Houghton Mifflin) were published, which shed important information on his life.

Overview of Critical Sources

With the exception of Signi Falk's *Archibald MacLeish* and Grover Smith's *Archibald MacLeish,* there are no full-length studies of the author. Therefore it is necessary to consult periodicals and works of general criticism. Critics that treat his poetry are especially interested in the works of the 1920's and 1930's. Dramatic criticism focuses on his Pulitzer Prize winning play, *J. B.*

Contemporary Authors (Detroit: Gale Research, 1974) gives a quick synopsis of various works that have critiqued MacLeish, mostly periodicals. It also includes a chronology and a bibliography of the author. *Dialogues in American Drama* by Ruby Cohn (Bloomington: Indiana University Press, 1971) is of interest because it deals with the plays of MacLeish, especially his most famous, *J. B.,* a prize-winning Broadway production. The analysis of the earlier plays is minimal, since Cohn dismisses them as mere transfers of MacLeish's poetry to drama, usually poorly done. There is a good though brief analysis of MacLeish in Hyatt H. Waggoner's *American Poetry from the Puritans to the Present* (Boston: Houghton Mifflin, 1968). The author notes MacLeish as always in touch with his times, although the analysis is mostly focused on earlier works in the tradition of T. S. Eliot. Horace Gregory's *A History of American Poetry* (New York: Gordian Press, 1969) gives a historical and biographical sketch, mainly of the earlier poetry of MacLeish.

Evaluation of Selected Criticism

Falk, Signi. *Archibald MacLeish.* New York: Twayne, 1965. This is the most complete study to date on MacLeish. It is however not a detailed study, but rather a worthy handbook of introduction to the author. It touches all his works, giving comments from the critics of all varieties, especially those who were current in other fields at the time MacLeish published his different works, such as Reinhold Niebuhr's comments on *J. B.*

Smith, Grover, *Archibald MacLeish.* Minneapolis: University of Minnesota Press, 1971. Smith gives a credible examination of MacLeish's important works, concentrating more on poetry than on drama, except for *J. B.* Smith offers a worthy comparison between T. S. Eliot's *Wasteland* and MacLeish's *The Pot of Earth.* There is a short biography and a bibliography of the author's works.

Selected Dictionaries and Encyclopedias

American Writers, Charles Scribner's Sons, 1983. The essay by Grover Smith contains much the same material as Smith's monograph by the University of Minnesota American Writers Series.

American Writers since 1900, St. James Press, 1983. Chronology of MacLeish's life and a complete list of publications; short evaluative essay by Robert K. Johnson.

Articles on American Literature, Duke University Press, Vol. 1. *1950–1967,* 1970; Vol. 2. *1968–1975,* 1979. Contains a comprehensive bibliography on articles in periodicals relating to MacLeish.

Magill's Bibliography of Literary Criticism, Salem Press, 1979. Gives references both in periodicals and books to MacLeish's poetry and drama, especially to *J. B.*

S. Catharine Christi

HUGH MACLENNAN
1907

Author's Chronology

Born March 20, 1907, Glace Bay, Nova Scotia, Canada, a coal mining company town in which his father was a surgeon; *1915* family moves to Halifax; *1917* much of Halifax destroyed in an explosion; *1928* receives B.A. from Dalhousie University, gets Rhodes scholarship to Oxford, plays varsity tennis there; *1932* graduates from Oxford, begins graduate studies at Princeton; *1935* awarded Ph.D in Roman history, takes position teaching Latin at Lower Canada College, a boys' school in Montreal; *1936* marries Dorothy Duncan, an American writer and painter; *1941 Barometer Rising,* set in Halifax at the time of the 1917 explosion, the third novel MacLennan wrote but the first to be published, appears and is a success; *1945* following another success with his second published novel, *Two Solitudes,* resigns post at Lower Canada College; works in journalism and broadcasting; *1951* takes part-time position in the English Department at McGill University (assumes full-time post in 1964; becomes professor emeritus in 1979); *1953* elected Fellow of the Royal Society of Canada; *1957* after a long illness, Dorothy Duncan dies; *1959* marries Frances Walker; *1967* after a period of producing non-fiction, publishes *Return of the Sphinx,* which receives generally unfavorable reviews; made Companion of the Order of Canada; *1980* publishes his latest novel, *Voices in Time,* another success.

Author's Bibliography (selected)

Barometer Rising, 1941 (novel); *Two Solitudes,* 1945 (novel); *The Precipice,* 1948 (novel); *Cross-Country* 1949 (essays); *Each Man's Son,* 1951 (novel); *Thirty and Three,* 1954 (essays); *The Watch That Ends the Night,* 1959 (novel) ; *Scotchman's Return* 1960 (essays); *Return of the Sphinx,* 1967 (novel); *The Colour of Canada,* revised edition, 1972 (non-fiction); *Rivers of Canada,* 1974 (non-fiction); *The Other Side of Hugh MacLennan: Selected Essays Old and New,* ed. Elspeth Cameron, 1978; *Voices in Time,* 1980 (novel).

Overview of Biographical Sources

Although MacLennan's life has been used by critics to illuminate his novels, and although there is a valuable collection of primary source materials, including his two unpublished novels, at McGill University, and other collections of his papers at the Universities of Toronto and Calgary, only one book-length biography has appeared.

Evaluation of Selected Biographies

Cameron, Elspeth, *Hugh MacLennan: A Writer's Life.* Toronto: University of Toronto Press, 1981. Cameron has done a thorough job of researching

MacLennan's life, examining letters and other primary sources, conducting interviews, and receiving cooperation from MacLennan himself, who has said that Cameron knows more about his life than he does. This is a definitive biography, not likely to be outdated by the emergence of any new material. Excellent for its factual details, it tends to slight critical analysis or imaginative use of biographical information to help interpret the novels. It is an extremely useful, if somewhat uninspired, book.

Duncan, Dorothy, *Bluenose: A Portrait of Nova Scotia.* New York: Harpers, 1942. MacLennan's first wife, in writing about Nova Scotia as seen by an American, includes interesting personal anecdotes and impressions about her marriage, her husband's character and writing, his family and his milieu.

Autobiographical Sources
MacLennan, as of 1985, has yet to publish the memoirs which he turned to after his latest novel. However, anyone familiar with the outline of his life will recognize autobiographical aspects in all of his novels. Notable examples include: the recurring doctor figure, variously modeled on his father: the Cape Breton mining community of MacLennan's childhood in *Each Man's Son,* Catherine in *The Watch That Ends the Night,* a characterization that owes a lot to MacLennan's wife Dorothy; and Paul in *Two Solitudes* and George in *The Watch That Ends the Night,* characters for whom MacLennan himself serves as something of a prototype.
Additionally, a great many of MacLennan's numerous essays are at least partially autobiographical; a good introduction to the autobiographical nature of his personal essays may be gained from *The Other Side of Hugh MacLennan.*

Overview of Critical Sources
As MacLennan pioneered the introduction of "nationalist" themes in Canadian fiction, critical emphasis has been on seeing him as a *Canadian* writer. Additionally, although his novelistic techniques and style have changed and developed, he has been generally a non-experimental realist, writing novels more notable for their ideas than for their plot, characterization or style. Thus, critical discussions tend to approach MacLennan's novels thematically. His dramatized ideas about history, nationalism and geography, the relationship between Quebec anglophones and francophones, the Odysseus-wanderer theme, religion, psychology, and politics has received more attention than his craft *per se.* Frequently speaking out, as a journalist as well as a novelist, on Canadian politics, MacLennan has been a controversial public figure. While they have been attacked as being simplistic or excessively didactic, generally his novels, while receiving limited critical attention outside of Canada, have been frequently, and favorably discussed in the Canadian press and scholarly journals. Although his reputation suffered something of a set-back with the publica-

tion of *Return of the Sphinx,* with *Voices in Time* he regained a secure position as one of Canada's most important men of letters.

Evaluation of Selected Criticism

Buitenhuis, Peter, *Hugh MacLennan.* Toronto: Forum House, 1971. A balanced summary and overview of MacLennan's works through *Return of the Sphinx.* Buitenhuis admires the intelligence and insight MacLennan brings to the novels, but finds fault with his "old-fashioned techniques of narration."

Cockburn, Robert, *The Novels of Hugh MacLennan.* Montreal: Harvest House, 1969. The most unfavorable of the books on MacLennan, this work, while conceding MacLennan's pioneering expression of Canadian experience, attacks the novels for being dominated by theme, showing a poverty of imagination and being excessively didactic. There is a germ of truth to Cockburn's adverse remarks, but they are overstated.

Goetsch, Paul, ed. *Hugh MacLennan.* Toronto: McGraw-Hill and Ryerson, 1973. Goetsch puts together twenty critical articles and reviews that give a good selection of different approaches to MacLennan criticism.

Lucas, Alec, *Hugh MacLennan.* Toronto: McClelland and Stewart, 1970. Lucas presents a generalized discussion of nationalism, autobiography, psychology, and social themes in MacLennan's work. He finds MacLennan to be essentially a religious novelist, and his novels to be parables of religious humanism. While Lucas's remarks are generally thoughtful, his attempt to find the "key" to the novels appears a bit forced.

Morley, Patricia, *The Immoral Moralists: Hugh MacLennan and Leonard Cohen.* Toronto: Clark Irwin, 1972. By focusing on MacLennan's role as an iconoclast attacking Victorian morality, Morley produces one of the most original and interesting discussions of MacLennan's work. Her ideas, such as comparing MacLennan and D. H. Lawrence, are not always convincing, but they are worth consideration. Morley's approach provides only a partial insight into MacLennan's novels, but a valuable one.

Woodcock, George, *Hugh MacLennan.* Toronto: Copp Clark, 1969. This pamphlet-length work remains the best brief introduction to MacLennan's work. It is a balanced discussion, quite favorable to MacLennan while recognizing his "manifest imperfections," such as a tendency to facile optimism. Woodcock discusses both MacLennan's ideas and techniques, and their connections; he finds *Each Man's Son, Barometer Rising, The Watch That Ends the Night* and the earlier half of *Two Solitudes* to be superior to the other novels. Woodcock is especially insightful in this work and in an earlier essay, "A Nation's Odyssey: The Novels of Hugh MacLennan," *Canadian Literature* 10

768Hugh MacLennan

(1961), 7–18, on the central importance of the Odysseus myth in MacLennan's novels.

Other Sources

Cameron, Donald, "Hugh MacLennan: The Tennis Racket is an Antelope Bone," *Journal of Canadian Fiction* 1 (1972) 40–46. A free-ranging interview in which MacLennan supplies various reminiscences and thoughts about the relation between his life and his novels.

Jones, D. G. *Butterfly on Rock.* Toronto: University of Toronto Press, 1970. Discusses MacLennan *passim,* comparing his novels to other Canadian works.

Mathews, Robin, "Hugh MacLennan: The Nationalist Dilemma," in *Canadian Literature: Surrender or Revolution.* Toronto: Steel Rail Educational Publishing, 1978. Discusses MacLennan's novels from a "class-struggle" perspective; sees both strengths and weaknesses.

Staines, David, "Mapping the Terrain," *Mosaic* XI (1978), 137–151. Sees MacLennan from his unpublished novels through *The Watch That Ends the Night,* moving from the international, to the national, to the character, novel.

Wilson, Edmund, "Hugh MacLennan," in *O Canada.* New York: Farrar, Strauss and Giroux, 1965. Praises *The Precipice* and *The Watch That Ends the Night;* attacks *Two Solitudes* and *Each Man's Son.* Generally very favorable to MacLennan.

Selected Dictionaries and Encyclopedias

Critical Survey of Long Fiction, Salem Press, 1983. A concise biography and overview of MacLennan's fiction, and brief analyses of selected novels.

An Oxford Companion to Canadian History and Literature, Oxford University Press, 1967. A very brief biography and discussion of the novels through *The Watch That Ends the Night.*

William B. Stone
Indiana University Northwest

THOMAS BABINGTON MACAULAY
1800–1859

Author's Chronology

Born October 25, 1800, Rothley Temple, Leicestershire, England; *1813–1818* attends boarding school; *1818* enters Trinity College, Cambridge; *1824* becomes a Fellow of Trinity College; *1826* called to the bar; *1830* elected to Parliament for Calne, Wiltshire; *1831* mother dies; *1831–1832* campaigns effectively for the Reform Bills; *1832* elected to Parliament for Leeds and becomes a Commissioner on the Board of Control for India; *1834* moves to India and becomes the Law Member of the Governor General's Supreme Council for India; sister Margaret dies and sister Hannah marries Charles Trevelyan; *1838* father dies; returns to England; *1839* elected to Parliament for Edinburgh and becomes Secretary-at-War; *1843* first authorized collection of essays appears; *1846* becomes Paymaster-General; *1847* loses Parliament seat for Edinburgh; *1848* volumes I and II of *The History of England from the Accession of James the Second* appear; *1852* regains Edinburgh seat in Parliament and has heart attack; *1856* resigns from Parliament because of illness; *1859* made Baron Macaulay of Rothley; *1859* dies December 28.

Author's Bibliography (selected)

Lays of Ancient Rome, 1842 (poetry); *Critical and Historical Essays Contributed to the Edinburgh Review,* 1843; *The History of England from the Accession of James the Second,* volumes I and II, 1848, volumes III and IV, 1855, and volume V (this last edited by Hannah [Macaulay], Lady Trevelyan), 1861; *Speeches of the Right Honorable T. B. Macaulay, M. P.: Corrected by Himself,* 1854; *Miscellaneous Writings of Lord Macaulay* (ed. T. F. Ellis), 1860; *The Works of Lord Macaulay* (ed. by Hannah [Macaulay], Lady Trevelyan), 1866 and 1898 (as the Albany edition).

Overview of Biographical Sources

G. O. Trevelyan's *The Life and Letters of Lord Macaulay* (1876; rev. 1908) has set the tone for all subsequent biographical studies. No one has, as yet, tried to supplant it as the definitive study of Macaulay's life. Most studies have either focused on a particular aspect of Macaulay's life or have been popularizations of the life. Earliest of the former is Frederick Arnold's *The Public Life of Lord Macaulay* (London: Tinsley Brothers, 1862), which presents a detailed account of Macaulay's political career; its description of the public aspect of Macaulay's life is more complete than that found in Trevelyan's biography. John Clive's *Macaulay: The Shaping of the Historian* (New York: Alfred A. Knopf, 1973) is a bio-critical work that focuses on the development of Macaulay's literary and public careers to 1839. It provides the fullest account of its subject's early life. R. C. Beatty's *Lord Macaulay: Victorian Liberal* (Norman: University of Oklahoma Press, 1938, revised 1979) has been severely criticized for its unsympathetic view of Macaulay; its independent point of view may make it worth reading for the contrast with commonly accepted interpretations by Macaulay's admirers.

Evaluation of Selected Biographies

Bryant, Arthur, *Macaulay.* London: Peter Davies, 1932. New York: D. Appleton, 1933. Revised edition: London: Weidenfeld and Nicolson, 1979. This book is the most successful of the popularizations of Macaulay's life. Bryant admires Macaulay as a "great master" of historical writing and clearly relishes discussing Macaulay's active life. *Macaulay* provides an interesting and reliable brief introduction to its subject's life.

Trevelyan, G. O. *The Life and Letters of Lord Macaulay,* two volumes. London: Longmans, 1876 (revised 1908). This book is the standard biography. It has been favorably compared with the best literary biographies in the English language; it discusses Macaulay's life with such grace and thoroughness that no other biography has come close to supplanting it. Most subsequent biographies have followed its lead in portraying Macaulay, including emphasizing the public man at the expense of the private one. All the significant facts of Macaulay's life are presented in elegantly readable language, but little of Macaulay's private character is examined.

Autobiographical Sources

An important autobiographical resource has been published in recent years: *The Letters of Thomas Babington Macaulay,* edited by Thomas Pinney in six volumes (London: Cambridge University Press, 1974–1981). This edition provides far more insight into Macaulay's character than do any of the biographies. Pinney's one-volume edition, *The Selected Letters of Thomas Babington Macaulay* (London: Cambridge University Press, 1982), presents many of the most interesting of Macaulay's letters.

Overview of Critical Sources

Macaulay wrote to reach a large audience; many critics have seemingly faulted him for this and have denigrated his work as decidedly middlebrow. Other critics have admired Macaulay's rhetorical skill and his vivid imagery. Most have focused on his historical writings while neglecting his literary criticism, political commentaries, and poetry. Typical of nineteenth-century critics is J. Cotter Morison, who in his *Macaulay* (London: Macmillan, 1882) declares that Macaulay's "narrative power among historians is quite unapproached, and on a level with that of the greatest masters of prose fiction." Twentieth-century admirers of Macaulay have generally followed the lead of the nineteenth-century critics in emphasizing his narrative style. Others have argued that his political beliefs made him color history with the middle-class values of the Whigs. The most recent and thorough examination of Macaulay's social values is J. Hamburger's *Macaulay and the Whig Tradition* (Chicago: University of Chicago Press, 1976).

Evaluation of Selected Criticism

Firth, Charles, *Commentary on Macaulay's History of England.* ed. Godfrey Davies. London: Macmillan, 1938. This is the most thorough study of Macaulay's methods as a historian. Firth discusses in detail the structure and literary style of the historical writings, while also examining their sources. His is a balanced point of view, noting Macaulay's stylistic strengths and weaknesses. For instance, he shows how Macaulay brings life to the past yet complains that Macaulay's historical portraits often produce mere caricatures.

Millgate, Jane, *Macaulay.* London: Routledge and Kegan Paul, 1973. This is the best general introduction to Macaulay's life and writings, including the criticism and poetry. Millgate's approach is biographical, tracing the development of Macaulay's art from youth to death. She attempts to distinguish between the continuing literary merits of the writings and Macaulay's importance as a historical figure. She is not entirely successful in this, although she makes a good case for Macaulay's literary merit lying in his following Samuel Johnson's dictum to "instruct by pleasing."

Other Sources

Jebb, R. C. *Macaulay.* Cambridge: Cambridge University Press, 1900. Jebb's discussion of Macaulay's style can help one to understand the author's literary skill.

Selected Dictionaries and Encyclopedias

The Victorian Experience: The Prose Writers, Ohio University Press, 1982. Provides a discussion of the paradoxes of Macaulay's writings: the contemplative versus active styles.

Kirk H. Beetz
National University, Sacramento

LOUIS MACNEICE
1907–1963

Author's Chronology

Born September 12, 1907, Belfast, Ireland of Anglo-Irish parents; *1914* mother dies of tuberculosis; *1921* attends Marlborough College on an entrance scholarship; *1926* enters Merton College, Oxford; *1928* takes a first in Honors Mods.; *1929* publishes his first collection of poetry, *Blind Fireworks; 1930* takes another first in Greats, marries Giovanna Marie Therese Babette Ezra, accepts position as assistant lecturer in classics at Birmingham University; *1935* publishes *Poems,* an important contribution to his reputation; his wife leaves him; *1936* publishes translation *The Agamemnon of Aeschylus;* travels to Iceland with W. H. Auden; divorces his wife; *1937* Group Theatre produces *The Agamemnon of Aeschylus; 1939* moves to America and gives a series of lectures at Cornell University; *1940* returns to England and tries to join the Armed Forces but is rejected due to poor eyesight; *1941* joins the Features Department of the BBC; *1943* marries Hedli Anderson, a singer from the Group Theatre; *1950* takes a leave of absence from the BBC to be the Director of the British Institute in Athens, Greece; *1957* awarded Commander of the Order of the British Empire; *1963* gives the Clark Lectures at Cambridge, later published as *Varieties of Parable* (1965); catches cold while doing underground recordings for radio drama for the BBC, develops pneumonia, dies September 3.

Author's Bibliography (selected)

Blind Fireworks, 1929 (poems); *Letters from Iceland* with W. H. Auden, 1937 (prose and poems); *The Agamemnon of Aeschylus,* 1936 (translation); *Modern Poetry,* 1938 (criticism); *Autumn Journal,* 1939 (poems); *The Poetry of W. B. Yeats,* 1941 (criticism); *The Dark Tower and Other Radio Scripts,* 1947 (radio drama); *Ten Burnt Offerings,* 1952 (poems); *The Strings Are False, An Unfinished Autobiography,* ed. E. R. Dodds, 1965; *One for the Grave,* 1968 (play).

Overview of Biographical Sources

There are few biographies of MacNeice that are not also studies of his poetry. His life, especially his childhood, played an important role in forming his concern for beliefs, and his difficulty in having any of his own. Few works even attempt to separate the man from his poetry. Terence Brown's *Louis MacNeice: The Skeptical Vision* (1975) is one of the more important biographical/critical studies. Brown has with Alec Reid collected personal reminiscences of MacNeice's friends for their *Time Was Away: The World of Louis MacNeice* (Dublin: Dolmen Press, 1974). Many of MacNeice's friends also wrote obituary tributes, including T. S. Eliot in *The Times,* 5 September 1963. W. H. Auden delivered an address at All Souls, Langham Place which has since been published as *Louis MacNeice: A Memorial* (London: Faber and Faber, 1963). One of the few works to deal extensively with the job that MacNeice held from 1941 until his death is Barbara Coulton's *Louis MacNeice in the BBC* (1980).

Evaluation of Selected Biographies

Brown, Terence, *Louis MacNeice: Skeptical Vision.* New York: Barnes and Noble, 1975. Brown combines MacNeice's biography with criticism of his poetry to establish what he terms MacNeice's "skepticism." MacNeice was known for seeming aloof and cold but was also witty and playful. Brown takes MacNeice's personal reserve and his philosophical reserve and suggests that they came from the same source, MacNeice's childhood and rejection of his father's (a Protestant Bishop) beliefs, and that they establish a skeptical core in the poetry. MacNeice's works are very personal and do reveal much about the poet; so Brown's approach works well, doing justice to both the man and the poetry.

Coulton, Barbara, *Louis MacNeice in the BBC.* London: Faber and Faber, 1980. Coulton presents the first major work on MacNeice's years with the BBC. This is a comprehensive survey of his radio career, emphasizing his value to the BBC. She does not discuss his poetry, leaving that for other critics. Her writing style is enjoyable, and her chapter on MacNeice's trip to India is especially well written.

Dodds, E. R. *Missing Persons.* Oxford: Clarendon Press, 1977. Dodd's autobiography is one of the many works about another writer which includes information about MacNeice. Dodds, MacNeice's long-time friend and editor, includes biographical information on MacNeice, W. H. Auden, and the friendship the three shared.

Autobiographical Sources

MacNeice never completed an autobiography and left only a manuscript in various stages of revision with his friend E. R. Dodds. Published posthumously, *The Strings Are False, An Unfinished Autobiography,* edited by Dodds (London: Faber and Faber, 1965; New York: Oxford University Press, 1966) is a loosely constructed book which presents a portrait of MacNeice as he matures as a person, a thinker, and as a writer. Covering his childhood until 1940, MacNeice reveals himself in many difficult situations: his mother's death when he was seven, and his first wife leaving him for another man. This book, together with his reminiscent-reflective poems such as *Autumn Journal* (1939) and *Autumn Sequel: A Rhetorical Poem* (1954), presents a persona of a complex and interesting man and artist.

Overview of Critical Sources

Most recent criticism of MacNeice's poetry aims to reestablish MacNeice as an important poet of the Modern period. Long overshadowed by the brilliance of his good friend W. H. Auden, MacNeice's poetry is finally being treated as works with significant philosophical content as well as having a technically smooth surface. Few see his work anymore as simply journalistic poetry, detached from the writer; it is now known that many of MacNeice's greater works are personal reminiscenses. The first major study of MacNeice as a serious thinker whose philosophical uncertainties added depth to his work was William T. McKinnon's *Apollo's Blended Dream: A Study of the Poetry of Louis Mac-Neice* (1971). McKinnon seems to have set the precedent of blending a biography and a critical study for the study of MacNeice's poetry to show how MacNeice the man, especially a man with doubts, influenced the surface and content of the poems. Since McKinnon, Brown published his *Skeptical Vision* (see above) following the same critical approach with more variation of emphasis than substance. The publication of Robyn Marsack's *The Cave of Making: The Poetry of Louis MacNeice* (London: Oxford University Press, 1982) demonstrates a growing critical appreciation of poetry that was once deemed detached and without depth because of its brilliant surface.

Despite the lack of full-length studies on MacNeice's poetry, MacNeice has always had a section of books that dealt with the poets of the 1930's. While this criticism is generally less favorable, MacNeice is consistently praised for his poetic skill, even when the critic thinks he has lost his poetic voice. One of the more important chapter-length studies of MacNeice is G. S. Fraser's "Evasive Honesty," in his *Vision and Rhetoric* (London: Faber and Faber, 1959).

Evaluation of Selected Criticism

McKinnon, William T. *Apollo's Blended Dream: A Study of the Poetry of Louis MacNeice.* London, New York, and Toronto: Oxford University Press, 1971. This major study of MacNeice's poetry focuses on MacNeice as a thinker, spending the first half of the book on MacNeice's philosophy and his lack of a system of belief even though he knew the importance of beliefs. The second part of the book presents how the problem of belief was expressed by MacNeice's imagery, structure, prosody, and voice.

Moore, Donald Best. *The Poetry of Louis MacNeice.* Leicester: Leicester University Press, 1972. The value of this work is more its lack of academic sophistication than its limited insights. Moore is a businessman who wrote the book in his spare time. He generally does a good job, but occasionally he makes major errors in his understanding of the poetry. The book's freshness comes from Moore's personal knowledge of MacNeice in the 1930's and his obvious enjoyment with his subject matter.

Other Sources

Armitage, Christopher and Neil Clark, *A Bibliography of the Works of Louis MacNeice.* London: Kaye and Ward, 1973.

McKinnon, William T. "Bibliography of Louis MacNeice," *Bulletin of Bibliography and Magazine Notes*. 27, nos. 2 and 3 (April-June 1970).

Southworth, James G. *Sowing the Spring: Studies in British Poets from Hopkins to MacNeice*. Oxford: B. Blackwell, 1940. Traces the development of modern British verse, especially the experiments in form and prosody within the English tradition of poetry.

Stanford, Derek, *Stephen Spender, Louis MacNeice, Cecil Day Lewis*. Grand Rapids, MI: Eerdmans, 1969. Evaluates MacNeice in relation to his immediate contemporaries.

Selected Dictionaries and Encyclopedias

Contemporary Authors, Gale Research, 1980. Lists of personal information and works. Very brief critical sketch and list of biographical and critical sources.

Contemporary Literary Criticism, Gale Research. A collection of excerpts from major critical works. A useful guide to the works on MacNeice and for a general approach to his poetry. MacNeice is included in vols. 1 (1973), 4 (1975), and 10 (1979).

Dictionary of Literary Biography, Gale Research, 1983. Biographical and critical overview of MacNeice's life and works. MacNeice is included in both "The British Poets, 1914-1945" and "Modern British Dramatists, 1900-1945." An excellent starting place for those new to MacNeice. Includes a strong selected bibliography

S. E. Jackson
Oklahoma State University

BERNARD MALAMUD
1914

Author's Chronology

Born April 26, 1914, Brooklyn, New York, to immigrant parents Max and Bertha Fidelman Malamud; *1928–1932* attends Erasmus Hall High School; *1936* receives B.A., City College of New York; *1940–1949* teaches English in New York evening high schools; *1942* receives M.A., Columbia University, thesis on Thomas Hardy; *1945* marries Ann De Chiara; *1949–1961* teaches English at Oregon State University; *1952* publishes first novel, *The Natural; 1956* spends year in Rome; *1956–1957 Partisan Review* fellowship in fiction; *1958* receives Rosenthal Foundation award for *The Assistant; 1959* receives National Book Award and a Ford Foundation Fellowship in humanities and arts; *1961* begins teaching at Bennington College, Vermont; *1965* visits Russia; *1966* publishes *The Fixer* and for it, in 1967, receives both a second National Book Award and a Pulitzer Prize; *1967* elected to American Academy of Arts and Sciences; *1966–1968* visiting lecturer at Harvard; *1982* publishes *God's Grace; 1983 The Stories of Bernard Malamud;* continues to teach at Bennington.

Author's Bibliography

The Natural, 1952 (novel); *The Assistant,* 1957 (novel); *The Magic Barrel,* 1958 (stories); *A New Life,* 1961 (novel); *Idiots First,* 1963 (stories); *The Fixer,* 1966 (novel); *A Malamud Reader,* 1967 (anthology); *Pictures of Fidelman: An Exhibition,* 1969 (novel); *The Tenants,* 1971 (novel); *Rembrandt's Hat,* 1973 (stories); *Dubin's Lives,* 1979 (novel); *God's Grace,* 1982 (novel); *The Stories of Bernard Malamud,* 1983.

Overview of Biographical Sources

There is no book-length biography of Malamud. A few of the book-length studies of his fiction contain a simple outline of essential biographical information, but all are quite minimal.

Autobiographical Sources

Malamud has not written an autobiography. He has always been reluctant to grant interviews and seems to have been consistently indifferent to establishing himself as a "literary personality." Several critics have pointed out connections between setting or theme in some of his novels and specific episodes or influences in Malamud's life—relating, for example, his experience at Oregon State to the action of *A New Life.* But no one has attempted to derive an "autobiography" from the contents of Malamud's novels.

Overview of Critical Sources

The lack of biographical/autobiographical resources on Malamud is more than offset by the abundance of critical appraisals of his fiction. Much of the criticism of Malamud's work focuses on several general themes: Malamud's place as one of the three major figures in Jewish-American fiction, along with Saul Bellow and Philip Roth; his use of myth and archetype; his style, including the influence on him of Yiddish writers Aleichem and Peretz; his portraits of characters who are "borderwalkers"—perpetually on the margins, not in the mainstream of life; his essentially romantic portrayal of characters—schnooks, schlemiels, schlimazels—who exhibit a strong determination to endure suffering and who are redeemed through love and commitment; and finally, Malamud's own humanistic commitment to ordinary people and ordinary lives, best summed up in this observation: "My work, all of it, is an idea of dedication to the human." There are now several hundred essays on Malamud's novels, published in a very wide range of magazines and journals. Fortunately, there are three volumes of essays that present selections of the best of this short criticism.

Evaluation of Selected Criticism

Astro, Richard and Jackson Benson, eds. *The Fiction of Bernard Malamud.* Corvallis: Oregon State University Press, 1977. This is the most recent collection of critical essays on Malamud's work. Many of the essays focus on various aspects of Jewishness as reflected in the novels. The book contains a comprehensive checklist of Malamud criticism compiled by Donald Risty, pp. 163–190.

Cohen, Sandy, *Bernard Malamud and the Trial by Love.* Amsterdam: Rodopi, 1974. Cohen concludes that the dominating theme in Malamud's first six novels is that of a trial by love that leads to self-transcendence. In each novel, at least one character realizes, after intense self-scrutiny, his own mistakes and his need to be concerned with other people. The novels express Malamud's belief in the inherent goodness and perfectability of man and his capacity to learn from suffering and to become better morally.

Ducharme, Robert, *Art and Idea in the Novels of Bernard Malamud.* The Hague: Mouton, 1974. Ducharme focuses on Malamud's use of myth and archetype as a structural device in his novels. For example, Ducharme contends, in *The Natural,* Roy Hobbs is a modern Sir Percival in search of the Grail (a baseball pennant).

Field, Leslie and Joyce W. Field, eds. *Bernard Malamud and the Critics.* New York: New York University Press, 1970. This useful collection gathers 21 essays originally published elsewhere between 1961 and 1970. The essays are suggestive of the wide range of topics Malamud critics have explored: myth and archetype, Jewish literary tradition, redemption through suffering, style and technique.

————, *Bernard Malamud: A Collection of Critical Essays.* Englewood Cliffs, NJ: Prentice-Hall, 1975. This second collection of essays contains studies, some original to this volume, published between 1970 and 1975. It also contains a long interview with Malamud, conducted by mail, in which the author discusses his work, particularly the literary and social influences he acknowledges.

Hershinow, Sheldon J. *Bernard Malamud.* New York: Frederick Ungar, 1980. Hershinow views Malamud as a moral activist who is also a humanist existentialist. He contends that Malamud's novels exalt the nobility of the human spirit and makes the interesting observation that only readers who respect human beings can respect Malamud's fiction.

Kosofsky, Rita N. *Bernard Malamud: An Annotated Checklist.* Serif Series of Bibliographies and Checklists, ed. W. White. Kent, OH: Kent State University Press, 1969. This checklist has essentially been superseded by the extensive checklist by Risty in Astro and Benson, pp. 163–190.

Meeter, Glen, *Bernard Malamud and Philip Roth: A Critical Essay.* Contemporary Writers in Christian Perspective Series. Grand Rapids, MI: Eerdmans, 1968. Meeter finds Roth and Malamud the "most Jewish" of modern Jewish American writers, especially in their treatment of man's relationship to God. More space is devoted to Roth than Malamud.

Richman, Sidney, *Bernard Malamud.* New York: Twayne: 1966. This entry in the U.S. Authors Series contains a very straightforward discussion of Malamud's work through 1966. It is still a good starting point for the reader unfamiliar with Malamud.

Other Sources

Several books on general literary themes or topics contain useful chapters or essays on Malamud.

Aldridge, John W. *Time to Murder and Create: The Contemporary Novel in Crisis.* New York: McKay, 1966, pp. 52–94.

Guttman, Allen, *The Jewish Writer in America: Assimilation and the Crisis of Identity.* New York: Oxford University Press, 1968, pp. 59–85.

Linguistics in Literature, II(3). Special Malamud issue, (Fall 1977). ed. Bates Hoffer. The special issue contains four essays that approach Malamud's fiction from the perspective of what might be called "new criticism." The authors analyze the works within their own contexts, focusing on words, metaphors, imagery, and not on sociological, historical, cultural, or personal aspects of the works.

Studies in American-Jewish Literature, IV(1). Special Malamud issue, (Spring 1978). The volume contains 13 essays about various aspects of Malamud as an American-Jewish writer. There is an excellent bibliographical essay by Robert Habich, pp. 78–84.

Wisse, Ruth, *The Schlemiel as Modern Hero*. Chicago: University of Chicago Press, 1971, pp. 110–118.

Selected Dictionaries and Encyclopedias

Dictionary of Literary Biography, 2, American Novelists Since World War II. Gale Research, 1978. Contains a useful overview of Malamud's works.

Dictionary of Literary Biography Yearbook 1980, Gale Research, 1981. The focus of the entry is on *Dubin's Lives*.

Dictionary of Literary Biography, 28, American-Jewish Fiction Writers. Gale Research, 1984. An excellent essay that attempts to place Malamud's work in the context of American-Jewish writing. Good short appreciations of the major fiction.

Contemporary Authors, 5–8, Gale Research, 1969. A brief entry that provides a concise overview of life and works through the 1960's.

Patricia A. Farrant
Coe College

THOMAS MALORY
?–?

Author's Bibliography (selected)

Malory's history of Arthurian chivalry exists in two early versions: the Winchester Manuscript, which probably dates from around 1480, and the volume entitled *Le Morte Darthur,* printed by William Caxton in London in 1485. There are two major modern editions. *The Works of Sir Thomas Malory.* ed. Eugene Vinaver. Oxford: Oxford University Press, 1947. 2nd edition, 1970. This is the definitive edition based on the Winchester MS. *Caxton's Malory.* ed. James W. Spisak. Berkeley and Los Angeles: University of California Press, 1983. This edition is newly prepared from Caxton's text.

Overview of Biographical Sources

The case of Thomas Malory poses the most fundamental problem of biography: identification. Caxton's preface to the 1485 edition attributes the work to "Syr Thomas Malorye" (a name confirmed by the colophons of the Winchester MS., discovered in 1934). It was not until 1894, however, that a firm identification of the author was made. George Lyman Kittredge, the famous Harvard scholar, assigned the work on the basis of chronology to a knight from Newbold Revel in Warwickshire. Research into the life of the Warwickshire knight culminated in Edward Hicks' 1928 biography, *Sir Thomas Malory,* and was extended by A. C. Baugh (see "Other Sources"). Yet the picture of criminal behavior that emerged seemed to many utterly inappropriate for the author of the greatest chivalric romance in English. Though there is no record of any conviction, Malory spent time in several prisons and was accused during his career of an extraordinary variety of crimes, from ambushing the Duke of Buckingham to cattle stealing, rape, and robbing the monastery of the Blessed Mary at Coombe. In 1966 William Matthews published *The Ill-Framed Knight,* which convincingly attacked the claim of the Warwickshire Malory on several grounds. Matthews' candidate, a man from Yorkshire, has in turn been rejected by scholars, who are once again left with no clear identification of the author of *Le Morte Darthur.*

Evaluation of Selected Biographies

Hicks, Edward, *Sir Thomas Malory: His Turbulent Career.* Cambridge: Harvard University Press, 1928. This biography of Sir Thomas Malory of Newbold Revel, Warwickshire, is the fruit of extensive documentary research in the Public Records Office and elsewhere. Hicks traces Malory's alleged criminal career in detail, but because he identifies his subject with the author of *Le Morte Darthur,* he is at pains to support Malory wherever possible. The book concludes with the defense of the authorship claim and a discussion of the author's prose style.

Matthews, William, *The Ill-Framed Knight.* Berkeley and Los Angeles: University of California Press, 1966. Matthews reviews all the claimants but focuses on the Warwickshire knight, convincingly detailing a variety of problems involved in attributing *Le Morte Darthur* to him. The most important of Matthews' objections are, first, that the Warwickshire Malory is unlikely ever to have had access to the vast Arthurian library used as sources in *Le Morte Darthur,* and, second, that the dialect of the Winchester MS. suggests an author from further north than Warwickshire. In a final chapter, Matthews proposes a new candidate: Thomas Malory of Hutton and Studley, Yorkshire.

Overview of Critical Sources

Modern Malory criticism begins with Eugene Vinaver's *Malory* (1929), which first focused attention on Malory's French sources and his techniques in adapting them. This remains the most prevalent concern in Malory studies. The discovery, in 1934, of the Winchester MS. and the publication, in 1947, of Vinaver's edition based upon it precipitated a thirty-year dispute over the "unity" of Malory's work. What Caxton had published as *Le Morte Darthur* in 1485 looked in the Winchester MS. less like one "book" than like eight separate "tales," and Vinaver presented them as *The Works of Sir Thomas Malory.* Angry rebuttals of Vinaver's thesis soon followed, the most notable being a collection of essays under the general editorship of R. M. Lumiansky, *Malory's Originality* (1963), while Larry Benson's discussion in *Malory's Morte Darthur* (1976) appears to have laid the question to rest. Apart from the unity issue, recent Malory criticism has focused on Malory's adaptation of his sources, on the development of his own artistry and vision, and on his relationship to the chivalric traditions of his time. A renewed interest in Caxton's text and on Malory's possible contact with Caxton has emerged recently.

Evaluation of Selected Criticism

Bennett, J. A. W. ed. *Essays on Malory.* Oxford: Oxford University Press, 1963. A number of distinguished English scholars contributed to this volume which consists of seven essays all prompted in one way or another by the theories espoused by Vinaver in his 1947 edition. D. S. Brewer's essay, " 'the hoole book'," addresses the question of unity but the high point of the volume is C. S. Lewis's "The English Prose *Morte.*" Perhaps the finest single essay in Malory studies, this piece addresses the various paradoxes raised by the career of the Warwickshire Malory and by Vinaver's position on the unity of the work and on Malory's treatment of his sources. It is a model of logic and eloquence.

Benson, Larry D. *Malory's Morte Darthur.* Cambridge: Harvard University Press, 1976. Benson has produced the most important and wide-ranging study of Malory to date. His discussion of 15th-century prose romance resolves the heated debate over "unity" by demonstrating that one-volume condensations of longer romance cycles were common at the time Malory wrote. In addition, the book explores Malory's thematic approach to narrative and his concern with the often overlooked 15th-century involvement with the forms and substance of chivalry. The concluding chapters offer an interesting, if controversial, reading of the last three tales. The book is beautifully written.

Brewer, D. S. and Toshiyubi Takamiya. eds. Totowa, NJ: Rowman and Littlefield, 1981. This is the most recent collection of essays on Malory, though another is due to appear in April, 1985 (see "Other Sources," below). The contributions cover a wide range of topics, including source studies, the history of the Winchester MS., and the identity of the author. This volume testifies to the growing sophistication of Malory studies, and most of the articles require a previous familiarity with both Malory's work and the standard scholarship.

Lambert, Mark, *Malory: Style and Vision in Le Morte Darthur.* New Haven and London: Yale University Press, 1975. This sophisticated discussion of Malory's prose style and its implications for the interpretation of his work is perhaps the most provocative of recent studies on Malory. Lambert explores both those features of style Malory shares with his sources and those which are uniquely his own. In addition, he offers a detailed discussion of Malory's last two tales, where he finds depicted "a particular country of the mind" (p 124). His reading is controversial but intriguing. This is a book for readers well-versed in Malory and Malory criticism.

Lumiansky, R. M. ed. *Malory's Originality: A Critical Study of Le Morte Darthur.* Baltimore: Johns Hopkins University Press, 1964. This collection of essays, produced in response to Vinaver's 1947 edition, is by various authors with a single purpose: to establish the "originality" with which Malory treats his sources and to emphasize the "unity" of his work. Each essay presents a detailed discussion of one of the eight tales, examining Malory's use of his source and relating the tale to larger patterns in the work. The essays are interesting and informative, although the work's partisan conception occasionally leads the writers into polemic.

Reiss, Edmund, *Sir Thomas Malory.* New York: Twayne, 1966. This book was the first full-length treatment of Malory since Vinaver's in 1929, and it remains the best introduction available. The opening chapter reviews the biography of the Warwickshire Thomas Malory—then the unchallenged candidate—and discusses Malory's sources. The remaining four chapters offer a sequential commentary on the text of Malory's work. Reiss is more concerned with Malory's own literary achievement than with his sources—a refreshing change from many Malory studies—and though his reading is occasionally superficial, he presents a coherent account readily accessible to the non-specialist.

Other Sources

Baugh, A. C. "Documenting Malory," *Speculum* VIII (1933), 3–29. Extends the Hicks biography through further information on the legal broils of the Warwickshire Malory.

Field, P. J. C. *Romance and Chronicle: A Study of Malory's Prose Style.* Bloomington and London: Indiana University Press, 1971. A sensitive and systematic analysis of the stylistic features of Malory's work.

Moorman, Charles, *The Book of Kyng Arthur: The Unity of Malory's Morte Darthur.* Lexington: University of Kentucky Press, 1965. A study stressing the unity of Malory's work and its focus on the fall of the Arthurian kingdom.

Pochoda, Elizabeth, *Arthurian Propaganda: Le Morte Darthur as an Historical Ideal of Life.* Chapel Hill: University of North Carolina Press, 1971. An approach to Malory through medieval political theory; includes an excellent annotated bibliography.

Studies in Malory. ed. James W. Spisak. Kalamazoo: Medieval Institute Publications, 1985. The most recent collection of essays.

Vinaver, Eugene, *Sir Thomas Malory.* Oxford: Oxford University Press, 1929. Chapters on a variety of topics, from biography to source study—still interesting but largely superseded by later studies.

Stephen C. B. Atkinson
Missouri Southern State College

KATHERINE MANSFIELD
1888–1923

Author's Chronology

Born October 14, 1888, Wellington, New Zealand, named Kathleen Mansfield Beauchamp, to parents of English descent born in Australia; grows up near Wellington; *1898* publishes first story in the *High School Reporter,* Wellington; *1903* sails with family to London, enters Queen's College; *1906* returns to New Zealand; publishes stories there and in Australia; *1908* goes back to London; never returns to New Zealand but lives thereafter in London and various parts of Europe; *1910* illness begins which affects the rest of her life; *1912* meets John Middleton Murry; publishes numerous stories under Katherine Mansfield; *1918* marries Murry; writes some of her best work during these last four years; *1922* undergoes radium treatment for tuberculosis; dies January 9, 1923, Fontainebleau, France.

Author's Bibliography (selected)

In a German Pension, 1911 (stories); *Prelude,* 1918 (novella); *Bliss and Other Stories,* 1920; *The Garden-Party and Other Stories,* 1922; *The Dove's Nest and Other Stories,* 1923; *Something Childish and Other Stories* (British title), *The Little Girl and Other Stories* (American title), 1924; *The Aloe,* 1930 (stories).

Overview of Biographical Sources

Although Katherine Mansfield's life was short, she lived it fully and left behind a small but substantial body of work, which made an impact on the modern short story. Biographers have found Mansfield's tragic life and her highly original work an interesting and significant subject, and have produced several excellent biographies. The first one, *The Life of Katherine Mansfield* (1933) by Ruth Elvish Kantz and John Middleton Murry (Mansfield's husband), focuses for the most part on the early years and contains some inaccurate information. Sylvia Berkman's *Katherine Mansfield: A Critical Study* (1951) and Antony Alpers' *Katherine Mansfield: A Biography* (1954) remain reliable, but have been superseded by Alpers' new book, *The Life of Katherine Mansfield* (1980), which is the definitive work now. Mansfield's husband wrote about their life together in his autobiography. In 1972 Mansfield's longtime friend, known as LM, published her memories of Mansfield, whom she first met at Queen's College.

Evaluation of Selected Biographies

Alpers, Antony, *The Life of Katherine Mansfield.* New York: Viking, 1980; Penguin, 1982. Alpers points out in the preface that this book is not a revision of his first biography (*Katherine Mansfield,* New York: Knopf, 1954), but altogether new, freed from constraint, based on twenty times as much material, including information from Mansfield's friends and contemporaries, and researched "at a suitable distance in time."

Meyers, Jeffrey. *Katherine Mansfield, A Biography*. New York: New Directions, 1978. Meyers' account of Mansfield, although true, seems to stress the subject's sexual and personal problems.

Moore, Leslie. *Katherine Mansfield, The Memories of LM*. New York: Taplinger, 1972. Because of her closeness to Mansfield, LM's "memories" open up yet another view, focusing on Mansfield as a woman.

Autobiographical Sources

In 1929 Murry published many of his wife's letters; later he published only those written to him, adding ones he had withheld previously and including passages he had omitted earlier, in *Katherine Mansfield's Letters to John Middleton Murry 1913–1922* (New York: Knopf, 1951). *The Letters and Journals of Katherine Mansfield, A Selection,* edited by New Zealand writer C. K. Stead (London: Allen Lane, 1977), provides a sampling of Mansfield's private writing, much of which had been published earlier by Murry in various volumes. Most of her letters, journals, and other papers are in the Alexander Turnbull Library, Wellington, New Zealand.

Overview of Critical Sources

Criticism on Mansfield began in earnest shortly after her death and has never let up, for her reputation seems only to grow. The critics have touched on all aspects of the stories, including the traditional elements of theme, character, setting and style, as well as the innovative techniques which have influenced modern fiction, the use of personal experience, and the psychological motivation behind some of the fiction. In addition to the major books listed below, numerous articles have appeared in US, British and Commonwealth journals, many dealing with single stories. Most of the critical works include extensive bibliographies of articles, but there is no complete bibliography of secondary sources.

Evaluation of Selected Criticism

Berkman, Sylvia, *Katherine Mansfield: A Critical Study*. New Haven: Yale, 1951. Berkman's greatest contribution lies in the way she makes clear the close relation between Mansfield's personal experience and her fiction.

Daly, Saralyn R. *Katherine Mansfield*. New York: Twayne, 1965. This book provides a concise and intelligent introduction to Mansfield's work, its sources, style, theme, concerns.

Hankin, C. A. *Katherine Mansfield and Her Confessional Stories.* New York: St. Martin's, 1983. Hankin places Mansfield in a long line of "confessional writers" and focuses his examination on the stories' personal and psychological revelations, an approach which makes an original contribution to Mansfield studies.

Hanson, Clare and Andrew Gurr. *Katherine Mansfield.* New York: St. Martin's, 1981. Although valuable in its concise and complete nature, the book does not add much that is new to Mansfield criticism. It would serve well as an introduction, especially the first chapter.

Other Sources

Gurr, Andrew. *Writers in Exile: the Creative Use of Home in Modern Literature.* Atlantic Highlands, NJ: Humanities Press, 1981. Gurr forms an evolutionary pattern for measuring exiled writers and places Mansfield alongside V. S. Naipaul and Ngugi Wa Thiong'o. Taking up the exile's inner concern with home, Gurr sees Mansfield's writing life as a struggle to come to terms with her memory of the New Zealand home she had fled to fulfill herself as an artist.

Hynes, Sam, "Katherine Mansfield: The Defeat of the Personal," *South Atlantic Quarterly,* LII (1953), 555–560. This appraisal takes a negative approach to the stories so often acclaimed. Hynes says that Mansfield's work lacks an adequate moral structure resulting from its immaturity and failure to compromise with reality.

Murry, John Middleton, *Between Two Worlds.* London: Jonathan Cape, 1936; *Katherine Mansfield and Other Literary Studies.* London: Constable, 1959. The first volume covers his life with the author; the second includes in Chapter 2 an evaluation of her literary achievement. Biographers and critics in later years have accused Murry of creating a Mansfield myth and a cult to perpetuate it.

Selected Dictionaries and Encyclopedias

Critical Survey of Short Fiction, Salem Press, 1981. Well-organized explication of several stories.

Encyclopedia of World Literature in the Twentieth Century, Frederick Ungar, 1967. Concise biography and analysis.

Robert L. Ross
Southern Methodist University

JOHN P. MARQUAND
1893–1960

Author's Chronology

Born November 10, 1893, Wilmington, Delaware, to a family whose roots go back to colonial days; *1911* enters Harvard College on a scholarship; *1917–1918* serves in France as an officer of the Fourth Division Artillery Brigade; *1921–1922* begins publishing fiction for mass-circulation magazines; *1922* marries Christine Sedgwick; *1935* divorces her; *1937* marries Adelaide Hooker whom he met on a trip to China; publishes *The Late George Apley,* the first of his serious novels; *1938* wins the Pulitzer Prize for *The Late George Apley; 1941* returns to Army Intelligence service; *1944* becomes a judge for the Book-of-the-Month Club; *1958* divorced by Adelaide; publishes his last novel, *Women and Thomas Harrow; 1960* dies in his sleep, July 16, at his home in Newburyport, Massachusetts.

Author's Bibliography (selected)

The Late George Apley, 1937 (novel); *Wickford Point,* 1939 (novel); *H. M. Pulham, Esquire,* 1941 (novel); *So Little Time,* 1943 (novel); *B. F.'s Daughter,* 1946 (novel); *Point of No Return,* 1949 (novel); *Melville Goodwin, U.S.A.,* 1951 (novel); *Thirty Years,* 1954 (collection of short stories, sketches, travel accounts, and lectures); *Sincerely, Willis Wayde,* 1955 (novel); *Women and Thomas Harrow,* 1958 (novel); *Timothy Dexter Revisited,* 1960 (revision of a biography, *Lord Timothy Dexter of Newburyport, Mass.,* first published in 1925).

Overview of Biographical Sources

Only one biography of Marquand appeared during his life-time, Philip Hamburger's brief profile, *J. P. Marquand, Esquire: A Portrait in the Form of a Novel* (1952); it had originally appeared as a series of profiles in the *New Yorker.* Until Stephen Birmingham's *The Late John Marquand* (1972), it was the fullest biographical study. The titles of both books suggest the titles of two of Marquand's novels: *The Late George Apley* (Subtitled "A Novel in the Form of a Memoir") and *H. M. Pulham, Esquire.* Not until nineteen years after his death and at a time when his reputation was at a low point did Millicent Bell's definitive biography, *Marquand: An American Life* (1979) appear, under the auspices of Marquand's long-time publisher and with full access to the Marquand papers and letters.

In addition to these three biographies, both *Time* and *Newsweek,* issues dated March 7, 1949, carried cover stories on the novelist. These articles, along with Roger Butterfield's story in *Life* (July 31, 1944, 64–73), contain a good deal of biographical information.

Evaluation of Selected Biographies

Bell, Millicent, *Marquand: An American Life.* Boston: Little Brown, 1979. A professor of English at Boston University who had written a biographical study of Edith Wharton and Henry James, Bell was quite familiar with the social world in which Marquand moved. She is impeccable in her scholarship and sympathetic in her understanding of the conflicts that lie behind his fiction. She sees him as a man with ambivalent feelings toward his background and his success. With his dream of success and with his longing for a departed innocence, Bell views his life as a typically American one. Her full access to the Marquand papers and letters and to the files of his publisher makes hers a book solidly packed with information. In a graceful prose style she moves effortlessly between the novelist's unhappy personal life and his successful public life. With penetrating insights into Marquand's mind, Bell's biography is both an intellectually stimulating experience and an enjoyable one.

Birmingham, Stephen, *The Late John Marquand.* Philadelphia: J. P. Lippincott, 1972. A novelist and social historian whose work covers the same territory that Marquand surveyed in his fiction, Birmingham is a most sympathetic biographer. The picture of Marquand that emerges, however, is that of a rather unattractive human being. Birmingham's thesis is that Marquand's unhappy childhood and adolescence account for the novelist's bitter personal adult life—two unhappy marriages and strained relations with the children of his second marriage—and for the emphasis on class distinction which pervades his work. This is an easy book to read, affording one the same pleasure to be had from reading a Marquand novel. The biography contains little evaluation of Marquand's work and no documentation. There is no bibliography of works consulted but there is a useful chronological list of Marquand's work. The book was written without the cooperation of Marquand's family.

Hamburger, Philip, *J. P. Marquand, Esquire.* Boston: Houghton Mifflin, 1952. This "portrait in the form of a novel" is a delight both as a pastiche of a Marquand novel and as a convincing profile of the novelist. Its satiric chapter titles, its long flashbacks, and its brilliant imitation of Marquand's urbane style make Marquand appear to be a character from one of his own novels. It is a very brief book and lacks the coverage of the two later biographies; still, it succinctly captures the essence of the man.

Autobiographical Sources

Marquand's fiction does contain autobiographical scenes—Charles Gray's boyhood and adolescence in *Point of No Return* and Thomas Harrow's marital experiences in *Women and Thomas Harrow*—but it would be unfair to label his fiction as autobiographical. There are, however, other autobiographical sources. During his lifetime Marquand gave many interviews. The two fullest appear in

Cosmopolitan, one by Robert Van Gelder, March 1947, 150–152, the other by Frederick Houghton and Richard Whitman August 1959, 46–50. In addition, there are Marquand's reflections on his first three novels, "Apley, Wickford Point, and Pulham: My Early Struggles," *Atlantic,* September 1956, 71–74, and his recollections of his formative years, "Hearsay History of Curzon's Mill," *Atlantic,* March 1957, 84–91.

Overview of Critical Sources

Marquand was widely reviewed by newspaper and magazine book reviewers, but was virtually neglected by literary and academic critics, a fact that rankled him. Because some critics found his work lacking in seriousness and too conventional in form and style, and because some critics could not forgive him his popular success, there are few critical studies.

Indeed there is only one full-length book—John J. Gross, *John P. Marquand* (1963)—and a pamphlet—C. Hugh Holman, *John P. Marquand* (1965)—devoted to Marquand as novelist. There are also a few perceptive critical articles and sections of books devoted to modern American writers.

Evaluation of Selected Criticism

Gross, John J. *John P. Marquand.* New York: Twayne, 1963. With the exception of the opening chapter which examines Marquand's relationship with literary critics, the bulk of this valuable study is an examination of Marquand's major novels. Gross traces the continuity of themes from novel to novel as well as providing an overview of Marquand's accomplishments as a novelist. He sees the major conflict in Marquand's fiction as one between traditional values of the past and the vulgarization of society in the present. This sound critical assessment with its useful annotated bibliography is important for anyone working on Marquand.

Holman, G. Hugh, *John P. Marquand.* Minneapolis: University of Minnesota Press, 1965. This is a polished essay that combines literary criticism with some biographical information. Unlike Gross who concentrates on Marquand's major fiction, Holman discusses the novelist's work prior to *The Late George Apley* as well. He concentrates on Marquand's themes and his craftsmanship, and sees him as a social historian of significant scope. This is a most sympathetic appraisal.

Other Sources

Brady, Charles A. "John Phillips Marquand: Martini-Age Victorian," in *Fifty Years of the American Novel: A Christian Appraisal,* ed. Harold C. Gardiner. New York: Scribner's, 1951, 107–134. A discerning evaluation that places Marquand in the tradition of Jane Austen, Thackeray, and Trollope.

Kazin, Alfred, "John P. Marquand and the American Failure," in *Contemporaries*. Boston: Little, Brown, 1962, 122–130. Kazin uses the publication of *Women and Thomas Harrow* to examine Marquand as a novelist of manners.

Prescott, Orville, *In My Opinion.* Indianapolis: Bobbs-Merrill, 1952, 173–179. The former distinguished book reviewer for the *New York Times* sees Marquand's novels as penetrating and comprehensive pictures of American upper-class life in the twentieth century.

Selected Dictionaries and Encyclopedias

Contemporary Authors, Vol. 85–88, Gale Research, 1980. Factual information on Marquand's life and career, an overall estimate of his work, and a sampling of critical opinion.

The Oxford Companion to American Literature, Oxford, 1984. A short overview of Marquand's themes and a thumbnail description of his major novels.

The Reader's Encyclopedia of American Literature, Crowell, 1962. A brief biography with a concise discussion of his fiction and a general estimate of his accomplishment. Major novels are discussed under separate title entries.

Richard B. Gidez
Pennsylvania State University

ANDREW MARVELL
1621–1678

Author's Chronology

Born March 31, 1621, Winestead-in-Holderness, England; *1624* moves to Hull where his father, the Rev. Andrew Marvell, is lecturer at Holy Trinity Church; *1633* enters Trinity College, Cambridge; *1637* contributes Greek and Latin poems to Cambridge volume on the birth of Princess Anne; *1638* becomes scholar of Trinity; *1640* leaves Cambridge, possibly becoming clerk for a while in trading house of brother-in-law, Edmund Popple; spends four years abroad in the early 1640's, and learns Dutch, French, Italian and Spanish; *1650–1653* tutor to Mary Fairfax at Appleton House, Yorkshire; *1653* recommended by Milton for government position, which he does not receive; becomes tutor to William Dutton, ward of Oliver Cromwell; *1659–1678* serves as M.P. for Hull; *1660* argues in Parliament for relief of Milton, who after Restoration was faced with prison and fined for his work under Cromwell; *1663–1665* goes to Russia as secretary for Earl of Carlisle's embassy; *1672* defends policy of religious toleration in first prose work, *The Rehearsal Transpros'd; 1678* dies August 18; *1681 Miscellaneous Poems* published by his landlady, who claims to be his widow.

Author's Bibliography

Only a few of Marvell's poems were published during his lifetime. His collected lyrics first saw print in the posthumous *Miscellaneous Poems* of 1681. During his life, his reputation was built on his activities as a Member of Parliament (from 1660 until his death) and as a prose controversialist. His prose includes *The Rehearsal Transpros'd* (1672), *The Rehearsal Transpros'd The Second Part* (1673), *Mr. Smirke, or The Divine in Mode* (1676), *Account of the Growth of Popery* (1677), and *Remarks upon a Late Disingenuous Discourse* (1678). The first two, by far his most significant prose, are available in a one-volume edition by D. I. B. Smith (London: Oxford University Press, 1971).

Evaluation of Selected Biographies

Hunt, John Dixon, *Andrew Marvell: His Life and Writings*. Ithaca: Cornell University Press, 1978. Pleasantly readable, with particular emphasis on the known details of Marvell's life, this is the newest good biography, and is valuable for its many portraits and other illustrations.

Legouis, Pierre, *André Marvell: Poetè, Puritan, Patriote, 1621–1678*. Oxford: Oxford University Press, 1928. In French, this is still the most substantial critical biography, though minor bits of new biographical evidence have emerged since it was written, and more recent scholarship has taken issue with some of Legouis' analysis of Marvell's works and thought. An appendix presents a fairly thorough summary of the publications involved in the pamphlet controversies in which Marvell was engaged during the last part of his life.

————, *Andrew Marvell: Poet, Puritan, Patriot.* Oxford: The Clarendon Press, 1968. This is Legouis' English translation, updated and streamlined, of the French original listed above. It lacks some of the documentation of the original version.

Autobiographical Sources

Marvell left no primarily autobiographical material. Over 300 letters, mostly connected with Marvell's business as an M.P., are published in Margoliouth's edition. They provide glimpses into his thought and way of life. Additionally, occasional comments in his prose pamphlets give biographical evidence, though these must be evaluated carefully because of the forensic nature of those publications.

Overview of Critical Sources

During his own day Marvell was known primarily for his prose. His lyric poems, upon which his modern reputation chiefly rests, were not published until after his death, and seem not to have been very widely read even then. Charles Lamb in 1818 urged Marvell's value as a lyric poet, and others from time to time commented upon the neglected excellencies of his lyrics and his Cromwell poems, or admired him as a nature poet or as a staunch parliamentary defender of liberty, but it was not until the 300th anniversary of his birth that his reputation as a lyric poet began to become really substantial. In that year, 1921, H. J. C. Grierson represented Marvell in his anthology of 17th century metaphysical poetry with poems that emphasized his wit and metaphysical qualities. T. S. Eliot, also in 1921, wrote an extremely influential essay to essentially the same end. Marvell has since come to be regarded as a major 17th century metaphysical poet, and indeed as a great lyric poet. Because most of his work is in a wide variety of eight-syllable stanza forms, he has been recognized as the "master of the octosyllabic."

Twentieth-century critics cannot be said to have reached a consensus on Marvell's political or religious beliefs. Rather they have tended to be fascinated by precisely those things that make his personal opinions elusive—his wit, irony, puns, personae and strikingly multivalent images, his ability to (for example) eulogize Charles I and Cromwell in the same poem. Studies also continue to place Marvell in historical context: to read his works in the light of emblem literature, political controversies, Ramist logic, landscape conventions, classical (especially Horatian) conventions and the works of his poetic contemporaries. In the last two decades there has been some scholarly interest in his prose pamphlets, both as adjuncts to interpreting the poetry and (for the two parts of *The Rehearsal Transpros'd*) as worthy of study in their own right.

Consultation of Donno, then Colie's preface, then Toliver (all listed below) will provide a useful review of significant Marvell criticism prior to 1980.

Evaluation of Selected Criticism

Bennett, Joan, *Five Metaphysical Poets*. Cambridge: Cambridge University, 1964. This is an expansion of Bennett's original *Four Metaphysical Poets* (1934) to include Marvell. Still a standard introduction to the metaphysicals, this book delineates those qualities which place Marvell among them, drawing parallels especially with Donne and Vaughan. Bennett also provides readings of the major lyric poems and of the "Horatian Ode Upon Cromwell's Return."

Colie, Rosalie, *"My Ecchoing Song": Andrew Marvell's Poetry of Criticism*. Princeton: Princeton University, 1970. Placing Marvell in the literary context of his day (genre, theme, etc.) and suggesting how he modified the traditions he received, Colie gives readings of all the major poems. She offers exceptionally lengthy treatments of "The Garden" and "Upon Appleton House." See her Preface, p. ix, for a capsule listing and evaluation of Marvell criticism from 1921 to 1968.

Donno, Elizabeth Story, *Andrew Marvell: The Critical Heritage*. London: Routledge & Kegan Paul, 1978. A superb survey of commentary on Marvell and his work, beginning with material from his own day and ending with Eliot's 1921 essay, this is a compilation of direct quotes excerpted from essentially every pertinent source during that period. The editorial comments are concise and helpful; browsing through this volume will give a very good picture of the fluctuations in Marvell's reputation.

Hodge, R. I. V. *Foreshortened Time*. Totowa, NJ: Rowman & Littlefield, 1978. Hodge approaches Marvell's poetry (with some notice of the prose) chiefly from the perspective of Ramist logic.

Hyman, Lawrence W. *Andrew Marvell*. New York: Twayne, 1964. Here are useful comments on most of Marvell's verse and prose; the emphasis is on the lyric poetry, approached through what is clearly one of Marvell's major themes: the question of action versus withdrawal.

Klause, John, *The Unfortunate Fall*. Hamden, CT: Archon Books, 1983. In this heavily footnoted book, Krause views Marvell's affinity for paradox as a reflection of his uncertainty about the problem of evil, and gives interesting readings of many of the poems, especially "Upon Appleton House" and the "Horatian Ode."

Patrides, C. A. *Approaches to Marvell*. London: Routledge & Kegan Paul, 1978. Containing fourteen papers delivered at the York tercentenary observance of Marvell's death, plus one additional article on Marvell and gardens, this volume provides an assortment of approaches to Marvell's poetry by some of the major modern Marvell scholars. It is probably better suited for advanced students of Marvell.

Toliver, Harold, "The Critical Reprocessing of Andrew Marvell," ELH, 47 (1980), 180–203. This essay provides an excellent overview and evaluation of the main currents of criticism of Marvell's poetry, especially the cluster of studies published in or around 1978, marking the 300th anniversary of the poet's death.

Wallace, John M. *Destiny His Choice: The Loyalism of Andrew Marvell.* Cambridge: Cambridge University Press, 1968. Wallace provides substantial readings of the poetry, especially the Fairfax and Cromwell poems, in their political context. Particularly concerned with Marvell's political posture, Wallace views him as one who supported a series of opposing governments out of genuine conviction rather than opportunism.

Other Sources

Marvell's Poems and Letters. ed. H. M. Margoliouth; rev. Pierre Legouis & Elsie Duncan-Jones. 2 vols. Oxford: Oxford University Press, 1978. Complete and well annotated.

Selected Dictionaries and Encyclopedias

Critical Survey of Poetry, Salem Press, 1983. Brief biography, and evaluation of Marvell's qualities as a poet, with readings of "Coy Mistress," "Upon Appleton House," and "The Garden."

Dictionary of National Biography, Macmillan, 1893. Still an accurate and fairly detailed biography and early publication history of the works.

C. Herbert Gilliland
U.S. Naval Academy

W. SOMERSET MAUGHAM
1874–1965

Author's Chronology

Born January 25, 1874, in Paris of English parents; *1884* lives with his uncle in England following death of parents; *1885–1889* attends King's School, Canterbury; *1890* travels to Germany; *1892* enrolls in St. Thomas Hospital, London, as a medical student; *1897* publishes first novel, *Liza of Lambeth;* awarded M.D.; *1907 Lady Frederick* launches his successful career as dramatist; *1915* serves in France as ambulance driver, then with British Intelligence; publishes *Of Human Bondage;* marries Syrie Bernardo Wellcome; *1916* travels extensively throughout South Pacific accumulating materials for fiction; *1926* purchases the Villa Mauresque; *1927* divorced by Syrie; *1940–1946* lives in United States during World War II; *1954* made Companion of Honour by the Queen; *1965* dies in Nice, France, 15 December.

Author's Bibliography (selected)

Liza of Lambeth, 1897 (novel); *Orientations,* 1899 (short stories); *Mrs. Craddock,* 1902 (novel); *Of Human Bondage,* 1915 (novel); *The Moon and Sixpence,* 1919 (novel); *The Painted Veil,* 1925 (novel); *Ashenden,* 1928 (short stories); *Cakes and Ale,* 1930 (novel); *The Narrow Corner,* 1932 (novel); *Don Fernando,* 1937 (essays); *The Summing Up,* 1938 (autobiography); *Christmas Holiday,* 1939 (novel); *The Razor's Edge,* 1944 (novel); *A Writer's Notebook,* 1949 (nonfiction); *The Complete Short Stories* 1951, (short fiction); *Collected Plays,* 1952 (dramas).

Overview of Biographical Sources

To many would-be biographers, Maugham has appeared the ideal subject. His long and highly successful career in several literary genres, his willingness to write about himself, his affluent and cosmopolitan lifestyle, and his drawing upon the lives of actual people for his characters—all made him a subject of intense interest. Yet he staunchly opposed a biography during his lifetime, and even the writers he encouraged in their efforts to evaluate his works were denied access to information about his personal life. While he lived, biographical accounts were most likely to be brief treatments of his literary career combined with literary criticism. With his death in 1965, people who had known Maugham began publishing accounts of their memories, meetings and conversations, and thereby added personal touches to the portrait of Maugham as a man of letters. A full-length scholarly biography emerged only after fifteen years had passed.

Evaluation of Selected Biographies

Kanin, Garson, *Remembering Mr Maugham.* London: Hamish and Hamilton, 1966. Kanin gives recollections of his and Ruth Gordon's friendship with

Maugham over more than twenty years. In a somewhat impressionistic account, filled with anecdotes, the book depicts Maugham as gracious and amiable in his friendships. It includes much conversation during infrequent dinner parties, with Maugham discoursing on his usual themes. Kanin makes use of a few Maugham letters and also stories from the press.

Maugham, Robin, *Conversations with Willie.* New York: Simon and Schuster, 1978. Robin, Maugham's nephew and a successful novelist in his own right, records conversations during his visits with his famous uncle at the Villa Mauresque. The words of Maugham reveal much about his perspective on life and his relationships with family and friends. They are particularly revealing about his work habits and his unhappy old age.

————, *Somerset and All the Maughams.* New York: The New American Library, 1966. The book provides details about the Maugham family and its origins. In the section on Somerset Maugham, the author relies on recollections, conversations, and Maugham's own published works. The conflict between Maugham and his brother Frederick, Robin's father, is illuminated.

Menard, Wilmon, *The Two Worlds of Somerset Maugham.* Los Angeles: Sherbourne Press, 1965. Menard sheds much light on Maugham's travels to the South Pacific, especially Tahiti and Samoa, and identifies characters used by Maugham in his short stories and novels. He gives accounts of people whom Maugham met and explains what happened to them.

Morgan, Ted, *Maugham.* New York: Simon and Schuster, 1980. Morgan writes a carefully researched, scholarly biography covering the entire range of Maugham's life, relying on Maugham's voluminous correspondence, interviews with his friends, family and acquaintances. He details the numerous journeys made by Maugham all over the world. More than any other account, Morgan's documents the author's difficult childhood, homosexual relationships, unfortunate marriage, and unhappy old age. Because sources were inaccessible, Morgan fails to unravel all the facets of Maugham's service with British Intelligence, nor does he discover why Gerald Haxton, Maugham's secretary, was expelled from England as an undesirable alien. He presents a portrait of a man of letters, highly professional, concerned with business matters and with his reading public.

Pfeiffer, Karl G. *W. Somerset Maugham: A Candid Portrait.* New York: W. W. Norton, 1959. Pfeiffer gives memorable characterizations of Maugham based upon selected periods during his life. He stresses Maugham's career as a man of letters, picturing him as a consummate professional.

Autobiographical Sources

In novels like *Of Human Bondage* and short stories like those in the *Ashenden* series, Maugham transmuted his own experiences and emotions into fiction, sometimes little changed, although truth cannot be clearly distinguished from fiction and so biographical portions of the fiction remain enigmatic. Maugham's numerous letters exist protected in library collections accessible only to serious scholars. The most reliable source of autobiography is *The Summing Up* (1938), written in Maugham's early sixties. He records some details of his early childhood and education, and discusses his service during World War I, his travels, and his illnesses. He devotes much more attention, however, to his literary views, philosophy of life, aesthetics, and quest for values in life, explaining that he has attempted to make his life conform to a pattern.

In *A Writer's Notebook* (1949) he expands upon the philosophical views outlined in his earlier autobiographical work but shows no significant change of opinion. In *Strictly Personal* (1941) Maugham narrates his escape to America from the imminent occupation of France, involving a flight that required him to abandon almost all of his possessions. He gives his theories about why France proved to be so ill prepared for the war. Later, in his eighty-ninth year he published serially an autobiographical account entitled *Looking Back* (1962). Maugham repeats some of his earlier information but gives a detailed and unfavorable account of his deceased former wife to the embarrassment of his friends.

Overview of Critical Sources

Maugham's preference for straightforward, lucid narrative; his precise, fluent, and idiomatic prose; and his adherence to traditional literary forms have led some critics to regard him as a popular author unworthy of serious attention and others to seek to discover where his chief merit lies. Much attention has been given to the autobiographical element in his fiction and the persona who often speaks for the author. Critics have explored his exotic settings, style, sources, and influences.

Maugham first achieved fame with the comedy of manners, a decidedly adult genre depicting upper class society, with wit and irony as major elements. Throughout his work, Maugham retained a sense of the dramatic moment and the ability to produce natural dialogue tempered by ironic detachment. One encounters a strong sense of irony, even of cynicism, and an adult world where faces and emotions are concealed, except on rare occasions. The usual critical study surveys the major works, relating them to the author's life and development, often reflecting a single point of view.

Evaluation of Selected Criticism

Burt, Forrest D. *W. Somerset Maugham.* Boston: G. K. Hall, 1985. The initial chapter provides a brief biography depicting Maugham sympathetically and emphasizing the significance of trauma in early life, an essentially Adlerian interpretation. The book finds value in the overall literary achievement of Maugham, seeing him as essentially a comic dramatist concerned with basic human themes. Burt examines the contribution of actual persons to the fiction and traces the development of the first person narrator, showing the extent of Maugham's use of this literary convention. He argues that the articulate, urbane, and detached first person represents a compensation for Maugham's overly reticent nature, a condition largely resulting from his stammer.

Calder, Robert L. *W. Somerset Maugham and the Quest for Freedom.* New York: Doubleday, 1973. Calder advances the thesis that the central concern of Maugham was the quest for physical and spiritual independence, as reflected in his central theme of escape from bondage. He points out that Maugham's beliefs and values did not alter during his long career. Finding that *Of Human Bondage* represents Maugham's greatest achievement, Calder concludes that Maugham's adherence to tradition in literature will ensure his survival.

Cordell, Richrad A. *Somerset Maugham: A Writer for All Seasons.* Bloomington: Indiana University Press, 1969. Cordell's work includes a biographical essay, extensive analysis of major works, and an account of Maugham's final years. Still perhaps the best introduction and overview, it clarifies the author's attitudes and values regarding religion, science, ethics, and civilization. Cordell includes as well a brief survey of important criticism of the works and makes a serious effort to assess Maugham's literary achievement.

Curtis, Anthony, *The Pattern of Maugham.* New York: Taplinger, 1974. The book provides a comprehensive account of Maugham's career emphasizing realism in Maugham's fiction. Curtis finds that Maugham's work represents a unified achievement or pattern, an outcome sought by the author himself. He places the works in relation to their backgrounds.

Jonas, Klaus W. ed. *The Maugham Enigma.* London: Peter Owen, 1954. Jonas has assembled a collection of book reviews, brief essays, and speeches by various critics, some eminent, devoted to all types of literary production represented in Maugham's works. By drawing upon previously published criticism, he brings together a variety of views on Maugham's achievement.

Naik, M. K. *W. Somerset Maugham.* Norman: Oklahoma University Press, 1966. Maugham's works, according to Naik, emerged from a conflict in his nature between cynicism and humanitarianism. He further suggests that Maugham's cynicism results from sentimentalism turning against itself. In a series of chapters the book traces Maugham's development and then considers separately his style and major themes.

Ward, Richard Heron, *William Somerset Maugham.* London: Geoffrey Bles, 1937. Ward attempts an impersonal approach to discover what lies at the center of Maugham's work. He finds that the works derive from an ethical ideal regarding the importance of human action. He minimizes the influence of realism and argues that Maugham upholds a platonic ideal.

Other Sources

Brophy, John, *Somerset Maugham.* London: Longmans, Green, 1952. In a pamphlet-length essay Brophy assesses Maugham's strengths and weaknesses as a creative writer, clarifying his values and attitudes and characterizing his style. After pointing out the disadvantages of popular success and after citing defects in the prose style, the work concludes that Maugham's best works will survive.

McIver, Claude S. *William Somerset Maugham: A Study of Technique and Literary Sources.* Folcroft Library Editions, 1973. McIver traces a variety of minor influences upon Maugham's work but finds major significance in the philosophical and ethical thought of Arthur Schopenhauer (1788-1860), whose works Maugham encountered while in Germany. They inclined him toward the cynical tone and pessimism that pervade Maugham's fiction. The book cites numerous similarities between the art of Maugham and of Guy de Maupassant (1850-1893), the fiction writer who exerted the strongest influence on him.

Selected Dictionaries and Encyclopedias

British Writers, Charles Scribner's Sons, 1981. Bibliography, biographical information, and analysis of Maugham's achievement as a writer.

Critical Survey of Long Fiction, Salem Press, 1983. Brief biography and discussion of selected novels.

Critical Survey of Short Fiction, Salem Press, 1981. Brief biography and analysis of Maugham's art of short fiction.

Dictionary of Literary Biography, Gale Research, 1983. Detailed biography and sources for biography.

Stanley Archer
Texas A&M University

CARSON McCULLERS
1917–1967

Author's Chronology

Born Lula Carson Smith, February 19, 1917, in Columbus, Georgia; educated at local schools and with private music teachers; *1934* moves to New York City, enrolls in college writing classes; *1937* marries Reeves McCullers, a Georgia soldier; *1938* completes her first novel; *1940* wins Houghton Mifflin Fellowship, publishes *The Heart Is a Lonely Hunter; 1941* hailed as a *Wunderkind* for her first novel, her second, *Reflections in a Golden Eye* is less well received; divorces Reeves McCullers; *1943* publishes *The Ballad of the Sad Cafe* in *Harper's Bazaar; 1945* remarries Reeves McCullers, now a wounded war hero, and settles in New York suburbs; *1946* publishes her most popular novel *Member of the Wedding; 1947* suffers serious strokes; *1950* Broadway production of *Member of the Wedding* wins several awards; *1953* Reeves McCullers commits suicide; *1957* second play, *The Square Root of Wonderful* proves a critical and commerical failure; *1958* enters psychiatric care; *1961* last novel, *Clock Without Hands,* appears to a negative press; *1965* long critical illness; dies on September 29, 1967 after another stroke.

Author's Bibliography (Selected)

The Heart is a Lonely Hunter, 1940 (novel); *Reflections in a Golden Eye,* 1941 (novel); *Member of the Wedding,* 1946 (novel); *The Ballad of the Sad Cafe,* 1951 (novella and stories along with three earlier novels); *Clock Without Hands,* 1961 (novel); *The Mortgaged Heart,* 1971 (uncollected stories, poetry, and essays).

Overview of Biographical Sources

The definitive biography of Carson McCullers is Virginia Spencer Carr's *The Lonely Hunter* (1977). Several other books and monographs on McCullers are called critical biographies, but the biographical information is generally scant and often inaccurate. McCullers was fond of fictionalizing her own experience, and several colorful but apocryphal incidents have attached themselves like barnacles to her biography. Carr's careful study documents the author's life, but unfortunately does not connect her experience to her fiction.

Evaluation of Selected Biographies

Carr, Virginia Spencer, *The Lonley Hunter.* Garden City, NY: Doubleday, 1977. Virginia Carr has written what undoubtedly will stand as the definitive biography of Carson McCullers. Although issued as a trade book, Carr's exhaustive research and careful citation (twenty pages of notes) insure the scholarly accuracy and usefulness of her book. Until 1975 biographical information on McCullers had been rather fragmented, scattered, and contradictory; Carr gathered and sorted these materials, added several years of her own research, and produced a careful, well organized, and interesting account of the life and times of Carson McCullers.

However, Carr scants her subject's most interesting aspect—the fiction which attracted the reader to the life in the first place. Without her novels and stories Carson McCullers would be an intriguing personality, but hardly one to be celebrated in six hundred pages of print. Yet Carr offers no analysis or interpretation of the fiction and comparatively little connection of the life and work in either its autobiographical genesis or its actual creation.

Autobiographical Sources

McCullers left no major autobiographical work, though an unpublished fragment exists. Several short autobiographical pieces are collected in *The Mortgaged Heart,* which also contains several critical essays and reviews. Her letters are uncollected and probably will remain so because of family control of the McCullers literary estate.

Overview of Critical Sources

McCullers criticism has varied in appreciation and evaluation, but presents a remarkable consensus in terms of analysis and interpretation. In this general view McCullers is a writer of talent, insight, and artistry, whose development was limited by her ill health and other personal circumstances, though her writing represents an interesting achievement. Most critics consider *The Heart Is a Lonely Hunter* and *The Ballad of the Sad Cafe* as her best works, with *The Member of the Wedding* (both novel and play) and *Reflections in a Golden Eye* following in that order of decreasing importance. *The Square Root of Wonderful* and *Clock Without Hands* are admitted failures, as are her later stories. About a half dozen of her early stories are considered fine work, as are a few of her essays, mostly concerned with her own writing; while her poetry is little regarded.

For the most part, McCullers' critics locate her fiction within the traditions of the Southern Gothic or grotesque schools; in particular, she is often compared with other Southern women writers. In most criticism McCullers is seen as a modern writer who uses the South as a telling symbol of a universal wasteland. Again and again the criticism finds the same motifs. In her works loneliness, alienation, and estrangement are created by the failure of love, religion, and communication, which are symbolized in sexual ambivalence, physical abnormality, and psychological aberration. Her people are losers, freaks, and gawky adolescents who fail to make social, personal, or sexual contact with one another. Her characters are lost in violent epiphanies, only partially redeemed by fitful flashes of human insight among the ruins of their dreams. Almost all of the criticism of McCullers has accepted this general consensus of analysis and interpretation.

Evaluation of Critical Sources

Cook, Richard, *Carson McCullers*. New York: Frederick Ungar, 1975. This monograph by Richard Cook provides an excellent introduction to McCullers criticism, though the author was unable to profit from Carr's biographical revelations. Cook's biographical introduction is adequate, however, and his critical readings of the individual works are both sensible and insightful. *The Heart Is a Lonely Hunter* is McCuller's most realistic work according to Cook, while *Reflections in a Golden Eye* is the most grotesque. *The Member of the Wedding* demonstrates pathos and humor, while *The Ballad of the Sad Cafe* counterpoints humor with tragic love. *Clock Without Hands* is McCuller's most ambitious novel, but it fails to realize its ambitions in terms of character, plot structure, and theme. In general, Cook's *Carson McCullers* does not go beyond earlier criticism, but it does create a synthesis that generally avoids the clichés of the earlier work while fulfilling the purpose of its series format quite nicely.

Edmonds, Dale, *Carson McCullers*. Austin: Steck-Vaughn, 1969. Although not widely known, Edmonds's work remains perhaps the best short introduction to the writer and her work. The interpretations are judicious and surprisingly free of the jargon that has limited McCuller's critics. In particular the connections with the Southern Renaissance prove illuminating.

Evans, Oliver, *Carson McCullers: Her Life and Work*. London: Peter Owen, 1965. Published in the United States as *The Ballad of Carson McCullers*. New York: Coward McCann, 1966. In the first book-length study of McCullers, Evans tried to trace the development of her fiction from her biography. Unfortunately, the biographical background is often inaccurate, and the critical estimates do not proceed beyond the consensus views presented in Evans's earlier articles. The book was probably most important for simply pulling together a good deal of information about McCullers in one volume for the first time.

Graver, Lawrence, *Carson McCullers*. Minneapolis: University of Minnesota, 1969. In this reliable introduction, Graver sees McCullers as a lyric artist, at her best when she balances mood and realism as in *The Member of the Wedding*. Graver's reading of *The Ballad of the Sad Cafe* also proves sensitive in the probing of that work's grotesque atmosphere.

McDowell, Margaret B. *Carson McCullers*. Boston: Little, Brown, 1980. McDowell takes advantage of the Carr biography and recent criticism to provide both a good general introduction to the writer and a scholarly analysis of the individual works. Although McDowell provides some new insights, especially in regard to *The Member of the Wedding, Clock Without Hands,* and the stories, most of her analysis does not go beyond the general consensus of McCullers criticism. McDowell underrates *The Heart Is a Lonely Hunter,* and she relies on critical generalizations in her chapters on *Reflections in a Golden Eye* and *The*

Ballad of the Sad Cafe. The later works are somewhat overrated, but some good points are made from feminist perspectives.

Other Sources

Millichap, Joseph R. "Carson McCuller's Literary Ballad," *Georgia Review* (Fall 1972). Views the narrator as an archetypal ballad maker, spinning a timeless tale of love and violence.

Presley, Delma Eugene, "Carson McCullers and the South," *Georgia Review* (Spring 1974). Argues cogently that McCuller's genius was Southern in origin, and declined when she cut herself off from her Georgian roots.

Reed, Rex, "Frankie Addams at 50," in *Do You Sleep in the Nude?* New York: New American Library, 1968. Perhaps the most memorable interview with McCullers.

Rubin, Louis, "Carson McCullers: The Aesthetic of Pain," *Virginia Quarterly Review* (Spring 1977). Defines McCuller's aesthetic in terms of the pain of literary creativity.

Williams, Tennessee, "Preface" to *Reflections in a Golden Eye.* New York: New Directions, 1950. An early appreciation of McCullers which did much to establish her critical reputation.

Joseph R. Millichap
Western Kentucky University

CLAUDE MCKAY
1889–1948

Author's Chronology

Born Festus Claudius McKay September 15, Clarendon Parish, Jamaica; *1907* meets Walter Jekyll, an English aristocrat who became mentor and patron; *1912* publishes two volumes of dialect verse; moves to United States; *1914* lives in New York, opens restaurant and marries—neither enterprise lasts long; *1918* meets Max Eastman, begins publishing poems and essays in *The Liberator; 1919* goes to England, co-edits *The Workers' Dreadnought; 1921* returns to New York, co-edits *The Liberator; 1922* publishes *Harlem Shadows,* his principal book of verse; *1922–1928* travels in Russia, Germany, France; publishes first novel, *Home to Harlem; 1931–1933* lives in Tangiers; *1934* returns to New York, financially ruined; is rescued by Max Eastman from government welfare camp; *1937* publishes autobiography, *A Long Way From Home; 1940* becomes American citizen; *1944* moves to Chicago, converts to Roman Catholicism; *1948* dies of heart failure; buried in Queens, New York.

Author's Bibliography (selected)

Songs of Jamaica, 1912 (poems); *Constab Ballads,* 1912 (poems); *Harlem Shadows,* 1922 (poems); *Home to Harlem,* 1928 (novel); *Banjo,* 1929 (novel); *Gingertown,* 1932 (short stories); *Banana Bottom,* 1933 (novel); *A Long Way From Home,* 1937 (autobiography); *Harlem: Negro Metropolis,* 1940 (social history).

Overview of Biographical Sources

Despite his important place in both Afro-American and West Indian literature, a definitive biography of Claude McKay has yet to be written. The closest thing to a book-length biographical source is Wayne F. Cooper's *The Passion of Claude McKay: Selected Poetry and Prose, 1912–1948* (1973). In fact, Cooper's book, McKay's autobiography, *A Long Way From Home* (1937), and James R. Giles' critical study, *Claude McKay* (1976), are to date the only book-length sources on McKay.

Evaluation of Selected Biographies

Cooper, Wayne F. *The Passion of Claude McKay: Selected Poetry and Prose: 1912–1948.* New York: Schocken Books, 1973. Cooper provides a sympathetic portrait of McKay both through a carefully researched biographical introduction, and through his notes to the chronologically arranged selections from McKay's writings. Cooper sets out to show McKay's relevance to contemporary currents in Afro-American literature, and in this he certainly succeeds. In this biographical anthology, McKay is allowed to speak for himself on the often bitter task of being a black man in a white society, with Cooper supplying additional background and a critical context for McKay's words. Of special interest is a selection of McKay's letters. Until a definitive biography is written, *The Passion of Claude McKay* will remain the best single biographical source. The generous sample of McKay's work makes the book a very useful one-volume introduction.

Autobiographical Sources

In *A Long Way From Home* (New York: Lee Furman, 1937) McKay does not attempt to be either comprehensive or conventional. He dispenses very briefly with his youth and early manhood, and chooses not to present an intimate portrait of his private life. What he does present is a chronicle of his development as a writer during the years of his greatest artistic output, from 1918 to 1937.

Of special interest are sections on his pilgrimage to Lenin's Russia, and on his uneasy relationship with the black intellectuals of the Harlem Renaissance. The final chapter, "On Belonging to a Minority Group," is one of McKay's most eloquent statements about black pride. There he speaks of the necessity "for the Negro race . . . to face the need to save itself."

An interesting glimpse at McKay's early life is provided by "Boyhood in Jamaica," posthumously published in the journal *Phylon* 14, (1953), pp. 134–145. This fragment from an unfinished work includes McKay's reflections on his African heritage, on British colonialism in Jamaica, and on his early impressions of America.

Overview of Critical Sources

There is but one book-length critical study of McKay, the bulk of critical commentary being scattered here and there in the form of journal articles and book reviews. Overall, he is probably studied less for his own sake than for his connection with the Harlem Renaissance of the 1920's and 1930's.

Evaluation of Selected Criticism

Giles, James R. *Claude McKay.* Boston: Twayne, 1976. Fortunately, this lone book-length critical study of McKay is a good one. Giles gives thorough and thoughtful attention to McKay's work, and strikes a good balance among poems, fiction and non-fiction. He argues persuasively that McKay's most significant contribution to literature is his fiction rather than his verse. Giles' analysis is all the more important in light of the fact that McKay's novels have not received a great deal of serious consideration. Giles also sheds light on the artistic and philosophical differences that distanced McKay from such black intellectuals as W. E. B. DuBois, and clarifies McKay's role in the Harlem Renaissance. The book includes a descriptive bibliography of important critical sources.

Other Sources

Lewis, David Levering, *When Harlem was in Vogue.* New York: Alfred A. Knopf, 1981. This excellent cultural history of the Harlem Renaissance includes a perceptive analysis of McKay's place in—and outside of—the Afro-American literary circle of the 1920's.

Perry, Margaret, *Silence to the Drums.* Westport, CT: Greenwood Press, 1976. Good introduction, with bibliography, to the writers and social background of the Harlem Renaissance. Considers McKay both as poet and novelist.

Tolson, Melvin B. "Claude McKay's Art," *Poetry* LXXXIII (February 1954), pp. 287–290. This review of *The Selected Poems of Claude McKay* by another notable black writer provides both a concise appraisal of McKay's poetic achievement and a good consideration of McKay's most famous poem, "If We Must Die."

Selected Dictionaries and Encyclopedias

Critical Survey of Poetry, Salem Press, 1982. Brief biography and short analysis of selected poems.

Dictionary of Literary Biography, Gale Research, 1980. Brief biography, with emphasis on McKay's years in Paris and Marseilles.

Richard A. Eichwald
McDonnell Douglas Corporation

HERMAN MELVILLE
1819–1891

Author's Chronology

Born August 1, 1819 in New York City to Allan and Maria Melvill; *1830* moves to Albany with family after father's business fails; attends Albany Academy; *1832* father dies; *1833* follows elder brother Gansevoort's example and adds final *e* to name; *1837* teaches at country school near Pittsfield, Mass.; *1838* studies surveying at Lansingburgh Academy; *1839* fails to find employment as surveyor and signs on as "boy" aboard *St. Lawrence* for voyage to Liverpool; *1840* signs on whaling ship *Acushnet; 1842* jumps ship at Nuka Hiva Bay; spends three weeks with natives reputed to be cannibals; picked up by whaler *Lucy Ann;* briefly imprisoned in Tahiti for joining with crew's rebellion; signs on whaler *Charles & Henry; 1843* discharged at Honolulu; joins U.S. Navy and sails on U.S. frigate *United States; 1844* discharged from navy; returns to Lansingburgh; *1847* marries Elizabeth Shaw; *1850* purchases "Arrowhead" near Pittsfield, Mass. where he becomes friends with Hawthorne; *1856–1857* tours Europe and Palestine; *1857–1860* unsuccessfully works lecture circuit; *1863* sells "Arrowhead" and moves to New York City; *1866* become customs inspector; *1867* son Malcolm commits suicide; *1885* resigns customs position after receiving small inheritance; *1886* son Stanwix dies in San Francisco; *1891* suffers fatal heart attack on September 28.

Author's Bibliography (selected)

Typee: A Peep at Polynesian Life, 1846 (novel); *Omoo: A Narrative of Adventures in the South Seas,* 1847 (novel); *Mardi and a Voyage Hither,* 1849 (novel); *Redburn: His First Voyage,* 1849 (novel); *White-Jacket; or, The World in a Man-of-War,* 1850 (novel); *Moby-Dick; or, The Whale,* 1851 (novel); *Pierre; or, The Ambiguities,* 1852 (novel); *Israel Potter: His Fifty Years of Exile,* 1855 (novel); *The Piazza Tales,* 1856 (stories); *The Confidence-Man: His Masquerade,* 1857 (novel); *Battle Pieces and Aspects of War,* 1866 (poems); *Clarel: A Poem and a Pilgrimage in the Holy Land,* 1876; *Billy Budd, Foretopman,* 1924 (novel).

Overview of Biographical Sources

Melville's biographers have faced special challenges. His first novels attracted considerable attention, but during the last 35 years of his life he published little and his literary reputation faded. The contemporary biographical material is collected in Mertons Sealts's *The Early Lives of Melville: Nineteenth-Century Biographical Sketches and Their Authors* (Madison: University of Wisconsin Press, 1974). When Raymond Weaver's pioneer biography *Herman Melville: Mariner and Mystic* (New York: George H. Doran Co., 1921) rekindled interest in Melville's work, many biographical resources were no longer available. Since then biographers have struggled to establish the facts of Melville's life, understand his psychological makeup, and relate his life and work. Lewis Mumford's *Herman Melville* (1929) stood as the authoritative biography for two decades. Charles Anderson's *Melville in the South Seas* (New York: Columbia University Press, 1939), a valuable study of Melville's seafaring years, envigorated the ongoing effort to establish the facts of Melville's life.

Interest in Melville increased dramatically after World War II, and three important biographies were published at mid-century: Newton Arvin's *Herman Melville* (1950); Jay Leyda's *The Melville Log: A Documentary Life of Herman Melville, 1819–1891* (1951); and Leon Howard's *Herman Melville: A Biography* (1951). These three books continue to provide the foundation for biographical study of Melville. The most comprehensive subsequent contribution is Edwin Haviland Miller's ambitious psychobiography *Melville* (1975).

Other important, though less comprehensive biographical resources are William Gilman's *Melville's Early Life and Redburn* (New York: New York University Press, 1951); Eleanor Melville Metcalf's *Herman Melville: Cycle and Epicycle* (Cambridge: Harvard University Press, 1953); Howard P. Vincent, ed. *Melville & Hawthorne in the Berkshires* (Kent, OH: Kent State University Press, 1968); and two texts by Merton M. Sealts Jr. *Melville as Lecturer* (Cambridge: Harvard University Press, 1957), and *Melville's Reading: A Check-List of Books Owned and Borrowed* (Madison: University of Wisconsin Press, 1966).

Evaluation of Selected Biographies

Arvin, Newton, *Herman Melville*. New York: William Sloane, 1950. Arvin's book is a balanced mixture of biography and criticism that offers psychological insights without becoming mired in excessive jargon.

Howard, Leon, *Herman Melville: A Biography*. Berkeley: University of California Press, 1951. Howard's authoritative biography was written in conjunction with Leyda. It includes literary criticism, but concentrates on establishing the facts of Melville's life. Its emphasis on detail makes it somewhat stiff reading, perhaps even reductive, but it gives the most credible account of Melville's life and provides a particularly clear picture of events surrounding the creation of his novels.

Leyda, Jay, *The Melville Log: A Documentary Life of Herman Melville, 1819–1891*. New York: Harcourt, Brace, 1951. Leyda's unique text is an invaluable resource that presents a chronological arrangement of documents pertaining to Melville. Leyda allows the documents to speak for themselves, avoiding the temptation to add intrusive commentary.

Miller, Edwin Haviland, *Melville*. New York: George Braziller, 1975. Miller's psychobiography portrays Melville as a neurotic orphan with an unresolved

Oedipal complex. Although this "inside narrative" often diminishes Melville, it is readable and presents a particularly thorough picture of Melville's one-sided friendship with Hawthorne.

Mumford, Lewis, *Herman Melville.* New York: Harcourt, Brace, 1929. Without the benefit of evidence that was discovered later, Mumford relied too heavily on the accuracy of Melville's autobiographical fiction. Nevertheless, this readable account continues to be important.

Autobiographical Sources

Typee (1846), *Omoo* (1847), *Redburn* (1849), and *White-Jacket* (1850) are all based on Melville's experiences, but early biographers accepted them too literally. Later biographers have established that Melville often altered the autobiographical facts in these novels to fit the demands of his fiction. The most complete collection of letters is Merrell R. Davis and William H. Gilman's *The Letters of Herman Melville* (New York: Yale University Press, 1960). Another useful autobiographical source is Howard G. Horsford's edition of *Journal of a Visit to Europe and the Levant* (Princeton: Princeton University Press, 1955). The discovery in 1983 of new material written in Melville's hand may eventually provide new autobiographical material.

Overview of Critical Sources

The mid-century explosion of interest in Melville has created a mature body of criticism that now comprises over 300 book-length studies and 1000 articles. Among the books are many comprehensive studies, applications of particular critical approaches, and detailed examinations of most of Melville's major works. The protean nature of Melville's art, however, has prevented the establishment of any critical consensus, and widely divergent interpretations of Melville's social, political, theological, metaphysical, and artistic beliefs continue to be vigorously presented.

Evaluation of Selected Criticism

Bernstein, John, *Pacifism and Rebellion in the Writings of Herman Melville.* The Hague: Mouton, 1964. Bernstein focuses on the conflict between Christian, humanistic acceptance of divine order and human limitations, on the one hand, and Promethean, idealistic defiance of powers stronger than man, on the other.

Dillingham, William B. *An Artist in the Rigging: The Early Work of Herman Melville.* Athens: University of Georgia Press, 1972. Dillingham mixes the factual, impressionistic, and archetypal to portray the protagonists of Melville's early novels as components of the author's emergent composite hero.

Dryden, Edgar A. *Melville's Thematics of Form: The Great Art of Telling the Truth.* Baltimore: John Hopkins University Press, 1968. Dryden argues that

Melville believed that only fiction could safely convey truth because it allows the reader an indirect revelation of existence.

Herbert, T. Walter, Jr. *Moby-Dick and Calvinism: A World Dismantled.* New Brunswick: Rutgers University Press, 1977. Herbert modifies Thompson's earlier study by suggesting that Melville's quarrel may have been with two equally unattractive religious traditions, Calvinism and liberalism, rather than God.

Karcher, Carolyn L. *Shadow Over the Promised Land: Slavery, Race, and Violence in Melville's America.* Baton Rouge: Louisiana State University Press, 1980. Influenced by H. Bruce Franklin, Karcher stresses Melville's reaction against race and wage slavery, and defines Melville's historical and political context. Concentrating on Moby-Dick and *The Confidence-Man,* Karcher shows Melville caught between hatred of oppression and fear of rebellion, using indirect "analogues" of slavery to express his rebellion.

Lebowitz, Alan, *Progress into Silence: A Study of Melville's Heroes.* Bloomington: Indiana University Press, 1970. Lebowitz's triadic groupings of nine novels into repeating patterns of (1) journey outward—*Typee, Redburn, Pierre* (2) return to land values *Omoo, White-Jacket, Israel Potter* and (3) resolution *Mardi, Moby-Dick, Confidence-Man* is somewhat forced, but his iconoclastic comparisons provide fresh insights.

Miller, James E., Jr. *A Reader's Guide to Herman Melville.* New York: Noonday, 1962. Miller's concise analysis of Melville's major works delineates a consistent pattern of compromising ideals in order to come to terms with evil. He explores Melville's use of masks, his duality, and his search for pragmatic balance. Miller appends a useful annotated bibliography.

Pops, Martin Leonard, *The Melville Archetype.* Kent, OH: Kent State University Press, 1970. Pops uses Jung, Freud, and primitive religious beliefs to argue that Melville was a heterodox Christian whose protagonists engage in primitive quests for the realization of the soul and sexual fulfillment.

Rosenberry, Edward H. *Melville.* London: Routledge & Kegan Paul, 1979. Rosenberry makes eclectic use of various critical approaches to construct a balanced, unpretentious introduction to Melville's writing. With its useful bibliography, this book is a logical place to begin a study of the author.

Seelye, John, *Melville: The Ironic Diagram.* Evanston: Northwestern University Press, 1970. Seelye defines two conflicting impulses in Melville: the drive to quest for ultimate truth and the realization that such truth cannot be attained. He argues that in Melville this conflict eventually resulted in literary stasis.

Stern, Milton, *The Fine Hammered Steel of Herman Melville.* Urbana: University of Illinois Press, 1957. Stern uses examples from *Typee, Mardi, Pierre,* and *Billy Budd* to argue that Melville's fiction is a prototype of naturalistic prose in America and that Melville eventually rejected idealism in favor of rationalism, empiricism, objectivity, and relativism.

Thompson, Lawrance, *Melville's Quarrel with God.* Princeton: Princeton University Press, 1952. Thompson documents Melville's rebellion against his mother's Calvinism, and demonstrates how Melville presented his unorthodox religious views indirectly to avoid offending his public.

Other Sources

Baird, James, *Ishmael.* Baltimore: Johns Hopkins Press, 1956. Reprinted, New York: Harper, 1960. The outcast, primitive art, and symbolism.

Bowen, Merlin, *The Long Encounter: Self and Experience in the Writings of Herman Melville.* Chicago: University of Chicago Press, 1960. The struggle between self and "other."

Bredahl, A. Carl, Jr. *Melville's Angles of Vision.* Gainesville: University of Florida Press, 1972. Melville's increasingly sophisticated use of perspective.

Chase, Richard, *Herman Melville: A Critical Study.* New York: Macmillan, 1949. Freudian interpretation of myth, symbol, and folklore.

Dillingham, William B. *Melville's Short Fiction 1853–56* Athens: University of Georgia Press, 1977. Meticulous scrutiny of the stories.

Feidelson, Charles, Jr. *Symbolism in American Literature.* Chicago: University of Chicago Press, 1953. Seminal study of Melville's symbolism.

Franklin, H. Bruce, *The Wake of the Gods: Melville's Mythology.* Stanford: Stanford University Press, 1963. Melville's use of Polynesian, Greek, Hindu, Egyptian, Druidic, and Christian myth.

Lawrence, D. H. *Studies in Classic American Fiction.* New York: Thomas Seltzer, 1923. Impressionistic commentary on *Typee, Omoo,* and *Moby-Dick.*

Matthiessen, F. O. *American Renaissance: Art and Expression in the Age of Emerson and Whitman.* New York: Oxford University Press, 1941. Important overview of Melville's art.

Rosenberry, Edward H. *Melville and the Comic Spirit.* Cambridge: Harvard University Press, 1955. Four phases of Melville's humor.

Sherrill, Rowland A. *The Prophetic Melville: Experience, Transcendence, and Tragedy.* Athens: University of Georgia Press, 1979. Melville's idea of the transcendent.

Shurr, William H. *The Mystery of Iniquity: Melville as Poet, 1857–1891.* Lexington: University Press of Kentucky, 1972. Thorough examination of the poetry.

Wright, Nathalia, *Melville's Use of the Bible.* Durham: Duke University Press, 1949. Authoritative study of biblical references.

Selected Dictionaries and Encyclopedias

Dictionary of American Biography, 1973. Concise biography and selected bibliography.

Dictionary of Literary Biography, Gale Research, 1983. Biographical essay, evaluation of some works, and selected bibliography.

Carl W. Brucker
Arkansas Tech University

THOMAS MERTON
1915–1968

Author's Chronology

Born January 31, 1915, Prades, Eastern Pyrenees, France; *1921* mother, an American artist, dies; *1931* father, an artist from New Zealand, dies; attends schools in America, France, and England; *1933* enters Clare College, Cambridge, on a scholarship but leaves after one year; *1935* enters Columbia University, living with American grandparents; *1938* graduates A. B.; converts to Roman Catholicism; *1939* earns a master's degree at Columbia; publishes reviews and an occasional poem; *1940–1941* English instructor at St. Bonaventure College; December 10, *1941* enters the Cistercian Order of the Strict Observance (the Trappists) at the Monastery of Our Lady of Gethsemani, near Bardstown, Kentucky, his home for the rest of his life; *1944* publishes first collection, *Thirty Poems; 1944* Simple Vows; *1947* Solemn Vows; *1948* publication of autobiography, *The Seven Storey Mountain,* brings fame and complicates vocation, followed by publication of works on the religious life, contemplation, and monastic reform, together with collections of poetry and further autobiographical books edited from journals; *1949* ordained priest; *1951–1955* Master of Scholastics; *1955–1965* Master of Novices; *1958–1960* work on *Hagia Sophia* and search for "hidden wholeness" brings a return to social issues and concern for those outside the monastery; *1962* forbidden to write on nuclear war; *1965* permitted to retire to hermitage on Gethsemani grounds; later writings on contemplation, eastern religion, social justice and civil rights; important international correspondence established with activists, writers, religious figures; becomes a visual artist and photographer, expands book reviews into literary essays and produces a major collection of poetry; *1966* receives honors, undergoes a crisis of vocation over his affection for a young woman; dies December 10, 1968, at a meeting of eastern and western monks in Bangkok, Thailand.

Overview of Bibliographical Sources

There are currently two bibliographies: Frank Dell'Isola's *Thomas Merton: A Bibliography* (Kent, OH: Kent State University Press, 1975) covers Merton's published work chronologically to 1975; Marquita Breit's *Thomas Merton: A Bibliography* (Metuchen, NJ: The Scarecrow Press, 1974) begins only in 1957, but includes more than 1800 items by and about Thomas Merton between that year and 1973. The Breit bibliography is in process of being brought up-to-date. The four selected bibliographies (pp. 655–674) of Michael Mott's *The Seven Mountains of Thomas Merton* (see below) are useful to 1983. Considerable bibliographical assistance is provided in the pages of *The Merton Seasonal,* edited by Robert E. Daggy, Director of the Thomas Merton Studies Center, published by Bellarmine College, Louisville, Kentucky.

Author's Bibliography (selected)

Thirty Poems, 1944; *The Seven Storey Mountain,* 1948 (autobiography); *The Sign of Jonas,* 1953 (autobiography); *Thoughts in Solitude,* 1958 (spiritual life); *Selected Poems,* 1959; *New Seeds of Contemplation,* 1962 (contemplation and spiritual life); *A Thomas Merton Reader,* 1962 (edited by Thomas P. McDonnell, revised 1974, includes *Hagia Sophia*); *The Way Of Chuang Tzu,* 1965 (translation, eastern thought); *Raids on the Unspeakable,* 1966 (essays); *Conjectures of a Guilty Bystander,* 1966 (autobiography, with essays on social issues); *The Geography of Lograire,* 1969 (poetry); *Collected Poems,* 1977; *Literary Essays,* 1981.

Overview of Biographical Sources

Where the wide range of Merton's talent as a writer was probably most concentrated in his skills as an autobiographer, he himself attracted early and unusual popularity as a subject for thesis writers and biographers. This occurred in spite of the disadvantage many of his biographers have been placed under by the terms of the legacy trust Merton established in the last two years of his life. Only one biographer, designated by the three trustees, was to have access to the journals Merton wrote from 1956 to 1968. The first designated biographer, John Howard Griffin, fell too ill to continue. The second, Michael Mott, began again on his own plan in 1978, completing his work with the publication of *The Seven Mountains of Thomas Merton* in 1984. This book makes full use of both restricted and unrestricted material. Before 1984 other biographers and critics had a very limited view of some of Thomas Merton's most revealing writing.

The first biographical essay in the field was by Merton's college friend Edward Rice, *The Man in the Sycamore Tree: The Good Times and Hard Life of Thomas Merton: An Entertainment, with Photographs* (Garden City, NY: Doubleday, 1970). Written first for older children as *Thomas Merton: The Daring Young Man on the Flying Belltower* (New York: Macmillan, 1976), the short, lively biography by Cornelia and Irving Süssman has been reissued as *Thomas Merton* (Garden City, NY: Doubleday Image, 1980). George Woodcock's *Thomas Merton: Monk and Poet: A Critical Study* (Vancouver: Douglas and McIntyre, 1978), while not a full biography, broke new and important ground. *Merton: A Biography,* by Monica Furlong (1980) was the first to attempt a rounded portrait. James Forest provided a brief, sharply focused essay to match the pictures in *Thomas Merton: A Pictorial Biography* (New York: Paulist Press, 1980). Anthony T. Padovano sought the spiritual and philosophic patterns in Merton's life in *The Human Journey—Thomas Merton: Symbol of a Century* (1982).

Evaluation of Selected Biographies

Furlong, Monica, *Merton: A Biography.* San Francisco: Harper and Row, 1980. Furlong begins with her conclusions, seeing Merton's life as a triumph over any number of obstacles. With some additions to the early period, this biographer accepts Merton's own account of his first thirty years, and struggles within the monastery are seen from Merton's view. Working within the restrictions of the legacy trust, Furlong presents a largely convincing portrait of the writer and personality, even if the religious figure remains enigmatic.

Mott, Michael, *The Seven Mountains of Thomas Merton.* Boston: Houghton Mifflin, 1984. Mott makes full use of his access to the restricted journals to illuminate the later years by comment and quotation. But he also employs early and unrestricted journals, fragments of Merton's early novels (believed lost), correspondence, and material from some eighty interviews to examine the first half of Merton's life from sources other than the autobiography. Generally in sympathy with his subject, Mott does not always agree with his views, or take Merton as the last word, even on Merton. He tries to keep a balance between attention to the monk-contemplative and the writer-artist-activist. This is the first full history of the complex situation developing over twenty years between Merton and his second abbot, as it is the first integrated account of Merton's love affair with a young woman in 1966. The notes and bibliographies are helpful, and this is clearly the definitive biography. Mott chooses to guide the reader, providing information, yet allowing the reader to form his or her own opinion.

Padovano, Anthony T. *The Human Journey—Thomas Merton: Symbol of a Century.* Garden City, NY: Doubleday, 1982. This study moves backwards and forwards in Merton's life, seeking links and connections, at times imposing patterns on the material. It is in part a matter of taste whether his method or Mott's provides the greater insight. Padovano attempts to set Merton's imaginative prose and his poetry within the context of themes in American Literature such as "the war between brothers"—Cain and Abel in the American Eden. If this is sometimes confusing, it is often stimulating, and little here is duplicated in the other two selected biographies.

Autobiographical Sources

In addition to writing a best-selling account of his first thirty years, *The Seven Storey Mountain,* Merton included an autobiographical element in the greater part of his published work. The strictly autobiographical line continues with *The Sign of Jonas, The Secular Journal,* and *Conjectures of a Guilty Bystander.* The content of these books was drawn from journals, reworked and edited. (Merton's methods are examined in Mott's biography.) Autobiographical elements are strong in his poetry from the beginning and in the early fiction. Much of this survives, and in the novel he himself preserved, retitled and published almost thirty years after it was written as *My Argument With the Gestapo* (1969), a character called Thomas Merton returns to England during the blitz and makes his way to Occupied France.

Both Furlong and Mott have done considerable detective work to reassemble the pieces of this larger, scattered autobiography, while Mott shows that Merton considered writing an all-inclusive autobiography (using *Finnegans Wake* as something of a model). Unpublished autobiographical works, such as "The Vow of Conversation" (which Merton held back) will soon be published; and Merton's own restriction on the publication of the later journals will run out within the decade. Merton's wide-ranging correspondence, another rich source, is housed at the Thomas Merton Studies Center. Five volumes of letters are projected to appear, the first in 1985.

Overview of Critical Sources

Many have seen Merton as a "born critic"—of institutions, of society, and much else. In his last years he was, among many other things, a literary critic (*Literary Essays*). Criticism of his own work on varied subjects is so large that it is surprising to find he is given only two lines in the Fifteenth Edition of the *Encyclopaedia Britannica,* where mention of Thomas Merton is confined largely to his role as a monastic reformer. The best single critical study, both of his own writing and of works about him, is Elena Malits's *The Solitary Explorer: Thomas Merton's Transforming Journey* (San Francisco: Harper and Row, 1980). There has yet to be a full critical evaluation of Merton's *The Geography of Lograire,* though both Mott and Padovano provide valuable approaches. See also Walter Sutton's article, "Thomas Merton and the American Epic Tradition: The Last Poems," *Contemporary Literature,* XIV, #1 (Winter 1973), 49–57. Short critical studies by two younger critics, George Kilcourse and Michael Higgins, have made contributions to the study of Merton as a poet.

Evaluation of Selected Criticism

Lentfoehr, Sister Thérèse, S.D.S. *Words and Silence: On the Poetry of Thomas Merton.* New York: New Directions, 1979. Lentfoehr provides much information on Merton's verse, from the poems of the 1930's to his major work in poetry, published posthumously, *The Geography of Lograire.* Unfortunately she strains to praise throughout, making too little of Merton's long struggle against being dominated by the influence of other poets.

Woodcock, George, *Thomas Merton, Monk and Poet: A Critical Study.* Vancouver: Douglas and McIntyre, 1978; New York: Farrar, Straus and Giroux. Woodcock presents a balanced critical view. He is especially insightful on the middle period (the poetry of the 1950's), and he draws a useful distinction between "the poetry of the cloister" and "the poetry of the desert."

Other Sources

Because the range of Merton criticism, and of the criticism of Merton's work, is enormous and growing, reference should be made to the bibliographies discussed above, especially to Briet and Dell'Isola. "Books and Articles about Merton," and "Extensive References to Merton: A Selective List," the third bibliography in Mott (pp. 661–668) are also useful starting points. On Merton as a religious writer, the following works are important.

Bailey, Raymond, *Thomas Merton on Mysticism.* Garden City, NY: Doubleday Image, 1976.

Higgins, John J., S.J. *Thomas Merton on Prayer.* Garden City, NY: Doubleday Image, 1975.

Shannon, William H. *Thomas Merton's Dark Path: The Inner Experience of a Contemplative.* New York: Farrar, Straus and Giroux, 1981.

On social issues and on Merton as "the conscience of his time," the following studies are indispensable.

Baker, James Thomas, *Thomas Merton, Social Critic.* Lexington, KY: University Press of Kentucky, 1971.

Forest, James H. *Thomas Merton's Struggle with Peacemaking.* Erie, PA: Benet Press, 1983.

Kelly, F. J., S.J. *Man before God: Thomas Merton on Social Responsibilities.* New York: Doubleday, 1974.

Michael Mott
Bowling Green State University

JOHN STUART MILL
1806–1873

Author's Chronology

Born May 20, 1806, at Pentonville, London; *1809* at age three, begins study of Greek under father's intense tutelage; *1811* studies Latin, Euclid, algebra; *1819* studies political economy; *1820–1821* lives in France with the family of Sir Samuel Bentham; *1823* forms Utilitarian society and clerks in East India Company, eventually becomes head of office; *1826–1827* suffers a mental crisis; *1830* meets and soon loves Mrs. Harriet Taylor; *1835* edits *London Review;* *1836–1840* owns and edits *London and Westminster Review; 1851* marries Harriet Taylor; *1858* retires from East India Company; his wife dies in Avignon; *1865–1868* serves as M.P. for Westminster; *1873* dies May 8 in Avignon.

Author's Bibliography (selected)

A System of Logic, 1843; *Principles of Political Economy,* 1848; *On Liberty,* 1859; *Thoughts on Parliamentary Reform,* 1859; *Dissertations and Discussions,* 1859; *Considerations on Representative Government,* 1861; *Utilitarianism,* 1863; *August Comte and Positivism,* 1865; *On the Subjection of Women,* 1869; *Autobiography,* 1873 (posthumously published); *Nature, the Utility of Religion, Theism, Being Three Essays on Religion,* 1874 (posthumously published); *Collected Works of John Stuart Mill,* ed. F. E. L. Priestley and J. M. Robson, 1963 on, in twenty-five projected volumes (the standard edition); *Bibliography of the Published Writings of John Stuart Mill,* (MacMinn, Hainds, and McCrimmon, eds.) 1945; rpt. 1970.

Overview of Biographical Sources

A major voice in the rich field of Victorian prose, and a major proponent of English liberal thought in philosophy, politics, sociology, ethics, logic, and economics, Mill has attracted much interest from various quarters. Most studies have been specialized articles, and relatively few full-blown biographical studies have appeared. The standard biography, perhaps not entirely definitive, is Michael St. John Packe's *The Life of John Stuart Mill* (New York: Macmillan, 1954). Despite occasional vagueness in dates due to Packe's concern to heighten Mill's reliance on his wife's advice, the biography is reliable, readable, and still current, despite the later appearance of some new facts. Although it is occasionally tentative in dealing with Mill's thought, and is a sometimes dramatized approach, Packe's study remains the best single account of Mill's life. An earlier study which still merits attention is Alexander Bain's *John Stuart Mill. A Criticism with Personal Recollections* (New York: Kelley, 1969 reprint of 1882 edition), not as full a treatment as Packe's because Bain was unfortunately alienated from Mill's heir and stepdaughter, Helen Taylor, and thus was denied

818

access to important materials. Perhaps Mill's closest disciple, Bain provides an invaluable first-hand account, enhanced by personal appreciation. Bain's superb rambling treatment, referring to conversations and quotes from now-lost letters, cannot be superseded. Alan Ryan's *John Stuart Mill* (Boston: Routledge and Kegan Paul, 1974), a sharply argued intellectual biography, is readable and accessible to beginning students of Mill, yet rewards professional scholars as well. Treatment of the historical setting informs Ryan's provocative study of Mill's personal concerns. A most winning biographer, Ryan offers a clear, insightful, and balanced picture of Mill's intellectual power and diversity.

Evaluation of Selected Biographies

Britton, Karl, *John Stuart Mill.* London: Penguin, 1953. This is a general life-and-works approach to Mill, critical yet sympathetic toward his subjects; a good broad introduction to Mill and his writing.

Hayek, F. A. *John Stuart Mill and Harriet Taylor.* Chicago: University of Chicago Press, 1951. Based on the correspondence between Mill and his wife, Harriet Taylor, this detailed and seminal study of Mill from 1830–1858 did much to shape later understanding of Mill and his remarkable wife. Hayek did much to stimulate later interest in Mill biography; his contention that Mill was greatly influenced by Harriet was developed further in Packe's study; later critics have sometimes disagreed.

Pappe, H. O. *John Stuart Mill and the Harriet Taylor Myth.* Melbourne: University of Melbourne Press, 1960. Pappe challenges Hayek and Packe, and argues that Mill in the *Autobiography* affectionately heightened the intellectual effect of his wife. Pappe remains unpersuaded that Harriet actually possessed the powerful abilities ascribed to her.

Autobiographical Sources

Mill's *Autobiography,* striking and at times wrenching in its effect, gives a vivid account of his rigorous fact-bound utilitarian education, and of his subsequent mental and spiritual growth. The most famous passages deal with "a crises in my mental history," which describe an emotional breakdown he suffered at age 25. Although Carlyle dismissed the work as the "autobiography of a steam-engine," it has proven to be a primary document in the development of nineteenth-century thought, and is also an important resource for biographers which has heavily influenced understanding of Mill's motivations.

The letters also provide invaluable autobiographical material—regrettably, some of them once in Bain's possession have been lost. The extant letters will be found in several volumes of the *Collected Works.*

The best treatment of Mill as critic is found in Francis Parvin Sharpless' *The Literary Criticism of John Stuart Mill* (Paris: Mouton, 1967), a broad summary of Mill's major critical writings which reveals three stages in Mill's critical development: first, a utilitarian interest in literature as vehicle for political and moral concerns; secondly, an attempt to formulate a synthesis of literary and philosophic realities; thirdly, a renewed emphasis on pragmatic uses of literature.

Overview of Critical Sources

As a major Victorian advocate of classical economics, empericism, and liberal thought, Mill figures in a large array of specialized studies of the Victorian period; many articles have appeared in journals concerned with nineteenth-century thought and culture. General book-length critiques are much less numerous. In Mill's lifetime his *Logic* (1843) produced most comment, followed by responses, often hostile, to his philosophic writings. After Hayek's study of the Mill-Taylor relationship, interest in Mill's life began to rise and with it growing appreciation of his literary significance.

Evaluation of Selected Criticism

Anschutz, R. P. *The Philosophy of J. S. Mill.* Oxford: Oxford University Press, 1953. Anschutz provides an acute and detailed critical study of the entire range of Mill's philosophic work. He notes the appearance of philosophic inconsistencies in Mill's thought, finding a mixture of experientialism and realism in his work.

McCloskey, H. J. *John Stuart Mill: A Critical Study.* London: Macmillan, 1971. McCloskey's treatment is largely unsympathetic to Mill, adducing that some of his arguments are "strange." McCloskey's study is more accessible than Anschutz's, offering a good overview of the general topics of Mill's thought.

Robson, John M. *The Improvement of Mankind: The Social and Political Thought of John Stuart Mill.* Toronto: University of Toronto Press, 1968. Robson, one of the pre-eminent Mill scholars, traces the growth of Mill's mind as he passed through the different stages of his career, illuminates Mill's thinking as a whole, and details the influence of Comte, Carlyle, Coleridge, de Tocqueville, and the Saint-Simonians on Mill. Readable and insightful, this study ably bridges the disparate fields of morals, politics, sociology, and scientific theory in Mill's intellectual development.

Ryan, Alan, *John Stuart Mill.* New York: Pantheon, 1970. Ryan argues that a consistent reliance on inductivism undergirds all Mill's writings; he investigates the philosophic issues, offering analysis of Mill's psychology and metaphysics. Noting inconsistencies, Ryan effectively argues the basic cohesion of Mill's intellectual approach; a sharply critical but nevertheless sympathetic study.

Other Sources

Duncan, Graeme, *Marx and Mill: Two Views of Social Conflict and Social Harmony*. Cambridge: Cambridge University Press, 1974. Rejects view of Mill as liberal philosopher; argues his commitment to an ideal of social harmony. Sees Marx and Mill as advocates of rival theories of society.

Halevy, Elie, *The Growth of Philosophic Radicalism*. trans. Mary Morris. London: Faber and Gwyer, 1928. Standard study of background of Mill's upbringing, placing Mill in the context of early utilitarianism.

Hamburger, Joseph, *Intellectuals in Politics: John Stuart Mill and the Philosophic Radicals*. New Haven: Yale University Press, 1965. Extended treatment beyond the early years into the 1830's. This is the fullest record of that period, and the best discussion of the effect of ideology on the school.

Himmelfarb, Gertrude, *On Liberty and Liberalism: The Case of John Stuart Mill*. New York: Alfred A. Knopf, 1974. Argues for two Mills, committed to different liberal traditions. An authoritative study which asserts a connection between *On Liberty* and women's liberation in Mill's time; sees *On Liberty* as a departure from Mill's characteristic Benthamite utilitarianism.

Mueller, Iris Wessel, *John Stuart Mill and French Thought*. Urbana: University of Illinois Press, 1956. Traces Mill's influence on French thought, and also seeks to demonstrate that French influence on Mill is second only to that of Bentham.

Selected Biographical Dictionaries

British Authors of the Nineteenth Century, H. W. Wilson, 1936. Short biography and brief bibliography for Mill and contemporary authors.

Dictionary of National Biography, Oxford University Press, 1885–1900. Biographies of virtually every noteworthy Britisher, including Mill; relatively full treatment.

Makers of Nineteenth Century Culture 1800–1914, Routledge and Kegan Paul, 1982. A biographical dictionary giving critical examination of leading figures of the century, including Mill.

Larry Brunner
Hardin-Simmons University

EDNA ST. VINCENT MILLAY
1892–1950

Author's Chronology

Born February 22, 1892, Rockland Maine; *1900* parents divorce; *1906* publishes first poems; *1912* gains national recognition with the publication of "Renascence;" *1913* attends Vassar College; begins acting; *1918* moves to Greenwich Village; affairs with Floyd Dell and Arthur Ficke; *1920* leaves for Europe; *1923* returns to U.S.; receives Pulitzer Prize for poetry; marries Eugen Boissevain; *1925* moves to Austerlitz, New York; *1927* protests the Sacco-Vanzetti case; *1935* begins association with George Dillon; *1940* begins propaganda writings; *1944* nervous breakdown, stops writing for two years; *1949* Eugen Boissevain dies; *1950* dies alone of heart failure on October 19th.

Author's Bibliography (selected)

Renascence and Other Poems, 1917; *A Few Figs from Thistles, Aria da Capo* 1920, (play); *Second April,* 1921 (poems); *The Harp-Weaver and Other Poems,* 1923; *The King's Henchman,* 1927 (play); *The Buck in the Snow,* 1928 (poems); *Fatal Interview,* 1931 (poems); *Wine from These Grapes,* 1934 (poems); *Flowers of Evil,* 1936 (translation of *Les Fleurs du Mal*); *Conversation at Midnight,* 1937 (poems); *Hunstman, What Quarry?* 1939 (poems); *Make Bright the Arrows,* 1940 (poems); *Invocation to the Muses,* 1941 (poems); *Collected Sonnets,* 1941; *The Murder of Lidice,* 1942 (poems); *Collected Lyrics,* 1943; *Poem and Prayer for an Invading Army,* 1944; *Mine the Harvest,* 1954 (poems); *Collected Poems,* 1956.

Overview of Biographical Sources

Much of the biographical material written on Millay is either overly simplistic and exuberant or overly concerned with her Greenwich village lovers. The earliest biography—Elizabeth Atkins' *Edna St. Vincent Millay and Her Times* (1936)—is a prime example of this hyperbole, juxtaposing Millay's name with Shakespeare's, Chaucer's, and Milton's. The latest biography—Anne Cheney's *Millay in Greenwich Village* (University: University of Alabama Press, 1975)—is representative of the narrowly focused Bohemian biographies. Another example of the simplistic type is Toby Shafter's *Edna St. Vincent Millay: America's Best-Loved Poet* (New York: Julian Messner, 1957). Written for a juvenile audience, Shafter's biography concentrates on Millay's childhood. The most complete biography to date is Jean Gould's *The Poet and Her Book: A Biography of Edna St. Vincent Millay* (1969).

Evaluation of Selected Biographies

Atkins, Elizabeth, *Edna St. Vincent Millay and Her Times.* Chicago: University of Chicago Press, 1936. Although Atkins presents an inflated view of Millay's poetic achievements, this biography is an important source of information because it is one of the few books that contains criticism on the poems, omitting only the Nancy Boyd stories. Atkins' ornate and didactic style may be too long-winded for the modern reader; yet, written when Millay was in her forties, it does reflect the favorable public response of Millay's contemporaries.

Gould, Jean, *The Poet and Her Book: A Biography of Edna St. Vincent Millay.* New York: Dodd, Mead, 1969. Stylistically, Gould's biography is the best written work on Millay's life. Its dramatic opening captures the reader's attention and without dwelling on insignificant anecdotes, Gould delves quickly into some pertinent details affecting Millay's life—her conflict between poetry and music, and the influences of the current literary milieu being two examples. In spite of a negative annotation by Judith Nierman, Millay's most significant bibliographer, Gould's biography is the major work on Millay's life. Also interesting are the book's many photographs.

Gurko, Miriam, *Restless Spirit: The Life of Edna St. Vincent Millay.* New York: Thomas Y. Crowell, 1962. Until publication of the Gould biography, this was the major source on Millay; however, Gurko's style is aimed toward a general audience, and her discussion of literary influences is quite simplistic. Descriptive chapter titles, short chapters, amusing anecdotes, and an approach that relates events in Millay's life to developments in her poetry make this book interesting, but not scholarly. Gurko's biography also contains exaggerated claims, labeling Millay's poetry as "some of the most spectacular love poems in the English language."

Sheean, Vincent, *The Indigo Bunting: A Memoir of Edna St. Vincent Millay.* New York: Harper & Bros., 1951. Sheean's book is a highly personal, nostalgic look at the Millay of the 1940's. Its unique approach—viewing Millay through her association with birds—concentrates more on Millay's personality than on her poems, though Sheean does discuss Millay's use of birds in her poetry to a limited extent. Containing snatches of dinner conversation, Sheean presents the "variable temperament" of Millay.

Autobiographical Sources

Edna St. Vincent Millay wrote no autobiography; however, because her poetry is so personal, much of it could be considered autobiographical. In prose, the closest source to an autobiography would be *Letters of Edna St. Vincent Millay,* edited by Allan Ross Macdougall (New York: Harper & Bros., 1952). Due to lack of space, Macdougall's collection is not complete, but it is a representative sampling of Millay's correspondence from age eight to just before her death fifty years later. Macdougall retains Millay's incorrect spelling and punctuation in the early letters and uses a row of three asterisks in places where he has omitted more than a sentence. Footnotes help identify correspondents and vague references in the letters. In these letters, the loving, coaxing, charming, and when necessary, adament and cutting Millay shine through, making this volume an invaluable source.

Overview of Critical Sources
Very few book-length critical studies have been done on Millay; in fact, there are but two—the Twayne series by Norman A. Brittin and the University of Minnesota Pamphlets on American Writers by James Gray—and both of these, though accurate and perceptive, are fairly brief. In addition to these sources, the Atkins and Gurko biographies contain some criticism but hardly an adequate, in-depth analysis.

Evaluation of Selected Criticism
Brittin, Norman A. *Edna St. Vincent Millay.* revised edition. Boston: Twayne 1982. Though short, this book is essential for a study of the complete Millay portfolio. After the author's chronology and a finely condensed biography, the book contains six chapters on criticism, adding evaluation of Millay's prose that was omitted in the 1967 edition. Chapters deal with Millay's early poetry, her prose, the plays, her poetry from *Buck in the Snow* to the posthumously published *Mine the Harvest,* Millay's feminism, and the critical reception of her work. Furthermore, Brittin's book contains an annotated selected bibliography that updates Nierman's and is more accurate in its assessment. Brittin's criticism of Millay's works is intelligent and honest, and he readily admits to the triteness of some of Millay's poems.

Gray, James, *Edna St. Vincent Millay.* St. Paul: University of Minnesota Press, 1967. Gray's pamphlet contains only 42 pages, but its criticism is significant. Citing recent scholarship that has made too much of Millay's love life, Gray claims that many of her other themes have been missed, particularly the search for the wholeness of the individual. Gray contends that Millay's poetry though highly personal is not trivial because this search for the soul's integrity continues to be important for the present. Although Gray treats but a dozen or so poems and a few plays and translations, his perceptive analysis demonstrates that Millay was not just a Greenwich village "nymph," but "a tragic figure" burdened with the world's problems, feeling "a scrupulous sense of responsibility toward her gift."

Other Sources
Dash, Joan, "Edna St. Vincent Millay," *A Life of One's Own: Three Gifted Women and the Men They Married.* New York: Harper and Row, 1973, pp. 116–227. A psychoanalytical biography, viewing Millay as a "neurotic woman."

Dell, Floyd, "Edna St. Vincent Millay," *Literary Spotlight.* New York: George H. Doran, 1924, pp. 77–90. A perceptive look at Millay's complex personality by one of her former lovers.

Hahn, Emily, "Mostly About Vincent," *Romantic Rebels: An Informal History of Bohemianism in America.* Boston: Houghton Mifflin, 1967, pp. 231–241. The only mention of Millay's drug addiction and abortion prior to Brittin's work.

Nierman, Judith, *Edna St. Vincent Millay: A Reference Guide.* Boston: G. K. Hall, 1977. An invaluable bibliography to Millay criticism through 1973, organized by year and category (books and shorter writings), and fully annotated. This guide also includes an excellent critical introduction and brief reviews of four Ph.D. dissertations on Millay.

Stanbrough, Jean, "Edna St. Vincent Millay and the Language of Vulnerability," *Shakespeare's Sisters: Feminist Essays on Women Poets.* eds. Sandra M. Gilbert and Susan Gubar. Bloomington: Indiana University Press, 1978, pp. 183–199. Traces Millay's "sense of vulnerability" in some of her poems, revealing a gulf between childhood dreams and adult realities and a concern over the victimization of women by "totalitarian powers."

Wilson, Edmund, "Epilogue, 1952: Edna St. Vincent Millay," *The Shores of Light: A Literary Chronicle of the Twenties and Thirties.* New York: Farrar, Straus and Young, 1952, pp. 744–793. A personal look at Millay during the Village period and later life.

Yost, Karl, *A Bibliography of the Works of Edna St. Vincent Millay.* New York: Harper & Bros., 1937. The earliest bibliography of Millay, sparsely annotated, and now superseded by Neirman and Brittin. Interesting for its inclusion of an essay by Harold Lewis Cook, written at the crescendo of Millay's work and drastically overrating her poetry.

Sandra Manoogian Pearce
Oklahoma State University

HENRY MILLER
1891–1980

Author's Chronology

Born December 26, 1891, Yorkville section of Manhattan to German-American parents; *1892–1908* lives in Williamsburg section of Brooklyn; *1909* enters City College of New York, drops out after two months; *1910* begins affair with first mistress, works in father's tailor shop, travels; *1917* marries Beatrice Wickens, a pianist; *1920* becomes employment manager of Western Union ("Cosmodemonic Telegraphic Company") of New York; *1923* falls in love with June Edith Smith; *1924* divorces first wife, marries June Smith; *1925* begins writing career, sells prose/poems door to door; *1928* tours Europe with Smith; *1930* returns to Europe alone, settles in Paris; *1931* meets Anais Nin, begins writing *Tropic of Cancer;* *1934* publishes *Tropic of Cancer* in Paris, divorces June Smith by proxy in Mexico; *1939* visits Lawrence Durrell in Greece; *1940* returns to New York; *1941* begins tour of United States; *1944* marries Janina Lepska, settles in Big Sur; *1953* marries Eve McClure after divorcing Lepska; *1961* Grove Press publishes *Tropic of Cancer* in United States; *1963* moves to Pacific Palisades; *1967* marries Hoki Tokuda after death of Eve McClure; *1968–1980* lives in California and continues publishing memoirs, essays, miscellany until death in Pacific-Palisades on June 7.

Author's Bibliography (selected)

Tropic of Cancer, 1934 (novel); *Black Spring,* 1936 (novel); *Tropic of Capricorn,* 1939 (novel); *The Colossus of Maroussi,* 1941 (travel journal); *The Air-Conditioned Nightmare,* 1945 (travel journal); *Remember To Remember;* 1947 (essays); *Sexus,* 1949 (novel); *Big Sur and the Oranges of Hieronymus Bosch,* 1957 (diary/reflections); *Nexus,* 1960 (novel); *Stand Still Like The Hummingbird,* 1962 (essays).

Overview of Biographical Sources

Henry Miller's life is so much the subject of his own writing that the task of separating the actual events and circumstances of Miller's nearly ninety years from the manner in which he used these incidents has been too overwhelming for anyone to even attempt a conventional biography. There are many accounts by Miller's friends, but these are mostly fragmentary and highly subjective. The only book that resembles a biography is Jay Martin's *Always Merry And Bright* (Santa Barbara, California: Capra Press, 1978), an attempt to "exhibit the process of Miller's life." Martin has consulted nearly every manuscript collection available, read all of the critical sources and interviewed many of Miller's acquaintances. His book is a vast source of information, but his attempts to describe some of the same scenes that are at the heart of Miller's best work are often clumsy and sometimes almost embarrassing. In addition, the book is very uneven since he covers some periods closely while being unable to get much material on others equally important. Still, there is a great deal of interesting Milleriana here, and his detailed account of the genesis of *Tropic of Cancer* is very illuminating.

Autobiographical Sources

Miller described his major works of prose-fiction as "auto-novels" or "auto-biographical romances," and in a sense, *all* of his writing, even the semi-critical essays, is part of an immense "autobiography." The major critical sources confront Miller's use of the "I" narrator and offer varying estimates of the reliability of Miller's versions of his life. The most accurate expression of the actual events of Miller's career is probably in the letters he exchanged with Lawrence Durrell, Wallace Fowlie, Harry Moore, J. Rives Childs and others. Anais Nin's multi-volume *Diary,* especially *Volume I: 1931-1934* (New York: Harcourt Brace Jovanovich, 1966) and *Volume II: 1934-1939* (New York: Harcourt Brace Jovanovich, 1968) provides another interesting if, inevitably, subjective account of Miller's world. All of Miller's many friends must be regarded, as must Miller himself, as *fabulists* in their recreations and recollections.

Overview of Critical Sources

For many years, the only commentary on Miller that existed took the form of enraged polemics by outraged people who thought of Miller as a swine, and exuberant, even rhapsodic defenses of the man and his work by acquaintances who regarded him as a secular saint. Even the serious critics like Edmund Wilson, Philip Rahv and George Orwell who wrote about Miller devoted themselves as much to a defense of his artistic integrity as to a discussion of his writing. William Gordon, who corresponded at length with Miller, wrote the first real critical study of Miller's entire output, *The Mind and Art of Henry Miller* (1967), and his work began the process of serious consideration of Miller's achievement as an artist. But the vociferous argument between Miller's acolytes and adversaries continues as well, notably in the clash between Kate Millett and Norman Mailer.

Evaluation of Selected Criticism

Gordon, William, *The Mind and Art of Henry Miller.* Baton Rouge: Louisiana State University Press, 1967. In this first full-length study of Miller's *oeuvre,* Gordon views Miller as the "ultimate romantic," whose autobiographically influenced fiction is a form of "progressive self-creation." He compares Miller to Whitman and Wordsworth, and regards Miller's use of obscene and erotic material as a part of a Freudian self-analysis in which repressed emotion is expressed symbolically and exorcised. His critical approach is strictly traditional and his judgments are generous and sympathetic.

Hassan, Ihab, *The Literature of Silence.* New York: Alfred A. Knopf, 1967. In striking contrast to Gordon's new-critical stance, Hassan's viewpoint is very much a product of the 1960's and he uses many facets of Post-Modern discourse in his discussion of Miller, concentrating on the concept of "silence" as a form of negative transcendence of an absurd universe. His elaborate formulations don't always apply to Miller's writing, but his comments on the shorter non-fiction pieces—the travelogue/essays and philosophical rambles—are penetrating as he locates Miller precisely with respect to Modernist thought.

Lewis, Leon, *Of Mighty Opposites.* New York: Schocken Books, 1985. This is the most contemporary examination of Miller and it extends significant insights of earlier scholarship as it focuses on seven books which the author contends are at the heart of Miller's achievement as an artist. Lewis challenges the claim that there is no order in Miller's work and demonstrates that there is a complex, revealing pattern of organization which Miller planned. In addition, this critical study evaluates and explains Miller's aims and accomplishments, clarifying Miller's struggle to understand his erotic impulses and his fascination with the "feminine" psyche, and demonstrating how Miller's "I" narrator parallels Albert Camus's man in rebellion. Miller's relationship to poets like Ezra Pound, William Carlos Williams and Charles Olson is also examined.

Mathieu, Bernard, *Orpheus In Brooklyn.* Paris: Mouton, 1976. In a book that is as much about Arthur Rimbaud as Miller, Mathieu concentrates on *The Colossus of Maroussi* to show how Miller's writing may be understood as a conscious retelling and updating of the Orpheus myth. His understanding of French Symbolist poetry enables him to identify the qualities of *music* and *song* that inform Miller's language, and to show how Miller utilizes the concept of the poet as seer to form a viable narrative consciousness.

Nelson, Jane, *Form and Image in the Fiction of Henry Miller.* Detroit: Wayne State University Press, 1970. Nelson claims that Miller organized all of his "fiction" according to a method that can be explained by the theories of Carl Jung and his disciples. Her book is as much an explication of Jungian psychology in terms of Miller's writing as a study of Miller, but her ideas about Miller's narrator and her conclusions concerning Miller's attitude toward women are carefully considered and illuminating.

Other Sources

Mailer, Norman, *Genius and Lust: A Journey Through the Major Writings of Henry Miller.* New York: Grove Press, 1976. This is a kind of maverick anthology in which Mailer selects his favorite excerpts from Miller's writing and intersperses them with brilliant, quirky comments about Miller's life and attitudes. Mailer, as always, is an extraordinary stylist and his perceptions on the nature of "narcissism" are exceptionally applicable and very incisive.

Mitchell, Edward, *Henry Miller: Three Decades of Criticism.* New York: New York University Press, 1971. This volume collects much of the important early criticism of Miller's work that appeared in various journals.

Wickes, George, *Henry Miller And The Critics.* Carbondale: Southern Illinois University Press, 1964. A collection which complements the Mitchell volume.

Selected Dictionaries and Encyclopedias

Critical Survey of Long Fiction, Vol. 5, Salem Press, 1983. An appreciation of Miller's achievements, a long list of publications other than fiction, and a short analysis of *Tropic of Cancer* and *Tropic of Capricorn.*

Leon Lewis
Appalachian State University

JOHN MILTON
1608–1674

Author's Chronology

Born December 9, 1608, at Bread Street, in Cheapside, London, first son and child of John Milton, scrivener; *1618(?)* tutored by Thomas Young; *1620(?)* enters St. Paul's School, London; *1625* enters Christ's College, Cambridge; *1626* suspension from Christ's College in the spring; *1629* takes A.B. degree; writes *Nativity Ode; 1632* takes A.M. degree; *1635* lives with his family at Horton; *1637* writes *Lycidas; 1638* on continental tour; *1639* becomes tutor of his nephews, John and Edward Phillips; *1641* anti-prelatical pamphlets; *1642* marries Mary Powell; *1643* first of the divorce tracts; *1644 Of Education* and *Areopagitica; 1645* first volume of poetry published; *1646* daughter Anne born; *1648* daughter Mary born; *1649* appointed Latin Secretary to the Council of State; *1651* goes totally blind, son John born; *1652* daughter Deborah born; wife Mary Powell and son John die; *1656* marries Katherine Woodcock; *1657* daughter Katherine born; *1658* wife Katherine and daughter Katherine die; *1660* publishes *The Ready and Easy Way to Establish a Free Commonwealth;* loses office; is imprisoned and released; *1663* marries Elizabeth Minshull; *1667* publishes *Paradise Lost; 1671 Paradise Regained* and *Samson Agonistes; 1673 Private Letters, Academic Prolusions,* and second edition of early poems; *1674* second edition of *Paradise Lost* published, dies of gout in London.

Author's Bibliography (selected)

Poems of Mr. John Milton, Both English and Latin, 1645; *Of the Tenure of Kings and Magistrates,* 1649; *Pro Populo Anglicano Defensio,* 1651; *Defensio Secunda,* 1654; *The Ready and Easy Way to Establish a Free Commonwealth,* 1660; *Paradise Lost,* 1667; *Paradise Regained* and *Samson Agonistes,* 1671; *Private Letters, Academic Prolusions,* and *Poems &c. Upon Several Occasions,* 1673; *Paradise Lost,* second edition, 1674; *The Poetical Works of John Milton,* ed. Henry J. Todd, 6 vols. 1809; *The Poetical Works of John Milton,* ed. David Masson, 3 vols. 1874; *The Works of John Milton,* Columbia edition, ed. Frank Allen Patterson, 18 vols. 1931–1938; *The Poems of John Milton,* ed. James Holly Hanford, 1936; *The Complete Poetical Works of John Milton,* ed. Harris F. Fletcher, 1941; *The Poetical Works of John Milton,* ed. Helen Darbishire, 2 vols., 1952–1955; *Complete Prose Works of John Milton,* Yale edition, ed. Don M. Wolfe, 8 vols. 1953–1982; *John Milton: Complete Poems and Major Prose,* ed. Merritt Y. Hughes, 1957; *The Complete English Poetry of John Milton,* ed. John T. Shawcross, 1963; *Poems,* ed. John Carey and Alastair Fowler, 2 vols. 1968; *Milton: A Bibliography for the Years 1624–1700,* compiled by John T. Shawcross, 1984.

Overview of Biographical Sources

Because of his controversial views on divorce, eloquent defense of the regicide position, and growing literary reputation, Milton was the subject of several contemporary and near-contemporary biographies. These have been collected by Helen Darbishire in *The Early Lives of Milton* (New York: Barnes and Noble, 1932). Much knowledge of Milton's character, physical person, and way of life is gathered from these early biographies. Next in importance is H. J. Todd's *Some Account of the Life and Writings of John Milton: Derived Principally from Documents in his Majesty's State-Paper Office* (1826). The most important breakthrough in Milton biography was the massive study by David Masson, *The Life of John Milton* 1859–1880. Other seminal studies included James Holly Hanford's study of Milton as a specifically English poet, *John Milton, Englishman* (New York: Crown Publishers, 1949); a critical biography, David Daiches, *Milton.* (London: Hutchinson, 1957); an essential collection of contemporary biographical materials in J. M. French's *The Life Records of John Milton* (1966); the standard, scholarly biography by Willard Riley Parker, *Milton: A Biography* (1968); a personal portrait of the poet by Edward Wagenknecht, *The Personality of Milton* (1970); a retrospective article by Leo Miller, "Milton's Contemporary Reputation: A Footnote to Parker and French," *Milton Quarterly,* 17 (1983), 56–57; a psycho-biography, James Thorpe's, *John Milton: The Inner Life* (San Marino, CA: Huntington Library, 1983); and a somewhat unsound but pleasingly written, popular biography, A. N. Wilson's *The Life of John Milton* (Oxford: Oxford University Press, 1983).

Evaluation of Selected Biographies

Fletcher, Harris Francis, *The Intellectual Development of John Milton.* 2 vols. Urbana, IL: University of Illinois Press, 1956–1961. Fletcher attempts to suggest how any person, place, or thing that Milton came in contact with might have had an effect on his mind.

French, J. M. *The Life Records of John Milton.* 5 vols. New York: Gordian Press, 1966. Although not a biography *per se,* French's reproduction of seventeenth-century Miltonia is very nearly exhaustive, and indispensable for any serious student of Milton's life.

Masson, David, *The Life of John Milton.* 7 vols. London: Macmillan, 1859–1880 (indexed 1894). Masson provides a comprehensive account of Milton's time in order to place the poet in an appropriately rich social and political context. All students of Milton's biography must know this work.

Parker, Willard Riley, *Milton: A Biography.* 2 vols. Oxford: Clarendon Press, 1968. This is the definitive biography, based on a lifetime of research, with one full volume devoted to documentation.

Wagenknecht, Edward, *The Personality of Milton.* Norman: University of Oklahoma Press, 1970. An interpretive, lucidly written portrait of Milton's personality and character by a distinguished literary scholar.

Autobiographical Sources

In a way, everything Milton wrote was autobiographical, for he made his own personality part of his great argument. One could single out the *Academic Prolusions* (1625-1632); the Latin letter to Charles Diodati (September 23, 1637); *Reason of Church Government* (1641); *Apology for Smectymnus* (1642); and *Defensio Secunda pro Populo Anglicano* (1654). These and other autobiographical abstracts from Milton's works have been arranged under periods and topics by John S. Diekhoff (*Milton on Himself,* New York: Oxford University Press, 1939). See also William B. Hunter, "John Milton: Autobiographer," *Milton Quarterly,* 8 (1974), 100-104.

Overview of Critical Sources

The ceaseless activity of the Milton industry has doomed any survey of critical sources to be both highly selective and subjective. Perhaps Milton's severest critic was Samuel Johnson, who objected both to Milton's method and his literary manner in his *Lives of the Poets* (1779). The atmosphere leading up to those views is documented by John T. Shawcross in *Milton: The Critical Heritage, 1732-1801* (New York: Barnes and Noble, 1972). Modern Criticism was sparked by T. S. Eliot's two essays, Milton I [1936] and Milton II [1947], collected in his *On Poetry and Poets* (New York: Farrar, Straus and Cudahy, 1957). In the first essay, Eliot accused Milton of being a bad model for all poetry, and of writing in a Latinate idiom that was remote from English poetic usage. In the second essay, Eliot conceded that Milton *might* be an appropriate model for some future poet. C. S. Lewis in *A Preface to 'Paradise Lost'* (London: Oxford University Press, 1942) defended Milton's concept of Satan along Christian lines, while William Empson combined an attack on Milton and on organized Christianity in his very odd book, *Milton's God* (Norfolk, CT: New Directions, 1962). E. M. W. Tillyard continued Milton's rehabilitation in *Milton* (London: Chatto & Windus, 1951), and Joseph A. Wittreich, Jr., placed the romantic poets' reservations about Milton in proper perspective in his edition, *The Romantics on Milton* (Cleveland: Case Western Reserve University, 1970). John Halkett objectified Milton's views of marriage in *Milton and the Art of Matrimony: A Study of the Divorce Tracts and Paradise Lost* (New Haven: Yale University Press, 1970). Since 1970, Milton scholarship has moved in a dozen interesting directions, including: a generic approach in Northrup Frye's, *The Return of Eden: Five Essays on Milton's Epics* (Toronto: University of Toronto Press, 1975); the reader-response view in Stanley E. Fish's, *Surprised by Sin: The Reader in 'Paradise Lost'* (Berkeley: University of California Press, 1971); the prophetic vision in Joseph A. Wittreich, Jr.'s, *Visionary Poetics: Milton's*

Tradition and his Legacy (San Marino, CA: The Huntington Library, 1979); the Marxist view in Christopher Hill's, *Milton and the English Revolution* (New York: Penguin, 1979), and in Andrew Milner's, *John Milton and the English Revolution: A Study in the Sociology of Literature* (New York: Macmillan, 1981); the iconographic in Roland Mushat Frye's, *Milton's Imagery and the Visual Arts* (Princeton: Princeton University Press, 1978); the structuralist approach in Donald F. Bouchard's, *Milton: A Structural Reading* (London: E. Arnold, 1974); the deconstructionist approach in Herman Rapaport's, *Milton and the Postmodern* (Lincoln: University of Nebraska Press, 1983); and the feminist view in Maureen Quilligan's, *Milton's Spenser: The Politics of Reading* (Ithaca, NY: Cornell University Press, 1983).

Evaluation of Selected Criticism

Barker, Arthur E. *Milton and the Puritan Dilemma, 1641–1660.* Toronto: University of Toronto Press, 1942. Barker traces the development of Milton's mind and the growing maturity of his poetical works against the background of his prose works and the sweep of political events in the seventeenth century. This is one of the most careful and rewarding historical and critical studies of Milton.

Lewalski, Barbara Kiefer, *Milton's Brief Epic: The Genre, Meaning, and Art of 'Paradise Regained.'* Providence, RI: Brown University Press, 1966. One of the finest generic studies of Milton, and one of the few book-length studies of *Paradise Regained,* Lewalski's book explores the relation of Milton's Christology to the theme of temptation and to Augustinian views of learning.

Radzinowicz, Mary Ann, *Toward 'Samson Agonistes': The Growth of Milton's Mind.* Princeton: Princeton University Press, 1978. This study, which argues for a late date of composition for *Samson Agonistes,* takes a contextual approach to Milton's great drama, covering in detail its relation to Milton's views of history, politics, poetics, theology, and logic, and asserting that most of those views reached their full maturity in this poem.

Rajan, Balachandra, *The Lofty Rhyme: A Study of Milton's Major Poetry.* London: Routledge & Kegan Paul, 1970. Despite its title, this major work of criticism covers both the minor and the major poems. In a highly metaphoric treatment of Milton, Rajan traces the changing vision of the poet from poem to poem, while at the same time showing how Milton maintains the essential continuity of the poems in a complex but consistent pattern.

Summers, Joseph, *The Muse's Method: An Introduction to 'Paradise Lost.'* Cambridge: Harvard University Press, 1962. Summers' study concentrates on the scope of Milton's great epic, and the differing ways events can be viewed from Earth, Heaven, and Hell. Such complex perspectives are united and synthesized in the great theme of love, which dominates Milton's vision in *Paradise Lost.*

Other Sources

Lieb, Michael and John T. Shawcross, eds. *Achievements of the Left Hand: Essays on the Prose of John Milton.* Amherst, MA: University of Massachusetts Press, 1974. Essays on Milton's prose works, together with a useful survey of the prose works and a selected bibliography.

McColley, Diane Kelsey, *Milton's Eve.* Urbana: University of Illinois Press, 1983. A persuasive attempt to disassociate Milton's Eve from an antifeminist tradition that denies her essential humanity, and fails to recognize her shared responsibility for the Fall with Adam.

Mulryan, John, ed. *Milton and the Middle Ages.* Lewisburg, PA: Bucknell University Press, 1982. An anthology of essays relating Milton's poetry and prose to the middle ages, from a variety of interdisciplinary perspectives.

Patrides, C. A. *Milton's 'Lycidas': The Tradition and the Poem.* revised edition. Columbia: University of Missouri Press, 1983. Includes the text of the poem, Milton's corrections, his companion poem in Latin, the *Epitaphium Damonis,* selected articles, and a comprehensive bibliography.

Webber, Joan Malory, "The Politics of Poetry: Feminism and *Paradise Lost,*" in Milton Studies, 14 (1980), 3–24. A summary and critique of feminist studies of the poem.

Selected Dictionaries and Encyclopedias

A Milton Dictionary, AMS Press, 1969. A discussion of "hard" words, Milton's works, and entries about Milton.

A Milton Encyclopedia, 9 vols. Lewisburg, PA: Bucknell University Press, 1978–1983. A monumental summary of all the information currently available about Milton, with indexes of names and subjects. Indispensable for serious students of Milton.

A Variorum Commentary on the Poems of John Milton, 6 vols. projected; 4 vols. currently in print. New York: Columbia University Press, 1970–1975. Keyed to the Columbia edition, this commentary brings all current information to bear on every line of Milton's poetry.

John Mulryan
St. Bonaventure University

GEORGE MOORE
1852–1933

Author's Chronology

Born February 24, 1852, Moore Hall, county Mayo, Ireland; *1861–1869* educated at Oscott College, Birmingham, England; *1873* studies painting at Academie Julian, Paris; *1875–1879* befriends Impressionist painters in Parisian café society; *1880* returns to London, working as art critic and overseeing affairs of family estate in Ireland; *1885* Zolaesque realism of *A Mummer's Wife* brings notoriety and censorship by commercial lending libraries; *1891–1895* art critic for the *Speaker; 1899* moves residence to Ireland in protest of England's actions in Boer War; *1901* becomes active member of the Irish Literary Revival; *1903* publicizes conversion from Catholicism to Protestantism; *1911* moves to final residence, Ebury Street, London; *1923* Moore Hall burned in Irish Civil War; dies January 20, 1933, in London.

Author's Bibliography (selected)

A Modern Lover, 1883 (novel); *A Mummer's Wife,* 1885 (novel); *A Drama in Muslin,* 1886 (novel); *Confessions of a Young Man,* 1888 (autobiography); *Esther Waters,* 1894 (novel); *The Untilled Field,* 1903 (stories); *The Lake,* 1905 (novel); *Memoirs of My Dead Life,* 1906 (autobiography); *Hail and Farewell,* 1914 (autobiography); *The Brook Kerith,* 1916 (novel); *Conversations in Ebury Street,* 1924 (criticism).

Overview of Biographical Sources

Without question one of the leading literary celebrities of Britain at the time of his death, George Moore has drawn little critical attention in the last fifty years. As a result, the wave of biographical memorabilia contemporary with his death has been followed by no careful biographical consideration. Joseph M. Hone's *The Life of George Moore* (1936) was an authorized biography that has much of the feel of a contractual obligation. The single ambitious biography published since, Jean C. Noel's *George Moore: L'Homme et l'Oeuvre* (1966) remains unavailable in English. During the first decade of this century, Moore was actively involved in the Irish Literary Revival. He figures prominently in virtually all of the memoirs of this movement.

Evaluation of Selected Biographies

Cunard, Nancy, *GM: Memories of Moore.* London: Hart-Davis, 1956. This is more an affectionate memoir than a true biography; the portrait is sympathetic, but of little critical value.

Goodwin, Geraint, *Conversations with George Moore.* London: Ernest Benn, 1929. Moore himself thought this odd recapitulation effective, and he wrote a complimentary letter as preface to the volume. Most modern readers, however, will be frustrated by this belletristic and circumlocutory approach to his thought.

Hone, Joseph M. *The Life of George Moore.* New York: Macmillan, 1936. This is by far the most important biography of Moore. It contains little documentation and much idle anecdote, however, and so seems badly dated by current critical standards. Hone, a biographer of Yeats and also author of the family history *The Moores of Moore Hall,* had first access to Moore's letters.

Noel, Jean C. *George Moore: L'Homme et l'Oeuvre.* Paris: Didier, 1966. Noel's voluminous, untranslated French study is the most impressive critical biography of George Moore. It is not at all heavily devoted to Moore's life in France or the French influences on his thought. Rather, it combines Hone's biographical chronology of the life with Noel's own convincing analyses of the works.

Autobiographical Sources

It now seems likely that George Moore's autobiographies will enjoy longer literary lives than his novels. In his three important autobiographies, Moore displayed an ingenious, venomous audacity that could find no place in the studied realism of his novels. In *Confessions of a Young Man* and *Memoirs of My Dead Life* Moore's persona is of a decadent, distinctly Parisian character who was shrewdly drawn to outrage his English readership. In *Hail and Farewell,* perhaps his single most important work, Moore pilloried W. B. Yeats and the other leaders of the Irish literary revival.

Overview of Critical Sources

The criticism that exists tends to focus on influences on Moore's work and his adaptations of several styles of narrative, most of them rooted in French, rather than English, assumptions about the priorities of the modern novel.

Evaluation of Selected Criticism

Brown, Malcolm, *George Moore: A Reconsideration.* Seattle: University of Washington Press, 1955. This is the most convincing attempt since Moore's death to resurrect his literary reputation. Brown draws on biographical information to build a case for Moore as an especially revealing instance of a writer caught in the shift from Victorian to modern cultures. He attaches great value to *A Mummer's Wife* and *Esther Waters* as late Victorian masterpieces of realism, and he also defends the more soporific experiments in style of Moore's last novels.

Dunleavy, Janet Egleson, *George Moore: The Artist's Vision, the Storyteller's Art.* Lewisburg, PA: Bucknell University Press, 1973. This cautious introduction to Moore's fiction catalogues successive influences on his prose style.

Freeman, John, *A Portrait of George Moore in a Study of His Work*. London: Laurie, 1922. This early study was completed with Moore's cooperation, but it never slips into unexamined adoration.

Jeffares, A. Norman. *George Moore*. London: Longmans, Green, 1965. This essay acknowledges the importance of *A Mummer's Wife* and *Esther Waters* but argues aggressively for more attention to Moore's other, less well-known, novels.

Other Sources

Gerber, Helmut, *George Moore in Transition*. Detroit: Wayne State University Press, 1968. A collection of letters dating from 1894 to 1910, with ample running commentary.

Hughes, Douglas A. *Man of Wax: Critical Essays on George Moore*. New York: New York University Press, 1971. A judicious selection of academic criticism, with reprinted remarks by such as W. B. Yeats and Virginia Woolf.

Owen, Graham, ed. *George Moore's Mind and Art*. Edinburgh: Oliver and Boyd, 1968. Critical essays focused on periods of Moore's career and on qualities consistent in all his works.

John P. Harrington
Rutgers University

MARIANNE MOORE
1887–1972

Author's Chronology

Born November 15, 1887, Kirkwood, Missouri; *1894* moves to Carlisle, Pennsylvania; *1905–1909* student at Bryn Mawr College, Pennsylvania; *1911–1915* teaches commercial subjects at U.S. Indian School, Carlisle; *1915* wins recognition as "new" poet; *1916–1918* keeps house for brother in Chatham, New Jersey; *1918* moves to Manhattan, employed as secretary and tutor; *1921* publishes *Poems; 1921–1925* assistant in New York Public Library; *1925* receives Dial Award, becomes acting editor *The Dial; 1926* appointed editor *The Dial; 1929* moves to Brooklyn, begins career as free-lance writer; *1951* publishes *Collected Poems; 1952* receives National Book Award, Pulitzer Prize, Bollingen Prize; *1955–1956* responds to request of Ford Motor Company with names for new line of cars, in correspondence that becomes celebrated; late *1950's* becomes public figure; *1972* dies in Manhattan.

Author's Bibliography (selected)

Collected Poems, 1951, *The Complete Poems of Marianne Moore,* 1967, *The Complete Poems of Marianne Moore,* 1981 (the 1981 book is authoritative, but all three should be consulted for revisions); *The Fables of La Fontaine,* 1954 (translations); *A Marianne Moore Reader,* 1961 (selected poems, essays, the Ford correspondence, selected *Fables*).

Overview of Biographical Sources

Although Moore was a meticulous saver of letters, manuscripts, and other papers, she wrote no autobiography, her letters have not been published, and no one has completed a biography. Most of her papers are in the Rosenbach Foundation, Philadelphia, under the care of Clive Driver, her literary executor. In journal articles she sometimes set down observations on people and experiences, but most of these are incidental to remarks on literature. Critical studies published before her death frequently contain material from interviews and correspondence; her papers did not become available until the mid-1970's. Remarks that occasionally include biographical information are scattered through the prose of T. S. Eliot, William Carlos Williams, Wallace Stevens, Ezra Pound, and other modernists. Additional material may be found in numerous essays and articles. Among the more useful are: Winthrop Sargeant, "Humility, Concentration, and Gusto," *New Yorker* 32 (February 16, 1957), pp. 38–40, 42, 44, 47–79; Moore, "Education of a Poet," *Writer's Digest* 43 (October 1963), pp. 35, 72; Moore, "Ten Answers: Letter from an October Afternoon, Part II," *Harper's* 229 (November 1964), pp. 91–92, 95–98; Donald Hall, "An Interview with Marianne Moore," *McCall's* 93 (December 1965), pp. 74, 182–186, 188, 190.

Overview of Critical Sources

Moore's status was confirmed by T. S. Eliot's observation in his introduction to her *Selected Poems* (1935) that she is "one of those few who have done the language some service in my lifetime." She was long considered a "poet's poet," however; only in the 1960's, after a surge of public recognition and the publication of book-length studies, did her work come to seem accessible to the general reader.

Evaluation of Selected Criticism

Costello, Bonnie, *Marianne Moore: Imaginary Possessions*. Cambridge: Harvard University Press, 1981. This is the first book that deals with themes and practices common in Moore's work rather than studying it poem by poem. Emphasizing the "sincerity and gusto" she finds, Costello discusses poems about poetry, descriptive poems, types of imagery, stanza forms, and Moore's prose. She keeps an eye on the way Moore's imagination "pursued the ecstatic momentum of detail rather than the measured progress of argument." Costello recognizes that Moore was an early feminist, but does not allow the sociopolitical to dominate. A feature is a reading of the poem "The Octopus" as an illustration of the way that Moore "borrows objects for the sake of vivid effects based on association, while maintaining an earnest celebration of their otherness."

Engel, Bernard F. *Marianne Moore.* New York: Twayne Publishers, 1964. Engel gives a reading of each of the pieces in *Collected Poems* (1951) and also of college publications and other poems omitted from the 1951 book. The study finds central a belief in unity of spirit and matter, with ethical and moral aims revivified by Moore's disciplined yet imaginative mind. The book divides her career into a period of guarded individualism, an era in which she shows more tolerance for mankind's flaws, and a later period in which she reasserts values comprehensively though often less vividly. This and other early books are now superseded to an extent by studies published since Moore's papers became available; moreover, in her last years Moore continued to publish new poems and revise early ones. The book is still useful, however, because it gives readings of all poems then available, begins the study of revisions, and contains material from interviews.

Hadas, Pamela White, *Marianne Moore: Poet of Affection.* Syracuse, NY: Syracuse University Press, 1977. This enthusiastic treatment focuses on individual poems and seconds what Hadas takes to be Moore's value system which, as Hadas says, argues that "Beyond all this fiddle . . . filling the place of the genuine, the soul is steadied for its efforts of affection."

Hall, Donald, *Marianne Moore: The Cage and the Animal.* New York: Pegasus, 1970. This appreciation draws on personal acquaintance and also on Hall's own considerable talents as a poet. Hall emphasizes feeling and color, and frequently refers to Moore's own understanding of a poem. He traces development of Moore's concern with danger and the consequent need for the protection that she images as armor and finds obtainable by independence, courage, and imagination. Hall shows development of her language from the precision and use of "astonishing images" in early work to the less startling imagery of the work of her middle period and of the late poems that often are in effect light verse.

Nitchie, George W. *Marianne Moore: An Introduction to the Poetry.* New York: Columbia University Press, 1969. Nitchie gives readings of many individual poems, emphasizing the rational though not omitting the emotional. He corrects earlier readings in some respects, and appraises the later poems as generally inferior to the earlier, even at times amounting to self-parody. Nitchie says that Moore moved from concern with esthetic and moral significance suggested by the objects of her attention to willingness to take them as they are in order to liberate emotion. He comes to a useful comparison of Moore with Wordsworth, seeing her as more cautious. Although she does not like the English poet, who presents the totality of "a mind in its operations," she does exercise "the courage of her peculiarities."

Stapleton, Laurence, *Marianne Moore: The Poet's Advance.* Princeton: Princeton University Press, 1978. Stapleton gives another set of readings, but one informed by use of notebooks, drafts of poems, correspondence, and other papers that had become available in the Rosenbach Foundation. She follows suggestions in this material but does not let it overwhelm her. She focuses on poems she finds of special merit or useful to her argument that Moore presents "a continuous undercurrent of feeling" together with "separate excitements of rhythmic arrangement and idiom proper to herself." The book is less comprehensive than earlier studies, but reliance on the papers makes it the most useful collection of readings of the poems it covers.

Other Sources

Abbott, Craig S. *Marianne Moore: A Descriptive Bibliography.* Pittsburgh: University of Pittsburgh Press, 1977. Abbott lists publishing details for each of Moore's books and other publications; these are often incidentally informative on life and opinions. He also lists drawings, printed letters, works Moore edited, records of her reading, and translations of her poems.

————. *Marianne Moore: A Reference Guide.* Boston: G. K. Hall, 1978. A first-rate resource, giving annotated listings of books and articles about Moore from 1916 through 1976.

Garrigue, Jean, *Marianne Moore.* University of Minnesota Press, 1965. An introductory pamphlet.

Phillips, Elizabeth, *Marianne Moore,* New York: Frederick Ungar, 1981. Brief critical survey, useful to students though not drawing on Moore's papers.

Tambimuttu, Thurairajah, ed. *Festschrift for Marianne Moore's Seventy-Seventh Birthday.* New York: Tambimuttu and Mass, 1964. This miscellany includes a preface by the editor, poems about, addressed to, or imitating Moore, and a selection of essays, letters, and comments.

Tomlinson, Charles, ed. *Marianne Moore: A Collection of Critical Essays.* Englewood Cliffs, NJ: Prentice-Hall, 1969. Tomlinson gives a letter from Moore to Ezra Pound, an interview with Moore by Donald Hall, eighteen essays on the poetry, and a chronology, notes, and bibliography.

Selected Dictionaries and Encyclopedias

American Women Writers, Frederick Ungar, 1981. Brief critical biography, and selected list of works by and about Moore.

Critical Survey of Poetry, Salem Press, 1982. Concise overview of Moore's life, discussion of style and of aims and themes, and selected bibliography.

Bernard F. Engel
Michigan State University

WILLIAM MORRIS
1834–1896

Author's Chronology

Born 24 March, 1834, Walthamstow, England into a middle-class family of comfortable means; *1847* father dies; *1853* enters Exeter College, Oxford, meets Edward Burne-Jones; *1856* is articled to architect G. E. Street; writes tales, articles, and poems for *The Oxford and Cambridge Magazine;* under the influence of Dante Gabriel Rossetti gives up architecture to try painting in London; *1857* paints frescoes with Rossetti, Burne-Jones, and others in Oxford; *1858* publishes *The Defence of Guenevere; 1859* marries Jane Burden; *1861* efforts made to furnish his new house—The Red House in Upton, Kent— lead to the founding of the decorative arts firm which becomes his chief vocation; birth of daughter Jenny; *1862* birth of daughter May; executes first wallpapers; *1865* moves family and the firm to London; *1867* rises to literary prominence with *The Life and Death of Jason; 1868–1869* solidifies his reputation with *The Earthly Paradise;* translates several Icelandic and Germanic legends; marital strain becomes acute and Jane forms a connection with Rossetti; *1871* leases Kelmscott Manor, Oxfordshire, as a country home and visits Iceland; *1873* second Icelandic tour; mid-1870's revives ancient techniques in dyeing and weaving; *1876* publishes his own version of the Niblung legend and makes his first entry into public affairs as Treasurer of the Eastern Question Association; *1883–1890* engages in a period of intense activism in the socialist movement; organizes, agitates, lectures and writes for the cause; *1888* composes *The House of the Wolfings,* the first of several prose romances which constitute his chief literary output over the last years of his life; *1890* founds the Kelmscott Press and begins collecting early printed books and illuminated manuscripts; *1896* the Kelmscott Press issues its masterpiece, *The Works of Geoffrey Chaucer;* visits Norway, dies on 6 October and is buried at Kelmscott.

Author's Bibliography (selected)

The Defence of Guenevere and Other Poems, 1858; *The Life and Death of Jason,* 1867 (narrative poem); *The Earthly Paradise,* 1868–1869 (narrative verse); *Love is Enough,* 1872 (masque); *The Story of Sigurd the Volsung and the Fall of the Niblungs,* 1876 (narrative poem); *The Dream of John Ball,* 1886 (socialist tale); *The Aims of Art,* 1887 (lectures); *Signs of Change,* 1888 (lectures); *News from Nowhere,* 1890 (utopian tale); *The Story of the Glittering Plain,* 1891 (prose romance); *Poems by the Way,* 1891; *The Wood Beyond the World,* 1894 (prose romance); *The Well at the World's End,* 1896 (prose romance); *The Collected Works of William Morris,* 24 vols., ed. May Morris, 1910–1915.

Overview of Biographical Sources

If, as his doctor claimed, Morris died simply from doing the work of ten men, then his life was packed with enough incident to employ ten biographers. He was a designer, craftsman, political activist, and writer; he had a complex mind and a fairly dramatic personal life. The superabundance of biographical material, perhaps, has made presenting an integrated, whole portrait difficult for biographers, who have attempted with partial success to correct the problem. The general trend has been toward a more sympathetic portrayal of Morris's later career, particularly his socialism, and toward an attempt to reconcile his artistic and political sides. The authorized biography is J. W. Mackail's *The Life of William Morris* (1899; reissued New York: Benjamin Blom, 1968). Lloyd Wendell Eshleman's *Victorian Rebel: The Life of William Morris* (New York: Charles Scribner's Sons, 1940) is widely accessible but should be avoided as a biographical source. Preoccupied with tracing ideas, it loses narrative continuity. Three major contemporary biographies are all dependable: Philip Henderson's *William Morris: His Life, Work, and Friends* (1967), Jack Lindsay's *William Morris: His Life and Work* (London: Constable, 1975), and E. P. Thompson's *William Morris: Romantic to Revolutionary*, 2nd ed. 1977.

Evaluation of Selected Biographies

Henderson, Philip. *William Morris: His Life, Work, and Friends.* New York: McGraw-Hill, 1967. Drawing upon previously unavailable manuscript material, Henderson was the first of Morris's biographers to discuss the problems in Morris's marriage. One noticeable flaw is its position that Morris's political and artistic views were incompatible.

Mackail, J. W. *The Life of William Morris.* London: Longmans, Green, 1899. Mackail's personal acquaintance with Morris gives this biography an authoritative voice. In part because of its elegant writing, Mackail's work will remain a classic biography, but it undervalues Morris's socialist period and deliberately conceals the unhappy marriage.

Thompson, E. P. *William Morris: Romantic to Revolutionary*, 2nd ed. New York: Pantheon Books, 1977. The most daring interpretation of Morris's life to date, this biography examines Morris's role in the British socialist movement. The book has the authority (and unfortunately the weight) of an historical treatise; Thompson meticulously details, for instance, the in-fighting which fractured socialist unity. Though emphasizing Morris's Marxist sympathies, Thompson also tries to show how the social concern grew out of artistic preferences, namely an attachment to literary Romanticism. Yet Thompson's historical focus has a built-in liability. Two thirds of the book is devoted to Morris's political career; the concentration inevitably leads to elevation of the social reformer at the expense of the artist.

Autobiographical Sources

Except for letters, Morris left few genuinely autobiographical sources. Fortunately, the definitive edition of his correspondence is near completion. *The Collected Letters of William Morris: Volume I, 1848–1880,* ed. Norman Kelvin (Princeton: Princeton University Press, 1984) is now available, and the second volume should appear shortly. In the meantime, *The Letters of William Morris to His Family and Friends,* ed. Philip Henderson (London: Longmans, Green, 1950) remains the primary source for Morris's later correspondence. His *Socialist Diary,* ed. Florence Boos (Iowa City, IA: The Windhover Press, 1981) records political activity—such as travel to speaking engagements—from late January to late April 1887.

Overview of Critical Sources

A recent upsurge in Morris criticism has performed an invaluable cultural service in establishing Morris as a writer of the first rank. In the case of Morris's poetry, the journals provide as important a source of critical opinion as do the book-length studies. Since 1970 *Victorian Poetry* alone has published over a dozen articles on Morris's poetry. The long narrative poems have been the chief beneficiaries of the recent poetry criticism. Recent books such as *Studies in the Late Romances of William Morris,* eds. Carole Silver and Joseph Dunlap (New York: William Morris Society, 1976) have established the artistic credibility of the prose tales, once deemed regressively escapist. The chief danger in Morris criticism is its tendency to use external matters as the instrument of interpretation. Rather than fully exploring the artistic merits of the work, critics tend to use the text as a means of discussing such concerns as Morris's manipulation of source material, his social conscience, and, most wearisome of all, his unhappy love life.

Evaluation of Selected Criticism

Calhoun, Blue, *The Pastoral Vision of William Morris: The Earthly Paradise.* Athens: University of Georgia Press, 1975. The quest for an earthly paradise is not an escapist flight from Victorian commercialism but rather a constructive pastoral vision. Using Morris's own terminology, Calhoun reads *The Earthly Paradise* as a dialectical interplay between two dominating moods: energy, which Calhoun aligns with the poem's heroic motifs, and idleness, aligned to the poem's pastoral elements.

Faulkner, Peter, *Against the Age: An Introduction to William Morris.* London: Allen and Unwin, 1980. A blend of biography and criticism, this book successfully fulfills its author's avowed purpose of interesting new readers in Morris's work. Faulkner's emphasis on rebellion somewhat underestimates Morris's conventionally Victorian traits, particularly his debt to the Romantic tradition, but he convincingly explicates Morris's counter-culture positions. Morris is against the age, for instance, in his unorthodox views of marriage and sex, and in his advocacy of revolution to redress social wrongs.

Kirchhoff, Frederick, *William Morris.* Boston: Twayne, 1979. The format of the Twayne series does not allow the author, an eminent Morris critic, full opportunity to prove his generalizations, but this survey is a handy introduction to Morris's literary canon. It gives succinct interpretations of many individual shorter poems and synopses of the longer narrative poems. According to Kirchhoff, a prevailing theme in Morris's work is the problem of reconciling the need for self-discovery with the need for social integration.

Oberg, Charlotte, *A Pagan Prophet: William Morris.* Charlottesville: University Press of Virginia, 1978. Focussing on the hero motif, Oberg applies modern folklore theory to show unity across Morris's *oeuvre.* The "Conclusion" contains an interesting application of Northrop Frye's generic labels: Morris's preference for myth ran counter to the taste for realism prevailing in the late nineteenth century.

Selected Dictionaries and Encyclopedias
British Writers, Charles Scribner's Sons, 1982. Contains a long summary of Morris's life and work, plus a substantial bibliography.

Critical Survey of Poetry, Salem Press, 1982. Contains a short biography, overview of Morris's artistic achievement, and analyses of major works.

Survey of Modern Fantasy Literature, Salem Press, 1983. Synopses and succinct interpretations of five of the late prose romances.

Michael Case
Boise State University

IRIS MURDOCH
1919

Author's Chronology

Born Jean Iris Murdoch, July 15, 1919 in Dublin, Ireland of Anglo-Irish parents; *1937* completes secondary education at Badminton School, Bristol; *1938* studies at Sommerville College, Oxford University; *1942* receives B.A. degree with first class honors in Classical Moderations and Greats; *1942-1944* serves as Assistant Principal in the British Treasury, London; *1944-1946* serves as Administrative Officer with the United Nations Relief and Rehabilitation Administration in London, Belgium, and Austria; *1947-1948* receives Sarah Smithson Studentship in Philosophy at Newnham College, Cambridge University; *1948* appointed Fellow of St. Anne's College, Oxford; *1948-1963* serves as University Lecturer in Philosophy at St. Anne's College, Oxford; *1956* marries John Oliver Bayley, a novelist, poet, and critic; *1959* accepts position as Lecturer at Yale University; *1963* named Honorary Fellow, St. Anne's College, Oxford; *1963-1967* joins Royal College of Art, London, as Lecturer; *1973* receives James Tait Black Prize for Fiction; *1974* receives Whitbread Literary Award for Fiction for *The Sacred and Profane Love Machine; 1975* receives Honorary D. Litt. degree from University of Washington; made Honorary Member of the American Academy of Arts and Letters; *1978* awarded Booker Prize for Fiction; *1985* continues to live in Oxfordshire, England.

Author's Bibliography (selected)

Sartre: Romantic Rationalist, 1953 (criticism); *Under the Net,* 1954 (novel); *The Flight from the Enchanter,* 1956 (novel); *The Sandcastle,* 1957 (novel); *The Bell,* 1958 (novel); *A Severed Head,* 1961 (novel); *An Unofficial Rose,* 1962 (novel); *The Unicorn,* 1963 (novel); *The Italian Girl,* 1964 (novel); *The Red and the Green,* 1965 (novel); *The Time of the Angels,* 1966 (novel); *The Sovereignty of Good over Other Concepts,* 1967 (philosophy); *The Nice and the Good,* 1968 (novel); *Bruno's Dream,* 1969 (novel); *A Fairly Honorable Defeat,* 1970 (novel); *The Servants and the Snow,* 1970 (play); *The Sovereignty of Good,* 1970 (philosophy); *An Accidental Man,* 1971 (novel); *The Three Arrows,* 1972 (play); *The Black Prince,* 1973 (novel); *The Sacred and Profane Love Machine,* 1974 (novel); *A Word Child,* 1975 (novel); *Henry and Cato,* 1976 (novel); *The Fire and the Sun,* 1977 (philosophy); *The Sea, the Sea,* 1978 (novel); *Nuns and Soldiers,* 1980 (novel).

Overview of Biographical Sources

Little biographical research has been done on Murdoch. The information that is available can be found almost exclusively in short entries in reference works. No book-length biographical studies have been made. Charles Osborne gives a brief biographical sketch in his entry "Murdoch, Iris (1919–) . . ." in *The Penguin Companion to Literature* (New York: McGraw-Hill, 1971), pp. 383–384. As do the majority of entries on Murdoch, the biographical information given consists of dates of major events in her life and of lists of her published works. Lindsey Tucker, in *Encyclopedia of World Literature in the 20th Century,* ed. Leonard S. Klein (New York: Frederick Ungar, 1983), pp. 333–334, provides the same biographical information and briefly discusses Murdoch's major novels.

Overview of Critical Sources

In recent years Murdoch has received increasing amounts of critical attention. Critics have attempted to analyze her novels in the light of her philosophical beliefs and have applied Murdoch's theories, as expressed in her lectures, critical essays, and philosophical works, to her own writing. Though many critics attempt to deal with the body of her work, there is no fully comprehensive study of all of her writing.

Evaluation of Selected Criticism

Baldanza, Frank, *Iris Murdoch.* New York: Twayne, 1974. Discusses major novels through *The Black Prince.* Good section on Murdoch's biographical and philosophical background.

Wolfe, Peter, *The Disciplined Heart: Iris Murdoch and her Novels.* Columbia: University of Missouri Press, 1966. Examines thematic relationship between Murdoch's philosophical work and her social comedies. Discusses the role of moral values in the chaotic worlds of her novels.

Other Sources

Byatt, A. S. *Degrees of Freedom.* New York: Barnes and Noble, 1965. Examination of Murdoch's novels as studies of the "degrees of freedom" available to individuals.

Dipple, Elizabeth, *Iris Murdoch: Work for the Spirit.* Chicago: University of Chicago Press, 1982. Analysis of individual novels and of Murdoch's work as a whole.

Gerstensberger, Donna, *Iris Murdoch.* Cranbury, NJ: Associated University Presses, 1975. Focus on *The Red and the Green.*

Todd, Richard, *Iris Murdoch: The Shakespearian Interest.* New York: Barnes and Noble, 1979. A study of Murdoch's use of symbols and patterns in her major novels.

Selected Dictionaries and Encyclopedias

Dictionary of Literary Biography, Gale Research, 1983. Murdoch's biography is briefly given and her philosophical/literary roots are discussed. The author examines the influence of the existential movement on Murdoch's writing and parallels the humor in her novels to the satiric wit of Beckett. Murdoch, though she espoused some of the beliefs of existentialism, argued against the current philosophies of the movement. The major concern of her novels is shown to be art, though the subject matter is generally love.

Contemporary Authors. New Revision Series, Gale Research, 1983. pp. 373–377. Donna Olendorf gives a short summary of biographical information and an overview of critical response to Murdoch's novels. She discusses the characters in the novels and their attempts to come to terms with a chaotic world. An interview with Murdoch, conducted by mail in 1981 by Jean W. Ross, is included.

Lisa A. Murray
Oklahoma State University

VLADIMIR NABOKOV
1899–1977

Author's Chronology

Born April 22, 1899, in St. Petersburg, Russia, the son of an eminent jurist and statesman; *1913–1916* attends Tenishev School; publishes verse; *1919* flees Russia with his family; enters Trinity College, Cambridge; *1922* B.A. in Romance and Slavic Languages; his father is murdered by right-wing terrorists in Berlin; Nabokov settles in Berlin, writes in Russian under the pseudonym V. Sirin, lives by teaching English and tennis; *1923* translates Lewis Carroll's *Alice in Wonderland* into Russian; *1925* marries Véra Evseevna Slonim; *1934* son Dmitri born; *1938* moves to Paris; *1940* writes *The Real Life of Sebastian Knight,* his first novel in English; sails for United States just ahead of German invasion; *1941–1948* lecturer in Russian at Wellesley College, Massachusetts; *1942–1948* research fellow in entomology at the Museum of Comparative Zoology at Harvard; *1945* receives U.S. citizenship; *1948–1959* teaches at Cornell University, eventually becoming Professor of Russian literature; *1959* with *Lolita* a best-seller, Nabokov leaves teaching and settles into a hotel in Montreux, Switzerland, taking frequent trips to chase butterflies; *1977* dies in Montreux on July 2.

Author's Bibliography (selected)

Dar, 1937 (*The Gift,* novel); *The Real Life of Sebastian Knight,* 1941 (novel); *Nikolai Gogol,* 1944 (critical biography); *Bend Sinister,* 1947 (novel); *Lolita,* 1955 (novel, Paris edition); *Pnin,* 1957 (novel); *Lolita,* 1958 (novel, U.S. edition); Nikolai Lermontov's *A Hero of Our Time,* 1958 (translation, with son Dmitri); *Nabokov's Dozen,* 1958 (stories); *Poems,* 1959 (English verse); *Pale Fire,* 1962 (novel); Aleksandr Pushkin's *Eugene Onegin,* 1964 (translation with notes); *Speak, Memory,* 1966 (autobiography); *Nabokov's Quartet,* 1966 (stories); *Ada,* 1969 (novel); *Poems and Problems,* 1970 (poems and chess problems); *Transparent Things,* 1972 (novel); *Strong Opinions,* 1973 (interviews, essays); *Tyrants Destroyed and Other Stories,* 1975 (stories); *Lectures on Literature,* 1980 (criticism); *Lectures on Russian Literature,* 1981 (criticism); *Lectures on Don Quixote,* 1983 (criticism).

Overview of Biographical Sources

Supplementing Nabokov's own recollections, there exist two outstanding biographical studies of Nabokov's life and works, both of them by Andrew Field. These curious volumes are as if sanctioned by the authority of Nabokov himself, who read them and otherwise participated in their production. However, there is as yet no single "definitive" biography of Nabokov. Brief biographical sketches of Nabokov have been published in Alfred Appel, Jr. and

Charles Newman, eds., *Nabokov: Criticisms, Reminiscences, Translations, and Tributes* (Evanston, IL: Northwestern University Press, 1970) and in Carl Proffer, ed., *A Book of Things About Vladimir Nabokov* (Ann Arbor: Ardis Publishers, 1973). More recently, some of Nabokov's former students have published their recollections of the author as lecturer. See, for example, John Updike's introduction to Nabokov's *Lectures on Literature* (New York: Harcourt Brace Jovanovich, 1980).

Evaluation of Selected Biographies

Field, Andrew, *Nabokov: His Life in Art*. Boston: Little, Brown & Company, 1967. This is a playfully written yet serious and thorough critical biography, using many of the same fictional devices, the same doublings of perspective and chronological shifts that Nabokov employed in his own biographies of Gogol and Nikolai Chernyshevsky (in *The Gift*). Field discusses all of Nabokov's major works in detail in both their Russian and English versions. This "critical narrative" remains an essential work; it also contains a useful bibliography of works by and about Nabokov up to 1967 (now superseded by Field's own 1973 bibliography). Nabokov himself liked this work enough to allow Field to return for a second biographical encounter.

Field, Andrew, *Nabokov: His Life in Part*. New York: Viking Press, 1977. If not exactly easy to use, this is certainly the most fascinating biography of Nabokov. Presented in the form of a biographical monologue overheard and frequently interrupted by the bold-face comments of Nabokov or his wife Véra, this work is at once a highly self-conscious and Nabokovian experiment to prove the ultimate impossibility of writing biography, while it also develops a suggestive and richly detailed portrait of Nabokov's personality as the facts of his past are recalled. Field also uses other historical sources describing Nabokov or his family. This remarkable book is utterly without notes, references, bibliography, or index, and provides no extended discussion of Nabokov's fiction, which Field discusses in his earlier critical biography.

Autobiographical Sources

Nabokov wrote one volume of autobiography, which first appeared as *Conclusive Evidence* (New York: Harper & Brothers, 1951), then in Russian as *Drugie berega* (*Other Shores*, New York: Chekhov Publishing House, 1954), and finally as *Speak, Memory: An Autobiography Revised* (New York: G. P. Putnam's Sons, 1966). Although some have hailed this work as one of the outstanding autobiographies of the century, it reflects Nabokov's preoccupation with atmospheres rather than facts, and despite their unquestionable accuracy and authority, the pictures Nabokov evokes remain oblique, opaque, as if fixed in the shimmering mounting of the author's inimitable style. *Speak, Memory: An Autobiography Revised* covers Nabokov's life up to his departure for America in 1940.

Many of the settings of Nabokov's fictions are distinctly autobiographical—the motels of *Lolita* and the campuses of *Pnin*—and Nabokov frequently makes autobiographical references in his criticism. The interviews collected in *Strong Opinions,* though frequently arrogant, contain interesting information about Nabokov's life and views since 1940. His correspondence with Edmund Wilson has been published as *Nabokov-Wilson Letters: Correspondence Between Vladimir Nabokov and Edmund Wilson, 1940–1971,* ed. Simon Karlinsky (New York: Harper & Row, 1979), which includes material concerning their public quarrel in the mid-1960's over Wilson's patronizing review of Nabokov's four-volume scholarly translation of Aleksandr Pushkin's *Eugene Onegin* (Bollingen Series; New York: Pantheon Books, 1964).

Nabokov's biography of *Nikolai Gogol* (New York: New Directions, 1944) remains still the liveliest English introduction to the grotesque life of the great Russian novelist. Much of Nabokov's criticism has appeared in the form of the footnotes and comments incidental to his translations of *Eugene Onegin,* of Nikolai Lermontov's *A Hero of Our Time* (Garden City: Doubleday, 1958), and of the Old Russian epic, *The Song of Igor's Campaign* (New York: Random House, 1960).

Nabokov's critical method begins by calling for a scrupulously accurate attention to the details of a given text, whether these be details of prosody, irony, or geography. His lecture notes have recently been prepared and published as a three-volume series of critical essays, edited by Fredson Bowers and published in New York by Harcourt Brace Jovanovich: *Lectures on Literature: British, French, and German Writers* (1980); *Lectures on Russian Literature* (1981); and *Lectures on Don Quixote* (1983). Nabokov typically organized his lectures around a drawing showing the setting of the work in question: the arrangement of the furniture in Gregor Samsa's room in Franz Kafka's *The Transformation,* for example, or the street layout of Dublin in 1904 for James Joyce's *Ulysses.*

Overview of Critical Sources

As with his biographers, many of Nabokov's critics have been constrained by their inability to follow him into Russian, French, and German, with the result that his earlier novels have received relatively little attention even though they are now available in English translation. Most criticism has focused on *Lolita, Pale Fire,* and *Ada.* The poems and stories have received scant attention to date, nor has Nabokov been recognized as a playwright (he wrote nine plays) and author of screenplays.

Evaluation of Selected Criticism

Appel, Alfred, Jr. ed. *The Annotated Lolita.* New York: McGraw-Hill, 1970. This volume contains the complete English text of *Lolita,* accompanied by a delightful and informative marginal commentary; an essential tool for anyone studying this novel.

Cancogni, Annapaola, *The Mirage in the Mirror: Nabokov's Ada and its French Pre-Texts.* New York: Garland Publishing, 1985. A formalist analysis of *Ada* with reference to Nabokov's French sources.

Page, Norman, ed. *Nabokov: The Critical Heritage.* London: Routledge & Kegan Paul, 1982. A useful chronological survey of reviews and articles about Nabokov's work, especially on the later English novels.

Proffer, Carl, *Keys to Lolita.* Bloomington: Indiana University Press, 1968. Contains helpful notes and a chronology of events in *Lolita.*

Rimmon, Shlomith, "Problems of Voice in Vladimir Nabokov's *The Real Life of Sebastian Knight,*" in *Poetics and Theory of Literature,* I (1976), 489–512. An important essay linking Nabokov's use of narrative perspective with recent developments in narratology.

Steiner, George, *Extra-Territorial: Papers on Literature and the Language Revolution.* New York: Atheneum, 1971. A stimulating and erudite comparison of Nabokov's work with that of Samuel Beckett and Jorge Luis Borges in terms of the role played in each author's work by his multi-lingual background.

Other Sources
Field, Andrew, *Nabokov: A Bibliography.* New York: McGraw-Hill, 1973. The most thorough and complete bibliography of works by and about Nabokov to date, including the Russian material.

Lee, L. L. *Vladimir Nabokov.* Boston: Twayne, 1976. A good basic introduction to Nabokov's life and works.

Rydel, Christine, *Nabokov's Who's Who: A Complete Guide to Characters and Proper Names in the Works of Vladimir Nabokov.* Ann Arbor: Ardis, 1984. A useful reference work.

Schuman, Samuel, *Vladimir Nabokov: A Reference Guide.* Boston: G. K. Hall, 1979. An excellent research tool with a chronological survey of works by and about Nabokov, including a bibliography current through 1977 and a checklist of selected Russian émigré criticism.

Gene M. Moore
Virginia Commonwealth University

V. S. NAIPAUL
1932

Author's Chronology

Born August 17, 1932, Trinidad to the descendants of Hindu immigrants from India; *1943-1948* educated at Queen's Royal College, Port of Spain, Trinidad; *1950* leaves Trinidad permanently for England and enters University College, Oxford on a scholarship from the Trinidadian government; *1953* awarded a B.A. (honors) in English; *1955* marries Patricia Ann Hale; *1954-1956* edits "Caribbean Voices," BBC, London; *1957-1961* reviews fiction for *New Statesman; 1958* awarded Rhys Memorial Prize for *The Mystic Masseur,* his first published novel; *1960-1961* receives a grant from the government of Trinidad for travel in the Caribbean; *1961* wins Somerset Maugham Award for *Miguel Street; 1962-1963* travels to his ancestral home, India, for the first time; *1964* awarded Hawthornden Prize for *Mr. Stone and the Knight's Companion; 1966* travels to Africa and teaches at Makerere University, Uganda; *1968* receives W. H. Smith Award for *The Mimic Men; 1969* awarded an Arts Council Grant and journeys to the United States and Canada; *1971* receives Booker Prize, Britain's most celebrated fiction award, for *In a Free State; 1980* receives Bennett Award for *A Bend in the River.*

Author's Bibliography (selected)

A House for Mr. Biswas, 1961 (novel); *The Middle Passage: Impressions of Five Societies—British, French and Dutch in the West Indies and South America,* 1962 (nonfiction); *An Area of Darkness,* 1964 (nonfiction); *The Mimic Men,* 1967 (novel); *In a Free State,* 1971 (novel); *Guerillas,* 1975 (novel); *A Bend in the River,* 1979 (novel); *The Return of Eva Peron,* 1980 (nonfiction); *Finding the Centre,* 1984 (nonfiction).

Overview of Biographical Sources

There is, as yet, no biography of Naipaul. The most detailed account of the events of his life and their bearing on his maturation as an author is to be found in the early chapters of Landeg White's *V. S. Naipaul. A Critical Introduction* (London: Macmillan, 1975). White is helpful in spelling out the early influence of Naipaul's father, both as a personality and as a writer. William Walsh's *V. S. Naipaul* (Edinburgh: Oliver and Boyd, 1973) is worth consulting for a more synoptic version of the life.

Autobiographical Sources

Naipaul writes about himself most fully in "Prologue To An Autobiography," one of the nonfictional narratives collected in *Finding The Centre* (1984). In it he describes his precarious mid-1920's when, freelancing for the BBC in

London, he was struggling both to make ends meet and to establish himself as a writer. Otherwise, he recounts little of his adult life. The focus is decidedly on his childhood days in Trinidad, a period in which his father, a talented journalist and a sporadic writer of fiction, loomed large in his life. Of particular interest is Naipaul's account of the childhood stirrings and growth of that sense of dislocation which was to become a hallmark of his mature writing.

"Prologue To An Autobiography" can be supplemented by autobiographical details gleaned from Naipaul's prodigious travel writings and essays, notably *The Middle Passage* (1962), *An Area of Darkness* (1964), and *The Overcrowded Barracoon* (New York: Deutsch, 1972). Here, too, his reflections about his adult life are scarce and muted, but he does return, time and again, to reflect on that cultural estrangement which has, as its source, his conflicting affinities with three diverse societies: Trinidad, India, and England.

Overview of Critical Sources

The bulk of the criticism is centered on the early novels, especially the comic irony of *A House for Mr. Biswas* (1961) and *The Mimic Men* (1967). Given Naipaul's shift towards producing more travel writing and fewer novels, the absence of a critical study devoted to his eight volumes of nonfiction is particularly striking.

Evaluation of Selected Criticism

Hamner, Robert D. ed. *Critical Perspectives on V. S. Naipaul.* Washington, D.C.: Three Continents Press, 1977. This is a most valuable book, bringing together many of Naipaul's essays, two interviews with him and a good spread of critical responses to his work. Hamner includes a very thorough annotated bibliography.

Gottfried, Leon and Hughes, Shaun F. ed. *Modern Fiction Studies.* Special Issue: V. S. Naipaul, XXX, #3 (Autumn 1984). This wide-ranging collection of twelve essays is especially useful in providing critical responses to Naipaul's later work.

Theroux, Paul, *V. S. Naipaul: An Introduction To His Work.* New York: Africana Publishing, 1972. Naipaul has written much since this critical work appeared, but it remains an important guide to his earlier writings, not least because of Theroux's personal affinity with Naipaul's subject matter. Himself a writer of travel books and novels set in the Third World, Theroux is one of the few critics to address the psychological and political dimensions of Naipaul's travel writing.

White, Landeg, *V. S. Naipaul. A Critical Introduction.* London: Macmillan, 1975. White provides a sound account of Naipaul's early life and his development as a writer up until *In a Free State* (1971).

Other Sources

Morris, Robert K. *Paradoxes of Order: Some Perspectives on the Fiction of V. S. Naipaul.* Columbia: University of Missouri Press, 1975. An accessible study that traces through Naipaul's fiction the idea of social order as necessarily grounded in contradictions.

Salmagundi #54 (Fall 1981). A special issue devoted to Naipaul. Contains an illuminating interview and four essays.

Walsh, William, *V. S. Naipaul.* Edinburgh: Oliver and Boyd, 1973. An early and very general study.

Selected Dictionaries and Encyclopedias

Contemporary Authors: New Revision Series, Vol. 1, Gale Research, 1981. Provides a sound sense of the development of Naipaul's writing and its reception by critics and reviewers.

Robert Nixon
Columbia University

THOMAS NASHE
1567–1601?

Author's Chronology

Born November, 1567, Lowestoft, England, one of three sons and four daughters of William Nashe, minister of St. Margaret's parish; *1573* family moves to All Saints, West Harling; *1583* matriculates sizar of St. John's College, Cambridge; *1586* awarded B.A. degree; *1588* moves to London where his first book, *Anatomie of Absurditie,* is registered by the Stationers' Company; *1592* visits the palace of Archbishop Whitgift in Croydon where his play *Summer's Last Will and Testament* is written and performed; *1593* visits the home of Sir Robert Cotton near Huntington; rescued by Sir George Carey from an action by the London City Council and sequestered at Carisbrooke Castle on the Isle of Wight; *1597* flight to Great Yarmouth after the manuscript of *The Isle of Dogs* is seized by the Privy Council; *1599* Archbishop Whitgift orders seizure of all books by Nashe and Gabriel Harvey; *1601* Nashe referred to as deceased in Fitzgeffrey's *Affaniae.*

Author's Bibliography (selected)

Preface to Greene's *Menaphon,* 1589 (criticism); *Anatomie of Absurditie,* 1590 (prose); *An Almond for a Parrat,* 1590 (prose); *Pierce Penilesse, His Supplication to the Divell,* 1592 (prose); *Summer's Last Will and Testament,* 1592 (play); *Strange Newes,* 1592 (prose); *The Terrors of the Night,* 1593 (prose); *Christ's Tears Over Jerusalem,* 1593 (prose); *The Unfortunate Traveller,* 1594 (fiction); *Have With Ye to Saffron-Walden,* 1596 (prose); *Nashe's Lenten Stuffe,* 1598 (prose); *The Works of Thomas Nashe,* edited by Ronald B. McKerrow, with notes by F. P. Wilson (Oxford: Basil Blackwell, 1966), 5 vols.

Overview of Biographical Sources

Because of the obscurity which cloaks much of the author's career and the difficulty of establishing his canon, Nashe's biographers have been forced to speculate about such crucial topics as his part in the Marprelate controversy, the initial causes of his quarrel with the Harveys, and his role in the performance of the infamous *Isle of Dogs* (1597). Of the thirty-three works variously attributed to Nashe, only fourteen have been credited to him with any degree of certitude. For 1589–1600, Nashe's most productive years, the only sources of biographical commentary are to be found in the polemical, and therefore unreliable, remarks of Richard and Gabriel Harvey and in Richard Lichfield's *The Trimming of Thomas Nashe, Gentleman* (1597), a mean-spirited attack upon the author after his humiliating flight to Great Yarmouth following the *Isle of Dogs* scandal. The most comprehensive biography is Charles Nicholl's *A Cup of Newes,* a genuinely definitive study which cuts through the legendary haze to present a clear picture of the author. Also important are the three impressive studies by Ronald B. McKerrow, "Introduction" to *Works* (V, 1–208); by G. R. Hibbard in *Thomas Nashe: A Critical Introduction;* and by Donald J. McGinn in *Thomas Nashe.* These four books are the first and last place to begin one's research on Nashe.

Evaluation of Selected Biographies

McGinn, Donald J. *Thomas Nashe.* Boston: Twayne, 1981. This bio-critical survey of Nashe's works presents a view of the author as a brilliant innovative satirist whose principal strategy was to achieve his polemical objectives through the use of shock tactics. Having discovered his real talent in the pamphlet war against Martin Marprelate, whose mordant wit he secretly admired, he thereafter plays constant variations upon a Martin-like persona. His true genius, however, lay in his ability to report with vivid clarity the sights, sounds, and colloquialisms of the Elizabethan underworld in "an extemporall vayne."

McKerrow, Ronald B. *The Works of Thomas Nashe.* Oxford: Blackwell, rpt. 1958. Although geared to problems of establishing the definitive Nashe canon, this circumspect treatment of specific issues sets the table for all subsequent biographical studies of the author. The lengthy discussion of the Marprelate controversy furnishes an excellent textual analysis of several anonymous pamphlets ascribed to Nashe but ultimately dismisses, on stylistic and textual grounds, his part in all extant pamphlets, even *An Almond for a Parrat.* McKerrow also rejects the "orthodox view" of the Harvey-Nashe dispute as a contest between "the brilliant young wit and the dull conceited pedant," suggesting that in a conflict of principles "it was the Harveys who stood for the future and Nashe for the past." His painstaking review of Nashe's reading as lacking in genuinely scholarly depth and as indebted to contemporary rather than classical sources is a good corrective against the critical enthusiasm which has inflated the Nashe "legend."

Nicholl, Charles, *A Cup of Newes: The Life of Thomas Nashe.* London: Routledge & Kegan Paul, 1984. Nicholl conducts a full-scale reexamination of Nashe's career as a social, religious and political arbiter of his times, essentially unmasking the man behind the legend to reveal a comic stylist whose satire contains rich veins of polemical commentary upon numerous contemporary issues. Each phase of Nashe's life is carefully explored to discover the fullest significance in each of his relationships, including those with Greene, Sir Robert Cotton, Sir George Carey, Lord Strange, Christopher Marlowe, and William Shakespeare. Penetrating analyses demonstrate that many of his works betray Catholic leanings and deep-seated fears and anxieties which explain what Hibbard calls "the Gothic Imagination" of Thomas Nashe.

Autobiographical Sources

Although it is wise to remember the author's penchant for self-dramatization, the best autobiographical sources for Nashe are his own works, particularly those in which he responds to attacks upon his reputation and beliefs. Otherwise, his only extant correspondence consists of one letter, dated August–September 1596, to William Cotton.

Overview of Critical Sources

Until recently, the principal interest in Nashe's works has been as a goldmine of editorial footnotes. While there has been some interest in Nashe as a prose stylist, no extensive examination of the author's contribution to the development of Elizabethan prose style appeared until Hibbard's landmark study. Since then, in several useful articles and books, considerable light has been shed on Nashe as dramatist, literary critic, and proto-novelist.

Evaluation of Selected Criticism

Hibbard, G. R. *Thomas Nashe: A Critical Introduction.* Cambridge: Harvard University Press, 1962. For Hibbard, Nashe is a jester, a comic artist of "Gothic imagination" which expresses itself in a juxtaposition of "the horrible and the humorous." Although there is usually very little genuine substance in his works, Nashe does reveal a number of consistent personal prejudices such as his literary conservatism and his deep aversion to Puritanism. His chief subject is himself, or the kind of persona he wishes to project and the kind of effects he seeks to achieve. In order to discover the real Thomas Nashe, therefore, the reader must try to penetrate the varied disguises through which he refracts his personality.

Wells, Stanley, ed. *Thomas Nashe and Selected Writings.* Stratford-upon-Avon Library, 1. London: Edward Arnold, 1964. Wells portrays Nashe as a miniaturist, an eccentric who, in spite of flashes of artistic genius, was incapable of sustaining a unified and comprehensive vision. He also insists that to see Nashe merely as a reporter is to accept "a deliberately distorted view of his subject matter," which must be understood in terms of the forms Nashe employs. Thus, *Pierce Penilesse* is best read as a social satire using the traditional framework of the Seven Deadly Sins, *Summer's Last Will* as a festive pageant "indissolubly linked with the occasion," *The Unfortunate Traveller* as a typical Elizabethan jest-book, and *Have With Ye* as mock biography.

Other Sources

Fehrenbach, Robert J. *The Predecessors of Shakespeare.* eds. T. P. Logan and D. S. Smith. Lincoln: University of Nebraska Press, 1973. A comprehensive bibliographical review of the critical, textual and biographical sources for Nashe.

Lanham, Richard H. "Tom Nashe and Jack Wilton: Personality as Structure in *The Unfortunate Traveller*," in *Studies in Short Fiction*, 4 (1967), 208–216. Interprets *The Unfortunate Traveller* as fictional autobiography which reflects the author's subconscious and "consistent pattern of anti-social violence."

Latham, Agnes M. C. "Satire on Literary Themes and Modes in Nashe's *Unfortunate Traveller*," in *Essays and Studies*, 1 (1948), 85–100. An interpretation of *The Unfortunate Traveller* as a spirited parody of such literary themes as revenge stories, sonneteering, Ciceronianism, and learned orations.

Schrickx, W. *Shakespeare's Early Contemporaries.* Antwerp: Nederlandsche Boekhandel, 1956. Interpretation of *Love's Labour's Lost* as a satire upon the Harvey-Nashe quarrel, with Harvey as a model for Armado and Nashe for Moth.

Stern, Virginia F. *Gabriel Harvey: His Life, Marginalia, and Library.* Oxford: Oxford University Press, 1979. A recent and useful overview of the Harvey-Nashe conflict.

Edward F. J. Tucker
The Citadel

ANAIS NIN
1903–1977

Author's Chronology

Born February 21, 1903, Neuilly, France and Cuban father and French-Danish mother; *1914* moves to New York, begins diary; *1923* marries Hugh Guiler in Cuba; *1924* sets up housekeeping in Paris; *1931–1939* publishes first three books in France, meets Henry Miller and Otto Rank; *1939* relocates to Greenwich Village; *1942* establishes Gemor Press, reissues *Winter of Artifice;* *1946* first commercial publication, *Ladders to Fire* with E. P. Dutton; *1947–1949* travels across country, visits Mexico and California; *1950's* California becomes primary residence; *1961* Allan Swallow becomes Nin's publisher; *1966* first volume of *Diary* published (Harcourt, Brace, Jovanovich); *1968* first work about Nin published; *1974* elected to National Institute of Arts and Letters; *1977* Nin dies (January 14), first volume of erotica published, first volume of *Early Diary* published.

Author's Bibliography (selected)

D. H. Lawrence: An Unprofessional Study, 1932 (criticism); *House of Incest,* 1936 (prose poem); *Winter of Artifice,* 1939, rev. 1942, 1961 (short fiction); *Under a Glass Bell,* 1944 (short fiction); *Children of the Albatross,* 1947 (novel); *A Spy in the House of Love,* 1954 (novel); *Cities of the Interior,* 1959, rev. 1974 (sequence of five novels); *Collages,* 1964 (fiction); *The Diary of Anais Nin 1931–1974,* 1966–1980 (in seven volumes); *Delta of Venus,* 1977 (erotica); *The Early Diary of Anais Nin 1914–1927,* 1978–1983 (three volumes to date).

Overview of Biographical Sources

No full-length biography is yet available, though Evelyn J. Hinz is preparing one. The critical studies reviewed below give some biographical information. Since Nin's major effort has been her diary, would-be biographers tend to be overwhelmed by the nature and extent of this material. Jay Martin's *Always Merry and Bright: The Life of Henry Miller* (Santa Barbara: Capra Press, 1978) is indispensable for the Nin-Miller relationship. See also Henry Miller's *Letters to Anais Nin,* ed. Gunther Stuhlman (New York: Putnam, 1965).

Autobiographical Sources

Because its many manuscript volumes have been severely edited and shaped, the published *Diary of Anais Nin* is best thought of as a retrospective work. Begun in childhood as a means of dealing with family dislocation and paternal abandonment, Nin's diary blossomed into her major work and the laboratory for her fiction. This record of an intelligent, sensitive woman's inner development treats facts casually and shouldn't be relied on for accuracy or thoroughness. Subjective truth is what Nin strives to grasp and articulate. In the diary, Nin practiced creating effects as well as a "self" that could contend with crisis, insecurity, and artistic ambition. An intriguing and unique literary document, the first two volumes are the most dynamic.

The Early Diary of Anais Nin is less heavily edited and thus more trustworthy both as to facts and to felt experience. While there is always an imaginative coloring to Nin's diary writing, these early volumes, in their mixture of innocence, exuberance, and transparent guile are more inviting than those of later years when propaganda and self-congratulation dominate.

Nin's critical views, scattered about in the diaries, are formulated in *D. H. Lawrence: An Unprofessional Study* and *The Novel of the Future* (1968). Commitment to psychological and lyrical modes of fiction is presented here enthusiastically, but Nin is not a disciplined critic. *A Woman Speaks* (1975, ed. Evelyn J. Hinz) blends materials from Nin's public addresses and interviews; the focus is on women's liberation. *In Favor of the Sensitive Man and Other Essays* (1976) contains reviews, prefaces, more feminist forays, and diary excerpts on exotic places. These two collections testify to Nin's status as a cult figure.

Overview of Critical Sources

There are six full-length studies of Nin's work, some of which are out of print. The more recent studies have had the advantage of access to more published diary material than the earlier ones. Some are conventional work-by-work approaches while others are arranged by critical issues. Much Nin criticism has been slanted toward advocacy and appreciation. The first collection of essays about Nin, Robert Zaller's *A Casebook on Anais Nin* (New York: New American Library, 1974) is part of the enthusiast tradition, though it reprints some important early commentary and provides a fine bibliographical essay by Benjamin Franklin, V. A collection of essays edited by Sharon Spencer is to appear in 1985.

Evaluation of Selected Criticism

Evans, Oliver, *Anais Nin.* Carbondale: Southern Illinois University Press, 1968. This is the first full-length study of Nin's fiction. Evans guides the reader through Nin's works one at a time, capturing the essential differences among them as Nin's art undergoes change and growth. Although he provides only minimal references to the *Diary* (the first volumes had just appeared) and none to Nin's critical works, Evans offers sound judgments from a traditional critical perspective.

Franklin, Benjamin, V, and Duane Schneider, *Anais Nin: An Introduction.* Athens: Ohio University Press, 1979. The plan here is similar to Evans', though these authors add chapters on six *Diary* volumes as well as on Nin's criticism and other non-fiction. Franklin and Schneider argue that the genuine merits of Nin's best fiction are often overlooked, while the diary volumes are often over-praised or praised for the wrong reasons. Factual and bibliographical reliability, common sense, and a balanced view characterize this joint effort. The brief "Conclusion" is probably the best short assessment of Nin's career and art.

Hinz, Evelyn J. *The Mirror and the Garden: Realism and Reality in the Writings of Anais Nin.* New York: Harcourt, Brace, Jovanovich, 1973 (first published in 1971). Hinz makes excellent use of Nin's book on Lawrence and her other critical prose to provide a clear view of Nin's artistic purposes. Stressing the unifying elements in Nin's art by examining themes, structure, characters, and language, this treatment is consistent with Nin's wish that her writings be viewed as a continuous whole. Hinz was the first to explore the range of influences upon Nin. Three *Diary* volumes are treated.

Knapp, Bettina, *Anais Nin.* New York: Frederick Ungar, 1978. This embryonic critical biography is highly laudatory without being compelling or thorough. There is little of Nin's life here, and some of her works are barely mentioned. Knapp's focus is on Nin's long fiction, which she sees as influenced by continental tendencies in music and painting, as well as literature. Knapp demonstrates this connection capably.

Scholar, Nancy, *Anais Nin.* Boston: Twayne, 1984. Scholar separates Nin's success as a model for feminists from her merit as an artist. She is more rigorous in pursuing Nin's faults than any of her predecessors, hence her work stands as a valuable corrective to the enthusiast tradition. Scholar gives the most effective analysis of the interaction between diary and fiction, elucidating and partially solving the interface of genres issue that is central to Nin studies. By sorting out Nin's various roles and examining Nin's limitations, Scholar has provided a provocative and courageous perspective.

Spencer, Sharon, *Collage of Dreams.* Chicago: Swallow Press, 1977. Spencer's firm grasp of modernist tendencies and her full engagement with the influential theories of Otto Rank give her book an authority that compensates for her partiality. Her particularly imaginative plan and evocative critical prose style provide an experience not unlike that of Nin's own writing. Nin's importance as a spokesperson for women receives significant attention, as do parallels between Nin and Proust. A pleasure to read, this book is an "appreciation" in the best sense.

Other Sources

Anais: An International Journal, now in its third year of annual publication, mixes recollections, commentary, and important primary materials.

Cutting, Rose Marie, *Anais Nin: A Reference Guide.* Boston: G. K. Hall, 1978. A detailed assessment of secondary sources.

Franklin, Benjamin, V. *Anais Nin: A Bibliography.* Kent, OH: Kent State University Press, 1973. Bibliographical descriptions of all printed primary sources; an indispensable guide through Nin's knotty publication history.

Hinz, Evelyn J. ed., *The World of Anais Nin.* This special issue of *Mosaic* (Winter 1978) is the best collection of critical essays on Nin.

Seahorse: The Anais Nin/Henry Miller Journal (1982–1983) and *Under the Sign of Pisces: Anais Nin and Her Circle* (1970–1981). Edited by Richard R. Centing, these periodicals are rich sources of commentary, biography, and trivia. Various issues update Franklin's *Bibliography* and Cutting's *Reference Guide.*

Selected Dictionaries and Encyclopedias

Critical Survey of Long Fiction, Salem Press, 1983. Brief analyses of *Winter of Artifice* and *Cities of the Interior.*

Critical Survey of Short Fiction, Salem Press, 1981. Brief analyses of representative short stories.

Dictionary of Literary Biography, Vol. 4, Gale Research, 1980. An excellent overview of Nin's life in Paris during the 1930's and of her first three publications.

Philip K. Jason
United States Naval Academy

FRANK NORRIS
1870–1902

Author's Chronology

Born Benjamin Franklin Norris, March 5, 1807 in Chicago, Illinois to Benjamin Franklin Norris and Gertrude Doggett Norris; *1878* travels to Europe with parents; *1885* moves to San Francisco; *1887–1889* studies art in the Atelier Julien, Paris; *1890–1894* attends University of California at Berkeley; *1894* studies creative writing under Lewis E. Gates at Harvard University; *1895* covers Boer War for the San Francisco *Chronicle*. *1896–1897* becomes junior editor for the San Francisco *Wave; 1898* moves to New York City and becomes a writer for *McClure's Magazine; 1899* becomes reader for Doubleday, Page and Company; *1900* marries Jeannette Black; *1902* Jeannette Norris born; family moves to ranch outside of Gilroy, California; plans tramp steamer trip around the world; dies October 25 of peritonitis following acute appendicitis.

Author's Bibliography

Yvernelle: A Legend of Feudal France, 1892 (poem); *Moran of the Lady Letty,* 1898 (novel); *McTeague: A Story of San Francisco,* 1899 (novel); *Blix* 1899, (novella); *A Man's Woman,* 1899 (novel); *The Octopus,* 1901 (novel); *The Pit,* 1903 (novel); *A Deal in Wheat and Other Stories,* 1903; *The Responsibilities of the Novelist,* 1903 (essays); *The Joyous Miracle,* 1906 (stories); *The Third Circle,* 1909 (short stories); *Vandover and the Brute,* 1914 (novel); *Frank Norris of the Wave,* 1931 (essays); *The Literary Criticism of Frank Norris,* 1964; *The Letters of Frank Norris,* 1965.

Overview of Biographical Sources

Norris's rather uninspiring, uneventful life has not been subject to biographical study with the same fervor as some of his contemporaries, such as Jack London. The paucity of subject matter is further complicated by a paucity of material, for most of Norris's personal papers were destroyed during the 1906 San Francisco earthquake and fire. The lack of numerous biographies is also explained by the excellence of the works which have been published, beginning with Franklin Walker's doctoral dissertation which was revised into *Frank Norris: A Biography* (1932). This work is still, today, the standard biography. Walker's neglect of a critical evaluation of Norris's work led to the 1942 *Frank Norris: A Study* by Ernest Marchand, who championed Norris's writings as no other critic has done. In addition, two short biographical essays have also been written: one by W. M. Frohock in 1974 for *American Writers: A Collection of Literary Biographies* (New York: Charles Scribner's Sons), and a straightforward summary of Norris's life written by John C. French in 1934 for *The Dictionary of American Biography* (New York: Charles Scribner's Sons).

Evaluation of Selected Biographies

Marchand, Ernest, *Frank Norris: A Study*. Stanford: Stanford University Press, 1942. Marchand attempts, with some success, to place Norris in the wider background of his period, with a good analysis and critical assessment of Norris's writings. The work is flawed by a sometimes overly sympathetic view of Norris's art, but nonetheless nicely complements the Walker biography with its focus more on Norris' writings than his life.

Walker, Franklin, *Frank Norris: A Biography*. Garden City, NJ: Doubleday, Doran & Company, 1932. Walker's straightforward biography contains a wealth of material, scrupulously researched, and carefully written. The book is flawed by some lengthy digressions, such as the passages of South African history, and by Walker's lack of critical analysis of Norris's work. Nonetheless, it has remained the standard Norris biography since its publication.

Autobiographical Sources

The few Norris letters still extant were published in a limited edition, ably edited and annotated by Franklin Walker. This book, *The Letters of Frank Norris* (San Francisco: Book Club of California, 1956) is now out of print.

Overview of Critical Sources

The American Naturalism Movement has commonly been attributed to Frank Norris, and much of the critical work—what little there is—has been devoted either to supporting this viewpoint, acknowledging it, or noting the inconsistencies in Norris's work. Possibly the best full-length critical work has been accomplished by Donald Pizer, whose study of Norris's novels, *The Novels of Frank Norris* (1966), and collection of Norris's critical works, *The Literary Criticism of Frank Norris* (Austin: University of Texas Press, 1964) have become classics.

Evaluation of Selected Criticism

Dillingham, William B. *Frank Norris: Instinct and Art*. Lincoln: University of Nebraska Press, 1969. This general study of Norris's life and works centers on the author's naturalism and his literary techniques.

French, Warren G. *Frank Norris*. New York: Twayne, 1962. French sees Norris as a romantic moralist in the tradition of the native American transcendentalist tradition, and likens Norris to Emerson. He claims that Norris's most popular work, *The Pit*, was also his most critically successful, because Norris was writing about the people he had known as a child.

Pizer, Donald, *The Novels of Frank Norris*. Bloomington: Indiana University Press, 1966. Pizer differs with French in his assessment of Norris's work, instead emphasizing the novels: *Vandover and the Brute, McTeague,* and *The*

Octopus. In this thorough and scholarly study, Pizer examines Norris's literary logic and artistry, and makes a strong case for his claim that all the novels are of a piece. Although Pizer doesn't believe, like Marchand, that Norris is a great novelist—primarily because of Norris's lack of human understanding—he does admire the themes in the author's work, and marvels at his creative imagination.

Other Sources

Hart, James D. *A Novelist in the Making.* Cambridge: Harvard University Press, 1970. A careful study of Norris's student themes, examining Lewis Gates's influence on the budding novelist.

Lynn, Kenneth S. *The Dream of Success: A Study of the Modern American Imagination.* Boston: Little Brown, 1955. Lynn claims that Norris, along with Jack London and others, accepted the American success myth as the primary meaning of life, and that the contradictions in Norris's work stem from this fatal conversion.

Selected Dictionaries and Encyclopedias

American Writers: A Collection of Literary Biographies, Charles Scribner's Sons, 1974. Critical essay, with weak biographical support, by W. M. Frohock, arguing that Norris did not understand French naturalism or the works of Zola.

Critical Survey of Long Fiction, Salem Press, 1983. Brief biography and short analysis of some of Norris's important novels.

Dictionary of American Biography, Charles Scribner's Sons, 1934. Contains a very straight-forward, factual biography of Norris, written by John C. French.

David Mike Hamilton
Palo Alto, California

FLANNERY O'CONNOR
1925–1964

Author's Chronology

Born Mary Flannery O'Connor on March 25, 1925, in Savannah, Georgia; attends St. Vincent Grade School; *1938* father becomes ill with lupus; family moves to Milledgeville, Georgia; attends Peabody (public) High School; *1941* father dies; *1942–1945* student at Georgia State College for Women; edits College Literary magazine; *1945* legally drops "Mary" from her name; enters the Writer's Workshop, State University of Iowa, on a scholarship; *1946* publishes first story, "The Geranium"; *1947* earns Master of Fine Arts degree and wins Rinehart-Iowa Fiction Award; *1948–1949* brief residence at Yadoo; meets Robert Lowell and other literary acquaintances; *1949* lives briefly in New York City; publishes several stories; *1949–1950* lives with Robert and Sally Fitzgerald in Connecticut; *1950* first major attack of lupus; *1951* returns to Milledgeville to live with her mother at the family estate, Andalusia; *1952* publishes first novel; *1953* receives *Kenyon Review* Fellowship in Fiction; *1954* receives first of several O. Henry Awards; *1955* publishes first collection of stories; *1956* first of several trips to colleges and universities; *1957* receives National Institute of Arts and Letters Grants; *1958* travels to Lourdes and Rome, has an audience with Pope Pius XII; *1959* Ford Foundation Grant; *1962* receives first Honorary Doctorate; *1964* undergoes surgery; dies in hospital in Milledgeville August 3.

Author's Bibliography (selected)

Wise Blood, 1952 (novel); *A Good Man Is Hard to Find and Other Stories,* 1955; *The Violent Bear It Away,* 1960 (novel); *Three By Flannery O'Connor,* 1964 (reprint of *Wise Blood, A Good Man Is Hard To Find,* and *The Violent Bear It Away*); *Everything That Rises Must Converge,* 1965 (stories); *Mystery and Manners,* ed. Robert and Sally Fitzgerald, 1969 (essays and occasional prose); *The Complete Stories of Flannery O'Connor,* ed. Robert Giroux, National Book Award, 1971; *The Habit of Being: Letters,* ed. Sally Fitzgerald, 1979; *The Presence of Grace and Other Book Reviews,* ed. Carter W. Martin, 1983 (book reviews).

Overview of Biographical Sources

There is no full-length biography of Flannery O'Connor, but many of the books listed under Critical Sources contain useful biographical summaries. Personal biographical sketches by Robert and Sally Fitzgerald, with whom O'Connor had a lasting personal friendship, are found in the introductions of *Everything That Rises Must Converge* and *The Habit of Being.* One autobiographical essay, concerning her legendary affection for peacocks, is reprinted in *Mystery and Manners.*

Evaluation of Biographical Sources

Fitzgerald, Sally, ed. *The Habit of Being.* New York: Farrar, Straus and Giroux, 1979. These letters, edited and introduced by one of O'Connor's long-time friends, provide important insights into the character and mind of this writer. Written between 1948 and O'Connor's death, the letters indicate an author who is at times irritable, humorous, serious, compassionate, and encouraging to both friends and new correspondents. O'Connor seems to have enjoyed the pose of the Southern hayseed, and often approximates dialect phonetically in her spelling. The letters also show the courage and dignity with which O'Connor faced her disease, and her unwillingness to use the disease as an excuse for not writing. Among the literary friendships included in the letters are Robert Lowell, John Hawkes, the Fitzgeralds, and Caroline Gordon. Fitzgerald's introduction, based on the year O'Connor stayed with the family and a lifetime of correspondence, is invaluable as a biographical resource.

Getz, Lorine M. *Flannery O'Connor: Her Life, Library and Book Reviews.* New York: Edwin Mellen Press, 1980. Getz has made the most progress of anyone to date in compiling a full-length biography. The essay on biography is very solid on the formative years, but becomes thin in discussing the complex period of O'Connor's illness and mature creativity. The discussions are least effective when treating literary influences. The listing of works in O'Connor's personal library significantly updates the list in Feeley (q.v.), and will be indispensable in future discussions of literary influences. Getz has also included all the reviews, published and unpublished, O'Connor wrote for Catholic periodicals. These show a mind at work on complex theological matters, but one seldom willing or able to take an ecumenical perspective on spiritual issues. The reviews have since been published, in a more attractive print format, in Carter Martin, ed., *The Presence of Grace and Other Book Reviews* (Athens: University of Georgia Press, 1983).

Walters, Dorothy A. *Flannery O'Connor.* New York: Twayne, 1973. Based on the premise that O'Connor's tragic life is an essential clue to understanding her work, Walters' biographical survey is useful, but thin in detail. The body of the book analyzes the stories and novels in interesting groupings, which permits Walters to reveal associations among the stories other than those customarily noted. The studies of the works focus on the religious dimension, and the readings sometimes seem arbitrary. The critical analysis depends heavily on O'Connor's published commentary on her own intentions in writing the stories. Walters' analysis is a perfect starting point in the systematic study of O'Connor's fiction. Every story from the major collections is treated in detail and with insight.

Overview of Critical Sources

Except for fellow novelist and correspondent John Hawkes, who suggests in "Flannery O'Connor's Devil" (*Sewanee Review,* 70 [1962]) that O'Connor's fiction reflects a fascination with the opposite of orthodox Christianity, all of the critics have sought to explain how, or to what degree, the work reflects a Christian vision. There has been no great critical controversy about the presence of orthodoxy in her fiction; there have been significant differences about the means and success of the communication of that vision.

Evaluation of Critical Sources

Asals, Frederick, *Flannery O'Connor: The Imagination of Extremity.* Athens: University of Georgia Press, 1982. A complex and subtle treatment of O'Connor's growth as a fiction writer, this study concentrates on the tensions that remain unresolved in the stories and novels. Asals offers fresh interpretations of the individual works as well as an overview of O'Connor's career that suggests the formative influence of the Christian existentialists. The chapters on the psychological double and the "aesthetics of incongruity" provide a valuable contribution to O'Connor criticism.

Feeley, Sister Katherine, S.S.N.D. *Flannery O'Connor: The Voice of the Peacock.* New Brunswick, NJ: Rutgers University Press, 1972. Feeley discusses the stories from the perspective of O'Connor as reader and Christian. This perspective casts interesting light on O'Connor's intentions and themes, but the readings are insistent on the anagogic levels of the stories, and at times tend to treat them as dogma rather than art—an intention O'Connor might have approved. Feeley studies O'Connor's personal library and quotes passages O'Connor marked to illustrate key themes and events in the fiction. This approach illuminates some important similarities in the thought of O'Connor and Teilhard de Chardin and Mircea Eliade. An indispensable work of scholarship.

Friedman, Melvin J. and Lewis A. Lawson, eds. *The Added Dimension: The Art and Mind of Flannery O'Connor.* New York: Fordham University Press, 1966; second edition, 1977. This is a collection of essays by several scholars. Most of the essays were written shortly after O'Connor's death. The principal concern is to assess O'Connor's achievement in the context of modern southern American fiction, and the collection makes a major contribution of studies of O'Connor and Southern writing.

Hendin, Josephine, *The World of Flannery O'Connor.* Bloomington: Indiana University Press, 1970. Proceeding from the thesis that O'Connor's stories and novels act out psychological conflicts within the author, Hendin argues that the central issues of the art defy the Southern lady, daughter, and Catholic stereotypes with which O'Connor's life and fiction are usually associated. Hendin finds that the real hero in O'Connor's fiction is one who has been able to escape from the trap of human involvement. These heroes are free because they can disassociate themselves from love, religion, the family, and social commitment. The later stories treat the recognition that the ultimate trap is the body itself. The violence in O'Connor's fiction is accordingly treated as an attempt to deny emotional commitment on the part of the hero. Hendin writes with full awareness that her approach does not conform with the mainstream of O'Connor criticism, and much of what she derives from the stories does not agree with O'Connor's stated intentions in *Mystery and Manners.*

Shloss, Carol, *Flannery O'Connor's Dark Comedies: The Limits of Inference.* Baton Rouge: Louisiana State University Press, 1980. Shloss attempts to apply the methods of reader-response criticism to seven of O'Connor's stories. The approach is very theoretical, but the objectives are indeed valuable. Shloss would like to determine what in the actual language of the stories creates the kinds of anagogic meaning the author spoke of in her own interpretations of the stories. How do the stories lead the non-Christian reader to the conclusions about Grace that were central to O'Connor's intentions? Asking the right questions of the stories, Shloss illuminates the method more than the stories.

Selected Dictionaries and Encyclopedias

American Women Writers, Frederick Ungar, 1981. Very general survey of O'Connor's life, fiction, and occasional writings.

Critical Survey of Long Fiction, Salem Press, 1983. A brief biography followed by a solid analysis of the two novels.

Critical Survey of Short Fiction, Salem Press, 1981. The biography is very brief; there is a general analysis of the major influences on O'Connor's short fiction, but only two of the stories are discussed in any detail.

Dictionary of Literary Biography, Gale Research, 1978; Yearbook, 1980. The main entry is a very general survey of the stories of the first collection, and a selective mention of stories from the second. The yearbook entry deals intelligently and in detail with *The Habit of Being.*

David C. Dougherty
Loyola College

FRANK O'CONNOR
1903-1966

Author's Chronology

Born Michael O'Donovan, September 17, 1903, Cork, Ireland; *1914* meets, as a student at St. Patrick's National School, Daniel Corkery, who becomes his mentor; *1918* joins First Brigade of Irish Republican Army; *1921-1923* works on the publicity staff of the IRA in their rebellion against the Free State government; *1923* captured and incarcerated by Free State soldiers in Gormanstown Internment Camp; *1923* released from Camp; *1925-1928* works as a librarian in Sligo, Wicklow, and Cork, successively; *1928* forms drama league in Cork, then moves to Dublin to assume librarianship in Pembroke; *1931* publishes first collection of short stories, *Guests of the Nation,* under the pseudonym of Frank O'Connor; *1935* appointed to the board of directors of the Abbey Theater; *1937* appointed Managing Director of Abbey Theater and produces, with Hugh Hunt, two of his own plays, *In the Train* and *The Invincibles; 1938* marries Evelyn Bowen; *1939* forced to resign from board of directors of Abbey Theater; *1940* appointed poetry editor of *The Bell; 1941* begins working at BBC and for the Ministry of Information in London; *1943* begins writing newspaper articles critical of Irish life under the pseudonym of Ben Mayo; *1948* separates from wife; *1951* moves to America; *1952* divorced from wife; teaches at Northwestern University and then at Harvard University; *1953* marries Harriet Rich, an American; *1961* teaches at Stanford University, suffers stroke, and then returns to Ireland; *1962* awarded honorary Litt. D. from Trinity College, Dublin; *1966* dies in Dublin on March 10.

Author's Bibliography (selected)

Guests of the Nation, 1931 (stories); *The Wild Bird's Nest: Poems from the Irish,* 1932 (verse translations); *The Saint and Mary Kate,* 1932 (novel); *Three Old Brothers and Other Poems,* 1936 (original poetry); *Bones of Contention,* 1936 (stories); *The Big Fellow,* 1937 (biography); *Dutch Interior,* 1940 (novel); *Crab Apple Jelly,* 1944 (stories); *The Common Chord,* 1947 (stories); *Irish Miles,* 1947 (travel book); *Traveller's Samples,* 1951 (stories); *The Mirror in the Roadway,* 1956 (literary criticism); *Domestic Relations,* 1957 (stories); *Kings, Lords, & Commons,* 1959 (Gaelic verse translations); *An Only Child,* 1961 (autobiography); *The Lonely Voice,* 1963 (literary criticism); *My Father's Son,* 1968 (autobiography); *A Set of Variations,* 1969 (stories).

Overview of Biographical Sources

James Matthews' *Voices: A Life of Frank O'Connor* (1983) is the only book-length biography of O'Connor, but there are several other biographical sources that readers will find valuable. *Michael/Frank: Studies on Frank O'Connor,* edited by Maurice Sheehy (1969), contains over a dozen brief portraits of O'Connor, written by friends and acquaintances. The opening chapter of *Frank O'Connor,* by William M. Tomory (Boston: Twayne, 1980), recounts the important events and experiences of O'Connor's early life—up to his release from Gormanstown Internment Camp—and then quickly sketches the remaining years until his death. Maurice Wohlgelernter makes extensive use of biographical materials in his critical study of O'Connor, entitled *Frank O'Connor: An Introduction* (New York: Columbia University Press, 1977).

Evaluation of Selected Biographical Sources

Matthews, James, *Voices: A Life of Frank O'Connor.* New York: Atheneum, 1983. Matthews finds the key to O'Connor's life and art in voices—both the many voices that O'Connor created in his literature and the voices of the people and places, especially of Ireland, that spoke to him. Although at least one of O'Connor's friends has pointed out minor factual errors in Matthews' account and has claimed that the biographer lacked sympathy for his subject, other friends of O'Connor have praised Matthews' work as an excellent and true portrait of O'Connor. Readers will find in Matthews' study a wealth of biographical detail and keen insights about the life and works of O'Connor. Despite the several minor errors, this work may prove to be the definitive biography.

Sheehy, Maurice, ed. *Michael/Frank: Studies on Frank O'Connor.* New York: Alfred A. Knopf, 1969. Sheehy has collected over a dozen personal portraits and reminiscences of O'Connor, written by friends and acquaintances. They depict O'Connor at different occupations and at various periods in his life—during the Irish Civil War, at the Abbey Theater, at the *New Yorker,* and so on. Because so many of these pieces were written by people who had intimate relationships with O'Connor, the work provides the best insight into his personal life.

Autobiographical Sources

O'Connor wrote two volumes of autobiography and had planned on a third. The first, *An Only Child* (1961), covers his childhood and youth up to age twenty-one. Much of it is devoted to his relationships with his mother, whom he greatly loved, and his alcoholic father. O'Connor also tells about his attempts to educate himself and about the influence which Daniel Corkery, the Irish writer and patriot, had on him. The last section of *An Only Child* describes his involvement in the Irish Civil War and his imprisonment in the Gormanstown Internment Camp. *My Father's Son* (1968), published posthumously from unfinished drafts, takes up where *An Only Child* leaves off and moves up through the 1930's. O'Connor focuses mostly on his public life (saying little, for example, about his marriage), explaining the succession of librarianships he held and his involvement in the Abbey Theater. He draws interesting portraits of his literary friends, notably W. B. Yeats, AE (George Russell), and Lennox Robinson. The third volume was to have moved from the early 1940's up to the 1960's, but it was never written. Of the two published volumes, the best is *An Only Child,* not only for its graceful and captivating style but also because it provides insights to the development of the young artist and to the genesis of many of O'Connor's stories.

Overview of Critical Sources

There were scattered reviews and brief critical analyses of O'Connor's works in the 1940's and 1950's, but no extended, serious commentary on him appeared until the 1960's. Since then there have been a number of articles and several books, most of them focusing primarily on his short stories. Growing critical interest in the art of the short story generally and, at the same time, diverging interest in O'Connor as a multi-genre writer are certain to lead to more studies of this Irish writer.

Evaluation of Selected Criticism

Matthews, James, *Frank O'Connor.* Lewisburg: Bucknell University Press, 1976. One of the *Irish Writer Series,* this monograph is a fine introduction to O'Connor. Though too brief to be comprehensive or to offer extensive analysis, Matthews' study does give an overview of O'Connor's life and works, including the novels, short stories, autobiographies, travel literature, and literary criticism. Matthews finds O'Connor to be a writer who practiced a realistic aesthetic while retaining a romantic way of seeing life.

Tomory, William M. *Frank O'Connor.* Boston: Twayne, 1980. Tomory's book is the most comprehensive and arguably the best study of O'Connor to date. He examines O'Connor's achievements in all the major genres: the short story, the novel, drama, poetry, verse translations, biography, autobiography, literary criticism, and travel literature. At the heart of the book is Tomory's perceptive analysis of O'Connor's short stories, conducted from several perspectives: the narratorial voice, character, theme, and O'Connor's literary theories as revealed in his books of literary criticism. In the course of his study, Tomory returns several times to the question of O'Connor's development as a writer, so that the reader is given a clear perception of O'Connor's complex literary career. Tomory also examines the literary influences of Daniel Corkery, Anton Chekhov, Sherwood Anderson, George Moore, and James Joyce on O'Connor. An extensive bibliography of primary and secondary works is included.

Wohlgelernter, Maurice, *Frank O'Connor: An Introduction.* New York: Columbia University Press, 1977. This illuminating book examines O'Connor's works for the purpose of finding in them the relationship of O'Connor's mind to certain Irish political, domestic, and religious realities of his time—most notably the violent struggle for Irish independence and the influence of Catholicism on Irish life. Wohlgelernter devotes most of his analysis to the short stories, but he also examines the novels, the biography of Michael Collins, the literary criticism, and O'Connor's involvement with the Abbey Theater. Not intended as either a comprehensive study or a "reader's guide" to O'Connor, this book fulfills its intention of discovering in O'Connor's works his ideas about contemporary life.

Other Sources

Sheehy, Maurice, ed. "Towards a Bibliography of Frank O'Connor's Writings," *Michael/Frank: Studies on Frank O'Connor.* New York: Alfred A. Knopf, 1969. Nearly-complete bibliography of O'Connor's works, including television, radio, and film productions of his writings.

Selected Dictionaries and Encyclopedias

Critical Survey of Short Fiction, Salem Press, 1981. Brief biography and concise commentary on O'Connor's literary characteristics and selected stories.

Dictionary of Irish Literature, Greenwood Press, 1979. Brief biography and concise analysis of O'Connor's literary characteristics.

Michael L. Storey
College of Notre Dame of Maryland

FRANK O'HARA
1926–1966

Author's Chronology

Born June 27, 1926, Baltimore, Maryland; *1927–1944* lives in Massachusetts; *1933–1944* studies piano privately and then at New England Conservatory; *1944–1946* serves as Sonarman on the destroyer U.S.S. Nicholas; *1946–1950* attends Harvard College, majors in English Literature and studies music; *1950* first publication in *The Harvard Advocate; 1950–1951* attends University of Michigan; *1951* receives M.A. in comparative literature; wins Hopwood Award for poetry; moves to New York and works at the Museum of Modern Art's information desk; *1952* publishes *A City and Other Poems* with drawings by Larry Rivers; *1953–1955* writes reviews as Editorial Associate of *Art News; 1955* becomes special assistant to Director of the International Program at Museum of Modern Art; *1956* poet-playwright-in-residence, the Poets Theater, Cambridge, Massachusetts; *1960* appointed Assistant Curator of Painting and Sculpture Exhibitions at the Museum of Modern Art; *1963* travels extensively in Europe arranging exhibitions; teaches poetry workshop at the New School for Social Research; *1965* appointed Associate Curator at the Museum of Modern Art and is featured in the National Education Television USA: Poetry Series; July 25, *1966* died when hit by a dune buggy on Fire Island, New York.

Author's Bibliography (selected)

A City Winter, 1952 (poems); *Oranges,* 1953 (poems); *Meditations In An Emergency,* 1957 (poems); *Jackson Pollock;* 1959 (art criticism); *Second Avenue,* 1960 (poem); *New Spanish Painting And Sculpture,* 1960 (Museum of Modern Art catalog); *Odes,* 1961 (poems); *Lunch Poems,* 1965 (poems); *Love Poems (Tentative Title),* 1965 (poems); *Robert Motherwell,* 1965 (Museum of Modern Art catalog); *Nakian,* 1966 (Museum of Modern Art catalog); *David Smith,* 1966 (Museum of Modern Art catalog); *In Memory of My Feelings,* 1967 (poems); *Collected Poems,* 1971; *Selected Poems,* 1974; *Early Writings,* 1977; *Selected Plays,* 1978.

Overview of Biographical Sources

Because Frank O'Hara's life was both brief and controversial, he has received only limited biographical attention. Editors Bill Berkson and Joe Le Sueur's *Homage To Frank O'Hara* (Berkeley: Creative Arts Book Co., 1980) is a collage of photographs, anecdotes, essays, notes, memoirs, poem-paintings, and poems collected from O'Hara's friends and admirers to acknowledge the profound effect O'Hara had on them. Although neither a biographical nor factual account of O'Hara's life, this collection gives much insight into O'Hara's enigmatic, vibrant and oftentimes melancholy personality. Jim Chap-

son's *A Biography of Frank O'Hara* (Corey, Ireland: Funge Art Centre, 1975) is
an eight page pamphlet available only at the University of Wisconsin Library
at Milwaukee, and the University of Connecticut Library.

Overview of Critical Sources
   O'Hara's critics argue the importance of his poems. O'Hara's work is discussed in the context of the post Robert Lowell generation, and much focus is
paid to his role as a New York School poet. Robert Altieri's *Enlarging the
Temple: New Directions in American Poetry During the 1960s* (Lewisburg: Bucknell University Press, 1979), devotes a chapter ("Varieties of Immanentist Experience: Robert Bly, Charles Olson, and Frank O'Hara") to describing why
poets of the sixties are often not good poets, but analyzes and defends O'Hara's
ability to de-mystify poetry through the use of real life experiences which are
vitalized with fantasy. Altieri discusses O'Hara's moral vision, humor, and
affirmative skepticism. Susan Holahan's chapter, "Frank O'Hara's Poetry," in
American Poetry Since 1960: Some Critical Perspectives (ed. Robert B. Shaw,
Chester Springs, PA: Dufour Editions, 1974), discusses the importance of New
York City on Frank O'Hara's poetry, and Holahan describes O'Hara's relationships with Surrealist and Abstract Expressionist painters, as it pertains to
O'Hara's poems. Holahan also provides an analysis of the development of
O'Hara's use of syntax as it relates to time and space. Richard Howard's chap-
ter, "Frank O'Hara," in *Alone With America: Essays on the Art of Poetry in the
United States Since 1950* (New York: Atheneum, 1965) uses O'Hara's tragic
death as a central motif, asserting that death was always central to O'Hara's
poems. Although not a believable argument, Howard's biographical readings of
O'Hara's poems are valuable. Paul Carroll's reading of "The Day Lady Died"
in *The Poem In Its Skin* (Chicago: Follett, 1968) is valuable as a paradigm of
how to read and understand the poetry of Frank O'Hara.

Evaluation of Selected Criticism
   Feldman, Alan, *Frank O'Hara.* Boston: Twayne, 1979. Feldman's study focuses on O'Hara's intentions as a poet. O'Hara's concern with the self, feelings,
and experiences is carefully explored. In explicating O'Hara's poetry, Feldman
also provides an in-depth study of O'Hara's diction, syntax, and imagery.

   Perloff, Marjorie, *Frank O'Hara: Poet Among Painters.* New York: George
Braziller, 1977. This is the first full length, and the most extensive critical study
of O'Hara's poems. Perloff chronologically explores the development of
O'Hara's poetics, seeing his work in historical context. In Perloff's close read-
ings of O'Hara's poems, various influences on O'Hara are explored, including
Dada, Surrealism and Abstract Expressionism, and Romanticism. Music, Ac-
tion painting and French poetry are also shown by Perloff to have influenced
O'Hara. Perloff provides an interesting study of O'Hara's involvement with the

visual arts, especially the poem-paintings O'Hara attempted with visual artists. Perloff's treatment of O'Hara as a poet among painters adds greatly to an understanding of his poetry.

Other Sources

Libby, Anthony, "O'Hara on the Silver Range," *Contemporary Literature,* 17 (Spring 1976), 140–162. Libby's study of O'Hara focuses on the relationship between poetry and modern painting. Willem de Kooning's abstract quality, and fleeting visual imagery is compared to that of O'Hara's. Libby discusses the influence of Surrealism on both Jackson Pollock and O'Hara, showing that Pollock's field paintings and drip paintings are similar to the shape of O'Hara's late poetry. Libby also provides an analysis of O'Hara's poetic style.

Selected Dictionaries and Encyclopedias

Dictionary of Literary Biography, Gale Research, 1980. Brief account of O'Hara's life, and a discussion of O'Hara's major poems.

Leslie Rebecca Bloom
University of Delaware

JOHN O'HARA
1905–1970

Author's Chronology

Born in Pottsville, Pennsylvania on January 31, 1905 to Irish Catholic parents, father a physician; *1911–1919* attends public and parochial schools; *1924* after being expelled from two preparatory schools is valedictorian at Niagara prep school; *1925* admitted to Yale, unable to attend because father's death reduces family money; *1925–1930* works on a number of newspapers as reporter and columnist; *1931* marries Helen Petit (divorce *1933*); *1930–1934* works in film publicity (RKO and Warners) and advertising; *1934 Appointment in Samarra,* first novel brings success; *1935–1940* works in Hollywood on screenplays, marries Belle Wylie (*1937*); *1940* Broadway play *Pal Joey* secures O'Hara wealth; *1940–1944* brief military career in OSS and as correspondent; *1945–1954* increasing fame, daughter born (*1945*), quits drinking (*1953*), wife dies (*1954*); *1955–1958* works in Hollywood, marrys Katherine Bryan (*1955*), elected to National Institute of Arts and Letters (*1957*), builds "Linebrook"; *1958–1969* writes various magazine columns, grandchildren, ill health; April 11, 1970 dies at Linebrook, New Jersey.

Author's Bibliography (Selected)

Appointment in Samarra, 1934 (novel); *The Doctor's Son and Other Stories,* 1934; *Butterfield 8,* 1935 (novel); *Hope of Heaven,* 1938 (novel); *Files on Parade,* 1939 (stories); *Pal Joey,* 1940 (stories); *Pipe Night,* 1945 (stories); *Hellbox,* 1947 (stories); *A Rage to Live,* 1949 (novel); *The Farmer's Hotel,* 1951 (novel); *Sweet and Sour,* 1954 (columns); *Ten North Frederick,* 1955 (novel); *A Family Party,* 1956 (novel); *From the Terrace,* 1958 (novel); *Ourselves to Know,* 1960 (novel); *Sermons and Soda-Water,* 1960 (novel); *Five Plays,* 1961; *Assembly,* 1961 (stories); *The Big Laugh,* 1962 (novel); *The Cape Cod Lighter,* 1962 (stories); *Elizabeth Appleton,* 1963 (novel); *The Hat on the Bed,* 1963 (stories); *The Horse Knows the Way,* 1964 (stories); *The Lockwood Concern,* 1965 (novel); *My Turn,* 1966 (columns); *Waiting for Winter,* 1966 (stories); *The Instrument,* 1967 (novel); *And Other Stories,* 1968; *Lovey Childs: A Philadelphian's Story,* 1969 (novel); *The Ewings,* 1972 (novel); *The Time Element and Other Stories,* 1972; *Good Samaritan and Other Stories,* 1974; *"An Artist Is His Own Fault," John O'Hara on Writers and Writing,* 1977 (literary essays); *Two by O'Hara,* 1979 (screenplay and play).

Overview of Biographical Sources

John O'Hara led a somewhat stormy public life. Celebrated for his drinking, he was a frequenter of night clubs and a member of several literary circles in New York. In many ways his public life has overshadowed his professional one, often obscuring his considerable literary talent.

Although there are six books which contain biographical material about John O'Hara, only three of them may properly be called biographies, each filling a place in the unfolding of O'Hara's life. The first to appear was Finis Farr's *O'Hara: A Biography* (1973) just three years after O'Hara's death. It is journalistic and reveals a lack of attention to detail; Farr pays little attention to O'Hara's published work. Matthew Bruccoli's *The O'Hara Concern: A Biography of John O'Hara* (1975) appeared two years later and does much to correct the factual errors and hastiness of its predecessor. Bruccoli admits that his biography is primarily literary, and he concentrates on O'Hara's career. As would befit O'Hara's bibliographer, Bruccoli carefully documents his biography and provides the reader with ample literary discussion while avoiding literary analysis. In 1977 Bruccoli edited the *Selected Letters of John O'Hara* which Frank MacShane made liberal use of for his biography *The Life of John O'Hara* (1980). Although less literary in scope than Bruccoli, MacShane is broader than Farr, including in his assessment of O'Hara a sense of the writer as a chronicler of American society during the first half of the twentieth century.

Evaluation of Selected Biographies

Bruccoli, Matthew J. *The O'Hara Concern: A Biography of John O'Hara.* New York: Random House, 1975. Bruccoli has written a critical biography and attempts to establish O'Hara's stature, in Bruccoli's words, in terms of his life and work. It is a career study, an examination of O'Hara's as a professional writer. Bruccoli believes that O'Hara is a major American talent who had been underestimated by the critical-academic literary establishment. A partisan biographer, he acknowledges the support of O'Hara's widow with obvious affection. Bruccoli's study is nevertheless well-written, if not distinguished, and well-researched, the best researched of the O'Hara biographies.

Farr, Finis, *O'Hara: A Biography.* Boston: Little, Brown and Company, 1973. This was the first study of O'Hara's life to be published and it suffers from a lack of careful research and an often gushy prose style. It is a journalistic job which while breezy and chatty, lacks depth and much insight.

MacShane, Frank, *The Life of John O'Hara.* New York: E. P. Dutton, 1980. This biography is a blend of its two predecessors. It does not follow Bruccoli's literary bent nor succumb to Farr's quick style. MacShane's study makes use of the former's scholarship while concentrating on the latter's social context. What emerges is an examination of O'Hara as a major chronicler of twentieth-century American life. This study does much to tie his often publicized public life into his literary works.

Autobiographical Sources

O'Hara left little of an autobiographical nature behind: a few letters, some unpublished manuscripts, mostly fiction, and not much else. Lacking were the intimate notebooks or diaries, or the surpressed, highly personal works which often reveal intimacies hidden from public view. O'Hara did use his personal life, as many writers do, more or less, in his fiction. For example, the fictional Gibbsville was a thinly disguised Pottsville, but drawing inferences from such materials is highly speculative. O'Hara was often autobiographical in his columns and interviews and a few of them have been brought together along with his public speeches in *"An Artist Is His Own Fault:" John O'Hara on Writers and Writing,* (Carbondale and Edwardsville: Southern Illinois University Press, 1977) edited by Matthew Bruccoli. It is the only easily accessible source of O'Hara's nonfictional writings. A second major source of autobiographical materials is the volume of letters also edited by Matthew Bruccoli, *Selected Letters of John O'Hara* (New York: Random House, 1978). These letters catch a glimpse of O'Hara denied elsewhere, and although many of the letters are concerned with literary matters, Bruccoli's choice presents a judicious cross-section of O'Hara's life.

Overview of the Critical Sources
There is yet to be written a comprehensive, full-length treatment of O'Hara's fiction. Several monographs exist but are necessarily brief, in some cases sketchy, when trying to assess O'Hara's fictional world. Because O'Hara wrote so voluminously and because he has not been academically fashionable, insufficient attention has been paid to his work. Currently only one collection of his short fiction and three of his novels are in print.

Evaluation of Selected Criticism
Carson, Edward Russell, *The Fiction of John O'Hara.* Pittsburgh: University of Pittsburgh Press, 1961. (Critical Essays in English and American Literature No. 7). This is the first monograph treatment of O'Hara's fiction and suffers from being overly brief in its analysis of both the stories and novels, even though the expressed purpose of this study is to concentrate on the "Gibbsville" or "Lantenengo County" stories and novels. Much of the analysis is solid and suggests areas for further study of O'Hara.

Grebstein, Sheldon Norman, *John O'Hara.* New York: Twayne, 1966. This monograph attempts too much as is often the case with such series volumes. It is a good introduction, however, to O'Hara's life and work with a general grouping of O'Hara's fiction by geographical location: Pennsylvania, New York, and Hollywood. The book suffers from a critical ambivalence towards its subject.

Long, Robert Emmet, *John O'Hara.* New York: Frederick Ungar, 1983. This is the most recent and the most balanced assessment to date. The book contains a judicious treatment of both the novels and the stories roughly grouped chronologically. Fine treatment of the primary themes in O'Hara's fiction.

Walcutt, Charles Child, *John O'Hara.* Minneapolis: University of Minnesota Press, 1969. (Pamphlets on American Writers Number 80). This is a sketchy tour through O'Haraland with too much plot summary and too little analysis.

Other Sources

Bassett, Charles W. "O'Hara's Roots," Pottsville *Republican,* March 20 1971–January 8, 1972. A biography of O'Hara's Pottsville experience in forty-four installments.

Bruccoli, Matthew J. *John O'Hara: A Descriptive Bibliography.* Pittsburgh: University of Pittsburgh Press, 1978. Supersedes Bruccoli's *John O'Hara: A Checklist.* New York: Random House, 1972.

Gary, Beverly, "A Post Portrait: John O'Hara," New York *Post,* May 18–22, 24, 1959. Contains a good overview biography.

Schanche, Don A. "John O'Hara Is Alive and Well in the First Half of the Twentieth Century," *Esquire,* 72 (August 1969), 84–86. Journalistic sketch of O'Hara's life and times.

Selected Dictionaries and Encyclopedias

Contemporary Authors, Gale Research, 1969. Summary of critical reception of O'Hara with brief biographical survey of life and career.

Critical Survey of Long Fiction, Salem Press, 1983. Overview of the fiction with short biographical sketch.

Dictionary of Literary Biography, Gale Research, 1981. Excellent discussion of both a biographical and critical nature. Covers most of the published work.

Charles L. P. Silet
Iowa State University

O. HENRY
1862–1910

Author's Chronology

Born William Sidney Porter, September 11, 1862, Greensboro, North Carolina, of a physician father and an educated mother; *1865* after his mother's death, moves with father to home of his aunt; *1882* moves to Texas; *1887* marries Athol Estes, daughter of a wealthy Austin family; *1891* becomes teller in Austin bank; *1894* begins publication of a weekly humor magazine, *The Rolling Stone;* indicted to stand trial for embezzlement of bank funds, released for lack of evidence; *1896* arrested but flees to Honduras; *1897* returns to Austin; Athol dies; *1898* found guilty and sentenced to five-year term in Federal Penitentiary where he begins his writing career; *1901* released on good behavior; *1902* moves to New York and becomes famous as a writer under the name O. Henry; *1903* signs newspaper contract for weekly short story; *1904* publishes first book, *Cabbages and Kings; 1907* marries Sara Lindsay Coleman; 1910 dies in New York, buried in Asheville, North Carolina.

Author's Bibliography (selected)

Cabbages and Kings, 1904; *The Four Million,* 1906; *The Trimmed Lamp,* 1907; *Heart of the West,* 1907; *The Voice of the City,* 1908; *The Gentle Grafter,* 1908; *Roads of Destiny,* 1909; *Options,* 1909; *Strictly Business,* 1910; *Whirligigs,* 1910; *Sixes and Sevens,* 1911; *Rolling Stones,* 1912; *Waifs and Strays,* 1917; *The Authorized Edition* (12 vols.), 1913; *The Complete Works of O. Henry* (2 vols.), 1953.

Overview of Biographical Sources

O. Henry was such a popular writer during the first two decades of the twentieth century, as well as such a mystery to his fans, that there are many early biographical treatments, especially by those who knew him personally. The first, C. Alphonso Smith's authorized biography, *O. Henry Biography* (1916), is still the standard source for much of what we know about O. Henry's life, although subsequent biographies have made it somewhat outdated by the discovery of new materials. More fictionalized, romanticized, and informal biographies and memoirs are: *Through the Shadows with O. Henry,* (London: Duckworth, 1923), written by Al Jennings who knew O. Henry in Honduras, where they were both fugitives, and later in prison; Frances G. Maltby's *The Dimity Sweetheart* (Richmond, VA: Dietz Publishing, 1930), which deals with his courtship and first marriage to Athol Estes; and William Walsh Williams, *The Quiet Lodger of Irving Place* (New York: E. P. Dutton, 1936), which focuses on O. Henry's literary and social life in New York. More authoritative studies are Ethel Stephens Arnett's *O. Henry From Polecat Creek* (1963), which gives new information about O. Henry's boyhood life; and the well-researched popular biography by Richard O'Connor, *O. Henry: The Legendary Life of William S. Porter* (1970), which focuses primarily on his life in New York. The two most recent scholarly biographical studies are: E. Hudson Long's *O. Henry, the Man and His Work* (1949), which makes use of previously unused information; and Gerald Langford's *Alias, O. Henry: A Biography of William Sidney Porter* (1957), the most documented, scholarly, and objective treatment O. Henry has yet received.

Evaluation of Selected Biographies

Arnett, Ethel Stephens, *O. Henry from Polecat Creek*. Greensboro, NC: Piedmont Press, 1963. Arnett interviewed people who either knew the young Porter in Greensboro or who had access to previously unpublished accounts. The result is the most thorough discussion of O. Henry before he went to Texas. Although this account of childhood is interesting, it has doubtful critical value, except to reveal the influence of "Miss Lina," Porter's first teacher, and to offer evidence of his early love of books and reading.

Langford, Gerald, *Alias O. Henry: A Biography of William Sidney Porter*. New York: Macmillan, 1957. Langford attempts to cut through the O. Henry legend to give a realistic and well-balanced picture of his life. He cites previously unused material in the public library of Greensboro to present a perspective from which to approach the large body of short fiction that O. Henry produced. The book is extensively footnoted and highly detailed. Along with Smith's early biography, it is the most authoritative source.

Long, E. Hudson, *O. Henry, The Man and His Work*. Philadelphia: University of Pennsylvania Press, 1949. This is primarily a biography with very little criticism of the stories except for references to some actual events that may have served as the bases for certain stories. Whereas it makes use of the Greensboro collection and thus is based on material not previously used by Smith and others, as a scholarly biography it is much less detailed than Langford's more extensive study.

O'Connor, Richard, *O. Henry: The Legendary Life of William S. Porter*. Garden City, NY: Doubleday, 1970. This is a very readable popular biography, less scholarly and academic than those of Langford and Long, focused primarily on O. Henry's New York literary life. Three fourths of the book recounts the last eight years of O. Henry's life during which he wrote most of his stories.

Smith, C. Alphonso, *O. Henry Biography*. New York: Doubleday, Page & Co., 1916. This is still the authoritative biography, written by a man who knew him. It is a formal and well-researched study by a professor of English who knows the conventions of literary biography quite well. The book is so filled with quotations, detailed facts, and primary material that all biographers of

O. Henry still use it as the basis for many of their assumptions and judgments. Smith also spends much of the text pointing out how many of the stories reflect O. Henry's particular interests. Especially helpful is a long chapter on his favourite themes, which represents the earliest criticism of O. Henry's works in book form.

Autobiographical Sources

There are no autobiographical sources of O. Henry's life, primarily because he wished to conceal his prison record from the public.

Overview of Critical Sources

Although O. Henry was extremely popular among the general reading public of his time, he has never been considered a serious writer by American critics. Indeed, because his stories seem primarily to depend on artificial plots, witty prose, and snap endings, he is often criticized for making the short story a cheap journalistic trick. Many of the short-story "How-To" books in America in the first quarter century focused on the O. Henry story as a kind of formula for writing success. Serious critical studies, except for a few Russian appreciations and analyses, are sparse.

Evaluation of Selected Criticism

Current-Garcia, Eugene, *O. Henry*. New York: Twayne, 1965. This study devotes the first few chapters to a summary of O. Henry's life, primarily drawn from other published sources, and then offers a sketchy and general discussion of O. Henry's basic themes and technical achievements. However, this is the only full-length study of O. Henry to offer a critical perspective of his work and to evaluate his reputation. It is an intelligent and well-informed work by a critic who knows the American short story genre thoroughly.

Éjxenbaum, B. M. *O. Henry and the Theory of the Short Story*. trans. I. R. Titunik. Ann Arbor: University of Michigan, 1968. Originally published in Russia in 1925, this study reflects both the Russian interest in O. Henry as a serious writer and the brand of criticism known as Russian Formalism. Because Formalism was more concerned with technical achievement than thematic profundity, O. Henry, who was a technical master, but perhaps a philosophic lightweight, is a perfect candidate for the exercise of this kind of analysis. Although this is only a short pamphlet, it is perhaps the most incisive discussion yet to be published on O. Henry's contribution to the short-story genre.

Other Sources

Brown, Deming, "O. Henry in Russia," *Russian Review, XII (1953)*, 253–258. Comments on O. Henry's popularity in Russia.

Courtney, L. W. "O. Henry's Case Reconsidered," *American Literature,* XIV (January 1943). Argues that the evidence shows O. Henry was indeed guilty of embezzlement.

Evans, Walter, " 'A Municipal Report': O. Henry and Postmodernism," *Tennessee Studies in Literature,* XXVI (1981), 101–116. Shows O. Henry's relationship to postmodernist fiction.

Harris, Richard C. *William Sydney Porter (O. Henry): A Reference Guide.* Boston: G. K. Hall, 1980. A bibliographical guide to O. Henry's works and criticism of his fiction.

McAllister, Dan, "Negligently, Perhaps; Criminally, Never," *South Atlantic Quarterly,* LI (October 1952), 562–573. Argues that O. Henry was innocent of the charges against him.

Pattee, Frederick Lewis, *The Development of the American Short Story* (New York: Harper and Brothers, 1923). The O. Henry chapter represents an influential negative criticism of the fiction.

Van Doren, Carl, "O. Henry," *Texas Review,* II (January 1917), 248–259. The first well-balanced critical analysis of O. Henry's work.

Selected Dictionaries and Encyclopedias

Critical Survey of Short Fiction, Salem Press, 1981. Brief discussion of O. Henry's life and work.

Charles E. May
California State University, Long Beach

JOHN OLDHAM
1653–1683

Author's Chronology

Born August 9, 1653 at Shipton Moyne, Gloucester, England; *1662* Oldham's father, ejected from his vicarage for non-conformity, opens a school which is attended by his son; *1668* enters the grammar school at Telbury; *1670* leaves Oxford and returns to Shipton Moyne, probably to teach at his father's school; *1676* becomes a master at Whitgrift School, Croydon; *1679* becomes tutor to the grandson of Sir Edward Thurland at Reigate; the first of the *Satyrs Upon the Jesuits,* "Garnet's Ghost," and "A Satyr Against Vertue" are pirated and published; *1680–1681* moves to London in order to establish himself as a writer; returns to tutoring in the household of Sir William of Rockwood; *1682* finds patronage with the Earl of Kingston; *1683* dies of smallpox and is buried at Kingston's estate, Holme Pierrepont, December 7.

Author's Bibliography

"Upon the Marriage of the Prince of Orange with the Lady Mary," 1677 (poem); *Satyrs Upon the Jesuits,* 1681 (poems); *Some New Pieces,* 1681 (poems); *Poems and Translations,* 1683; *Remains of Mr. John Oldham in Verse and Prose,* 1684.

Overview of Biographical Sources

The present sources of Oldham's biography are meager. Aside from a handful of recent periodical notes and a brief summary of Oldham's life that is part of a larger essay upon Oldham's poetry by Harold F. Brooks, the main sources are the anonymous biography which prefaced the 1772 edition of Oldham's works and the anecdotal materials supplied by Oldham's contemporary, Anthony À Wood, in *Athenae Oxonensis* (1691–1692). The only two books devoted to the study of Oldham, both published in 1983, contribute little to the study of Oldham's life. Harold Brooks has promised that a separate biography of Oldham will accompany the publication of his long-expected critical edition. Without such a biography, there exists no definitive book-length version of the poet's life.

Evaluation of Selected Biographies

Brooks, Harold F. "The Poetry of John Oldham" in *Restoration Literature.* ed. Harold Love. London: Methuen, 1972. The brief treatment of Oldham's life with which Brooks begins his discussion of the poet has not been significantly extended by further research. Brooks examines, in a roughly chronological fashion, Oldham's practice in various genres and his debt to previous poets. His emphasis is upon contextual evaluation rather than explication.

Zigerell, James, *John Oldham.* Boston: Twayne, 1983. This biographical and critical study, aimed at the "nonspecialist reader," begins with a biographical summary. Although the general outline of Oldham's life is accurate, much of his introductory biographical chapter and some of the biographical speculations which are joined to his considerations of individual poems seem questionable. For the most part, however, Zigerell's treatment of Oldham's poetry is confined to quotation and paraphrase. For a poet, most of whose work is not readily available, such a procedure has some warrant. Indeed, that nearly a third of the book is devoted to a discussion of the *Satyrs Upon the Jesuits* seems justified, in part, by the fact that a modern critical text of these poems does exist. Moreover, Zigerell's extended discussion of the literary, political, and religious contexts of the *Satyrs Upon the Jesuits,* if not his analyses of the individual satires, allows a reader unfamiliar with the Restoration period to approach them without some historical awareness.

Overview of Critical Sources

Until very recently, criticism of Oldham's poetry was to be found only in scholarly journals, in collections of articles, or in portions of general studies of Restoration and eighteenth-century poetry. In 1972, Harold Brooks could recommend only the short appreciations of Oldham by Rachel Trickett and Roger Sharrock. Since Oldham's poetry, with the exception of the *Satyrs Upon the Jesuits,* has not subsequently become more readily available, it is not surprising to find that the number of valuable brief treatments has not substantially increased. Indeed, the appearance of two books devoted to Oldham, both in 1983, is a surprise. Nevertheless, a reader who has found usable texts of Oldham's poetry and is seeking some guidance is not likely to be well-served by either, even if he already possesses some familiarity with Restoration poetry. It remains the case that several shorter studies are the most useful introductions to Oldham as a Restoration poet whose major accomplishments were his satires.

Evaluation of Selected Criticism

Hammond, Paul, *John Oldham and the Renewal of Classical Culture.* Cambridge: Cambridge University Press, 1983. Hammond's book is primarily concerned with the genesis of Oldham's poetry, and with an investigation of how English, French, and Latin sources found a voice in his translations, imitations, and occasional poems. Oldham's poetic statements are constantly weighed against those of others; consequently, readers looking for an overview of any individual poem may be disappointed. Nevertheless, although Hammond has framed his entire book as a study of influences and their transformations, he does establish Oldham's poetic originality.

Korshin, Paul J. *From Concord to Dissent: Major Themes in English Poetic Theory, 1640–1700.* Menston, Yorkshire, 1973. In his illuminating chapter on

Oldham, Korshin considers the poet as a satirist whose work evolved through three stages: an early poetics of excess, in which Oldham's sheer vituperation constituted a poetic dissent from the orthodoxies of John Dryden's poetry; the poetic mode of the *Satyrs Upon the Jesuits,* in which distortion replaced vituperation as the primary satirical device; Oldham's final poetic achievements, in which his use of implication and indirection indicate a respect for moderation.

Sharrock, Roger, "Modes of Satire," in *Restoration Theatre.* Stratford-Upon-Avon Studies 6. London: Edward Arnold, 1965. A valuable general discussion of Restoration poetic satire which views Oldham as an innovator in "heroic satire" and "classical imitation."

Trickett, Rachel, *The Honest Muse: A Study of Augustan Satire.* Oxford: Oxford University Press, 1967. A chapter of this study discusses the satires of Rochester and Oldham as contemporary alternatives to the poetic style of Dryden and Oldham's use of satiric voice and poetic imitation as an anticipation of certain aspects of the poetry of Pope.

James Maloney
Humber College, Ontario
Toronto

CHARLES OLSON
1910–1970

Author's Chronology

Born December 27, 1910, Worcester, Massachusetts; *1915* his mother and father began renting a summer place in Gloucester, Massachusetts, in the working-class area known as Stage Fort, near the sea; *1932* receives a B.A. from Wesleyan University and an M.A. in *1933*, with a thesis on Melville; *1934* Instructor in English, Clark University; *1935* father dies; *1936* meets Edward Dahlberg; *1938* completes coursework for a Ph.D. at Harvard University; *1939* is awarded a Guggenheim Foundation grant; meets Constance Wilcock, whom he will marry; moves to New York City; begins writing poems a few months after outbreak of WWII; *1940–1944* works for American Civil Liberties Union, and, subsequently, for The Foreign Languages Division of Office of War Information; *1944* works for the Democratic Party as a Director of the Foreign Nationalities Division; *1946* begins visiting Ezra Pound in St. Elizabeths; publishes his first poems; *1947* publishes *Call Me Ishmael;* *1949* publishes *Y & X,* his first collection of poetry, with Caresse Crosby's Black Sun Press; *1950* his mother dies; writes first *Maximus* poem as a letter to Vincent Ferrini; begins correspondence with Robert Creeley; begins formal teaching at Black Mountain College, where he will remain as Rector until the closing of the School in 1956; *1951* daughter, Katherine Mary, is born; *1954* while at Black Mountain meets Elizabeth Kaiser, who will become his second wife; *1955* a son, Charles Peter, is born; *1956* moves back to Gloucester, continues to write, publish, and give readings; *1960–1961* participates in experiments with consciousness-expanding drugs; *1963* attends Vancouver Poetry Conference; becomes Professor of English at The State University of New York at Buffalo; *1964* wife dies; Olson is hospitalized in Buffalo; *1966* leaves for London and remains in Europe about a year; *1967* publishes *Selected Writings* and continues to travel; *1969* enters hospital after Thanksgiving and dies in New York City, January 10, 1970 of cancer of the liver.

Author's Bibliography (selected)

Call Me Ishmael, 1947 (criticism); *Selected Writings* (edited by Robert Creeley), 1966; *Human Universe & Other Essays,* 1967 (philosophy); *Archaelogist Of Morning,* 1970 (poetry); *Poetry & Truth: The Beloit Lectures,* 1971; *Additional Prose,* 1974; *Charles Olson & Ezra Pound: An Encounter at St. Elizabeths,* 1975; *The Post Office,* 1975; *The Fiery Hunt & Other Plays,* 1977; *Muthologos: Collected Interviews and Lectures,* 2 volumes, 1978–1979; *The Maximus Poems,* 1983.

Overview of Biographical Sources

Most of the literary snapshots of Olson, many in the form of poems addressed to him by other poets, have been published in little magazines and small press editions. A bibliographical guide listing all publications pertaining to Olson is being prepared, but until it is completed, the best guide to this voluminous material so far is in the ten issues of the journal *OLSON* published by The University of Connecticut, whose Wilber Cross Library houses the literary archives of the Olson Estate. Other biographical sources include the reminiscences of Olson's life at Black Mountain College, written by one of his students, Fielding Dawson (*The Black Mountain Book.* New York: Croton Press, 1970). Also useful is Chapter 13 of Martin B. Duberman's mammoth study of Black Mountain College titled *Black Mountain: An Exploration In Community* (New York: Doubleday, 1972). George F. Butterick's Introduction to *A Guide to THE MAXIMUS POEMS* (Berkeley: University of California Press, 1978) and Robert Creeley's Introduction to *The Selected Writings Of Charles Olson* (New York: New Directions, 1967) are both more formal writings which also serve as "entrances" into the poet's life and work.

Evaluation of Selected Biographies

Boer, Charles, *Charles Olson in Connecticut.* Chicago: Swallow Press, 1975. Boer, whom Olson came to Storrs to visit and subsequently appointed his Literary Executor, presents a readable, impressionistic, yet factual memoir of the last months of Olson's life. This book remains the best biographical source, especially of Olson's last few months.

Autobiographical Sources

In his letters to Robert Creeley, Olson wrote at great length about the problems facing a poet. There are now six volumes of the Creeley-Olson correspondence (*Charles Olson and Robert Creeley: The Complete Correspondence.* Santa Barbara: Black Sparrow Press, 1980–Present). *Mayan Letters,* comprising volumes 5 and 6 of the Olson-Creeley Letters, describe the poet's perceptions and life on the Yucatan coast of Mexico, where he had journeyed with his first wife, Constance.

Olson visited Ezra Pound when Pound was living in St. Elizabeths and "conducting America's foremost literary salon." *Charles Olson and Ezra Pound: An Encounter at St. Elizabeths,* edited by Catherine Seelye (New York: Grossman Publishers, 1975), makes available a rich source of valuable information. Other sources for letters are *Letters For Origin, 1950–1956,* (Albert Glover, ed. New York: Cape Goliard Press, in association with Grossman Publishers, 1970) and the correspondence between Olson and Edward Dahlberg published in the magazine *Sulfur.*

In addition to autobiographical materials in *Muthologos, volumes 1 & 2. The Collected Interviews and Lectures* (George F. Butterick, ed. Bolinas, California:

Four Seasons Foundation, 1978–1979), and in *Poetry & Truth: The Beloit Lectures and Poems* (George F. Butterick, ed. San Francisco: Four Seasons Foundation, 1971), the best autobiographical source is the marathon Berkeley Poetry Conference Reading known as *The Reading At Berkeley*. The definitive edition of *The Reading* was transcribed by Ralph Maud (English Department, Simon Fraser University, British Columbia), available on tape from The Language Laboratory, University of California at Berkeley.

The poet's life is also encoded in his long series poem, *The Maximus Poems,* though Olson himself decried the suggestion that he was Maximus or that the figure of Maximus was a *persona,* insisting that Maximus "the man in the word" was a Middle Voice.

Overview of Critical Sources

A Guide to THE MAXIMUS POEMS of Charles Olson by George F. Butterick is a major indispensable text. Olson said of the turgidity of his work, that his references were not references but inner inherences. Butterick's "guide" traces these inner inherences through each volume of *The Maximus Poems,* a Herculean task for which every reader of the work is indebted. It is an invaluable source for the range and depth and quality of its information, but also for an excellent cross-indexing referencing system.

Books of criticism began to proliferate not long after Olson's death in 1970, but the best critical work remains the earliest, originally published in little journals by other poets who were among the first to respond to Olson's work. Articles like Ed Dorn's "What I See In *The Maximus Poems*" and special issues of other little magazines like the Black Mountain issue of *The Review* (Oxford, England) and *Boundary 2* (SUNY Binghamton), and *Maps* (English Department, Shippensburg State College, Pennsylvania), explore the issues raised by Olson's work.

Evaluation of Selected Criticism

Charters, Ann, *Olson/Melville: A Study in Affinity.* Berkeley: Oyez Press, 1968. This was the first book-length study to be published, and it attempts to be faithful to the kind of methodological problems which Olson himself raised in *Call Me Ishmael,* Olson's own book on Melville. Ann Charters also edited *The Special View Of History* (Berkeley: Oyez Press, 1970). Her Introduction to these lectures and notes for lectures Olson was presenting to his students at Black Mountain College not only contains interesting critical and biographical statements from Robert Creeley and Robert Duncan, but also argues for a view of Olson as anti-existentialist, a view which can be supported not only by *Special View Of History,* but also by Olson's essay, *Proprioception,* reprinted in *Additional Prose,* and the essays in *Human Universe.*

Meachen, Clive, *Charles Olson, His Only Weather.* London: Spanner, 1979. Meachen's is the most adventuresome book published. A long monograph, it is an "active engagement with what the work proposes". Meachen's one hundred page essay, good on specifics but weakest when trying to generalize about American Literature, nevertheless manages to understand part of the vision of Olson's work rather than taking a more Thucididean or analytic approach.

Other Sources

Byrd, Don, *Charles Olson's MAXIMUS.* University of Illinois Press, 1980. Christensen, Paul, *Charles Olson: Call Him Ishmael.* University of Texas Press, 1979. Merrill, Thomas F. *The Poetry of Charles Olson: A Primer.* University of Delaware Press, 1982. Paul, Sherman, *Olson's Push: Origin, Black Mountain, and Recent American Poetry.* Louisiana State University Press, 1978. Von Hallberg, Robert, Charles Olson: *The Scholar's Art.* Harvard University Press, 1979. These were the first full-length books to be published after Olson's death, which attempted to deal with Olson's work and the traditions in which it occurred. All of these five critical studies are more-or-less formalist and generic. Within that analytic framework, all of these works offer sometimes illuminating insights and may prove useful to students of Olson's work.

Sherman, William D. "Beyond Parataxis: Notes Toward Synchronic Verse," in *A Gregynog Lecture in American Literature,* Wales 1970; available on tape from The Board of American Studies, University College of Wales, Aberystwyth. Olson's use of Notopoulis and Eric Havelock in relation to Jung.

OLSON: The Journal Of The Charles Olson Archives. Storrs: The University of Connecticut Library, 1974, continuing. Ten issues so far have been issued. Enlightening for its checklists and bibliographical information, it is also an important aid for more advanced Olson studies and scholarship.

William David Sherman
Margate, New Jersey

GEORGE ORWELL
1903-1950

Author's Chronology

Born Eric Arthur Blair June 25, 1903, Bengal, India; *1904* returns to England, but father remains in India until *1912,* as a British official in Customs and Excise; *1911-1916* attends St. Cyprian's private school; *1917* wins scholarship to Eton, which he attends until 1921; *1922-1927* serves in the Indian Imperial Police in Burma; *1927* spends six months as a tramp in London's East End; *1928* lives for eighteen months among poor and outcasts in Paris; *1929-1939* returns to England; supports himself by working in a bookstore, teaching, and writing; *1933* publishes his first book, *Down and Out in Paris and London; 1936* marries Eileen O'Shaughnessy; goes to Spain as a journalist but joins P.O.U.M. militia; *1937* suffers a neck wound; 1938 enters a sanitorium for tuberculosis; *1941-1943* works as Talks Assistant and producer at BBC; *1943* adopts a son, Richard; becomes literary editor of the *Tribune; 1945* wife dies after a minor operation; publishes *Animal Farm; 1946* moves to Jura in the Hebrides; *1949* enters Gloucestershire sanitorium; *Nineteen Eighty-Four* published; January 21, 1950 dies following a hemorrhage.

Author's Bibliography (selected)

Down and Out in Paris and London, 1933 (autobiography); *Burmese Days,* 1934 (novel); *A Clergyman's Daughter,* 1935 (novel); *Keep the Aspidistra Flying,* 1936 (novel); *The Road to Wigan Pier,* 1937 (documentary); *Homage to Catalonia,* 1938 (documentary); *Coming Up for Air,* 1939 (novel); *Inside the Whale,* 1940 (criticism); *Animal Farm,* 1945 (novel); *Dickens, Dali, and Others,* 1946 (criticism); *Nineteen Eighty-Four,* 1949 (novel); *The Collected Essays, Journalism and Letters of George Orwell,* 1968.

Overview of Biographical Sources

Because Orwell requested that no biographies be written about him, no book-length biographies appeared for twenty years after his death. Several friends and colleagues did, however, write critical studies that included substantial biographical accounts. Two of these early books express views of Orwell no longer current: Lawrence Brander's *George Orwell* (London: Longmans and Green, 1954) and Christopher Hollis' *A Study of George Orwell: The Man and His Works* (London: Hollis and Carter, 1956). Richard Rees, Orwell's friend and first literary executor, wrote one of the more reliable and insightful early biographical and critical studies: *George Orwell: Fugitive from the Camp of Victory* (Carbondale: Southern Illinois University Press, 1961). Rees views Orwell as heroic, his actions motivated by an exaggerated sense of honor. While Rees recognizes that the writer and his work are closely interrelated, Rees avoids the pitfall of other early Orwell biographers who confused his characters with the author.

Evaluation of Selected Biographies

Buddicom, Jacintha, *Eric and Us: A Remembrance of George Orwell.* London: Leslie Frewin, 1974. A friend of Orwell's since childhood, Buddicom recreates his life from 1914 to 1922. Her biography is pleasurable reading since she emphasizes the positive aspects of Orwell's early years. Her account of the young Orwell's reading tastes and his aspiration to be a writer are interesting and informative.

Crick, Bernard, *George Orwell.* Boston: Little, Brown, 1980. This is the first complete biography of Orwell, the first whose author had access to nearly all of Orwell's writing, published and unpublished. Crick eschews psychological analysis, focusing instead on the external Orwell. Crick acknowledges that this approach creates a distance between himself as biographer and his subject. The result, however, is an objective and judicious study of Orwell's life and writing. Footnotes correct minor inaccuracies in earlier biographies, such as Stansky and Abrahams'. Crick also argues convincingly that Orwell exaggerated the harshness of life at St. Cyprian's. The school nurtured Orwell's hostility toward British imperialism but not his fear of totalitarianism as expressed in *Nineteen Eighty-Four.* Crick analyzes Orwell's gradual and inconsistent maturation as a writer. Crick focuses on the coherence of the novels and non-fiction, and the relationship between Orwell's life and writings. Crick is not blind to the limitations of Orwell as a writer and a political thinker, but the reader is left with a clear portrait of a man who genuinely sought to live by his principles. The lucid, colloquial style of Crick's biography would have pleased its subject.

Stansky, Peter and William Abrahams, *The Unknown Orwell.* New York: Alfred A. Knopf, 1972. This biography spans the first twenty years of Orwell's life, up to his publication of *Down and Out in Paris and London.* The biography's thesis is that Orwell, in adopting a pseudonym, changed his entire personality, both as a writer and as an individual. The chapters on Orwell's childhood through his years at Eton provide richly detailed discussions of the forces that shaped his character. The account of his Burma years is well documented by interviews and letters.

———, *Orwell: The Transformation.* New York: Alfred A. Knopf, 1980. A sequel to *The Unknown Orwell,* this volume traces his development as a writer and a socialist from 1933 to 1936. Especially informative are the detailed analyses of the influences that contributed to the evolution of George Orwell: his friends, his wife Eileen O'Shaughnessy, and the Spanish Civil War. His war experience is viewed as the catalyst needed to transform Blair into Orwell. The authors offer insights into Orwell's daily life as well as his struggle to write and be published. This biography is regarded as generally reliable, but lacking a clear explanation of Orwell's transformation.

Woodcock, George, *The Crystal Spirit: A Study of George Orwell.* Boston: Little, Brown, 1966. This is generally considered the best biographical and critical study by a friend of Orwell. Woodcock examines four sides of Orwell: his life, as Woodcock remembers it; themes in Orwell's writing; his contradictory but consistent ideas; his penetrating criticism and crystalline prose style. Woodcock's study is illuminating.

Autobiographical Sources

Orwell's four books that recount his own experiences have been classified variously as dramatic autobiography, documentary, and memoir, because each unites elements of fact and fiction. The first such work published by Orwell is *Down and Out in Paris and London,* a vivid recreation of his months living in the slums of both European cities. The book is important as a dramatic record of Orwell's first attempt to break out of his middle class prejudices. He claimed that all the episodes recorded actually happened to him, though not in the order presented. He also said that he changed individual characters into representative types.

The Road to Wigan Pier records Orwell's second attempt to submerge himself in lower class life. The first half of this book presents Orwell's experiences among the working class, especially the miners, in Lancashire and Yorkshire, in Northern England. These experiences cause him, in the second half of the book, to examine his middle class prejudices and to articulate his ideas about socialism. Like *Down and Out in Paris and London, The Road to Wigan Pier* can be enjoyed for its graphic descriptions and clear journalistic style.

Orwell's fictionalized documentary *Homage to Catalonia* narrates his experiences in the Spanish Civil War. The book reveals the origins of Orwell's disillusionment with the Communist party and his distrust of political journalism. *Homage to Catalonia* also describes Orwell's experience of comradeship among militia men, which strengthened his belief in socialism and his faith in the common man.

"Such, Such Were the Joys" is an autobiographical essay published posthumously. Once again Orwell blends fact and fiction, here to focus on his snobbish, oppressive private school. Although Orwell's picture of St. Cyprian's is now regarded as exaggerated, the essay is illuminating in showing Orwell's early sense of alienation from England's middle class.

Overview of Critical Sources

Although *Animal Farm* and *Nineteen Eighty-Four* have received the most critical attention, studies of the complete fiction and of Orwell's entire output are numerous. His books, essays, and journalism are analyzed from various perspectives: psychological, political, sociological, historical, and literary. Critics tend to emphasize the relationship between his life and work, or between his politics and his aesthetics.

Evaluation of Selected Criticism

Atkins, John, *George Orwell: A Literary Study.* London: Calder, 1954; New York: Frederick Ungar, as, *A Literary and Biographical Study,* 1971. A friend and colleague of Orwell, Atkins provides an insightful study of both the man and his works. After a substantial chapter on biography, Atkins focuses on subjects that concerned Orwell: imperialism, poverty, morality, freedom, class, language, and socialism. Atkins argues convincingly that a key word in comprehending Orwell is "decency."

Hammond, J. R. *A George Orwell Companion.* New York: St. Martin's Press, 1982. After a brief biography and an overview of Orwell's literary achievement, Hammond provides an Orwell Dictionary which briefly describes the poems, books, and essays. The reviews are simply listed, but the number and breadth of topics is impressive. Detailed discussions of the novels and documentaries follow. The last chapter is a key to significant characters and locations in Orwell's work. An appendix lists film versions of the novels.

Kubal, David, *Outside the Whale: George Orwell's Art and Politics.* Notre Dame, IN: University of Notre Dame Press, 1972. Part One of Kubal's study explores Orwell's quest for a political myth after his disillusionment with romantic liberalism and communistic socialism. Part Two focuses on Orwell's goal of combining fiction and polemic, art and politics.

Lee, Robert A. *Orwell's Fiction.* Notre Dame, IN: University of Notre Dame Press, 1969. This is the first book devoted solely to textual criticism of the novels, omitting the non-fiction except for *Homage to Catalonia.* Lee focuses on the Spanish Civil War as the turning point in Orwell's development from a minor to a major novelist, a novelist who deserves to be ranked alongside E. M. Forster.

Steinhoff, William, *George Orwell and the Origins of* 1984. Ann Arbor: University of Michigan Press, 1975. Steinhoff's thesis is that *Nineteen Eighty-Four* represents the culmination of the experiences and reading of a lifetime. Therefore Steinhoff discusses the literary forerunners of *Nineteen Eighty-Four* and explores Orwell's other novels for themes and attitudes that are repeated in *Nineteen Eight-Four.* The last third of the book focuses on the atmosphere, themes, and significance of the novel. The book is informative both on background and on the novel itself.

Zwerdling, Alex, *Orwell and the Left.* New Haven: Yale University Press, 1974. Zwerdling argues that Orwell's criticism of socialism was always from within, since he never abandoned his commitment to socialism. This book provides an excellent discussion of Orwell's criticism of socialism, Marxism, and the Labor Party. Zwerdling also analyzes Orwell's experiments in writing, viewing them as his quest for a form that would express his political ideas. Rejecting documentary and realistic fiction as inadequate, Orwell found didactic fantasy the best vehicle in his last two novels.

Other Sources

Bal, Sant Singh, *George Orwell: The Ethical Imagination.* New Delhi: Arnold-Heinemann, 1981. A study of Orwell's Puritan imagination as the force shaping his aesthetics.

Bolton, W. F. *The Language of 1984: Orwell's English and Ours.* Knoxville: University of Tennessee Press, 1984. A study of Orwell's principles of prose style and language, and his views on technology.

Howe, Irving, ed. *1984 Revisited: Totalitarianism in Our Century.* New York: Harper & Row, 1983. A collection of essays examining the political implications of *Nineteen Eighty-Four.*

Jensen, Ejner J., ed. *The Future of Nineteen Eighty-Four.* Ann Arbor: University of Michigan Press, 1984. A collection of essays that illuminate the novel from various perspectives: feminist, literary, historical, psychological, sociological, and political.

Meyers, Jeffrey, *A Reader's Guide to George Orwell.* London: Thames and Hudson, 1975. A helpful chronological guide to Orwell's works and ideas.

Patai, Daphne, *The Orwell Mystique: a Study in Male Ideology.* Amherst: University of Massachusetts Press, 1984. A feminist reassessment of Orwell's writing that focuses on his treatment of misogyny, male power, and traditional gender roles.

Smyer, Richard L. *Primal Dream and Primal Curse.* Columbia: University of Missouri Press, 1979. The first book-length psychological study of Orwell's fiction, in particular, the surrealistic, grotesque, and sensational elements.

Selected Dictionaries and Encyclopedias

British Writers, Charles Scribner's Sons, 1984. A survey of the life and concise analyses of the works.

Dictionary of Literary Biography, Gale Research, 1983. A clear narrative of Orwell's life and brief critical comments on his writings.

Margaret K. Schramm
Hartwick College

WILFRED OWEN
1893–1918

Author's Chronology

Born March 18, 1893, at Oswestry, Shropshire, England; *1900* enters Birkenhead Institute; *1907* attends Shrewsbury Technical School; *1911* matriculates at London University but is unable to attend classes; goes to Dunsden, Oxfordshire, as the vicar's lay assistant; *1913* becomes a Berlitz tutor in English at Bordeaux; *1914* leaves the Berlitz school to become a private tutor in Bordeaux; meets Laurent Tailhade, an elderly French symbolist poet; *1915* returns to England; joins the Artist's Rifles; *1916* is commissioned in the Manchester Regiment; sails for France and active duty; *1917* participates in heavy fighting; is sent home to be treated for shell shock; at Craiglockhart War Hospital meets Siegfried Sassoon; publishes his first poem; *1918* returns to active service; receives the Military Cross; is killed in action November 4 at the Sambre Canal near Ors, France; is buried at Ors.

Author's Bibliography

"Song of Songs," 1917 (poem) in *The Hydra* (magazine edited by Owen); "Miners," 1918 (poem); "Futility," 1918 (poem); "Hospital Barge at Cérisy," 1918 (poem)—the only works by Owen published in his lifetime; *The Collected Poems of Wilfred Owen*, ed. C. Day Lewis, 1963; *Wilfred Owen: Collected Letters*, ed. Harold Owen and John Bell, 1967.

Overview of Biographical Sources

Although no book-length biographies of Owen were to appear for many years after his death, a very brief sketch of the poet's life was published in 1920, just two years after the war, when Sassoon, a fellow war poet and close friend, wrote an introduction to his edition of the *Poems of Wilfred Owen* (London: Chatto and Windus, 1920). Another war poet, Edmund Blunden, published a much longer memoir of Owen in *The Poems of Wilfred Owen* (London: Chatto and Windus, 1931); based largely on letters from Owen to his mother, Blunden's account was the best available for several decades, and it was reprinted in the edition of Owen's verse prepared by Lewis (London: Chatto and Windus, 1963). Memoirs of the entire Owen family began to appear that same year, and in 1974 a full-length biography of Owen finally appeared. Accounts of Owen's life have all been written by open worshippers, and some of the accounts are slightly suspect. However, Owen wrote a great many letters, most faithfully kept by family and friends, and these serve as the basis of many elements in the life story.

Evaluation of Selected Biographies

Owen, Harold, *Journey from Obscurity: Wilfred Owen 1893–1918. Memoirs of the Owen Family*. 3 vols. London: Oxford University Press, 1963–1965. Harold

Owen, the poet's brother, exhibits a good memory for detail as he traces the joys and sorrows of the Owen family over a period of about twenty years, ending shortly after World War I. The relationship of the two brothers—love and sibling rivalry mixed—is a significant addition to biographical knowledge of the poet; and the information on the poet's dissatisfaction with theology is valuable. Unfortunately, the subtitle misleads: the three volumes are not concerned with the life of the poet nearly as much as with the chronicle of the family and particularly of Harold. In searching for information about the poet, the reader will frequently be disappointed. Also, readers may question the memory of someone writing of events and emotions fifty years or more after the occurrence; particularly suspect would be the writer's strange account of a psychic experience aboard his cruiser shortly after Armistice Day—an incident in which he found his brother's ghost waiting for him when he walked into his cabin.

Stallworthy, John, *Wilfred Owen*. London: Chatto and Windus, 1974. Stallworthy's account differs from that of Harold Owen, his close friend, in the attention given to the war years, during which both brothers were on active duty and had few actual meetings with each other. Different, too, is the attention given to the poems; Stallworthy connects many of the poems to specific events of the war years. Several photos of manuscript versions of the poem appear in the volume, and it is possible to trace Owen's revisions of certain poems through several stages.

Autobiographical Sources

Many of Owen's poems, particularly the war poems, are the records of intense personal experiences. Owen was also a prolific writer of letters, most of them to his mother, Susan, who saved every one of them. Both the poems and the letters present vivid accounts of the slaughter in France in 1917–1918, fully indicating Owen's disillusionment. They also present a picture of an interesting human being: a man with intelligence, humor, sensitivity, immense concern for others, and a great desire to be a poet.

Overview of Critical Sources

Appreciation of Owen's war poems began early. He has been praised for the truth of his grim pictures of trench warfare, and for the impersonal quality of these poems, in which he never asks pity for himself, but rather always shows the misery of others. He has been lauded, also, for the technical decision to write many of his war poems in pararhyme, the use of which is considered a stroke of genius by critics and, indeed, by other war poets, who see the incompleteness of the rhyme ("killed" with "cold," for example) as emblematic of the sense of loss, futility, and failure occurring in war. Attempts to fix the chronology of the poems have also been a significant element in Owen scholarship; the chronology seems now to have been determined about as well as it can be. Recent criticism has elevated Owen to a very high position in twentieth-century English verse: he is called the best of the War Poets, a founder of English modernism, an important influence on the early W. H. Auden, Stephen Spender, and others, as well as a poet whose untimely death—along with the deaths of Isaac Rosenberg and Edward Thomas—left English poetry undefended and vulnerable to its unhealthy Americanization by T. S. Eliot and Ezra Pound.

Evaluation of Selected Criticism

Bäckman, Sven, *Tradition Transformed.* Lund: CWK Gleerup, 1979. Bäckman analyzes the directions taken by English verse since World War I. In the first of two major sections of his book, Backmän studies Owen in connection with nineteenth-century poetic traditions and maintains that Owen either rejected or transformed many of these. The second major section discusses Owen's knowledge of music and musical language, analyzing the poet's use of half-rhyme, pararhyme, and other sound effects in his verse.

White, Gertrude M. *Wilfred Owen.* New York: Twayne, 1969. White's overview of Owen's life and work echoes much that had been stated in the previous few decades of Owen criticism but offers concise critical perceptions in support of her views. White analyzes the poems written before Owens became a soldier, concludes that they are weak imitations of much nineteenth-century verse and therefore disagrees with J. Loiseau's "A Reading of Wilfred Owens' Poems," *English Studies* XXI (June 1939), 97–108, which argues that the war tragically diverted the true greatness of Owen's artistry. Of special interest to students, Chapter V traces the growth of Owen's poetic reputation; the Selective Bibliography also will aid the student greatly.

Other Sources

Fairchild, H. N. "Toward Hysteria," *Religious Trends in English Poetry, 1880–1920.* Vol. V. New York: Columbia University Press, 1962. Good analysis of the views of Owen and other war poets toward Christianity.

Hibberd, Dominic, *Wilfred Owen: Writers and Their Work,* 246. London: Longman Group Limited, 1975. Discussion of Owen's career with the focus on the *annus mirabilis* following his first meeting with Sassoon; by one of the major researchers on Owen's works.

Masson, David J. "Wilfred Owen's Free Phonetic Patterns: Their Style and Function," *Journal of Aesthetics and Art Criticism,* XIII (March 1955), 360–369. Analysis of Owen's technical qualitites: alliteration, assonance, and varied rhymes.

Walsh, T. J. comp., *A Tribute to Wilfred Owen.* Birkenhead: Birkenhead Institute, 1964. Collection containing a number of brief essays on Owen's verse as well as several reminiscences and tributes by people who knew him, all commemorating the opening of the Wilfred Owen Memorial Library in Birkenhead.

Welland, D. S. R. *Wilfred Owen: A Critical Study.* London: Chatto and Windus, 1960. The initial monograph on Owen and still a very substantial study, repeating much of Welland's earlier scholarship on Owen's manuscripts and on the sources of his poetic technique.

Selected Dictionaries and Encyclopedias

Critical Survey of Poetry, Salem Press, 1982. Brief biography, statement of the poet's achievements (including a recognition of his mastery of the form of the sonnets and the mood of the elegy), and analysis of a few major poems.

A Library of Literary Criticism: Modern British Literature, Vol. II, Frederick Ungar, 1966. Seven excerpts from criticism of Owen dating from 1921 to 1964; Vol. IV, 1975, three more excerpts from the period 1964 to 1969.

Howard L. Ford
North Texas State University

WALTER PATER
1839–1894

Author's Chronology

Born August 4, 1839, London, England; *1853* enters King's School, Canterbury; *1858* enters Queen's College, Oxford (B.A., *1862*); *1864* gains non-clerical fellowship, Brasenose College; *1865* receives Oxford M.A.; *1873* publishes epoch-making collection of essays, *Studies in the History of the Renaissance; 1885* publishes first novel, *Marius the Epicurean: His Sensations and Ideas; 1886* moves, with his two sisters, to London while remaining fellow of Brasenose; *1887* publishes *Imaginary Portraits,* four short romances; *1889* publishes *Appreciations: With an Essay on Style; 1893* moves household back to Oxford from London; *1894* dies at Oxford, buried in the cemetery of St. Giles.

Author's Bibliography (selected)

Studies in the History of the Renaissance, 1873 (essays); *Marius the Epicurean: His Sensations and Ideas,* 1885 (novel); *Imaginary Portraits,* 1887 (fiction); *Appreciations: With an Essay on Style,* 1889 (essays); *Plato and Platonism: A Series of Lectures,* 1893; *Greek Studies: A Series of Essays,* 1895; *Miscellaneous Studies: A Series of Essays,* 1895; *Essays from the "Guardian,"* 1896; *Gaston de Latour: An Unfinished Romance,* 1896.

Overview of Biographical Sources

Walter Pater's diffidence, his reluctance to become a public figure, and the concerted efforts of his sisters, Hester and Clara, to honor after his death the privacy he had sought in life account for the lack of an authorized biography and the dearth of biographical information about him. Several of Pater's friends and self-styled disciples wrote reminiscences of him in 1894 and the years immediately following his death, among them Edmund Gosse, Lionel Johnson, George Moore, William Sharp, and Arthur Symons. The first biography, Arthur C. Benson's *Walter Pater* (London and New York: Macmillan, 1906), is a sensitive and partisan but unscholarly and limited view of Pater's life. Thomas Wright's *The Life of Walter Pater* (London: Everett, 1907) is an unauthorized, highly unreliable, flawed work that for seventy years remained the only full biographical treatment of Pater in English. Germain d'Hangest focuses on Pater's work in relation to his life and included some new biographical material in *Walter Pater: l'homme et l'oeuvre* (1961). Gerald C. Monsman's *Walter Pater* (1977) is an accurate, readable, biographical and critical account that is an excellent introduction to Pater and his work. Michael Levey, in *The Case of Walter Pater* (1978), presents a popular biography that relies on copious, if exaggerated, use of Pater's fiction as a key to his views, philosophy, and life. Gerald Monsman's *Walter Pater's Art of Autobiography* (1980) breaks new ground by assessing Pater's *oeuvre* as mirroring the artist's self-conscious creation of a separate order of reality. The mix of biography with an examination of Pater's fiction and essays as autobiographical fables of identity makes Monsman's a highly interesting, subtle, and well-wrought rendering of his subject.

Evaluation of Selected Biographies

d'Hangest, Germain, *Walter Pater: l'homme el l'oeuvre.* 2 vols. Paris: Didier, 1961. This is the first study to explore Pater's work in relation to his life and to emphasize the man behind the fiction, essays, and lectures. Volume I deals with Pater's childhood, student days, and maturity as the author of *The Renaissance* and *Marius the Epicurean.* Volume II treats of Pater's later life and work (1885–1894) and contains an analysis of Pater's revision of his work. This study, the first truly complete scholarly study of Pater's life and work, remains an invaluable resource to scholars and students of Pater and his times.

Levey, Michael, *The Case of Walter Pater.* London: Thames and Hudson, 1978. Levey's strengths lie in providing a more detailed version of Pater's family and immediate ancestry than has any other writer and revealing new information about the young Pater and his friends at Canterbury and Oxford. The early chapters (1–7) offer new material, or material newly re-shaped, and are more valuable than the remaining chapters on Pater's life after 1873. The work is flawed by an over-identification of Pater with his fictional characters and by undocumented, unverifiable speculative elements.

Monsman, Gerald C. *Walter Pater.* Boston: Twayne, 1977. In this broadly appealing biographical/critical study of Pater, Monsman adds to the biographical record in English several fruits of d'Hangest's research at Oxford and corrects some of Thomas Wright's more serious flaws that led to several popular misconceptions about Pater. Monsman's accuracy of information is greatly helped by access to *Letters of Walter Pater,* ed. Lawrence Evans (Oxford: Oxford University Press, 1970).

―――. *Walter Pater's Art of Autobiography.* New Haven and London: Yale University Press, 1980. Advancing beyond his earlier studies, Monsman applies the critical methodology of deconstruction to Pater's fiction and essays. He asserts that Pater underwent a creative crisis in 1887–1888 and explores the ramifications of that crisis in the self-referential frames of Pater's work.

Autobiographical Sources

Pater's fictions have been generally taken to be autobiographical, especially "The Child in the House" (1878) and *Marius the Epicurean.* Both Michael Levey and Gerald Monsman have explored these works in great detail; Monsman has extended his admittedly Freudian analysis to include Pater's *Imaginary Portraits* and *Gaston de Latour.* Pater's fictional characters, temporally and spatially distanced from their creator, contend with the very issues of identity and self-definition in a world of conflicting philosophical, artistic, religious, and social claims Pater and his generation contended with.

The autobiographical concerns that suffuse Pater's non-fictional works have received copious attention, especially his choice of topics in the continental Renaissance and the classical world, and the philosophy of "art for art's sake" he made explicit in the "Conclusion" to *The Renaissance.* Suppressed in a second edition and modified in a third, this "Conclusion" suggested many thoughts Pater elaborated in *Marius the Epicurean.*

The only explicitly autobiographical materials Pater left behind are his letters, nearly three hundred of which Lawrence Evans edited and published in *Letters of Walter Pater* (Oxford: Oxford University Press, 1970). Several other letters have since been found and some have been published by George P. Landow, Peter J. Vernon, and John J. Conlon.

Overview of Critical Sources

Walter Pater's wide-ranging interests in and writing about the Renaissance, the classical world, and the literature of his own age have been the subject of an increasingly large body of criticism in the ninety years since his death. In the past twenty-five years Pater's place as a major figure in the late-Victorian age has received considerable attention; and the many recent essays and books on him have rehabilitated his literary reputation which had declined early in this century.

Evaluation of Selected Criticism

DeLaura, David J. *Hebrew and Hellene in Victorian England: Newman, Arnold, and Pater.* Austin: University of Texas Press, 1969. DeLaura presents an extended analysis of Pater's adaptation of received philosophical and religious thought to the needs of his own era by transforming them into the fabric of aestheticism.

Fletcher, Iain, *Walter Pater.* London: Longmans, Green, 1959. Fletcher's incisive and influential pamphlet remains a good introduction to Pater and his works and helped set the tone of most contemporary Pater studies.

Monsman, Gerald C. *Pater's Portraits: Mythic Pattern in the Fiction of Walter Pater.* Baltimore: Johns Hopkins University Press, 1967. In one of the first and best detailed examinations of Pater's fiction Monsman discusses Pater's treatment of the mythic brothers, Apollo and Dionysius, in *The Renaissance* and the fictive portraits he subsequently wrote.

————. *Walter Pater.* Boston: Twayne, 1977. This brief study of Pater's "life and works" is useful for undergraduates, graduate students, and Victorianists alike. Using a standard chronological approach to Pater's work Monsman combines biography with deft literary criticism.

————. *Walter Pater's Art of Autobiography*. New Haven and London: Yale University Press, 1980. Monsman applies the criticism of deconstruction to Pater's fiction and examines it from the perspectives of artistic self-consciousness and veiled autobiography.

Other Sources

Conlon, John J. *Walter Pater and the French Tradition*. Lewisburg: Bucknell University Press, 1982. A study of French influences on Pater's work and his role as interpreter of French Romantic literature, history and criticism.

Court, Franklin, ed. *Walter Pater: An Annotated Bibliography of Writings about Him*. DeKalb: Northern Illinois University Press, 1979. Court and the contributors list and annotate 1168 works on Pater published between 1871 and 1973.

Dale, Peter A. *The Victorian Critic and the Idea of History: Carlyle, Arnold and Pater*. Cambridge: Harvard University Press, 1977. Dale emphasizes the positivist influence on Pater's historicism.

Dodd, Philip, ed. *Walter Pater: An Imaginative Sense of Fact*. London: Frank Cass, 1981. A collection of essays on most aspects of modern Pater studies including a survey of works published 1970–1980.

Inman, Billie Andrew, *Walter Pater's Reading: A Bibliography of His Library Borrowings and Literary References, 1858–1873*. New York and London: Garland Publishing, 1981. More than a bibliography, this is a history of Pater's intellectual development.

Wright, Samuel, *A Bibliography of the Writing of Walter H. Pater*. New York and London: Garland Publishing, 1975. The most comprehensive and detailed primary bibliography of Pater's work.

Selected Dictionaries and Encyclopedias

Critical Survey of Long Fiction, Salem Press, 1983. Concise overview of Pater's life and discussion of his fiction.

Dictionary of National Biography, Oxford University Press, 1950. Brief biography and list of works.

John J. Conlon
University of Massachusetts at Boston

COVENTRY PATMORE
1823–1896

Author's Chronology

Born July 23, 1823, Woodford Green, Essex, England; *1839–1840* studies in Paris, where he falls in love with Miss Gore; *1844* publishes first collection of poetry, *Poems,* at his father's urging; *1846* start of friendship with Tennyson; receives British Museum appointment through Monckton Milnes; *1847–1862* marries Emily Augusta "The Angel" Andrews; *1849–1853* associates with the Pre-Raphaelite Brotherhood; *1864* travels to Italy; converts to Roman Catholicism; break with Tennyson; *1864–1880* marries second wife, Marianne (Mary) Caroline Byles, after Emily's death; *1881–1896* marries third wife, Harriet Robson, after Marianne's death; *1882* daughter, Emily Honoria (Sister Mary Christina, SHCJ), dies; ceases to write poetry, turning exclusively to prose; *1892–1895* has a passionate "literary" friendship with Alice Meynell; dies November 26, 1896, at Lymington, Hampshire, England.

Author's Bibliography (selected)

Tamerton Church-Tower and Other Poems, 1854; *The Angel in the House,* 1858 (poem); *The Victories of Love,* 1863 (poem); *Amelia and Other Poems,* 1878; *The Unknown Eros, I–XLVI,* 1878 (poems); *Principle in Art,* 1889 (prose); *Religio Poetae,* 1883 (prose); *The Rod, The Root, and The Flower,* 1895 (prose); *Poems of Coventry Patmore,* 1949 (standard edition).

Overview of Biographical Sources

The biographies on Coventry Patmore were written, by and large, by friends and admirers; consequently, their point of view is partisan. The official, and the standard, biography of Patmore, upon which all of the others largely rely upon, is Basil Champneys' *Memoirs and Correspondence of Coventry Patmore* (1900). The other biographies are comparatively brief. Edmund Gosse's *Coventry Patmore* (New York: Charles Scribner's Sons, 1905) is a critical biography that is sketchy as biography and deficient as criticism. Derek Patmore's *The Life and Times of Coventry Patmore* (London: Constable, 1949) is a revised version of his earlier *Portrait of My Family* (London: Cassell, 1935). These popular biographies by Patmore's great-grandson essentially are guided tours through the Patmore family album. E. J. Oliver's *Coventry Patmore* (New York: Sheed and Ward, 1956) is a short, insightful critical biography for the general reader.

Evaluation of Selected Biographies

Champneys, Basil, *Memoirs and Correspondence of Coventry Patmore.* 2 vols. London: George Bell and Sons, 1900. Champneys, Patmore's friend and literary executor, was commissioned to write the memoir by Patmore's widow.

Memoirs and Correspondence is a solid piece of old-style biography, often overly elaborate but balanced and fair in its judgments. Champneys' approach is thematic rather than chronological. The first volume contains the actual biography of Patmore. The biography deals very thoroughly with Patmore's relationships with women, with his children, and with his friends. The second volume contains Champneys' intellectual portrait of Patmore, Patmore's own "Religious Autobiography," a selection of his correspondence with his family and his friends, and a selection of his unpublished prose fragments. This extremely full collection of primary materials, coupled with the detailed biography, makes Champneys' work the prime biographical source for the student of Patmore.

Weining, SHCJ, Sister Mary Anthony, *Coventry Patmore.* Boston: Twayne, 1981. Like other biographers of Patmore, Sister Mary relies heavily upon Champneys in her critical biography. Unlike her predecessors, however, she blends a perceptive appraisal of the poetry with her account of the life. In fact, her examination of the poetry quite eclipses that of the life. As a biography, her study is general, sketchy in places, and inaccurate on a few points. Her main focus is upon Patmore's relationships with women and with their influence upon his thought. Her view of Patmore is sympathetic but not biased. Sister Mary Anthony Weining's critical biography ought to be treated as a supplement to that of Champneys.

Autobiographical Sources

Although many of Patmore's poems contain elements of autobiography, the only real source of autobiography is the correspondence and the "Religious Autobiography" contained in the second volume of Champneys' *Memoirs and Correspondence of Coventry Patmore.*

Overview of Critical Sources

Patmore rose to fame then sunk into disfame on the wings of *The Angel in the House.* Consequently, much of the criticism focuses upon that poem. The few book-length critical studies of the entire *oeuvre* are early and of an appreciative rather than an analytic nature. At least one half of Osbert Burdett's *The Idea of Coventry Patmore* (London: Oxford University Press, 1921) is devoted to an appreciation of *The Angel In the House,* and the whole reads like a vindication of Patmore's poetry. Frederick Page's *Patmore. A Study In Poetry* (London: Oxford University Press, 1933), although in many ways surpassed by more recent studies, is still of some value to a serious study of the poetry.

Evaluation of Selected Criticism

Reid, J. C. *The Mind and Art of Coventry Patmore.* London: Routlege and Kegan Paul, 1957. Reid's study of the poetry and prose grows out of his examination of the nature of Patmore's thought. At least half of Reid's study is devoted to a close examination of the personal and the literary influences that have shaped Patmore's poetic vision. Reid consistently draws connections between the influence and the poetry and prose. Reid's critical approach, that of solid textual analysis, sheds new light on Patmore and on his poetry.

Other Sources

Abbott, Claude Colleer, *Further Letters of Gerard Manely Hopkins.* 2nd. ed. London: Oxford University Press, 1956. Contains the Patmore-Hopkins correspondence.

Evans, Ifor, *English Poetry in the Later Nineteenth Century.* London: Methuen, 1933; rpt. New York: Barnes and Noble, 1966. Contains a chapter on Patmore.

Meynell, Viola, *Alice Meynell: A Memoir.* London: Burns, Oates, and Washbourne, 1929. Contains a chapter on Alice Meynell's friendship with Patmore.

Selected Dictionaries and Encyclopedias

Dictionary of National Biography, Oxford University Press, 1917; rpt. 1963–1964. A brief biography of Patmore.

Critical Survey of Poetry, Salem Press, 1983. A concise overview of Patmore's life, and a brief consideration of his major poems.

Stella Maloney
York University, Ontario

THE *PEARL*-POET (*GAWAIN*-POET)
fl. 1380–1400

Author's Chronology

The author, or authors, responsible for the four untitled alliterative poems found in a single manuscript in the Cotton Collection of the British Museum has never been convincingly identified. None of the four poems is known in any other manuscript and no contemporary references to them survive. Critics who are convinced that more than one poet was involved with the writing of the four poems continue to amass evidence for their side of the argument. The question of single or multiple authorship is compounded by the ascription to the *Pearl*-Poet of another alliterative poem, *St. Erkenwald,* by scholars who have edited or translated it and one or more of the poems in the *Pearl*-MS. These bibliographical problems will probably continue to receive attention despite the reasonableness of A. C. Spearing's conclusion (in *The "Gawain-Poet",* Cambridge: Cambridge University Press, 1970) that it is more likely for one great poet to have lived in a small dialect area in the late fourteenth century than for two or three or four of such poets to have done so. The limits of the dates of the writing of the four alliterative poems, *Pearl, Cleanness, Patience,* and *Sir Gawain and the Green Knight,* in the British Museum manuscript Cotton Nero A.x. are tentatively set at c. 1360–1395 by E. V. Gordon in his edition of *Pearl,* London, Oxford University Press; 1953. The most authoritative evidence about the poet has come through the identification of the location of the dialect by Angus McIntosh in "A New Approach to Middle English Dialectology," *English Studies* XLIV (1963), 1–11, as a small area, either in S.E. Cheshire or just over the border in N.E. Staffordshire.

Overview of Critical Sources

In the past ten years, the traditional assumption that the fourteenth century alliterative poets were an offshoot of the rise of English nationalism based on baronial discontent in the northwest midlands against the corrupt and Frenchified court in London has been scrutinized and reappraised by a couple of scholars. In "The Origins of the Alliterative Revival," in *The Alliterative Tradition in the Fourteenth Century,* edited by B. Levy and P. Szarmach, (Kent, OH: Kent State University Press, 1981) Derek Pearsall decries the standard explanation as dynamic, evolutionary, and xenophobic, a conception of the development of poetry as a battle between French and English elements. Elizabeth Salter also challenges the historical basis of the traditional assumption, showing in (*Fourteenth Century Alliterative Poetry.* London: Oxford University Press, 1983) that such a political movement in the northwest simply did not exist. W. A. Davenport in *The Art of the "Gawain"-Poet* (London: Athlone, 1978) gives detailed analyses of all four poems, argues that the poet's art is one of antithesis and conflict, and suggests that the order of the poems in the manuscript is the order of their composition. Probably the most significant work on all four poems is A. C. Spearing's *The "Gawain"-Poet: A Critical Study* (Cambridge: Cambridge University Press, 1970), which includes detailed discussions of all four poems, an account of the poet's cultural milieu, the alliterative tradition, and the recurring pattern of confrontation between man and a superhuman power.

Much more critical attention has been given to *Sir Gawain and the Green Knight* than to the other three poems together. The poem has variously been thought of as an historical allegory, a vegetation or solar myth, a satire on romances, an attack on the degradation of Arthur and his court, or an expression of the poet's ambiguous response to the oppositions of courtly and chivalric values. There has been an equally wild disagreement about the characters in the poem; Bercilak, for example, has been taken as a devil, a friendly guide, a fertility deity, and even the Word of God. Early work on the poem studied the source and analogues and influence of the Irish myths, the best still being George Kittredge's *A Study of "Sir Gawain and the Green Knight"* (Cambridge: Harvard University Press, 1916), in which he argues for a non-surviving French source in which the two motifs, the Temptation and the Challenge, were fused. R. F. Dossetor in *"Sir Gawain and the Green Knight": The Myth of an Intuitive* (London: Guild of Pastoral Psychology, 1942) maintains that Gawain's progress can be seen as one of the Jungian classifications. Henry Savage's recognition of the parallels between the hunting and bedroom scenes in "The Significance of the Hunting Scenes in 'Sir Gawain' " (in *Journal of English and Germanic Philology* 27, 1928, 1–15), has often been modified and restated, for it marked the early demonstration of the poet's care for structure, which, along with the number symbolism suggested by the description of Gawain's shield, has led several structuralist critics to write on *Gawain,* such as A. Kent Hieatt in *"Sir Gawain: Pentangle, Luf-Lace, Numerical Structure"* (*Papers on Language and Literature* 4, 1968, 339–359). The moral aspect of the poem has continued to receive attention, especially the identification of Gawain's fault and the validity of his confession. Hans Schnyder gives an exegetical reading in *"Sir Gawain and the Green Knight": An Essay in Interpretation* (Bern: Francke, 1961), in which he argues that Gawain's arrival at the castle is his discovery of Jerusalem within himself. Bernard Levy sees Gawain's adventures as an imitation of Christ in "Gawain's Spiritual Journey: Imitatio Christi *in Sir Gawain and the Green Knight,"* (*Annuale Medievale* 6, 1965, 65–106).

Two books devote considerable space to *Pearl:* James Wimsatt's *Allegory and Mirror* (New York: Pegasus, 1970) differentiates between the allegorical, or personification allegory, and the mirror. He concludes that the Pearl maiden goes beyond Boethius's Lady Philosophy in that she is not symbolic of the rational but of the suprarational. In *The Visionary Landscape* (London: Arnold, 1971) Paul Piehler discusses patterns of transformation, and relates the Pearl maiden to the Jungian archetype of the child. Structuralists have celebrated the *Pearl's* numerical circularity with almost as much joy as that of the *Divine Comedy*. Maren-Sofie Røstvig, in "Numerical Composition in *Pearl:* A Theory" (*English Studies* 48, 1967, 326–332), shows the circular structure, in that a time-bound man of the first part returns to God in the second part. Cary Nelson, in *The Incarnate Word: Literature as Verbal Space* (Urbana: University of Illinois Press, 1973) emphasizes the close relationship between form and meaning, and identifies images of circularity—pearls, seeds, grapes, cycles of growth, even water and light images—which dominate the meaning.

The most important work on purity is Charlotte Morse's *The Pattern of Judgment in the "Queste" and "Cleanness"* (Columbia and London: University of Missouri Press, 1978), in which the paradigm of the vessel as an image of man is central to the poem. Belshazzar's sacrilege is comparable to sexual uncleanness, and the three major narratives adhere to the model established by the parable of the wedding feast.

The main critical issue of *Patience* is whether the Jonah story is structurally an *exemplum* in a sermon, as is argued by Charles Mooreman in "The Role of the Narrator in *Patience*" (*Modern Philology* 61, 1963, 90–95). David Williams expresses reservations about treating the poem as a sermon in "The Point of *Patience*" (*Modern Philology* 68, 1970, 127–136). William Vatuono has countered with "The Structure and Sources of *Patience*" (*Medieval Studies* 34, 1972, 401–421), in which the five-fold division of the poem is shown to follow the traditional structure of a sermon.

Evaluation of Selected Criticism

Benson, Larry D. *Art and Tradition in "Sir Gawain and the Green Knight."* New Brunswick, NJ: Rutgers University Press, 1965. Presenting a thematically oriented analysis of the evolution of the "beheading game," Benson argues that the poet's modification of both the beheading and temptation stories derives from his change of underlying theme. In Benson's words, "the subject of this romance is romance itself," and the poem criticizes the romantic ideal, playing noble but rarified Courtesy against vigorous, sometimes undignified Nature; that is, playing Arthur and Sir Gawain against the Green Knight.

Borroff, Marie, *"Sir Gawain and the Green Knight": A Stylistic and Metrical Study.* New Haven and London: Yale University Press, 1962. An authority on the metre of *Sir Gawain and the Green Knight,* Borroff discusses the relationship between style and meaning as they affect the expressive value of words, as well as the relationship between alliterative status and expressive values in vocabulary. She concentrates on such words as those for "man, warrior" and "earth, field," and analyzes the effects of narrative viewpoint. In the second half, she considers metrical aspects of the poetry, such as the phonological evidence for the accentuation of romance words, the pronunciation of the final -e, and a metrical pattern for the "wheels." She reviews four- and seven-stress theories, favoring the latter.

Gardner, John, *The Complete Works of the "Gawain"-Poet.* Chicago: Chicago University Press, 1970. Gardner offers close verse translations of the four poems, and in the introduction discusses the poet, alliterative verse, number symbolism, the use of sources and conventions, four-fold exegesis, and general analyses of all the poems. Gardner argues that all the poems deal with the discrepancy between earthly and heavenly values.

Haines, Victor, *The Fortunate Fall of Sir Gawain: The Typology of "Sir Gawain and the Green Knight."* Lanham, MD: University Press of America, 1982. Synthesizing the two tendencies in *Gawain* criticism—the *culpa* school which emphasizes the Gawain's sin without being able to explain the final laughter at Camelot, and the *felix* school, which sees the comedy without being able to face the fact of Gawain's sin. Haines argues for the similarity of the sin of Gawain to the sin of Adam, each a *felix culpa.*

Madeleva, Sr. M. *"Pearl": A Study in Spiritual Dryness.* New York and London: Appleton, 1925. After a review of interpretations of *Pearl,* Sister Madeleva argues that the poem is a spiritual autobiography and a study of spiritual dryness, typical of spiritual desolation found in the writings of medieval mystics. In her interpretation, spiritual desolation is followed by spiritual initiation, in which the Maiden stands for the dreamer's soul. She believes the poem is about the dynamic growth of the soul of a mystic.

Shoaf, R.A. *The Poem as Green Girdle: Commercialism in "Sir Gawain and The Green Knight."* Gainesville: University of Florida Press, 1984. Relating the commercial imagery of *Sir Gawain and the Green Knight* to the Feast of Circumcision setting and the commercial language of England in the late fourteenth century, Shoaf shows the way moral theology and liturgy affect the meaning of the poem.

Judith Weise
State University College at Potsdam New York

SAMUEL PEPYS
1633–1703

Author's Chronology

Born February 23, 1633 London; *c. 1644* educated at Huntington; *c. 1646–1650* St. Paul's School; *1651–1654* Magdalene College, Cambridge; *?1654* enters the service of Sir Edward Mountagu; *1655* marries fifteen-year-old Elizabeth St. Michel; January 1, *1660* begins diary; sails with fleet to Holland to bring back Charles II; begins work at Navy Office; *1660–1662* Clerk of the Privy Seal; *1662* appointed to Tangier Committee; *1665* appointed Surveyor-General of the Victualling; *1668* defends Navy Board in House of Commons; May 31, *1669* ends diary because of eyestrain; *1669* wife dies; *1673* becomes Secretary to the Admiralty; May 21, *1679* resigns; May 22 committed to the Tower for supposed complicity in Popish Plot; July 9 released; *1680* charges against him are dropped; *1683* goes to Tangier with Lord Dartmouth and writes "Tangier Diary"; *1684* re-appointed Secretary to the Admiralty; *1684–1686* President of the Royal Society; *1689* resigns Secretaryship after accession of William and Mary; *1690* imprisoned briefly "on suspicion of being affected to King James"; *1701* retires to Clapham Common (London); May 26, 1703 dies; buried June 4 at St. Olave's Church, London.

Author's Bibliography

Memoirs Relating to the State of the Royal Navy of England for Ten Years Determined December 1688, 1690 (ed. J. R. Tanner, 1906); *An Account of the Preservation of King Charles II After the Battle of Worcester,* 1766 (ed. Sir D. Dalrymple), 1954 (ed. W. Rees-Mogg); *Diary,* 1825 (ed. Lord Braybrooke), 1875–1879 (ed. Mynors Bright), 1893–1899 (ed. Henry B. Wheatley), 1970–1983 (ed. Robert Latham and William Matthews); *Samuel Pepys's Naval Minutes,* 1926 (ed. J. R. Tanner); *The Tangier Papers of Samuel Pepys,* 1935 (ed. Edwin Chappell); *Mr. Pepys upon the State of Christ's Hospital,* 1935 (ed. Rudolf Kirk).

Overview of Biographical Sources

Pepys has been the subject of numerous biographies, varying considerably in quality and scope. These include two nineteenth-century and many twentieth-century works, ranging from J. R. Tanner's scholarly *Mr. Pepys: An Introduction to the Diary together with a Sketch of his Later Life* (1925) and John Drinkwater's readable *Pepys: His Life and Character* (Garden City, NY: Doubleday, 1934) to John Harold Wilson's sensationalized *The Private Life of Mr. Pepys* (New York: Farrar, Straus and Cudahy, 1959), emphasizing Pepys's promiscuity and the general atmosphere of libertinism in the Restoration. Among the more recent biographies are Ivan E. Taylor's *Samuel Pepys* (New York:

Twayne, 1967), a short but solid book with chapters on music, theatre, and some of the great events Pepys witnessed; Geoffrey Trease's brief, heavily illustrated *Samuel Pepys and His World* (New York: G. P. Putnam's Sons, 1972); John E. N. Hearsey's *Young Mr. Pepys* (London: Constable, 1973); and Richard Ollard's *Pepys: A Biography* (1974), the best of the recent works. Still recognized as the authoritative biography is Sir Arthur Bryant's three-volume *Samuel Pepys* (1933–1938).

Evaluation of Selected Biographies

Bryant, Sir Arthur, *Samuel Pepys.* Cambridge: Cambridge University Press. 3 vols. *The Man in the Making.* 1933. *The Years of Peril.* 1935. *The Saviour of the Navy.* 1938. Though it omits the last 14 years of Pepys's life, this is otherwise the most thorough and detailed biography of Pepys and is recognized as the standard one. It is superbly written—clear though complex, vivid, sometimes moving—and is based on solid scholarship, including extensive research into manuscript sources. Bryant, who has been accused of hero worship and Tory bias, is sometimes excessive in his praise of Pepys and denigration of his opponents. But generally this is an accurate and balanced, as well as highly readable, work. Besides offering an exceptionally vivid portrait of Pepys, this biography effectively places him in his historical setting.

Ollard, Richard, *Pepys: A Biography.* London: Hodder and Stoughton, 1974. Though not as thorough as Bryant's, Ollard's biography is scholarly and capably written, and corrects a few errors found in Bryant's work. The last 30 pages cover Pepys's 14 final years, which Bryant never reaches. Ollard deals intelligently with the various sides of Pepys's personality, without sensationalism or exaggeration. He does, however, give undue emphasis to the years of the *Diary,* those nine years receiving as much attention as the other 61.

Tanner, J. R. *Mr. Pepys: An Introduction to the Diary together with a Sketch of his Later Life.* London: G. Bell, 1925. Despite its age, this is still one of the most valuable books on Pepys's life. It emphasizes the *Diary* years, but has a brief chapter on Pepys's earlier life and a long one on the years after the *Diary.* Most of the material, though divided into topics, is presented as straightforward narrative, with little interpretation. Exceptions include an insightful discussion of Pepys's character and a cogent analysis of the *Diary* and of Pepys's motives in writing it. Perhaps the book's greatest weakness is Tanner's reticence in discussing Pepys's extramarital affairs and his overly generous evaluation of this aspect of Pepys's life.

Autobiographical Sources

For few writers is there such a wealth of autobiographical material as for Pepys, though he probably intended much of it—the extraordinarily revelatory *Diary* in particular—to remain secret. The *Diary,* written in shorthand, was first deciphered in the early nineteenth century by John Smith, whose transcription, edited by Richard Lord Braybrooke, was published in part in 1825. This first edition covered about one-fourth of the *Diary;* later editions by Lord Braybrooke included about two-fifths. The *Diary and Correspondence,* edited by Mynors Bright (6 vols. London: Bickers, 1875–1879), covered about four-fifths of the original. Henry B. Wheatley's edition (10 vols. London: Bell, 1893–1899) was nearly complete, but still left out about 30 of the most offensive or embarrassing pages. Not until recent years has an unexpurgated edition been published: *The Diary of Samuel Pepys: A New and Complete Transcription,* ed. Robert Latham and William Matthews (11 vols. London: G. Bell; Berkeley: University of California Press, 1970–1983). This is an excellent scholarly edition, with useful footnotes and, in the first volume, a long introduction discussing Pepys's life and the *Diary.* Volumes 10 (Companion) and 11 (Index) are especially helpful, the first of these consisting of reference materials on the people, places, events, and customs of Pepys's time.

Besides the *Diary,* autobiographical sources for Pepys include *Samuel Pepys's Naval Minutes, The Tangier Papers of Samuel Pepys,* and Pepys's correspondence: *Private Correspondence and Miscellaneous Papers of Samuel Pepys, 1679–1703.* 2 vols. (London: G. Bell, 1926); and *Further Correspondence of Samuel Pepys, 1622–1679.* (London: G. Bell, 1929), both edited by J. R. Tanner; *Letters and the Second Diary of Samuel Pepys.* ed. R. G. Howarth (London: J. M. Dent, 1932); *Shorthand Letters of Samuel Pepys.* ed. Edwin Chappell (Cambridge: Cambridge University Press, 1933); and *Letters of Samuel Pepys and His Family Circle.* ed. Helen T. Heath (Oxford: Clarendon, 1955), with 162 new letters. None of these equals the *Diary* in literary value or depth of personal revelation, but they do shed light on periods of Pepys's life the *Diary* does not cover.

Overview of Critical Sources

Apart from brief comments by Pepys's contemporaries, there was little comment that could be called "criticism" until the *Diary* was transcribed in the nineteenth century. The *Diary* brought Pepys fame as an embodiment of Restoration practicality and good spirits, and as the writer of an invaluable historical source. But as the successive nineteenth-century editions revealed more and more of the seamier side of his life (his sensuality, his sexual escapades, his occasional hot temper), his reputation began to suffer. During the twentieth century, most critics have come to a fairly balanced view of Pepys, admitting his weaknesses but admiring his zest for life, his immense honesty, and the vividness of his writing.

Critics of Pepys have approached him in several ways: as a source of information about Restoration England, its public affairs, its arts and studies, and especially its everyday life; as a prose stylist; and as a pioneer in the field of autobiography.

Evaluation of Selected Criticism

Fothergill, Robert A. *Private Chronicles: A Study of English Diaries.* London: Oxford University Press, 1974. Though not exclusively about Pepys, this is one of the most perceptive and sophisticated books dealing with him and is a must for any serious student of Pepys's *Diary.* Fothergill traces changes in sensibility, language, and literary form in English diaries from the seventeenth to the twentieth century and locates Pepys in this line of development. He discusses his motives for writing the *Diary,* his subject matter, and his style of self-presentation. He credits Pepys with having found a form and style that allowed him to become the first great English diarist.

Hunt, Percival, *Samuel Pepys in the Diary.* Pittsburgh: University of Pittsburgh Press, 1958. This is a sensible and detailed discussion of Pepys, dealing with various aspects of his life and personality. Perhaps the most useful chapters for students of literature are those dealing directly with the *Diary:* "Substance in the Diary," on the importance of home life and work in the *Diary;* "Prose of the Diary," which discusses Pepys's style; and the "Envoy," which offers a perceptive evaluation of the *Diary* as a personal and literary document.

McAfee, Helen, *Pepys on the Restoration Stage.* New Haven: Yale University Press, 1916. Now about seven decades old, this is still a useful source of information on Pepys and the Restoration stage. Preceding the main body of the book, which consists of entries from Pepys's *Diary* on the plays he saw and on actors, playwrights, audiences, and theatres, is a section with useful background and a general estimate of Pepys's contribution to stage history. McAfee sets Pepys in the context of Restoration attitudes and corrects the inaccurate impression—which still persists—that Pepys was without moral sensitivity and without appreciation for Shakespeare.

Other Sources

Abbott, Wilbur Cortez, "The Serious Pepys," in *Conflicts with Oblivion.* New Haven: Yale University Press, 1924. 1–33. A useful survey of Pepys's reputation from his own day to the early twentieth century.

Emden, Cecil S. *Pepys Himself.* London: Oxford University Press, 1963. Emphasizes Pepys's character—his qualities as an administrator, his inner life, his relationship with his wife—rather than the events of his life.

Lee, Sidney, *Pepys and Shakespeare.* London: Bedford Press, 1906. A brief discussion of Pepys's playgoing, especially his response to Shakespeare, which Lee finds inadequate.

Matthews, William, "Samuel Pepys, Tachygraphist," in *Modern Language Review* 29 (1934), 397–404. A discussion of the shorthand Pepys used in writing his diary.

Nicolson, Marjorie Hope, *Pepys'* Diary *and the New Science*. Charlottesville: University of Virginia Press, 1965. Though mainly concerned with the Royal Society, this book frequently turns to Pepys, especially in the first chapter, where his varied scientific interests are explored.

Stevenson, Robert Louis, "Samuel Pepys," in *Familiar Studies of Men and of Books*. London: Chatto and Windus, 1882. Engagingly written, this early essay presents a frank but sympathetic picture of Pepys and praises his prose style.

Tanner, J. R. *Samuel Pepys and the Royal Navy*. Cambridge: Cambridge University Press, 1920. Discusses Pepys's contribution to the Royal Navy, which his reforms helped raise to distinction from its lowest state since the Middle Ages.

Taylor, Ivan E. "Mr. Pepys's Use of Colloquial English," in *CLA Journal* 7 (1963), 22–36. Discusses what the *Diary* reveals about colloquial English of the seventeenth century.

Weiss, David G. *Samuel Pepys, Curioso*. Pittsburgh: University of Pittsburgh Press, 1957. Emphasizes Pepys's interest in music.

Willy, Margaret, *English Diarists: Evelyn & Pepys*. Writers and Their Work #162. London: British Council, 1963. Briefly discusses Pepys's life, *Diary*, character, and interests.

Selected Dictionaries and Encyclopedias
The Concise Oxford Dictionary of English Literature, 2nd ed. Clarendon Press, 1970. Contains a brief but perceptive article on Pepys and the *Diary*.

Encyclopaedia Britannica: Macropaedia, 1974. Contains an extensive article discussing Pepys's life and character, the *Diary*, and his style.

Bruce W. Young
Brigham Young University

SYLVIA PLATH
1932–1963

Author's Chronology

Born October 27, 1932, Jamaica Plain, Massachusetts to Aurelia and Otto Plath; *1940* father dies; *1942* family moves to Wellesley, Massachusetts; *1950* enters Smith College on scholarship; *1952* publishes "Sunday at the Mintons" in *Mademoiselle; 1953* summer guest managing editor for *Mademoiselle* in New York City; August 24 suicide attempt at home in Wellesley; *1954* re-enrolls in Smith; attends Harvard University summer school; *1955* graduates summa cum laude with prizes for poetry; begins Fulbright year at Newnham College, Cambridge University; *1956* meets Ted Hughes; June 16 marries Ted Hughes; *1957* returns to United States and teaches English at Smith College; *1958* begins serious involvement in psychotherapy; attends Robert Lowell's poetry class; *1959* returns to England; *1960* birth of daughter Freida Rebecca; publishes *The Colossus; 1961* miscarriage followed by an appendectomy; receives Saxon Fellowship and Cheltenham Festival award; *1962* birth of son, Nicholas Farrar; separates from Ted Hughes; *1963* publishes *The Bell Jar* in England under the pseudonym Victoria Lucas; February 11 commits suicide in London.

Author's Bibliography (selected)

The Colossus, 1960 (poems); *The Bell Jar,* 1963 (novel); *Uncollected Poems,* 1965; *Ariel,* 1965 (poems); *Three Women: A Monologue for Three Voices,* 1968 (radio play); *Fiesta Melons,* 1971 (poems, with eleven drawings by Sylvia Plath); *Crystal Gazer,* 1971 (poems); *Lyonesse,* 1971 (poems); *Crossing the Water,* 1971 (poems); *Winter Trees,* 1971 (poems); *Letters Home: Correspondence 1950–1963,* 1975 (letters, edited and with introduction by Aurelia Plath); *The Bed Book,* 1976 (children's stories); *Johnny Panic and the Bible of Dreams, and Other Prose Writings,* 1977 (short stories and essays); *Collected Poems,* 1981 (awarded Pulitzer Prize); *The Journals of Sylvia Plath,* 1982 (personal diaries).

Overview of Biographical Sources

The highly personal imagery and corresponding intensity of vision in Sylvia Plath's work have provided ample, if uncertain, territory for biographical research. Because the reasons behind her suicide seem so firmly rooted in the poetry itself, Plath's biographers are necessarily critics. A. Alvarez contributed an early, but important, biographical article, "Sylvia Plath," in *The Review,* I:9, October 1963, the first study to directly relate stages in Plath's poetic development to specific biographical events. His research on Plath continued and is more extensively dealt with in *The Savage God: A Study of Suicide* (London: Weidenfield and Nicolson, 1971). Plath's college friend, Nancy Hunter Steiner, published *A Closer Look at Ariel: A Memory of Sylvia Plath* (New York: Harper

Magazine Press, 1973), and in the same year Eileen Aird published *Sylvia Plath: Her Life and Work* (1973). This important study identifies the biographical knowledge significant to effective criticism, and places Plath in a contemporary literary context. In 1976 Edward Butscher published *Sylvia Plath: Method and Madness,* and in the next year published the less strictly biographical study *Sylvia Plath: The Woman and Her Work* (New York: Dodd, Mead, and Company, 1977). Carolyn Barnard wrote the pamphlet-length study of Plath for the United States Authors Series, *Sylvia Plath* (New York: G. K. Hall, 1978). More recently, Margaret Uroff published the first full length study of Plath's relationship with Hughes, *Sylvia Plath and Ted Hughes* (1979).

Evaluation of Selected Biographies

Aird, Eileen, *Sylvia Plath: Her Life and Work.* New York: Harper and Row, 1973. Aird presents a concise biographical introduction to Plath's life and works, examining in some detail the biographical elements of *The Colossus, Crossing the Water, Winter Trees,* and *Ariel.* The study is most useful for its explanation of Plath's need for autobiographically-based writing and consequent motives for turning to the novel. Aird's study also includes an informative synopsis of Plath's imagery.

Butscher, Edward, *Sylvia Plath: Method and Madness.* New York: The Seabury Press, 1976. Butscher presents an extensively detailed and sympathetic study of Plath's life, with general references to her major works. His information is accurate, but, because his central focus is on Plath's obsession with her father, the study's factual basis is obscured with psychoanalytic overtones. Nonetheless, Butscher is consistently careful to distinguish between Plath as public figure and Plath as private person, relying to a great extent on Alvarez's research. Butscher depicts the creative impulse both nurtured and destroyed by Plath's marriage, and, in doing so, attempts to account for her suicide.

Uroff, Margaret D. *Sylvia Plath and Ted Hughes.* Urbana: University of Illinois Press, 1979. Uroff attempts to dispel unjustified mythic qualities attributed to both Plath and Hughes. Familiar with the works of both poets, she studies closely their individual working methods, their common interest in the subconscious, and the poetic interests each supported in the other.

Autobiographical Sources

While many critics maintain that *The Bell Jar* is autobiographical in nature, the most direct source of Plath's experiences are her personal writings. Plath maintained close correspondence with her mother and brother Warren during her school years and throughout her experiences in England. These letters are collected in *Letters Home: Correspondence 1950–1963.* While these letters recount much of Plath's personal and literary frustrations, they are most useful for what they reveal of Plath's often self-imposed roles brought about through a complicated and often bitter relationship with her mother.

Plath's journals, collected by Ted Hughes in *The Journals of Sylvia Plath,* come still closer to a true autobiography of the poet in all of her hidden and unhidden complexities. The journal entries reveal Plath's struggle to evaluate herself honestly as daughter, friend, wife, mother, and poet. For Plath, the struggle was devastatingly real, and the journals reflect her painful effort to come to grips with life itself.

Overview of Critical Sources

Although public interest in Plath's work initially grew out of a fascination with its bearing on her suicide, critics have gradually come to appreciate the poetry for its intrinsic literary merit. While she continues to be valuable for feminist criticism, Plath has increasingly become the focus of wider critical movements not restricted to specific poetic category. Her poetry is at once confessional, lyrical, and symbolic; the best existing criticism synthesizes these facets of Plath's work without overemphasizing the inextricable, and often frightening, bonds between her work, creative impulse, and personal life.

Evaluation of Selected Criticism

Bundtzen, Lynda K. *Plath's Incarnations: Woman and the Creative Process.* Ann Arbor: University of Michigan Press. Bundtzen's study is essential to anyone wishing to understand Plath's place in current feminist criticism. Bundtzen presents a "generous" view of Plath's achievement as an artist while explicating many of Plath's difficult poems through a consistent, if not always agreeable, theory of the feminine creative impulse.

Holbrook, David, *Sylvia Plath: Poetry and Existence.* London: The Athlone Press, 1976. Holbrook's study makes extensive use of psychoanalytic interpretation to understand Plath's poetry in an effort to diagnose her death as a "schizoid suicide." Considered by many scholars to be an essential of Plath criticism, the study effectively analyzes her major works both for their intense personal vision and for their falsification of problems. Holbrook remains sympathetic to Plath throughout.

Newman, Charles, *The Art of Sylvia Plath: A Symposium.* Bloomington: Indiana University Press, 1970. Newman's important study brings together significant critical essays. Four essays in the first section place Plath's work in an intellectual and cultural framework; the three essays in the second section elucidate Plath's poetry through imagery and metre studies; part three is biographical and reminiscent in nature; part five contains essays which deal with single works but specifically discussed in preceding contributions.

Other Sources

Alvarez, A. *The Savage God: A Study of Suicide.* London: Weidenfield and Nicolson, 1971. Monumental study of Plath's psychology, based, to a large extent, on personal encounters.

Broe, Mary L. *Protean Poetic: The Poetry of Sylvia Plath.* Columbia: University of Missouri Press, 1980. A useful summary of *The Colossus, Crossing the Water, Ariel,* and *Winter Trees.* Broe attempts to demythologize Plath by discussing her developing poetic within a wider range of emotions than most criticism suggests.

Butscher, Edward, *Sylvia Plath: The Woman and Her Work.* New York: Dodd, Mead, 1977. Collection of nine biographically oriented essays on Plath, most of which are based on personal recollections. The study also includes eight essays on her poetry which are, again, reminiscent in nature.

Kroll, Judith, *Chapters in a Mythology: The Poetry of Sylvia Plath.* New York: Harper and Row, 1976. A good introduction to thematic meanings in Plath's later poetry.

Selected Dictionaries and Encyclopedias

Critical Survey of Poetry, Salem Press, 1982. Concise overview of pertinent biographical data and brief, but useful, analysis of Plath's poetic technique.

Great Writers of The English Language, St. Martin's Press, 1983. Brief overview of Plath's life, selected publications, and a useful critical discussion of *The Bell Jar* and major poems.

Maria B. Hinkle
University of Delaware

EDGAR ALLAN POE
1809–1849

Author's Chronology

Born Edgar Poe, January 19, 1809, Boston, Massachusetts, of American-English parents; *1810–1811* father disappears and mother dies in Richmond, Virginia; Poe enters home of John and Frances Allan; *1815–1820* family to Great Britain; *1826* attends University of Virginia; *1827* quarrels with Allan; joins army; publishes *Tamerlane and Other Poems; 1829* discharged; *1830* enters West Point briefly; *1830–1832* obscure years in New York, Baltimore; first tales appear; *1834* Allan dies, leaving Poe nothing; *1835* Poe begins editorial career at *Southern Literary Messenger; 1836* marries cousin Virginia E. Clemm; *1837* lives in New York; *1838–1841* works in Philadelphia for *Burton's Gentleman's Magazine* and *Graham's Magazine;* hopes to found his own magazine; *1842* to New York for journalistic work; *1845–1846* works with *Broadway Journal; 1847* Virginia dies; *1848* lectures; romances several women; *1849* dies October 7, Baltimore, Maryland.

Author's Bibliography (selected)

Tamerlane and Other Poems, 1827; *Al Aaraaf, Tamerlane and Minor Poems,* 1829; *Poems,* 1831; *The Narrative of Arthur Gordon Pym,* 1838 (novel); *Tales of the Grotesque and Arabesque,* 1839, 1840; *Tales,* 1845; *The Raven and Other Poems,* 1845; *Eureka,* 1848 (poems).

Evaluation of Selected Biographies

Much misinformation has obscured Poe's biographies. Two are reliable: Arthur Hobson Quinn's *Edgar Allan Poe: A Critical Biography* (1969) and G. R. Thompson's "Edgar Allan Poe." Accurate biographical outlines appear in Thomas Ollive Mabbott's "Annals," in *Collected Works of Edgar Allan Poe, Volume I: Poems* (1969).

The misinformation and sensationalizing about Poe's life began during his life. He romanticized his own biography, notably in accounts to Henry B. Hirst, whose "Edgar A. Poe," in the *Philadelphia Saturday Museum,* March 4, 1843, pp. 1–2, began many inaccuracies. More significant, and more injurious, was the "Death of Edgar Allan Poe," signed "Ludwig," by Rufus W. Griswold, Poe's literary executor and editor, which appeared in the New York *Tribune,* October 9, 1849 (rpt. in *The Complete Works of Edgar Allan Poe,* New York: AMS Press, 1965, 1979, I, pp. 348–359). Rebuked by Poe's friends, Griswold expanded and prefixed his memoir to *The Works of the Late Edgar Allan Poe* (New York: J. S. Redfield, 1850–1856, III, pp. v–xxix). Griswold's forging of letters and other damage to Poe's image—one of the ironies that dog Poe's biography—and the ensuing battles between Poe's detractors and defenders persist into this century. Three more weighty defenses of Poe appeared late in the nineteenth century, William F. Gill's *The Life of Edgar Allan Poe* (New York: Dillingham, 1877; rev. ed. London: Chatto & Windus, 1878), John Henry Ingram's *Edgar Allan Poe: His Letters and Opinions* (1880, rpt. New York: AMS, 1965), and George E. Woodberry's *Edgar Allan Poe* (1885, rpt. with an introduction by R. W. B. Lewis, 1980). Hervey Allen's *Israfel: The Life and Times of Edgar Allan Poe* (1926, rpt. 1956) used correspondence between Poe and John Allan, plus material in the Allan-Ellis papers at the Library of Congress. The book offers more on Poe in Philadelphia than previous works, but, overall, Allen's inaccuracies lessen the reliability. As Arthur Hobson Quinn regularized correspondence that Griswold had altered, he discovered numerous facts overlooked by previous biographers. Quinn's critical perceptions were not brilliant, and they have become outmoded. For factual narrative biography, however, his book continues to be the best life of Poe after more than forty years. Mabbott's "Annals" are valuable because they represent informed, careful consideration of Poe's life and literary career. Mabbott is more prone to accept oral accounts about Poe than many others. Thompson's account combines clear vision concerning Poe's life with lively, broad-minded opinions of his writings.

Evaluation of Selected Biographies

Allen, Hervey, *Israfel: The Life and Times of Edgar Allan Poe.* 2 vols. New York: George H. Doran, 1926; rpt. New York, Rinehart, 1956. Allen's novelist's procedures often romanticize Poe's life, although he first drew substantially on letters between Poe and John Allan and the Ellis-Allan papers in the Library of Congress, which shed light on Poe's life. Poe's Philadelphia years receive good coverage.

Mabbott, Thomas Ollive, "Annals," in *The Collected Works of Edgar Allan Poe,* Vol. I. Cambridge: Belknap Press of Harvard University Press, 1968, pp. 527–572. Mabbott's peerless command of Poe scholarship makes the "Annals" important biographical information. His no-nonsense approach to Poe the man, who is not viewed as synonymous with any of Poe's literary characters, counters much that is "legendary" in lightweight biographies.

Quinn, Arthur Hobson, *Edgar Allan Poe: A Critical Biography.* New York: Appleton-Century-Crofts, 1941; rpt. New York: Cooper Square Publishers, 1969. Quinn spent over twenty years amassing material for this biography, used and corrected available correspondence, unearthed information about Poe's parents, and undercut much shaky speculation derived from psychoanalysis about Poe's sexuality. He also knew much more about the backgrounds for the writings than many other biographers, as well as about the nineteenth-century literary scene in general. Quinn's interpretations and judgments are not always perceptive as to literary artistry, and they negatively date the book.

Thompson, G. R. "Edgar Allan Poe," in "Antebellum Writers in New York and the South," Vol. III, *Dictionary of Literary Biography.* Detroit: Gale Research, 1979, pp. 249–297. Because of its recent date, this account draws upon more materials than Mabbott and Quinn had available, particularly in the way of correspondence to and from Poe. Thompson's critical ideas also surpass those of his predecessors, not merely because he employed a greater wealth of interpretations but also in terms of his larger literary view—as opposed to Quinn's outdated perceptions and Mabbott's aim for factuality. Brief and readable, this essay best integrates Poe's life with his writings.

Woodberry, George E. *Edgar Allan Poe.* Boston: Houghton Mifflin, 1885; revised and expanded to 2 vols. as *The Life of Edgar Allan Poe, Personal and Literary, With His Chief Correspondence With Men of Letters.* Boston: Houghton Mifflin, 1909; rpt. New York: Chelsea House, 1980. Woodberry never realized the extent of Griswold's tamperings with facts of Poe's life. He attempted however, to give accurate biographical portraiture and his literary criticism is more discriminating than that by earlier biographers.

Autobiographical Sources

Hirst, Henry B. "Edgar Allan Poe," in the *Philadelphia Saturday Museum* (March 4 1843), pp. 1–2. This sketch stems from information by Poe. Several of the deliberate inaccuracies—trips by young Poe to Russia and Greece, his relations to John Allan and comments on Allan's character, the writing of the first "To Helen" at age 14—persist through indiscriminate biographical accounts. Mention of autobiographical origins for the story "William Wilson" prepared the way for speculations about just how much of Poe the man was incorporated into his imaginative writings.

Ostrom, John Ward, ed. *The Letters of Edgar Allan Poe.* 2 vols. New York: Gordian Press, 1966. This is a revision of volumes originally published by Harvard University Press in 1948, to which Ostrom adds new letters. Poe's correspondence provides information about his thoughts, whereabouts, relationships with others, and his literary work. Ostrom's editing superbly compliments by means of the notes the texts of the correspondence.

Overview of Critical Sources

Two broad divisions of critical opinion about Poe exist. First is the conception that Poe's writing offered well-wrought and serious presentations of lovely but perishing women, in verse and prose; that his poems centered on beauty and succeeded or failed in conveying vagueness through imagery and sound effects; that his protagonists exemplified lofty or criminal artist-figures; that he created detective fiction; and that his criticism was generally just if at times harsh. Second, and more recent, emerge analyses of Poe's comic impulses, lying just below the surfaces of his tales in particular. Within both schools, source studies aim to shed light on Poe's intentions. Edward H. Davidson combined both attitudes, and his work during the 1950's stimulated much additional study. Poe's contemporaries had perceived humor in his fiction, but the comic was ignored for many years, or else it was deplored as mere fumbling in an area where Poe had no business.

Evaluation of Selected Criticism

Buranelli, Vincent, *Edgar Allan Poe*. Boston: Twayne, 1977. Poe's place as a world writer is highlighted by chapters addressing varied categories of his creative efforts. Offering a good explication of texts, Buranelli provides a satisfying introduction to Poe's reputation and writings.

Carlson, Eric W. ed. *The Recognition of Edgar Allan Poe: Selected Criticism Since 1829*. Ann Arbor: University of Michigan Press, 1966. This collection provides a good spectrum of opinions about Poe, especially those by artists and writers. Carlson's introduction tersely charts shifting attitudes toward Poe as a man and writer.

Davidson, Edward H. *Poe: A Critical Study*. Cambridge: The Belknap Press of Harvard University Press, 1957. Davidson's "philosophic inquiry into the mind and writings" of Poe reveals Davidson's great grasp of background material, combined with a keen analytical sense of Poe's work. Chapter divisions focus on the poems, short fiction, and the criticism. Discussion of Poe's comic tales as worthwhile artistry appears for the first time in twentieth-century criticism about Poe. This book has probably had greater influence upon subsequent Poe criticism than any earlier one.

Eddings, Dennis W. ed. *The Naiad Voice: Essays on Poe's Satiric Hoaxing*. Port Washington, NY: Associated Faculty Press, 1983. Twentieth-century critiques of Poe's humorous fiction are reprinted. The book provides good perspectives on this growing branch of Poe studies, as well as on his satiric, punster, and parodic tendencies.

Fisher, Benjamin Franklin IV. ed. *Poe at Work: Seven Textual Studies*. Baltimore: The Edgar Allan Poe Society, 1978. After an overview treating Poe's practices in revising, essays follow which discuss *Tales of the Folio Club*, "Bon-Bon," "Silence—A Fable," "William Wilson," "The Murders in the Rue Morgue," and "The Mystery of Marie Roget." Robert W. Burns lists studies pertinent to Poe's habits of composition and revision.

Hoffman, Daniel, *PoePoePoePoePoePoePoe*. Garden City, NY: Doubleday, 1972. Hoffman's personal approach, replete with colloquial language, borrows heavily from Freudian psychology. He groups Poe's works according to type, with the greatest portion of the book centering on the tales.

Jacobs, Robert D. *Poe: Journalist & Critic.* Baton Rouge: Louisiana State University Press, 1969. This lengthy book examines Poe's career in the periodical world of his time, arguing that his critical principles and the backgrounds for his imaginative writings are closely linked with magazines, gift books and annuals, and newspapers of his times. Scottish Commonsense Philosophy underlies many of Poe's theories and practices. Jacobs analyzes Poe's links with and differences from Romantic aesthetics.

Pollin, Burton R. *Discoveries in Poe.* Notre Dame and London: University of Notre Dame Press, 1970. The twelve chapters, some reprinted from professional journals, concentrate on sources for Poe's works. Pollin develops the traditional source study into analyses of Poe's art. There are factual inaccuracies, but nevertheless this is a book necessary for interpretive work on Poe.

Regan, Robert, ed. *Poe: A Collection of Critical Essays.* Englewood Cliffs, NJ: Prentice-Hall, 1967. This collection assembles some of the best critiques of Poe's major pieces, moving from essentially unfavorable to positive responses to them.

Thompson, G. R. *Poe's Fiction: Romantic Irony in the Gothic Tales.* Madison: University of Wisconsin Press, 1973. The thesis of the book—that Poe derived much from Romantic irony and that he consciously gauged his tales as hoaxes upon readers—is provocative and has stimulated great response.

Veler, Richard P. ed. *Papers on Poe: Essays in Honor of John Ward Ostrom.* Springfield, OH: Chantry Music Press at Wittenberg University, 1972. The seventeen essays address varied aspects of Poe's life and work. His Gothicism; international reputation; relations with contemporaries like Thomas Dunn English and W. G. Simms; his humor; several features in *Pym:* all these and more receive treatment by Poe specialists.

Wagenknecht, Edward, *Edgar Allan Poe: The Man Behind the Legend.* New York: Oxford University Press, 1963. Wagenknecht attempts to link Poe's life with his work, organizing his criticism under such categories as "Learning," "Art," "Love," and "God."

Benjamin Franklin Fisher IV
University of Mississippi

ALEXANDER POPE
1688–1744

Author's Chronology

Born May 21, 1688 in London, England of a Roman Catholic family, his father being a linen merchant; c. *1696* enters Twyford School near Winchester; later attends Thomas Deane's school in London; *1700–1716* family settles in Windsor Forest at Binfield; c. *1705* develops tuberculosis, causing stunted growth (Pope was 4′6″ tall in manhood), curvature of the spine, and lifetime recurrence of ill-health; *1706–1711* meets Addison, Steele, Congreve, Wycherley, William Walsh, and c. *1711* joins many writers at Button's Coffee House; *1712* forms close friendships with brilliant Tory writers—Swift, Gay, Arbuthnot, Parnell, and Prior; these form the Scriblerus Club; *1714–1726* at work upon translations of Homer and an edition of Shakespeare; *1716* resides briefly in Chiswick; *1718* acquires villa and grotto at Twickenham, his home for the rest of his life; *1727–1738* commences to develop his satiric major phase as a writer; becomes increasingly political, playing a role in the opposition to Walpole, the Whig prime minister; *1744* dies on May 30 from dropsy and asthma.

Author's Bibliography (selected)

Pastorals, 1709 (poems); *Essay on Criticism,* 1711 (poem); *The Rape of the Lock,* 1712, 1714, 1717 (poem); *Windsor Forest,* 1713 (poem); *Three Hours After Marriage,* 1717 (theatrical farce, written with Arbuthnot and Gay); *Iliad* of Homer, 1715-1720 (translation); *Odyssey* of Homer, 1725-1726 (translation); *Works of Shakespeare,* 1725 (edition); *Peri Bathous, or Of The Art of Sinking in Poetry,* 1727 (prose satire); *The Dunciad,* 1728–1743; *Imitations of Horace,* 1733–1738; *Essay on Man,* 1733–1734; *Memoirs of Martinus Scriblerus,* 1741 (prose satire, with Swift and Arbuthnot, mostly composed 1712–1714). The standard authoritative edition of the poems is *The Twickenham Edition of the Poems of Alexander Pope.* 11 vols. ed. John Butt. London: Methuen & New Haven: Yale University Press, 1939-1969. A convenient 1-volume version is also available: *The Poems of Alexander Pope.* 1 vol. ed. John Butt. New Haven: Yale University Press, 1963.

Overview of Biographical Sources

Because Pope was Catholic, deeply political (on the losing side, for the most part), and capable of being ferociously Juvenalian as a satirist, he has been the frequent recipient of calumniation, rumor, and gossip. In addition, nineteenth-century writers doubted his "sincerity," "simplicity," and capacity for genuine emotion altogether; he was hardly considered poetic. Only well into the twentieth century have critics rendered favorable readings of his life and work. Hence, William Ayre's *Memoirs of the Life and Writings of Alexander Pope, Esq.*

(1745) and Owen Ruffhead's *The Life of Alexander Pope* (1769) are of minimal importance and none too reliable. On the other hand, Samuel Johnson's essay, "Pope," in his *Lives of the Poets* (1781) does provide a favorable reading, with intelligent comments on Pope's life and writings. Similarly, Joseph Warton's *An Essay on the Writings and Genius of Mr. Pope* (i, 1756; ii. 1782) is largely favorable and of some value. But far too many subsequent studies have routinely found Pope's life, his morals, and his satires objectionable. For example, Leslie Stephen, in *Alexander Pope* (1880), cannot conceal the fact he considers Pope something of a spiteful monster, labelling him at one point, "the cruel little persecutor." Edith Sitwell's *Alexander Pope* (London, 1930), although not scholarly, is noteworthy for being at least sympathetic to its subject. G. Wilson Knight's *Laureate of Peace: On The Genius of Alexander Pope* (London, 1954) is similarly favorable, if a bit mystical. Peter Quennell's *Alexander Pope: The Education of a Genius,* 1688–1723 (London: Faber & Faber, 1968) has been overrated in the popular press; its author is frequently careless, and far from scholarly, using minimal documentation. Most biographies in the present century are sketchy general introductions, too brief to be weighty or significant, though respectable and well-meaning. Such is the case with Ian Jack's *Pope* (London: Longmans, Green, 1954) in the "Writers and Their Work" series, Bonamy Dobrée's *Alexander Pope* (London: Sylvan Press, 1951), and George S. Sutherland's *Alexander Pope* (London: Routledge & Kegan Paul, 1978); this last is written by a non-specialist for the general reader and aimed at sharing the author's own "amateur enjoyment" of Pope's poetry.

Evaluation of Selected Biographies

Clark, Donald B. *Alexander Pope.* New York: Twayne, 1967. Part of the Twayne English Authors series, this volume gives succinct treatment of Pope's life and writings, stressing his variety and his employment of metaphor and allusion in his creative work. It includes a useful Selected Bibliography with brief evaluative comments.

Mack, Maynard, *The Garden and the City: Retirement and Politics in the Later Poetry of Pope, 1731–1743.* Toronto: University of Toronto Press, 1969. Virtually completing Sherburn's biography of Pope's early years, Mack's study explores the last years of Pope's life, and the great period of his satires and imitations of Horace. The volume is first-rate, dealing exhaustively with two sides of Pope's character—his devotion to the bucolic, the genteel, the withdrawn, the innocent, and the virtuous ideal of retirement to villa and grotto but also his commitment to politics, to angry and gloomy condemnation, as a leader of the opposition, of Walpole and the Whig government in power. The volume is accompanied by a host of handsome plates.

Sherburn, George, *The Early Career of Alexander Pope.* Oxford: Clarendon Press, 1934. This is the most admirable, well-written, and complete of available biographies, although it only traces Pope's career to the year 1727. Sherburn never published the concluding sequel. Rich in facts, careful in judgements, and, remarkably free of gross prejudices against Pope's personality, the book is satisfying. Sherburn is best in tracing Pope's early involvement with men like Addison, Dennis, and Curll.

Autobiographical Sources

Pope is seldom explicitly autobiographical. He does at times in his poetry deal overtly with topics that concern his life—his Twickenham country home, his parents, his hopes and ideals—as in the poem from the *Imitations of Horace* called "An Epistle to Dr. Arbuthnot" (1735), and to be sure a number of poems are prefaced by prose "letters," "introductions," "Arguments," and are even accompanied occasionally with "notes." Nevertheless, Pope seldom speaks to his contemporaries directly. Like Jonathan Swift, the other great ironist and satirist of the period, and his close friend, Pope adores deviousness, mystery, and indirection. He will often exaggerate or fictionalize himself and his status. Even in his letters (*The Correspondence of Alexander Pope,* ed. George Sherburn. 5 vols. Oxford: Clarendon Press, 1956, which contains over 2,100 letters), Pope all too often is rather self-consciously playing roles. In addition, anecdotes and quotations (Joseph Spence, *Observations, Anecdotes, and Characters of Books and Men, Collected from Conversation,* ed. James M. Osborn. Oxford: Clarendon Press, 1966) of Pope's casual remarks by one of his friends who transcribed such data has proven of the first importance.

Overview of Critical Sources

Because Pope is considered to be the major poet of the Augustan era in England (1700-1745) and even of the entire eighteenth century, he naturally has received a considerable amount of critical attention. His poetic output was enormous, however, and no single literary study has been able to circumscribe this creative *oeuvre.* Moreover, Pope's letters, prose essays and satires present an additional area for study that, if anything, has been less carefully assessed. Most studies tend to isolate some specific poetic strategy (imagery, allusions, imitations) or period of creativity in Pope's life (his early pastoral poetry; the translations; the Horatian poems).

Evaluation of Selected Criticism

Brower, Reuben Arthur, *Alexander Pope: The Poetry of Allusion.* Oxford: Clarendon Press, 1959. A book broadly committed to rendering Pope's poetry more accessible to the modern reader, this sensitively analyzes the poems by demonstrating how much Pope assimilated into himself (as the last great poet to do so) the classic and European literary traditions. Brower demonstrates how Pope reshapes materials drawn widely from Homer, Theocritus, Virgil, Ovid, Spenser, Boileau, Milton, Racine, Dryden, and particularly Horace. This book builds upon but goes much further than the earlier, impressive study of Pope's debt to French influences by E. Audra, *L'influence francaise dans l'oeuvre de Pope* (Paris: Champion, 1931).

Fairer, David, *Pope's Imagination*. Manchester: Manchester University Press, 1984. A slender volume but a well-written book that further assaults romantic and Victorian prejudices by urging that Pope in no sense frowned upon or eschewed the imagination. On the contrary, his major literary work is rife with enormous imaginative creativity. The volume studies in particular several specific writings: "Eloisa to Abelard," "The Rape of the Lock," "Epistle to a Lady," and "The Dunciad Variorum."

Jones, John A. *Pope's Couplet Art*. Athens: Ohio University Press, 1969. This is the most thorough study of Pope's variety, flexibility, and artistry in utilizing the heroic couplet. Jones does much, with plentiful illustrations, to shed light upon Pope's variousness, his development, and his couplet-artistry's significance.

Spacks, Patricia Meyer, *An Argument of Images: The Poetry of Alexander Pope*. Cambridge: Harvard University Press, 1971. Spacks presents an uneven but ambitious attempt to survey Pope's great variety in employing imagery to reflect ideas and content in his verse. The early portion of the book scans widely different major poems: the "Essay on Criticism," the "Essay on Man," and "The Dunciad." The latter portion studies major image clusters, such as the imagery of madness and the altogether different imagery of limitation and control that pervade much of the verse.

Tillotson, Geoffrey, *On the Poetry of Pope*. Oxford: Clarendon Press, 1938, 2nd ed. 1950. Tillotson's is one of the first new-critical studies of Pope's verse that takes the poetry seriously as art—controverting the traditional assumptions of the nineteenth century that Pope was unpoetical, even prosaic. Tillotson thoroughly explores Pope's diction, meter, allusions, and imitations, and discusses the ambiguities in Pope's poetry. This is clearly an influential study and a turning-point that marks growing respect for Pope's poetic artistry. In the same year, a similar interest in Pope's artistry is also revealed in Robert Kilburn Root's *The Poetical Career of Alexander Pope* (Princeton: Princeton University Press, 1938); Root's is a less impressive, but nonetheless attractive and informative volume.

Wasserman, Earl R. *Pope's "Epistle to Bathurst": A Critical Reading with an Edition of the Manuscripts*. Baltimore: Johns Hopkins Press, 1960. A close reading of the poem that traces both Horatian and Christian backgrounds, Wasserman supplies an extremely lengthy and effective *explication de texte*. This book complements Wasserman's earlier reading of "Windsor Forest" in Chapter IV of his book, *The Subtler Language: Critical Readings of Neoclassic and Romantic Poems* (Baltimore: Johns Hopkins Press, 1959).

Weinbrot, Howard D. *Alexander Pope and the Traditions of Formal Satire*. Princeton: Princeton University Press, 1982. A careful, studied, and persuasive survey of satiric traditions and of Pope's practice in the 1730's, Weinbrot's volume shows clearly that Pope could "use" the form and tone of Horatian satire quite often as a mask or shell that would conceal his more caustic Juvenalian and Persian ideas and tones. Containing careful studies of the *Imitations of Horace,* this volume goes further than John M. Aden's *Something Like Horace: Studies in the Art and Allusion of Pope's Horatian Satires* (Nashville: Vanderbilt University Press, 1969).

Williams, Aubrey, *Pope's Dunciad: A Study of Its Meaning.* Baton Rouge: Louisiana State University Press, 1955. Williams' is the most thorough critical exposition of the *Dunciad,* revealing its backgrounds, its literary debts, and tracing the thread of its historical and ethical meanings. This major study overturns conventional assumptions that the *Dunciad* was an aberrant aside in the poet's career and nothing but a demeaning exercise in spite and malice.

Other Sources

Bedford, Emmet G. and Robert J. Dilligan, eds. *A Concordance to the Poems of Alexander Pope.* 2 vols. Detroit: Gale Research, 1974. Thorough concordance to all the poetry.

Kowalk, Wolfgang, *Alexander Pope: An Annotated Bibliography of Twentieth-Century Criticism 1900-1979.* New York: Peter Lang Publications, 1981. Most useful annotated bibliography of Pope criticism.

Lopez, Cecilia L. *Alexander Pope: An Annotated Bibliography 1945-1967.* Gainesville: University of Florida Press, 1970.

Mack, Maynard, ed. *Essential Articles for the Study of Alexander Pope.* Hamden, CT: Archon Books, 1964; revision and enlargement, 1968. Selection of forty-nine essays on every aspect of Pope and his poetry.

Tobin, James, *Alexander Pope: A List of Critical Studies Published from 1895-1944.* New York: Cosmopolitan Science and Art Service, 1945. Early and useful bibliography of Pope studies in this century.

Selected Dictionaries and Encyclopedias

Critical Survey of Poetry, Salem Press, 1982. Overview of Pope's life and work, with brief bibliography.

Great Writers of the English Language: Poets, St. Martin's Press, 1979. Brief biography, bibliography, and assessment of Pope's career and achievement.

The New Cambridge Bibliography of English Literature, Cambridge University Press, 1969-1977. Extensive bibliography.

John R. Clark
University of South Florida

KATHERINE ANNE PORTER
1890–1980

Author's Chronology

Born Collie Russell Porter, May 15, 1890 in Indian Creek, Texas; attends various schools; *1906* runs away from home; marries; *1909* divorces; *1914–1917* holds various jobs in Texas and Louisiana; *1918* works as a reporter in Denver; becomes severely ill; *1919* recovers; goes to New York; supports herself by writing-for-hire; *1920* studies art in Mexico; *1921* returns to Fort Worth; *1922* writes *María Concepción; 1931* receives Guggenheim Fellowship (and again in 1938); lives in Mexico; sails from Veracruz to Bremerhaven; lives in Paris; marries again; *1939* publishes *Pale Horse, Pale Rider; 1944 The Leaning Tower and Other Stories; 1965* wins Pulitzer Prize for *Katherine Anne Porter's Collected Short Stories;* first novel, *Ship of Fools,* published in 1962, became a best seller; dies September 18, 1980 in Silver Spring, Maryland.

Author's Bibliography (selected)

Flowering Judas and Other Stories, 1930; *A Book of French Songs with Translations,* 1933; *Hacienda,* 1934 (short novel); *Noon Wine,* 1937 (novella); *Pale Horse, Pale Rider,* 1939 (three short novels); *The Itching Parrot,* 1942 (translation, with introduction, of novel by José Joaquín Fernandez de Lizardi); *The Leaning Tower and Other Stories,* 1944; *The Days Before,* 1952 (essays); *Ship of Fools,* 1962 (novel); *A Christmas Story,* 1967; *The Collected Essays and Occasional Writings of Katherine Anne Porter,* 1970; *The Never-Ending Wrong,* 1977 (on the Sacco-Vanzetti case).

Overview of Biographical Sources

Before Joan Givner's *Katherine Anne Porter: A Biography* (1982), few facts about Porter's life had been documented, mainly because of her own tendency to romanticize her past. Even interviews had not been satisfactory, and contain much that is repetitious. Barbara Thompson's interview with Porter is one of the most valuable, as is Glenway Wescott's *Katherine Anne Porter Personally.* Both of these articles may be found in *Katherine Anne Porter: A Critical Symposium* edited by Lodwick Hartley and George Core (Athens: University of Georgia Press, 1969). There are a number of other interviews with Porter that have been published in periodicals, such as "A Country and Some People I Love," Harper's, September, 1965, dealing with the role of Mexico in her life. A more complete list is given by George Hendrick in *Katherine Anne Porter* (New York: Twayne, 1965). This work also contains biographical data obtained from unpublished dissertations. John Edward Hardy's monograph *Katherine Anne Porter* (New York: Frederick Ungar, 1973), on the themes in Miss Porter's stories, has taken what was known of her life to give insight into her works. Hardy's work is available and readable.

Evaluation of Selected Biographies

Givner, Joan, *Katherine Anne Porter: A Biography*. New York: Simon and Schuster, 1982. In this book commissioned by Porter herself at age eighty-six "to get at the truth," Givner has compiled the only complete biography. With indefatigable zeal she assembled mountains of material, much of which she presents uncritically, resulting in occasional lack of precision. She attempts to relate Porter's creative work to her life, again a problem, since often neither the chronology nor the details correspond. Givner's love of detail leads her to lengthy descriptions of Porter's many sufferings, both physical and spiritual. As a result the quality of the person Katherine Anne Porter is often blurred by the straightforward facts. Mrs. Givner imputes Porter's sufferings to her longing for love, to her unfortunate marriages and love affairs, and to her early rejection by her father. It is, however, a great contribution to literary research that Givner established a reliable chronology and presented facts that will surely lead to a new interpretation of Porter's works.

Autobiographical Sources

Other than Glenway Wescott's edition of *The Selected Letters of Katherine Anne Porter* (Boston: Seymour Lawrence, 1970), and the interviews referred to in biographical materials, there are no autobiographical sources for Porter. Critics, however, believe there is a great deal of autobiography in her works, especially in the Miranda stories analyzed by William Nance as examples of the rejection theme in *Katherine Anne Porter and the Art of Rejection* (1964).

Overview of Critical Sources

Critics tend to observe first and foremost that while Porter exhibits technical perfection, her literary output is very small. She is ranked as a major American short story writer, although the greatest number of critical works addresses her only novel *Ship of Fools*. Most critical works are articles in periodicals, for which Edward Schwartz's *Katherine Anne Porter: A Critical Bibliography* (Bulletin of the New York Public Library, LVII, May 1953) and Louis Waldrip and Shirley Ann Bauer's *A Bibliography of the Works of Katherine Anne Porter, and a Bibliography of the Criticism of the Works of Katherine Anne Porter* (Metuchen, NJ: Scarecrow Press, 1969) are excellent sources. Although Porter published her most significant works in the 1920's and 1930's, full-length critical works do not appear until the 1960's, probably because of the attention aroused by *Ship of Fools*. Some of the most important critics of Katherine Anne Porter are Robert Penn Warren, Ray West, Jr., Glenway Wescott, George Core, M. M. Liberman, and more recently, Joan Givner.

Evaluation of Selected Criticism

DeMouy, Jane Krause, *Katherine Anne Porter's Women*. Austin: University of Texas Press, 1983. In this study DeMouy defines Porter's central theme as a basic psychological conflict in the women protagonists. It is on the one hand a desire for independence and freedom, and on the other, a desire to fulfill the traditional role of woman as wife and mother. In this context DeMouy examines all of Porter's major stories except "Noon Wine" and "The Leaning Tower," with special emphasis on the Miranda figure. She sees *Ship of Fools* as Porter's *magnum opus* in which she universalizes her observations on collective loneliness and failure to love. The whole work centers on feminine psychology and draws on such sources as Freud, Karen Horney, and archetypal imagery.

Hartley, Lodwick and George Core, *A Critical Symposium: Katherine Anne Porter.* Athens: University of Georgia Press, 1969. This is probably one of the best works on Miss Porter. It contains Robert Penn Warren's "Irony with a Center," to which future critics regularly defer, and "The Eye of the Story" by Eudora Welty, whom Miss Porter influenced. Each of the editors, eminent Porter critics, has a work worthy of notice.

Hendrick, George, *Katherine Anne Porter.* New York: Twayne, 1965. As is usual in this series, Hendrick's work is a general biographical introduction to the author and a chronological approach to her works. It is a good departure point, since it gives a brief résumé and critical evaluation of each short story and of the novel *Ship of Fools.* The book contains a good bibliography of Porter's works as well as an annotated bibliography of secondary sources.

Nance, William L., S.M. *Katherine Anne Porter and the Art of Rejection.* Chapel Hill: University of North Carolina, 1964. As the title indicates, the book is devoted to the theme of rejection in Katherine Anne Porter's works. The first of the few full-length monographs on Porter, this study explores her stories according to two groups: the presence or absence of the semi-autobiographical protagonist often portrayed as Miranda. Consequently he studies the Miranda stories in greatest detail, without, however, eliminating any of her works. Nance sees an organic unity in all of Porter's work, which he calls a "profoundly true testimony to the truth as she sees it," but which is in reality "a blind instinctive flight from it." The study is strongly rooted in previous criticism, especially Robert Penn Warren's concept of irony. It is a very readable, well-documented book, though subjective in the divisions of Porter's work.

Warren, Robert Penn, ed. *Katherine Anne Porter: A Collection of Critical Essays.* Englewood Cliffs, NJ: Prentice Hall, 1979. Edited by the eminent poet, novelist, and critic, this book contains an excellent biographical and bibliographical overview by Warren himself. The articles are by notable Porter critics. It also contains the famous interview with Katherine Anne Porter: "A Country and Some People I Love," relating her fondness for Mexico and the genesis of her Mexican stories, and "Noon Wine: the Sources," considered one of her best essays. The articles represent the best of what has already appeared in reviews and books, most during the 1950's and 1960's; therefore, despite the publication date of 1979, there is little recent material.

West, Ray, Jr. *Katherine Anne Porter.* Minneapolis: University of Minnesota Press, 1963. This short study deals with Porter's memories, though not in the sense in which one usually speaks of memory; rather, the imprint that events leave through the manner in which they are experienced.

Selected Dictionaries and Encyclopedias

American Writers since 1900, Chicago: St. James Press, 1983. Bibliography and chronology.

American Women Writers, Frederick Ungar, 1983. Works, bibliography, and commentary on works.

S. Catharine Christi

EZRA POUND
1885-1972

Author's Chronology

Born October 30, 1885, Hailey, Idaho; *1905* awarded Ph.B. Hamilton College; *1906* M.A. University of Pennsylvania; travels in Europe as a Fellow in Romanics; *1908* begins first instructorship in Wabash College after six months of travel in Italy; *A Lume Spento* published in Venice; *1910* publishes *The Spirit of Romance,* a reworking of his abandoned doctoral thesis; *1912* becomes foreign editor of Harriet Monroe's Chicago-based *Poetry; 1914* marries Dorothy Shakespear; *1915* begins work on the *Cantos; 1917* publishes first three *Cantos* in *Poetry; 1920* moves to Paris; publishes *Hugh Selwyn Mauberly* and his editing of Fenollosa's work on the Chinese character; *1921* publishes *Poems 1918–1921;* edits Eliot's "The Wasteland"; *1924* moves to Italy; *1925* daughter born to Pound and Olga Rudge; *1926* son born to Pound and Dorothy Shakespear; *1930–1940* years of high productivity and many publications; *1941* begins broadcasts over Rome Radio which lead to U.S. indictment for treason in 1943; *1945* arrested and incarcerated in Pisa for six months; *1946* declared unfit for trial by reason of insanity; committed to St. Elizabeth's Hospital, Washington, DC; *1949* awarded Bollingen prize for *The Pisan Cantos; 1958* returns to Italy after indictment dismissed; *1959* publishes *Thrones: 96–109 de los cantares; 1972* dies on November 1 in Venice, Italy.

Author's Bibliography (selected)

The Spirit of Romance, 1910 (criticism); *Personae: The Collected Poems of Ezra Pound,* 1926; *The ABC of Reading,* 1934 (criticism); *Social Credit: An Impact,* 1935 (economic and social criticism); *Guide to Kulchur,* 1938 (social criticism); *The Translations of Ezra Pound,* 1953; *Literary Essays of Ezra Pound,* 1954; *The Cantos of Ezra Pound,* 1970; *Selected Cantos,* 1970.

Overview of Biographical Sources

Ezra Pound led a long and controversial life which tends to polarize not only his readers but his biographers; thus, most treatments of Pound's life are strained by the decision to support or oppose him. Apart from Stock's *Life of Ezra Pound* and Norman's *Ezra Pound,* the major biographies, there are several other works of note. Most recent is C. David Heymann's *Ezra Pound: The Last Rower: A Political Profile* (New York: Viking, 1976) which contributes a perspective augmented by access to previously unavailable material and explores in some detail the relationship of politics and poetry in Pound's work. Though criticized for its organization and approach, the information and analysis is solid. Michael Reck's *Ezra Pound: A Close-Up* (New York: McGraw-Hill, 1967) is a fairly complete biography which also correlates the poetry and life of

Pound. Part IV of the book contains a lucid assessment of Pound's work and a fine short chapter on reading the *Cantos*. Harry M. Meacham's *The Caged Panther: Ezra Pound at Saint Elizabeth's* (New York: Twayne, 1967) focuses on Pound's incarceration in the asylum and his efforts to remain in contact with the world, his work and his sanity as well as the efforts of his friends and advocates toward getting him released. Eustace Mullins' *This Difficult Individual, Ezra Pound* (New York: Fleet Publishing, 1961) provides a rather sardonic account of Pound's residence in St. Elizabeth's and the efforts to release him. This work is still valuable for the personal and immediate perspective which Mullins maintains throughout.

Evaluation of Selected Biographies

Norman, Charles, *Ezra Pound.* New York: Macmillan, 1960. Norman relates Pound's life until shortly after his release from St. Elizabeth's and return to Italy, and the book contains a substantial and powerful political theme as a result. Carefully organized and well written, the book became a source for Stock's later biography, yet still contains significant readings of Pound's poetry concurrent with the events of his life. Norman's other book, *The Case Of Ezra Pound* (New York: Funk and Wagnall's, 1968), delves more deeply into Pound's politics through focusing on the sources and circumstances of Pound's trial and indictment for treason. Read in conjunction, they provide an exceedingly thorough account of those years of Pound's life.

Stock, Noel, *The Life of Ezra Pound: An Expanded Edition.* San Francisco: North Point Press, 1982. This carefully documented biography deals thoroughly with the events of Pound's life. Written by an intimate friend and associate of Pound, it remains probably the most important and complete account. Though it deals exhaustively with Pound's biography, the book has been criticized for failing to present a more personal side of the public man. The expanded edition includes some clarifications of facts reported in the first edition and a short and useful survey of scholarship which appeared in the ten years between the editions.

Autobiographical Sources

As one of the most public poets of the twentieth century, Pound leaves a large void with respect to autobiographical materials. This may occur because the *Cantos* are, in their own way, more autobiographical than anything else he might have written. Pound as correspondent does allow a view of the articulate, irrepressible crusader and man of great personal feeling in D. D. Paige's edition of *The Letters of Ezra Pound: 1907–1941* (New York: Harcourt, Brace, 1950), and Pound's volume, *Indiscretions,* is acknowledged as a fictional account of a boy's early relationship with his father drawn from his own life. It is certain, however, that Pound's vigorous merging of the public and the private man in his life and work provides an adequate explanation of his neglect of this area.

Overview of Critical Sources

The bulk of Pound's work and the nature of his personal, political and poetic theories tends to discourage attempts to treat the whole of Pound's life and work in one critical assessment. Critical studies of Pound generally focus on one aspect of the man: his biography, politics, or poetry. They tend to demonstrate correspondences between these elements of Pound's influence, or to substantiate a reading of Pound's work for a particular purpose. In fact, much of the critical work on Pound takes the form of providing guides that identify and explicate the references in the poetry so that readers may attempt their own understanding of Pound with some assistance concerning the fundamentals of Pound's work and methods.

Evaluation of Selected Criticism

Kenner, Hugh, *The Pound Era.* Berkeley: University of California Press, 1971. This book continues the research Kenner began twenty years earlier with his study, *The Poetry of Ezra Pound* (Norfolk, CT: New Directions, 1951), and demonstrates Pound's place in the cultural and intellectual flux of the world during his life and times. Though somewhat impressionistic, it is a thoroughly readable and insightful account of Pound's intellectual and poetic dialogue with the world he sought to change.

Knapp, James F. *Ezra Pound.* Boston: Twayne, 1979. Knapp makes a general critical introduction to Pound's life and work by assuming an essential and progressive thematic coherence which he pursues through a chronological exploration of selected poetry and criticism of Pound. He sees the evolution of Pound's thought as the result of a consistent quest to realize a vision of artistic and cultural unity and integrity. He identifies and demonstrates essential aspects of Pound's poetic method and offers solid readings of much of the early poetry as well as the *Cantos.* The book provides a starting place for serious research or an overview of Pound for the general reader.

Stock, Noel, *Reading the Cantos: The Study of Meaning in Ezra Pound.* New York: Pantheon, 1966. Reacting against impressionistic readings of earlier critics, Stock determines that a hard look at the text of the *Cantos* before discussing them is the best way to understand them. Noting Pound's method of associating and developing ideas through juxtaposing images, Stock provides some solid close readings of the poetry. The book deals with the *Cantos* up to and including *Thrones.*

Wilhelm, James J. *The Later Cantos of Ezra Pound.* New York: Walker and Co., 1977. Wilhelm provides a useful though not complete thematic survey of the final *Cantos* and demonstrates some connections with the earlier work, as well as making some remarks about the conclusion of the *Cantos* and the work as a whole.

Other Sources

Edwards, John Hamilton and William W. Vasse, *Annotated Index to the Cantos: Of Ezra Pound: Cantos 1–84.* Berkeley: University of California Press, 1957. This reference guide identifies various figures and events to which Pound alludes. Superseded by Carroll F. Terrell's, *Companion to the Cantos of Ezra Pound,* Vol. 1. (Cantos 1–71). Berkeley: University of California Press, 1980.

Kearns, George, *Guide to Ezra Pound's Selected Cantos.* New Brunswick, NJ: Rutgers University Press, 1980. Kearns provides an interpretive guide through the *Cantos* Pound selected as an introduction to the entire work.

Rosenthal, M. L. *A Primer of Ezra Pound.* New York: Macmillan, 1960. Rosenthal gives a brief, still useful survey of Pound's work and thought from the early poetry through *Canto* 109.

Selected Dictionaries and Encyclopedias

American Writers: A Collection of Literary Biographies, Vol. III. Charles Scribner's Sons, 1974. William Van O'Connor provides a brief, cogent summary of Pound and his work as well as a helpful bibliography.

Eric Paul Shaffer
University of California—Davis

E. J. PRATT
1882–1964

Author's Chronology

Born Edwin John Pratt, 1882, Western Bay, Newfoundland; father a Methodist minister; family moves from one fishing and whaling outport to another at almost regular four year intervals. After graduating from St. John's Methodist College, Pratt served as a preacher and then as a teacher in several remote Newfoundland villages. His experiences in these outposts strongly influenced his early poetry. *1909* attends University of Toronto; studies philosophy; awarded Victoria Gold Medal for Old Testament Studies; *1911* granted B.A.; *1912* M.A., with thesis on demonology; *1913* B.D.; *1917* Ph.D., with thesis on Pauline Eschatology; *1918* marries Viola Whitney, a staunch member of the United Church; fathers one daughter, Mildrid Claire; *1920* while working as a demonstrator in the Department of Psychology, joins English department, University of Toronto; *1930* elected to Royal Society of Canada; *1940* wins Lorne Pierce Medal; *1946* made a Commander of the Order of Saint Michael and Saint George; *1961* receives Canada Council Medal; granted LL.D. by the University of Toronto; *1964* dies in Toronto.

Author's Bibliography (selected)

Newfoundland Verse, 1923 (poems); *The Witches' Brew*, 1925 (narrative poem); *The Titans*, 1926 (narrative poems); *The Iron Door: An Ode*, 1927 (poem); *The Roosevelt and the Antinoe*, 1930 (narrative poem); *Many Moods*, 1932 (poems); *The Titanic*, 1935 (narrative poem); *The Fable of the Goats and Other Poems*, 1932; *Brebeuf and his Brethren*, 1940 (narrative poem); *Still Life and Other Verse*, 1943 (poems); *Behind the Log*, 1947 (narrative poem); *Collected Poems*, 1944; *Towards the Last Spike*, 1952 (narrative poem); *The Collected Poems of E. J. Pratt*, 1958.

Overview of Biographical Sources

The results of a detailed biographical analysis of Pratt's life and work are only now coming into print. Until 1984, only a one monograph-length treatment of Pratt's life and accomplishment was available to the non-specialist: Karl F. Klinck's "A Biography", included in *E. J. Pratt: The Man and His Poetry*. Since then, however, the first of a two-volume biographical study has appeared: David G. Pitt's *E. J. Pratt: The Truant Years, 1882–1927*. Regrettably, the main body of this biography is still in preparation; only the first volume has been published, and it ends its study a little more than half-way through the poet's career. Therefore, if a reader wishes to gain a "sense" of the poet's overall life, he must be content with the sketch offered in Klinck's brief monograph.

Evaluation of Selected Biographies

Klinck, Karl F. "A Biography," in *E. J. Pratt, The Man and His Poetry.* Toronto: Ryerson Press, 1947. This study presents an overview of Pratt's life and writings. It does not give material in great length, nor does it include commentary drawn from confidential sources. The information is accurate about facts and details, and the book stresses Pratt's public image of a well-loved teller of tall tales. Its strength, in other words, is its ability to draw a broad character sketch of the man.

Pitt, David G. *E. J. Pratt: The Truant Years, 1882–1927.* Toronto: Ryerson, 1981. Although still incomplete, this study promises to be the definitive work of the poet. It discusses information in detail, and often relies on letters or private documents to reveal the poet. The overall picture is sympathetic, penetrating and insightful. Pitt, in particular, is able to reveal the often elusive personality of the man. Although Pitt does discuss some of Pratt's major poems, he generally prefers to describe the poet's experiences, actions and thoughts as revealed in documents.

Autobiographical Sources

Susan Gingel has edited *E. J. Pratt on His Life and Times* into a solid and readable work which gives insight into the writer and his aims. The book is ordered chronologically and follows Pratt's commentary on his own poems in their order of composition. The main flaw of this method, of course, is that the reader interested in autobiographical material rather than the poet's critical commentary must be content to be his own biographer.

Overview of Critical Sources

Pratt is primarily recognized as a narrative and lyric poet who, with a strong sense of irony, develops a unique poetic vision which blends humanism, Christianity and evolutionary theory. Until recently, he has been neglected or under-estimated as a poet. It is not surprising, therefore, that there is no extended study of the man and his works. Furthermore, given this situation, it is to be expected that the writings about him focus primarily on the achievements of his poems and the various interrelationships between them. Often the most convincing and worthwhile commentaries about Pratt are confined to short introductions to his collected or selected poems, written by the people who undertook the arduous task of editing Pratt's collected and selected editions. Of particular value are the "Introductions" by William Rose Bennet in *Collected Poems of E. J. Pratt* (1945); Northrop Frye, *Collected Poems of E. J. Pratt*, 2nd ed. (1958); Peter Buitenhuis, *Selected Poems of E. J. Pratt* (Toronto: Macmillan, 1968). In recent years Pratt studies have increased. Of particular importance is Sandra Djwa's *E. J. Pratt: The Evolutionary Vision*, a complete and helpful guide to a study of Pratt's poetry and the cultural forces which have influenced it. Djwa offers sound, helpful readings of the poems while carefully linking these readings to the intellectual forces of the poet's time.

Evaluation of Selected Criticism

Bennet, William Rose, "Introduction" in *Collected Poems of E. J. Pratt*. New York: Alfred A. Knopf, 1945, pp. xi–xv. A crucial short commentary, it outlines Pratt's powers as a narrative poet and it describes the merits of this Canadian poet for an American audience.

Djwa, Sandra, *E. J. Pratt: The Evolutionary Vision*. Montreal: McGill-Queen's University Press. In this first full-length study of the poetry and criticism, Djwa focuses on the "holistic vision" of Pratt. She traces with careful detail the early, middle and late periods of Pratt's writing while also discussing the literary, historical and cultural forces that shaped Pratt's art.

Frye, Northrop, "Introduction" in *The Collected Poems of E. J. Pratt*. 2nd ed. Toronto: Macmillan, 1958, pp. xii–xxviii. Frye's central argument that Pratt has mastered a disarmingly simple style in order to be an effective narrative poet is crucial to anyone who hopes to understand Pratt's work.

Pacey, Desmond, "E. J. Pratt," in *Ten Canadian Poets*. Toronto: Ryerson Press, 1958, pp. 165–193. Undoubtedly, this is the best essay available for anyone new to Pratt. The account is balanced, usually focusing on the interrelationship of theme and style. Pacey deliberately restricts himself to poems that relate to his main subject, and he consistently points out the weaknesses of any thesis that holds Pratt is a straightforward humanist.

Pitt, David, ed. *E. J. Pratt*. Toronto: Ryerson, 1969. Pitt has collected major reviews and essays that offer an excellent general survey of the secondary material which deals with Pratt's reception as a poet in Canada and the United States.

Sutherland, John, *The Poetry of E. J. Pratt: A New Interpretation*. Toronto: Ryerson Press, 1956. This first extended study of some of Pratt's early work is flawed by Sutherland's effort to impose upon Pratt a rather narrow Christian philosophy.

Other Sources

Birney, Earle, "E. J. Pratt and His Critics," in *Our Living Tradition*. ed. Robert McDougall. Toronto: Ryerson Press, 1958, pp. 123–174. Birney lucidly describes the misdirections and misunderstandings of Pratt's works up to 1958.

Clever, Glenn, ed. *Reappraisals: The E. J. Pratt Symposium*. Ottawa: University of Ottawa Press, 1977. A collection of papers that dramatically changes earlier readings of Pratt. The general aesthetics of Pratt's artistry receives particular emphasis.

New, William, H. "The Identity of Articulation: Pratt's *Towards the Last Spike,*" in *Articulating West: Essays of Form in Modern Canadian Literature.* Toronto: New Press, 1972, pp. 32–42. Although New places emphasis on a single long narrative, he makes a convincing case for the subtle interrelationship of language and act in Pratt's poetry. New's essay is a concise example of the recent directions of Pratt criticism.

Wilson, Milton T. *E. J. Pratt.* Toronto: McClelland and Stewart, 1971. Although a short book, Wilson offers a solid introduction to Pratt's shorter and longer poems. It's wit often makes it very entertaining reading.

Selected Dictionaries and Encyclopedias
Critical Survey of Poetry, Salem Press, 1983. Brief Biography and short analysis of Pratt's major accomplishments as a poet.

The Oxford Companion to Canadian Literature, Oxford University Press. A concise overview of Pratt's life, and a discussion of the main books.

Ed Jewinski
Wilfrid Laurier University

MATTHEW PRIOR
1664–1721

Author's Chronology

Born July 21, 1664, Westminster, Middlesex, the son of a joiner; attends Westminster School until death of father; employed in uncle's London tavern; returns to Westminster under patronage of Earl of Dorset; *1681* elected King's Scholar; *1683* enters St. John's College, Cambridge; *1686* earns bachelor's degree; *1688* appointed Fellow; *1690* appointed secretary to Lord Dursley, Ambassador at The Hague; *1697* active in negotiations leading to Treaty of Ryswick; *1699* appointed Under-Secretary of State; *1701* sits briefly in Parliament; *1707* publishes first collection of poems; serves as plenipotentiary in negotiations leading to signing of the Treaty of Utrecht in *1713; 1715–1716* political prisoner in England; *1718* publishes financially rewarding folio edition of poems; spends last years at Down Hall, Essex; dies September 18, 1721, and is buried in Westminster Abbey at Spenser's feet.

Author's Bibliography (selected)

Collected poems, variously assembled, appeared in editions of 1707, 1709, 1716, 1718 under the title *Poems on Several Occasions.* Since Prior's works are numerous and often brief, the full bibliographic listing (including the Latin) should be consulted in *The Literary Works of Matthew Prior,* ed. H. Bunker Wright and Monroe K. Spears, 2nd ed., 2 vols. (Oxford: Clarendon Press, 1971). Following is a select list: *Carmen Seculare,* 1700; "Hans Carvel," 1701; "The Ladle," 1704; "An English Padlock," 1704; *Solomon,* 1718; *Alma, or, the Progress of the Mind,* 1718; *Down-Hall,* 1723; *Dialogues of the Dead* (prose), 1907.

Overview of Biographical Sources

Samuel Johnson's biographical essay in the *Lives of the English Poets* (1781) stood as the closest thing to a biography of Prior until the twentieth century. During this century three book-length studies have appeared. Francis Bickley's *Life of Matthew Prior* (1914) is the least specialized and authoritative. L. G. Wickham Legg's *Matthew Prior: A Study of His Public Career and Correspondence* (1921) is particularly useful, as the title indicates, with reference to Prior's active public service years. The third, Charles Kenneth Eves' *Matthew Prior: Poet and Diplomatist* (1939), though outdated in its scholarship is regarded as the standard life and devotes more attention to Prior's literary career than do its biographic predecessors. Currently in progress is a bio-critical life of Prior by Frances Mayhew Rippy for the Twayne English Authors Series.

Evaluation of Selected Biographies

Bickley, Francis, *The Life of Matthew Prior.* London: Isaac Pitman, 1914; rpt. Folcroft Press, 1970. This, the first twentieth-century biography of Prior to see print, is also the most pedestrian. Written without the benefit of scholarly precision in a style that tends to dullness, the work has little to recommend it as a reading text. As a reference text it fares little better: the indexing is thin and the attention to the literary works minimal.

Eves, Charles Kenneth, *Matthew Prior: Poet and Diplomatist.* New York: Columbia University Press, 1939; rpt. New York: Octagon, 1971. Eves' biography is both the fullest and most useful of the three available, but its scholarship is outdated by almost fifty years. Although its text must be double-checked for particular assurance of authority, in general it serves as a sound resource. Length of text exceeds Bickley by over 40% and Legg by 25%. The index is broader in scope and more extensive than those of the other two. Eves sets Prior's writing into the context of his life, whereas Bickley and Legg rarely attempt this. As a comparative gauge, Eves' index under the heading 'Matthew Prior' devotes 3¼ columns to literary titles; Bickley and Legg employ fewer columns than this for their complete 'Prior' entries, with no separate headings for literature. In brief, Eves, if handled circumspectly, is a useful, readable, and often stimulating biography and should be consulted.

Johnson, Samuel, "Prior," *Lives of the English Poets,* ed. George Birkbeck Hill. Oxford: The Clarendon Press, 1905; rpt. New York: Octagon, 1967 Vol. II. This biographical essay from Johnson's famous collection consists of a life sketch together with critical commentary. The critical focus is both particular and general. Though the views are often biased, no one, after gaining familiarity with Prior's writing and twentieth-century assessments of it, can afford to by-pass a critic of Johnson's stature.

Legg, L. G. Wickham, *Matthew Prior: A Study of His Public Career and Correspondence.* Cambridge: The University Press, 1921; rpt. New York: Octagon, 1972. Legg's work is superior to Bickley's in content, style, and usefulness. The indexing is fuller, the text much more incisive and readable. Although perhaps no real advantage is gained with respect to the literary focus, it is Legg's expressed aim, as the title suggests, to write of Prior's public career. Eves' biography generally supersedes that of Legg; however, two points should be made. First, Legg's attention to major political events in Prior's life is full and should be consulted in conjunction with Eves. Secondly, Legg reprints a number of Prior's letters and other MS notations in his text, plus appendices, that are unavailable elsewhere.

Autobiographical Sources

There is no autobiographical material readily available outside of selected letters in L. G. Wickham Legg's biography. However, a scholarly edition of Prior's correspondence is currently being prepared by H. Bunker Wright and Richard B. Kline.

Overview of Critical Sources

Although no book-length critical work has yet appeared, Prior's contemporary literary reputation and influence, his active public life, and the varied nature of his writings have occasioned many scholarly essays. Most are traditionally specific in their focus: source studies, printing histories, tracings of influence, genre analyses. Others are of a more general cast, concerned with overviews of literary personality or achievement. The value of individual essays within such a heterogeneous collection is difficult to assess; however, three essays by Monroe K. Spears stand apart. In combination they probe the broad intellectual nature of Prior's poetry as viewed against the late seventeenth and early eighteenth-century background and have influenced all subsequent studies.

Evaluation of Selected Criticism

Spears, Monroe K. "Matthew Prior's Attitude toward Natural Science," in *Publications of the Modern Language Association,* LXIII (1948), 485–507. Spears shows Prior to be skeptical of scientific systems (and other systems based solely upon human reason). While the contemporary intellectual climate coupled with his own intellectual vitality prevented Prior from holding to the older faith with unquestioned assurance, he could not accept the implications of 'natural religion' as evidenced in nature and codified by the new science.

————. "Some Ethical Aspects of Matthew Prior's Poetry," in *Studies in Philology,* XLV (1948), 606–629. Spears attempts to show the impact of eighteenth-century ethical theories on a "writer of receptive but independent mind." Prior, for example, refuses to be swayed by the growing popularity of the belief in natural benevolence. According to Spears, Prior can neither accept nor completely reject man's intellectual attempts to avoid facing the realities of life's misery, a misery which he believes to be fundamental.

————. "Matthew Prior's Religion," in *Philological Quarterly,* XXVII (1948), 159–180. In his previous two essays Spears considers science and ethics as they influence Prior's writing, but throughout there exists evidence of a bond of religious thinking. In the present essay Prior's religious beliefs form the primary focus, unifying the essays into a central study. Formal manifestations of Prior's religion are introduced along with a survey of religious problems that concerned him.

Other Sources

Bronson, Bertrand Harris, "On Choosing Fit Subjects for Verse; or, Who Now Reads Prior?" *Facets of the Enlightenment.* Berkeley: University of California Press, 1968. Imagined conversation between Prior and Dr. Johnson, cast in the mode of Prior's own *Dialogues of the Dead.* Two voices receive their blendings from the context of Prior's poems, Johnson's recorded criticism of Prior, and twentieth-century scholarship.

Jack, Ian, "The 'Choice of Life' in Johnson and Matthew Prior," *Journal of English and Germanic Philology,* XLIX (1950), 523–530. Argues that Johnson, though critical of Prior in general, was directly influenced by his *Solomon.*

Rippy, Frances Mayhew, "Matthew Prior as the Last Renaissance Man," *Studies in Medieval, Renaissance, American Literature.* ed. Betsy Colquitt. Fort Worth: Texas Christian University Press, 1971. A most readable and informative biocritical essay that suggests the influence exerted by the classics, nationalism, and religious questioning on Prior's poetry. Stresses Prior's sometimes undervalued versatility.

Spears, Monroe K. "The Meaning of Matthew Prior's *Alma,*" *ELH,* XIII (1946), 266–290. Examines the nature of Prior's thought in *Alma* with particular attention to the influence of Montaigne.

Wright, H. Bunker, "Matthew Prior's Funeral," *Modern Language Notes,* LVII (1942), 341–345. The lavish London funeral described.

Selected Dictionaries and Encyclopedias

Dictionary of National Biography, Oxford University Press, 1921–1922. Although outdated in its scholarship, still a useful source for general biographical orientation.

English Literature in the Early Eighteenth Century: 1700–1740. Vol. VII of *The Oxford History of English Literature,* Oxford University Press, 1959. A standard brief reference for someone approaching Prior initially. Well focused critical assessment of Prior as writer. Little biographical attention. Provides selective bibliography.

Edward P. Willey
Clemson University

ANN RADCLIFFE
1764–1823

Author's Chronology

Born July 9, 1764, Holborn, England, the only child of William and Ann Oates Ward; *1769* Thomas Bentley, uncle and partner with Josiah Wedgwood, rents a house in Chelsea which Ann visits frequently as a child; *1771* William Ward becomes the Wedgwood representative at Bath; family takes up residence there; *1787* marries William Radcliffe; moves to London where William reports on parliamentary proceedings as a journalist; *1789–1794* period of publications; *1794* William and Ann tour Holland and Germany and the English Lake region; move residence to Southwark; *1798* father dies; *1800* mother dies; *1802* Ann writes *Gaston de Blondeville,* but has decided to no longer write for publication; *1800–1812* Ann and William travel extensively in England; Ann writes a travel diary and poetry; *1823* dies of asthma and respiratory problems on February 7.

Author's Bibliography

The Castles of Athlin and Dunbayne, 1789 (short story); *A Sicilian Romance,* 1790 (novel); *The Romance of the Forest,* 1791 (novel); *The Mysteries of Udolpho,* 1794 (novel); *A Journey made in the Summer of 1794 through Holland and the Western Frontiers of Germany, with a return down the Rhine, to which are added Observations during a tour to the Lakes of Lancashire, Westmoreland and Cumberland,* 1795 (travel journal); *The Italian, or the Confessional of the Black Penitents,* 1797 (novel); *Gaston de Blondeville, or the Court of Henry III keeping Festival in Ardenne,* 1826 (novel); *St. Alban's Abbey,* 1826 (narrative poem).

Overview of Biographical Sources

Radcliffe was the foremost novelist of her day. This status persisted from the publication of her first popular success, *The Romance of the Forest,* in 1791 to well into the nineteenth century, even though she wrote nothing for publication after 1797. She was sought after by the rich and famous. In the face of this acclaim, Radcliffe persevered in leading an exceptionally private and uneventful life. However, in retreating from notoriety in her own time, Radcliffe succeeded too well; she left behind very little biographical information for posterity. In fact, Radcliffe's admirer, Christina Rossetti, relinquished her plan to write a biography because Radcliffe's life was so uneventful.

The major source of biographical information was published posthumously, by all evidence under the aegis of her surviving husband, journalist and newspaper owner William Radcliffe. The *Annual Biography and Obituary* for 1824 (Vol. 8. London, 1824) indicates its source as the person best qualified to give information about the author. The entry gives information about Radcliffe's parentage and her childhood, although Clara McIntyre in *Ann Radcliffe in Relation to her Time* (New Haven: Yale University Press, 1920) points out some inconsistencies. It also corrects rumors about what Radcliffe was paid for her two most famous novels. Nineteenth century "Memoirs" by Sir Walter Scott and Mrs. Julia Kavanagh draw from this source.

Because of the dearth of biographical information about Radcliffe, no definitive biography has been written. In fact, although books about Radcliffe's writing contain sections on her life, only *Ann Radcliffe* by Aline Grant (1920; rpt. 1951) is exclusively devoted to biography. Clara Frances McIntyre includes the salient biographical facts and quotes from documents in the chapter on Radcliffe's life in her *Ann Radcliffe in Relation to her Time* (New Haven: Yale University Press, 1920). The central problem of Radcliffe's biography is why she chose to stop publishing at the height of her popularity. Common speculations include: she was revolted by Matthew Lewis' extension of her literary ideas in the sexually explicit *The Monk;* she was injured by criticisms of her weaknesses as an author; she was in such a financially sound position that she no longer needed to write. The evidence supplied by Aline Grant's biography implies that she was melancholy over the death of her parents, and that as owner of the *English Chronicle,* her husband had free time to travel with her.

Evaluation of Selected Biographies

Grant, Aline, *Ann Radcliffe.* New Haven: Yale University Press, 1920; rpt. Denver: Swallow, 1951. Grant solves the problem of source information in a way Radcliffe herself might have approved: she provides an almost lyrical description of the life of the ordinary tenant of London and Bath, paying particular attention to the daily patterns a tradesman's family like Radcliffe's would have engaged in. Where biographical information exists, Grant embroiders it with the minutia of daily life—the plants her Uncle Bentley might have lovingly cultivated in his garden in Chelsea when the child Ann paid one of her many visits, or the people he might have entertained and introduced the 12-year-old to. Grant elaborates beyond the literal facts, but is not irresponsible. She provides original research and notes legal documents about Radcliffe's father's business, family connections and events. Her investigation of such tangential subjects as the appearance of Wedgwood china, which Radcliffe's father merchandised, give this brief biography charm and substance.

Autobiographical Sources

Autobiographical material is limited to the travel journals Radcliffe published and the diary excerpts published after her death. In lieu of other evidence about the inner workings of this very private writer, Clara McIntyre sees clues in Radcliffe's poem, "December's Eve at Home," a celebration of the domestic delight of a fire in a cosy parlor on a cold winter night.

Overview of Critical Sources

Current trends in critical theory and the interest in the female literary tradition have heightened appreciation for the once denigrated Gothic novel, and consequently for Ann Radcliffe, the genre's first major practitioner. The seminal critical work exemplifying this new trend is Ellen Moers' *Literary Women: The Great Writers* (1976); she names Radcliffe's contribution to a trend in women's literature "traveling heroinism." A significant collection of essays called *The Female Gothic,* edited by Juliann E. Fleenor (Montreal: Eden Press, 1983), contains two essays devoted to Radcliffe exclusively and several which include discussions of her. A Twayne series publication, *Ann Radcliffe* by E. B. Murray (New York: Twayne, 1972) is marred by a sneering attitude toward its subject, but contains a succinct summary of the Gothic novel before Radcliffe. Malcolm Ware, in *Sublimity in the Novels of Ann Radcliffe* (Copenhagen: Lundequistska Bokhandln, 1963) correlates Radcliffe's and Edmund Burke's ideas of the sublime.

The most important criticism from the early decades of this century is Clara Frances McIntyre, *Ann Radcliffe in Relation to her Time* (1920). McIntyre summarizes the facts known about Radcliffe's life, considers sources for some of her material, and assesses her contemporary popularity by quoting extensively from reviews, and enumerating translations and dramatizations. She also argues Radcliffe's significant contribution to the structure of the novel. A. S. S. Weiten's *Mrs. Radcliffe, Her Relation towards Romanticism* (Amsterdam: H. J. Paris, 1926) shows Radcliffe's direct influence on Romantic writers.

Evaluation of Selected Criticism

McIntyre, Clara, *Ann Radcliffe in Relation to her Time.* New Haven: Yale University Press, 1920. McIntyre claims that Radcliffe created the structure of suspense in the novel form, arguing that Fielding, in spite of his emphasis on the novel as "a comic epic in prose," and Richardson were both interested primarily in characterization. Walpole explicitly applies the structure of drama to the novel. Radcliffe, like Walpole, is mainly interested in plot. Unlike Walpole, she "gave new emphasis to action—not action in and for itself as in the picaresque novel, but action as bringing about complications and resolving them" (p. 89). McIntyre notes Radcliffe's superficial characterizations and connects them to Radcliffe's shyness and reclusiveness.

Moers, Ellen, *Literary Women: The Great Writers.* Garden City, NY: Doubleday, 1976. Moers calls Radcliffe the greatest practitioner of the Gothic novel, and suggests that in her hands the genre became the form which served the needs for women that the picaresque serves for men. The female heroine travels to distant and exciting places and, under extreme danger, demonstrates energy, resourcefulness, and courage. She is both persecuted and heroic. By these means, Radcliffe is able to accommodate the social directive toward feminine passivity and meekness with women's natural longing for movement, change, and adventure. Moers discusses Radcliffe's contribution to the themes in women's literature of travel, indoors and outdoors, and tomboyism. She compares Radcliffe's heroines, who find security in property, with Fanny Burney's, who find security in a social circle.

Other Sources

Two works helpful in situating Radcliffe in her time are J. M. S. Tompkins' *The Popular Novel in England 1770–1800* (London: Constable & Co., 1932; rpt. Lincoln: University of Nebraska Press, 1961), and Volume XI of *The Smith College Studies in Modern Languages:* Joyce M. Horner's *The English Women Novelists and their Connection with the Feminist Movement, 1688–1797* (rpt. Folcroft Library Editions, 1973). Studies of the Gothic include Mario Praz, *The Romantic Agony* (London: Oxford University Press, 1933), Montague Summers, *The Gothic Quest: A History of the Gothic* (London: Fortune Press, 1938), and Devendra P. Varma, *The Gothic Flame* (New York: Russell & Russell, 1957). See also Sandra M. Gilbert and Susan Gubar, *The Madwoman in the Attic: The Woman Writer and the Nineteenth-Century Literary Imagination* (New Haven and London: Yale University Press, 1979) for an influential statement of uses of Gothicism by later writers.

Charmaine Wellington
University of Illinois

SIR WALTER RALEIGH
c. 1552–1618

Author's Chronology

Born c. 1552, Hayes Barton, Devon, England, of West Country family; educated Oxford University; arrives in mid *1570's* in the Court of Queen Elizabeth; rapidly became a leading courtier, soldier, explorer; *1584* founds the first settlement in Virginia; remains a favorite of the Queen until *1592* when he secretly marries one of her Maids-of-Honor, Elizabeth Throckmorton and is imprisoned; the same year, released and regains some of his popularity; leads a naval attack on Cadiz, 1596; *1603* is arrested by newly crowned James I, tried for treason, sentenced to death, later commuted to life imprisonment; *1603–1616* lives in the Tower of London, confined but comfortable; becomes a close associate of Henry, Prince of Wales until Henry's death in 1612; during his imprisonment becomes a voluminous writer working especially on *The History of the World; 1614 History* is published; *1616* released from prison in the hope he could discover treasure in South America; *1617* expedition fails, his son dies on the venture; returns to England, is executed on October 29, 1618, on the basis of the 1603 death sentence.

Author's Bibliography (selected)

A Report about the Iles of Azores, 1591 (pamphlet); *The Discovery of the Empire of Guiana,* 1596 (pamphlet); *History of the World,* 1614 (history); *Works of Sir Walter Raleigh,* 1827 (Complete Works); *Poetry of Sir Walter Raleigh,* 1951, *Selected Prose and Poetry,* 1965; *The History of the World,* 1971 (a selection).

Overview of Biographical Sources

Because of his flamboyant life as a courtier under Queen Elizabeth and King James, Raleigh excited many envious and scurrilous comments during and after his lifetime, most notably by John Aubrey in *Brief Lives* (modern selection by O. L. Dick, New York: Secker and Warburg, 1949). Modern biographies have often tended to be romantic, near-fictional accounts of a man whose acts were not only larger than life but for whom, like most Elizabethans, the records are often scanty. Pierre Lefranc's *Raleigh, Ecrivain, l'oeuvre et les idees* (Quebec: Les Presses de l'Universite Laval, 1968) is the most reliable biographical survey, but Robert Lacey's *Sir Walter Raleigh* (New York: Atheneum, 1973) is a more readable account. Walter Oakeshott's *The Queen and the Poet* (New York: Barnes and Noble, 1960) is a lively, but highly romantic treatment of what the author takes as the love story in Raleigh's poems. Part of the problem of constructing an accurate biography of Raleigh is that while many parts of his public life were well-publicized, his writings, especially his poetry were not published in his lifetime. Some of the poems ascribed to him may not even be his own.

Evaluation of Selected Biographies

Aubrey, John, *Brief Lives.* New York: Secker and Warburg, 1949; rpt. Harmondsworth: Peregrine Books, 1962. The brief account of Raleigh is one of the most flamboyant in Aubrey's fascinating mixture of gossip and history. It focuses on the brilliance of Raleigh's life, his personal appearance, reputation, and intrigues at court.

Bradbrook, M. D. *The School of Night: a study in the literary relationships of Sir Walter Raleigh.* Cambridge: Cambridge University Press, 1936. A pioneering study of the intellectuals of the 1590's, especially between the poets Raleigh knew well—Spenser, Marlowe and Chapman. Shakespeare's nickname for the group was "the school of night," and it also included the Earl of Northumberland, known as the Wizard Earl, mathematicians, philosophers and others interested in the occult.

Lacey, Robert, *Sir Walter Raleigh.* New York: Atheneum, 1973. A detailed, but readable and lively bio-critical introduction, and probably the best modern popular account of Raleigh's life. It draws on Pierre Lefranc's massive and scholarly *Sir Walter Raleigh, Ecrivain,* adding various more recent biographical details. Like most Raleigh biographers, Lacey speculates on the place of the poems in Raleigh's life, though more judiciously than Oakeshott.

Oakeshott, Walter, *The Queen and the Poet.* New York: Barnes and Noble, 1960. A lively, but highly romanticized reading of Raleigh's handful of poems in terms of a narrative account of the affection (never sexual, but highly intense) between the Queen and Raleigh. He builds his case largely on the belief (highly dubious) that Raleigh's poems are directly autobiographical. Although much of his speculations are conjectural, there is a lively and tantalizing story in his study.

Strathmann, E. A. *Sir Walter Raleigh: A Study in Elizabethan Skepticism.* New York: Columbia University Press, 1951. A still useful account of Raleigh's relationships with the intellectuals in the 1590's who were reputed to be interested in skeptical philosophy, religious speculation, atheism and magic. These associates included the poet and playwright Christopher Marlowe, and scientists like Thomas Harriott.

Autobiographical Sources

While Raleigh left no direct account of his own life, nonetheless there are many autobiographical references in his works. His poems have been scoured for references to his life but there are only a handful that can definitely be seen as autobiographical: four poems found in the Cecil Papers in Hatfield House, and associated with his imprisonment in 1592, one of which, usually called "the Oceans love to Cynthia" is a barely disguised plea to the Queen for a return to favour; and a verse reliably ascribed to the night before his execution in 1618 in which he calls on God to save him. More substantial autobiographical references can be found in the *History of the World* which (despite its subject) Raleigh used partly for therapy and partly to give vent to what he saw as his own mistreatment by King James. They are most particularly found in the moving preface to the work.

Overview of Critical Sources
Raleigh's importance as a writer, especially as a poet, is despite the slimness of his poetic output—little more than two dozen short and one long poem. Modern criticism has focused not only on his most interesting life but also on his connections with the age's major intellectual movements, and most especially on his role in the Court and his struggles within its power.

Evaluation of Selected Criticism
Greenblatt, Stephen J. *Sir Walter Raleigh: The Renaissance Man and His Roles.* New Haven: Yale University Press, 1973. The most important modern study of Raleigh, Greenblatt's book focuses on the way Raleigh created different selves for himself according to the different roles he filled—explorer, poet, courtier, soldier. He raises the fascinating question of whether there was a 'real' Raleigh behind all the masks the man wore.

Hill, Christopher, *Intellectual Origins of the English Revolution.* Oxford: Clarendon Press, 1965. Hill looks at Raleigh's contribution to the developing social and political changes of the period, and especially on the ways the Puritan and Country factions used his skepticism about the monarchy to develop a theory of republicanism.

Racin, John J., Jr. *Sir Walter Raleigh as Historian: An Analysis of the History of the World.* Salzburg: Institut fur Englische Sprache und Literature/Humanities Press, 1974. This is the most substantial study of Raleigh's *History,* focusing on his unsuccessful desire to follow a traditional Christian understanding of history. In particular, Racin focuses on his skepticism about a final, providential direction to history.

Waller, Gary, *Sixteenth Century Poetry.* London: Longman, 1985. Waller provides an account (chapter four) of Raleigh as a court poet, with some mention of his role as a historian. He looks at ways Raleigh was, not always consciously, a spokesman for oppositional tendencies in the period.

Other Sources
Garrett, George P. *Death of the Fox.* New York: Doubleday, 1972. Long, lively, fictionalized biography of Raleigh's entire life, focusing on Raleigh's division between poet and politician.

Tennenhouse, Leonard, "Sir Walter Raleigh and the Literature of Client-age," in *Patronage in the Renaissance.* ed. Guy Fitch Lytle and Stephen Orgel. Princeton: Princeton University Press, 1981. An excellent account of Raleigh's problems as a writer struggling to achieve his reputation in the Court.

Selected Dictionaries and Encyclopedias

Critical Survey of Poetry, Vol. 6, Salem Press, 1983. An account of Raleigh's poetry, his connections at court and his modern reputation.

Gary F. Waller
Carnegie-Mellon University

JOHN CROWE RANSOM
1888–1974

Author's Chronology

Born April 30, 1888, Pulaski, Tennessee; *1903* matriculates at Vanderbilt University at age 15; *1907* returns to Vanderbilt after teaching positions in Taylorsville, Mississippi, and Lewisburg, Tennessee; *1909* graduates Phi Beta Kappa and first in class from Vanderbilt; *1913* graduates as Rhodes Scholar from Oxford University; *1914* joins faculty of Vanderbilt; *1918* commissioned First Lieutenant Field Artillery and stationed in France, returning to Vanderbilt two years later; *1919* publishes *Poems About God; 1922* joins the Fugitive group of poets and cofounds the *Fugitive; 1924* publishes *Chills and Fever* and *Grace after Meat; 1927* publishes *Two Gentlemen in Bonds; 1930* publishes *God Without Thunder: An Unorthodox Defense of Orthodoxy,* in which he argues for the need of a God of mystery, magnificence, and thunder and contributes to the agrarian manifesto, *I'll Take My Stand; 1937* moves from Vanderbilt to Kenyon College, Oberlin, Ohio; *1938* publishes *The World's Body; 1939* founds and edits until *1959* the *Kenyon Review; 1941* publishes *The New Criticism; 1945* publishes *Selected Poems; 1951* awarded Bollingen Prize for Poetry; *1955* publishes *Selected Poems and Essays; 1963* publishes *Selected Poems; 1969* publishes a controversial and enlarged revision of *Selected Poems; 1972* publishes *Beating the Bushes,* a collection of previously unpublished essays; 1974 dies in Gambier, Ohio.

Author's Bibliography (selected)

Poems about God, 1919; *Chills and Fever,* 1924 (poems); *Grace After Meat,* 1924 (poems); *Two Gentlemen in Bonds,* 1927 (poems); *God Without Thunder: An Unorthodox Defense of Orthodoxy,* 1930 (prose); *The World's Body,* 1938 (critical essays); *The New Criticism,* 1941 (critical essays); *Selected Poems,* 1945; *Poems and Essays,* 1955; *Selected Poems,* 1963; *Selected Poems,* revised and enlarged, 1969; *Beating the Bushes,* 1972 (critical essays).

Overview of Biographical Sources

Fortunately, scholars interested in Ransom's life have a splendid source in Thomas Daniel Young's *Gentleman in a Dustcoat: A Biography of John Crowe Ransom* (1976). As the definitive biography, it is readily available. Other sources only peripherally treat Ransom's life and often limit themselves to Ransom as either Fugitive poet or Nashville Agrarian. But still helpful, for example, are John M. Bradbury, *The Fugitives: A Critical Account* (Chapel Hill: University of North Carolina Press, 1958); Louise Cowan, *The Fugitive Group: A Literary History* (Baton Rouge: Louisiana State University Press, 1959); and especially John L. Stewart, *The Burden of Time: The Fugitives and the Agrarians* (Princeton: Princeton University Press, 1965). Also of interest to a student of

Ransom as a Fugitive poet and as a member of the Nashville Agrarians are Rob Roy Purdy, ed., *The Fugitive's Reunion: Conversations at Vanderbilt, May 3-5, 1956* (Nashville: Vanderbilt University Press, 1959) as well as William C. Havard and Walter Sullivan, eds., *A Band of Prophets: The Vanderbilt Agrarians After Fifty Years* (Baton Rouge: Louisiana State University Press, 1982). Interesting personal memoirs of Ransom include one by his granddaughter, Robb Forman Dew, "Summer's End," *Mississippi Quarterly,* XXX (Winter 1976-1977), 137-153, and by Robert Penn Warren in Floyd C. Watkins and John T. Hiers, eds., *Robert Penn Warren Talking: Interviews 1950-1978* (New York: Random House, 1980). Some of Ransom's literary correspondence with Allen Tate is available in Thomas Daniel Young and George Core, eds., "Art as Adventure in Form: Letters of John Crowe Ransom, 1923-1927," *Southern Review,* XII (Autumn 1976), 776-799.

Evaluation of Selected Biographies

Stewart, John L. *John Crowe Ransom: University of Minnesota Pamphlets on American Writers, No. 18.* Minneapolis: University of Minnesota Press, 1962. Stewart introduces the neophyte scholar to Ransom's general literary themes and critical theories. Biographical information is only a secondary concern, but Stewart does give pertinent biography when necessary.

Young, Thomas Daniel, *Gentleman in a Dustcoat: A Biography of John Crowe Ransom.* Baton Rouge: Louisiana State University Press, 1976. Young presents a detailed, accurate account of Ransom's life. With access to family papers, Young in this generally readable biography comes closer to the inner man than any other scholar to date. Although some of Young's discussions of Ransom's aesthetics might be difficult at times, his biography is definitive. Any comprehensive study of Ransom must begin here.

Overview of Critical Sources

For years considered an excellent, yet minor regional poet of relatively narrow interests, Ransom only in the last two decades has begun to receive significant critical attention. Discussions of Ransom's controversial role as one of the Nashville Agrarians and of his influence as editor and critic have generally given way to serious attention to Ransom as poet. Because Ransom abruptly ceased to write poetry in 1927, seemingly at the height of his powers, he was relatively ignored as a poet during the last half of his long life, except by such fellow poets as Allen Tate, Robert Penn Warren, and Randall Jarrell, and by such sympathetic critics as Cleanth Brooks. The 1960's and the 1970's, however, saw several relatively good book-length studies of his poetry appear.

Evaluation of Selected Criticism

Buffington, Robert, *The Equilibrist: A Study of John Crowe Ransom's Poems, 1916-1963.* Nashville: Vanderbilt University Press, 1967. Buffington's work remains one of the most useful and readable books on Ransom's poetry. Concentrating throughout on Ransom's dualism, his thematic insistence on a balance between reason and mystery, mind and body, Buffington also explores the connections between Ransom's aesthetic principles and his poetry.

Knight, Karl R. *The Poetry of John Crowe Ransom: A Study in Diction, Metaphor, and Symbol.* London: Mouton, 1964. Knight helps with Ransom's symbolism and prosody.

Magner, James E., Jr. *John Crowe Ransom: Critical Principles and Preoccupations.* The Hague: Mouton, 1971. Magner considers the philosophical bases of Ransom's critical theories. He emphasizes the various structural "tensions" in several of Ransom's better known poems and also devotes some space to Ransom's assessments of a few of his contemporary poets and critics.

Parsons, Thornton H. *John Crowe Ransom.* New York: Twayne, 1969. In this work Parsons dwells almost exclusively on the poetry of Ransom, and in the process analyzes several poems largely ignored by other critics, some of which Ransom himself excluded from his *Selected Poems.* Parsons especially does the student of Ransom a valuable service in his final chapter, which discusses Ransom's later revisions of his three *Selected Poems,* many of which remain very controversial.

Williams, Miller, *The Poetry of John Crowe Ransom.* New Brunswick: Rutgers University Press, 1972. Williams believes that Ransom's ultimate themes or questions as a poet are theological. In this very readable and provocative volume, he finds that as a poet, Ransom reflects the stoical traditions of Southern Calvinism, especially in his attitudes toward mortality. The strength of Williams' study, however, may be his analysis of Ransom's poetic diction, which, he says, has origins in "the classics, the King James Bible, medieval ballads, and Southern preachers."

Other Sources

Brooks, Cleanth, "The Doric Delicacy," *Sewanee Review,* LVI (Summer 1948), 402–415. Draws parallels between Ransom's and Milton's use of Latinate diction.

Core, George, "A Naturalist Looks at Sentiment," *Virginia Quarterly Review,* LIII (Summer 1977), 455–474. Discusses Ransom's friendships with Allen Tate, Donald Davidson, and Robert Penn Warren.

Hough, Graham, "John Crowe Ransom: The Poet and the Critic," *Southern Review,* I (January 1965), 1–21. Especially helpful on the relationships between Ransom's criticism and his poetry.

Kock, Vivienne, "The Achievement of John Crowe Ransom," *Sewanee Review,* LVIII (Spring 1950), 227–261. A comprehensive analysis of much of Ransom's best verse.

Rubin, Louis D., Jr. "The Wary Fugitive John Crowe Ransom," *Sewanee Review,* LXXXII (Fall 1977), 502–618. Argues that Ransom's poetry is some of the twentieth century's best.

Warren, Robert Penn, "John Crowe Ransom: A Study in Irony," *Virginia Quarterly Review,* XI (January 1935), 93–112. Ransom's irony discussed in light of modern science and religion.

Wasserman, G. R. "The Irony of John Crowe Ransom," *University of Kansas City Review,* XXIII (Winter 1956), 151–160. Discusses Ransom as a modern ironist.

Young, Thomas Daniel, ed. *John Crowe Ransom: Critical Essays and a Bibliography.* Baton Rouge: Louisiana State University Press, 1968. Helpful bibliography of earlier secondary criticism on Ransom. Contains the above essays by Brooks, Koch, Warren, and Wasserman.

Selected Dictionaries and Encyclopedias
American Writers: A Collection of Literary Biographies, Charles Scribner's Sons, 1974. Concise summary of Ransom's life, including major poetical, critical, and social concerns.

Contemporary Poetry, St. Martin's Press, 1975. Brief biographical and critical introduction to Ransom's poetry.

Southern Writers: A Biographical Dictionary, Louisiana State University Press, 1979. Brief chronological sketch of Ransom's life and works.

John T. Hiers
Valdosta State College

SIR JOSHUA REYNOLDS
1723-1792

Author's Chronology

Born 16 July 1723 in Plympton, Devonshire, England, son of clergyman and schoolmaster; *1740* goes to London for three years apprenticeship under portrait painter Thomas Hudson; *1749* sets off for almost three years to study in Italy; *1753* returns to London and produces portraits of lesser nobility; *1756* meets Samuel Johnson; *1760* settles in house and studio in Leicester Fields; *1764* with Johnson founds Literary Club; *1768* helps organize and becomes president of Royal Academy; *1769* knighted; *1769-1790* delivers fifteen famous *Discourses; 1773* made Doctor of Civil Laws by Oxford; *1784* appointed His Majesty's Principal Painter in Ordinary; left lonely at Johnson's death; *1789* loses sight of left eye and more or less gives up painting; *1790* quarrels with Academy; dies February 23, 1792 and buried in St. Paul's.

Author's Bibliography (selected)

Three letters to the *Idler,* nos. 76, 79, 82, 1759-1761 (essays); *The First Discourse,* 1769 (lecture); *The Second Discourse,* 1769 (lecture); *The Third Discourse,* 1771 (lecture); *The Fourth Discourse,* 1772 (lecture); *The Fifth Discourse,* 1773 (lecture); *The Sixth Discourse,* 1775 (lecture); "Character of Mrs. Parker," 1775-1776 (character sketch); *The Seventh Discourse,* 1777 (lecture); *The Eighth Discourse,* 1779 (lecture); *The Ninth and Tenth Discourses,* 1781 (lectures); *The Eleventh Discourse,* 1783 (lecture); annotations to *The Art of Painting* by Charles Alphonse du Fresnoy, 1783 (criticism); *The Twelfth Discourse,* 1785 (lecture); *The Thirteenth Discourse,* 1787 (lecture); *The Fourteenth Discourse,* 1789 (lecture); *The Fifteenth Discourse,* 1791 (lecture); *Portraits by Sir Joshua Reynolds,* 1952 (character sketches and other papers).

Overview of Biographical Sources

A number of biographies of Reynolds as a painter have been produced, including the still standard *The Life and Times of Sir Joshua Reynolds* by Charles Robert Leslie and Tom Taylor, two volumes (London: J. Murray, 1865). The first biography with discussions of Reynolds' literary aspirations and achievements is F. W. Hilles' *The Literary Career of Sir Joshua Reynolds* (1936). A more recent biography is Derek Hudson's *Sir Joshua Reynolds: A Personal Study* (1958).

Good biographical material on Reynolds can also be found in the works of his friends: Boswell's *Life of Johnson,* edited by G. B. Hill, revised and enlarged by L. F. Powell (Oxford: Oxford University Press, 1934); *Private Papers of James Boswell from Malahide Castle,* 19 volumes (Mt. Vernon, NY: W. E. Rudge, 1929-1936) [Vol. 3 contains Reynolds' "Ironical Discourse"]; and *John-*

sonian Miscellanies, edited by G. B. Hill, 2 volumes (Oxford: Clarendon Press, 1897) [contains Reynolds' dialogue "Johnson and Garrick"].

Evaluation of Selected Biographies

Hilles, Frederick Whiley, *The Literary Career of Sir Joshua Reynolds.* New York: Macmillan, Cambridge: Cambridge University Press, 1936. The pioneer work in describing Reynolds outside of his studio, this biography details Reynold's education, reading, and association with great men of letters. The book is based largely on Reynolds' manuscripts preserved in the Royal Academy. By profession a painter, Reynolds' ambition was to be considered an equally proficient writer, and this work examines the success of those ambitions. It does not, however, analyze in depth the problems and issues of aesthetic theory.

Hudson, Derek, *Sir Joshua Reynolds: A Personal Study.* London: Geoffrey Bles, 1958. Readable and gossipy, this biography concentrates not chiefly on Reynolds as a painter or a critic but as a man. It also includes illustrations with assessments of Reynolds' paintings. Though Hudson draws on the earlier biographies of Reynolds, he also presents his own theory that Reynolds really was tense, restless and sensitive under his legendary calm exterior. Hudson also prints new material such as Reynolds' "Journey from London to Brentford" and a piece in which Reynolds discusses Hogarth's theory of beauty.

Autobiographical Sources

Reynolds' personal writings are not many and are not readily available. Most easy to obtain are his letters, collected and edited by F. W. Hilles (Cambridge: Cambridge University Press, 1929). The collection is small—only 161 letters. Reynolds wrote sparingly and what he did write was often written carelessly and hastily. Most of the letters are from the middle part of his life: in his youth he was too busy studying, and in his later years he was threatened with blindness.

More difficult to obtain is *Gleanings—Sir Joshua Reynolds, and His Works. Gleanings from his Diary, unpublished Manuscripts, and from other Sources,* by William Cotton, edited by John Burnet (London: Longmans, 1856). Reynolds made sketchy entries in his diary—short phrases describing what he had observed—and a little fuller, though still scanty, remarks on paintings in his notebooks.

Overview of Critical Sources

Reynolds' status as a literary figure, an aesthetician, and critic has within the last fifty years begun to receive scholarly attention. There is, though, no book-length study of his *Discourses.* Hilles' biography prints "The Discourses in Embryo" and looks at their making but does not evaluate them. Important comments on Reynolds have, however, appeared in books with larger scope and in articles.

Evaluation of Selected Criticism

Bate, Walter Jackson, *From Classic to Romantic: Premises of Taste in Eighteenth-Century England.* Cambridge: Harvard University Press, 1946, pp. 79–92. According to Bate, Reynolds' *Discourses* contain the most broadly representative expression of English neo-classicism. Bate examines Reynolds' views on such aesthetic issues as imitation, the sublime, reason, and general nature and compares Reynolds' ideas to Samuel Johnson's. Like Johnson, Bate believes, Reynolds was convinced that art's province is to imitate the objective and unchanging truths of "general nature": art's end is the ethical enlargement of man's character.

Hipple, Walter, "General and Particular in the *Discourses* of Sir Joshua Reynolds: A Study in Method," *Journal of Aesthetics and Art Criticism,* 11 (March 1953), 231–247; reprinted in his *The Beautiful, the Sublime, and the Picturesque in Eighteenth-Century British Aesthetic Theory.* Carbondale, IL: Southern Illinois University Press, 1957. In defining the ground of Reynolds' theory and practice in his lectures, Hipple tries to show that the neoclassic concern with the general and the particular underlies the *Discourses.* Attacking earlier critics like William Hazlitt who accused Reynolds of inconsistency, Hipple claims that the paradoxes in the *Discourses* can be reconciled if allowance is made for Reynolds' methodological devices. Hipple also notes the influence of Edmund Burke's ideas of the beautiful and the sublime on Reynolds.

Waterhouse, Ellis K. *Reynolds.* Boston: Boston Book & Art Shop, 1955; and *Reynolds.* London: Phaidon, 1973. These are basically art books containing selected paintings done by Reynolds. Both include a biographical summary of Reynolds' life, a chronological catalogue of his paintings, a selected bibliography, and the collections in which the paintings are now kept. The earlier work (first published in 1941) provides a nine page discussion of Reynolds as a writer, including summary and commentary on each of the *Discourses.*

Other Sources

Bevilacqua, Vincent M. "Ut Rhetorica Pictura: Sir Joshua Reynolds' Rhetorical Conception of Art," *Huntington Library Quarterly,* 34 (1970), 59–78. Emphasis on traditional relationship between rhetoric and visual arts.

Burke, Joseph, *Hogarth and Reynolds: A Contrast in English Art Theory.* The William Henry Charlton Memorial Lecture, November 1941; London: Oxford University Press, 1943. Resemblance of Reynolds' philosophical approach to Aristotle, and the contradictions in Reynolds' theories.

Mahoney, John L. "Reynolds' *Discourses on Art:* The Delicate Balance of Neoclassic Aesthetics," *British Journal of Aesthetics,* 18 (1978), 126–136. The *Discourses* as part of the liberal tradition of neoclassic theory.

Northcote, James, *The Life of Sir Joshua Reynolds.* ed. R. W. Lightbown (rpt. of 1819 ed.; London: Cornmarket Press, 1971). Main source for first-hand information about Reynolds.

Olson, Elder, *Longinus: On the Sublime; and Sir Joshua Reynolds: Discourses on Art.* Chicago: Packard, 1945. Reynolds' differentiation of phases through which artists pass to develop their faculties.

Parke, Catherine Neal, "The Image of the Good Man in Sir Joshua Reynolds' *Discourses,*" *Thought,* 53 (1978), 151–173. The *Discourses* as moral and intellectual education.

Selected Dictionaries and Encyclopedias

Chambers's Cyclopaedia of English Literature, Vol. 2, J. B. Lippincott, 1902. Brief biography and extract from *Discourses.*

Everyman's Dictionary of Literary Biography, English and American, E. P. Dutton, 1969. Brief biography with very few dates.

The New Century Handbook of English Literature, rev. ed. Appleton Century Crofts, 1967. Short but fairly complete biography.

Ann W. Engar
University of Utah

JEAN RHYS
1890–1979

Author's Chronology

Born Ella Gwendoline Rees Williams, August 24, 1890, Roseau, Dominica, West Indies of a Welsh father and a Creole mother; *1907* travels to England, attends school and joins a touring company as a chorus girl; *1910* has a love affair with an older man who leaves her after a year but who supports her for almost a decade; *1919* marries Jean Lenglet, a Dutch-French journalist, and moves to Paris; *1920* son William is born and dies three weeks later; *1922* daughter Maryvonne is born; *1923* Lenglet is imprisoned on a charge of illegal entry into France and for currency violations; he is extradited to Holland; Rhys is befriended by Ford Madox Ford who encourages her writing and becomes both her patron and lover; *1924* first story is published; *1927* estranged from Lenglet, meets Leslie Tilden Smith who becomes her literary agent; *1932* is divorced from Lenglet and marries Tilden Smith; *1945* Tilden Smith dies; *1947* marries Max Hamer; *1952* Hamer is sentenced to six months' imprisonment for embezzlement; *1956* moves to Devonshire where she spends the rest of her life; *1964* Hamer dies; *1966 Wide Sargasso Sea* is published to critical and popular acclaim; *1978* is awarded the CBE by Queen Elizabeth; *1979* dies on May 14.

Author's Bibliography (selected)

The Left Bank, 1927 (sketches); *Postures* (later entitled *Quartet*), 1928 (novel); *After Leaving Mr. Mackenzie,* 1930 (novel); *Voyage in the Dark,* 1934 (novel); *Good Morning, Midnight,* 1939 (novel); *Wide Sargasso Sea,* 1966 (novel); *Smile, Please,* 1979, (autobiography).

Overview of Biographical Sources

Rhys made it clear in her will that she did not wish a biography written, in great part because of her fear of inaccuracy. There is no full-scale biography of Rhys, though this is not entirely due to a respect for her wishes. Rhys's life was essentially an obscure one, lived out of the public eye; facts are difficult to verify. David Plante's chapter on Rhys in *Difficult Women: A Memoir of Three* (New York: Atheneum, 1983) illustrates this vividly. He tried to help the elderly Rhys organize an autobiography, but her reticence, faulty memory, and erratic interest in the project made his task impossible. Some biographical information may be found in the critical studies of her novels; on the whole, however, the richest source of biographical information is *Jean Rhys Letters 1931–1966* (1984). The letters, selected and edited by Rhys's literary executor, Francis Wyndham, represents his compromise between Rhys's wish that nothing be written and the increasing interest in Rhys as a writer whose novels are based in great part on her own life. To date, the definitive biography of Jean Rhys has not been written.

Evaluation of Selected Biographies

Plante, David, *Difficult Women: A Memoir of Three*. New York: Atheneum, 1983. The chapter on Rhys is a harrowing picture of her old age. Frail, alcoholic, paralyzed by loneliness, Rhys nevertheless emerges as a powerful personality of enormous charm. Plante vividly depicts Rhys's distrust of biography and her valiant attempt to complete an autobiography.

Staley, Thomas F. *Jean Rhys: A Critical Study*. Austin: University of Texas Press, 1979. This critical study contains a chapter of Rhys's life. It is very good and shows to advantage Mr. Staley's personal acquaintance with Rhys, who answered his questions about her life and work.

Wolfe, Peter, *Jean Rhys*. Boston: Twayne, 1980. A bio-critical introduction to Rhy's life and work. Wolfe's study is even-handed and fair. He is particularly good in examining the autobiographical content of the novels and the limits of biography. Wolfe consistently shows how Rhys transformed her own experiences into art.

Wyndham, Francis and Diana Melly, eds. *Jean Rhys Letters 1931–1966*. London: Andre Deutsch, 1984. Wyndham is the most trustworthy source for biographical information. Additionally, he is consistently sympathetic to Rhys, who, on the evidence, was demanding in her dependence on friends. The letters illuminate the fiction, particularly *Wide Sargasso Sea*, in valuable ways. Rhys's letters to her editors on the drawn-out writing and rewriting of *Sargasso* provide important information about her life on Dominica. Wyndham would seem to be the ideal biographer of Jean Rhys; perhaps, in the future, he will undertake the task.

Autobiographical Sources

Rhys's fiction is itself a tantalizing, yet finally elusive, source of autobiography. *Quartet* is a fictionalized account of her affair with Ford Madox Ford. *Voyage in the Dark* uses Rhys's early experiences in England, vividly portraying her sense of exile from Dominica and her unease in European society. *Wide Sargasso Sea* beautifully invokes her West Indian childhood and adolescence. The fiction, though acknowledged by Rhys to be grounded in her own experience, is finally both more than, and different from, her life.

In her last years, Rhys began work on an autobiography. The first part of *Smile, Please* is a brilliant evocation of her West Indian childhood, but there are only random notes and fragments written about her life in England and on the continent. The book is disappointing; nevertheless, it remains a fascinating fragment, indispensable to a critical understanding of Rhys's master work, *Wide Sargasso Sea.*

Overview of Critical Sources

The existing criticism of Rhys's work is, on the whole, traditional. Much attention has been paid to what Ford identified as her greatest strength, her "singular instinct for form." Most critics focus on *Wide Sargasso Sea,* her strongest and most perfectly realized work. All of the novels have been analyzed and interpreted in a variety of useful ways, and almost every critical work recognizes the importance of autobiography in the works. Recently, Rhys has been receiving attention from feminist critics, and she is beginning to attract notice as a Third World writer. Long forgotten, since the publication of *Wide Sargasso Sea,* Rhys's reputation has been growing steadily.

Evaluation of Selected Criticism

Nebeker, Helen, *Jean Rhys: Woman in Passage.* Montreal: Eden Press Women's Publications, 1981. A feminist reading of the five novels. Not entirely trustworthy as to biographical information.

Staley, Thomas F. *Jean Rhys: A Critical Study.* Austin: University of Texas Press, 1979. The first and best full-length critical study of Rhys's work. A stimulating and sensitive reading of the novels. One of the strengths of this very good book is a full bibliography that is extremely helpful to any student of Rhys.

Wolfe, Peter, *Jean Rhys.* Boston: Twayne, 1980. A valuable introduction to Rhys's life and work. Wolfe summarizes plot and analyzes technique in familiar but still useful ways. A good place to begin a study of Rhys.

Other Sources

James, Selma, *The Ladies and the Mammies: Jane Austen & Jean Rhys.* Bristol, England: Falling Wall Press, 1983. An impressionistic reading of two of Rhys's novels. James makes a persuasive case for seeing Rhys as a Third World writer.

Selected Dictionaries and Encyclopedias

Contemporary Novelists, St. Martin's Press, 1976. Lists publications, gives a brief biography and summary of criticism.

Elizabeth Buckmaster
The Pennsylvania State University
Delaware County Campus

DOROTHY RICHARDSON
1873–1957

Author's Chronology

Born May 17, 1873, in Abingdon, Berkshire; *1884–1890* attends private day school in London; *1891* spends six months as pupil-teacher in Hanover; *1891–1895* teaches in private school and works as governess; *1895* mother commits suicide; *1896* moves to London lodgings and begins work as dental assistant, also meets novelist H. G. Wells; *1902* begins contributing articles and reviews to minor magazines; *1907* ends affair with Wells, suffers miscarriage, and leaves London for Sussex; *1908–1914* writes sketches for *Saturday Review;* *1913* begins work on *Pilgrimage,* her long series of "connected novels"; *1915* publishes first section, *Pointed Roofs; 1917* marries artist Alan Odle, whom she supports by proofreading, reviewing, writing for *Dental Record,* translating, and so forth; *1938* publisher advertises four-volume edition of *Pilgrimage* as "complete in twelve parts"; *1948* Alan Odle dies; *1957* dies June 17 at Beckingham, Kent; *1967 Pilgrimage* reissued with the previously unpublished thirteenth part, *March Moonlight.*

Author's Bibliography (selected)

The Quakers Past and Present, 1914 (nonfiction); *Gleanings from the Work of George Fox,* 1914 (anthology); *Pilgrimage,* 1938, 1967 (novel series which includes *Pointed Roofs,* 1915; *Backwater,* 1916; *Honeycomb,* 1917; *The Tunnel,* 1919; *Interim,* 1919; *Deadlock,* 1921; *Revolving Lights,* 1923; *The Trap,* 1925; *Oberland,* 1927; *Dawn's Left Hand,* 1931; *Clear Horizon,* 1935; *Dimple Hill,* 1938; *March Moonlight,* 1967.)

Overview of Biographical Sources

Richardson was extremely reticent about the facts of her life; even her birthdate (which was apparently not known to her husband) was not revealed until 1950. The first account of Richardson's life to appear in print was an essay by Gloria Glikin in *PMLA* in 1963. The same scholar, writing as Gloria G. Fromm, produced the authoritative biography of Richardson in 1977. Some letters about Richardson from people who knew her are reproduced in the appendix to Gillian E. Hanscombe, *The Art of Life: Dorothy Richardson and the Development of Feminist Consciousness* (London: Peter Owen, 1982).

Evaluation of Selected Biographies

Fromm, Gloria G. *Dorothy Richardson: A Biography.* Urbana: University of Illinois Press, 1977. Written with the cooperation of Richardson's relatives, friends and literary executor, Fromm's book provides accurate information about Richardson's life and supplies a detailed bibliography, including stories, poems, translations, articles (many of them previously unidentified), and contemporary reviews of Richardson's work. Fromm also carefully traces the correspondence between Richardson's experience and the incidents which appear in *Pilgrimage*.

Rosenberg, John, *Dorothy Richardson: A Critical Biography*. New York: Alfred A. Knopf, 1973. A "joint biography" of the writer and her books uses the central characters, incidents and issues of *Pilgrimage* for information about Richardson's attitudes and feelings. Though Rosenberg has less information than Fromm, his biographical reading of the novels is clear and convincing.

Autobiographical Sources

Richardson deliberately and adamantly refused to supply any biographical information to publishers or interviewers. Only after her death did it become evident that her major work, the thirteen-part novel *Pilgrimage,* reflects the essence of her own life, not only in details such as family background, event, experience and setting but also in the effort to create conscious existence and new modes of perceiving reality. The novel is often difficult because of its technical innovation and its focus on consciousness rather than incident; many readers find it helpful to follow a biography in conjunction with the novel. The bibliography in Gloria G. Fromm's *Dorothy Richardson: A Biography* describes the location and contents of Richardson's letters and papers, which have not been published.

Overview of Critical Sources

There has been surprisingly little critical discussion of Richardson, considering her place in literary history as one of the major innovators in twentieth-century fiction and the writer to whom the phrase "stream of consciousness" was first applied. With the biographical facts now at last available and with the reexamination of women writers and feminist consciousness that is currently underway, it seems certain that a number of critical and analytical studies of Richardson will be published in the coming years. Of the books already in print, some are almost wholly devoted to exploring the interplay between Dorothy Richardson, the author, and Miriam Henderson, the central character of *Pilgrimage*. Others focus on the novel's literary and stylistic innovations.

Evaluation of Selected Criticism

Blake, Caesar R. *Dorothy Richardson*. Ann Arbor: University of Michigan Press, 1960. In a study written before the biographical basis of *Pilgrimage* was evident, Blake comments on the book's mystical elements, analyzes Richardson's use of language, viewpoint and imagery to create Miriam Henderson's subjective reality, and discusses the book as an experimental novel. He emphasizes Richardson's attempt to create a consciousness which is the "feminine equivalent" of the "current masculine realism."

Gregory, Horace, *Dorothy Richardson: An Adventure in Self-Discovery*. New York: Holt, Rinehart and Winston, 1967. One of the most perceptive reviewers of *Pilgrimage* when the four-volume edition was published in 1938, Gregory here undertakes a psychological study of the novel in light of Richardson's letters and the manuscript (still unpublished at the time he wrote) of *March Moonlight*. He proclaims that the "essential truths" of Richardson's life must be sought in *Pilgrimage* and traces her literary roots to Charlotte Brontë. Although the biographical information has been superseded, Gregory's critical analysis is a useful help in reading the novel.

Hanscombe, Gillian E. *The Art of Life: Dorothy Richardson and the Development of Feminist Consciousness*. London and Boston: Peter Owen, 1982. In a close analysis of *Pilgrimage* that centers on language and theme, Hanscombe tries to elucidate what Richardson meant by "feminine" and argues that the conflict between personhood and womanhood in Richardson's life created a bipolar world view. Although she considers *Pilgrimage* a "unique and definitive example of autobiographical fiction," Hanscombe's study is organized thematically rather than chronologically.

Kaplan, Sydney Janet, *Feminine Consciousness in the Modern British Novel*. Urbana: University of Illinois Press, 1975. The chapter on Richardson in Kaplan's discussion of five novelists emphasizes the significance of her emergence as a novelist in a period of feminist struggle for independence and equality. Analyzing Miriam Henderson's beliefs and perceptions, Kaplan finds her ambivalent towards her a role as a woman. Richardson is important because she used "traditional attitudes about the female psyche" to provide the basis for "a new method of character development."

Staley, Thomas F. *Dorothy Richardson*. Boston: Twayne, 1976. Brief biography and a summary and explanation of each section of *Pilgrimage* provide the clarity many readers need to help them through a first encounter with the work. Staley also evaluates Richardson's technical innovation (especially her narrative technique and use of time) in the context of developments in the novel during the twentieth century.

Other Sources

Bryher, Winifred, *The Heart to Artemis: A Writer's Memoirs*. New York: Harcourt, Brace and World, 1962. Some information about Richardson and a good picture of her times in memoirs by a woman contemporary who was also an experimental writer.

DuPlessis, Rachel, *Writing Beyond the Ending: Narrative Strategies of Twentieth-Century Women Writers*. Bloomington: Indiana University Press,

1985. Within the context of an ideological and narrative critique of romance, the chapter on *Pilgrimage* argues that Richardson ruptured narrative conventions and developed a strategy allowing the individual to dissolve into social groups in order to remove herself from the heterosexual love plot.

Edel, Leon, *The Modern Psychological Novel, 1900–1950.* New York: Lippincott, 1955. Edel's identification of Richardson, Marcel Proust and James Joyce as three novelists who, unknown to each other, simultaneously sought techniques for expressing inner reality was probably the critical mention that began the rescue of Richardson's work from obscurity and neglect. His book remains an essential background study.

Friedman, Melvin, "Dorothy Richardson and Virginia Woolf: Stream-of-Consciousness in England," in *Stream of Consciousness.* New Haven: Yale University Press, 1955. Discusses Richardson's technique in some detail but believes *Pilgrimage* is of interest only to literary historians. Rose, Shirley, "Dorothy Richardson's Theory of Literature: The Writer as Pilgrim," *Criticism,* XII (Winter 1970), 20–37. Explains concept of collaboration between reader and writer, which Rose believes is essential to Richardson's working method.

Showalter, Elaine, *A Literature of Their Own: British Women Novelists from Brontë to Lessing.* Princeton: Princeton University Press, 1977. Considers Richardson the prime example of a relatively unsatisfactory female aesthetic created by British women novelists in the early years of the century.

Woolf, Virginia, "Romance and the Heart," *Nation and Athenaeum,* 19 May 1923, 229. In a review of *Revolving Lights,* Woolf calls Richardson the first novelist to create a language for expressing feminine consciousness.

Selected Dictionaries and Encyclopedias

Critical Survey of Long Fiction, Salem Press, 1983. Brief biography, analysis of literary innovation and achievement, and short commentary on *Pilgrimage.*

Encyclopedia of World Literature in the 20th Century, Frederick Ungar, 1971. Discusses literary influences, themes and techniques; provides summary evaluation.

A Library of Literary Criticism, Frederick Ungar, 1966. Short critical extracts about Richardson's work, many of them quoted from brief passages in books on larger topics.

Sally Mitchell
Temple University

SAMUEL RICHARDSON
1689–1761

Author's Chronology

Born July 31(?), 1689, Mackworth(?), Derbyshire, England; *1698(?)* family moves to London; *1706–1713* apprenticed to John Wilde, printer; *1713–1719(?)* continues to work for Wilde as overseer and corrector; *1715* is made Freeman of the Stationers' Company and citizen of London; *1721(?)* works for John Leake, printer, and then establishes his own printing business; *1721* marries Martha Wilde, daughter of his former master; *1722* is admitted to the livery of the Stationers' Company; *1722–1731* fathers six children, all of whom died by 1731; *1723* is involved in printing an opposition journal, *The True Briton;* *1731* first wife dies; *1733* marries Elizabeth Leake, daughter of former employer (four daughters survive), and publishes *The Apprentice's Vade Mecum;* *1739* begins composition of *Pamela;* *1740* completes and publishes *Pamela;* *1741* publishes *The Familiar Letters* and *Pamela II;* *1744(?)–1746* writes and revises *Clarissa;* *1747* publishes *Clarissa,* volumes I and II; *1748* publishes *Clarissa,* volumes III–VII; *1749–1761* printing business flourishes; *1750* begins writing *Sir Charles Grandison;* *1753* publishes *Sir Charles Grandison,* volumes I–VI; *1754* completes publication of *Sir Charles Grandison,* volume VII, and is elected Master of the Stationers' Company; July 4, *1761,* dies as a result of a stroke.

Author's Bibliography (selected)

The Apprentice's Vade Mecum, or Young Man's Pocket-Companion, 1733; *Pamela, or Virtue Rewarded,* 1740 (novel); *Pamela in her Exalted Condition* [*Pamela II*], 1741 (novel); *Letters Written to and for Particular Friends* [*Familiar Letters*], 1741; *Clarissa, or the History of a Young Lady,* 1747–1748 (novel); *The History of Sir Charles Grandison,* 1753–1754 (novel); *A Collection of the Moral and Instructive Sentiments, Maxims, Cautions, and Reflexions, Contained in the Histories of Pamela, Clarissa, and Sir Charles Grandison,* 1755.

Overview of Biographical Sources

There is a wealth of information about the life and times of Samuel Richardson, resulting from records of his printing business, published remarks from his friendships with other prominent persons of the age (such as Aaron Hill, Samuel Johnson, and Henry Fielding), and his own voluminous correspondence. This data has been painstakingly collected and lucidly organized in the definitive study by T. C. Duncan Eaves and Ben D. Kimpel, *Samuel Richardson: A Biography* (1971). Their work supplements and corrects earlier biographies with an intensive examination of all available sources. The biography narrates the complete story of Richardson's printing business, private life, and writing career. An appendix provides a complete list and description of the correspondence. Although all earlier biographies have been superseded by Eaves and Kimpel, other useful works are still available. The first full biography, authorized by Richardson's daughters, appeared in the *Universal Magazine* of January 1786. Anna L. Barbauld's edition of *The Correspondence of Samuel Richardson* (London: Phillips, 1804), includes a biography prefixed to the first volume. Clara L. Thomson's *Samuel Richardson: A Biographical and Critical Study* (London: Horace Marshall and Son, 1900), was the first major study, a mixture of criticism and biography. Austin Dobson's *Samuel Richardson* (1902), another early twentieth-century study, combines a narrative of the life with examination of the novels and the correspondence. Brian W. Downs' *Richardson* (London: George Routledge and Sons, 1928) provides a one-chapter biography at the beginning. Alan Dugald McKillop's *Samuel Richardson, Printer and Novelist* (1936) was the first fully-detailed and documented study, containing important new information about the printing business. McKillop's study was the most complete until the appearance of Eaves and Kimpel.

Evaluation of Selected Biographies

Dobson, Austin, *Samuel Richardson*. London: Macmillan, 1902. Dobson uses Richardson's correspondence to flesh out the narrative of his writing career, but the study gives little insight to either the business or personal sides of Richardson's life. There are brief summaries of the life before *Pamela* and after *Sir Charles Grandison*, but the main emphasis is on the process of composition of the novels. Dobson evaluates the novels and Richardson's letters, concluding that they are not suitable for modern readers.

Eaves, T. C. Duncan, and Ben D. Kimpel, *Samuel Richardson: A Biography*. Oxford: Clarendon Press, 1971. Eaves and Kimpel provide a comprehensive and fully-documented narrative of Richardson's life, as well as criticism of the fiction. The biography demonstrates the relationships among Richardson's career as a printer, his private life, and his development as a novelist. It builds a portrait of Richardson's character through the evidence of his own words and the words of his contemporaries, rather than through psychological analysis. Because so much of Richardson's life was devoted to the printing business (*Pamela* first appeared when Richardson was fifty-one), there is an abundance of detail that is of more use to the scholar than of interest to the general reader. Although the criticism of the novels is, as the authors intend, "old-fashioned" (biographical), the narrative of Richardson's life stresses the connections between the development of the novels and the author's personal and professional friendships.

McKillop, Alan Dugald, *Samuel Richardson, Printer and Novelist*. Chapel Hill: University of North Carolina Press, 1936; rpt. Shoe String Press, 1960. McKillop does not attempt to give a complete biography of Richardson, but concentrates instead on the author's life during the writing of the novels, 1739-1754. There is only a brief survey of Richardson's life prior to 1739, and the work focuses on those aspects of the life that specifically relate to the composition of the novels. An appendix provides a useful summary and description of the records of Richardson's private life and business career.

Autobiographical Sources

Richardson's public and private letters are available in manuscript and collected formats. These letters provide a unique glimpse of Richardson's life, personal opinions, views of his contemporaries, and the spirit of the times. Since Richardson was a middle-class businessman as well as a novelist, the letters reveal characteristics of both aspects of his life. Richardson's only specific comments about his early years are in a letter to Johannes Stinstra, his Dutch correspondent, dated June 2, 1753. Anna L. Barbauld's edition of *The Correspondence of Samuel Richardson* (London: Phillips, 1804), is the most complete collection of the letters. It is not entirely reliable because it includes letters only from persons not living in 1804 (with one exception), and the letters are often edited and abridged. John Carroll's edition of the *Selected Letters of Samuel Richardson* (Oxford: Clarendon Press, 1964), is of most interest to the general reader. The selection is based on the relevance of the letters to the fiction, as opposed to concerns with private or business affairs. William C. Slattery's edition of *The Richardson-Stinstra Correspondence and Stinstra's Prefaces to Clarissa* (Carbondale and Edwardsville: Southern Illinois University Press, 1959), contains the autobiographical letter cited above. A complete list of Richardson's letters appears in the appendix to Eaves and Kimpel's *Samuel Richardson: A Biography* (Oxford: Clarendon Press, 1971).

Overview of Critical Sources

Criticism of Richardson's fiction has traditionally centered on several major issues: style and epistolary technique, characterization (especially in *Clarissa*), representation of social and moral issues of the mid-eighteenth century, and the interplay of realism and romance. Richardson's contemporaries often compared his works with Fielding's, but Richardson's enormous popular appeal colors much of that criticism. In the nineteenth century most critics focused on the moral sentiments. Modern criticism takes a more analytic and pluralistic approach, examining language and style, structure, and characterization. Although there is much useful material on *Pamela I* and *Clarissa, Pamela II* and *Sir Charles Grandison* remain largely neglected.

Evaluation of Selected Criticism

Golden, Morris, *Richardson's Characters*. Ann Arbor: University of Michigan Press, 1963. Starting from an acceptance of traditional views of Richardson's moral purposes and aesthetic techniques, Golden classifies and describes the major character types in the three novels: the Bold Young Man, the Mild Young Man, Girls, Older People, and Bourgeois Aristocracy. He uses these types to demonstrate conflict as the central focus in the novels: conflict within and between individuals, and conflict between the desires of the individual ego and the demands of society.

Kinkead-Weekes, Mark, *Samuel Richardson: Dramatic Novelist.* Ithaca, NY: Cornell University Press; London: Methuen, 1973. This major study demonstrates Richardson's debt to drama for the development of his fictional technique and his dramatic imagination in creating characters. Kinkead-Weekes differentiates between Richardson as a dramatic novelist and Fielding as an epic novelist. Although the longest part of the work centers on *Clarissa,* Kinkead-Weekes examines all the fiction as well and presents a theory of the dramatic novel.

McKillop, Alan Dugald, *The Early Masters of English Fiction.* Lawrence: University of Kansas Press, 1955, pp. 47–97. McKillop gives an overview of Richardson's novels, emphasizing their intrinsic qualities and their relationship to the time in which they were written. He places Richardson squarely in the tradition of eighteenth-century literature through an examination of all the major novelists. This work remains a fine introduction to Richardson.

Watt, Ian, *The Rise of the Novel: Studies in Defoe, Richardson, and Fielding.* Berkeley: University of California Press; London: Chatto and Windus, 1957; rpt. 1967. By focusing primarily on Richardson, Watt develops his theory that "formal realism" marks the beginning of the novel as a modern genre. He demonstrates that Richardson's presentation of middle-class values sparked the formalization of the genre. Watt emphasizes *Pamela I* and *Clarissa* as Richardson's major works, and carefully examines the elements of realism in theme, plot, and structure; he pays less attention to characterization than other critics do.

Other Sources

Ball, Donald L. *Samuel Richardson's Theory of Fiction.* The Hague and Paris: Mouton, 1971. An analytic study of Richardson's statements about his art and the language and style of the novels. The appendix contains tables of the correlations between theory and practice.

Brissenden, R. F. *Samuel Richardson.* Writers and Their Work, no. 108. London and New York: The British Council, 1958; revised 1965. A brief survey of Richardson's works, with a selective critical bibliography.

Downs, Brian W. *Richardson.* London: George Routledge and Sons, 1928. An early biographical-critical study that covers the novels and Richardson's influence on later writers.

Flynn, Carol H. *Samuel Richardson: A Man of Letters.* Princeton: Princeton University Press, 1982. A study of the tension between moral and aesthetic principles in the novels and letters.

Kearney, Anthony M. *Samuel Richardson.* Profiles in Literature Series. London: Routledge and Kegan Paul, 1968. A brief overview of Richardson's career as a novelist, this work uses numerous extracts from the works to illustrate the author's themes and techniques.

Wolff, Cynthia, *Samuel Richardson and the Eighteenth-Century Puritan Character.* Hamden, CT: Shoe String Press, 1972. An in-depth examination of Richardson's conception of character, emphasizing both his literary sources and his own fictional technique.

Selected Dictionaries and Encyclopedias
British Authors Before 1800: A Biographical Dictionary, H. W. Wilson, 1952; rpt. 1965. Brief biography and selective primary and secondary bibliographies.

Critical Survey of Long Fiction, Salem Press, 1983. Brief biography and analysis of the novels.

Dictionary of National Biography, Oxford University Press, 1917; rpt. 1973. Standard biography and brief description of career.

Lawrence F. Laban
Virginia Commonwealth University

ELIZABETH MADOX ROBERTS
1881–1941

Author's Chronology

Born October 30, 1881, Perryville, Kentucky, of Welsh, Irish and Germanic ancestry; *1884* moves to Springfield, Kentucky, which remains her lifelong home and setting of most of her fiction; *1900* studies briefly at State College of Kentucky (now the University of Kentucky); *1900–1914* teaches school intermittently in and around Springfield; *1915* publishes first volume of poetry; *1917–1921* takes Ph.D. degree at the University of Chicago, studies with Robert Morse Lovett, associates with writers such as Glenway Westcott, Yvor Winters, Janet Lewis, and Harriet Monroe; *1922* returns to Springfield; *1926 The Time of Man,* her first novel, wins great popular and critical acclaim; Book-of-the-Month selection; *1928* wins John Reed Memorial Prize of *Poetry* magazine; *1930 The Great Meadow* adapted for film by MGM; *1931–1941* deteriorating health; continues to publish fiction and poetry; *1941* member, National Institute of Arts and Letters; too ill to attend the reception; dies in Orlando, Florida March 13; returned to Springfield for burial.

Author's Bibliography (selected)

In the Great Steep's Garden, 1915 (poems); *Under the Tree,* 1922 (poems); *The Time of Man,* 1926 (novel); *My Heart and My Flesh,* 1927 (novel); *Jingling in the Wind,* 1928 (novel); *The Great Meadow,* 1930 (novel); *A Buried Treasure,* 1931 (novel); *The Haunted Mirror,* 1932 (stories); *He Sent Forth A Raven,* 1935 (novel); *Black Is My Truelove's Hair,* 1938 (novel); *Song in the Meadow,* 1940 (poems); *Not By Strange Gods,* 1941 (stories).

Overview of Biographical Sources

No full-length biography of Roberts has yet been published. During her lifetime, she insisted on her personal privacy and maintained that all that mattered of her life went into her fiction. The definitive study to date of her life is the unpublished Ph.D. dissertation (University of Kentucky, 1953) by Woodbridge Spears, "Elizabeth Madox Roberts: A Biographical and Critical Study." This has served, along with the Roberts papers in the Library of Congress, as the basis for most studies of her life and work. Harry Modean Campbell's and Ruel Foster's *Elizabeth Madox Roberts: American Novelist* (1956) includes a long biographical chapter by Foster based on the author's first-hand knowledge of Springfield and acquaintance with Miss Roberts and her neighbors. Other biographical materials include Glenway Westcott and others, *Elizabeth Madox Roberts: A Personal Note* (New York, 1930) and J. Donald Adams and others, *Elizabeth Madox Roberts: An Appraisal* (New York, 1938). The recent Roberts Issue of the *Southern Review* (Autumn 1984) contains some Roberts letters and journal entries as well as reminiscences by Janet Lewis and others who knew her.

Evaluation of Selected Biographies

Campbell, Harry Modean and Ruel E. Foster, *Elizabeth Madox Roberts: American Novelist.* Norman: University of Oklahoma Press, 1956. Foster's long biographical chapter yields a vivid if somewhat impressionistic portrait of Roberts and her home town of Springfield. There is much useful material here, and Foster's account is generally sound and reliable, but the documentation could be more thoroughgoing.

McDowell, Frederick P. W. *Elizabeth Madox Roberts.* New York: Twayne, 1963. Little new material concerning Roberts' life is presented here, but this brief, well-organized study offers a good introduction. It also includes critical analyses of *The Time of Man* and *A Buried Treasure.* There is an annotated (selected) bibliography.

Overview of Critical Sources

Although some attention was paid to Roberts as an important poet in her lifetime (e.g., Allen Tate, who mentions her in his *Memoirs* as one of the few "first-rate Southern poets of the twenties and thirties"), she is known primarily for her novels. Often compared with Faulkner, she is correctly perceived (for example, by the Nashville Agrarians—Davidson, Tate, Warren) as the first important novelist of the Southern Renascence. Her variety of sound regionalism lacks even the faintest trace of "local color" or exploitation of quaintness, and speaks to the universal condition of humankind in the fashion of the best southern writers. This quality, together with the poetic realism of her style, has exerted a seminal influence on later southern writers. Although she has suffered inexplicably from critical neglect since her death, it appears that a Roberts revival and revaluation is now in progress, and critics predict that literary history will accord her work its appropriate central place in the Southern Renascence.

Evaluation of Selected Criticism

Campbell, Harry Modean and Ruel E. Foster, *Elizabeth Madox Roberts: American Novelist.* Norman: University of Oklahoma Press, 1956. The first full-length critical treatment of Roberts, this includes chapters on the novels, the short stories and the poetry. While the commentary is sometimes content to stop short of full analysis and rest in celebration—not to say adulation—of Roberts' work, this is nevertheless a good introduction to Roberts, with many illuminating observations.

Rovit, Earl H. *Herald to Chaos: The Novels of Elizabeth Madox Roberts.* Lexington: University of Kentucky Press, 1960. Concerned strictly with the novels, this volume offers penetrating analyses and valuable commentary on style. Rovit argues convincingly that Roberts is among "the finest half-dozen novelists in this century."

Other Sources

Adams, J. Donald, "Elizabeth Madox Roberts," *Virginia Quarterly Review,* XII (1936), 80–90. Adams celebrates the affirmative and universal vision of Roberts' work, and finds *The Time of Man* one of the very best novels, one that "stands alone" like *Moby Dick* or *The Scarlet Letter.*

Buchan, Alexander M. "Elizabeth Madox Roberts," *Southwest Review,* XXV (1940), 463–481. Good study of Roberts' "poetic style."

"Roberts Issue," *Southern Review,* Autumn, 1984. A touchstone in Roberts studies, this issue includes fresh biographical material as well as important essays by Lewis Simpson, William Slavick and others.

Slavick, William H. "Ellen Chesser: A Journey of the Mind," in *The Time of Man.* Lexington: University Press of Kentucky, 1982. Excellent introduction to the novel, with useful background materials.

Warren, Robert Penn, "Elizabeth Madox Roberts: Life is From Within," in *The Time of Man.* Lexington: University Press of Kentucky, 1982. First published in 1963, Warren's essay is still the best brief treatment. He reminds the reader that in 1930 "it was impossible to discuss American fiction without reference to Elizabeth Madox Roberts" and suggests why that should still be so today.

Selected Dictionaries and Encyclopedias

Dictionary of Literary Biography, Gale Research 1981. Biographical overview, with brief commentary on individual works.

American Women Writers, Frederick Ungar, 1981. Concise sketch of career. Observes that "Roberts' penetrating analysis of the female consciousness" was ahead of her time and should be of special interest today.

H. R. Stoneback
State University of New York
New Paltz

EDWIN ARLINGTON ROBINSON
1869–1935

Author's Chronology

Born December 22, 1869, Head Tide, Maine; *1870* moves to Gardiner, Maine, the "Tilbury Town" of his poems; *1891* matriculates at Harvard; *1893* leaves Harvard without degree to return to Gardiner; *1896* privately publishes his first book of poetry; *1899* moves to New York; *1903–1904* works for eight months as time keeper on New York subway project; *1905* accepts President Theodore Roosevelt's appointment as Customs Agent in New York, receives publicity with Roosevelt's review of *The Children of the Night* in *Outlook; 1911* spends the first of the next twenty-four summers in residence at the MacDowell Colony in Peterborough, New Hampshire; *1914* publishes *Van Zorn*, his first prose play; *1922* receives the Pulitzer Prize for *Collected Poems; 1923* visits England; *1925* receives the Pulitzer Prize for *The Man Who Died Twice; 1927* enjoys the phenomenal success of *Tristram* which is a Literary Guild offering; *1928* receives the Pulitzer Prize for *Tristram; 1935* dies from cancer in New York on April 6th.

Author's Bibliography (selected collections)

The Torrent and the Night Before, 1896; *Captain Craig,* 1902; *The Town Down the River,* 1910; *Van Zorn,* 1914; *The Man Against the Sky,* 1916; *Merlin,* 1917; *Avon's Harvest,* 1921; *The Man Who Died Twice,* 1924; *Tristram,* 1927; *Sonnets 1889–1927,* 1928; *Collected Poems,* 1929; *Nicodemus,* 1932; *Amaranth,* 1934; *King Jasper,* 1935.

Overview of Biographical Sources

Since Edwin Arlington Robinson's death in 1935, there have been seven book-length biographical studies of the Maine poet. However, Robinson's acute introversion, resulting in a complete lack of "public image," has exacerbated the task of writing a definitive biography. While Hermann Hagedorn's *Edwin Arlington Robinson* (1938) is not definitive, it is the only authoritative biography. It continues to be the main reference source for most subsequent biographies such as: Emery Neff's *Edwin Arlington Robinson* (New York: William Sloane Associates, 1948, rpt. 1968), Chard Powers Smith's *Where the Light Falls: A Portrait of Edwin Arlington Robinson* (1965), and Louis O. Coxe's *Edwin Arlington Robinson: The Life of Poetry* (1969). Since much of Robinson's poetry is autobiographical, frequent critical attention is given to various poems in each of these biographies. In 1947, an indispensable biographical source was published entitled *Untriangulated Stars: Letters of Edwin Arlington Robinson to Harry De Forest Smith 1890–1905,* ed. by Denham Sutcliffe (Cambridge: Harvard University Press, 1947). These letters illustrate Robinson's vast knowledge of literary genres. The Poet's sensitivity and humor revealed in this correspondence has not been as successfully conveyed in any third person biographical narrative.

Evaluation of Selected Biographies

Coxe, Louis O. *Edwin Arlington Robinson: The Life of Poetry.* New York: Pegasus, 1969. In this critical biography, Coxe's account of Robinson's life is accurate although less sympathetic than most. While the biography is not particularly focused, attention is given to previously "sensitive" material such as Robinson's chronic drinking problem and his tormenting periods of being unable to write. Political and social events and their impact on Robinson's poetry are discussed with Coxe citing the Arthurian trilogy as being the direct result of the Poet's aversion to World War I. Coxe's academic style is quite readable.

Hagedorn, Hermann, *Edwin Arlington Robinson.* New York: Macmillan, 1938. Hagedorn was a very close friend of Robinson who persuaded the Poet to attend the MacDowell Colony. A detailed account of Robinson's life and renewed inspiration for writing at the Colony is depicted. Hagedorn also gives close attention to Robinson's attempts at writing drama, a medium in which the Poet strived to be successful but failed. Letters and poems are often quoted to support autobiographical details, but Hagedorn has not provided any formal documentation to reveal his sources. Although the tone and style of the biography are occasionally reminiscent of fiction, it is well written and quite sympathetic. The life of Robinson is divided into chronological sections and discussed accordingly. However, more than three-fourths of the book is dedicated to Robinson's life before 1916.

Smith, Chard Powers, *Where the Light Falls: A Portrait of Edwin Arlington Robinson.* New York: Macmillan, 1965. This bio-critical "Portrait" is comprised of Smith's reminiscence of his friendship with Robinson as well as a critical analysis of his poetry. However, two-fifths of the book is biographical and is centered upon Smith's "Legend of Emma." Through analysis of letters, usually to Harry De Forest Smith, and conversations with unrevealed sources, Smith argues that Robinson was in love with Emma Shepherd Robinson, the wife of his brother Herman. While occasionally resorting to conjecture, Smith's depiction of Emma as apex of a fraternal lovers' triangle is convincing. He cites numerous passages from Robinson's poetry which seem to verify the "Legend" and his premise that this conflict lies at the center of many of Robinson's poems. Smith's book is well written in a journalistic style, enjoyable to read, and enhanced by precise documentation.

Overview of Critical Sources

The first major work of criticism to appear on Robinson was Charles Cestre's *An Introduction to Edwin Arlington Robinson* (New York: Macmillan, 1930), a study which Robinson personally acknowledged as providing an accurate analysis of his poetry. Since Cestre's publication, nine book-length critical studies have been published. However, much of this attention has been given to Robinson's more "popular" writing involving the "Cory-like" protagonists of his earlier poems and sonnets and his Arthurian trilogy. Robinson's longer poems, especially those written after *Tristram,* are frequently omitted from thorough critcism. With the exception of his centenary in 1969, overall critical studies of Robinson's poetry have waned since the poet's death in 1935.

Evaluation of Selected Criticism

Barnard, Ellsworth, *Edwin Arlington Robinson: A Critical Study.* New York: Macmillan, 1952; rpt. New York: Octagon Books, 1969. In this lengthy critical study, Barnard examines representative poetry from each of Robinson's books. Particular attention is given to style, poetic form, and thematics. Robinson's personal "philosophy," centered upon anti-materialism, and its assimilation into his poetry is discussed. Since Robinson created more than two hundred characters, Barnard's classification of certain character traits is very beneficial.

Fussell, Edwin S. *Edwin Arlington Robinson: The Literary Background of a Traditional Poet.* Berkeley: University of California Press, 1954. Fussell provides a thorough examination of Robinson's numerous literary influences, giving equal attention to American, English, and Classical sources. Focusing primarily on earlier poems, the emphasis of this study is the analysis of these influences on Robinson's thematic and stylistic structures. The importance of Zola and Ibsen is discussed in detail with Fussell citing *Captain Craig* as being the most Ibsenesque work in the Robinson canon. Much of Fussell's study is based upon Robinson's literary criticism in *Untriangulated Stars: Letters of Edwin Arlington Robinson to Harry De Forest Smith 1890–1905.*

Robinson, W. R. *Edwin Arlington Robinson: A Poetry of the Act.* Cleveland: Western Reserve University Press, 1967. While the deeply philosophical nature of this major critical study often makes for difficult reading, W. R. Robinson's discussion of the poet's aesthetics and its application to his poetry is particularly insightful. Alienation of self from society in E. A. Robinson's earlier poems is discussed in detail. Tilbury Town is depicted as a dramatic character representing the materialistic whole of modern man's alienation from the spiritual realm. Attention is given to the longer poems, from *Roman Bartholow* to *King Jasper,* with W. R. Robinson stating these poems should be read as a group since they all possess a protagonist who has faced spiritual death and yet achieves a spiritual reawakening and inner peace.

Other Sources

Barnard, Ellsworth, " 'Of This or That Estate': Robinson's Literary Reputation," *Edwin Arlington Robinson's Centenary Essays.* ed. by Ellsworth Barnard.

Athens: University of Georgia Press, 1969. A discussion of Robinson's vacillation between fame and obscurity with regard to popular and critical reception.

Joyner, Nancy Carol, *Edwin Arlington Robinson: A Reference Guide.* Boston: G. K. Hall, 1978. In more than 1400 bibliographical entries, Joyner briefly describes each bio-critical writing (books, pamphlets, articles) which has been published between 1894–1976. From 1916–1976, she has attempted a comprehensive listing of works.

Zabel, Morton Dauwen, ed. *Selected Poems of Edwin Arlington Robinson.* New York: Collier, 1966. James Dickey's introduction to this collection provides an insightful perspective on how one should read Robinson's poetry.

Selected Dictionaries and Encyclopedias

American Writers: A Collection of Literary Biographies, Charles Scribner's Sons, 1974. Contains a lengthy critical discussion of selected poems and depicts Robinson as a Romantic who was completely isolated from poets and poetry of the twentieth century.

Dictionary of American Biography, Charles Scribner's Sons, 1948. Presents a brief discussion of Robinson's lineage, a full overview of the Poet's life, and comments upon Robinson's artistry.

The National Cyclopaedia of American Biography, James T. White, 1947. Accurately depicts Robinson's entire life while focusing on the popular and critical reception of his poetry.

Joseph R. Taylor
University of Delaware

EARL OF ROCHESTER
1647–1680

Author's Chronology

Born April 1, 1647, at Ditchley, near Woodstock, Oxfordshire, son of a Puritan mother and a royalist general under Charles I; *1660* matriculates at Wadham College, Oxford; *1661* receives a pension of 500 pounds a year from the King; at age thirteen receives the courtesy degree of M.A.; November *1661* leaves England for a four-year tour of France and Italy to complete his education with a tutor appointed by Charles II, Sir Andrew Balfour, a distinguished Scottish physician and scholar; *1664* at court earns a reputation for wit and notoriety for libertinism; becomes a favorite of Charles II, often rebuked and exiled from court, but as often pardoned and recalled for his charm; May *1665* abducts the beautiful heiress, Elizabeth Malet, because her family opposes their marriage, and is imprisoned in the Tower for several weeks; July *1665* volunteers for the Second Dutch War and sees action at sea; *1666* is made Gentleman of the Bedchamber to the King, distinguishes himself under fire at sea; *1667* marries Elizabeth Malet to her family's surprise, and eventually fathers three daughters and a son in a happy union; *1667* takes his seat underage in the House of Lords; *1668* is appointed Gamekeeper for the county of Oxford; *1669* succeeds in talking his way out of a duel with the Earl of Mulgrave; *1670* to *1675* gradually develops as a poet; *1674* secures the coveted offices of Ranger and Keeper of Woodstock Park, with its fine High Lodge as his residence; March *1676* Etherege brings more fame to Rochester by drawing his character as Dorimant in *The Man of Mode;* June *1676* is involved in the brawl at Epsom, in which Captain Downs is killed; *1679–80* has a series of conversations on religion with Gilbert Burnet, later Bishop of Salisbury; July 26, 1680, dies at Woodstock at age 33 after a dramatic conversion to Christianity witnessed by his mother's chaplain, Robert Parsons.

Author's Bibliography (selected)

Poems on Several Occasions (1680); *Poems on Several Occasions* (1685); *Poems Etc. on Several Occasions, with Valentinian, a Tragedy* (1691); *The Miscellaneous Works* (1707, 1709); *The Works* (1714); *The Collected Works of John Wilmot, Earl of Rochester,* ed. John Hayward (1926); *Poems by John Wilmot, Earl of Rochester,* ed. Vivian de Sola Pinto (1953; rev. ed. 1964); *The Complete Poems of John Wilmot, Earl of Rochester,* ed. David M. Vieth (1968).

Overview of Biographical Sources

The first place Rochester's biographers traditionally turned for his life was to Gilbert Burnet's *Some Passages of the Life and Death of the Right Honorable John Earl of Rochester* (London, 1680). This is an account of Rochester's early life, his beliefs, and his final repentance and conversion. Another contemporary account often cited is Robert Parsons, *A Sermon Preached at the Funeral of the Right Honorable John Earl of Rochester* (Oxford 1680). Samuel Johnson's largely unsympathetic "Life of Rochester" in his *Lives of the Most Eminent English Poets* (London, 1781) is widely available. Serious scholarship into Rochester's life begins in the twentieth century with Johannes Prinz's, *John Wilmot, Earl of Rochester: His Life and Writings* (Leipzig: Mayer and Müller, 1927), followed by Vivian de Sola Pinto's *Rochester: Portrait of a Restoration Poet* (London: John Lane the Bodley Head, 1935), which was corrected and revised into a better book, retitled *Enthusiast in Wit.*

Evaluation of Selected Biographies

Greene, Graham, *Lord Rochester's Monkey, Being the Life of John Wilmot, Second Earl of Rochester.* New York: Viking, 1974. Because Prinz's biography is not easily accessible to contemporary students, Greene's serves as an alternative book-length biography. Greene's biography is replete with long quotations of Rochester's verse, letters to and from the poet, and photographs, paintings, and drawings relating to his life. It is a solid book, even when Greene's artistic imagination prevails and he explores out-of-the-way stories and rumors about Rochester.

Pinto, Vivian de Sola, *Enthusiast in Wit: A Portrait of John Wilmot Earl of Rochester, 1647–1680.* Lincoln: University of Nebraska, 1962. Pinto surrounds his subject with Rochester's intellectual, social, and political milieu. He devotes space to the better known poems, and faces squarely problems for a biographer of Rochester, like the Downs affair at Epsom and the conversations with Burnet and the conversion to Christianity. Although two and a half decades old, this study remains definitive on the life of the poet.

Autobiographical Sources

Because critical opinion is hardly in agreement on the possible autobiographical elements of his poems, the letters of Rochester, including *The Rochester-Savile Letters,* ed. J. H. Wilson (Columbus: Ohio State University Press, 1941), are as close to autobiography as one can find. The letters of his wife reveal a side not often emphasized, the frank yet tender and affectionate husband, side by side with the remorseful husband. He seems to have revealed himself to his wife as to no one else, except to his friend Henry Savile. Pinto and Greene provide many of the letters.

Overview of Critical Sources

The change in Rochester studies from the older biographical and historical to the newer critical mode has been slow in this century compared with the abrupt change in approach to other seventeenth-century poets like the Metaphysicals. As late as the 1980's many articles deal with sources, influences, and textual ascriptions, indicators of beginning scholarly and critical interest in an author. Even with what is often considered as the definitive edition of the poems, scholars question the approach, and critical views seem to sway in the uncertain winds of critical fashion. Nonetheless, a body of criticism mounts in journals, and recent books view Rochester more seriously as a poet than he has been regarded in almost three hundred years.

Evaluation of Selected Criticism

Farley-Hills, David, *Rochester's Poetry.* London: Bell and Hyman, 1978. The author bases his interpretation not on the Vieth edition or the first edition of Pinto, both of which he finds unsatisfactory, but largely on the Scholar facsimile reprint of *Poems on Several Occasions,* 1680. He places Rochester's lyrics in the tradition of seventeenth-century love lyrics, and finds him an unusual blend of aristocrat and philosopher in his lyrics, writing platonic, anti-platonic, and libertine verse. His chapters on burlesque and satire prepare for the concluding chapter on Rochester's literary and social satires, and his satires upon Nothing, in which he includes both "Upon Nothing" and the "Satyr against Reason and Mankind."

Griffin, Dustin H. *Satires Against Man: The Poems of Rochester.* Berkeley: University of California Press, 1973. Griffin contrasts Dryden, the middle class and professional writer of the age, with Rochester, the aristocrat and amateur poet. As a result of his philosophical mind, his withdrawing to the country for intervals, and his directing a rake's energy into poetry, Rochester surpassed all noble poets of the age, and except for Dryden, all professionals. Griffin discusses the poet's skeptical mind, his libertine and overtly sexual poems, gives the background of the "Satyr against Mankind" and a reading of the poem, and places Rochester in the Augustan age in relation to Dryden, Swift, and Pope.

Vieth, David M. *Attribution in Restoration Poetry: A Study of Rochester's "Poems" of 1680.* New Haven: Yale University Press, 1963. Part I is a detailed examination of the manuscript and printed versions of Rochester's *Poems of 1680,* and Part III is 112 pages of Lists of Early Texts and Ascriptions. Part II is partly a close, New-Critical analysis of poems like the "Epistolary Essay" contrasted with "A very Heroical Epistle," and of "Timon" and "Tunbridge Wells," and partly an analysis of scholarly problems surrounding Rochester and his poetry.

Other Sources

Farley-Hills, David, *Rochester: The Critical Heritage.* London: Routledge and Kegan Paul, 1972. The reception of Rochester and his poetry from contemporary comments, through acclamation (1700–1750), growing disapproval (1750–1800), the poet in eclipse (1800–1850), to the beginnings of reassessment (1850–1903).

Johnson, Ronald W. "Rhetoric and Drama in Rochester's 'Satyr Against Reason and Mankind,'" *Studies in English Literature, 1500-1900,* 15 (1975), 365-373. A look beyond the usual quest for sources of Rochester's most famous satire to a consideration of the poem as debate and drama, wherein lie the fundamental principles of the poem's construction.

Treglown, Jeremy, ed. *Spirit of Wit: Reconsiderations of Rochester.* Hamden, CT: Archon Books, 1982. Essays by well-known critics on Rochester's poetry, his philosophy, and his age.

Selected Encyclopedias
British Writers, Charles Scribner's Sons, 1979. Pinto's essay in "The Restoration Court Poets" is a well-balanced view of the place of Rochester and his friends in the period.

The Critical Temper: A Survey of Modern Criticism on English and American Literature, ed. Martin Tucker, II, Frederick Ungar, 1969. Passages on Rochester's life and writing from twentieth-century publications.

James A. W. Rembert
The Citadel

THEODORE ROETHKE
1908–1963

Author's Chronology

Born May 25, 1908 in Saginaw, Michigan, the son of first-generation immigrants from Prussia; *1913* enters John Moore School; *1921* enters Arthur Hill High School; *1921* his speech praising the Junior Red Cross is translated into twenty-six languages; *1923* death of his father after prolonged illness; *1925* enters the University of Michigan; graduates *magna cum laude; 1929* studies criminal law for one semester; *1931* enters graduate school at Harvard; *1931* first poem published; joins staff of English department, Lafayette College; coaches tennis team; *1935* accepts position in English at Michigan State University; November *1935* first episode of mental illness requiring hospitalization; *1936* accepts post at Pennsylvania State University; coaches tennis team; *1945* second serious episode of mental illness; receives shock therapy; *1946* receives first of two Guggenheim fellowships; *1947* receives Eunice Tietjiens Prize; October *1949* third hospitalization for mental illness; *1951* Levinson Prize; *1953* Ford Foundation Grant; *1953* marries Beatrice O'Connell of Winchester, Virginia; *1954* Pulitzer Prize in Poetry; *1955-1956* lectures in Italy on a Fulbright Grant; *1957* attack of manic depression requires extensive treatment; *1959* Bollingen Award; National Book Award; three month confinement for depression; *1959* begins Ford Foundation Grant abroad; requires hospitalization in Ireland; *1962* Shelley Memorial Poetry Award; Honorary Doctorate, University of Michigan; *1963* dies while swimming at Bainbridge Island, Washington.

Author's Bibliography

Open House, 1941 (poems); *The Lost Son and Other Poems,* 1948; *Praise to the End!* 1951 (poems); *The Waking: Poems 1933-1953,* 1953; *Words for the Wind: The Collected Verse of Theodore Roethke,* 1958; *I Am! Says the Lamb, 1961* (poems for children); *Party at the Zoo,* 1963 (poetic fantasy for children); *Sequence, Sometimes Metaphysical,* 1963 (poems); *The Far Field: Last Poems,* 1964; *On the Poet and His Craft: Selected Prose of Theodore Roethke,* ed. Ralph J. Mills, Jr., 1965; *The Achievement of Theodore Roethke: A Comprehensive Selection of his Poems with a Critical Introduction.* ed. Louis Martz, 1966; *The Collected Poems of Theodore Roethke,* 1966; *Selected Letters of Theodore Roethke.* ed. Ralph J. Mills, Jr., 1968; *Theodore Roethke: Selected Poems,* selected by Beatrice Roethke, 1969; *Dirty Dinkey and Other Creatures: Poems for Children.* ed. Beatrice Roethke and Stephen Lushington, 1973.

Evaluation of Biographies

Seager, Allan, *The Glass House: The Life of Theodore Roethke.* New York: McGraw-Hill, 1968. A sympathetic biography, written by a novelist and long-time acquaintance of the poet, *The Glass House* covers the entire life of a complex and enigmatic man. Although Seager tries to present an objective view of Roethke's bouts with mental illness, his fantasies of power, and his delusions of persecution, it is impossible to form an independent judgment about the relative weights of these elements of personality because of the lack of annotation. Many materials from Roethke's notes and letters from academic and literary colleagues are available here. The book offers excellent reading, but the scholarship fails to unlock the keys to the personality of this unique genius.

Autobiographical Sources

The poems of Theodore Roethke are insistently autobiographical. Like his students Carolyn Kizer and James Wright, Roethke made his personality, as well as his personal experiences, the subject of his poetry. At least some of his historical importance must be traced to his willingness to accept the risks of poetic autobiography. The power of *The Lost Son,* along with that of his friend Robert Lowell's *Life Studies,* contributed to the break with the objectivity of the school of T. S. Eliot. Working out his ambiguous feelings about his father dominates the second and third books, and Roethke claimed that the central character of "Meditations of an Old Woman" is an archetypal version of his own mother. The most famous adaptation of personal experience to poetry is his eloquent "Elegy for Jane: My Student, Thrown by a Horse."

Besides the poetry, Roethke left three important autobiographical materials. His letters, edited by Ralph Mills, cover the period from 1931 through his death. These contain witty and perceptive comments on his own work, on his life, and on fellow writers. Of particular interest are his extensive correspondence with William Carlos Williams and Kenneth Burke, both of whom Roethke respected and loved as father figures. The letters also contain revealing comments on his dedication to, and frustration with, his vocation as teacher. Of particular interest are his communications with the people he really loved about his mental illness, and the way he learned to deal with his affliction.

Many of the essays collected in *On the Poet and His Craft* are autobiographical. Some of these reveal the intentions of certain poems, such as "Open Letter," written originally for *Mid-Century American Poets.* Other essays treat Roethke's concept of himself as person, poet, and teacher. One, "An American Poet Introduces Himself and His Poems," was broadcast by the British Broadcasting System on 30 July, 1953. Two essays illustrate prose adaptations of Roethke's famous wit; unlike the wit of the poetry, the humor of "Last Class" or "A Tirade Turning" is caustic. This collection of essays may be the most effective method, in addition to the poems, of understanding the personality of this author.

David Wagoner has edited *Straw from the Fire: From the Notebooks of Theodore Roethke, 1943–1963,* a judicious selection of materials from the poet's nearly three hundred notebooks and more than eight thousand loose leaf sheets. In these notes, Roethke comments on his own work, that of other poets, poetry in general, and preparations for class lectures.

Overview of Critical Sources

Roethke's critics have generally agreed on the Romantic influence, the crucial effect on the history of modern poetry, the autobiographical and mythic sources of the poems, the creative uses of the greenhouse as metaphor, and the degree to which Roethke's poems assimilate the works of past poets. There have been disagreements on which Romantic poet or group exerts the greatest influence and on the degree to which Roethke merges the autobiographical with the mythic.

Evaluation of Selected Criticism

Blessing, Richard Allen, *Theodore Roethke's Dynamic Vision.* Bloomington, Indiana: Indiana University Press, 1974. Disdaining line-by-line anaylsis as inappropriate to Roethke's poems, Blessing attempts to treat the poems in terms of dynamics, or tensions. For Blessing, the attempt to locate a meaning in Roethke's poems is to accept the poem as a protean experience like reality itself, something that is always in a process of becoming. The study makes sharp contrasts between the tightly formal poems of *Open House* and the poem sequences. The chief value of the study is its attempt to illuminate some of the linguistic and thematic tensions. Although specific interpretations are often obscure because of the critic's belief that the longer poems "de-create" their own form as a prelude to creating a new form, the thematic implications of this process are worth exploring.

Burke, Kenneth, "The Vegetable Radicalism of Theodore Roethke," in *The Sewanee Review,* 58 (1950); rpt. in *Language as Symbolic Action: Essays on Life, Literature, and Method.* Berkeley: University of California Press, 1968, 254–281. Burke, a friend of Roethke's from their term at Bennington College, has written the most influential study of the psychological and aesthetic keys to Roethke's work. By exploring the meanings of the greenhouse as the central symbol of the poetry, Burke is able to discuss the emotive power and the psychological origins of Roethke's imagery with original insight. In this way, Burke lays the groundwork for most future understandings of the unique lyrical power of Roethke's poems.

La Belle, Jenijoy, *The Echoing Wood of Theodore Roethke.* Princeton: Princeton University Press, 1976. A former student of Roethke's, La Belle attempts to trace the echoes of former poets in the Roethke's poems. Although the stated purpose is not to determine literary influences, this book is indispensable for such study. La Belle traces echoes of the metaphysical and Romantic poets, but comes to the surprising conclusion that the chief influence on Roethke's concepts of poetry and tradition is T. S. Eliot, whom Roethke often called "Tiresome Tom."

Malkoff, Karl, *Theodore Roethke: An Introduction to the Poetry*. New York: Columbia University Press, 1962. This sound introduction studies the poems in terms of the author's artistic development, and treats them chronologically, with special attention to the difficult sequences. Malkoff also argues for certain psychological, philosophical, theological, and literary influences on Roethke's development. The approach is systematic and comprehensive, but occasionally sexual or Freudian readings are forced, especially in the discussion of *The Lost Son* sequence. Most of the poems, except those written for children, are discussed; at the same time, few of the poems are discussed in revealing detail.

Mills, Ralph J., Jr. *Theodore Roethke*. Minneapolis: University of Minnesota Press, 1963. Still the best general introduction to the poetry, this study balances a sensible overview with insightful analyses of poems.

Parini, Jay, *Theodore Roethke: An American Romantic*. Amherst: University of Massachusetts Press, 1979. The central premise is that Roethke can be best understood and appreciated in the context of Romanticism, specifically visionary American Romanticism. In this area, the study is a disappointment, for the discussion of the Romantic presence adds little to the general knowledge of influences on Roethke's life and work. The assertions of a Romantic influence are seldom handled in a way that casts a unique light on the poems. Parini offers an original and convincing explanation of the relation between a general Romantic disposition and the influence of psychoanalytic method that enables Roethke to grow to the point at which he is able to write *The Lost Son*. Parini's discussion of that sequence in relation to the archetype of the journey is excellent and original criticism, among the very best analysis of Roethke's poetry available.

Stein, Arnold, ed. *Theodore Roethke: Essays on the Poetry*. Seattle: University of Washington Press, 1965. Nine essays evaluate Roethke's achievement from a variety of perspectives, and there is no significant area of agreement among the contributors. The collection therefore is distinguished by the variety of approaches it offers the reader. Two essays are by fellow poets Stephen Spender and W. D. Snodgrass, the other seven by distinguished critics. The collection contains few actual explications of individual poems, but because of the variety of approaches and the perceptiveness of the contributors, this book contains indispensable evaluations of Roethke's overall achievement.

Sullivan, Rosemary, *Theodore Roethke: The Garden Master*. Seattle: University of Washington Press, 1975. A subtle and complex analysis of the poetry, Sullivan considers Roethke's claim that he willed his manic episodes in order to explore the widest range of human experience. Sullivan studies the poems as attempts to generalize the personal psychic experience to a universal archetype. By this logic, she shows that the poems are not autobiographical, but paradoxically objective. This casts an important light on the uniqueness of Roethke's work, as well as on his debt to Eliot.

Selected Dictionaries and Encyclopedias

Critical Survey of Poetry, Salem Press, 1982. The concise biography is followed by an analysis that emphasizes the Romantic presence in the poems. This discussion is supported by brief analyses of selected poems.

Dictionary of Literary Biography, Gale Research, 1980. Although analysis of the poems is judgmental, the connections between the poems and the biography are illuminating. The biography is the best available brief study of Roethke's life.

David C. Dougherty
Loyola College

CHRISTINA ROSSETTI
1830–1894

Author's Chronology

Born December 5, 1830, London, England of English-Italian parents; *1847* publishes her first collection of poems, privately printed by her maternal grandfather, Gaetano Polidori; *1848* receives offer of marriage from James Collinson; *1850* contributes seven poems to *The Germ* under the pseudonym of Ellen Alleyne; *1853* moves to Frome in Somerset where she assists her mother in teaching a day school; *1854* her father, Gabriele, dies; *1866* refuses the marriage proposal of Charles Bagot Cayley; *1871* suffers from Graves's disease; *1873* her sister joins an Anglican religious order; *1876* her sister dies; *1882* her brother, Dante Gabriel, dies; *1886* her mother dies; *1892* suffers from and is operated on for cancer; *1894* dies in London on the morning of December 29.

Author's Bibliography

Verses, 1847; *Goblin Market and Other Poems,* 1862; *The Prince's Progress and Other Poems,* 1866; *Commonplace and Other Short Stories,* 1870; *Sing-Song: A Nursery Rhyme Book,* 1872; *Annus Domini: A Prayer for Each Day of the Year,* 1874; *Speaking Likenesses,* 1874 (prose); *Goblin Market, The Prince's Progress, and Other Poems,* 1875 (first collected edition, containing 37 new pieces); *Seek and Find: A Double Series of Short Studies of the Benedicite,* 1879; *A Pageant and Other Poems,* 1881; *Called to Be Saints: The Minor Festivals Devotionally Studied,* 1881 (contains 13 poems); *Letter and Spirit: Notes on the Commandments,* 1883; *Time Flies: A Reading Diary,* 1885 (contains 130 poems); *Poems,* 1890 (second collected edition, contains 13 new poems); *The Face of the Deep: A Devotional Commentary of the Apocalypse,* 1892 (contains several hundred verses and fragments); *Verses Reprinted from Called to Be Saints, Time Flies, The Face of the Deep,* 1893 (contains modifications and additions); *New Poems Hitherto Unpublished or Uncollected.* Edited by W. M. Rossetti, 1896; *Maude: A Story for Girls,* 1897 (contains six poems); *The Poetical Works of Christina Georgina Rossetti, with Memoir and Notes.* Edited by W. M. Rossetti, 1904; *The Complete Poems of Christina Rossetti.* Edited by R. W. Crump, vol. 1, 1979.

Overview of Biographical Sources

Even though Christina Rossetti lived a relatively uneventful life, a considerable amount of biographical material has been written about her. There are to date eight biographies and numerous shorter biographical studies. The first full-length biographical treatment was written by Mackenzie Bell (1898), and many commentators maintain that it is still the best. Written with the close cooperation of the poet's brother, William Michael, Bell's book is exhaustive, factual and detailed and is free of speculation about the sources of the emotional turmoil apparent at times in Rossetti's poetry that plays a role in subsequent biographies. Bell's book and William's "Memoir" are the basic sources of information for a host of biographical studies that have followed them, including Mary F. Sandar's *The Life of Christina Rossetti* (London: Hutchinson, 1930); Dorothy Stuart's *Christina Rossetti,* English Men of Letters Series (London: Macmillan, 1930); Eleanor Thomas's *Christina Georgina Rossetti* (New York: Columbia University Press, 1931); Marya Zaturenska's *Christina Rossetti: A Portrait with Background* (New York: Macmillan, 1949); and Margaret Sawtell's *Christina Rossetti: Her Life and Religion* (London: A. R. Mowbray, 1955). The first important biography based on a significant number of new materials is that written by Lona Mosk Packer (1963). Though meticulously researched and generally considered to be the best biography, Packer's book, according to some scholars, is flawed by a thesis concerning her romantic life, which facts cannot adequately support. Georgina Battiscombe's biography of Rossetti (1981) seeks to correct Packer's thesis and also utilizes previously unpublished materials. Battiscombe's *Christina Rossetti,* Writers and Their Work Pamphlet No. 189 (London: Longmans and Green, 1965) is perhaps the most worthwhile shorter biographical study. It should also be noted that much biographical information about Rossetti can be found in works concerning her famous brother and in studies of the Pre-Raphaelite Brotherhood. Her letters, for example, are a case in point. Only one volume, *The Family Letters of Christina Georgina Rossetti, with Some Supplementary Letters and Appendices,* ed. W. M. Rossetti (London: Brown, Langham, 1908), has been published. Others appear in volumes concerned with Dante Gabriel and the Rossetti family.

Evaluation of Selected Biographies

Battiscombe, Georgina, *Christina Rossetti: A Divided Life.* New York: Holt, Rinehart and Winston, 1981. This biography, which makes use of material which came to light subsequent to the publication of Packer's book, seeks to correct that author's thesis that the tensions and frustrations evident in Rossetti's love poems resulted from her love for William Bell Scott, a thesis derived mainly from the poetry itself rather than from factual documentation. Battiscombe's thesis maintains that the tensions in the poet's work are the result of a division between her passionate nature and her religious beliefs. The book is beautifully written and highly readable.

Bell, Mackenzie, *Christina Rossetti: A Biographical Study.* London: Hurst and Blackett, 1898. Bell's book is both biographical and critical. He devotes five chapters, about two thirds of the book, to Rossetti's life. Based upon the poet's letters and written with the aid of her brother, the book contains factual, accurate, and thorough information. Bell, who was a close acquaintance of Rossetti, presents a sympathetic portrait of the poet. His criticism focuses on her style rather than on revelations pertaining to her inner life that the poems might contain. The book includes a bibliography by J. P. Anderson. It is an indispensable source.

Bellas, Ralph, *Christina Rossetti.* Boston: Twayne, 1977. This brief introduction to the poet's life and work is an excellent starting point for those doing research on Rossetti. Giving some attention to Rossetti's prose, the author focuses on the poetry. Acknowledging the psychological emphasis of contemporary Rossetti criticism, the author concerns himself with the degree to which the poet's "inner life" is "reflected in her works." The book also contains a convenient chronology and an excellent, briefly annotated bibliography.

Packer, Lona Mosk, *Christina Rossetti.* Berkeley: University of California Press, 1963. Although this book is widely considered to be the best and most scholarly biography to follow Bell's, the author's thesis concerning Rossetti and Scott remains extremely controversial. However, like Bell's biography, it is an essential source for students of Rossetti because of the new materials utilized by the author and because of Packer's penetrating and original readings of the poems. As commentators have observed, Packer's Scott theory may be wrong, but her perception that something profoundly affecting underlies Rossetti's poetry is surely correct.

Overview of Critical Sources

Because of the relationship between Rossetti's life and work that the recent scholarship has emphasized, much of the best criticism is incorporated into the biographical works previously discussed, particularly in the biographies of Packer, Battiscombe, and Bellas. Also, because of her status as an important but minor poet, many good treatments of Rossetti's work are part of more general studies on the Pre-Raphaelite movement, or are published as essays in scholarly journals. However, three full-length studies—books by Fredegond Shove, Edith Birkhead, and Thomas Burnett Swann—are worth mentioning. Both Birkhead's and Shove's books are bio-critical.

Evaluation of Selected Criticism

Birkhead, Edith, *Christina Rossetti and Her Poetry.* London: Harrap, 1930. Birkhead argues that Rossetti was not influenced by the currents of her times. She maintains that the poet chose spiritual love over human contact.

Shove, Fredegond, *Christina Rossetti: A Study.* Cambridge: Cambridge University Press, 1931; rpt. New York: Octagon, 1969. The critical portion of this book includes discussions of "Goblin Market," "The Prince's Progress," "Maiden Song," and the sonnet sequence, "Monna Innominata." The author sees parallels between Rossetti's religious beliefs and her work; rates the sonnets lower than the children's poems; and places the literary quality of the poetry above that of the prose.

Swann, Thomas Burnett, *Wonder and Whimsey: The Fantastic World of Christina Rossetti.* Francestown, NH: Marshall Jones, 1960. The author's thesis is that Rossetti was most successful as a poet when her subject matter concerned wonder and whimsey, the strange and the charming. He analyzes selections from *Sing-Song: A Nursey Rhyme Book* and *Speaking Likenesses,* as well as "Goblin Market," "The Prince's Progress," and other works. The author also draws useful parallels between Rossetti's writings and the works of Tennyson and Arnold.

Other Sources

Bowra, C. M. "Christina Rossetti," in *The Romantic Imagination.* Cambridge: Harvard University Press, 1949, pp. 245–270. This critique posits the idea of a duality in Rossetti's nature that is reflected in her poetry.

Fredeman, William E. "Christina Rossetti," in *The Victorian Poets: A Guide to Research.* ed. Frederick E. Faverty, 2d ed. Cambridge: Harvard University Press, 1968, pp. 284–293. An excellent survey of and commentary on the editions of poetry and letters and the major biographies and critical works.

Packer, Lona Mosk, "Symbol and Reality in Christina Rossetti's *Goblin Market,*" in *PMLA,* 73 (1958), 375–385. A very important analysis of the poem, which includes Packer's Scott thesis.

Weathers, Winston, "Christina Rossetti: The Sisterhood of Self," in *Victorian Poetry,* 3 (1965), 81–89. While discussing the characteristic tension in Rossetti's poetry, Weathers suggests that her "sister" poems indicate a progression from division to integration.

Zasadinski, Eugene, "Christina Rossetti's 'A Better Resurrection' and 'Up-Hill: Self-Reliance and Its Limitations,'" in *The Journal of Pre-Raphaelite Studies,* 4 (May 1984), 93–99. The author argues that these poems contain heterodox religious views.

Selected Entries in Dictionaries and Encyclopedias

British Writers, Charles Scribner's Sons, 1982, Vol. 4, pp. 247–260. An excellent bio-critical introduction to Rossetti. Includes bibliography.

Eugene Zasadinski
St. John's University

DANTE GABRIEL ROSSETTI
1828–1882

Author's Chronology

Born 1828 in London, England; *1836–1841* attends a day school and then King's College School; *1841–1845* attends Sass's drawing school, enters the Antique School of the Royal Academy; *1847* writes "The Blessed Damozel;" *1848* forms the Pre-Raphaelite Brotherhood with John Millais, Holman Hunt and others; *1849* displays first painting, "The Girlhood of the Virgin Mary;" *1850* publishes *The Germ,* the Pre-Raphaelite journal; *1852* becomes engaged to Elizabeth Siddal; *1854* begins his never-finished painting "Found;" develops close relationship with John Ruskin; *1856* becomes friends with William Morris; *1857* the Pre-Raphaelite Exhibition opens; meets A. C. Swinburne; *1860* marries Elizabeth Siddal; *1861* Elizabeth delivers a stillborn child; publishes *Early Italian Poets; 1862* wife dies from an overdose of laudanum; buries manuscript of many poems with his wife; *1866* health begins to worsen; *1870 Poems* published; *1871* faces attack from R. W. Buchanan about belonging to the "Fleshly School of Poetry;" *1872* attempts suicide; *1874* breaks with William Morris; *1876–1880* declines physically and mentally, increases reliance on opium and alcohol; *1881* publishes *Ballads and Sonnets* and a new edition of *Poems,* despite decline; *1882* dies April 9, Easter.

Author's Bibliography (selected)

The Early Italian Poets, 1861 (translations; published as *Dante and his Circle,* 1874); *Poems,* 1881; *Ballads and Sonnets,* 1881.

Overview of Biographical Sources

Rossetti himself sensed that his life would be appealing to biographers given the legendary and sensational aspects of his life, and his premonition has proved correct. Well over ten biographies have appeared since his death. Hall Caine's biography, *Recollections of Rossetti* (London: Cassell and Company, 1928, first published in 1882) was the first to appear and is based on firsthand contact with Rossetti but is, however, overly dramatic and not completely reliable. Another contemporary, Henry Treffrey Dunn, an art assistant to Rossetti, capitalized on his relationship with Rossetti by writing *Recollections of Dante Gabriel Rossetti and his Circle* (London: Elkin Matthews, 1904), but the work is limited in being merely recollections. Rossetti's brother William also gave his impressions in *Some Reminiscences,* two volumes (New York: Charles Scribner's Sons, 1906). This work deals with the whole Rossetti family. Also in the same period, a friend, Joseph Knight, published a highly flattering biography, *Lie of Dante Gabriel Rossetti* (London: Walter Scott, 1887).

While the early biographies are decorous and err on the side of dullness, those which followed the centenary of Rossetti's birth err on the side of sensationalism. Violet Hunt's *The Wife of Rossetti* (London: John Lane, 1932) deals with Elizabeth Siddal and sensationalizes the Rossetti relationship. Francis Winwar's *Poor Splendid Wings: The Rossettis and Their Circle* (Boston: Little Brown, 1933) tells a good story but is not particularly accurate. One work of this period does bear special mention: Evelyn Waugh's *Rossetti: His Life and Works* (London: Duckworth, 1928). Waugh stresses the relationship of life and works and gives the reader valuable insights from an important modern writer.

Modern scholars have carefully researched the life and have produced significant biographies. Despite objections to it, the major biography is clearly by Oswald Doughty, *Dante Gabriel Rossetti: A Victorian Romantic* (1949). Doughty deals fully with Rossetti and uses the poetry to explain him. Also, Doughty suggests that there was an affair between Jane Morris and Rossetti. This assertion is rejected by other studies. Rosalie Glyn Grylls reassesses Rossetti's life in *Portrait of Rossetti* (1964); using recently released letters, Grylls rejects the Rossetti-Jane Morris affair. Also of note is a study done by Rossetti's niece, Helen Rossetti Angeli. Her book, *Dante Gabriel Rossetti: His Friends and Enemies* (London: Hamish Hamilton, 1949) is an attempt to set the record straight about many issues surrounding the Rossetti legend. Finally, William E. Fredeman's study, *Prelude to the Last Decade: Dante Gabriel Rossetti in the Summer of 1872* (Manchester: John Rylands Library, 1971), shows the extent to which scholarship still must go to understand Rossetti's life. Narrowly focused, Fredeman's monograph covers one year of Rossetti's decline by evaluating all the available material from Rossetti's life at that time.

Evaluation of Selected Biographies

Doughty, Oswald, *Dante Gabriel Rossetti: A Victorian Romantic.* London: Frederick Muller, 1949. In a complete but controversial account, Doughty demonstrates how the poetry provides autobiographical insights. To some critics, he overstresses Rossetti's psychotic tendencies, and his contention that there was a love affair between Jane Morris and Rossetti is not corroborated by the recently available letters. The controversial elements present in Doughty's work are typical of the difficulty of dealing with other sensational issues of Rossetti's life.

Grylls, Rosalie Glyn, *Portrait of Rossetti.* London: McDonald, 1964. A newer study but more limited in scope than Doughty's, Grylls focuses on the effect of women and the concept of woman on Rossetti's career. She bases some of her assertions on material not available to Doughty.

Autobiographical Sources

Rossetti's *House of Life,* a sequence of sonnets, can be termed autobiographical in only a general way. It reveals the inner life of Rossetti, providing philosophical insights into his ideas about physical and spiritual love. However, readers should consult the letters, diaries and papers to understand his life and career fully. William Rossetti, Rossetti's brother, edited several volumes, all of which are important: *Dante Gabriel Rossetti: His Family Letters with a Memoir,* two volumes (London: Ellis, 1895), *Rossetti Papers 1862–1870* (London: Sands, 1893), and *Preraphaelite Diaries and Letters* (London: Hurst and Blackett, 1900). Two modern scholars have produced an edition of the letters which to date is the most complete: Oswald Doughty and J. R. Wahl, eds. *The Letters* of *Dante Gabriel Rossetti,* four volumes (London: Oxford University Press, 1965–1967). This edition is controversial both for its incompleteness and its lack of an index. Since the Doughty-Wahl project, other scholars have edited smaller portions of the whole correspondence of Rossetti: John Bryson, ed. *Dante Gabriel Rossetti and Jane Morris: Their Correspondence* (Oxford: Clarendon Press, 1976); Francis J. Fennell, Jr. ed. *The Rossetti-Leyland Letters* (Athens: Ohio University Press, 1978). Also of note is Odette Bornand, ed. *The Diary of W. M. Rossetti,* 1870–1873 (Oxford: Clarendon Press, 1977).

Overview of Critical Sources

Anyone studying Rossetti must be aware of two important factors which have profoundly influenced the available scholarship about him. Rossetti is both poet and painter, and no scholar has tried in one single study to come to terms with his two careers. Second, Rossetti is part of the Pre-Raphaelite movement in art and poetry and cannot actually be studied without placing him in the context of his group. Thus no one study can treat every aspect of Rossetti. Students must be prepared to consult different types of studies to develop a full understanding.

Evaluation of Selected Criticism

Howard, Ronnalie Roper, *The Dark Glass: Vision and Technique in the Poetry of Dante Gabriel Rossetti.* Athens: Ohio University Press, 1972. This book is the first complete treatment of all of Rossetti's poetry. Howard's approach is a formal list approach which pays close attention to explication. Unlike some studies, Howard focuses on the poems with little emphasis on the poems as autobiography.

Johnstone, Robert D. *Dante Gabriel Rossetti.* New York: Twayne, 1969. This book is a helpful general guide and probably the best book for the beginning reader. While the book is organized by the familiar Twayne format, Johnstone gives especial emphasis to the *House of Life,* Rossetti's elaborate sonnet sequence.

Rees, Joan, *The Poetry of Dante Gabriel Rossetti.* Cambridge: Cambridge University Press, 1981. Rees tries to see Rossetti as typical of the divided Victorian consciousness and in Rossetti's case, the split is between medievalism and modernism. In this respect, Rees sees Rossetti as part of the mainstream of Victorianism rather than alien to it. Rees deals with both the life and poetry.

Stevenson, Lionel, *The Pre-Raphaelite Poets.* Chapel Hill: University of North Carolina Press, 1972. Stevenson's book is the best book for placing Rossetti in the poetic context of the Pre-Raphaelite movement. Stevenson provides valuable introductory material and a sixty-page biographical and critical discussion of Rossetti. He also discusses Christina Rossetti, Morris and Swinburne.

Surtees, Virginia, ed. *Dante Gabriel Rossetti: 1828–82, The Paintings and the Drawings.* 2 vols. London: Oxford University Press, 1965–1967. This work gives information about 750 paintings and sketches, and provides reproductions of some of Rossetti's paintings. It is the best source for information on Rossetti as a painter.

Other Sources

Bowra, C. M. *The Romantic Imagination.* New York: Oxford University Press, 1961. Bowra places Rossetti in the context of the Romantic movement and provides one chapter on *The House of Life.*

Fredeman, William, *Pre-Raphaelitism; a Bibliocritical Study.* Cambridge: Harvard University Press, 1965. Fredeman provides a complete bibliography for the movement through 1865.

Hough, Graham, *The Last Romantics.* London: Methuen, 1947. In one chapter, Hough deals with the theory of Pre-Raphaelitism and Rossetti's poetry.

Vogel, Joseph F. *Dante Gabriel Rossetti's Versecraft.* Gainesville: University Presses of Florida, 1971. Vogel restricts his study to verse form and pays especial attention to "The Blessed Damozel."

Selected Dictionaries and Encyclopedias

British Writers, Charles Scribner's Sons, 1982. This work has a thorough article on Rossetti's life and poetry by Oswald Doughty.

Critical Survey of Poetry, Salem Press, 1982. This survey presents a thoughtful analysis of Rossetti's life and selected works.

Dennis Goldsberry
College of Charleston

PHILIP ROTH
1933

Author's Chronology

Born March 19, 1933, Newark, New Jersey of lower-middle-class Jewish parents; father an insurance salesman; *1950* graduates from Weequahic High School; *1950–1951* attends Newark campus, Rutgers University; *1951–1954* attends Bucknell University, edits its literary magazine, and receives B.A. *magna cum laude* in English; *1955* receives M.A. in English from University of Chicago; enlists in the U.S. Army, working in the Public Information Office in Washington; medical discharge for back injury during basic training; *1956* Ph.D. candidate and instructor in English at Chicago; "The Contest for Aaron Gold," published in *Epoch,* selected for inclusion in *The Best Short Stories of 1956; 1959 Goodbye, Columbus* wins Houghton Mifflin Literary Fellowship and National Book Award; *1959* marries Margaret Martinson Williams, from whom he is separated in *1963* and divorces in *1966* and who dies in an automobile accident in *1968; 1960–present* part-time teaching at the universities of Iowa, Princeton, SUNY, Stony Brook, and Pennsylvania; *1969 Portnoy's Complaint* achieves enormous commercial success, provokes controversy, makes Roth a celebrity; *1972* first visits Czechoslovakia; *1975* becomes editor of the Penguin series "Writers from the Other Europe"; alternates residence between rural New England and England.

Author's Bibliography (selected)

Goodbye, Columbus, 1959 (stories); *Letting Go,* 1962 (novel); *When She Was Good,* 1967 (novel); *Portnoy's Complaint,* 1969 (novel); *Our Gang,* 1971 (novel); *The Breast,* 1972, revised 1980 (novel); *The Great American Novel,* 1973 (novel); *My Life as a Man,* 1974; *Reading Myself and Others,* 1975 (essays); *The Professor of Desire,* 1977 (novel); *The Ghost Writer,* 1979 (novel); *Zuckerman Unbound,* 1981 (novel); *The Anatomy Lesson,* 1983 (novel); *Zuckerman Bound,* 1985 (novel).

Overview of Biographical Sources

Still quite productive and still, presumably, in mid-career, Roth has not yet been the subject of a book-length biography. Much of his fiction is ostensibly drawn from details of his own life, but Roth has attempted to discourage speculation over what the correspondences are. Biographical information on him is available only in encyclopedia entries, and, either in passim or in brief sections, in studies whose focus is literary analysis.

Autobiographical Sources

There are evident parallels between Roth's principal characters and various stages of his own life. He has been reticent about discussing these and insistent that, though written in the first person, the notorious *Portnoy's Complaint,* for example, is a work of fiction. *Zuckerman Unbound* examines the personal consequences to its fictive author of the kind of scandalous success Roth achieved with *Portnoy's Complaint.* Both *My Life as a Man* and *The Ghost Writer* are fictional attempts to examine the transmutation of life into art. In their reflexive commentary, the essays and interviews collected in *Reading Myself and Others* constitute an artistic inventory and testament. An interview conducted by Hermione Lee (*The Paris Review,* 93, Fall 1984, pp. 215–247) allows Roth to continue his self-scrutiny through the period of *The Anatomy Lesson.*

Overview of Critical Sources

Roth began receiving serious critical notice with his first book, though assessments of this steadily productive author must continually be readjusted to new developments in his career. Roth helped to foster, and benefitted from, the growth of ethnic awareness during the 1960's and is widely regarded as, with Saul Bellow and Bernard Malamud, one of the triumvirate of major American Jewish novelists. Hence studies like Allen Guttmann's *The Jewish Writer in America: Assimilation and the Crisis of Identity* (New York: Oxford University Press, 1971) and Irving Malin's *Jews and Americans* (Carbondale: Southern Illinois University Press, 1965) are useful in situating Roth within an ethnic context. Norman Podhoretz's "Laureate of the New Class" and Irving Howe's "Philip Roth Reconsidered," both in the December, 1972 *Commentary,* are influential attacks on Roth from a Jewish perspective.

Roth has been accepted into the contemporary American canon, and attempts to define it, like Frederick R. Karl's *American Fictions: 1940–1980* (New York: Harper & Row, 1983), Alfred Kazin's *Bright Book of Life* (Boston: Little, Brown, 1973), Raymond M. Olderman's *Beyond the Waste Land* (New Haven: Yale University Press, 1972), and Tony Tanner's *City of Words* (New York: Harper & Row, 1971) give him prominent attention. Several book-length treatments of Roth, focusing on him as social commentator, Jew, and analyst of character, are of necessity provisional.

Evaluation of Selected Criticism

Jones, Judith Paterson, and Guinevera A. Nance, *Philip Roth.* New York: Frederick Ungar, 1981. This is a chronological retrospective of Roth's first eleven books in terms of recurring conflicts: between the individual and society, men and women, adventure and security, and American myths and realities.

Lee, Hermione, *Philip Roth.* London & New York: Methuen, 1982. Lee's is a short, thematically organized overview of the Roth canon, by a British critic.

McDaniel, John N. *The Fiction of Philip Roth.* Haddonfield, NJ: Haddonfield House, 1974. The first book-length study, this work analyzes the fiction through *My Life as a Man* via categories of "victim-hero" and "activist-hero."

Pinsker, Sanford, *The Comedy That "Hoits": An Essay on the Fiction of Philip Roth.* Columbia: University of Missouri Press, 1975. Pinsker's short introduction depicts Roth in terms of tensions between his public and private lives, and between laughter and pain.

Rodgers, Bernard F., Jr. *Philip Roth.* Boston: Twayne, 1978. Rogers presents a useful chronological survey of Roth's career, combining some biography with a general critical reading.

Other Sources

Kellman, Steven G. "Philip Roth's Ghost Writer," *Comparative Literature Studies,* 2 (Summer 1984), 175–185. Argues that Roth's fiction has been shaped by his obsession with the writings and the life of Franz Kafka.

Raban, Jonathan, "The New Philip Roth," *Novel,* 2 (Winter 1969), 155–163. Analyzes Roth's relationship between formal structures and the chaos of modern experience.

Shechner, Mark, "Philip Roth," *Partisan Review,* 41 (Fall 1974), 410–427. Roth read psychoanalytically, through the themes of fathers, sons, and manhood.

Solotaroff, Theodore, "The Journey of Philip Roth," *Atlantic,* 223 (April 1969), 64–72. Biographical and critical overview by Roth's friend and editor.

Wisse, Ruth, "Requiem in Several Voices," *The Schlemiel as Modern Hero.* Chicago: University of Chicago Press, 1971, 118–123. Examines *Portnoy's Complaint* as a reversal of the schlemiel formula that exposes the pain beneath laughter.

Selected Dictionaries and Encyclopedias

Critical Survey of Long Fiction, Vol. 6, Salem Press, 1983. Brief biography, and short analysis of Roth's novels.

Dictionary of Literary Biography, Vol. 2. Gale Research, 1978. Overview of Roth's life, and a discussion of the principal works to 1978.

Steven G. Kellman
The University of Texas
San Antonio

SUSANNA ROWSON
1762–1824

Author's Chronology

Born Susanna Haswell in 1762, Portsmouth, England; *1786* publishes first novel, *Victoria,* in London; marries William Rowson; *1791* publishes *Charlotte: A Tale of Truth* (published in the United States as *Charlotte Temple,* 1797); *1793* brought to America as an actress with her husband and sister-in-law by Thomas Wignell; *1795* publishes four-volume novel, *Trials of the Human Heart;* *1797* opens Young Ladies' Academy in Boston, where she teaches until 1822; *1824* dies in Boston on March 2.

Author's Bibliography

Charlotte: A Tale of Truth, 1791 (novel); *Mentoria; or The Young Lady's Friend,* 1791 (novel); *The Inquisitor; or, The Invisible Rambler,* 1794 (novel); *Rebecca, or the Fille de Chambre,* 1794 (novel); *Trials of the Human Heart,* 1795 (novel); *Sarah, or the Exemplary Wife,* 1813 (novel); *Charlotte's Daughter: or, The Three Orphans,* 1828 (novel).

Overview of Biographical Sources

True scholarly appreciation of Mrs. Susanna Haswell Rowson has been relatively recent and sparse. The earliest complete outline of her life was Elias Nason's *A Memoir of Mrs. Susanna Rowson* (Albany, NY: Joel Munsell, 1870). Although Nason consulted several sources close to Rowson, the word "memoir" indicates the depth of his revelations. Besides the useful and concise article by R. W. G. Vail "Susanna Haswell Rowson, The Author of Charlotte Temple: A Bibliographical Study," *Proceedings of the American Antiquarian Society* XLII (20 April 1932) pp. 47–160, the only substantial biographical source about Rowson is Ellen B. Brandt's *Susanna Haswell Rowson, America's First Best-Selling Novelist* (1975). Brandt's work stands above all others for details about Rowson's life and an accurate assessment of her skill as an author. In Brandt's book, Rowson most clearly comes to life as a talented, energetic, loving and concerned individual.

Evaluation of Selected Biographies

Brandt, Ellen B. *Susanna Haswell Rowson, America's First Best-Selling Novelist.* Chicago: Serba Press, 1975. Brandt's work is designed to bring more scholarly attention to Rowson as an important American individual and author. Presented in a chronological structure, the study demonstrates the tremendous amount of energy and diversity of Rowson. Brandt analyzes Rowson's works as revealing the nature and morality of both European and American society and the status of and opportunities for women during that era. Through careful analysis, Brandt clearly defines Rowson's skillful use of such techniques as multiple perspectives and humor and places her within the scope of literary history. The book thus contains an insightful and clearly presented blending of biography, social and literary history, and textual analysis.

Autobiographical Sources

Rowson's *Rebecca, or the Fille de Chambre* contains an account of experiences from her young life in Massachusetts, including a shipwreck, from 1767 to 1778. Her novel *Sarah: Or, the Exemplary Wife* is prefaced with the motto "Do not marry a fool," which is thought to be a personal reference.

Overview of Critical Sources

As with the biographical sources, truly useful critical works about Rowson only finally emerged in the 1970's. Prior to that time, Herbert Ross Brown defined Rowson's similarities to other writers of her era in *The Sentimental Novel in America 1789–1860* (1940). But Rowson does not emerge as a distinct artist in Browns' study. Two scholars with distinctly opposite opinions of Rowson are Patricia L. Parker, "*Charlotte Temple:* America's First Best-Seller," *Studies in Short Fiction* 13 (Fall 1976), 518–520, and Kathleen Conway McGrath, "Popular Literature as Social Reinforcement: The Case of *Charlotte Temple,*" in *Images of Women in Fiction: Feminist Perspectives,* ed. Susan Koppelman Cornillon (Bowling Green, OH: Bowling Green University Popular Press, 1972). Parker sees Rowson as a skillful and compassionate writer while McGrath finds her distinctly unfeminist and a supporter of the status quo. Although both studies are useful, McGrath's suffers from taking Rowson out of the context of her times and other writings. The most comprehensive analysis of Rowson's work is Dorothy Weil's *In Defense of Women: Susanna Rowson (1762–1824)* (1976). Weil fully documents Rowson's use of ten major themes, but fails to adequately consider the contradictions inherent in some of the writer's opinions.

Evaluation of Selected Criticism

Brown, Hebert Ross, *The Sentimental Novel in America 1789–1860.* Durham, NC: Duke University Press, 1940. Brown provides examples of Rowson's morals, themes, and concerns within the context of outlining these same issues in all early American novels. He also comments on her use of the epistolary form in *Trials of the Human Heart, Sarah; or, the Exemplary Wife,* and *Mentoria; Or, The Young Lady's Friend.* Brown writes clearly, with the intention to describe rather than to analyze.

Weil, Dorothy, *In Defense of Women: Susanna Rowson (1762–1824).* University Park: Pennsylvania State University Press, 1976. Using a thematic organization that incorporates each of Rowson's ten novels, her plays, pedagogical works, and much of her poetry and song lyrics, Weil demonstrates that the writer's intention was the complete education of young women and argues that there is a direct relationship between her and modern feminists. The basis for Rowson's beliefs, Weil concludes, is that the Christian is the ideal human type and that democracy should rule in both the home and in politics. The weakness of this volume is that Weil attempts to demonstrate each of Rowson's attitudes by providing long lists of quotations from her works, which are thus taken out of context and lack excitement.

Selected Dictionaries and Encyclopedias

Critical Survey of Long Fiction, Salem Press, 1983. This summary of Rowson's life and work provides a brief assessment of her literary achievement, a short biography, and an analytical essay that characterizes Rowson as an educator and moral instructor and examines three representative novels to show how she attempted to create fiction that taught useful values. The essay explains how Rowson created her main characters as an example of the value of virtuous living.

Thomas J. Slater
Oklahoma State University

JOHN RUSKIN
1819–1900

Author's Chronology

Born 8 February 1819, London; his father a wine merchant; *1833–1835* European travels; first look at the Alps; *1837–1840* attends Oxford; *1840* first physical and mental crises (as throughout his life); foreign travel (as throughout his life); begins art collection; *1848* marries; studies architecture; *1851* champions Pre-Raphaelites; meets Thomas Carlyle; *1854* marriage annulled; *1855* studies social and political economy; *1858* meets Rose La Touche; abandons Evangelical beliefs; declining responsiveness to nature; *1864* inherits paternal wealth; *1866* unsuccessfully proposes marriage to Rose; *1870* named Slade Professor, Oxford; lectures on art; *1871* buys Brantwood, in the English Lake District; *1874* at Assizi, recovers some religious feeling; *1875* Rose dies, insane; *1878* Whistler trial; *1878–1885, 1889–1900* mental instability, debility; *1900* dies at Brantwood, 21 January.

Author's Bibliography (all nonfictional prose)

Modern Painters (1843–1860); *The Seven Lamps of Architecture* (1849); *The Stones of Venice* (1851–1853); *Unto This Last* (1860); *Sesame and Lillies* (1865); *The Crown of Wild Olives* (1866); *Lectures on Art* (1870); *Fors Clavigera* (1871–1884); *The Eagle's Nest* (1872); *Deucalion* (1875–1883); *The Storm Cloud of the Nineteenth Century* (1884); *Praeterita* (1885–1889).

Overview of Biographical Sources

Being not only one of the most voluminous authors in English but also one of the most personal, Ruskin left behind an unusually full record. His letters, by no means fully collected, include some of his most appealing passages. Those appearing in the last volumes of E. T. Cook and Alexander Wedderburn, eds. *The Works of John Ruskin,* 39 vols. London, 1903–1912, will suffice for many purposes; other collections, also valuable, are limited to single recipients or periods of time. *The Ruskin Family Letters.* ed. Van Akin Burd (2 vols. Ithaca, NY: Cornell University Press, 1973) have influenced subsequent biographies. Joan Evans and John Howard Whitehouse, eds. *The Diaries of John Ruskin* (3 vols. Oxford, 1956) and Helen G. Viljoen, ed. *The Brantwood Diary of John Ruskin* (New Haven: Yale University Press, 1971) are necessary sources. Many of Ruskin's publications also include biographical information.

Evaluation of Selected Biographies

Collingwood, W. G. *The Life and Works of John Ruskin.* 2 vols. London: Metheun, 1893. Collingwood emphasizes Ruskin's poetry more than later biographies do; it also includes a number of Ruskin's drawings and some useful appendices. Written by a former student of Ruskin's and published while he was still alive (but revised in 1900), Collingwood's biography is gracious, reticent, and largely obsolete.

Cook, E. T. *The Life of John Ruskin.* 2 vols. London: George Allen, 1911. By one editor of the monumental *Works,* this is a major biography of permanent interest. Like Collingwood, Cook deals gently with Ruskin's emotional aberrations. Chary of speculation, and emphasizing facts, he attributed the same particularity to Ruskin.

Evans, Joan, *John Ruskin.* New York: Oxford University Press, 1955. Evans begins with comments upon earlier biographies. A balanced, well written account of reasonable length, hers also utilized Ruskin's diaries (which she edited). While no single title can be recommended unreservedly, Evans' is still the best general biography, with much sensitivity, fine insights, and good footnoting throughout.

Hunt, Dixon John, *The Wider Sea: A Life of John Ruskin.* New York: Viking, 1982. An intellectual biography, emphasizing Ruskin's mind and imagination. His life, therefore, is not only presented but interpreted thematically, facts becoming symbols.

Leon, Derrick, *Ruskin: The Great Victorian.* London: Routledge and Kegan Paul, 1949. Published posthumously, and despite its being only a first draft, Leon's adulatory life is exceptionally well written and has remained one of the important biographies, largely because of its splendid comprehension and abundant new material.

Quennell, Peter, *John Ruskin: The Portrait of a Prophet.* New York: Viking, 1949. Quennell's is a graceful, undocumented summary of what had been known prior to Leon, together with insights regarding Ruskin's writing life and new material about his marriage. As an introduction to Ruskin, it still has some value.

Wilenski, R. H. *John Ruskin: An Introduction to the Further Study of His Life and Work.* London: Faber and Faber, 1933. An important art critic who opposes Collingwood, Wilenski asserts that Ruskin had little to do with the Victorian period's Gothic Revival and was far less influential in his earlier years than Collingwood had supposed. Wilenski deals candidly with Ruskin's mental quirks—his obsession with young girls especially. He also addresses such issues as Ruskin's theory of art, his success as an art critic, his relations with artists, his economic theories, his thinking on war and religion, and his habits as a writer.

Autobiography

Ruskin's incomplete autobiography, *Praeterita,* has been described as the most charming in English. Perhaps no other evokes an oppressive childhood so poignantly and with so little malice. All other accounts of Ruskin's early years should be compared with it. Written at the very end of Ruskin's mental capability, the book was a struggle that eventually failed. Nothing whatever of Ruskin's marriage appears within it, but the child Rose La Touche is tenderly evoked.

The first two chapters of *Praeterita* (Latin for "Things Passed Over") are derived from earlier reminiscences in *Fors Clavigera*. As well documented biographies (like Evans') reveal, many other autobiographical passages have also been collected. In "The Mystery of Life and Its Arts" (1868), Ruskin summarized what he had learned. He also left numerous comments upon art, and a few upon fiction, but very little helping to explain his own literary works.

Overview of Critical Sources

Most of the worthwhile commentary upon Ruskin appears within the major biographies cited above or in specialized journal articles. His life has naturally attracted great attention and his ideas about art and society were obvious topics from the beginning. As a writer, however, Ruskin seldom constructed formal works. He wrote some interesting poetry (minor and usually neglected), a few well-structured essays ("Traffic," for example), and perhaps two conventional books (*The Seven Lamps of Architecture* and *The Stones of Venice*). But the unity of *Modern Painters* is debatable, *Praeterita* is a fragment, and most of Ruskin's other works are fairly miscellaneous collections. *Fors Clavigera* and *Unto This Last* have seldom been approached from any generic point of view. As a result, little has been done to clarify what principle of order, if any, underlies the long, sprawling, and seemingly shapeless works for which Ruskin is best known. Even his famous prose style has not been adequately investigated.

Evaluation of Selected Criticism

Fitch, Raymond E. *The Poison Sky: Myth and Apocalypse in Ruskin.* Athens, OH and London: Ohio University Press, 1982. This is a long, thoroughly impressive discussion of Ruskin's pessimistic assumption that everything he valued was deteriorating through time (of which his double lecture *The Storm-Cloud of the Nineteenth Century* was a classic statement). As the first extensive study to make Ruskin's theory of history central, Fitch offers a number of useful insights—and might even explain why so many of Ruskin's endings go astray.

Rosenberg, John D. *The Darkening Glass: A Portrait of Ruskin's Genius.* New York and London: Oxford University Press, 1961. This remains the standard, or at least the introductory, work on most aspects of Ruskin's thought. Extensive treatment is limited to five books: *Modern Painters, The Stones of Venice, Unto This Last, Fors Clavigera,* and *Praeterita.*

Other Sources

Helsinger, Elizabeth K. *Ruskin and the Art of the Beholder.* (Cambridge and London: Harvard University Press, 1982). Explores Ruskin's writing, art and landscape from a common viewpoint—how Ruskin admonishes us to perceive.

Hewison, Robert, *John Ruskin: The Argument of the Eye.* Princeton: Princeton University Press, 1976. Influenced by Rosenberg, Hewison attempts to unify Ruskin's mind around the concept of visual imagination.

Hough, Graham, *The Last Romantics.* London: Metheun 1947. Includes an influential chapter on Ruskin, who has nowhere been summarized more brilliantly.

Wilenski, R. H. *John Ruskin: An Introduction to the Further Study of His Life and Work.* London: Faber and Faber, 1933. This is the earliest critical work still of major interest today.

Dennis R. Dean
University of Wisconsin—Parkside

SAKI
1870–1916

Author's Chronology

Born Hector Hugh Munro, December 18, 1870, Akyab, Burma, the son of a senior official in the Burma police; *1872* in the peaceful Devonshire, England countryside, his mother is charged by a cow, suffers a miscarriage and dies; three children sent to their strict spinster aunts; *1887* father retires and takes over Hector's education by traveling with him in Europe; *1893* Hector accepts an appointment with the Burma police; *1894* resigns because of ill health; contributes Tory sketches, "The Westminster Alice" to the *Westminster Graphic; 1900* publishes his first and only serious work, *The Rise of the Russian Empire; 1902–1908* foreign correspondent in the Balkans and in Paris for the right-wing paper, the *Morning Post; 1912* publishes his first novel; *1914* publishes a pro-war fantasy of England under German domination; enlists as a private in the Royal Fusiliers, refusing offers of a commission; *1915* goes to France; *1916* suffers from an attack of malaria; returns to the field too soon and is killed in the attack on Beaumont-Hamel, November 13.

Author's Bibliography (selected)

The Rise of the Russian Empire, 1900 (history); *The Westminster Alice,* 1902 (sketches); *Reginald,* 1904 (stories); *Reginald in Russia,* 1910 (stories); *The Chronicles of Clovis,* 1911 (stories); *The Unbearable Bassington,* 1912 (novel); *When William Came,* 1914 (fantasy novel); *Beasts and Super-Beasts,* 1914 (stories); *The Square Egg and Other Sketches,* 1924 (patriotic sketches).

Overview of Biographical Sources

Saki's first biographer, his sister Ethel Munro made it her lifelong commitment to expunge from the record any facet of her beloved brother's life that did not conform to her conception of him. So thorough was she in her attempts that subsequent biographers found little new evidence with which to recreate the facts of his life. A. J. Langguth's *Saki: A Life of Hector Hugh Munro with Six Stories Never Before Collected* (1981) is a valiant attempt to fill this void for the modern reader, but the author is forced to pad his biography with so much unessential information (e.g., long and frequent quotations from the stories of Saki, negative information, such as the fact that Saki did not play golf, and quotations from the memoirs of people who might have mentioned Saki but did not) that the work can hardly be called definitive. The strengths of Langguth's biography lie in his source material from Saki's two surviving nieces who possessed numerous papers, notebooks, letters and photographs relating to their uncle's life; and his discovery and attempted interpretation of certain cryptological squiggles used by Saki in his 1904 diary.

Evaluations of Selected Biographies

Langguth, A. J. *Saki: A Life of Hector Hugh Munro with Six Stories Never Before Collected.* New York: Simon and Schuster, 1981. Working under the incredible handicap of Ethel Munro's vigilance, Langguth seeks to sympathetically isolate the obsessions that fueled Saki's imagination: a bloodlust, a liking for cruel practical jokes, misogyny and traces of what Langguth characterizes as a "genuine, if faintly nasty desire" for young boys. Langguth quotes and paraphrases from Ethel Munro extensively, and despite extensive quotations directly from the stories of Saki, he includes little criticism. Langguth posits the influence of Oscar Wilde on Saki the Edwardian dandy; but does little more than list the few writers who wrote of Saki subsequent to his death when assessing his literary influence on posterity.

Munro, Ethel, "Biography of Saki" in *The Square Egg and Other Sketches.* London: John Lane the Bodley Head, 1924. A mere 118 pages, this is basically an anecdotal memoir of their childhood together. She emphasizes his humor and his flippancy, his love of animals, his pride in their Scots Highland ancestry, and his indifference to the rewards of financial gain.

Overview of Critical Sources

Although no anthology of the twentieth century short story seems complete without a selection from Saki, criticism of him as a literary artist does not abound, and although such figures as G. K. Chesterton, A. A. Milne, Noel Coward and Graham Greene wrote of him after his death, their words are not easily accessible to readers two or three generations later except when they have been enshrined as introductions or prefaces to his various editions. It seems certain that this lack of critical focus on Saki stems most from his relegation to the superficial status of writer as entertainer rather than the Edwardian ideal of writer as social analyst. To classify him thus, however, in the words of George James Spears (*The Satire of Saki,* 1963), is to "bypass wantonly one of the most efficacious and mordant artists the world has ever seen," and he cites the elusiveness of Saki's satiric humor as the prime deterrent to literary critics. Yet Spears concedes that even the most mature of his male creations have a touch of the *enfant terrible;* and a modern reviewer such as Rhoda Koenig suggests the subtitle, "The Boy Who Would Not Grow Up," for his 1981 biography ("A Genius for Revenge," *The New York Review of Books,* XXVIII, #15, October 8, 1981).

Evaluation of Selected Criticism

Spears, George James, *The Satire of Saki: A Study of the Satiric Art of Hector H. Munro.* New York: Exposition Press, 1963. Spears analyzes the means by which Saki satirizes human stupidity and social and intellectual snobbery, demonstrating that many of his "animus-ridden" stories are the wish fulfillment of a boy's dream to free himself from the thrall of his tyrannical aunts. Spears points out that Saki's young male characters demonstrate far more outright cruelty than Oscar Wilde endowed to his characters, and suggests that Saki tempers his Juvenalian *saeva indignatio* with the urbanity of Horace. Admiring of Saki and immensely readable, this analysis concludes with four letters addressed to the author from the octagenarian Ethel Munro (1952).

Selected Dictionaries and Encyclopedias

Critical Survey of Short Fiction, Salem Press, 1982. Brief biography and short analysis of some of Saki's important short stories.

Who's Who in Twentieth Century Literature, Holt, Rinehart and Winston, 1976. Martin Seymour-Smith challenges the long-standing critical comparison of Saki with Ronald Firbank.

Jack Shreve
Allegany Community College

J. D. SALINGER
1919

Author's Chronology

Born Jerome David Salinger January 1, 1919, New York City, second child and only son of Sol and Miriam Jillich Salinger; *1934-1936* attends Valley Forge Military Academy, Pennsylvania; *1937-1938* tours in Austria and Poland, then enrolls for one semester at Ursinus College; *1939* attends Whit Burnett's short-story writing class at Columbia University; *1940* first short story, "The Young Folks," appears in Burnett's *Story* magazine; *1942-1945* serves in U.S. Army in Europe; *1946* "Slight Rebellion Off Madison" first contribution to *New Yorker; 1949* "A Perfect Day for Bananafish" begins long exclusive association with *New Yorker* (January 31); *1951* publishes *The Catcher in the Rye* July 16; *1953* moves to Cornish, New Hampshire; *1955* marries Claire Douglas, February 17; daughter Margaret Ann, born December 10; *1960* son Matthew born February 13; *1965* "Hapworth 16, 1924" last story published in *New Yorker* (June 19); *1967* divorce granted Claire; *1985* continues to reside in Cornish.

Author's Bibliography

The Catcher in the Rye, 1951 (novel); *Nine Stories,* 1953; *Franny and Zooey,* 1961 (novellas); *"Raise High the Roof Beam, Carpenters"* and *"Seymour: An Introduction,"* 1963 (stories); "The Complete Uncollected Stories of J. D. Salinger" (1974) is an unauthorized piracy.

Overview of Biographical and Autobiographical Sources

Salinger has steadfastly declined to write any autobiographical accounts, to authorize any biographies or even to grant interviews which may be quoted. Most of the critical books listed below contain brief biographical summaries of what can be gleaned about his life from the public record. He has maintained a complete silence about his life and works and has imposed a similar silence on relatives and friends since November 13, 1953 when teenager Shirlie Blaney reported a record party that Salinger held for neighborhood high school students in the Claremont (New Hampshire) *Daily Eagle.* His last communication with the public was a telephone call from New England to a *New York Times* representative in San Francisco, Lacey Fosburgh, reported in the *Times* November 3, 1974, denouncing the unauthorized publication of his uncollected stories. During the conversation he described publishing as "a terrible invasion" of his privacy.

Overview of Critical Sources

While there have been hundreds of articles produced by what George Steiner called "The Salinger Industry," analyzing in detail the thirteen stories and one short novel that Salinger allowed to be published, there have been relatively few book-length studies of his provocative work, largely because of his implacable opposition to publicity of any kind, especially criticism. Even these few books have tended for several decades to cover the same ground. At the height of the critical enthusiasm for Salinger in the early 1960's, a number of then fashionable "source books," collecting criticism of his works, were published, but most of these have disappeared.

Evaluation of Selected Criticism

Alsen, Eberhard, *Salinger's Glass Stories as a Composite Novel.* Troy, NY: Whitston Publishing Co., 1983. The first important movement in a new direction in Salinger criticism in the twenty years since it peaked, Alsen argues that Salinger is a Neo-Romantic rather than a Post-Modernist writer. He concentrates on the six stories about the Glass family to demonstrate that together they constitute a "composite novel." When read in the order Buddy Glass claims to have written them, they focus on his effort to understand his brother Seymour; when read in the chronological order of the events described, they focus on "Seymour's quest for God."

French, Warren, *J. D. Salinger.* New York: Twayne, 1963; 2nd edition, Boston: Twayne Publishers, 1976. The text of these two editions is the same, but the revision contains a long new preface and an updated bibliography. This close reading of all Salinger's published writings focuses on the social criticism in the early stories and his switch, beginning with his withdrawal to New Hampshire, to the search for a seer in the Glass family stories.

Grunwald, Henry Anatole, ed. *Salinger: A Critical and Personal Portrait.* New York: Harper and Brothers, 1962. This largest collection of early criticism, reprinted and specially commissioned, of Salinger's work also remains valuable for Jack Skow's biographical sketch, "Sonny: An Introduction," from which most subsequent accounts have derived.

Hamilton, Kenneth, *J. D. Salinger: A Critical Essay.* Grand Rapids, MI: Eerdmans, 1967. Part of a series of pamphlets on "Contemporary Writers in a Christian Perspective," this sensitive reading is the fullest account of Salinger's relationship to Christian and other religious traditions.

Lundquist, James, *J. D. Salinger.* New York: Frederick Ungar, 1979. This book is valuable for long analyses of the influence of Zen Buddhism on Salinger's work, especially an interpretation of the nine collected stories as "verses" commenting on the Zen koan quoted as an epigraph for the book. Lundquist also points out Salinger's relationship to post-modernist writing, but fails to provide any overall focus that unifies his five chapters.

Miller, James E., Jr. *J. D. Salinger.* Minneapolis: University of Minnesota Pamphlets on American Writers No. 51, 1965. This outstanding appreciation by a distinguished humanist finds alienation the dominant theme in Salinger's fiction. Miller argues that Salinger deserves perhaps "the pre-eminent position" among post-World-War II American fiction writers.

Selected Dictionaries and Encyclopedias

Critical Survey of Long Fiction, Vol. 6, Salem Press, 1983. Short biography and analysis of *The Catcher in the Rye.*

Critical Survey of Short Fiction, Vol. 6, Salem Press, 1981. Analysis of the stories from *Nine Stories,* and of *Franny and Zooey.*

Dictionary of Literary Biography, Vol. 2: "American Novelists Since World War II," 1978. Illustrated account that contains a reading of *Nine Stories* as a "short-story cycle," not published elsewhere.

Warren French
Indiana University-Purdue University
at Indianapolis

CARL SANDBURG
1878–1967

Author's Chronology

Born January 6, 1878, Galesburg, Illinois, of Swedish immigrant parents; *1898* served with 6th Illinois Regiment in Puerto Rico; enrolls in Lombard College; *1907* associate editor of Chicago's *The Lyceumite; 1908* marries Lillian Steichen (they had three daughters); *1909* reporter for Milwaukee *Journal; 1912–1917* works on Chicago's *World, Day Book, System* and *Daily News;* nine "Chicago poems" published in *Poetry;* Levison Prize; *1919* and *1921* shares Poetry Society of America prize; *1928* Phi Beta Kappa poet at Harvard; honorary degree from Lombard (14 others over the years); *1940* Pulitzer Prize for History (for poetry in *1950*); elected to American Academy of Arts and Letters; *1943* Phi Beta Kappa poet at College of William and Mary; *1952* American Academy of Arts and Letters gold medal for history and biography; *1953* Order of the Northern Star (Sweden); Poetry Society of America gold medal; *1955* Boston Arts Festival poetry prize; *1956* Humanities Award, Albert Einstein College; *1959* addresses both Houses of Congress; receives "Litteris et Artibus" medal (Sweden); dies July 22, 1967.

Author's Bibliography (selected)

Chicago Poems, 1916 (poems); *Cornhuskers,* 1918 (poems); *Smoke and Steel,* 1921 (poems); *Slabs of the Sunburnt West,* 1922 (poems); *Abraham Lincoln: The Prairie Years,* 1926 (biography); *The American Songbag,* 1927 (edited); *Good Morning, America,* 1928 (poems); *Steichen the Photographer,* 1929 (biography); *Mary Lincoln, Wife and Widow,* 1932 (biography); *The People Yes,* 1936 (poetry); *Abraham Lincoln: The War Years,* 1939 (biography); *Remembrance Rock,* 1948 (novel); *Complete Poems,* 1950 (poems); *The New American Songbag,* 1950 (edited); *Always the Young Strangers,* 1953 (autobiography); *The Sandburg Range,* 1957 (poems and prose); *Harvest Poems,* 1960 (poems); *Honey and Salt,* 1963 (poems).

Overview of Biographical Sources

At the time of his death in 1967 there were four books that might be loosely described as biographies of Carl Sandburg. Of these four, Bruce Weirick's *From Whitman to Sandburg* (New York: Macmillan, 1924), which considered him a leading poet in the Midwest and a "humanitarian revolutionist," is out of print. The same is true of Karl Detzer's *Carl Sandburg* (New York: Harcourt Brace, 1941), a "study in personality and background." The other two consist of Harry Golden's *Carl Sandburg* (Cleveland: World Publishing, 1961), more of a collection of friendly anecdotes than an in-depth biography, and Richard Crowder's *Carl Sandburg* (1964), an erudite and significant reference of considerable scope on Sandburg's life and works, which includes a sampling of critical appraisals. Since Sandburg's death, North Callahan's *Carl Sandburg: Lincoln of Our Literature* (1970) is probably the closest thing to a book-length biography, though not a definitive one, while Helga Sandburg's *A Great and Glorious Romance* (1978) is essentially a loving daughter's account of the married life of Carl and Lillian Sandburg, with some biographical gems. Gay Wilson Allen's *Carl Sandburg* (1972) is a short but excellent and well balanced biographical study. Mark Van Doren's *Carl Sandburg* (1969) is another pamphlet study by a poet which includes a comprehensive bibliography. Of considerable importance in the study of Sandburg is *The Letters of Carl Sandburg* edited by Herbert Mitgang (New York: Harcourt Brace and World, 1968).

Evaluation of Selected Biographies

Allen, Gay Wilson, *Carl Sandburg.* Minneapolis: University of Minnesota pamphlet #101, 1972. Allen presents a favorable review of Sandburg's work. The 48-page pamphlet contains the sort of analysis of Sandburg's writing that is prerequisite to a full appraisal of his achievements. Allen feels Sandburg suffered from too much recognition or, as he put it, the "curse of success," and that the critics found the poet's "love affair with the people" a source of irritation.

Callahan, North, *Carl Sandburg: Lincoln of Our Literature.* New York: New York University Press, 1970. Callahan's volume might be considered the closest thing to a book-length biography, though hardly the comprehensive work Sandburg's prose and verse deserve. The biographer had Sandburg's help in writing this biography; so it is primarily sympathetic. Secondary sources were used to a great degree, and there is very little discussion of any of Sandburg's works in any detail. Callahan is content to quote critics, earlier books, reviews, and articles rather extensively.

Crowder, Richard, *Carl Sandburg.* New York: Twayne, 1964. Crowder presents an introduction to Sandburg's life and work that is surprisingly inclusive despite its 176 page length. His assessment is rather thorough and even-handed. Along with the essential biographical material—well handled in a revealing though sparse way—Crowder considers Sandburg's prose and poetry, agrees or disagrees with the critics, brings his own considerable knowledge of literature to the discussion of Sandburg's writing, and concludes with a thoughtful judgement of his own. "To have read Sandburg," he says, "is to have been in the company of a profoundly sincere American and of a craftsman of communicating pity, scorn, brawn, beauty, and an abiding love."

Golden, Harry, *Carl Sandburg.* Cleveland: World Publishing, 1961. Golden's book was written with the help of Sandburg and can be regarded as a tribute to a friend. It is essentially a collection of anecdotes and quotations headed by captions such as "Who reads Sandburg?" or "Fifty-two years of evolution." Inaccuracies managed to find their way into what appears to be newspaper pieces and fillers brought to book. The book is useful for the details it provides.

Sandburg, Helga, *A Great and Glorious Romance, The Story of Carl Sandburg and Lilian Steichen.* New York: Harcourt Brace Jovanovich, 1978. A daughter's account of the married life of her father and mother containing a wealth of interesting details about Sandburg's earlier years. Her recollections shed light on his home life and on his development as a writer. There are some portraits of Sandburg as husband and father that reveal a sensitive and compassionate man, as well as one who believed he was destined to achieve greatness.

Van Doren, Mark, *Carl Sandburg.* Washington: The Library of Congress, 1969. In this pamphlet study, Van Doren brings a poet's insight to his view of Sandburg's life and works, and pointedly suggests the need for further study. The pamphlet contains an extensive bibliography.

Autobiographical Sources

While there may be truth to Crowder's observation that "every poet is to some degree autobiographical" there is only one readily accessible, though limited, Sandburg autobiography. *Always the Young Strangers* covers only the first twenty years of his life. Sandburg regarded it as an account of Galesburg, Illinois, "filtered through the life of a boy." Of considerable value, as autobiographical material, is *The Letters of Carl Sandburg.* Among the 640 letters Mitgang has selected can be found examples of Sandburg's originality and ready humor.

Overview of Critical Sources

There are no books in print that offer a comprehensive critical analysis of the full range of Sandburg's prose and poetry. Crowder and Allen manage to round up a respectful sampling of both unstinted praise as well as unfavorable criticism of the poet's work. Some of the criticism appeared in such periodicals as *The Dial,* The London *Times Literary Supplement, Vanity Fair, New York Times Book Review, The Little Review, The Bookman, Saturday Review of Literature,* and so on. Most of the appraisals are marked more by petulance than serious evaluation. John Crowe Ransom, along with the "New Critics," discounted Sandburg altogether as a poet. A growing body of criticism appeared to take its cue from flippant remarks rather than scholarly judgements. Ezra Pound called Sandburg "a lumberjack who taught himself all he knows." Edmund Wilson's *Patriotic Gore* (New York: Oxford University Press, 1962) discusses Sandburg's Lincoln biography but without the detachment it merits. Wilson believes that "the cruellest thing that has happened to Lincoln . . . has been to fall into the hand of Carl Sandburg." By way of contrast, other critics view the poet and his works as important. Archibald MacLeish has called him the "poet of the

American affirmation." Thomas Lask has observed that through everything Sandburg wrote was a strong awareness or "sense" of "being American." Amy Lowell has hailed his *Chicago Poems* as being "one of the most original books this age has produced." Allen believes the poet was an "enormously productive writer," and the "question of his 'minor' or 'major' status can wait for time to answer."

Evaluation of Selected Criticism

Crowder, Richard, *Carl Sandburg*. New York: Twayne, 1964. Crowder explores the difficulty in assessing Sandburg's output. He says that critics "are of two minds" over the literary quality in the poet's work. The estimates of him, as a creative artist, range from "tiresome, unreadable, and beneath notice," to praise over how he has "managed clarity, color, suggestion, emotional energy and melodic variety."

Durnell, Hazel, *The America of Carl Sandburg*. Washington: The University Press of Washington, D.C., 1965. Durnell's book, while limited as a critical study of Sandburg's work, does make a few telling points. The author feels the poet's "revolutionary style" is the principle reason for the disparity between the conclusions of many of his critics. Until his new viewpoint finds some acceptance among the "New Critics," Durnell says, they will continue to see Sandburg's work as "an assault on the English language."

Other Sources

Bradley, Sculley, ed. "Carl Sandburg" in *American Tradition in Literature*. 5th edition in one volume. New York: Random House, 1981. A brief but useful summary of Sandburg's life and output.

Selected Dictionaries and Encyclopedias

American Writers, A Collection of Literary Biographies, Vol. III, Charles Scribner's Sons, 1974. Pages 575–598.

Contemporary Authors, A Bio-Bibliographical Guide to Current Authors and Their Works, Gale Research, 1969. Three pages which serve quite credibly to summarize Sandburg's life, accomplishments, honors, and philosophy.

Robert A. Gates
St. John's University

WILLIAM SAROYAN
1908-1981

Author's Chronology

Born August 31, 1908 in Fresno, California, of Armenian immigrant parents; *1911-1916* placed with siblings in the Fred Finch Orphanage, Oakland, California, then reunited with family; returns to Fresno and enters public school; *1925* ends his formal education in the second year of high school; begins a succession of menial jobs; *1926-1928* employed as clerk, telegraph operator, then office manager for Postal Telegraph Company, San Francisco, California; abandons the workaday world to pursue a career as a writer; publishes first story in *Overland Monthly* magazine; *1933* begins a lifelong literary involvement with the Armenian Hairenik Association of Boston; initially publishes under the pseudonym "Sirak Goryan"; *1934-1939* publishes "The Daring Young Man on the Flying Trapeze" in *Story* magazine to critical acclaim; produces by his own estimate over five hundred stories; *1940* wins and rejects the Pulitzer Prize for his play *The Time of Your Life; 1942* enters the United States Army; *1943* marries Carol Marcus; birth of son Aram; *1945* discharged from military service; *1946* birth of daughter Lucy; *1949* divorces Marcus; *1951* remarries Marcus; *1952-1958* divorces a second time; resides in Malibu, California, then departs for Europe; *1966* establishes the William Saroyan Foundation; begins to divide his time between residences in Paris, France, and Fresno; continues to write as a means of livelihood; dies of cancer May 18, 1981 in Fresno.

Author's Bibliography (selected)

The Daring Young Man on the Flying Trapeze and Other Stories, 1934; *Three Times Three,* 1936 (stories); *My Heart's in the Highlands,* 1939 (play); *The Time of Your Life,* 1939 (play); *My Name Is Aram,* 1940 (stories); *The Human Comedy,* 1943 (novel); *The Adventures of Wesley Jackson,* 1946 (novel); *Tracy's Tiger,* 1951 (novel); *The Bicycle Rider in Beverly Hills,* 1952 (autobiography); *The Whole Voyald and Other Stories,* 1956; *The William Saroyan Reader,* 1958; *Here Comes, There Goes, You Know Who,* 1961 (autobiography); *Not Dying,* 1963 (autobiography); *Days of Life and Death and Escape to the Moon,* 1970 (autobiography); *Obituaries,* 1979 (autobiography); *My Name Is Saroyan,* 1983 (stories; published posthumously).

Overview of Biographical Sources

William Saroyan represents for biographers one of the most intriguing and complex subjects in American literature. Although flavored by his Armenian heritage, Saroyan's life and work illustrate a distinctly American vision. During his literary career, Saroyan published hundreds of short stories, essays, plays, novels, autobiographical sketches, and miscellaneous items in well over fifty books. Emerging as a populist voice during the Depression era, often turning personal experiences into allegorical events, Saroyan's seemingly overnight success and rapid decline as a writer capture what one critic termed "the history of American optimism" in the twentieth century. Interestingly, prior to Saroyan's death in 1981, a full length biography was never published. Attributing to this is undoubtedly the role Saroyan created for himself in a unique attempt by an author to chronicle his own life. This is illustrated by Saroyan's autobiographical materials intermittently published over a thirty year period.

After his death, several biographical treatments on Saroyan were published in rapid succession, initiated by Aram Saroyan's *Last Rites* (New York: Morrow, 1982). Written as a journal covering the last five weeks of his father's life, this brief but engaging account offers a bittersweet portrait of an estranged father-son relationship, while opening the door to an otherwise untold story of the private Saroyan in contrast to the public persona. This aspect of Saroyan's eccentric and often bizarre behavior surfaces as one of the most challenging questions concerning Saroyan but will remain unanswered until biographers have the opportunity to consult the Saroyan archives presently being catalogued at the Bancroft Library, University of California at Berkeley.

Evaluation of Selected Biographies

Lee, Lawrence and Barry Gifford, *Saroyan: A Biography*. New York: Harper & Row, 1984. Although Lee and Gifford provide an informative overview of biographical material, their efforts focus mostly on the second half of Saroyan's life. Introducing Saroyan at the peak of his literary career, the authors follow him to Hollywood, and through his military service during World War II, an experience the authors contend permanently altered Saroyan's personality and literary ambitions. Relying heavily on information gathered from conversations with personal and professional sources close to Saroyan, Lee and Gifford analyze what they consider Saroyan's post-War period of self-destruction that produced a growing estrangement from his family and a depreciating literary reputation. Written in a polished, journalistic style, this represents an important addition to the study of Saroyan's life, but suffers from a narrow and consequently limited perspective of Saroyan, resulting in what one critic termed "not so much a biography as a chronicle of failure."

Saroyan, Aram, *William Saroyan*. San Diego: Harcourt Brace Jovanovich, 1983. Employing biography to serve a cathartic purpose, this is an uneven attempt to resolve the paradox of Saroyan the legend and the man. Utilizing familiar family background, Aram Saroyan focuses primarily on his father's concern with his public image. The author also develops a theory that the psychological implications of Saroyan's childhood continued to haunt and affect his personality throughout his life. Lacking in objectivity, a large portion of this study is devoted to analyzing Saroyan's relationship with the author's mother, Carol Marcus. Of value in the work is the author's insight into the inherent need, insistence, and aftermath of Saroyan's literary recognition.

Autobiographical Sources

Beginning in 1952 with the publication of *The Bicycle Rider in Beverly Hills,* Saroyan turned increasingly to the exploration of his past through a series of autobiographical memoirs and journals. Although Saroyan continued to publish fiction and plays, autobiography became his main form of self-expression. Similar to his fiction, the autobiographies are structured with limited organization and form, unfolding by the association of memories in an anecdotal, colloquial style. Although it is often difficult to distinguish between Saroyan the fictional narrator and Saroyan himself, most critics agree that Saroyan produced at least ten volumes of autobiography including the critically important *Here Comes, There Goes, You Know Who* (1961), *Not Dying* (1963), *Days of Life and Death and Escape to the Moon* (1970), *Obituaries* (1979), and *Births* (1983), published posthumously. Although Saroyan's autobiographical works suggest a candid and often confessional tone, many critics argue that Saroyan embellished the events of his life to insure the endurance of his literary reputation.

Overview of Critical Sources

A literary nonconformist Saroyan represents an original and unorthodox subject for criticism. Consequently, although Saroyan's body of literature has been widely reviewed, it has rarely received serious critical analysis. In structure and philosophy, Saroyan's writing is often defined as simplistic, nostalgic, and naively optimistic in celebrating the human experience, characteristics for which he has been both praised and scorned. Many critics contend that Saroyan did not develop as an artist after reaching a period of popular recognition and that his subject material and outlook became entrenched in a proven formula of success. Late in his career, critics were almost unanimous in calling Saroyan's work overly sentimental and superficial, charges that were strongly denied by Saroyan in defense of his literary reputation. Conflicting with the predominant post-War theory of criticism interested in craftsmanship and formal analysis, the absence of symbolic and ironic textures in Saroyan's writing often resulted in labelling his work as escapist literature.

The majority of existing criticism is devoted to Saroyan's plays, offered by the leading theatrical critics of his generation including Brooks Atkinson, John Mason Brown, Harold Clurman, John Gassner, George Jean Nathan, and Stark Young. However, the growing body of criticism attempts to incorporate all genres of Saroyan's writing, generally in agreement that the short story was Saroyan's most successful medium. Of additional importance is the major bibliographic work on Saroyan to date: David Kherdian's *A Bibliography of William Saroyan 1934–1964* (San Francisco: Howell, 1965).

Evaluation of Selected Criticism

Floan, Howard R. *William Saroyan.* New York: Twayne, 1966. In the first full-length bio-critical study of Saroyan, Floan incorporates a chronological account of Saroyan's writing with a detailed explanation of Saroyan's popular appeal. Convincing in his viewpoint that Saroyan is deserving of serious critical attention, Floan provides a valid assessment of Saroyan's use of language, stylistic devices, and unique quality of writing while recognizing the limitations of his indifference to plot, lack of technical development, and overplaying of sentimentality. Confronting the most complex critical question concerning Saroyan, Floan successfully identifies Saroyan's autobiographical "impulse" as an attempt to illuminate his affection and sympathy for mankind, and offers valuable insight into the separation of the ubiquitous "I" of the fiction from the identity of the author. Although published without access to the complete range of Saroyan's work, this continues to be regarded as one of the most accurate and influential critical studies on Saroyan.

Calonne, David Stephen, *William Saroyan: My Real Work Is Being.* Chapel Hill: University of North Carolina, 1983. The first full-length critical study to appear since Saroyan's death, this represents a useful and well written survey of the major themes and subject matter of Saroyan's work. Incorporating significant details from Saroyan's life to enhance his analysis, Calonne demonstrates the literary influences of Walt Whitman, Sherwood Anderson, and George Bernard Shaw on Saroyan's work while illuminating Saroyan's literary affinities with Thomas Wolfe, Henry Miller, and Samuel Beckett. Least effective in textual analysis, Calonne has been criticized for his overinsistence in clarifying Saroyan's status as a "major" writer.

Other Sources

Burgum, Edwin Berry, "The Lonesome Young Man on the Flying Trapeze," in *The Novel and the World's Dilemma.* New York: Russell and Russell, 1963. Enlightening account analyzing Saroyan's war experience and its relationship to the publication of *The Human Comedy,* emphasizing Saroyan's ability in regaining the literary strength of his earlier short stories in the form of the novel.

Carpenter, Frederic I. "The Time of Saroyan's Life," in *American Literature and the Dream.* Freeport, NY: Book for Libraries, 1968. Acknowledging Saroyan's artistic faults, Carpenter identifies Saroyan's versatility and idealism as an extension of the "transcendental" tradition in American literature.

Grace, Carol (Carol Marcus Saroyan Matthau), *The Secret in the Daisy.* New York: Random House, 1955. Autobiographical novel by Saroyan's former wife recounting in part her early relationship with Saroyan.

Krickel, Edward, "Cozzens and Saroyan: A Look at Two Reputations," in *Georgia Review,* Fall, 1970, pp. 281–296. Critical of Saroyan's lack of development as a writer, Krickel provides valuable insight by means of comparison into Saroyan's literary contribution and his artistic philosophy concerning his purpose of writing.

Peden, William, *The American Short Story: Continuity and Change 1940–1975.* Boston: Houghton Mifflin, 1975. Emphasizing the importance of Saroyan's literary contributions of "simplicity, gaiety, and sympathetic understanding" of the common man, Peden recognizes Saroyan as "part of the permanent literature of the American short story."

Schulberg, Budd, "Ease and Unease on the Flying Trapeze," in *Writers in America: The Four Seasons of Success.* New York: Stein and Day, 1983. An affectionate account of early friendship with Saroyan exploring the circumstances leading to Saroyan's withdrawal into his own world while identifying Saroyan as a victim of the American syndrome of "overnight success and intolerance of subsequent failure."

Selected Dictionaries and Encyclopedias

Critical Survey of Short Fiction, Salem Press, 1981. Biographical background supplementing a brief analysis of Saroyan's short stories.

Dictionary of Literary Biography, Gale Research, 1981. Informative overview of Saroyan's life and analysis of the major works in all genres.

Steven Serafin
Long Island University

MAY SARTON
1912

Author's Chronology

Born May 3, *1912*, Wondelgem, Belgium, daughter of historian of science George Sarton and Mabel Elwes Sarton, artist; *1916* during World War I the Sarton family flees Belgium, moving first to England, then to the United States, settling in Cambridge, Massachusetts; *1917–1926* attends Shady Hill School; *1929* graduates from The High and Latin School, Cambridge, finishing formal education; *1930–1936* apprentice with Eva Le Gallienne's Civic Repertory Theater, then directs own company, The Apprentice Theater; *1937* publishes *Encounter in April; 1937–1940* teaches at the Stuart Fenway School, Boston; *1938* first novel, *The Single Hound,* is published; *1944–1945* writes scripts for documentary films for the U.S. Office of War Information; *1940–1965* lectures on poetry and holds teaching appointments at several colleges and universities throughout the United States; *1954* receives Guggenheim Fellowship in poetry; *1958* moves to Nelson, New Hampshire, and renovates an old farmhouse; *1973* moves to "a house by the sea," in York, Maine, where she resides today.

Author's Bibliography (selected)

Encounter in April, 1937 (poems); *The Single Hound,* 1938 (novel); *A Shower of Summer Days,* 1952 (novel); *The Land of Silence,* 1953 (poems); *Faithful are the Wounds,* 1955 (novel); *The Fur Person,* 1956 (novel); *In Time Like Air,* 1958 (poems); *I Knew a Phoenix,* 1959 (autobiography); *Cloud, Stone, Sun, Vine,* 1961 (poems); *The Small Room,* 1961 (novel); *Joanna and Ulysses,* 1964 (novel); *Mrs. Stevens Hears the Mermaids Singing,* 1965 (novel); *A Private Mythology,* 1966 (poems); *Plant Dreaming Deep,* 1967 (autobiography); *Kinds of Love,* 1970 (novel); *A Grain of Mustard Seed,* 1971 (poems); *A Durable Fire,* 1972 (poems); *Journal of a Solitude,* 1973 (non-fiction); *As We Are Now,* 1973 (novel); *Collected Poems, 1930–1973,* 1974; *Crucial Conversations,* 1975 (novel); *A World of Light,* 1976 (autobiography); *The House by the Sea,* 1977 (non-fiction); *A Reckoning,* 1978 (novel); *Halfway to Silence,* 1980 (poems); *At Seventy: A Journal,* 1982 (non-fiction); *Letters from Maine,* 1984 (poems).

Overview of Biographical Sources

No full-length biography of May Sarton has been written. Sarton has only recently been widely recognized by critics and scholars; she has not authorized a biography, and her published journals and memoirs give the most complete information about her life. Besides Sarton's own writings, the best account is a chapter in Agnes Sibley's *May Sarton,* which provides an autobiographical framework for her discussion of the novels and poems. A number of articles about the writings make use of autobiographical information, and several interviews with Sarton supplement the journals and memoirs.

Evaluation of Selected Biographies

Sibley, Agnes, *May Sarton.* New York: Twayne, 1972. Sibley provides an overview of Sarton's major writings to 1972, concentrating on the basic facts of the author's life and works. A brief chronology opens the book, and the first chapter is biographical in focus, following Sarton's memoirs, *I Knew a Phoenix.* Since *Plant Dreaming Deep* is the only other nonfictional work Sarton had published by 1972, it is the only work Sibley cites that describes Sarton's mature life. Four volumes of journal writings and another collection of essay-memoirs have appeared since Sibley's book was written; so the account is clearly dated. Sibley sees in both the novels and poems a tension between detachment and communion, themes that Sarton has emphasized in her own autobiographical and literary works.

Autobiographical Sources

May Sarton has completed two volumes of memoirs: *I Knew a Phoenix* (1959) and *A World of Light* (1976). While not autobiography in the strictest sense of explanatory chronological narrative, these two works describe Sarton's childhood, her parents' youth, and her education; *A World of Light* is a series of "Portraits and Celebrations," biographical sketches of people who have influenced her most deeply. *I Knew a Phoenix* begins similarly, with chapters on George Sarton and Mabel Elwes in their youth. Later chapters describe Wondelgem and the important stages in Sarton's education: Shady Hill School, Eva Le Gallienne's Civic Repertory Company, and Sarton's early visits to Paris and England. *I Knew a Phoenix* is justly subtitled *Sketches for an Autobiography,* for it documents the gradual development of a young poet, focusing on profoundly influential experiences and personalities. It is, by definition, a selective account.

Sarton's published nonfiction, in the form of essay series (*Plant Dreaming Deep*) and journals (*Journal of a Solitude, The House by the Sea, Recovering,* and *At Seventy*) describe Sarton's life since 1958, first in the small town of Nelson, New Hampshire, and later in York, Maine. The impulse for these journals springs from Sarton's decision to buy an old house and property and live by herself in the country. Exploring the joys and tribulations of living in solitude and of the coming of old age, these journals also form an ongoing spiritual biography, as Sarton describes her experience with isolation, an encounter with cancer, and finally, the clamor of critical and popular acclaim.

Overview of Critical Sources

For most of her publishing life, Sarton has been unjustly ignored by literary critics; most of the serious critical attention has come since the 1970's, in part due to the development of women's studies programs at American universities. Only two full-length studies are currently available: Agnes Sibley's *May Sarton* (1972) and Constance Hunting's collection of essays, *May Sarton: Woman and Poet* (1982). In the ten years between the two works' publication dates, Sarton has produced at least ten volumes, and most of the critical appraisal of her work has also appeared during this time. Consequently, Hunting's collection is more useful today than Sibley's, though the Twayne volume is more readily available in library collections. Other criticism is scarce.

Evaluation of Selected Criticism

Hunting, Constance, ed. *May Sarton: Woman and Poet.* Orono, ME: The National Poetry Foundation, University of Maine at Orono, 1982. This work, a volume in the *Man and Poet* series, is an indispensable collection of critical articles, appreciative essays, interviews with Sarton, and an updated bibliography. Eight of the sixteen pieces have been published elsewhere; since these constitute much of the serious scholarly work on Sarton, their collection in one volume is useful. Hunting, in her introduction, notes that as scholars are coming to appreciate Sarton's work, they are learning to see it as a consistent *oeuvre,* the novels, poems, essays, and journals returning to the same themes: alienation and detachment, the need for human relationships, the attempt to construct a meaningful life. Critical approaches of the essays vary. Among the issues raised by the contributors are: patterns of friendship in Sarton's novels; the concept of balance in Sarton's writings; justice as a theme in the novels; patterns of metaphor in the poems; Sarton's use of traditional Christian emblems and ideas; paradox in "A Divorce of Lovers;" and Sarton's use of poetic form. George Bailin's tribute to Sarton's work is a fitting final essay.

Sibley, Agnes, *May Sarton.* New York: Twayne, 1972. Major chapters are concerned with *I Knew a Phoenix,* with Sarton's poems, and with two groups of novels which Sibley dubs "early" and "later." She sees a progression in Sarton's works, from a desire for detachment to a yearning for communion with others. While she does not treat the novels and poems in detail, Sibley does view Sarton's work in three major genres as unified by common themes of exile and of the joys and pains of being human.

Other Sources

Blouin, Lenora, *May Sarton: A Bibliography.* Metuchen, NJ: Scarecrow Press, 1978. A very thorough listing of works by and about May Sarton.

Springer, Marlene, "As We Shall Be: May Sarton and Aging," *Frontiers* 5 (Fall 1979), 46–49. Springer notes that Sarton draws portraits of strong and individual elderly women; like them, Sarton is attempting to "grow into" old age.

Woodward, Kathleen, "May Sarton and Fictions of Old Age," in *Women and Literature: Gender and Literary Voice.* Janet Todd, ed. New York: Holmes and Meier Publishers, 1980, 108–127. Woodward sees Sarton's view of aging as basically romantic, though, as she grows older herself, Sarton's depiction of aging has become increasingly realistic, aware of the problems that beset the elderly.

Selected Dictionaries and Encyclopedias

American Women Writers, Frederick Ungar, 1982. Brief bibliographic entry and overview of Sarton's works in three major genres.

Contemporary Authors, Vol. 4. Gale Research, 1973. Personal information, outline of career, list of published writings, and sample of reviews.

Contemporary Literary Criticism, Gale Research, 1975, Vol. 4; 1980, Vol. 14. Quotations from selected reviews of Sarton's major novels and volumes of poetry.

Twentieth Century Authors, H. W. Wilson, 1955. Brief bibliographic information and overview of works of fiction and poetry.

Pamela J. Clements
College of Charleston

DOROTHY L. SAYERS
1893–1959

Author's Chronology

Born June 13, 1893, Oxford, England; *1912* enters Somerville College, Oxford University; *1915* awarded title to a degree in Modern Languages, First Class; *1916* publishes her first collection *Op. 1; 1920* receives Master of Arts in Modern Languages as one of the first women to be awarded an Oxford degree; *1922* begins work as a copywriter for Benson's Advertising Agency in London; *1923* publishes first detective novel, *Whose Body?; 1924* gives birth to an illegitimate son, John Anthony; *1926* marries Captain Oswald Arthur (or Atherton) Fleming, known as "Mac"; *1929* moves to Witham, Essex; cofounds the Detection Club in London; *1939* turns from detective fiction to other literary forms; *1950* Mac Fleming dies; *1959* Sayers dies December 17 in her home in Witham.

Author's Bibliography (selected)

Op. 1, 1916 (poems); *Whose Body?,* 1923 (novel); *Clouds of Witness,* 1926 (novel); *Unnatural Death,* 1927 (novel); *Lord Peter Views the Body,* 1928 (short stories); *The Unpleasantness at the Bellona Club,* 1928 (novel); *Strong Poison,* 1930 (novel); *Murder Must Advertise,* 1933 (novel); *Gaudy Night,* 1935 (novel); *The Comedy of Dante Alighieri,* 1949 (translation).

Overview of Biographical Sources

Despite Sayers' request that no biography of her be published until fifty years after her death, several biographies have been written since 1975. The first, Janet Hitchman's *Such a Strange Lady* (1975), is highly speculative because of the author's inability to gain access to Sayers' personal papers. Two subsequent biographies, Ralph E. Hone's *Dorothy L. Sayers: A Literary Biography* (Kent, Ohio: Kent State University Press, 1979) and Nancy M. Tischler's *Dorothy L. Sayers: A Pilgrim Soul* (Atlanta: John Knox Press, 1980), rely heavily on Hitchman's work. The most recent of the biographies, James Brabazon's *Dorothy L. Sayers* (1981), benefits from the cooperation of Sayers' son, Anthony Fleming, who wrote the book's introduction. Brabazon was also able to make use of the correspondence between Sayers and her family and friends, most of which has only recently been released by Sayers' correspondents. At this point, Brabazon's must be considered the definitive biography, but some information about the author's life has not yet been released because of her son's desire for privacy.

Evaluation of Selected Biographies

Hitchman, Janet, *Such a Strange Lady.* New York: Harper and Row, 1975. Hitchman makes clear from the beginning of her biography that she was hampered by her lack of access to Sayers' papers. Undaunted by her lack of material, however, Hitchman creates a biography from public records, Sayers' works, and interviews with Sayers' acquaintances. Her book is readable but marred by its substitution of speculation for fact.

Brabazon, James, *Dorothy L. Sayers*. New York: Charles Scribner's Sons, 1981. Brabazon, who knew and worked with Sayers, corrects some inaccuracies in Hitchman's biography. In addition to being more complete and correct, Brabazon's biography is also more sympathetic than Hitchman's. Brabazon uses Sayers' personal papers to contradict Hitchman's portrait of an eccentric, unstable woman. Brabazon is quick to point out, however, that his biography is not "authorized" in the sense of having to have Sayers' son's approval; sympathetic though he may be, Brabazon does not omit or attempt to excuse details which might reflect badly on his subject. Brabazon, a television producer, deals briefly but well with Sayers' literary work.

Autobiographical Sources
Sayers began work on an autobiography, *My Edwardian Childhood,* about 1932, but she completed only about 33 pages before abandoning the project. Two years later, she began writing a novel, *Cat o' Mary,* which clearly is based on the autobiographical fragment. Although she wrote over 200 pages of the novel, it, like the autobiography, was never completed or published.

Overview of Critical Sources
Critical interest in Sayers' work has remained steady since the author's lifetime. Her detective fiction claims most of this interest, but Sayers has also been recognized for her talents as a translator and playwright. Other than the literary biographies of Hone and Tischler, (discussed above), the critical works do not generally attempt to deal with the entire, diverse body of work.

Evaluation of Selected Criticism
Gaillard, Dawson, *Dorothy L. Sayers*. New York: Frederick Ungar, 1981. Like other recent but less fully developed criticism, this book traces Sayers' development as a detective writer and also briefly discusses various ideologies associated with Sayers and her work.

Hall, Trevor H. *Dorothy L. Sayers: Nine Literary Studies*. Hamden, CT: Archon Books, 1980. Focusing on the detective novels and on Sayers' life, Hall in these essays presents the results of exhaustive research. Two essays deal with Conan Doyle's influence on Sayers; two others shed light on two mysterious men in Sayers' life, her husband and her collaborator, Robert Eustace.

Hannay, Margaret P. ed. *As Her Whimsey Took Her*. Kent, OH: Kent State University Press, 1979. Various essays in this important collection focus on

Sayers' detective fiction, drama, and translations. The final section of the book, a comprehensive bibliography of Sayers' work, includes lists and detailed descriptions of the contents of U.S. collections of Sayers' manuscripts and letters.

Other Sources

Heilbrun, Carolyn, "Reappraisals: Sayers, Lord Peter, and God," in *American Scholar,* 37 (Spring 1967), 324–334. An examination of the enduring appeal of Sayers' works and her detective hero, Lord Peter Wimsey.

Scott-Giles, C. W. *The Wimsey Family: A Fragmentary History Compiled from Correspondence With Dorothy L. Sayers.* New York: Harper and Row, 1977. A family history of the fictional Wimseys as written by Sayers and her friends.

Whelpton, Eric, *The Making of a European.* London: Johnson, 1974. The autobiography of Sayers' college friend and later employer which includes discussion of Sayers and her writing.

Selected Dictionaries and Encyclopedias

Critical Survey of Long Fiction, Salem Press, 1983. Brief biography and analysis of several of the detective novels.

Dictionary of National Biography, 1951–1960 Supplement, Oxford University Press, 1971. Focus on Sayers' literary work along with brief mention of biographical information.

Claire Clements Morton
Huntingdon College

DELMORE SCHWARTZ
1913–1966

Author's Chronology

Born December 8, 1913, Brooklyn, New York; *1931* attends University of Wisconsin; *1932–1935* attends New York University; graduates with a Bachelor of Arts degree in philosophy; *1935* graduate student at Harvard in philosophy; *1937* leaves Harvard without a degree; *1938* marries Gertrude Buckman; *1940* wins Guggenheim Fellowship; becomes Briggs-Copeland Instructor of English Composition at Harvard; *1941* second Guggenheim Fellowship; *1943* assumes editorship of the *Partisan Review,* a position he holds until 1955; *1944* divorces Buckman; *1947* resigns position at Harvard; *1949* marries Elizabeth Pollet; *1949–1950* lectures at Princeton; *1955–1957* becomes poetry editor and film critic of the *New Republic; 1957* separates from Pollet; *1962–1965* teaches at Syracuse University; *1966* dies in New York City of a heart attack on July 11.

Author's Bibliography (selected)

In Dreams Begin Responsibilities, 1938 (a story, poems, a play); *Shenandoah,* 1941 (play); *Genesis,* 1943 (poem); *The World is a Wedding,* 1948 (stories); *Vaudeville for a Princess,* 1950 (poems); *Summer Knowledge: New and Selected Poems 1938–1958,* 1959; *Successful Love,* 1961 (stories); *Selected Essays,* 1970; *Last and Lost Poems of Delmore Schwartz,* 1979.

Overview of Biographical Sources

Accounts of Delmore Schwartz's life are abundant and rich with information. The New York intellectual milieu of Schwartz's experience provides a catalog of famous names, many of which are associated with memoirs. Notable among these are Philip Rahv's article, "Delmore Schwartz: The Paradox of Precocity" in the *New York Review of Books* (May 20, 1971), which examines Schwartz's precocity as a critic; William Barrett's two memoirs in *Commentary:* "The Truants: *Partisan Review* in the 40's" (June 1974), and "Delmore: A 30's Friendship and Beyond" (September 1974); and Irving Howe's article, "Delmore Schwartz: An Appreciation," in his book *Celebrations and Attacks: Thirty Years of Literary and Cultural Commentary* (New York: Horizon Press, 1979). Of special note is Saul Bellow's affectionate, fictionalized borrowing from Schwartz's life as transformed into the character of Von Humboldt Fleisher in his novel *Humboldt's Gift* (1975). There are two book-length biographies of Schwartz available: Richard McDougall's, *Delmore Schwartz* (1974), which emphasizes a critical analysis of Schwartz's work, and James Atlas' more definitive *Delmore Schwartz: The Life of an American Poet* (1977), which follows his personal life and associations. In 1982, a detailed, informal, book-length memoir of Schwartz and his contemporaries was published by the first wife of poet John Berryman, Eileen Simpson; it is titled *Poets in Their Youth: A Memoir* (New York: Random House).

Evaluation of Selected Biographies

Atlas, James, *Delmore Schwartz: The Life of an American Poet.* New York: Farrar, Straus, and Giroux, 1977. This "definitive" biography examines Schwartz's complicated character and follows his movement from being one of the most promising writers in America to the chaos of his last years. Atlas emphasizes the tragedy of a talent burned out. The work is divided into three sections: 1913-1945, 1946-1957, and 1958-1966. The author conducted extensive research, most notably with interviews and letters from Schwartz's friends, colleagues, and family. Although it is generally acknowledged that much of Schwartz's life involved emotional turmoil, it should be said that Philip Rahv, in his article in the *New York Review of Books,* sees a life-long productivity which provides a contrast to Atlas' thesis. Atlas' biography includes a fine assortment of photographs.

McDougall, Richard, *Delmore Schwartz.* New York: Twayne, 1974. Although McDougall thinks that the disorder of Schwartz's personal life kept him from completely realizing his poetic intentions, he keeps information which is strictly biographical to a minimum. The emphasis here is on criticism—the alienation or isolation of poets in the modern world and the Jewish experience are related to Schwartz's work. There is an excellent selected bibliography included.

Overview of Critical Sources

The critical analyses of Schwartz's work are scattered, for the most part. When individual texts were published, they were analyzed by many of the author's distinguished contemporaries, and the bibliography included in Richard McDougall's book *Delmore Schwartz* lists many of them. McDougall's volume, in fact, is probably the most fruitful source for critical information on all the major stories, poems, and plays.

Evaluation of Selected Criticism

Politzer, Heinz, "The Two Worlds of Delmore Schwartz: Lucifer in Brooklyn," *Commentary,* X (December 1950), 561-568. This excellent critical overview covers Schwartz's work through the publication of *Vaudeville for a Princess.* Politzer examines Schwartz's characters as middle-class Jews, and addresses the pervasive theme of the self-conscious ego and its attempts to reach beyond itself, the consciousness which informs Schwartz's best work.

Zucker, David, "Self and History in Delmore Schwartz's Poetry and Criticism," *Iowa Review,* VIII (1977, iv), 95-103. Zucker was a student of Schwartz at Syracuse University, and sees the man as a brilliant poet and critic caught by the contradictions of his own personality and his consciousness of them. Zucker views the Schwartz of the 1960's as a writer still determined to express himself as a poet. This article is notable for its discussion of Schwartz's critical writings.

Kathleen Massey
University of Southern California

SIR WALTER SCOTT
1771–1832

Author's Chronology

Born August 15, 1771, Edinburgh, Scotland; *1773* suffers from infantile paralysis, which leaves him lame; *1779* enters second year class at Edinburgh Royal High School; *1783* enters Edinburgh College; *1786* signs indentures with his father to become a Writer to the Signet; *1792* becomes an Advocate; *1796* suffers when the woman he loves, Williamina Belsches, becomes engaged to another; publishes adaptations of two German ballads by Bürger; *1797* marries Charlotte Carpenter; *1799* translates Goethe's tragedy, *Goetz of Berlichingen;* becomes Sheriff of Selkirkshire; *1802* publishes two-volume *Minstrelsy of the Scottish Border* to great applause; *1804* moves to Ashestiel, on south bank of Tweed; *1805* publishes *The Lay of the Last Minstrel,* his first great success as an original poet; *1806* becomes Clerk to the Court of Session; *1808* publishes *Marmion,* another poetic success; publishes his 18-volume edition of *The Works of John Dryden;* *1810* publishes *The Lady of the Lake,* which shatters all records for the sale of poetry; *1812* buys Abbotsford, which he extends and cultivates throughout his life; *1814* publishes *Waverley,* the first in the series of remarkably successful and influential "Waverley Novels"; publishes his 19-volume edition of *The Works of Jonathan Swift;* 1819 becomes a Baronet; publishes *Ivanhoe,* his first English and medieval romance; *1822* arranges and manages the visit to Scotland of King George IV; *1823* publishes *Quentin Durward,* his first Continental novel; *1826* suffers bankruptcy, and struggles throughout the remainder of his life to make restitution; wife dies; *1827* acknowledges publicly his authorship of the Waverley Novels; publishes *The Life of Napoleon Buonaparte,* a 9-volume historical study; *1829* begins publication of the "Magnum Opus," a 48-volume edition of the Waverley Novels; *1830* suffers a paralytic stroke; *1831* begins trip to Mediterranean and Italy for his health; *1832* returns to Abbotsford where he dies on September 21.

Author's Bibliography (selected)

The Lay of the Last Minstrel, 1805 (poetry); *Marmion,* 1808 (poetry); *The Lady of the Lake,* 1810 (poetry); selected Waverley novels: *Waverley,* 1814; *Old Mortality,* 1816; *Rob Roy,* 1817; *The Heart of Midlothian,* 1818; *The Bride of Lammermoor,* 1819; *Ivanhoe,* 1820; *Quentin Durward,* 1823; *St. Ronan's Well,* 1824; *Redgauntlet,* 1824; "The Highland Widow," 1827 (short story); "The Two Drovers," 1827 (short story).

Overview of Biographical Sources

Sir Walter Scott was a giant of European Romanticism, so there is an abundance of biographical materials. In *A Bibliography of Sir Walter Scott* (London:

Oliver and Boyd, 1943), James C. Corson lists nearly 200 biographical items, including twenty-eight books. Serious biographical study begins with John Gibson Lockhart's *Memoirs of the Life of Sir Walter Scott* (1837–1838). Lockhart, the son-in-law, friend, and admirer of Scott, had unique access to the documents, as well as verbal communications of his subject. Before Lockhart, biographies of Scott are skimpy and inaccurate; afterwards, all biographers of Scott are Lockhart's dependents. Nevertheless, several later studies make valuable contributions to the biographical tradition. John Buchan's *Sir Walter Scott* (1932) offers a delightfully readable condensation of Lockhart's monumental narrative. Sir Herbert J. C. Grierson's *Sir Walter Scott, Bart* (1938) provides a well documented supplement to and correction of Lockhart's biography. Arthur Melville Clark's *Sir Walter Scott: The Formative Years* (Edinburgh: Blackwood, 1969) examines Scott's first thirty years in fresh detail. Finally, Edgar Johnson's *Sir Walter Scott: The Great Unknown* (1970) combines a thorough reexamination of Scott's life with a deep appreciation of his accomplishments to provide a worthy modern successor to Lockhart's masterpiece.

Evaluation of Selected Biographies

Buchan, John, *Sir Walter Scott.* London: Cassell, 1932. Buchan offers the easiest and most enjoyable introduction to the life and works of Scott. He cuts Lockhart's full-length picture severely but still retains the essential portrait. In addition, being a disciple of Scott in fiction of adventure, Buchan has a sympathetic insight into Scott's works. His remarks stimulate the reader to return to Scott himself. As usual, Buchan writes with considerable charm.

Grierson, Sir Herbert J. C. *Sir Walter Scott, Bart.* London: Constable, 1938. The editor of the 12-volume *Letters of Sir Walter Scott* (1932–1937), Grierson brings a fresh expertise to the study of Scott's life. He corrects misrepresentations and omissions in Lockhart and provides an especially well documented analysis of Scott's financial difficulties throughout his life.

Johnson, Edgar, *Sir Walter Scott: The Great Unknown,* 2 vols. New York: Macmillan, 1970. Johnson is the modern Lockhart. Benefiting from over a century of additional scholarship, he adds to and corrects Lockhart's biography. Despite many differences in detail, however, the two chief biographies present the same fundamental picture of Scott: a great writer and a good man. Johnson also offers considerable literary discussion, although he is more of a sensitive "appreciator" than a critic.

Lockhart, John Gibson, *Memoirs of the Life of Sir Walter Scott.* 7 vols. Edinburgh: Cadell, 1837–1838. This is the starting point; all biographies of Scott are footnotes to Lockhart. Modern scholarship may have shown that Lockhart falsified, omitted, added, and rearranged material, that he was "creative" rather than factual. Nevertheless, his picture of Scott remains the established one. Its venial offenses as a biography may even contribute to its stature as an independent work of art, for this is one of those rare biographies that takes on a life of its own. Among literary biographies, it may be second only to James Boswell's *Life of Samuel Johnson.*

Autobiographical Sources

Scott provided abundant autobiographical materials, but they are scattered among many volumes. The best place to begin is the Ashestiel Memoirs, a "Memoir of the Early Life of Sir Walter Scott, Written by Himself," which appears at the beginning of Lockhart's *Memoirs of the Life of Sir Walter Scott.* This delightful reminiscence covers the first twenty-one years of Scott's life. He continues his own story in the numerous prefaces to his literary works. Scott actually wrote two kinds of preface. The first prefaces appeared upon initial publication of several of his works: they are witty, ironic, oblique, and written behind various masks. The final prefaces were written for the "Magnum Opus" during the last years of Scott's life: they are more straightforward, documentary, reminiscent, and personal. Although a student may examine all of these prefaces by going through a complete set of Scott's works, the most relevant have been conveniently gathered together in Mark A. Weinstein's *The Prefaces to the Waverley Novels* (Lincoln: University of Nebraska Press, 1978). Within Scott's works themselves, the most important autobiographical documents are the introductions to each of the six cantos of *Marmion* and, more obliquely, the description of Alan Fairford's life in the opening volume of *Redgauntlet.* Sir Herbert J. C. Grierson's *The Letters of Sir Walter Scott,* 12 vols. (London: Constable, 1932–1937), has become much easier to use since the publication of James C. Corson's *Notes and Index to Sir Herbert Grierson's Edition of The Letters of Sir Walter Scott* (Oxford: Clarendon Press, 1979). Still, it is recognized that Grierson's edition is seriously incomplete, and a new edition of Scott's letters is being planned in Scotland. The now standard edition of the "Gurnal" is W.E.K. Anderson's *The Journal of Sir Walter Scott* (Oxford: Clarendon Press, 1972). This remarkable book covers much of Scott's life from November 20, 1825, to his death in 1832. It provides little literary information but presents Scott's heroic struggles against financial ruin, his wife's death, and his own sickness. Finally, David Hewitt's *Scott on Himself: A Selection of the Autobiographical Writings of Sir Walter Scott* (Edinburgh: Scottish Academic Press, 1981) incorporates within one volume many of the most important autobiographical documents.

Overview of Critical Sources

Criticism of the Waverley Novels falls into three broad but distinct periods. From 1814 to the 1880's, Scott was considered one of the greatest of European novelists. For the next half century, his reputation suffered a serious decline, epitomized best by the mocking attack in E. M. Forster's *Aspects of the Novel*

(1927). For the last half century, many critics have attempted to rehabilitate his reputation as a novelist, but the jury is still out. The Waverley Novels do not seem to be widely read today, and contemporary criticism does not seem to consider Scott among the first rank of novelists. With regard to Scott the poet, the critical tradition has made its decision: it does not so much belittle Scott's poetry as ignore it.

Evaluation of Selected Criticism

Hart, Francis R. *Scott's Novels: The Plotting of Historic Survival.* Charlottesville: The University Press of Virginia, 1966. In this scholarly study of all of the novels, Hart takes "cultural survival and fulfillment" to be the underlying thematic problem and pattern of the novels. Yet he is flexible enough to divide the corpus into four major categories—"The Quixotic Tragicomedy of Jacobitism," "Opposing Fanaticisms and the Search for Humanity," "The Historical Picturesque and the Survivals of Chivalry," and "The Falls and Survivals of Ancient Houses"—and to examine each novel on its own terms.

Hayden, John O. *Scott: The Critical Heritage.* New York: Barnes and Noble, 1970. Hayden prints the texts of the most important criticisms of Scott from 1805 to 1883, his heyday.

Hillhouse, James T. *The Waverley Novels and Their Critics.* Minneapolis: University of Minnesota Press, 1936. In this invaluable critical aid, Hillhouse shows what was thought about the novels, and why, from 1814 to 1932, and also gauges their position with successive reading publics.

Hillhouse, James T. and Alexander Welsh, "Sir Walter Scott," *The English Romantic Poets and Essayists.* ed. Carolyn Houtchens and Lawrence Houtchens. New York: New York University Press, 1966, pp. 115–154. This important critical aid updates Hillhouse's discussion of the novels to 1963 and adds sections on criticism of the poems, special problems, questions of influence, political and religious views, and Scott's miscellaneous writing and editing.

Lukács, Georg, *The Historical Novel.* 1937; rpt., trans. Hannah and Stanley Mitchell, London: Merlin, 1962. Doctrinaire in approach, incorrect in detail, Lukács still provides the most enlightening and influential essay on Scott in modern criticism. He ranks Scott among the greatest writers and shows how he transformed the social novel of the eighteenth century into a genuine history of the present.

Welsh, Alexander, *The Hero of the Waverley Novels.* New Haven: Yale University Press, 1963. Although he reduces Scott's nearly thirty novels to a neat abstract pattern and Scott's individual characters to oversimplified types, like "the passive hero," "the dark hero," "the dark heroine," "the blond," Welsh still offers the most exciting and challenging book on the Waverley Novels in modern criticism. He claims that the passive hero is the most important feature of the novels and that his progress stresses the projection of conservative moral ideals.

Other Sources

Cockshut, A. O. J. *The Achievement of Walter Scott.* New York: New York University Press, 1969. A persuasive argument that the way to save Scott is to concentrate on the "five books that form the core" of his achievement—*Waverley, Old Mortality, Rob Roy, The Heart of Midlothian,* and *Redgauntlet.*

Devlin, D. D. *Walter Scott.* London: Macmillan, 1969. A collection of thirteen of the best modern essays on Scott.

Fleishman, Avrom, *The English Historical Novel.* Baltimore: The Johns Hopkins Press, 1971. A fascinating attempt to read the Waverley Novels in chronological sequence as a sustained history of certain European institutions.

Selected Dictionaries

A Dictionary of the Characters in The Waverley Novels of Sir Walter Scott. Husband, M. F. A. 1910; rpt. New York: Humanities Press, 1962. An identification and description of the 2836 characters, including 37 horses and 33 dogs, created by Sir Walter Scott.

A Key to the Waverley Novels. Grey, Henry, 1882; rpt. New York: Haskell House, 1973. Brief sketches of all of the novels in chronological sequence, with an index of the principal characters.

Mark A. Weinstein
University of Nevada, Las Vegas

ROBERT SERVICE
1874–1958

Author's Chronology

Born January 16, 1874, Preston, England; *1880–1895* studies and works in Scotland; *1895* journeys to British Columbia; wanders U.S. west coast; *1903* joins the Canadian Bank of Commerce, allowing him to travel British Columbia and the Yukon; aspires to be "the Bret Harte of the Northland;" *1907* publishes "The Shooting of Dan McGrew" and "The Cremation of Sam McGee," securing his literary fortune; *1912* covers the Balkan War for the Toronto *Star; 1913* marries Germaine Bourgoin of Paris; *1914* serves with American and Canadian units in World War I; *1924* Hollywood begins film productions of his work; lives leisurely, making two journies to Russia; *1945* moves to Brittany where he lives until his death, September 11, 1958.

Author's Bibliography (selected)

Songs of a Sourdough, 1907; *The Spell of the Yukon,* 1907 (American title for *Songs of a Sourdough*); *Ballads of a Cheechako,* 1909; *The Trail of '98,* 1910 (novel); *Rhymes of a Rolling Stone,* 1912; *The Pretender, A Story of the Latin Quarter,* 1914 (novel); *Rhymes of a Red Cross Man,* 1916; *The House of Fear,* 1927 (novel); *Why Not Grow Young? or, Living for Longevity,* 1928 (prose); *The Complete Poems of Robert Service,* 1933; *Bar-Room Ballads,* 1940; *Ploughman of the Moon: An Adventure Into Memory,* 1945 (autobiography); *Harper from Heaven: A Record of Radiant Living,* 1948 (autobiography); *Rhymes of a Roughneck,* 1950; *Songs For My Supper,* 1953; *More Collected Verse,* 1955; *Later Collected Verse,* 1960.

Overview of Biographical Sources

Despite his enormous popularity, only one full-length biography of Service has appeared. Carl F. Klinck's *Robert Service* (1976) is written by a scholar well-acquainted with the vast history of Canadian literature.

Evaluation of Selected Biographies

Klinck, Carl F. *Robert Service.* New York: Dodd, Mead, 1976. This is a vigorously paced account of a full life. Writing clearly and crisply, Klinck does more than draw upon autobiographical sources; he also draws upon subjective elements of Service's work, showing how the poems themselves provide clues for revealing an inner life, hidden within those poems. Letters from Mrs. Service and others are quoted; numerous photographs included. Authoritative, without being ponderous, this biography reveals a man whose life is richly textured.

Autobiographical Sources

Two autobiographical volumes encompass the range of Service's experience. *Ploughman of the Moon: An Adventure Into Memory* (New York: Dodd, Mead, 1945) describes his early life in Scotland, his immigration to America, his wanderings in the Northwest and aspirations to write. He re-tells his experiences in the Yukon with exhilaration. *Harper of Heaven: A Record of Radiant Living* (New York: Dodd, Mead, 1948) presents the later years of his life in Europe and his travels to Russia. Largely undramatic, it does, however, describe a number of amusing incidents.

Overview of Critical Sources

Since Robert Service has been popularly regarded as a writer of "verse," and not a producer of serious literature, there is yet no full-length critical study of his work. In recent years, however, several perceptive articles have appeared, revealing the complexity and craftsmanship of his work, previously unacknowledged.

Evaluation of Selected Criticism

Atherton, Stanley S. "The Klondike Muse," *Canadian Literature,* 47 (1971), 67–72. Claiming that Service's poems are seldom simply descriptive, Atherton sees them as an attempt to mythologize the northern environment, although Service fails to create a coherent mythic vision. While his poems evoke the mystery of the north, demonstrating a macabre humor in the face of a hostile environment, they present only contradiction, rather than ambiguity. This brief, but informed interpretation provides a good beginning point for discussing Service's poems sensibly.

Hirsch, Edward, "A Structural Analysis of Robert Service's Yukon Ballads," *Southern Folklore Quarterly,* 40 (1976), 125–140. This essay is clearly the most authoritative and the most persuasive critical study of Service's work. Recognizing the immense popularity of Service's poems, Hirsch argues that they must be judged, not as literary artifacts, but as successful monologues. Hirsch demonstrates the integrity of form and content, meter and story, in the Yukon ballads, through examining what he calls "binary oppositions," both metric and thematic. Furthermore, these juxtapositions and tensions serve also to implicate middle class values. Hirsch's brilliant study contributes much toward a recognition of Service's poetic stature.

Other Sources

Hamer-Jackson, Celesta, "Robert Service," in *Leading Canadian Poets,* ed. W. P. Percival. Toronto: Ryerson Press, 1948. A whimsical glimpse of Service's early years, written by a personal acquaintance.

Reyburn, Wallace, "He Created Dan McGrew and Cremated Sam McGee," *Reader's Digest,* 59 (October 1951), 105–107. A light account of Service's literary beginnings.

Roberts, F. X. "A Bibliography of Robert William Service," *Four Decades of Poetry, 1890–1930,* 1 (1976), 76–85. A comprehensive list of primary and secondary material.

Selected Dictionaries and Encyclopedias

Critical Survey of Poetry, Salem Press, 1982. A "reasonable approach" to the life and work of Robert Service, describing his poetry as reflecting his experience.

Dictionary of National Biography, Oxford University Press, 1971. A brief synopsis of his life and work.

Thomas Becknell
Bethel College,
Minnesota

ANNE SEXTON
1928–1974

Author's Chronology

Born Anne Gray Harvey, November 9, 1928, Newton, Massachusetts of upper-middle-class parents; *1948* met and eloped with Alfred Muller Sexton II, a Colgate University student who later worked for the Harvey woolen business; did some professional modeling; *1953* daughter Linda Gray Sexton born; suffers increasingly severe depressions; *1955* daughter Joyce Ladd Sexton born; *1956* first suicide attempt; daughters sent to live temporarily with grandparents; begins to write and study poetry; *1957* enrolls in poetry seminar conducted by poet John Holmes; meets Maxine Kumin and they became lifelong friends; begins to publish poems in magazines; *1959* mother dies of cancer and father dies of a cerebral hemorrhage; *1960* first book of poems published; *1962* *All My Pretty Ones* published; *1963* travels through Europe on a grant from the American Academy of Arts and Letters; *1964* begins a series of visits and stays at the psychiatric ward of Massachusetts General Hospital; *1966* travels on safari in Africa; *1967* Pulitizer Prize for *Live or Die;* serious suicide attempt; *1968* honorary Phi Beta Kappa from Harvard; *1969* Guggenheim Fellowship; *1970* begins teaching at Boston University; *1973* divorced from Sexton; *1974* commits suicide at her home.

Author's Bibliography (selected)

To Bedlam and Part Way Back, 1960 (poems); *All My Pretty Ones,* 1962 (poems); *Live or Die,* 1966 (poems); *Love Poems,* 1969 (poems); *Transformations,* 1971 (poems); *The Book of Folly,* 1972 (poems and prose); *The Death Notebooks,* 1974 (poems); *The Awful Rowing Toward God,* 1975 (poems); *45 Mercy Street,* 1976 (poems); *Words for Dr. Y.,* 1978 (poems and prose); *The Collected Poems,* 1981.

Overview of Biographical Sources

To date, there has been no published book-length biography of Anne Sexton. However, since so much of Sexton's poetry is directly entwined with the actual events of her life, biographical sketches and insights are provided in numerous articles, essays and reviews available at most libraries and in both scholarly and popular indexes. Most of the biographical information included in articles, essays and reviews has been taken from interviews conducted with the poet and from the poet's letters. Some such useful biographical information may be found in newspaper reports as well.

Evaluation of Selected Biographies

Berg, Beatrice, "Oh, I Was Very Sick," *New York Times.* (November 9, 1969), pp. 1, 7. Berg presents a biographical account based on an interview with

Sexton. The material is not discussed in great detail, but the article does include information regarding Sexton's involvement with the theatre as well as her work as a poet.

Middlebrook, Diane, "Becoming Anne Sexton," *The Denver Quarterly*. 18:4 (Winter 1984), pp. 23–34. Working from a biographical basis, Middlebrook examines in depth certain aspects of Sexton's life as they relate to and influence many of the poet's poems.

Mood, John J. "A Bird Full of Bones," *Chicago Review*. 23:1, (1972), 107–123. Mood presents a well-detailed account of a poetry reading delivered by Sexton in Muncie, Indiana. Included in the article are interesting observations and examples of Sexton's phobias, dependencies, as well as her strengths as a speaker and reader of poems.

Sexton, Linda Gray and Lois Ames, eds. *Anne Sexton: A Self-Portrait in Letters*. Boston: Houghton Mifflin, 1977. The editors are Sexton's elder daughter and Sexton's close friend and official biographer. Therefore, the editors offer detailed accounts of the author's childhood, adolescence and adulthood. Provided in the text is a chronology of her bouts with mental illness, the rise of her stature as a poet, and the complex relationships she had with family, friends, and colleagues. The biographical additions to the book serve well to provide a cohesive element to the many, often manic, letters Sexton wrote.

Autobiographical Sources
The close relationship that exists between Sexton's life and her poems has caused the great body of her work to be labeled "confessional" by many readers and critics. However, close examinations of her ideas and thought processes must include Sexton's own words about her life and her art. Most of the views she expressed as autobiography are contained in recorded interviews and in the volume of letters published after her death.

Most notably is the book, *Anne Sexton: A Self-Portrait in Letters* (see above). The letters themselves trace her personality from childhood through adulthood. Many of the letters, particularly the earlier ones, present her as a spoiled child and adolescent, rebellious in school, impetuous, and romantic. As she discovered her talent for writing poems, her ambition and emotional instabilities are reflected in the many letters she wrote to other poets such as Robert Lowell, W. D. Snodgrass, and George Starbuck. In addition, the letters written to family members and close friends reveal her urgent need to express her love for them and to assuage much of the guilt she experienced by being separated for any length of time from her daughters and husband. The letters, as a whole, are at times deeply personal in nature and do provide a plethora of information and insight into the poet's psyche.

Of the interviews conducted with Sexton, three are of particular note because of their accessibility and their critical importance: Patricia Marx's "Interview with Anne Sexton" (*Hudson Review,* 18, Winter 1965–1966, 560–570); "The Craft Interview With Anne Sexton" (*New York Quarterly,* 3, Summer 1970, 8–12); and Barbara Kelves' "The Arts of Poetry XV: Anne Sexton" (*Paris Review,* 52, 1971, 159–191).

Overview of Critical Sources

The great volume of criticism of Sexton's poems exists primarily in essays, articles and book reviews. It is difficult at times to determine if Sexton's life is the subject of criticism or if the poems are the objects of examination. These problems often occur in the general criticism written on her work because the personae and the subject matter of her work so often parallel the realities of her life. Although her first three books of poems received, for the most part, critical acclaim, many critics felt Sexton and her poetry were becoming melodramatic and sloppy. Nevertheless, some critics were beginning to apply more psycho-analytic and feminist theory to her work. Feminist criticism, particularly, added new dimensions and fresh approaches to Sexton's work that allows her work to be examined more closely today and affords her poems another critical light. The first book-length critical study of Sexton's work is due in 1985 or 1986 (Diana Hume George. *Oedipus Anne: The Poetry of Anne Sexton.* Urbana: University of Illinois Press). The text is a psychoanalytic and feminist critical study.

Evaluation of Selected Criticism

George, Diana Hume, "Beyond the Pleasure Principle: Anne Sexton's 'The Death Baby,' " *University of Hartford Studies in Literature.* 15:2 (1983), 75–92. George's article explores the controversy among the psychoanalytic theorists regarding the pleasure principle and applies successfully these ideas to Sexton's sequence of six poems, "The Death Baby."

Juhasz, Suzanne, "The Excitable Gift: The Poetry of Anne Sexton," in *Naked and Fiery Forms: Modern American Poetry by Women.* New York: Harper Colophon, 1976, 117–142. Juhasz's analysis of Sexton's work surveys most of the major poems in terms of the personae established in the works, and treats the collective body of poems much like the process of becoming a whole person.

Phillips, Robert, "Anne Sexton: The Blooming Mouth and the Bleeding Rose," in *The Confessional Poets.* Carbondale: Southern Illinois University Press, 1973, 73–91. Phillips closely presents selected poems of Sexton in terms of her established personae and in relation to the "confessional poets" of her time.

Other Sources

McClatchy, J. D. ed. *Anne Sexton: The Artist and Her Critics.* Bloomington: Indiana University Press, 1978. McClatchy presents several essays and interviews about Sexton, some serving as criticism of her work and others as insights into the poet. The book is an anthology of critical works written by several critics.

Northouse, Cameron and Thomas P. Walsh, eds. *Sylvia Plath and Anne Sexton: A Reference Guide.* Boston: G. K. Hall, 1974. This guide contains a useful and comprehensive reference listing of all of Sexton's work that appeared in magazines and book form from 1958 to 1971. It also includes reference listings of writings about Sexton and her work from 1960 to 1971.

Michael S. Tkach
The Pennsylvania State University,
The Behrend College

WILLIAM SHAKESPEARE
1564-1616

Author's Chronology

Born April 23, 1564, Stratford-upon-Avon, England, of John Shakespeare, a glover, and Mary Arden Shakespeare; *1582* married Anne Hathaway; May 26, *1583* first child (Susanna) baptized; February 2, *1585* twins Hamnet and Judith christened; *c. 1590* goes to London; *1592* Greene's attack against "upstart crow"; *1593 Venus and Adonis* published; *1596* coat of arms granted, Hamnet dies; *1597* buys New Place in Stratford; *1603 Hamlet* Q1 published; *1612* retires to Stratford; April 23, 1616 dies, buried in Holy Trinity Church, Stratford; *1623* collected plays published.

Author's Bibliography (selected)

The Comedy of Errors, 1591 (comedy); *Romeo and Juliet,* 1596 (tragedy); *Henry IV, Parts I and II,* 1597–1598 (history); *Julius Caesar,* 1599 (tragedy); *Twelfth Night,* 1600 (comedy); *Hamlet,* 1601 (tragedy); *Othello,* 1603 (tragedy); *King Lear,* 1605 (tragedy); *Macbeth,* 1606 (tragedy); *The Tempest,* 1612 (romance).

Overview of Biographical Sources

Although actual documents and verifiable facts directly concerning Shakespeare's life are far from abundant—they are totally lacking for the period between 1585 and 1592—biographies of the English National Poet are legion. Initiating a practice that has endured to the present day, Shakespeare's first editor, Nicolas Rowe, prefaced a "Life" of the dramatist to his edition of the plays in 1709. Seventeenth century biographical notices aside, this is the first true biography, and it incorporates some of the traditions, such as Shakespeare's attendance at Stratford Grammar School, that have since been generally accepted. It also incorporates less likely legends, such as the story of young Shakespeare's deer poaching at Charlecote Manor or Queen Elizabeth's asking him to write a play about Falstaff in love (*The Merry Wives of Windsor*). This mixture of fact, tradition, and myth is discernible in almost every biography and is carefully detailed in S. Schoenbaum's extensive and invaluable volume, *Shakespeare's Lives* (Oxford: Clarendon Press, 1970). This was followed by his *William Shakespeare: A Documentary Life* (1975), supplemented by *William Shakespeare: Records and Images* (New York: Oxford University Press, 1981). Until the publication of Schoenbaum's work, the most authoritative biography was Sir E. K. Chambers, *William Shakespeare: A Study of Facts and Problems* (1930), 2 vols. This is still a very useful study. Of the anti-Stratfordians—those who refuse to accept William Shakespeare as the author of the plays and poems—little need be said. Sir Francis Bacon, Christopher Marlowe, and many others have been put forward as the true author, but all of these various claimants have been answered decisively by scholars such as Frank Wadsworth, whose book, *The Poacher from Stratford* (Berkeley: University of California Press, 1958), exposes the snobbery underlying the views of Baconians and their ilk.

Evaluation of Selected Biographies

Alexander, Peter, *Shakespeare's Life and Art*. New York: New York University Press, 1961. After a brief introduction on life in Shakespeare's Stratford and the publishing history of Shakespeare's plays, Alexander traces the development of the playwright through four main periods, giving the relevant data for each play in chronological order. On the basis of an allusion to Henry of Navarre as heir to the French throne, he dates *The Comedy of Errors* from before 1589, and he carefully considers the circumstances surrounding Shakespeare's departure from the Pembroke's Men in 1592 and his joining the Chamberlain's Men.

Bentley, Gerald Eades, *Shakespeare: A Biographical Handbook*. New Haven: Yale University Press, 1961. This compact volume presents the significant documents relating to Shakespeare's life and career in the context of other similar documents and the background of Elizabethan customs and prejudices to give a fuller understanding of both the documents and Shakespeare's life as it is reflected by them. Bentley reviews Shakespearean biography in the seventeenth and twentieth centuries, then Shakespeare in Stratford, in London as actor, playwright, and poet, and finally his reputation. He chronicles the legends of the "lost years"—Shakespeare as schoolmaster, actor, deer poacher—and carefully analyzes the famous will, explaining the true meaning of the bequest to his wife of the "second best bed."

Bradbrook, Muriel C. *Shakespeare: The Poet in His World*. New York: Columbia University Press, 1978. Bringing a wealth of knowledge about Elizabethan literature and the age to bear, Bradbrook offers a sociological approach in her biography, as her subtitle suggests. For all its great learning, the book is written in clear and readable style, free of jargon. What emerges is a detailed picture of Shakespeare and his milieu, as well as still another candidate for the identity of Shakespeare's Dark Lady of the Sonnets, Winifred Burbage, wife of Shakespeare's colleague, Richard Burbage.

Chambers, Sir Edmund Kerchever, *William Shakespeare: A Study of Facts and Problems*. Oxford: Clarendon Press, 1930, 2 vols. This is the culmination of Chambers's earlier work, *The Mediaeval Stage* and *The Elizabethan Stage*, and his still earlier editions of the plays for the Red Letter Shakespeare. The actual biography of the playwright takes only some ninety pages; the rest of the first volume covers the state of the stage in 1592, Shakespeare's company and his part in it as actor and shareholder, the composition and publication history of the plays and the problems of authenticity (for example, in *Pericles*), and the bibliographical and textual information on each composition, including those ascribed to Shakespeare. Volume 2 contains extensive appendices of documents and records, a list of contemporary allusions, discussion of what Chambers calls the "Shakespeare-Mythos," and other data. In 1933 Clarendon Press published an abridged version of this monumental work, *A Short Life of Shakespeare with the Sources* by Charles Williams.

Eccles, Mark, *Shakespeare in Warwickshire.* Madison: University of Wisconsin Press, 1961. A supplement to Chambers's *William Shakespeare,* this study carries objective biography to the extreme, as Schoenbaum notes, refusing to augment the bare record of facts with imaginative speculation or conjecture. But true to its title, it provides the information available concerning Shakespeare's native environment, his ancestors and family members, Stratford's school, Anne Hathaway, Shakespeare's friends in the town, and other items of note.

Reese, M. M. *Shakespeare: His World and His Work,* revised ed. London: Edward Arnold, 1980. This, one of the best of the "popular" biographies, is a somewhat shortened as well as updated version of the first edition of 1953. Reese arranges his material by theme rather than strict chronology, with the avowed intention of offering the general reader acquainted only with the plays the fruits of more erudite scholarship. Largely dependent upon Chambers for his facts, Reese writes in a clear and attractive style, rejecting such myths as the deer-stealing episode on the basis of known facts, namely, that Sir Thomas Lucy of Charlecote had no park and no deer in it, as the scholar J. S. Smart proved.

Rowse, A. L. *William Shakespeare: A Biography.* New York: Harper and Row, 1963. An eminent historian of the Elizabethan age, Rowse has for the last twenty years also busied himself in Shakespearean scholarship and criticism. In this biography, he boasts of bringing new and certain light to problems "hitherto intractable" through "historical investigation, by proper historical method." But he is essentially a popularizer, and his claim to have resolved, for example, all the problems of the sonnets, except for the identity of the Dark Lady, is inadequately justified, just as his certainty concerning the date and occasion of the first performance of *A Midsummer Night's Dream* is based entirely on circumstantial evidence. A subsequent work, *Shakespeare the Man* (New York: Harper and Row, 1973), proclaims the discovery of the true identity of Shakespeare's Dark Lady, Emilia Bassano Lanier, but other scholars have demonstrated that Rowse misread Dr. Simon Forman's casebooks, the source of the discovery, regarding her physical description.

Schoenbaum, Samuel, *William Shakespeare: A Documentary Life.* New York: Oxford University Press, 1975. Schoenbaum claims to offer "a straightforward account of Shakespeare's life" together with supporting documents in faithful facsimiles in this folio-sized volume, "not shirking vexatious issues like the significance of the marriage records and the second-best bed." He is as good as his word, and his biography is at once as engaging as it is lucid and informative. The narration of events involving the curious circumstances of Shakespeare's marriage, for example, takes the reader to the diocesan court at Worcester for the special license and discusses the reasons for the license without sensationalism but with an honest recognition of the fact that young Will was still a minor, needing his father's approval, and Anne was pregnant. In this discussion as in others, Schoenbaum refers to other biographies, agreeing, amending, or rejecting views as facts and reason dictate. In 1977 Oxford Press published a shorter version, *William Shakespeare: A Compact Documentary Life,* in a smaller and handier format with fewer of the facsimiles and some revisions of the original text. In 1981 a supplementary volume, *William Shakespeare: Records and Images,* again folio-sized, appeared with sections on Shakespeare's handwriting, the various portraits (none reproduced in color, however), and other materials.

Wilson, John Dover, *The Essential Shakespeare: A Biographical Adventure.* Cambridge: Cambridge University Press, 1932. Well to the other extreme of "objective" biographies such as those by Chambers and Eccles, this one is appropriately subtitled. Wilson gives the reader a frankly subjective appraisal, drawn from a study of the plays, the known facts, and the period, of the kind of man he believes Shakespeare really was. He emphasizes the young Shakespeare, the writer of comedies, as against the Victorian Olympian, the writer of tragedies.

Autobiographical Sources

Many biographers have sought to find in Shakespeare's plays and poems clues or at least hints concerning his private life, since he wrote no autobiography as such. The closest approximation to actual autobiography is his sonnet sequence, published in 1609 by Thomas Thorpe and dedicated "To the Only Begetter . . . Mr. W. H." Most of the sonnets were written at least a decade or more earlier and circulated privately among Shakespeare's friends. Unlike *Venus and Adonis* and *The Rape of Lucrece,* which Shakespeare dedicated to his then patron, the Earl of Southampton, and published in 1593 and 1594 through his friend, the printer Richard Field, the sonnets were not authorized for publication, and the mystery still surrounds the identities of the young man (to whom the majority of them are addressed), "Mr. W. H.," the Dark Lady who appears late in the sequence, and the Rival Poet who competes with the speaker of the sonnets for the young man's affection. Finally, astute critics have reminded biographers that the sonnets, like the poems, may have been written as purely imaginative works, and the stories they tell are simply products of Shakespeare's invention. But the poet's devotion to his young friend, his arguments persuading him to marry, the emotions generated by rivalry and competition, his feelings about his mistress, all have the ring of something much closer to lived experience, and so the hunt continues for the key to unravel the mystery.

Overview of Critical Sources

Approaches to Shakespeare's work are many and varied, and they wax and wane with the times: to understand Shakespeare better, but also itself, each age discovers new interpretations, or believes it does. For this reason, the articles and books, in addition to the critical introductions that preface editions of the poems and plays, seem endless. A series of book-length bibliographies—one for each play and several for *Hamlet*—have recently begun to appear from Garland Publishing Company with hundreds of annotated entries designed to facilitate research in Shakespearean scholarship and criticism for the period since 1940. These volumes supplement and update earlier bibliographies, such as those by Walter Ebisch and L. L. Schücking (Oxford: Clarendon Press, 1931, 1937) or Gordon Ross Smith (Pennsylvania State University Press, 1963), and are more complete than selective bibliographies, like James G. McManaway and Jeanne Addison Roberts' *A Selective Bibliography of Shakespeare* (Charlottesville: University Press of Virginia, 1974) or Stanley Wells's *Select Bibliographical Guides* (London: Oxford University Press, 1975), useful as these are.

Historical criticism of Shakespeare, that is, criticism that attempts to interpret his work in and from the context of the age in which it was written, is a perennial favorite among scholars deeply versed in sources that derive from the late sixteenth and early seventeenth centuries. The work by Hardin Craig, E. M. W. Tillyard, and Virgil Whitaker are notable examples of this approach. A sub-category of historical criticism includes studies of Shakespeare's language—his pronunciation, use of rhetoric, changing meanings of words—as exemplified in Helge Kökeritz's *Shakespeare's Pronunciation* (New Haven: Yale University Press, 1953) and Sister Miriam Joseph's *Shakespeare's Use of the Arts of Language* (New York: Columbia University Press, 1947). Yet another sub-category concentrates on the conditions of Elizabethan theaters and stagecraft as they may have influenced Shakespeare's composition, as in Bernard Beckerman's *Shakespeare at the Globe 1599–1609* (New York: Macmillan, 1962).

Character studies are another perennial favorite among critics, for a while falling into disfavor as the New Criticism analyzed the fallacies of the approach, notably in L. C. Knights's landmark essay, "How Many Children Had Lady Macbeth?" (1933). Although approaches from the standpoint of psychological realism inevitably involve the critic in methodological and other problems, psychoanalytical criticism of Shakespeare's works remains attractive to some scholars, and has produced books like Norman Holland's *Psychoanalysis and Shakespeare* (London: Chatto and Windus, 1966). Studies of Shakespeare's use of imagery may also lead to insights about Shakespeare the man, as Caroline Spurgeon's pioneer work, *Shakespeare's Imagery and What It Tells Us* (London: Cambridge University Press, 1935), claims. More often, investigations of this sort properly limit themselves to showing how image patterns reflect thematic developments or are otherwise involved in Shakespeare's skills as a poet and dramatist, as in Wolfgang Clemen's *The Development of Shakespeare's Imagery* (Cambridge, MA: Harvard University Press, 1936, 1951).

Thematic studies have recently been criticized as reductivist, and the call for a more comprehensive approach has gone out, one that includes the experience of both reading and witnessing the plays in the theater. Thus, performance criticism has lately gained in favor, stimulated by the work of John Styan, Marvin Rosenberg, John Russell Brown, and others. As more and more film and television productions of the plays have become available, articles and books on Shakespeare in the media have increased in number. Social commentaries provide still another approach and are by no means limited to such Marxist studies as Terence Eagleton's *Shakespeare and Society* (New York and London: Chatto and Windus, 1967) or Robert Weimann's *Shakespeare and the Popular Tradition in the Theater* (1967; English tr., Baltimore: Johns Hopkins Press, 1978). Anthropology has lent its discipline also to Shakespearean scholarship, as in Marjorie Garber's *The Coming of Age in Shakespeare* (London: Methuen, 1981), and for many years studies of myth and ritual have yielded useful insights.

Music and the other arts have not been ignored in Shakespeare studies. As critics have become competent in more than one field, interdisciplinary approaches have gained steadily. Shakespeare loved music and used it frequently in his plays, both directly and in his imagery. Genre studies—those that focus primarily on the comedies or tragedies or histories—continue to attract attention and have gained in depth from such seminal works as Northrop Frye's *The Anatomy of Criticism* (Princeton University Press, 1957) and C. L. Barber's *Shakespeare's Festive Comedy* (Princeton University Press, 1959). Finally, the important advances made in this century in textual and bibliographical scholarship, as in the work of Alfred W. Pollard, Ronald B. McKerrow, W. W. Greg, Fredson Bowers, and Charlton Hinman, have helped scholars understand more clearly what Shakespeare actually wrote and how it came into print in the copies that survived. Some of the most exciting as well as controversial work now going on is in this special area of Shakespeare studies, which quite literally provides the foundation for all other work.

Evaluation of Selected Criticism

Bethell, S. L. *Shakespeare and the Popular Dramatic Tradition.* London: King and Staples, 1944. This is one of the first studies to discuss the self-reflexive aspects of Shakespeare's drama and relate them both to earlier drama and later forms, including films. The analysis of Shakespeare's use of "planes of reality" is enlightening and instructive.

Bradley, A. C. *Shakespearean Tragedy.* 2nd ed. London: Macmillan, 1905. Although sometimes criticized for its character-oriented approach, this landmark of criticism brings the nineteenth-century psychological approach to full fruition. The chapter on "The Substance of Shakespearean Tragedy" contains many useful insights. Bradley treats only *Hamlet, Othello, King Lear,* and *Macbeth*—the greatest of the tragedies in his view.

Doran, Madeleine, *Endeavors of Art.* Madison: University of Wisconsin Press, 1954. By no means limited to Shakespeare's achievements though extensively treating them, this essay in historical and esthetic criticism provides a broad context for understanding what Shakespeare and his contemporaries accomplished in drama as an art in all its variety of forms.

Granville-Barker, Harley, *Prefaces to Shakespeare.* Princeton: Princeton University Press, 1946, 2 vols. Originally published as a series beginning in 1930, these "Prefaces" provide detailed studies of the plays *as plays,* not overlooking important considerations such as versification, characterization, and textual problems in addition to the staging, costumes, music, and overall dramatic structure of the works treated.

Knight, G. Wilson, *The Wheel of Fire: Interpretation of Shakespeare's Tragedy.* rev. ed. London: Methuen, 1949. For Knight, Shakespeare's plays are dramatic *poems;* hence, a study of their imagery and other poetic techniques is of the greatest importance. This is the first of several volumes on Shakespeare that Knight has written; here, he concentrates upon the major tragedies but includes essays on the problem comedies, *Timon of Athens,* and other subjects. "On the Principles of Shakespeare Interpretation" introduces the book and explains his approach.

Rabkin, Norman, *Shakespeare and the Common Understanding.* New York: The Free Press, 1967. As the title indicates, Rabkin borrows from theoretical physics the concept of "complementarity" in his approach to interpreting Shakespeare. The approach stresses divergent and sometimes even contradictory ways of looking at the same phenomena so that a fuller apprehension of reality in all its complexity becomes possible. Shakespeare does this, and competent critics should do the same in attempting to understand his work. Rabkin's book, organized under thematic headings such as "Eros and Death," ranges widely over the entire corpus of Shakespeare's plays and poems.

Traversi, Derek A. *An Approach to Shakespeare.* 3rd rev. ed. New York: Doubleday, 1969. Traversi's work, here expanded from the second edition of 1956 to include the entire canon, has influenced a whole generation of critics.

Its focus is primarily on a close reading of the texts, with particular attention to Shakespeare's linguistic techniques and his growth as a poet and dramatist.

Other Sources

Booth, Stephen, *An Essay on Shakespeare's Sonnets.* New Haven: Yale University Press, 1969. Close readings of the sonnets with particular attention to individual structure and patterns.

Bullough, Geoffrey, *Narrative and Dramatic Sources of Shakespeare.* 8 vols. New York: Columbia University Press, 1957–1974. Contains the known and probable sources and analogues of Shakespeare's plays and poems prefaced by analytical and explanatory introductions.

Coghill, Nevill, "The Basis of Shakespearean Comedy," *Essays and Studies,* new series, III (1950), 1–28. Contrasts the comedies with those of Ben Jonson and shows how they derive from basically two different traditions stretching back to classical times.

Jay L. Halio
University of Delaware

MARY SHELLEY
1797–1851

Author's Chronology

Born August 30, 1797 near London, England to William Godwin and Mary Wollstonecraft Godwin; complications of childbirth cause death of mother September 10; *1812* first meets Percy Bysshe Shelley; goes to live in Dundee for two years; *1814* further meetings with Percy initiated in May, leading to European travels in company with Mary's stepsister Claire Clairmont; *1816* son William born; Percy, Mary and Claire take a four-month trip to Switzerland; in Geneva, spending time with Lord Byron and Dr. Polidori, they initiate a ghost-story contest to pass the time, resulting in the first version of *Frankenstein;* Percy Shelley's legal wife, Harriet, commits suicide; Mary and Percy marry in London; *1817 Frankenstein* is rejected by two publishers, accepted by third; daughter Clara born; publishes *History of a Six Weeks' Tour* with Percy; *1818 Frankenstein* published anonymously; Shelleys go to Italy; daughter Clara dies; *1819* son William dies; son Percy Florence born; *1822* Percy Shelley drowns while sailing in Gulf of Spezia; *1823* Mary returns to England; *1851* dies Februrary 1.

Author's Bibliography

History of a Six Weeks' Tour (with Percy Shelley), 1817 (travel); *Frankenstein*, 1818 (novel); *Valperga,* 1823 (novel); *The Last Man,* 1826 (novel); *Perkin Warbeck,* 1830 (novel); *Proserpine,* 1831 (closet drama); *Lodore,* 1835 (novel); *Lives of the Most Eminent Literary and Scientific Men of Italy, Spain and Portugal,* 1835–1837 (biography); *Falkner,* 1837 (novel); *Lives of the Most Eminent Literary and Scientific Men of France,* 1838–1839 (biography); *Rambles in Germany and Italy,* 1843 (travel); *Mathilda,* written 1819 but not published until 1959 (novel).

Overview of Biographical Sources

That Mary Shelley was the child of two famous parents and the wife of one of England's most illustrious poets, as well as the friend or acquaintance of a number of important literary figures of her day, would be sufficient to ensure that a good deal of material illuminating those around her be preserved. An unfortunate side-effect has been the virtual impossibility of viewing her purely in her own light. Her activity as a letter-writer and a diarist have resulted in a considerable mass of extant biographical raw material. A large portion of her correspondence and nearly all of the material in her diaries (5 manuscript volumes usually referred to collectively as her *Journal*) was first edited by her son (and the heir to the family baronetcy) Sir Percy Florence Shelley, and his wife Lady Jane Shelley. Twelve copies of this four-volume set, titled *Shelley and*

Mary, were printed privately in 1882. *Shelley and Mary* was the primary source for early biographers of the Shelleys, even those who had access to the original manuscripts from which it was drawn. This is clearly the case for Mrs. Julian Marshall, whose *The Life and Letters of Mary Wollstonecraft Shelley* (2 vols. 1889), was an official biography "undertaken at the request of Sir Percy and Lady Shelley." More recently scholars have made full use of the original manuscripts.

Evaluation of Selected Biographies

Dunn, Jane, *Moon in Eclipse.* New York: St. Martin's Press, 1978. For the general reader and derived from previous biographies, this focuses on the years with Percy.

Grylls, Rosalie, Glynn, *Mary Shelley: A Biography.* London: Oxford University, 1938. A good biography, primarily devoted to the period with Percy Shelley, but with some useful comments about the later novels.

Neumann, Bonnie Rayford, *The Lonely Muse: A Critical Biography of Mary Wollstonecraft Shelley.* Salzburg: Institute fur Anglistik und Amerikanistik, Universitat Salzburg (Salzburg Studies in English Literature), 1979. A critical biography focusing on a single theme, this "exploration of that single condition which came to dominate [Shelley's] personal emotional life and her writing as well—the condition of loneliness," treats all of the major works. It provides a useful reading of *Frankenstein,* and is especially valuable in that Neumann devotes half the book to the post-Percy period and writings.

Nitchie, Elizabeth, *Mary Shelley: Author of "Frankenstein."* New Brunswick, NJ: Rutgers University Press, 1953. This is a useful and well documented critical biography.

Autobiographical Sources

Mary Shelley never wrote an autobiographical composition as such, but the store of autobiographical material is nevertheless rather rich. It falls into four categories. First is her *Journal,* a diary kept in five successive volumes between 1814 and 1840. The entries are especially copious during the first ten years and so are very valuable for that which has moved most people to consult them— Percy Shelley's activities and Mary's relationship with him. Next are the *letters,* of which over 1,300 either to or from Mary are extant. A third category of autobiographical material encompasses works published by Mary Shelley which, although not autobiographies, are nevertheless overtly autobiographical in nature. Chief among these are the two travel books: *History of a Six Weeks' Tour* (based heavily upon her *Journal* for that period, plus some letters, and essentially Mary's work, although Percy was credited as co-author); and *Rambles in Germany and Italy,* describing her travels in the early 1840's. To these must be added her biographical notes on Shelley for her editions of his work, *Poetical Works* and *Essays, Letters from Abroad.* There is also her preface to the 1831 edition of *Frankenstein,* in which she describes the circumstances surrounding her initial composition of that tale. Finally, her novels are biographically important for the way they reveal Mary's attitudes, especially her attitudes toward people important in her life. She admitted, for example, that a character in *The Last Man* was really Percy Shelley. It is clear, too, that a major character in that novel and others in *Valperga, Lodore,* and *Falkner* are patterned closely on Byron.

Overview of Critical Sources

By far her best received work, in her own day and since, has been *Frankenstein.* Critical attention to Mary Shelley, which has been steadily growing in recent years, has also focused primarily on that work. Her stature has grown considerably since the time when Sir Walter Scott could permit himself to believe Percy Shelley had written the famous novel for her. Though critics do not call *Frankenstein* a great book, critics do agree it is an "important" book. A variety of studies have sought to delineate its importance as a quintessentially Romantic artifact, or to answer the question of why it is so popular, and why the Frankenstein story has become a myth in its own right.

Evaluation of Selected Criticism

Bloom, Harold, "Afterword," in Mary Shelley, *Frankenstein.* New York: New American Library, 1965. A major literary critic addresses the Romantic qualities of the novel.

Ketterer, David, *Frankenstein's Creation: The Book, The Monster, and Human Reality.* Victoria: University of Victoria Literary Studies, 1979. This study of the monster's ontology emphasizes the novel's dream-like quality, and raises questions about the "Chinese-box" narrative structure, while making a very useful comparative analysis of the first edition, the 1831 edition, and those portions of the manuscript still extant.

Levine, George and U. C. Knoepflmacher, eds. *The Endurance of "Frankenstein."* Berkeley: University of California, 1974. This very well edited volume contains ten essays on the novel and two on its cinematic offspring. The spread of approaches to the novel plus a fairly detailed chronology of Mary Shelley's life, an annotated bibliography, and a good index, make this one of the handiest single volumes devoted to *Frankenstein.*

Small, Christopher, *Mary Shelley's "Frankenstein": Tracing the Myth.* Pittsburgh: University of Pittsburgh, 1973. Small very usefully examines the novel in the context of 19th century forms of the Prometheus myth and of the ideas of Godwin and Shelley.

Walling, William, *Mary Shelley*. New York: Twayne, 1972. Walling gives a good general survey of the life and works.

Other Sources

Bennett, Betty T. ed. *The Letters of Mary Wollstonecraft Shelley*. 3 vols. Baltimore: Johns Hopkins University, 1980+. Perhaps the finest piece of scholarship associated with Mary Shelley. When complete (2 volumes are in print as of 1985) will include 1,300 letters from and to Mary Shelley. Remarkably readable and informative.

Florescu, Radu, *In Search of Frankenstein*. Boston: New York Graphics Society, 1975. One of the authors of *In Search of Dracula* describes Mary Shelley's early life and the circumstances surrounding the composition of *Frankenstein*. Useful chiefly for the many illustrations and the final section on the novel's cinematic progeny.

Jones, Frederick L. ed. *Mary Shelley's Journal*. Norman: University of Oklahoma, 1947. Still the standard edition of the *Journal*, though based not upon the manuscript volumes but upon the material in *Shelley and Mary*.

Lyles, W. H. *Mary Shelley: An Annotated Bibliography*. New York: Garland Publishing, 1975. Lists items pertaining to Mary Shelley and her writings.

Selected Dictionaries and Encyclopedias

Critical Survey of Long Fiction, Salem Press, 1983. Brief biography plus a balanced brief survey of *all* the novels.

Dictionary of National Biography, Macmillan, 1897. Lively biography, though perhaps dated in attitudes.

C. Herbert Gilliland
U. S. Naval Academy

PERCY BYSSHE SHELLEY
1792–1822

Author's Chronology

Born August 4, 1792, near Horsham, Sussex, England; *1804* enters Eton; *1810* enters University College, Oxford; *1811* expelled as co-author of *The Necessity of Atheism;* elopes with Harriet Westbrook; *1812* works in Dublin for Catholic emancipation and Irish independence but fails to have any impact; moves to Wales where he falls under government scrutiny as a seditious reformer; *1813* publishes first significant poem, *Queen Mab; 1814* abandons his wife and elopes with Mary Wollstonecraft Godwin; after a short tour of the continent returns to England where he is hounded by debt and suffers poor health; *1816* meets Byron and spends the summer in almost daily contact with him; writes "Hymn to Intellectual Beauty" and "Mont Blanc"; returns to England and marries Mary Godwin after Harriet Shelley drowns herself; *1817* loses custody of his children by Harriet in a bitter court battle; *1818* publishes *The Revolt of Islam* and leaves England, spending the rest of his life in Italy; *1819* publishes *Rosalind and Helen* and enjoys the beginning of a great surge of creative activity; *1822* drowns with two others on July 8 when his sailboat founders in a storm; cremated by Byron and friends.

Author's Bibliography (selected)

Queen Mab, 1813 (poem); *Alastor,* 1816 (poem); with Mary Shelley, *History of a Six Weeks' Tour,* 1817 (travel) *Laon and Cythna* (reissued slightly revised as *The Revolt of Islam*), 1818 (poem); *Rosalind and Helen,* 1819 (poem); *The Cenci,* 1819 (dramatic poem); *Prometheus Unbound,* 1820 (verse drama); *Epipsychidion,* 1821 (poem); *Adonais,* 1821 (poem); *Hellas,* 1822 (poem); *Posthumous Poems,* edited by Mary Shelley, 1824; *Poetical Works,* edited by Mary Shelley, 1839.

Overview of Biographical Sources

Shelley's brief, unorthodox, eventful life has provoked a great number of biographical studies, though all have not proved helpful or reliable. Potentially the most valuable source of information, Mary Shelley herself wanted to write a biography, but Shelley's father used the threat of withdrawing his meagre allowance for her maintenance to prevent her from doing so. Still, her preface to *Posthumous Poems* (1824) and her notes to her edition of *Poetical Works* (1839) provide essential details about the circumstances under which Shelley wrote. Though each has its limitations of perspective, four biographical accounts by men who knew the poet represent the first significant studies and remain essential sources: Thomas Medwin's *Life of Percy Bysshe Shelley* (2 vols., London: Thomas Cantley Newby, 1847) concentrates on literary matters;

Thomas Jefferson Hogg's *The Life of Percy Bysshe Shelley* (2 vols., London: Edward Moxon, 1858), though begun as an authorized biography with the cooperation of Shelley's family, presents a factually unreliable but nonetheless important and lively account, most useful concerning the younger Shelley; Edward John Trelawny's *Recollections of the Last Days of Shelley and Byron* (London: Edward Moxon, 1858) is readable and fairly accurate except as concerns Trelawny himself; Thomas Love Peacock's *Memoirs of Shelley* (originally in *Fraser's Magazine,* 1858–1862; later ed. H. F. B. Brett-Smith, London: Oxford University Press, 1909) corrects some earlier views and is the most reliable among these early accounts. The early biographies have all been reprinted and remain widely available.

Though constrained by the sensitivities of the Shelley family, who gave him invaluable access to manuscripts and letters in their possession, Edward Dowden in *The Life of Percy Bysshe Shelley* (London: Kegan Paul, Trench, 1886) produced an authorized biography that remained the standard for over half a century. Dowden did not tell all the truth, but all he told was true so far as he could ascertain. The standard biography is Newman Ivey White's *Shelley* (1940), a model of meticulous research and scholarly objectivity. Except for a slight reticence concerning sexual matters, White's biography presents the poet's life and career in full detail and documents virtually every statement, always relying on primary sources wherever possible. This monumental biography has not been superseded by subsequent works. In two separate studies Kenneth Neill Cameron chronicles Shelley's development and examines the relevant biographical background. *The Young Shelley: Genesis of a Radical* (New York: Macmillan, 1950) treats Shelley's intellectual development up to the publication of *A Refutation of Deism* (1814). *Shelley: The Golden Years* (Cambridge: Harvard University Press, 1974) treats the rest of Shelley's career, especially the biographical background relevant to each of the poet's important works. Richard Holmes' *Shelley: The Pursuit* (1974), the most recent attempt at a fully comprehensive biography, provides a readable account of Shelley's life, but its surmises concerning several controversial events in Shelley's life and its idiosyncratic estimations of Shelley's poetry have not met with widespread acceptance.

Evaluation of Selected Biographies

Holmes, Richard, *Shelley: The Pursuit.* London: Weidenfeld and Nicolson, 1974; New York: E. P. Dutton, 1975. Holmes provides a lively and readable full-scale study that attempts to present not only a detailed and accurate account of Shelley's life but also a portrait of his personality. Holmes' major efforts at original investigation revolve around two episodes in Shelley's life never fully understood by earlier biographers: a supposed assassination attempt made against Shelley in 1813 and the evidence of Shelley's adopting a daughter in Naples in 1818. Holmes' explanations have not met with wide acceptance. Holmes also offers a revision of the prevailing critical estimate of Shelley's poetry and prose. Unfortunately, his own critical estimates seem to be made without a thorough acquaintance with the standard critical literature and are, therefore, idiosyncratic. Holmes also makes factual errors in his account. Nevertheless, this study usefully complements Newman Ivey White's *Shelley*, fulfilling better the expectations of readers who look to a biography for a vivid interpretive portrait of a man's personality and motives.

White, Newman Ivey, *Shelley*. 2 vols. New York: Alfred A. Knopf, 1940; rpt. New York: Octagon Books, 1972. White's full-scale scholarly biography remains the standard for serious students of Shelley's life. Its publication marked the end of a long, slow decline in Shelley's reputation, corrected the false impression of Shelley as a sentimental dreamer that popular biographies had created, and provided the first reliable attempt to chronicle every aspect of Shelley's life. Though White treats most of Shelley's works in passing, criticism is of secondary importance to White, who above all strives for factual accuracy and objective judgments. White relies wherever possible on primary sources, not other biographies, and furnishes references for his every statement, making his notes an invaluable mine of information. The cautious approach means there is no amateur psychoanalyzing, no moralizing, and no attempts to make a good story out of Shelley's life. These strengths constitute the biography's weakness, if it be one: White himself makes few sweeping generalizations and offers no profound insights into Shelley's personality. Such work is left to the reader. Though this exemplary biography remains standard, later scholarship has brought to light information unavailable to White and requires that the serious student consult more recent sources if seeking the latest word on very specific matters in Shelley's life.

Overview of Critical Sources

Shelley's reputation underwent a decline in the late nineteenth and early twentieth centuries, largely due to injudicious anthologizing and to unsympathetic attacks by Matthew Arnold, T. S. Eliot, and F. R. Leavis; consequently, very little criticism from before World War II is important today. Since then, however, Shelley's work has received generous attention. A student of Shelley will find an abundance of excellent studies on his individual works, certain phases of his career, his political vision, his poetic dramas, his style, his imagery, and his general achievement. For an extensive overview of critical sources see *The English Romantic Poets: A Review of Research and Criticism*, third revised edition, ed. Frank Jordan (New York: Modern Language Association, 1972).

Evaluation of Selected Criticism

Baker, Carlos, *Shelley's Major Poetry: The Fabric of a Vision*. Princeton: Princeton University Press, 1948. First among the critical studies that began the rehabilitation of Shelley's reputation, this fine book takes up each major poem in turn, offers a sound and balanced reading, and tries to show how each fits into the developing fabric of his vision. Baker calls Shelley a most "literary" poet and strikingly demonstrates Shelley's conscious indebtedness to his artistic forbears—Plato, Dante, Milton, and Wordsworth among them. This is still the best book to serve as antidote against thinking Shelley an eccentric or isolated poet.

Bloom, Harold, *Shelley's Mythmaking*. New Haven: Yale University Press, 1959; rpt. Ithaca, NY: Cornell University Press, 1969. This ground-breaking examination does more to make Shelley's endeavor seem important than any other study. Bloom reveals a Shelley who takes up an ironically conscious prophetic stance and who seeks to create new myths for his own time. Shelley is profitably compared with William Blake as trying to harness the mythmaking power of poetry to create a revitalized vision of the cosmos. Though not an easy book, *Shelley's Mythmaking* poses none of the inordinate difficulties of Bloom's later criticism.

Cameron, Kenneth Neill, *Shelley: The Golden Years*. Cambridge: Harvard University Press, 1974. Interweaving biographical and critical materials adroitly, Cameron explores all of Shelley's major works, as well as several biographical problems that have plagued scholars. Shelley is treated as a radical and original political poet best understood in his historical context. The book is authoritative in matters of biographical and scholarly detail, but its readings of the poetry are perhaps too bound by such concerns.

Curran, Stuart, *Shelley's Annus Mirabilis: The Maturing of an Epic Vision*. San Marino, CA: Huntington Library, 1975. Curran treats the works produced in the amazing flourish of activity that began shortly after Shelley took up residence in Italy. This study explores the varied genres, styles, and audiences the poet addressed in his conscious search for a voice and an impact. The book is especially strong in examining the intellectual and artistic influences upon the poet's work.

Reiman, Donald H. *Percy Bysshe Shelley*. New York: Twayne, 1969; corrected paperback edition, New York: St. Martin's Press, 1974. Both brief and authoritative, this study is without doubt the best starting point for any student of Shelley. Reiman's unparalleled familiarity with both the scholarly and critical tradition in Shelley studies enables him to offer a sound, balanced introduction valuable even to advanced students. The chronological arrangement puts each work in its biographical context and proceeds with a brief analysis and evaluation.

Wasserman, Earl, *Shelley: A Critical Reading*. Baltimore: Johns Hopkins University Press, 1971. Wasserman carefully applies the techniques of close reading, aided by the wealth of his own prodigious learning, to explicating almost all of Shelley's important works. The book's overarching arguments about Shelley's maturing philosophy seem of less import than the persuasive and illuminating individual readings. This massive study is essential for every serious student.

Other Sources

Cameron, Kenneth Neill and Donald H. Reiman, eds. *Shelley and His Circle: 1773–1822.* 6 vols. (10 vols. projected). Cambridge: Harvard University Press, 1961–. A catalog and edition of the manuscripts in The Carl H. Pforzheimer Library, this contains editions of and extensive commentaries on manuscripts by the poet and his circle. It provides a wealth of biographical detail that has not found its way into a full-scale biography.

Chernaik, Judith, *The Lyrics of Shelley.* Cleveland: Press of Case Western Reserve University, 1972. The best analysis of the lyric poetry Shelley is most widely known for. Contains authoritative editions of many important poems.

Clairmont, Mary Jane Clara, *The Journals of Claire Clairmont.* ed. Marion K. Stocking. Cambridge: Harvard University Press, 1968. Valuable records by Mary Shelley's half-sister who lived with the Shelleys on and off over several years. A well edited and annotated resource.

Shelley, Mary Wollstonecraft, *The Letters of Mary Wollstonecraft Shelley.* 2 vols. (3 vols. projected). ed. Betty T. Bennett. Baltimore: Johns Hopkins University Press, 1981–.

Shelley, Mary Wollstonecraft and P. B. Shelley, *The Shelley Journals.* 2 vols. ed. Paula R. Feldman and Diana Pugh. Oxford: Oxford University Press, 1984. Though intermittently maintained, this journal contains invaluable information about the poet's daily life.

Shelley, Percy Bysshe, *The Letters of Percy Bysshe Shelley.* ed. Frederick L. Jones. 2 vols. Oxford: Clarendon Press, 1964. The only significant autobiographical materials are contained in these letters.

David L. Ackiss
Missouri Southern State College

SIR PHILIP SIDNEY
1554–1586

Author's Chronology

Born November 30, 1554, at Penshurst, Kent, England, of aristocracy on mother's side; *1568* enters Corpus Christi College, Oxford; *1572* in Paris with Sir Francis Walsingham; witnesses St. Bartholomew's Day Massacre; begins friendship with Hubert Languet; *1576* becomes cupbearer to Queen Elizabeth; campaigns in Ireland; *1578* presents *The Lady of May* for Queen Elizabeth's visit with his uncle Lord Leicester; begins *Old Arcadia; 1579* argues with the Earl of Oxford; receives dedications of Stephen Gosson's *The School of Abuse* and Edmund Spenser's *The Shepheardes Calender; 1580* finishes *Old Arcadia; 1581* is elected to Parliament; finishes *The Defence of Poesie,* in answer to Gosson; possibility of marriage to Penelope Devereux ends; begins *Astrophel and Stella; 1582* finishes *Astrophel and Stella;* begins *New Arcadia; 1583* is knighted; marries Frances Walsingham; begins translation of Philippe Mornay's *The Truth of the Christian Religion; 1584* becomes governor of Flushing; *1586* wounded at Zutphen; dies on October 17 at Arnheim, the Netherlands.

Author's Bibliography (selected)

The Lady of May, 1578 (play); *The Old Arcadia,* 1580 (novel); *The Defense of Poesie,* 1581 (criticism); *Astrophel and Stella,* 1582 (poem); *The New Arcadia,* begun 1582, published 1590 (novel); *The Arcadia,* revised, 1593 (novel).

Overview of Biographical Sources

Sir Philip Sidney's art, personality, and statesmanship have attracted several biographers. Among accounts by his contemporaries, the most notable is that written about 1612 by his close friend and fellow soldier Fulke Greville, Lord Brooke; Greville's *The Life of the Renowned Sir Philip Sidney,* ed. Newell Smith (Oxford: Clarendon Press, 1907) treats Sidney as a soldier, statesman, and thinker and not as a writer. Many of Sidney's later biographies have a similar limitation, emphasizing Sidney as either the statesman-soldier or the poet-lover. In the second half of the nineteenth century the standard authority on Sidney's life was H. R. Fox Bourne, of whose studies the most readily available for libraries was *Sir Philip Sidney: Type of English Chivalry in the Romantic Age* (New York: G. P. Putnam's Sons, 1891). Bourne's work was far better than John Addington Symond's *Sir Philip Sidney* (London: Macmillan, 1886), a volume in the English Men of Letters series which was reprinted in 1909, before any good twentieth-century biographies had appeared, but then unaccountably reprinted in 1968, when its errors in fact and interpretation could no longer be excused on any grounds. Another inadequate biography is Percy Addleshaw's *Sir Philip Sidney* (London: Methuen, 1909); its almost complete lack of scholarly apparatus is one of its limitations, and Addleshaw's religious biases make him incapable of appreciating certain aspects of Sidney's works and personal relationships. An outstanding biography, Malcolm W. Wallace's *The Life of Sir Philip Sidney* (1915), offered new insights into Sidney's early life and his later relationships with the Dutch, both resulting from discoveries made by Wallace on a trip to Europe; Wallace's work was for a time relatively unknown and insufficiently appreciated (undoubtedly because it appeared during World War I), but Wallace, with his superior scholarship, has the best biography available today. The thorough documentation in Mona Wilson's *Sir Philip Sidney* (London: Gerald Duckworth and Company, 1931) has been complimented highly by several other writers on Sidney, but the objection is frequently made that Wilson romanticizes her subject too much. C. Henry Warren's *Sir Philip Sidney: A Study in Conflict* (New York: Thomas Nelson and Sons Limited, 1936) pays tribute to the work of both Wallace and Wilson, but then justifies its own existence by claiming that previous biographies have not viewed Sidney first and foremost as a poet. Although admitting that Wilson has stressed Sidney's important position at the beginning of Elizabethan literature, Warren wants more emphasis on Sidney as a poet of extraordinary accomplishments. Alfred H. Bill's *Astrophel, or The Life and Death of The Renowned Sir Philip Sidney* (New York: Farrar and Rinehart, 1937) suffers from an absence of documentation; it is conjectural, impressionistic, and at times, as in the discussion of Penelope Devereux, pages 223–235, absurdly fanciful. F. S. Boas' *Sir Philip Sidney, Representative Elizabethan: His Life and Writings* (1955) is a very general study of Sidney's life in relation to his works; Boas, acknowledging his indebtedness to Wallace and Wilson, writes a very readable book that touches upon most of the major events of Sidney's life but one that contains little in-depth investigation. At the other extreme is James M. Osborn's *Young Philip Sidney, 1572–1577* (New Haven: Yale University Press, 1972), which devotes more than 500 pages to the period in which Sidney traveled widely on the Continent. Although it is unlikely that much new biographical information on Sidney will be discovered in the future, it is quite likely that several new interpretations of Sidney, particularly of his religious thought, will be made. Sidney's biographies are of particular importance because Sidney's life, to a greater extent than is the case with many other writers, is of vital importance to an understanding of his works.

Evaluation of Selected Biographies

Boas, F. S. *Sir Philip Sidney, Representative Elizabethan: His Life and Writings.* London: Staples Press Limited, 1955. This is a literary biography which because of its brevity (fewer than 200 pages) and easy style serves as a good general introduction to Sidney's life and works. Its sketchiness is sometimes annoying. In the account of the Battle of Zutphen and the remaining days of Sidney's life, it may actually be misleading, for Boas states that Sidney "lingered for sixteen days" before dying on October 17, and a work published in 1960 actually gives October 2 as the date of the fatal battle rather than the fully authenticated date of September 22. The work has only scanty documentation, and the index provides no titles or place names.

Wallace, Malcolm W. *The Life of Sir Philip Sidney.* Cambridge: Cambridge University Press, 1915. Wallace replaced Bourne as the standard biographical authority on Sidney. Wallace reexamined the known manuscript sources for Sidney's life and discovered a new one, Thomas Marshall's account book, which records Sidney's expenses from December 1565 to September 1566 and which provides information about such things as Sidney's books and travels during those months. Wallace also introduced some valuable findings on Sidney's relationship with Prince William of Orange, leader of the Dutch opposition to Spanish domination of the Netherlands, and several other interesting historical notes. Wallace analyzes the thought of Sidney in detail, paying attention to Sidney's visit to France, where he possibly was influenced by the Pléiade; he also thinks it likely that Sidney was influenced by the Ramists. The work is lengthy, informative, and readable. Intelligent scholarship is evident; fanciful guesswork is lacking. It is possible to wish for more documentation (even though much is provided), and the index is very slight; but the work is sound and dependable.

Autobiographical Sources

Sidney's sonnet sequence, *Astrophel and Stella,* purports to be autobiographical; Astrophel (Sidney) laments the loss of a lady whom he loves very much but who has been forced to marry another. Many scholars believe that Sidney's laments are not the result of frustrated passion for Penelope, but rather the mere echoing of the theme of unrequited love, traditional in sonnet sequences since Petrarch.

Sidney's *Defence of Poesie* is the major English critical work of the entire sixteenth century. In it Sidney expresses his theories of literary art, his knowledge of its forms, and his concern for the ability of the English language to be the vehicle for a great literature.

Sidney had many friends in England and on the Continent with whom he corresponded; much of this correspondence is still extant, more than for any other writer of the age. Selected letters appear in *The Prose Works of Sir Philip Sidney* (ed. Albert Feuillerat, 4 vols. Cambridge: Cambridge University Press, 1962). Sidney's Latin correspondence with Hubert Languet appears in translation in *The Correspondence of Sir Philip Sidney and Hubert Languet,* ed. S. A. Pears, London: W. Pickering, 1845. The letters present important evidence of the character and intelligence of Sidney.

Overview of Critical Sources

For a long while effective literary critcism of Sidney was hindered by various factors: the magnetic personality and adventurous exploits of the youthful courtier led to very romantic and impressionistic criticism of his works; the autobiographical question concerning Sidney's true relationship with Penelope Devereux dominated analysis of *Astrophel and Stella;* and the presence of different versions of *Arcadia* created major difficulties for those wishing to analyze Sidney's political and religious beliefs. In the past few decades Sidney criticism has improved greatly; modern analyses of form, sources, and technique are not affected by the facts of Sidney's personal charm, bravery in battle, and noble behavior as he lay dying; considerable doubt currently exists about the presence of a significant autobiographical element in the sonnets, and they may now be analyzed and appreciated as works of literary art; the publication of well-edited texts has made the study of other works less formidable, and one of the phenomena of the past decade has been the appearance of a large number of full-length works on *Arcadia.*

Evaluation of Selected Criticism

Myrick, K. O. *Sir Philip Sidney as a Literary Craftsman.* Cambridge: Harvard University Press, 1935. This classic study of Sidney's literary art insists that Sidney is a well-read and well-trained artist. Myrick, concentrating primarily on the prose, maintains that *The Defence of Poesie* and *The Arcadia* should be studied together, the latter work simply exemplifying what the former had established in theory. The book is famous for its discussion of *sprezzatura,* the nonchalance of the courtier.

Rudenstine, Neil L. *Sidney's Poetic Development.* Cambridge: Harvard University Press, 1967. Rudenstine deals with Sidney's poetic techniques and style as Sidney tries to escape the limitations of Petrarchanism. Rudenstine finds an unbroken pattern of development in Sidney's verse. The work is valuable for the student because of its effective organization: numerous short chapters deal specifically with precise areas of Sidney's works. Some discussion of the prose is included.

Zandvoort, R. W. *Sidney's Arcadia: A Comparison Between The Two Versions.* Amsterdam: N. W. Swets and Zeitlinger, 1929. Zandvoort is valuable for any study of the *Arcadia* texts. He analyzes the various manuscripts, explains the causes of variant readings, discusses source material, compares stylistic elements, and traces Sidney's development as a thinker and as a narrative writer. Zandvoort concludes that the second version shows a significant growth of literary power and provides valuable insights into the maturing Sidney's mind.

Other Sources

Buxton, John, *Sir Philip Sidney and the English Renaissance.* New York: St. Martin's Press, 1954. Analysis of patronage system as central to much of Sidney's life and writing.

Danby, John F. *Elizabethan and Jacobean Poets: Studies in Sidney, Shakespeare, Beaumont and Fletcher.* London: Faber and Faber, 1964, previously published as *Poets on Fortune's Hill.* London: Faber and Faber Limited, 1952. Two influential chapters on Sidney with thesis that he, like Shakespeare, had the ability to express firm moral viewpoints in great art.

Kimbrough, Robert, *Sir Philip Sidney.* New York: Twayne, 1971. A brief, well-organized, easily readable overview with a useful annotated bibliography.

Montgomery, Robert L., Jr. *Symmetry and Sense: The Poetry of Sir Philip Sidney.* Austin: University of Texas Press, 1961. Discussion of Sidney's verse within the rhetorical theory of the age, with a glossary of rhetorical terms.

Purcell, James M. *Sidney's Stella.* New York: Oxford University Press, 1934. Conclusion that romantic interpretations of true love between Sidney and Penelope are highly questionable, some sonnets having been written before the pair ever met.

Selected Dictionaries and Encyclopedias

British Authors Before 1800: A Biographical Dictionary, H. W. Wilson Company, 1952. Overview of Sidney's life with brief comments on his major works.

Critical Survey of Poetry, Vol. 6, Salem Press, 1982. Concise biography with analysis of Sidney's literary career.

Howard L. Ford
North Texas State University

WILLIAM GILMORE SIMMS
1806–1870

Author's Chronology

Born April 17, 1806, Charleston, South Carolina; *1808* mother dies, and father leaves him with grandmother; *1824* makes first trip to the Mississippi frontier to visit his father; *1826* marries Anna Malcolm Giles; *1827* admitted to bar; publishes two books of verse; *1832* wife dies, leaving him with infant daughter; sells his Unionist newspaper; travels to Northeast and establishes friendships with Northern literati; *1833* publishes first novel, *Martin Faber;* *1834* publishes his first border novel; *1835* publishes first Colonial and first Revolutionary romances; *1836* marries Chevillette Roach and moves to Woodlands plantation; *1844–1846* serves term in South Carolina legislature; *1849–1854* edits *Southern Quarterly Review;* *1854* misjudges Northern audiences and cuts short lecture tour of the North; becomes increasingly involved in defending Southern interests and in secessionist movement; *1861* witnesses bombardment of Fort Sumter; *1863* wife dies suddenly; *1864* eldest son wounded in battle; *1865* Woodlands burns completely in fire set by men from Sherman's army; *1870* dies June 11, with six of his fifteen children surviving him.

Author's Bibliography (selected)

Guy Rivers, 1834 (novel); *The Yemassee,* 1835 (novel); *The Partisan,* 1835 (novel); *Richard Hurdis,* 1838 (novel); *Border Beagles,* 1840 (novel); *Beauchampe,* 1842 (novel); *The Life of Francis Marion,* 1844 (biography); *The Wigwam and the Cabin,* 1845 (short stories); *Views and Reviews,* 1846 (criticism); *The Sword, and the Distaff,* 1852, later renamed *Woodcraft* (novel); *Poems Descriptive, Dramatic, Legendary and Contemplative,* 1853; *The Forayers,* 1855 (novel); *Eutaw,* 1856 (novel); *The Cassique of Kiawah,* 1859 (novel); *Voltmeier* 1969 (novel); *Paddy McGann,* 1972 (novel); "How Sharp Snaffles Got His Wife," 1974 (*Stories and Tales*).

Overview of Biographical Sources

With his extraordinary energies, his wide range of interests, and his eighty-plus books, William Gilmore Simms poses a challenge to the biographer. Although scholars agree on Simms' position as the most important writer in the antebellum South, only four books devoted to him have appeared in print. No new biography has yet superseded William Peterfield Trent's *William Gilmore Simms* (1892). Despite obvious limitations and errors, Trent's scholarship generally remains sound; and his work includes material otherwise unavailable since he interviewed and corresponded with people who had known Simms personally. Subsequent commentary relied heavily on Trent and perpetuated some of his errors and conclusions until the publication of *The Letters of William Gilmore Simms* (see below), the most reliable and comprehensive source for a complete portrait of the man. A. S. Salley's "Biographical Sketch" in the first volume of letters counters several of Trent's statements and misinterpretations. Even with the benefit of the published letters, scholarship continues to deal with the life only briefly or selectively. For example, Jon Wakelyn in *Politics of a Literary Man* (Westport, CT: Greenwood Press, 1973) focuses on Simms' polemical activities. The study contains errors in fact and spelling and contends that even the imaginative literature was politically motivated, but Wakelyn places Simms in his local and national historical context.

Evaluation of Selected Biographies

Ridgely, J. V. *William Gilmore Simms.* New York: Twayne, 1962. Though he includes a chronology and occasional brief summaries of events in Simms' life, Ridgely subordinates biographical data to his theory that the South stimulated rather than hindered Simms' creative writing. The critic examines the Revolutionary and Border romances as illustrations of Simms' development of a Southern myth incorporating the author's views of an ideal society. Despite his limiting thesis, Ridgely contributes the most readable and readily available book-length consideration of Simms.

Salley, A. C. "William Gilmore Simms," in *The Letters of William Gilmore Simms.* ed. Mary C. Simms Oliphant *et al.* Columbia: University of South Carolina Press, 1952–1982, 1:1ix–1xxxix. Salley presents an enthusiastic, sympathetic summary of the life with emphases and details to rebut Trent's interpretations concerning Simms' father's bankruptcy, the author's early poverty, and his neglect by contemporaries and by the social aristocracy of Charleston.

Trent, William P. *William Gilmore Simms.* Boston: Houghton Mifflin Company, 1892. Trent presents a sympathetic, readable account of the man, if not of the work. His book combines interesting narrative with outmoded digressions and criticism of Simms' fiction. A "New South" Reconstructionist, Trent stresses the detrimental effect of Simms' southern environment on his work. A "genteel" reader, he disapproves of Simms' "vulgar" realism and "repulsive" low-life characters. His interpretations of the Old South and of the author's neglect by his own society became repeated subjects of critical discussions.

Autobiographical Sources

The Letters of William Gilmore Simms furnish a running account of the life of the multifaceted Simms from 1830 until his death. Correspondence with editors and authors such as Edgar Allan Poe and William Cullen Bryant provide an inside look at the publishing and literary history of the period, while those to other friends and to family reveal the daily life and personal traits of the author. Invaluable material about the composition of specific works provides a major source for critical interpretation. Some of the letters become autobiographical, literary, or political essays. Most give informal, honest expressions of the conflicts and events in a long, full career.

Prefatory material in Volume 1 includes useful biographical information in the "Introduction," "Biographical Sketch," "Simms' Circle," and "The Family Circle." Volume 5 contains indexes to the first five volumes and to Simms' works, as well as corrections of errors in previous volumes. Volume 6 supplements the letters published in the earlier volumes. Throughout the collection, the editors annotate with admirable precision and accuracy, providing dates and details otherwise unavailable. Another valuable source is *Views and Reviews in American Literature, History and Fiction* (ed. C. Hugh Holman. Cambridge: Harvard University Press, 1962). This edition makes convenient a sampling of Simms' essays in the 1840's and includes important discussions of his theories of the romance and novel and his use of history for the purposes of art.

Much of Simms' critical theory appears in reviews, essays, and prefaces difficult to locate. His 1853 Preface to *The Yemassee,* containing his theory of romance as epic, often accompanies modern editions of that work.

Overview of Critical Sources

Except for the four books on Simms, the criticism is found in general essays in articles focusing on sources or specific topics. Following Trent's work, critics argued over whether Simms' southern environment influenced him for good or ill, whether he wrote romantic realism or realistic romance. More recently, critics examine his fiction as works of inherent literary merit and integrity. Valuable contributions to interpretations of Simms' works appear in the explanatory notes to the Bicentennial Edition of the Revolutionary Novels (Spartanburg, South Carolina: The Reprint Company, 1976). Important introductions and explanatory notes also accompany the texts of the Centennial Editions of *The Writings of William Gilmore Simms* (Columbia: University of South Carolina Press), which include *Voltmeier,* Vol. 1 (1969) and *As Good as a Comedy and Paddy McGann,* Vol. 3 (1972).

Evaluation of Selected Criticism

Holman, C. Hugh, *The Roots of Southern Writing.* Athens: University of Georgia Press, 1972, pp. 1–86. Besides his useful introduction to his edition of *Views and Reviews,* which describes Simms' role in the "Young America" controversy of the 1840's, this book also reprints earlier scholarly articles by Holman dealing with influences and with Simms' use of history. Though some of the critic's generalizations are arguable, an examination of Simms' activities during the "American Renaissance" details events in Simms' life between 1850 and 1855.

Hubbell, Jay B. *The South in American Literature 1607–1900.* Durham: Duke University Press, 1954, pp. 572–602, 958–961. Hubbell balances Simms' role as a Southerner with his importance as a national author. He provides a concise summary of the life and of Simms' theories of the romance and the novel. Subsequent critics praise Hubbell's balanced perspective and reliability.

Parks, Edd Winfield, *William Gilmore Simms as Literary Critic.* Athens: University of Georgia Press, 1961. Chapters on Simms' theories of the novel, poetry, drama, and national and sectional literature provide glimpses of the life and include liberal quotations and paraphrases from essays and reviews now difficult of access. Though somewhat stiffly presented, the study provides a springboard for further investigation.

Other Sources

Hetherington, Hugh H. *Cavalier of Old South Carolina: William Gilmore Simms's Porgy.* Chapel Hill: University of North Carolina Press, 1966, pp. 3–74. In his introduction to texts dealing with Porgy, Hetherington compares Porgy to Falstaff, discusses *Woodcraft* as fictional rebuttal to *Uncle Tom's Cabin,* and argues that Porgy is in part a self-portrait of his author.

McHaney, Thomas L. "William Gilmore Simms," in *The Chief Glory of Every People.* ed. Matthew J. Bruccoli. Carbondale: Southern Illinois University Press, 1973, pp. 173–190. Focuses on the elements of southwest and folk humor in Simms' fiction and emphasizes the realistic portrayals in the Border novels and short stories.

Watson, Charles S. "William Gilmore Simms: An Essay in Bibliography," *Resources for American Literary Study,* 3 (Spring 1973), 3–26. A review of critical opinions of Simms with citations and brief commentary.

Selected Dictionaries and Encyclopedias

Critical Survey of Long Fiction, Salem Press, 1983. Brief biographical sketch followed by general summaries of selected works.

Dictionary of Literary Biography, Vol. 3, Gale Research, 1979. A balanced, reliable review of the life and the works.

Linda E. McDaniel
University of South Carolina

UPTON SINCLAIR
1878–1968

Author's Chronology

Born 20 September 1878 in Baltimore, Maryland; *1897* graduates from City College of New York; *1900* marries Meta Fuller; *1901* son David born; *1903* publishes *The Journal of Arthur Stirling;* becomes a Socialist; *1906* publishes most famous work *The Jungle; 1912* divorces Fuller; *1913* marries Mary Craig Kimbrough; *1916* moves to Pasadena; *1917* favors American intervention in WWI and opposes Soviet Communism; *1920's–1930's* famous in Europe as *the* American Socialist; *1926* Socialist candidate for governor of California; *1927 Oil!* banned in Boston; *1930* Socialist candidate for Governor of California; *1932 The Wet Parade,* about the evils of alcohol, becomes a motion picture; *1934* Democratic candidate for governor of California; *1940* popular "Lanny Budd" Series begun with *World's End; 1942 Dragon's Teeth* wins Pulitzer Prize; *1960* Mary Craig Sinclair dies; *1961* at age 83 marries Mary Willis; *1968* dies 25 November in Rockville, Maryland.

Author's Bibliography (selected)

Springtime and Harvest, 1901, reissued as *King Midas,* 1901 (novel); *The Journal of Arthur Stirling,* 1903 (novel); *The Jungle,* 1906, 1973 (novel); *The Moneychangers,* 1908, 1969 (novel); *King Coal,* 1917 (novel); *The Brass Check: A Study in American Journalism,* 1919, 1970 (nonfiction); *100%: The Story of a Patriot,* 1920 (novel); *Goose-Step—A Study in American Education,* 1923 (nonfiction); *The Goslings: A Study of the American Schools,* 1924 (nonfiction); *Mammonart,* 1925 (nonfiction); *Oil!,* 1927 (novel); *Boston,* 1928, reissued as *August Twenty-Second,* 1965 (novel); *American Outpost: A Book of Reminiscences,* 1932; *The Wet Parade,* 1932 (novel and motion picture); *No Pasaran,* 1937 (novel); "The Lanny Budd" Series begun with *World's End,* 1940; *Dragon's Teeth,* 1942 (novel); *The Autobiography of Upton Sinclair,* 1962.

Overview of Biographical Sources

Because Sinclair saved everything he wrote, biographical material is not hard to find. The problem is selecting that which is important from among the plethora of material. Almost all scholarly articles about Sinclair are biographical. In the earliest biography, *Upton Sinclair: A Study in Social Protest* (1927), Floyd Dell, himself a Socialist, sees Sinclair as the primary interpreter of that period in American history. The book is accurate, but slanted. It is now hard to find, but worth finding, as Dell was a fine writer and a better stylist than Sinclair. Leon Harris, in the most complete biography, *Upton Sinclair: American Rebel,* quotes extensively from Sinclair and others, using hundreds of thousands of letters, books, and articles.

Evaluation of Selected Biographies
Bloodworth, William, *Upton Sinclair*. Boston: Twayne, 1977. While this book is both critical and biographical, both rely heavily on psychological interpretation.

Dell, Floyd, *Upton Sinclair: A Study in Social Protest,* 1927. This biography has authority for several reasons: Dell knew Sinclair well, Sinclair gave Dell anything he wanted, Dell was an experienced reporter and knew how to research his subject. It is insightful not only because Dell knew Sinclair, but also because Dell was not above disagreeing with him. It has the weaknesses of biographies written by one persuaded of the faith espoused by the subject. It is also very Freudian, in keeping with the avant-garde knowledge of the day. The book is far more sympathetic to Sinclair than the letters of Dell to Sinclair, in which he is forthright and sometimes cruel in his appraisals of Sinclair's life and works. One must remember that when Dell's biography was published, Sinclair still had more than forty years to live.

Harris, Leon, *Upton Sinclair: American Rebel.* New York: Thomas Y. Crowell, 1975. This must be considered the definitive biography to date. Included for the first time are detailed descriptions of Sinclair's horror of having children, his cruel treatment of his son, David, and of the probable abortions undergone by at least his first wife. Because so much of the book is quotation, Harris's views are sometimes omitted. Yet one comes away feeling that Sinclair has been as well served as an energetic life of ninety years may be served in fewer than four hundred pages. The book has no bibliography, but the notes are extensive, and this is the starting point for any study of Sinclair.

Autobiographical Sources
Nearly all of Sinclair's papers written before March 16, 1907 were destroyed by fire. The Lilly Library at Indiana University, however, contains more than eight tons of Sinclair materials, including more than 250,000 letters. One may look in almost any literary or popular magazine of the day and find a letter to the editor from Sinclair on subjects ranging from diet to death, socialism to sophistry, birth control to booze. In addition, the collected letters of nearly every literary, and many political, contemporaries are preserved. Many small collections may be found in universities as far afield as The University of Amsterdam. In short, primary materials for the study of Sinclair are everywhere, and everywhere in abundance.

The primary autobiographies are *American Outpost* (1932) and *The Autobiography of Upton Sinclair* (1962). Many of Sinclair's novels are thinly disguised autobiography combined with his latest theories. These include *The Journal of Arthur Stirling* (1902), and *Love's Pilgrimage* (1911). Sinclair wrote ninety books and thousands of essays on hundreds of subjects, articles, reviews, and letters to editors, and nowhere is the author's life far from the words on his pages.

Overview of Critical Sources

Because Sinclair was so active politically, his life and times and friends so interesting, and because his work, as literature, is almost uniformly bad, most critical evaluations are to be found in the biographies. His work is viewed critically from two related perspectives: as marxist literature and the literature of muckraking. As marxist literature, Sinclair's work becomes a vehicle for the political rhetoric of others. Marxist critics believe Sinclair's work to be great because it is concerned more with politics than art, and is an example of the inevitable stage in history during which the "workers of the world" rise against their oppressors.

Much less insistent, socialistic criticism often remains political, but not so blinded by marxist polemics. Floyd Dell fits into this category, writing as he did at a time when the intelligencia of the United States had great hopes for socialist reform. Leon Harris, almost fifty years later, belongs to this category, and writes during a similar time of great social change.

Of writers of social protest—those whom Teddy Roosevelt labeled "muckrakers"—Sinclair was clearly the leader. His indefatigible energy, exhaustive research, and frenzied writing kept him in the forefront of the "muckraking school" for nearly six decades. Evaluations of Sinclair's influence may be found in any book written about twentieth century American social movements.

Evaluation of Selected Criticism

There is little purely critical work on Sinclair. Because he was an important writer, not a great one, the emphasis has been on the biography, and is concerned largely with his politics and his influence as the great American muckraker. That Sinclair is not dismissed by the literati "merely" as a muckraker is demonstrated by the words of many contemporary literary critics. Van Wyck Brooks gives a sympathetic portrayal in *The Confident Years* (New York: E. P. Dutton, 1952). In addition, Granville Hicks ("Warmakers and Peacemakers," *The New Republic,* 1940) and H. L. Mencken, the most widely read American literary critic of the period, praised Sinclair. H. L. Mencken's letters and reviews (*Prejudices,* 3rd Series. New York: Alfred A. Knopf, 1922) are worthy of attention, not only because they give Mencken's views, but because Sinclair valued them in spite of their being almost always negative.

Evaluation of Selected Criticism

Bloodworth, William, *Upton Sinclair.* Boston: Twayne, 1977. Bloodworth's book is intelligent, well-researched (deriving from Bloodworth's Ph.D. dissertation), and one of the few books on Sinclair attempting to overcome political positions espoused by the author. Bloodworth sees Sinclair as "a progressive

Christian Socialist" and is better able than most to reconcile the seeming contradictions implied by those terms. It has the advantage also of blending Sinclair's life and works without a disproportionate emphasis on one or the other.

Yoder, Jon A. *Upton Sinclair*. New York: Frederick Ungar, Modern Literature Monograph, 1975. This short critical and biographical work covers much territory in little space, and stresses Sinclair's enormous influence on the writers of his and a later generation. It does, however, concern itself with Sinclair's three best books: *The Jungle, Oil!*, and *The Brass Check*.

Chester L. Wolford
The Pennsylvania State University
Behrend College

ISAAC BASHEVIS SINGER
1904

Author's Chronology

Born November 21, 1904, Leoncin, Poland; *1908* family moves to Warsaw and father becomes rabbi of Krochmalna Street; *1917* moves to Bilgoray with his mother and remains for four years; *1923* becomes proofreader for a Warsaw journal, *Literary Pages; 1927* signs one of his stories Isaac Bashevis to distinguish his works from his brother's; *1929* his only child, Israel, is born to Runya, an avid Communist; *1935* publishes his first book, *Satan in Goray,* in Warsaw; follows his brother, Joshua, to the United States; *1937* becomes a United States citizen and meets Alma (Haimann) Wasserman whom he marries in 1940; *1944* his brother Joshua dies; *1953* "Gimpel the Fool," translated by Saul Bellow, appears in *Partisan Review; 1955* his son, living in Israel, visits him after a separation of twenty years; *1966* publishes his first children's book, *Zlateh the Goat; 1964* is elected to the National Institute of Arts and Letters with the distinction of being the only American member to write in a language other than English; *1970* wins National Book Award for *A Day of Pleasure; 1975* wins National Book Award for *A Crown of Feathers and Other Stories; 1978* wins Nobel Prize for Literature.

Author's Bibliography (selected)

The Family Moskat, 1950 (novel); *Satan in Goray,* 1955 (novel); *In My Father's Court,* 1956 (memoir); *Gimpel the Fool and Other Stories* (1957); *The Magician of Lublin,* 1960 (novel); *The Spinoza of Market Street,* 1961 (short stories); *The Slave,* 1962 (novel); *Short Friday and Other Stories,* 1964; *Zlateh the Goat,* 1966 (children's stories); *The Manor,* 1967 (novel); *When Shlemiel Went to Warsaw and Other Stories,* 1968 (children's stories); *The Estate,* 1969 (novel); *Enemies, A Love Story,* 1972 (novel); *A Crown of Feathers and Other Stories,* 1973; *Shosha,* 1978 (novel); *Love and Exile,* 1984 (memoir).

Overview of Biographical Sources

There are only two biographical works on Isaac Bashevis Singer. The first is a sprawling four-hundred page montage by Paul Kresh, *Isaac Bashevis Singer: The Magician of West 86th Street* (New York: The Dial Press, 1979). The second treatment, *The Brothers Singer* by Clive Sinclair (London: Allison and Busby, 1983), deals not only with Singer, but with his brother, Israel Joshua, as well as Singer's sister, Esther Kreitman, the first writer among the Singer siblings and the least known. Neither of these works fills the need of a definitive biography of Isaac Bashevis Singer.

Evaluation of Selected Biographies

Kresh, Paul, *Isaac Bashevis Singer: The Magician of West 86th Street.* New York: The Dial Press, 1979. This is a treasure of biographical information, combined with summaries and brief critical analyses of most of Singer's novels and tales. Included are Singer's relationships with his translators, his publishers, and even photographs of Singer and literary and familial associates. The information concerning Singer's early life as a young man in Warsaw is recorded by the author in many of his works and is readily available. His life in the United States is gleaned from interviews with Singer and Singer's family and close associates. The major problem of Kresh's biography is organization: its loose construction, haphazard organization, and its equal attention to Singer's older brother, Israel Joshua. Consequently this work is accurate but flawed and limited in its usefulness.

Autobiographical Sources

Many of Singer's works are memoirs of his life in the Polish shtetl and provide biographers with most of their material concerning his youthful years. The first of these, *In My Father's Court,* consists of short pieces originally published under the pseudonym, Isaac Warshawsky—Warshawsky meaning man of Warsaw—in the *Jewish Daily Forward.* Although the work follows a chronological order, the sketches are not necessarily sequential. Singer's writings, while they entertain, attempt to recreate a destroyed world. *In My Father's Court* is important for its sense of place, and for its revitalization, however briefly, of the East European shtetl. Peering into Warsaw in the first decade of the twentieth century, the reader is also privy to the views of the narrator as they relate to family, friends, religion, and vocation. The work concludes with the end of the First World War and Singer, at the age of fifteen moving away from the restrictive teachings of his father into the enlightened world of literature and love.

The novel, *Shosha,* which also originally appeared in the *Jewish Daily Forward,* in 1974 under the title, *Soul Expeditions,* is an enlarged and fictionalized rendering of the memoir, *A Young Man in Search of Love.* (1978). Much of the work is autobiographical, and Aaron Greidinger, the protagonist, shares many—but not all—of the characteristics, experiences, and concerns of his author.

The most recent autobiographical work to date, *Love and Exile,* conjoins three previous works, *A Little Boy in Search of God* (1975), *A Young Man in Search of Love,* and *Lost in America* (1981). It is, however, as the author states in his "Note" which precedes the work, "not the complete story of my life from childhood to my middle thirties, where the book ends." Nevertheless, it is a straightforward, chronological account of his life beginning with his childhood in Warsaw and concluding with his estrangement in America. Three years after he followed his brother, Israel Joshua, to the United States Singer still had difficulty adjusting to life in this strange world.

The first part deals with his home life, his youthful spiritual problems, his search for answers to questions in the Holy Books of his father, and in the secular/philosophical works found in the library, his emulation of his older brother, his growing awareness of his own talents, and his introduction to the diverse intellectual life of Warsaw. The second part begins in Warsaw at the time when he is proofreader for the journal, *Literary Pages.* It is also a time of heightened sexual awakening for him, and in the midst of political turmoil, Singer's various love escapades together with his literary trials unfold. The third part deals with the worsening situation in Poland, the difficulties he encounters in getting to America and in America itself.

All the autobiographical works deal with the same time period: they scan Singer's youthful life in Poland and conclude with his first few years in the United States. The only written record of his later years is to be found in the many interviews that he has granted throughout his lifetime. These are also important for the statements of his critical views.

A recent interview conducted by professors Paul Rosenblatt and Gene Koppel, has been published in book form, *Isaac Bashevis Singer on Literature and Life* (Tucson, AZ: The University of Arizona Press, 1978). In it Singer states his theories concerning modern literature: There is too much discourse in contemporary literature. Fiction, like journalism, should state only the facts. The reader can fill in the explanation for himself. A fiction writer cannot and should not become a spiritual leader. The writer's job is to entertain his readers. Singer believes in Providence, in a world that is not chaotic, and in a God that is good.

Overview of Critical Sources

As popular a writer as Singer is, and for all the interviews, lectures, and articles about him, there are only four book-length studies of his works and two books of critical essays. Of the book-length studies, two are monographs. All the books except one have been published between the years 1968–1972. Only one was published in 1980. While the quality of these works is good, there obviously is much room for current and detailed analyses of this prolific Nobel Laureate.

Evaluation of Selected Criticism

Alexander, Edward, *Isaac Bashevis Singer.* Boston, Twayne, 1980. Alexander's is the most recent study of Singer and is intelligent, sensitive, and well-written. Although his focus is on Singer's novels, there is a chapter devoted to his short stories, as well.

Buchen, Irving H. *Isaac Bashevis Singer and the Eternal Past.* New York: New York University Press, 1968. By far the best critical work, Buchen's study is limited because of its early date. Buchen focuses on Singer's works in relation to biography, Jewish history and literature, and Singer's aesthetics. He suggests that "all Singer's works . . . are informed by the parable of the prodigal son."

Malin, Irving, *Isaac Bashevis Singer.* New York: Frederick Ungar, 1972. Malin, in his monograph, sees the scope of Singer's novels in terms of "open" and "closed." The family sagas belong to the first category because the entire range of human experience in its panoramic expanse and cosmic conception is considered. The "closed" novels telescope a specific "center of consciousness" and are more "claustrophobic and concentrated" in design, focusing on the protagonists' spiritual choices. Malin deals with Singer's early works and devotes a chapter to what he considers the best tales.

Siegel, Ben, *Isaac Bashevis Singer.* Minneapolis: University of Minnesota Press, 1969. Siegel's prose is eminently readable and his criticism is insightful. In this monograph Siegel notes the universal quality in Singer's parochial presentation.

Other Sources

Buchen, Irving H. *Isaac Bashevis Singer and the Eternal Past.* New York: New York University Press, 1958. A well-written, accurate, although brief, biographical treatment of Singer is presented in the first chapter.

Howe, Irving, ed. *Selected Short Stories of Isaac Bashevis Singer.* New York: The Modern Library, 1966. Howe's prefatory essay to this edition is both biographical and critical and is a useful introduction to this selection of stories.

Malin, Irving, ed. *Critical Views of Isaac Bashevis Singer.* New York: New York University Press, 1969. This excellent collection of essays includes two interviews with Singer as well as a vignette by one of his translators.

Studies in American Jewish Literature. Vol. 1, 1981. This issue is devoted to a reconsideration of Isaac Bashevis Singer. The articles, by many noted scholars, cover almost every facet of his work. Of special interest, are the five interviews included at the end of this volume.

Selected Dictionaries and Encyclopedias

Critical Survey of Long Fiction, Salem Press, 1983. Concise biography and brief but incisive analysis of four novels: *Satan in Goray, Magician of Lublin, Enemies, A Love Story,* and *Shosha.*

Dictionary of Literary Biography, Vol. 6. American Novelists Since World War II, Second Series. Gale Research, 1982. A lengthy, thorough article which includes biography, summaries, and analyses of novels.

Dictionary of Literary Biography, Volume 28: Twentieth-Century American-Jewish Fiction Writers. Gale Research, 1984. Concentrates on Singer's "American tales."

Liela H. Goldman
Michigan State University

JOHN SKELTON
1460?–1529

Author's Chronology

Born probably in 1460, perhaps of a Yorkshire family; *1480* a "Skelton" who may be the poet is registered as about to take his B.A. at Cambridge, but is not recorded as receiving it, and may have left for Oxford; *1488* the title of "laureate" may have been granted to him by Oxford, and in the same year he enters the royal service of Henry VII; *1490?* Caxton's Preface to *Eneydos* praises him for skill in translation; *1492* the title of "laureate" conferred on him by Louvain University; *1493* he is crowned "laureate" by Cambridge; *1495* lives chiefly in London or Westminster and begins to assemble the *Garlande of Laurell; 1496* while tutor to Prince Henry he writes several pedagogical works; *1498* he is ordained sub-deacon on March 31, deacon on April 14, and priest on June 9, attached to the Abbey of St. Mary of Graces; *1499* he is praised as the "light and glory of English letters" by Erasmus, whom he may have met; *1502* imprisoned as surety for William Guy, Prior of St. Bartholomew, a debtor; *1503?–1512* resides in Diss, Norfolk, a rector until his death; *1504–1505* probably given another honorary degree by Cambridge; *1509* upon accession of Henry VIII, his former student, he writes *A Lawde and Prayse Made for Our Sovereigne Lord the Kyng,* and presents a copy of *Speculum Principis* to him hinting that he would like to return to court; *1512* writes epitaph for Henry VII to hang as a scroll over his tomb, and he is named "Orator Regius," the king's orator; *1514* engages in debate with Garnesche and is attacked in Barclay's *Eclogues; 1518* lives within the sanctuary of Westminster; *1519* participates in "Grammarians' War" and is described as "neither learned nor a poet" by William Lily, whom he ridiculed; *1521–1522* composes satirical attacks on Cardinal Wolsey; *1523* reconciled with Wolsey; *1529* dies on June 21 and is buried before high altar in St. Margaret's Westminster.

Author's Bibliography (selected)

Upon the Dolorus Dethe and Muche Lamentable Chaunce of the Mooste Honorable Erle of Northumberlande, 1489 (poem); *The Bowge of Courte,* 1498 (poem); *Phyllyp Sparowe,* 1505? (poem); *Calliope,* 1512 (poem); *Magnyfycence,* 1515–1516 (play); *Speke Parott,* 1521 (poem); *Collyn Clout,* 1521–1522 (poem); *Why Come Yet Nat to Courte?,* 1522 (poem); *The Garlande of Laurell,* 1523 (poem).

Overview of Biographical Sources

Through the painstaking efforts of recent literary historians current knowledge of Skelton's life has been greatly enlarged and freed from a number of false assumptions and myths generated in the sixteenth century. Unfortunately

W. L. R. Edwards' often informative work *Skelton, The Life and Times of an Early Tudor Poet* (1949) repeats too many of these errors and is misleading in places. New ground was broken by William Nelson's *John Skelton, Laureate* (1939), in an effort to reexamine documentary evidence, and later biographers have benefited immensely from this study. The two best works by Nelson's successors are Gordon Ian's *John Skelton, Poet Laureate* (Melbourne and London: Melbourne University Press, 1943) and Maurice Pollet's *John Skelton: Poet of Tudor England* (1971). Both biographies combine a sceptical reappraisal of historical evidence with a comprehensive survey of the poet's social and cultural milieu.

Evaluation of Selected Biographies

Edwards, W. L. R. *Skelton.* London: Jonathan Cape, 1949. It is a shame that Edwards accepted at face value far too much of the legendary Skelton that is preserved in the Tudor jest-books, suggesting that he was a renegade priest, disliked by his parishioners at Diss. The author, apart from these difficulties, has written an eminently readable text that carefully integrates Skelton's life and work for general readers. Edwards manages to cover the whole of the poet's career from his days as a "prentice poet" at Cambridge, through his quarrels with literary associates and his satires on Wolsey, up until his final years as a courtier, completing his poetic apology *The Garlande of Laurell.* The biographer modernizes all spelling and also provides translations of Latin quotations. An appendix lists early lives of the poet.

Gordon, Ian, *John Skelton: The Life and Times of an Early Tudor Poet.* Melbourne and London: Melbourne University Press, 1943. This excellent and sympathetic study contains newly discovered biographical information. It focuses on an attempt to relate the poet's life and work to the historical movements of his day—Humanism, the Reformation, and the Renaissance, using the concrete evidence of cathedral and public records. The religious poetry is explored in an attempt to show the orthodox side of the legendary "rebel," and the tale of Skelton's flight from Wolsey to the sanctuary of Westminster is modified. Gordon characterizes Skelton as a man living in an age of transition, between the Middle Ages and the Renaissance, who shows modes of thought linked to both epochs. The chapter on "Skelton and Humanism" is consequently followed by another, "The Faithful Son," which dramatizes the poet's hatred for theologians such as Luther, who argued the need for new creeds. The paradox of Skelton's remaining loyal to the established church and yet attacking current practices of the clergy is then delineated in the following chapter "The Goliard." The concluding sections of this book manage to cover a wide range of topics, including Skelton's morality play, *Magnyfycence,* and his satiric poems against Wolsey. The final chapter traces "The Re-Discovery of Skelton," showing how he has recently emerged from neglect, and it also includes an appreciation of the poet's characteristic verse form—the "Skeltonic" short line. All classes of readers will find this book useful.

Nelson, William, *John Skelton.* New York: Columbia University Press, 1939. This book, written in a remarkably clear style is a model of scholarship aimed at both general readers and specialists. Ian Gordon has called it the "greatest advance in a century of research." Nelson is always cautious about the status of his biographical assertions and has meticulously researched archival materials. Attempting to rescue the poet from the claim that he was an arrogant but incompetent craftsman and scholar, Nelson places him in the context of Renaissance Humanism. He accomplishes this by documenting the circle of scholars at the court of Henry VII, who were Skelton's associates, and manages to make such obscure pedants as Andre, Carmeliano, and Opiciis come to life. The volume itself is actually a collection of essays that follows the poet's career chronologically, emphasizing its major phases. It follows his progress from Diss, to his service at court, the quarrel with other grammarians and with Wolsey, and ends with his final attack on two heretics at Cambridge. Like Gordon, he ends by treating Skelton's reputation, but also adds commentary on his influence. A chronology of the poet's works is appended.

Pollet, Maurice, *John Skelton: Poet of Tudor England.* London: J. M. Dent, 1971. Translated from the French by John Warrington, this volume furnishes yet another valuable survey of Skelton's life and achievements. One of the virtues of Pollet's account, especially valuable for scholars, is his interest in presenting both positive and negative aspects of the poet's accomplishments. Pollet judges Skelton to be situated at an important juncture in literary history between Chaucer and Spenser, in the generation of Caxton, writing under the last Plantagenet monarch. He also considers him to be a "national" poet, symbolic of England's awakening between the War of Roses and the Reformation. Viewed essentially as a cleric-poet, Skelton's learning is seen as extensive rather than profound. His satire both lashes his contemporaries in an aggressive manner and serves as a branch of didactic literature, reasoned in a way that is both logical and harsh, orthodox and excessive. This attention to the extremes in Skelton's method of self-presentation gives this rendering of his life both depth and persuasiveness. Pollet's historical detective-work contributes to a clearer sense of the poet's geographical and social settings as well as placing his reconciliation with Wolsey in the context of a more specific political situation.

Autobiographical Sources

Much of Skelton's work appears to have been triggered by actual events in his own life, but it is always important to keep in mind the difference between historical events and their reconstruction within a literary medium. Romantic biographers, for instance, interpret *The Bowge of Courte* literally, as the poet's farewell to the corrupt court that attempted to undo him. The leap overboard in this sense represents his retirement to Diss. But this fails to account for the fact that Skelton continued to live within the same society he would still deride for five years. Other poems, like that *Agenst Garnesche* (1514), supply important information about the poet, such as his receiving the "laureate" status for which he prides himself. But, by far the most central work in this vein is *The Garlande of Laurell,* a poetic defense of his learning and literary achievement that includes a lengthy list of his works, some now lost, and an unabashed hymn to his own accomplishments. Through it, he places himself in literary history, in the tradition of Geoffrey Chaucer, John Gower, and John Lydgate.

Overview of Critical Sources

From the Elizabethan period to the beginning of the twentieth century, critical estimation of Skelton's poetry has been so severe that renewed interest in his work is a small miracle. Those sympathetic to his vigorous and creative wit have had to labor against Pope's condemnation of "beastly Skelton." This has caused much of the scholarship to be apologetic, in an attempt to prove his classical knowledge and define the Humanist traditions he employs. Literary analysis has centered specifically on the sources of his satire in both classical and medieval prototypes. The extent to which topical allusions appear in his writing has also constituted one of the fundamental questions for literary historians. The formal analysis of the "Skeltonic" line and the technical question of its derivation and use by the poet is the third question that has engaged his critics. The definition of his poetics is for the most part still a matter of debate, and questions of the poems' structural integrity are vital to scholarship.

Evaluation of Selected Criticism

Edwards, Anthony, *Skelton, The Critical Heritage.* London: Routledge and Kegan Paul, 1981. Edwards has collected a large selection of commentary on Skelton's life and work from his time to our own.

Fish, Stanley, *John Skelton's Poetry.* New Haven: Yale University Press, 1965. Fish analyzes the philosophical aspects in Skelton's poems, seeing them as a verbal dramatization of the problem of moral action. By explicating Skelton's use of lyrics and rhetoric, Fish demonstrates how Skelton's poetry is a psychological or spiritual history of its protagonist, doubt-torn and questing, but returning to an order reasserted by the process.

Harris, William, *Skelton's* Magnyfycence *and the Cardinal Virtue Tradition.* Chapel Hill: University of North Carolina Press, 1965. Harris argues that the two morality conflicts in the play—temptations in prosperity and adversity—are based on the cardinal virtue of Fortitude, sometimes called Magnificence or Magnanimity. The tradition clarifies Skelton's term which is often related to an Aristotelian category in the *Ethics.* Harris rejects this premise and the notion that the play contains Wolseyan satire. By perceptively re-examining the play and placing its terms in a medieval rather than a classical context, Harris sees the play as organically conceived, and resolves certain cruxes of interpretation.

Heiserman, Anthony, *Skelton and Satire.* Chicago: Chicago University Press, 1961. In this historical critique of Skelton's satires and critical history of the traditions of medieval satire from which they derived, Heiserman fuses criticism with history, and controls both with a concept of poetic form. His systematic overview of Skelton's major works demonstrates a discernible mixture of structural devices, appropriate personae, and diction. Heiserman shows how Skelton relies on conventions to control his audience, and proves that Skelton begins and ends as an "official" poet whose office is to attack national enemies while entertaining and informing the court. This is a masterful study necessary for a richer reading of Skelton's often difficult allusions.

Other Sources
Kinsman, Robert and Theodore Young, *John Skelton: Canon and Census.* NY: Published for the Renaissance Society of America by Monographic Press, 1967. Compiled to supply a satisfactory account of Skelton's writings and early printed editions of his work to 1600.

Kinsman, Robert, *John Skelton, Early Tudor Laureate, An Annotated Bibliography, c. 1488–1977.* Boston: G. K. Hall, 1979. Extensive listing of scholarly research with comments.

Selected Dictionaries and Encyclopedias
Dictionary of National Biography, Smith, Elder, and Company, 1893. Concise summary of Skelton's career that is often useful, but which contains some inaccuracies. Most university libraries have an edition of this work.

James P. Bednarz
Long Island University

C. P. SNOW
1905–1980

Author's Chronology

Born Charles Percy Snow, October 15, 1905, Leicester, England, in a lower middle-class family; *1925* entered University College of Leicester on a scholarship; *1927* graduates with First Class Honours in chemistry; *1928* receives Master of Science degree in physics; *1930* receives Ph.D. from Christ's College, Cambridge and is elected Fellow of the College; *1932* publishes first novel, *Death Under Sail; 1939* appointed to a committee that organized scientists for the war effort; continues this work with the Ministry of Labour during World War II; *1940* publishes *Strangers and Brothers,* the first volume of a series of novels; *1943* made a Commander of the Order of the British Empire; *1945* becomes a Civil Service Commissioner; *1950* marries the novelist Pamela Hansford Johnson; leaves position at Cambridge; *1952* son Philip born; *1957* knighted; *1959* gives the Rede Lectures at Cambridge, published as *The Two Cultures and the Scientific Revolution; 1964* made a Life Peer, Baron Snow of the City of Leicester, and serves the Labour Government for two years as Parliamentary Secretary of the Ministry of Technology; *1970* publishes *Last Things,* the final volume in the series; *1979* publishes his last novel, *A Coat of Varnish;* July 1, 1980 dies in London.

Author's Bibliography (selected)

Novels: *Death Under Sail,* 1932; *New Lives for Old,* 1933; *The Search,* 1934; *Strangers and Brothers,* 1940, retitled *George Passant,* 1972; *The Light and the Dark,* 1947; *Time of Hope,* 1948; *The Masters,* 1951; *The New Men,* 1954; *Homecomings,* American edition titled *Homecoming,* 1956; *The Conscience of the Rich,* 1958; *The Affair,* 1960; *Corridors of Power,* 1964; *The Sleep of Reason,* 1968; *Last Things,* 1970; *The Malcontents,* 1972; *In Their Wisdom,* 1974; *A Coat of Varnish,* 1978. Non-Fiction: *The Two Cultures and the Scientific Revolution,* 1959; *Trollope: His Life and Art,* 1975; *The Realists. Portraits of Eight Novelists: Stendhal, Balzac, Dickens, Dostoevsky, Tolstoy, Galdós, Henry James, Proust,* 1978.

Overview of Biographical Sources

Snow's life was unusual in its combination of work in science, public administration, political administration, political activity and controversy, and literary creativity. Nevertheless, in spite of this mixture, and the interesting relationship between his life and his novels, relatively little biographical work has appeared. Typically, books about Snow discuss his work rather than his life. There is yet no definitive biography. However, three books are important for an understanding of Snow's life: the memoirs by his wife, Pamela Hansford Johnson, the informal biography by his brother, Philip Snow, and John Halperin's edited interviews with Snow. Additionally, certain novels by Snow's close friend William Cooper (Harry Hoff) use the younger Snow as a prototype; he is, e.g., the basis for Robert in *Scenes from Provincial Life* (1950).

Evaluation of Selected Biographies

Halperin, John, *C. P. Snow: An Oral Biography*. New York: St. Martin's, 1983. Based on some sixteen hours of taped conversations, between March 1978 and June 1980, Halperin's work gives Snow's responses to a wide-ranging series of questions and comments. Topics include Snow's life, his writing practices and theories, each of his novels, and prototypes of his fictional characters. Halperin provides a preface, some footnotes, and a conversation with Lady Snow. As Halperin brings understanding, curiosity, and his own ideas to the interviews, he evokes many interesting comments from Snow. One must remember that Snow's memory, while generally excellent, is capable of some lapses and of being self-serving; with this caveat, this book is an indispensable source of biographical information.

Johnson, Pamela Hansford, *Important to Me: Personalia*. New York: Macmillan, 1974. In this collection of autobiographical essays, Johnson touches on such matters as her marriage to Snow, their travels together, Snow's eye operations, and his attitude towards his son. Her candid recollections provide a useful source for some comparisons between Snow and his fictional persona Lewis Eliot.

Snow, Philip, *Stranger and Brother: A Portrait of C. P. Snow*. New York: Charles Scribner's Sons, 1982. This book is very useful as an "informal picture" of Snow by his youngest brother. As the two were close throughout much of Snow's life, and as Philip Snow is quite forthcoming with a balanced view of his older brother, this account seems accurate and truthful. It contains photographs, letters written by Snow, and a valuable list of identifications of the real-life sources for characters in Snow's novels.

Autobiographical Sources

Although Snow wrote no autobiography as such, in his extensive output of non-fiction and in published interviews, various autobiographical recollections occasionally emerge. They are too brief and scattered to cite here; the interested reader may attempt to track them down with the help of Paul Boytinck's *C. P. Snow: A Reference Guide* (1980). Additionally, Halperin's work is "autobiographical" in that it presents Snow's own words about his life.

The novels themselves provide the major autobiographical source, especially as Lewis Eliot, the central figure in the *Strangers and Brothers* series, is modeled on Snow himself (as is, to a lesser extent, Arthur Miles in *The Search*). One must always remember, though, that Eliot is a fictional creation who cannot be automatically equated with Snow; Philip Snow's *Stranger and Brother* is a useful guide in comparing the fictional Eliot to the actual Snow.

Overview of Critical Sources

Throughout his long career, Snow remained a controversial figure; criticism of his work has tended to be more partisan than objectively analytical. No general agreement as to his abilities and standing appears imminent. Much of the dispute that Snow engendered was related to his views on politics and society, and much debate was produced over the still unresolved issues he raised in *The Two Cultures*. The criticism of Snow as novelist has raised a similar disagreement about his worth.

The quality of Snow's psychological insight, manifested in his characterization, and the effectiveness of his generally unadorned style, have been the major points at issue. The division is between critics who find Snow a worthy continuer of the realistic tradition, and those who consider both his techniques and subject matter second-rate. The former critics, such as Jerome Thrale, defend Snow's insight into socially conditioned character and the clarity of his style; his detractors, such as Rubin Rabinovitz, attack Snow's flat style, his lack of technical innovation, and the over-simplification of his characterization.

Evaluation of Selected Criticism

Boytinck, Paul, *C. P. Snow: A Reference Guide*. Boston: G. K. Hall, 1980. Boytinck provides an introduction that discusses "Snow's Literary Credo," "The Reception of His Fiction," and "The Question of Style," then followed by a bibliography listing both Snow's own work, including book reviews, and works about Snow. The entries are briefly annotated. The work is generally quite accurate and complete, and invaluable to anyone doing serious work on Snow.

Karl, Frederick R. *C. P. Snow: The Politics of Conscience*. Carbondale: Southern University Press, 1963. Karl sees a "moral principle" as the center of Snow's work, and discusses structure and style in the novels. Although generally favorable to Snow, Karl recognizes stylistic problems and some social and psychological over-simplification in the novels. This is a serious and insightful early study.

Rabinovitz, Rubin, "C. P. Snow as Novelist," in *The Reaction Against Experiment in the English Novel, 1950–1960*. New York: Columbia University Press, 1967. Rabinovitz attacks Snow's "flat" style, deterministic themes, superficial characterization, and banal plotting. Rabinovitz has read Snow carefully; his criticisms, as the most thoughtful of the attacks on Snow's novels, should not be ignored.

Shusterman, David, *C. P. Snow*. New York: Twayne, 1975. Useful for its summaries of Snow's work, this short study avoids taking a clear critical stance, or making significant or controversial interpretations.

Thrale, Jerome, *C. P. Snow*. Edinburgh and London: Oliver and Boyd, 1964. Thrale sees Snow's main appeal to be his "wordly pragmatism." The overall structure of the series, through *The Affair,* is discussed. This brief book is particularly interesting for its defense, in some detail, of Snow's "clear" style.

Other Sources
Cooper, William, *C. P. Snow*. London: Longmans, Green, 1957. A pamphlet, written by an old friend of Snow's, that defends the "verbal texture" of Snow's style.

Morris, Robert K. "C. P. Snow, Strangers and Brothers: The Morality of History," in *Continuance and Change: The Contemporary British Novel Sequence.* Carbondale: Southern Illinois University Press, 1972. Brief but interesting comments on Snow's "resonance" technique, and the role of morality and reason in the *Strangers and Brothers* series.

Ramanthan, Suguna, *The Novels of C. P. Snow*. New York: Charles Scribner's Sons, 1978. Although written from a hero-worshipping approach, this study has some interesting insights mixed in.

Selected Dictionaries and Encyclopedias
Critical Survey of Long Fiction, Salem Press, 1983. Concise biography, and overview of Snow's fiction, and brief analyses of selected novels.

Dictionary of Literary Biography, Gale Research, 1983. Snow's life and works summarized; illustrated.

William B. Stone
Indiana University Northwest

ROBERT SOUTHWELL
1561–1595

Author's Chronology

Born 1561 at Horsham St. Faith's in Norfolk, England of Sir Richard and Bridget (Copley) Southwell; *1576* sent secretly to the English College, Belgian Netherlands to be educated at the nearby Jesuit school; *1577* requests admission to the Society of Jesus (Jesuits); rejected because of his youth; transfers to Rome where he is admitted to the Society the next year (1578); *1579* studies at the Roman College; *1580* makes vows in the Society; *1581* transfers to the English College at Rome; *1584* ordained priest; *1586* serves at the English College as tutor, later as prefect of English students; *1586* accepts the English mission; July 7, *1586* lands secretly with fellow-Jesuit Henry Garnet near Folkestone, England; *1586–1592* ministers to English Catholics using Arundel House in London as a base; writes several prose works and sixty poems of devotional and didactic character; supervises publication of some from a secret press; *1592* betrayed and captured by government agents; *1592–1595* tortured ten times and imprisoned for three years in the Tower of London; February 20, *1595* tried and condemned to death; executed the following day at Tyburn; *1970* declared a saint by Pope Paul VI.

Author's Bibliography (selected)

An Epistle of Comfort, 1587–1588 (prose); *Mary Magdalens Funerall Teares,* 1592 (prose); *The Triumphs over Death,* 1596 (prose); *A Four-fold Meditation on the Four Laste Things,* 1606 (prose); *The Dutiful Advice of a Loving Son to His Aged Father,* 1632 (prose); *A Short Rule of Good Life,* 1598 (prose); *The Poems of Robert Southwell, S. J.,* 1967.

Overview of Biographical Sources

Christopher Devlin's *Life of Robert Southwell, Poet and Martyr* (1956), is a scholarly biography of a brother-Jesuit. His account reaches a peak of inspiration that may call into question the author's objectivity. But the life Southwell was heroic in the extreme. His preoccupation with moral perfection, his yearning for the hazardous mission to England, his passion for martyrdom, lure the biographer to heights where only superlatives suffice.

Biographers of Southwell owe a great debt to Henry More's *Historia missionis Anglicanae Societatis Jesus,* translated by Francis Edwards under the title, *The Elizabethan Jesuits of Henry More* (1981). More describes Southwell's missionary activities on behalf of Elizabethan Catholics. More uses eye-witness accounts of the trial and death of Southwell.

Evaluation of Selected Biographies

Devlin, Christopher, *The Life of Robert Southwell, Poet and Martyr.* New York: Farrar, Cudahy and Straus, 1956. Devlin reveals in his foreword his predominant interest in Southwell as a person. It is an heroic figure that emerges from the page. Devlin justifies every encomium through careful documentation. He emphasizes too the literary aspects of Southwell's career, because Southwell casts his teaching in poetic form for the religious education and spiritual nourishment of his Catholic compatriots, so sorely deprived of religious literature. The vogue his works enjoyed after his execution—there were sixteen editions within forty years of his death—demonstrates his popularity among Catholics and Protestants alike.

Devlin makes a plausible case for connections between Southwell's *Mary Magdalens Funerall Teares* and Thomas Nashe's *Christ's Tears over Jerusalem.* Thomas Lodge in his poem, "Tears of the Mother of God" (1596), openly acknowledges his familiarity with Southwell's poems. More interesting still, Devlin explores the similarities between Southwell's and Shakespeare's verses. While Shakespeare's are clearly superior, Southwell's verses, Devlin suggests, seem to have "roused Shakespeare to a loftier conception of the divine spark within himself."

More, Henry, *The Elizabethan Jesuits of Henry More.* trans./ed. Francis Edwards. London: Phillimore, 1981. Henry More is Sir Thomas More's great grandson. He was a Jesuit, sometime provincial of the English provinces, always a scholar. Historians are in More's debt for his study of the Jesuit archives in Rome. In regard to Southwell, he discovered two letters of Henry Garnet, Southwell's superior in the English mission, who gives an eye-witness account of Southwell's death at Tyburn.

Tierney, M.A. "Of Father Southwell's Coming to Live with Her." ed. C. A. Newdigate, S. J. *The Month,* 57 (March 1931), 246–254. This account of Southwell's sojourn in the Arundel household is contained in *The Lives of Philip Howard, Earl of Arundel and of Anne Dacres, His Wife,* compiled by the family chaplain several years after Southwell's death. It reveals the straitness of Southwell's life in the Arundel household, probably in their London home close to the Tower. Only two or three of the most trusted servants were aware of the small, secret room constructed especially for him. His presence was a constant danger to Anne, for it was a capital offense to shelter a priest. The Earl himself was a prisoner in the Tower and ultimately died there for the same offense. Southwell probably wrote most of his poems during his period of confinement, as well as his *Epistle of Comfort for the Earl* and the *Short Rule for a good Life* for the Countess.

Autobiographical Sources

Southwell left no autobiography, but his letters in the Jesuit archives in Rome reveal his activities, especially during the English mission (1586–1592). They are translated and published in volume five of the *Catholic Record Society Publications.*

The Spiritual Exercises and Devotions of Blessed Robert Southwell, S. J., ed.

J. M. de Buck, S. J. (London, 1931), with English translation by P. E. Hallet, covers the period from Southwell's entrance into the Society of Jesus (1578) to his departure for the English mission (1586).

Overview of Critical Sources

Southwell's critics universally recognize that his life as a Jesuit and his mission to beleagured Catholics in England determine the use of his gifts as a writer. He is credited with initiating religious, meditative verse which would be developed more fully by Donne and Crashaw.

Southwell's critics note how he was limited by the poetic style of the day; he was preoccupied with conceits, inversions and alliteration. He was further limited by the didactic character of his writings. Likewise, his prose too reflects the literary fashion of his time. "Its euphuistic redundancy and artificial constructions," Sidney Lee claims, "deprive it of permanent literary value."

Evaluation of Selected Criticism

Janelle, Pierre, *Robert Southwell, the Writer: A Study in Religious Inspiration.* Mamaroneck, NY: P. P. Appel, 1971. Janelle gives a competent account of Southwell's life, using the sources adequately. He recognizes that Southwell's poetry and most significant prose all fall within the narrow space of six years. As a consequence, and doubtless as a result of adhering closely to the meters, vocabulary and style of the day, there is not evidence of any striking development of style.

Janelle states that "from the date of Southwell's arrival in England, none of his manuscripts are extant; his works were generally published long after being written." Their appearance in print, Janelle points out, does not correspond to the order of their composition. With the exception of *An Humble Petition to Her Majesty* which can be dated with considerable certainty in December 1591, there are no helpful references to contemporary events to ascertain the date of composition.

McDonald, James H. C.S.C. and Nancy Pollard Brown. *The Poems of Robert Southwell, S.J.* Oxford: Clarendon Press, 1967. In addition to a critical edition of Southwell's poetry, the primary focus of the work, Brown gives extensive introductions which describe and evaluate Southwell under the headings of "General Introduction," an excellent biographical account; "Textual Introduction," describing the manuscripts and editions. The first edition of the poems appeared in March, 1595, immediately following Southwell's death. No authoritative edition appeared among the sixteen early editions mentioned by Morton. It is impossible however, to distinguish between the work of the editor and the plans Southwell had made. The surviving manuscripts "preserve a record of spiritual teaching set in an effective order to guide the English Catholic . . . The printed books are designed for a wider public . . . for ecclesiastical approval and for their appeal to their purchasers."

Morton, Sister Rose Anita, S.S.J. *An Appreciation of Robert Southwell, S.J.* Philadelphia: University of Pennsylvania Press, 1929. In this first full-length study of Southwell's writings, Morton analyzes in careful detail his style, his subject matter, his strengths and weaknesses as a religious poet. She considers Shakespeare's use of Southwell's images as merely another example of his free use of any author's ideas, chronicles and plots. She does not distinguish between wholesale borrowing and the more subtle and flattering imitation of Southwell's images which Shakespeare often enough develops to a higher poetic level.

Consuelo M. Aherne, S.S.J.
Chestnut Hill College

MURIEL SPARK
1918

Author's Chronology

Born 1918 in Edinburgh, Scotland of a Jewish father and Presbyterian mother; attends James Gillespie's Girls' School in Edinburgh, forming impressions later to be used in *The Prime of Miss Jean Brodie; 1937* moves to Africa where she marries and has son, Robin; *1944* after divorce, returns to England; works for British Intelligence Service based in London; after the war she joins jewelry trade magazine, *Argentor; 1947* becomes Secretary and Editor for the Poetry Society; *1949* publishes her own magazine, *Forum,* which fails after only two issues; *1949* collaborates with poet Derek Stanford on editions of Cardinal Newman and Mary Shelley, and books on Wordsworth and Emily Brontë in a partnership lasting until 1956; *1951* wins the *Observor* short story contest with her first fictional publication, "The Seraph and the Zambesi;" *1952* prints her first collection of poems, *The Fanfarlo and Other Verse; 1954* received into the Roman Catholic Church by Father Philip Caraman, editor of *The Month; 1957* publishes her first novel, *The Comforters; 1960* Thomas More Association awards medal to J. B. Lippincott Company for publishing Spark; *1961* on a visit to Israel observes the Adolf Eichmann trial which serves as a central motif in *The Mandelbaum Gate; 1962* wins Italia Prize for radio adaptation of *The Ballad of Peckham Rye; 1962* goes to the United States for a period of three years; *1966* takes up residence in Rome; *1966* receives James Tait Black Memorial Prize for *The Mandelbaum Gate; 1967* honored by inclusion in the Order of the British Empire.

Author's Bibliography (selected)

Child of Light: A Reassessment of Mary Wollstonecraft Shelley, 1951 (criticism); *The Fanfarlo and Other Verse,* 1952; *John Masefield,* 1953 (criticism); *The Comforters,* 1957 (novel); *The Go-Away Bird and Other Stories,* 1963; *Memento Mori,* 1959 (novel); *Voices at Play: Stories and Earpieces,* 1962; *The Prime of Miss Jean Brodie,* 1961 (novel); *Doctors of Philosophy,* 1963 (play); *The Mandelbaum Gate,* 1965 (novel); *Collected Poems I,* 1967; *Collected Stories I,* 1967; *The Very Fine Clock,* 1969 (children's literature); *The Driver's Seat,* 1970 (novel); *The Hothouse by the East River,* 1973 (novel); *The Abbess of Crewe,* 1974 (novel); *The Takeover,* 1976 (novel); *Loitering with Intent,* 1981 (novel); *The Only Problem,* 1984 (novel).

Overview of Biographical Sources

A few of the critical books and articles on Spark's fiction offer brief biographical details, but no attempt at a full-length study of her life has yet been made. Although Spark is certainly prolific, with thirty-one books to her credit, she is still relatively young, and without doubt biographers at some time will gather enough material for extended examination. The Washington University Libraries in St. Louis, Missouri have begun a Muriel Spark Collection of Letters which should prove to be invaluable to researchers.

Evaluation of Selected Biographies

Stanford, Derek, *Muriel Spark: A Biographical and Critical Study*. London: Centaur Press Ltd., 1963. The publisher's apologetic Foreward clearly indicates his reticence to produce a book by someone displaying such considerable personal admiration for his subject. Stanford admits that he is not writing a biography, but a highly subjective memoir or reminiscence, and he is committed more to his own feelings than to accuracy of dates or scholarly criticism. The book, however, reveals Spark in her formative literary years and gives many insights into her commitment as a creative writer. In a chatty, off-handed style, Stanford also tells of Spark's relationships with such authors as George Fraser, John Heath-Stubbs, Gabriel Fielding, and George Woodcock. Although Stanford acknowledges the stylistic influences of Scottish Border Ballads, Max Beerbohm, Marcel Proust, Cardinal Newman, and John Stuart Mill, he insists that much of Spark's fictional substance is autobiographical and constitutes "an imaginative denial of her roots."

Autobiographical Sources

Unlike many writers, Muriel Spark takes great care in hiding her personal life and is reluctant either to write or speak about it. In her book *The Faith and Fiction of Muriel Spark* (New York: St. Martin's Press, 1982), Ruth Whittaker argues that Spark hoards the material of her life to use it sparingly in her fiction. Certainly *The Comforters, The Prime of Miss Jean Brodie,* and *Loitering with Intent* are obvious attempts at transforming the impressions and incidents of her past into the realm of art.

Spark's most significant confession is found in "My Conversion," *Twentieth Century,* CLXX (Autumn 1961), 58–63. In this brief monologue prompted by W. J. Weatherby, she credits Cardinal Newman and the Catholic Church for giving her a definite location and a norm from which to write. Before the conversion, she claims her mind was in disorder, but within the security of the Church is able to produce her best work.

Overview of Critical Sources

Much of the critical analysis of Spark has been individual articles, which often focus on the triviality and insincerity of her work. Some books and monographs, however, treat her as an important novelist deserving more serious consideration.

Evaluation of Selected Criticism

Kemp, Peter, *Muriel Spark*. London: Paul Elek, 1974. The first substantial examination of Spark's novels, it still remains the best in the field. Rather than seeing Spark as merely a fine technician, concerned mainly with form, Kemp realizes that her controlling metaphysical viewpoint gives unusual depth and variety to her fiction.

Whittaker, Ruth, *The Faith and Fiction of Muriel Spark*. New York: St. Martin's Press, 1982. Whittaker regards Spark as a religious but non-doctrinaire social satirist who dissects the absurdity of the temporal world. She focuses more on the humanity of Spark's characters than Kemp does, and makes many astute observations.

Other Sources

Bold, Alan, ed. *Muriel Spark: An Odd Capacity for Vision*. Totowa, NJ: Barnes & Noble, 1984. A comprehensive set of essays covering Spark's early work, an analysis of her female characters, her use of the apologia, and the distinctive nature of the supernatural in her writing.

Bradbury, Malcolm, *Possibilities: Essays on the State of the Novel*. London: Oxford, 1973. Includes an essay on Spark's metaphysical modernism and formal detachment which separates her from traditional Catholic humanism.

Kermode, Frank, *Modern Essays*. London: Fontana, 1971. Three extensive reviews of *The Girls of Slender Means, The Mandelbaum Gate,* and *The Public Image*. One of the first major critics to treat Spark as a serious writer, Kermode argues that her integration of technique and meaning gives the novels formidable power even to a secular audience.

Lodge, David, *The Novelist at the Crossroads and Other Essays on Fiction and Criticism*. London: Routledge & Keegan Paul, 1971. A long, detailed article on *The Prime of Miss Jean Brodie* which emphasizes the subtlety of the prose.

Malkoff, Karl, *Muriel Spark*. New York and London: Columbia University Press, 1968. Monograph with selected bibliography and short biography. Focuses on the compatibility of Spark's method and her religious views.

James C. MacDonald
Humber College

STEPHEN SPENDER
1909

Author's Chronology

Born February 28, 1909, London, England, to Harold Spender, a liberal journalist, and Hilda Spender, a poet and painter; *1928* attends University College, Oxford; meets W. H. Auden and Christopher Isherwood; prints first collection of poems, *Nine Experiments; 1930* leaves Oxford without a degree; travels to Germany with Isherwood; *1936* briefly joins Communist Party; marries Agnes (Inez) Pearn, an Oxford student; *1937* travels to Spain during the Civil War to promote the anti-Fascist cause; *1939* separates from his wife; *1939–1941* joins Cyril Connolly as co-editor of *Horizon; 1941* marries Natasha Litvin, a pianist; *1942* joins the Auxiliary Fire Service; *1953–1966* co-editor of *Encounter;* resigns upon disclosure of CIA funding given to the journal; *1971* receives Queen's Gold Medal for Poetry; *1973* receives Honorary Fellowship to University College, Oxford; *1970–1975* holds Chair of English Literature at University College, London; *1985* continues to hold visiting positions in both England and America.

Author's Bibliography (selected)

Nine Experiments, 1928 (poems); *Twenty Poems,* 1930; *Poems,* 1933, revised and enlarged, 1934; *Vienna,* 1934 (poems); *The Destructive Element: A Study of Modern Writers and Beliefs,* 1935 (criticism); *The Still Centre,* 1939 (poems); *Selected Poems,* 1940; *Ruins and Visions,* 1942 (poems); *Poems of Dedication,* 1947; *The Edge of Being,* 1949 (poems); *World Within World,* 1951 (autobiography); *Collected Poems, 1928–1953,* 1955.

Biographical Sources

There is no complete biography of Spender. Biographical information can be gathered from the book-length criticism, which without exception draws on the events of the poet's life—particularly during the 1930's—to support its analyses. Most of the information in this criticism, though, is itself drawn from Spender's autobiography, *World Within World,* which remains the most complete source of information about his life. Additional material can be found in the reminiscences of Spender's contemporaries, like Louis MacNeice's *The Strings Are False: an Unfinished Autobiography* (1966), and Christopher Isherwood's *Lions and Shadows* (1947).

Autobiographical Sources

Spender makes it clear that the motivation behind writing his autobiography, *World Within World,* is related closely to the concerns of his poetry; autobiography, for him, becomes a kind of affirmation of the "I," a statement of faith in the individual conscience and its significance in the modern world. Spender argues that making moral decisions requires this acceptance of personal identity and responsibility, and his book is both a product of this idea and a description of the events in his life that led him to it.

World Within World covers the years between 1928 and the early 1940's, years that include his attendance at Oxford, his travels in Germany, his journey to Spain during the Civil War, his two marriages, and his duty with the Fire Service. This information is mixed with reminiscences of figures like Auden and Virginia and Leonard Woolf, and the whole makes for engaging reading and an interesting picture of the literary atmosphere of the 1930's. The autobiography should be supplemented by *The Thirties and After: Poetry, Politics, People 1933–1970* (New York: Random House, 1978). Spender devotes each section of this book to a decade in his life, and prefaces each with a "Background" essay that discusses his own activities during the years covered by that particular section.

Overview of Critical Sources

The book-length studies of Spender that have emerged in the last fifteen years agree in calling the 1930's the most productive and interesting years of his long career, and in citing *Poems* and *The Still Centre* as his strongest work. He is commonly grouped with Auden, Louis MacNeice, and C. Day Lewis in discussions of "the thirties poets" who, it is argued, moved away from the more pastoral and introspective verse of their immediate predecessors toward a poetry of greater social urgency and commitment. Much of the criticism draws on Spender's prose writings in describing his struggle to define the proper relationship between the poet and the world; and because Spender is concerned with connecting poet and world, his own work tends to be discussed in the context of his age. Though the critical reception of the poems is sometimes lukewarm, Spender is admired for the integrity with which he explores the place of the poet in the modern world.

Evaluation of Selected Criticism

Kulkarni, H. B. *Stephen Spender: Poet in Crisis.* London: Blackie & Son, 1970. The first complete study of Spender's work in the context of the age, Kulkarni's discussion centers on the conflict between the artist's individualism and the demands of social responsibility. The first section is largely a biographical account of how this conflict came to have its place in Spender's poems, while the following sections draw on Spender's prose to demonstrate his resolution of that conflict.

Pandey, Surya Nath, *Stephen Spender: A Study in Poetic Growth.* Atlantic Highlands, NJ: Humanities Press, 1982. Like Kulkarni, Pandey identifies a tension between the poet as visionary and the poet as a man of social commitment. He divides Spender's career into three phases, the first marked by an emotional lyricism, the second by public turmoil and the appeal of Marxism, and the third by an increasing introspection. Pandey begins with a chapter on the climate of the thirties and traces Spender's development through *The Generous Days* (1971).

Weatherhead, A. Kingsley, *Stephen Spender and the Thirties.* Lewisburg, PA: Bucknell University Press, 1975. This is the most thorough study of Spender to date. Weatherhead provides an in-depth look at the literary thirties by examining a number of the periodicals and anthologies of the day, and by considering Spender's relationship to some of the decade's more minor poets like Michael Roberts and Geoffrey Grigson. His chapter on "Repudiating the Georgians" provides an interesting background to the thirties poets' attitude toward nature. Spender's poems, in Weatherhead's view, are more "pure," more divorced from the objective, external world, than is commonly supposed.

Other Sources

Connors, J. J. *Poets and Politics: A Study of the Careers of C. Day Lewis, Stephen Spender, & W. H. Auden in the 1930's.* New Haven: Yale University Press, 1967. Emphasizes Spender's prose and his involvement with Communism.

Daiches, David, *Poetry and the Modern World.* Chicago: University of Chicago Press, 1940. Contrasts Spender's lyric simplicity with Auden's more interesting use of ambiguity.

Hynes, Samuel, *The Auden Generation: Literature and Politics in England in the 1930s.* New York: Viking, 1977. Places Spender among his contemporaries in describing the major literary and political developments of the 1930's.

Stanford, Derek, *Stephen Spender, Louis MacNeice, Cecil Day Lewis: A Critical Essay.* Grand Rapids: William B. Eerdmans, 1969. A contribution to the "Writers in a Christian Perspective" series, this essay speaks of Spender's imaginative and emotional charity as the characteristic of his poetry most appealing to the Christian mind.

Selected Dictionaries and Encyclopedias

Critical Survey of Poetry, Salem Press, 1982. Brief biography, summary of achievements, and analysis of major poetry and prose.

Dictionary of Literary Biography. Gale Research, 1983. Selected bibliography of primary and secondary works, brief biography, and discussion of major poetry and prose.

Steven Reese
University of Delaware

EDMUND SPENSER
1552? – 1599

Author's Chronology

Born probably in 1552 to Elizabeth and John Spenser, a clothmaker; *1561* is likely to be the year in which he enters the Merchant Taylors' school; *1569* six of his translations from Petrarch and fourteen of Du Bellay are published in Van der Noodt's *A Theatre for Worldings;* in the same year he goes up to Pembroke Hall, Cambridge, as a "sizar" or scholarship student; *1576* M.A. from Cambridge, visits the north country of his family, and falls in love with "Rosalind" of *The Shepheardes Calender;* *1578* serves as Latin secretary to John Young, Bishop of Rochester; *1578* he temporarily becomes a member of the household at Leicester House; *1579* expects to be sent abroad, and meets Sir Philip Sidney, who is experimenting with classical meters in poetry; begins *The Faerie Queene;* *1580* appointed secretary to Lord Grey de Wilton, lord deputy of Ireland, views the Smerwick massacre in that country; *1582* signs himself as being "of New Abbey," in county Kildare for the next two years; *1583* commissioner for musters in the same county; *1588* resigns post as clerk of the court of chancery and becomes clerk of the council of Munster; settles on the Kilcolman estate; *1589* Lord Roche accuses him of mistreating neighboring servants; visits England with Sir Walter Raleigh and licenses *The Faerie Queene;* *1591* leaves England, having received a pension and lease from Queene Elizabeth; *1594* marries Elizabeth Boyle in Youghal (she is his second wife); *1596* James VI of Scotland complains of the treatment of his mother as "Duessa" in the second part of *The Faerie Queene;* Spenser returns to England as associates with the Earl of Essex; *1597* returns to Kilcolman; Hugh O'Neill rises in rebellion; Spenser appointed sheriff of Cork, but never serves; *1598* Kilcolman burnt and he flees to Cork; *1599* dies on January 16, entombed next to Chaucer in Westminster Abbey.

Author's Bibliography (selected)

The Shepheardes Calender, 1579 (poem); *The Faerie Queene,* 1590 and 1596 (epic); *Colin Clouts Come Home Againe,* 1591 (poem); *Complaints,* 1591 (collection of poems); *Epithalamion* and *Amoretti,* 1595 (wedding song and sonnet sequence); "Mutability Cantos," 1609 (fragment of *The Faerie Queene*).

Overview of Biographical Sources

Much valuable information concerning Spenser's life, attitudes, literary models, and historical background can be gleaned from the standard edition of Spenser's writing: *Works, A Variorum Edition,* edited by Charles Osgood and Frederick Padelford (Baltimore: Johns Hopkins Press, 1932–1949). The *Variorum* consists of nine volumes of text and commentary, including line-by-line annotation and short essays, many on "historical allusions." The best full-length biography was published with the *Variorum:* Alexander Judson's *The Life of Edmund Spenser* (Baltimore: Johns Hopkins Press, 1945). Although there are some difficulties in ascertaining the facts of the poet's life, Judson does a remarkable job of posing the most likely events, or lists alternative interpretations. The narrative is clear and thorough, appealing to both students and experts. It is divided into twenty-eight chapters, beginning with discussion of Spenser's relation to the wealthy "Spencers" of Althorp. The introduction to G. C. Smith and Ernest De Selincourt's *The Poetry of Edmund Spenser* (Oxford: Clarendon Press, 1912) successfully integrates the chronology of the poet's life and his literary themes and structures. Donald Cheney brings out some of the problems facing literary historians in "Spenser's Fortieth Birthday and Other Related Fictions," *Spenser Studies,* IV (1984), 3–31.

Evaluation of Selected Biographies

Bayley, Peter, *Edmund Spenser: Prince of Poets.* London: Hutchinson, 1971. Bayley provides a good treatment of Spenser's life and career for general readers.

Church, Richard, *Spenser.* London: Macmillan, 1880. This early study has many excellent suggestions about the connection between *The Faerie Queene* and the poet's experience in Ireland and England.

Henley, Pauline, *Spenser in Ireland.* Dublin and Cork: Cork University Press, 1928. This is the most thorough study yet of Spenser's existence in Ireland, mentioning his role as a soldier and settler as well as a man of letters.

Judson, Alexander, *A Biographical Sketch of John Young, Bishop of Rochester with Emphasis on His Relations with Edmund Spenser.* Bloomington: Indiana University Studies, 1935. Judson creates a vivid background for Spenser's activities in 1578, when he was living in Kent and writing *The Shepheardes Calender.* Young appears as the shepherd "Roffy" in that work, and his friends are given prominence as well.

Nelson, William, *The Poetry of Edmund Spenser: A Study.* New York: Columbia University Press, 1963. This volume is perhaps the best introduction to the works of Spenser for undergraduates. Nelson skillfully integrates biography, cultural history, and thematic analysis to present a comprehensive view of the poetry. The opening chapters are explicitly biographical. Later chapters elucidate individual books of *The Faerie Queene.* Nelson is cautious about questions of historical allegory, but is extremely suggestive.

Oakeshott, Walter, *The Queen and The Poet.* London: Faber and Faber, 1960. The second section of this book uses evidence from Spenser's poetry to interpret Sir Walter Raleigh's relation with Queen Elizabeth. The "poet" in its title refers to Raleigh, but this study links the poetry of these two major writers in several credible ways.

Autobiographical Sources

In *The Shepheardes Calender* Spenser created a poetic persona, and he glanced at his own unhappiness and skill in that of the poet-shepherd Colin Clout. The popularity of this work sealed the identification. Spenser again refers to himself in this manner in *Colin Clouts Come Home Againe,* an account of his return to England and audience with Queen Elizabeth and his friendship with Raleigh. At the end of "The Book of Courtesy," the last complete book of *The Faerie Queene,* Colin Clout suddenly appears only to have his vision of the graces interrupted by Sir Calidore, as Spenser comments on the limits of his art. *Epithalamion* and the *Amoretti* can also be read as a fictionalized rendition of his courtship of Elizabeth Boyle. Richard Helgerson examines the writer's conception of his mission in "The New Poet Presents Himself: Spenser and the Idea of a Literary Career," *PMLA,* XCIII (1978), and *Self-Crowned Laureates: Spenser, Jonson, Milton, and the Literary System* (Berkeley: University of California Press, 1983).

Overview of Critical Sources

There has been a renewed interest in Spenser's work in the last twenty years, and studies cluster around a wide variety of topics. Debate often centers on the nature of Spenser's allegory and the kind of universe it presupposes. Northrop Frye's essay, "The Structure of Imagery in *The Faerie Queene,*" in *Fables of Identity* (New York: Harcourt, Brace & World, 1963), epitomizes a conservative reading of the epic as a work that is unified both morally and esthetically. But Paul Alpers' study, *The Poetry of* The Faerie Queene (Princeton: Princeton University Press, 1967), finds much more ambivalence and poetic disjunction than Frye admits. Alpers' insistence on the open-ended quality of the poem has been explored by a number of important critics, who have paid attention to the problematic and paradoxical dimension of his work. Scholarship has also expanded our knowledge of the political milieu in which Spenser flourished.

Evaluation of Selected Criticism

Alpers, Paul, ed. *Elizabethan Poetry: Modern Essays in Criticism.* New York: Oxford University Press, 1967. Section III, on *The Faerie Queene,* contains excellent essays on subjects from style to sources, by G. Wilson Knight, A. S. P. Woodhouse, Thomas Roche, and others.

Arthos, John, *On the Poetry of Spenser and the Form of Romance.* London: Allen & Unwin, 1956. Arthos accounts for the apparent lack of unity in *The Faerie Queene* by showing the tradition of medieval romance from which it evolved.

Berger, Harry, ed. *Spenser: A Collection of Critical Essays.* Englewood Cliffs: Prentice-Hall, 1968. These essays contain selections that cover the poet's career: his minor poems; *Epithalamion;* the hero's dual identity; the mythology of Venus and Diana; and "The Mutability Cantos."

Cullen, Patrick, *Spenser, Marvell, and Renaissance Pastoral.* Cambridge, MA: Harvard University Press, 1970. Cullen examines Spenser's contribution to the pastoral tradition, his sources in Greek and Latin antiquity, and his influence on seventeenth-century writers.

Evans, Maurice, *Spenser's Anatomy of Heroism.* Cambridge: Cambridge University Press, 1970. Evans sees the theory of unified opposites as the basis of *The Faerie Queene* and supplies a close reading of all its books in sequence. This is an excellent introduction.

Hamilton, A. C. *The Structure of Allegory in* The Faerie Queene. Oxford: Clarendon Press, 1961. In a thorough, reasoned approach that avoids historical allusions, Hamilton analyzes the underlying moral assumptions, literary models, and major themes of the epic.

Lewis, C. S. *The Allegory of Love.* Oxford: Clarendon Press, 1936. Sometimes misleading, but still instructive, Lewis traces Spenser's connection with the literature of courtly love, especially in The Book of Chastity.

————. *English Literature in the Sixteenth Century Excluding Drama.* Oxford: Clarendon Press, 1954. Lewis presents a generally sympathetic study of Spenser's position at the pinnacle of Elizabethan literature and a good synthesis of Spenser's place in literary history.

Nohrnberg, James, *The Analogy of* The Faerie Queene. Princeton: Princeton University Press, 1976. Confusing in organization and filled with digressions, this book is still a fascinating tome for the initiated Spenser reader.

Roche, Thomas, *The Kindly Flame: A Study of the Third and Fourth Books of Spenser's* Faerie Queene. Princeton: Princeton University Press, 1964. Roche discusses Spenserian allegory and then shows the philosophical aspects of the poet's celebration of married love.

Tonkin, Humphrey, *Spenser's Courteous Pastoral, Book Six of* The Faerie Queene. Oxford: Clarendon Press, 1972. In this comprehensive treatment of an individual book of the poem, Tonkin relates pastoral poetry in the epic to courtesy book literature popular in the period.

Williams, Kathleen, *Spenser's World of Glass: A Reading of the* Faerie Queene. Berkeley: University of California Press, 1966. Outstanding and sensitive discussion of Spenserian poetics. Highly readable, this is an enlightening explication of the unifying processes behind the poet's work and his desire to be broadly comprehensive, often at the risk of logical unity.

Other Sources

Carpenter, Fredric I. *A Reference Guide to Edmund Spenser.* Chicago: University of Chicago Press, 1923. Extremely useful tool for finding out about Spenser's background. Carpenter has arranged his book to facilitate reference to many different areas of interest. Indispensable for historical research.

Heffner, Ray and Fredrick Padelford, eds. *Spenser Allusions in the Sixteenth and Seventeenth Centuries.* Chapel Hill: University of North Carolina Press, 1972. Catalogues responses to Spenser's work by his contemporaries and successors in chronological order.

Lotspeich, Henry, *Classical Mythology in the Poetry of Edmund Spenser.* Princeton: Princeton University Press, 1932. The introduction characterizes Spenser's debt to Renaissance dictionaries of mythography. Major figures of myth are arranged alphabetically with description and citation of Spenser's use and its probable sources.

McNeir, Waldo and Foster Provost, *Edmund Spenser: An Annotated Bibliography, 1937–1972.* Pittsburgh: Duquesne University Press, 1975. Abstracts of biographies, list of editions, as well as criticism in books and articles are gathered together in this convenient volume.

Osgood, Charles, *Concordance to the Poems of Edmund Spenser.* Gloucester, MA: Peter Smith, 1963; reprint of 1915 edition. Enables reader to trace words and themes dispersed throughout Spenser's collected works.

James P. Bednarz
Long Island University

CHRISTINA STEAD
1902–1983

Author's Chronology

Born July 17, 1902, Rockdale, New South Wales, Australia, only child of first generation Australian parents of English and Scottish descent; mother dies two years later; *1907* father remarries; family moves to Sydney; grows up in Sydney along with six younger brothers and sisters; receives education there, teaches, then works in NSW Department of Education; *1925* leaves teaching, learns typing and shorthand, takes up secretarial work; *1928* sails for England, works in a London bank where she meets American banker and writer William James Blake, whom she later marries; *1929* goes to Paris with Blake, works in a bank; *1934* publishes in London *The Salzburg Tales* in January, and *Seven Poor Men of Sydney* in October; 1935 travels to United States, then to Spain and France; *1937* settles in US, first in New York, then in Hollywood briefly as a Senior Writer with MGM; returns to New York; *1940* publishes *The Man Who Loved Children;* 1946 leaves New York to live in France, then The Hague; *1953* settles in England; *1965 The Man Who Loved Children* reissued in U.S., receives praise, revives and creates new interest in Stead's work, sets off reprints of earlier novels; *1968* William Blake dies; *1969* returns to Canberra, Australia, for the first time in 40 years as Creative Arts Fellow at the National University; *1974* lonely and feeling on the fringe of European life, takes up residence in Sydney permanently; first Australian author to receive Patrick White award; *1976* publishes last novel, *Miss Herbert (The Suburban Wife)*; dies March 31, 1983 in Sydney.

Author's Bibliography (selected fiction)

The Salzburg Tales, 1934; *Seven Poor Men of Sydney,* 1934; *The Beauties and Furies,* 1936; *House of All Nations,* 1938; *The Man Who Loved Children,* 1940; *For Love Alone,* 1945; *Letty Fox: Her Luck,* 1947; *A Little Tea, A Little Chat,* 1948; *The People with the Dogs,* 1952; *Dark Places of the Heart,* 1966 (U.S. title; *Cotter's England,* British title, 1967); *The Puzzleheaded Girl, Four Novellas,* 1967; *The Little Hotel: A Novel,* 1973; *Miss Herbert (The Suburban Wife)*, 1976.

Overview of Biographical Sources

At this time no major biography of Christina Stead exists, only articles, interviews, and biographical portions of critical books. One will be sure to appear before long, now that she is no longer living but did in the last few years of her life establish herself as a major writer on three continents. Such a work will prove valuable, for Stead based much of her fiction on personal experience.

Evaluation of Selected Biographies

Beston, John B. "A Brief Biography of Christina Stead," *World Literature Written in English,* XV (April 1976), 79–86. Prepared with the assistance of Stead, this account gives some new information on her Australian background.

Geering, R. G. *Christina Stead.* New York: Twayne, 1969. Geering provides a detailed chronology through 1967, as well as biographical details as they relate to Stead's development as a writer.

Autobiographical Sources

Because Stead was an international resident and virtually unacknowledged in the United States until the 1960's, the sources are few and scattered. In the 1970's she gave several interviews, including one with Beston, printed along with his biographical sketch in *WLWE,* and another with Lidoff, included in her book. Other important interviews appeared in *London Magazine,* XI (Feb. 1970), 70–77; and in *Australian Literary Studies,* III (May 1974), 230–248. Stead's reviews and articles, published over a long period in the US and abroad, give insight into her critical and political stance.

Overview of Critical Sources

As a result of Stead's late discovery by American critics, most of the critical work is recent and found in journals. Articles appeared earlier and continue to do so in Australia, whose critics claim her though she spent most of her productive years elsewhere. Some critics have hailed her as a feminist writer, a label she denied.

Evaluation of Selected Criticism

Geering, R. G. *Christina Stead.* New York: Twayne, 1969. In this first full-length study, Geering focuses on the major themes of the fiction; she also surveys briefly Stead's nonfiction.

Lidoff, Joan, *Christina Stead.* Frederick Ungar, 1982. This more recent book sets forth an overview of all Stead's fiction and a detailed analysis of her two most highly regarded novels, *The Man Who Loved Children* and *For Love Alone.* The discussion of Stead's complex style, although far from a comprehensive analysis, displays refreshing insight.

Other Sources

Hardwick, Elizabeth, "The Neglected Novels of Christina Stead," in *A View of My Own,* London: Heineman, 1964, 41–48; originally appeared as an essay in *New Republic,* CXXXIII (Aug. 1, 1955), 17–19. When Hardwick wrote this essay, all of Stead's work was out of print and even her whereabouts were unknown. Hardwick, well ahead of her time, points out that many of the novels are great ones, unlike anything else in English fiction.

Jarrell, Randall, "An Unread Book," Introduction to *The Man Who Loved Children*. New York: Holt, Rinehart & Winston, 1965. This detailed introduction to a novel which Jarrell predicted would be read by people in the future served as an impetus to what has been called the "resurrection" of Stead's work.

Jean B. Read, ed. *A Christina Stead Reader*. New York: Random House, 1976. These selections, each introduced, acquaint the reader with the breadth of Stead's fiction.

Selected Dictionaries and Encyclopedias

Contemporary Authors, Vol. 15, Gale Research. Biography, survey of critical reputation, and analysis of theme and method.

Contemporary Novelists, 3rd ed. St. Martin's. Concise biography and analysis.

Robert L. Ross
Southern Methodist University

RICHARD STEELE
1672–1729

Author's Chronology

Born 1672 in Dublin, Ireland; *1684* enters Charterhouse School in London; *1686* meets Joseph Addison at Charterhouse; *1689* enters Christ Church, Oxford; *1691* enters Merton College, Oxford; *1692* joins the Second Troop of Life Guards; *1695* publishes *The Procession. A Poem on Her Majesties Funeral; 1695* leaves the Second Troop of Life Guards and joins the Coldstream Regiment; *1701 The Christian Hero; 1701 The Funeral, or Grief a la Mode; 1703 The Lying Lover; 1705 The Tender Husband; 1705* marries Margaret Ford Stretch; *1705* leaves his commission in the Coldstream Regiment; *1706* becomes Gentleman-Waiter to Prince George; *1707* a year after the death of his first wife, marries Mary Scurlock; *1707* is writer of *The London Gazette,* an official government paper; *1708* socializes with Addison and Swift; *1708* Prince George dies; *1709* publishes *The Tatler* under the name of Isaac Bickerstaff; *1711* concludes *The Tatler* and begins *The Spectator; 1712* concludes *The Spectator; 1713* writes *The Guardian* and *The Englishman,* and is elected to Parliament; *1714* is expelled from Parliament, but appointed governor of Drury Lane Theatre under the new king, George I; *1715* is elected to Parliament and knighted by King George I; *1718* wife dies; *1720* publishes *The Theatre; 1722 The Conscious Lovers; 1724* retires to Carmarthenshire, Wales; *1729* dies on September 1.

Author's Bibliography (selected)

"The Procession, 1695 (poem); *The Christian Hero,* 1701 (prose); *The Funeral, or Grief a la Mode,* 1701 (comedy); *The Lying Lover,* produced in 1703 (comedy); *The Tender Husband,* 1705 (comedy); *The Tatler,* with Joseph Addison, 1709–11 (essays); *The Spectator,* 1711–12 (essays); *The Guardian,* 1713 (essays); *The Englishman,* in two series, 1713–14, 1715 (essays); *The Theatre,* 1720 (essays); *The Conscious Lovers,* produced in 1722 (comedy).

Overview of Biographical Sources

Richard Steele's flamboyant personality has received varied treatments at the hands of biographers. Early nineteenth century biographers emphasized his drinking and contrasted him to the dignified Joseph Addison. Steele was demeaned as Addison was exalted. With George Aitken's biography, *The Life of Richard Steele* (1889), Steele began to receive fairer treatment. A two volume biography by Calhoun Winton appeared in 1964 and 1970, so there is now available a "definitive," accurate, and dispassionate presentation of Steele's life.

Evaluation of Selected Biographies

Aitken, George A. *The Life of Richard Steele.* 2 vols. 1889; rpt. New York: Greenwood Press, 1968. With the information available to him, Aitken provides a fair and informative biography. Today it is only of passing interest, since a later biography exists.

Goldgar, Bertrand A. *The Curse of Party*. Lincoln: The University of Nebraska Press, 1961. Goldgar offers considerable insight into the relationship between Richard Steele and Jonathan Swift from 1705 to 1714. With clarity and grace Goldgar explains how the warm friendship of the "triumvirate" deteriorated into the bitter opposition of Whig Richard Steele and Tory Jonathan Swift. Political differences separated them, and they became apologists for their respective political parties.

Winton, Calhoun, *Captain Steele: The Early Career of Richard Steele*. Baltimore: The Johns Hopkins Press, 1964; Winton, Calhoun. *Sir Richard Steele, M.P.: The Later Career*. Baltimore: The Johns Hopkins Press, 1970. The "definitive" biography of Richard Steele studies its subject with precision and accuracy. While showing a sensitivity to and an understanding of Richard Steele, Winton is not a Steele idolator. He analyzes strengths and weaknesses dispassionately, placing Steele's character in an historical context.

Autobiographical Sources

In 1714 there appeared *Mr. Steele's Apology for Himself and His Writings, Occasioned by his Expulsion from the House of Commons*. Written as a defense of his character after his expulsion from Parliament, this tract also attacks his political opponents. While not a complete autobiography, Steele's self-defense does provide significant glimpses of his self-perception.

Overview of Critical Sources

The reading public knows Richard Steele as a dramatist and an essayist. While his four comedies are rarely produced today, *The Tatler* and *The Spectator* are read frequently by scholar and general reader alike. Except for *The Tatler*, his plays and essays have appeared in definitive twentieth century editions with full scholarly apparatus. With the anticipated publication of *The Tatler*, all of Steele's work will have appeared in current editions.

Evaluation of Selected Criticism

Blanchard, Rae, ed. *Tracts and Pamphlets by Richard Steele*. Baltimore: The Johns Hopkins Press, 1944. Blanchard provides a clear, precise criticism and evaluation of Steele's prose works.

————. *The Christian Hero*. London: Humphrey Milford, 1932. In the Introduction Blanchard provides insightful criticism on Steele. Tracing Steele's "sensibility," Blanchard places him in a context with other writers at the beginning of the eighteenth century.

Bond, Donald F. ed. *The Spectator.* 5 vols. Oxford: Clarendon Press, 1965. The commentary by Bond provides a sound introduction to *The Spectator* and an overview of important contemporary issues.

Dammers, Richard H. *Richard Steele.* Boston: Twayne, 1982. This study of Steele's works presents a critical discussion of his major literary achievements. It serves as an introduction to Steele for both student and teacher.

Kenny, Shirley Strum, ed. *The Plays of Richard Steele.* Oxford: Clarendon Press, 1971. The introduction and commentary offer the reader sound information and judgment about Steele's four comedies.

Other Sources
Otten, Robert M. *Joseph Addison.* Boston: Twayne, 1982. Richard Steele and Joseph Addison are among the most famous literary teams in English history; as a result the reader interested in the accomplishments of Richard Steele is likely to be interested in this critical introduction to Joseph Addison and his works.

Selected Dictionaries and Encyclopedias
Critical Survey of Short Fiction, Salem Press, 1981. Brief biography, and analysis of Steele's major periodical essays.

The Cambridge History of English Literature, Cambridge University Press. Overview of Addison and Steele and their literary achievement.

Richard H. Dammers
Illinois State University

GERTRUDE STEIN
1874–1946

Author's Chronology

Born February 3, 1874, Allegheny, Pennsylvania; *1893–1897* studies psychology at Radcliffe College under William James and conducts experiments with automatic writing; *1897* enters Johns Hopkins Medical School; leaves Johns Hopkins in *1901* without degree; *1903* moves to France, lives with brother Leo at 27, Rue de Fleurus, Paris; *1906* poses for Pablo Picasso and finishes *Three Lives; 1909* publishes *Three Lives;* Alice Toklas moves into Stein's apartment; *1912–1920's* Stein and brother become patrons of avant-garde painters, Picasso, Matisse, Braque, Cezanne; *1914* publishes *Tender Buttons,* influenced by Picasso's cubism; *1916–1919* Stein and Toklas work for the American Fund for French Wounded; *1922* Stein receives Medaille de la Reconnaissance for work in the war; *1920's* Stein's home becomes a center for writers, such as Sherwood Anderson, Ernest Hemingway, F. Scott Fitzgerald, whom she termed "the lost generation"; *1933* publishes *Autobiography of Alice B. Toklas,* which becomes a best-seller; *1934–1935* lectures in United States and in England in 1936; *1939–1944* Stein and Toklas remain in French countryside during war; *1944* after German occupation ends Stein returns to Paris with Toklas and opens home to soldiers; *1944* depicts soldiers' lives in *Brewser and Willie,* published in 1946; dies of cancer July 27, 1946.

Author's Bibliography (selected)

Three Lives, 1909 (short novels); *Tender Buttons,* 1914 (prose poems); *The Making of Americans,* 1925 (essays); *Composition as Explanation,* 1926 (essay); *The Autobiography of Alice B. Toklas,* 1933 (biography); *Four Saints in Three Acts,* 1934 (play); *Lectures in America,* 1935 (essays); *Ida,* 1941 (novel); *Things As They Are (Q.E.D.,* 1903), 1950 (novel).

Overview of Biographical Sources

Gertrude Stein's life—in the center of the Parisian artistic scene of the 1920's—is often thought to be as interesting as her literary work. Distinguishing between her reputation and the quality of her work is often difficult. Biographers and critics alike tend to divide themselves into those sympathetic to Stein's lifestyle and attitudes and those critical of them. Donald Sutherland, for example, in *Gertrude Stein: A Biography of Her Work* (New Haven: Yale University Press, 1951) offers an energized personal defense of Stein as an innovative artist while Kingsley Widmer in *The Literary Rebel* (Carbondale: University of Illinois Press, 1965) finds Stein to be nothing more than an "avant-kitsch writer." Recently, discussions of Stein have become less polemical as seen in the lively and sensitive biography by James Mellow, *Charmed Circle: Gertrude*

Stein and Company (1974), and in the number of recently published popular biographies of Stein such as W. G. Rogers' *Gertrude Stein is Gertrude Stein is Gertrude Stein: Her Life and Work* (1973) and Ellen Wilson's *They Named Me Gertrude Stein* (New York: Farrar, Straus, and Giroux, 1973).

Evaluation of Selected Biographies

Brinnan, John M. *The Third Rose*. Boston: Little Brown, 1959. This is provocative bio-critical introduction, attempting to distinguish the legends from the facts about Stein's personality, aesthetic standards, and role in Parisian artistic circles. While always interesting, it's at times biased against Stein's attitudes.

Hobhouse, Janet, *Everybody Who Was Anybody: A Biography of Gertrude Stein*. New York: G. P. Putnam's Sons, 1975. Although not as interesting and detailed as Mellow, this account nonetheless provides a straightforward introduction to Stein. Hobhouse frequently uses Stein's own texts to elaborate and substantiate her points about Stein's life. The book contains a number of fine reproductions and photographs.

Mellow, James R. *Charmed Circles: Gertrude Stein and Company*. New York: Praeger, 1974. This lively, sympathetic biography, rich in local detail, provides an extensive study of Stein's life as a writer. The focus of this work is Stein's sense of her own work, its general reception, her relationship with her family, particularly her brother Leo, her fellow artists, and her companion of forty years, and Alice Toklas. These are recreated with accuracy and sensitivity, and it is always enjoyable as well as informative.

Rogers, W. G. *When This You See Remember Me: Gertrude Stein in Person*. New York: Rinehart, 1948. A chatty, personal memoir with a few interesting anecdotes but relatively insignificant discussions of Stein's work.

Spriggs, Elizabeth, *Gertrude Stein: Her Life and Work*. New York: Harper, 1957. This is a rather mechanical and somewhat superficial discussion of Stein's life, intellectual relationships, and literary development which tends to summarize rather than analyze Stein's work.

Autobiographical Sources

Perhaps more than any literary figure of the twentieth century, Stein was obsessed with telling the story of her own life and work. She did this with narrative sophistication in her most popular work, *The Autobiography of Alice B. Toklas* (New York: Harcourt, Brace, 1933). Ostensibly writing in Toklas' voice, Stein fictionalizes and lengendizes their early lives before they came to Paris, their life during World War I, and the years after until 1932. *The Autobiography of Alice B. Toklas* was initially popular because of the scandalous information it contained about Stein's artist companions, but it has remained popular as a subjective account of a woman whose egotism allowed her to see herself at the center of the modernist movement.

Overview of Critical Sources

Because of the difficulty of Stein's canon, most critics have attempted to devise systems whereby it can, if not be understood, at least be explained aesthetically. The systems critics devise vary from those tracing patterns and developments in Stein's own texts as they relate to cubist painting to those using modern theories of interpretation such as psychoanalysis, linguistics, or structuralism to explain Stein's use of language.

Evaluation of Selected Criticism

Bridgman, Richard, *Gertrude Stein in Pieces*. New York: Oxford University Press, 1970. The first book-length study of the whole Stein canon, this perceptive book distances itself from Stein's own comments about her career and provides a detailed examination of continuities, development, and changes in Stein's work. This is the most stimulating and complete study of Stein to date, essential for any student of Stein.

Dubnick, Randa, *The Structure of Obscurity: Gertrude Stein, Language, and Cubism*. Urbana: University of Illinois Press, 1984. Dubnick uses structuralist theories of Saussure, Barthes, and Jakobson to suggest that Stein's writing contains two linguistically consistent obscure styles, one emphasizing *selection* (vocabulary), the other, *combination* (ordering). Dubnick argues that these two styles parallel two major phases of cubist painting—analytic and synthetic—and attempts to establish that Stein's linguistic imitations of cubism are appropriate to literature, a point that many of Stein's critics have debated. Dubnick presents a fascinating, well-argued approach to Stein's work.

Hoffman, Michael J. *Gertrude Stein*. Boston: Twayne, 1976. Hoffman locates Stein in the context of avant-garde movements in literature and painting from 1900–1950. Half the book studies Stein's work from 1902–1913 as it developed from realism to cubism, focusing on *Three Lives, The Making of Americans,* and *Tender Buttons*. The remainder analyzes Stein's later work more selectively. Hoffman provides an excellent, lively introduction to Stein's work and intellectual contexts.

Reid, B. J. *Art by Subtraction: A Dissenting Opinion of Gertrude Stein*. Norman: University of Oklahoma Press, 1958. Arguing that "the strangeness of Gertrude Stein debilitates and paralyzes," Reid onesidedly dismisses Stein's literary work in an interesting, though unfair, argument against Stein.

Steiner, Wendy, *Exact Resemblance to Exact Resemblance*. New Haven: Yale University Press, 1978. A detailed study of Stein's literary portraits in relation to modernism and to Stein's knowledge of psychology and philosophy, this is an interesting, though at times reductive, attempt to explain Stein's theoretical framework.

Other Sources

Stewart, Allegra, *Gertrude Stein and The Present.* Cambridge, MA: Harvard University Press, 1967. Relates Stein's thinking to various philosophers such as James, Santayana, Bergson, and Whitehead, and then performs a provocative Jungian analysis of Stein's work, focusing on *Tender Buttons* and *Doctor Faustus Lights the Lights.*

Weinstein, Norman, *Gertrude Stein and the Literature of Modern Consciousness.* New York: Frederick Ungar, 1970. Relates Stein's work to theories of speech pathology, psycho-linguistics, and structural linguistics. Often formulaic, this book does little to elucidate Stein's work.

Wilson, Edmund, *Axel's Castle.* New York: Scribner's, 1931. Wilson's chapter on Stein represents the first substantive study of Stein's work. Wilson emphasizes Stein's humor and originality.

Selected Dictionaries and Encyclopedias

Twentieth-Century Literary Criticism, Gale Research, 1982. Excerpts from criticism on Stein's work.

American Women Writers, Frederick Ungar Publishing Company, 1982. Brief biography, and discussions of Stein's major works.

Kathleen McCormick-Leighty
Carnegie-Mellon University

JOHN STEINBECK
1902–1968

Author's Chronology

Born John Ernest Steinbeck, Salinas, California, February 29, 1902; *1919* graduates from Salinas High School; enrolls at Stanford University; *1925* leaves Stanford permanently, without degree; visits New York City; *1929 Cup of Gold,* first novel; *1930* marries Carol Henning; meets Ed Ricketts, lifelong friend and mentor; *1935 Tortilla Flat,* first successful novel; travels to Mexico; *1936 In Dubious Battle* begins major social novels; *1939* wins Pulitzer Prize for *The Grapes of Wrath; 1942* divorces Carol Henning; *1943* marries Gwyn Conger; visits the European war zone for the New York *Herald Tribune; 1950* marries Elaine Scott; *1962* receives Nobel Prize for literature; *1968* dies in New York City, December 20.

Author's Bibliography (selected)

Cup of Gold, 1929 (novel); *The Pastures of Heaven,* 1932 (novel); *To a God Unknown,* 1933 (novel); *Tortilla Flat,* 1935 (novel); *In Dubious Battle,* 1936 (novel); *Of Mice and Men,* 1937 (novella); *The Long Valley,* 1938 (stories); *The Grapes of Wrath,* 1939 (novel); *The Moon is Down,* 1942 (novel); *Cannery Row,* 1945 (novel); *The Wayward Bus,* 1947 (novel); *The Pearl,* 1947 (novel); *East of Eden,* 1952 (novel); *The Winter of Our Discontent,* 1961 (novel); *The Acts of King Arthur and His Noble Knights,* 1976 (translation).

Overview of Biographical Sources

Despite his considerable success and popularity, Steinbeck remained a very private person who jealously guarded the details of his personal life. His artistic philosophy also favored privacy, as he believed his works of fiction should be judged on their intrinsic merit without connection to his life. Steinbeck wrote no autobiography, as such, refused interviews, withheld information from the standard references, and even destroyed letters and other documents. Since his death, his family has continued to withhold a considerable amount of biographical information.

Therefore, an accurate, comprehensive Steinbeck biography did not appear until 1984. Jackson J. Benson's *The True Adventures of John Steinbeck, Writer,* should prove to be the definitive biographical work; yet it still leaves many questions unanswered, especially in regard to Steinbeck's literary decline in his later books. Other biographical works, including Thomas Kiernan's earlier effort, *The Intricate Music: A Biography of John Steinbeck* (1979), suffer by comparison with Benson's more accurate, detailed, and focused book. However, *The Intricate Music* and several critical biographies found below under the Evaluation of Selected Criticism provide adequate sources for the general reader.

Evaluation of Selected Biographies

Benson, Jackson J. *The True Adventures of John Steinbeck, Writer.* New York: Viking Press, 1984. Benson's biography of Steinbeck proves a work of formidable scholarship, critical acumen, and lively style. Benson labored for over thirteen years in the production of his volume, a prodigious 1,116 page effort, and like several contemporary biographies of modern writers, this one is simply too long.

Benson has uncovered a great mass of factual information previously unknown or misunderstood. His study lays to rest many of the myths which attach themselves like barnacles to a major writer's reputation—for example, Steinbeck's alleged trip to Oklahoma to research Okie life for *The Grapes of Wrath.* More importantly, Benson carefully traces the evolution of individual works, a particularly complex process in Steinbeck's early career. His scholarship presents a complete picture of the novelist's development from an awkward, posturing romantic to the realistic, successful artist of the late 1930's.

Kiernan, Thomas, *The Intricate Music: A Biography of John Steinbeck.* Boston: Little Brown, 1979. Until the publication of Benson's book in 1984, *The Intricate Music* was the only full-length biography of Steinbeck. It is a popular, rather than a scholarly work, which is better on personal anecdote than literary insight. While Benson's account contains some inaccuracies, it provides a good sense of the flow of Steinbeck's life, and his book may be more accessible to the general reader.

Autobiography

Steinbeck wrote no autobiography as such, but several of his non-fiction works include journalistic reporting of his own experiences. The more notable of these include: *Sea of Cortez* (New York: Viking Press, 1941), the narrative of a voyage in the Gulf of California; *A Russian Journal* (New York: Viking Press, 1948); *Travels with Charley in Search of America* (New York: Viking Press, 1962), and *Journal of a Novel* (New York: Viking Press, 1969), which chronicles the writing of *East of Eden. Steinbeck: A Life in Letters* (New York: Viking Press, 1975) is a chronologically arranged selection of edited letters compiled by the writer's third wife, Elaine Steinbeck, and Robert Wallsten.

Overview of Critical Sources

Steinbeck remains an enigmatic figure in the mosaic of modern American fiction. A writer of immense popularity and public recognition during a career which spanned four decades, Steinbeck's critical reputation waned after his masterwork, *The Grapes of Wrath* (1939), and plummeted after his epic, *East of Eden* (1952). Despite his Nobel Prize for Literature in 1962, Steinbeck's post Depression fiction proved wildly uneven and generally disappointing. Steinbeck thus remains a writer of the 1930's, perhaps the most representative novelist of that decade, and he is still widely read and appreciated.

The stark contrast between the major phases of his career creates critical confusion about the Steinbeck canon. Recent scholarship, however, has done much to create a balanced view of this important novelist. The books discussed here make substantial contributions to a better understanding of Steinbeck and his artistic background, and each suggests further bibliography for consideration.

Evaluation of Selected Criticism

DeMott, Robert, *Steinbeck's Reading: A Catalogue of Books Owned and Borrowed.* New York: Garland Publishing, 1984. DeMott's catalogue of Steinbeck's reading makes a useful contribution to the study of the novelist. His introductory essays carefully trace the influence of other authors and books on the writer's development; in Steinbeck's case this becomes a history of ideas. Some of these connections have been made in other places, such as Benson's biography, but many are new, and the others are documented by the evidence of the catalogue.

French, Warren, *John Steinbeck.* Boston: Twayne, 1961; rev. 1975. French's compact, intelligent, and readable introduction was the second volume in the Twaynes United States Authors Series in 1961; it was revised and updated in 1975. Although the series format somewhat restricts the analysis of a voluminous writer like Steinbeck, French provides a solid base for critical understanding. The book accurately locates Steinbeck within the American traditions of idealism and pragmatism. French also acknowledges Steinbeck's decline, which he explains by the author's separation from California in his later life. The later edition of this study remains perhaps the best introduction to Steinbeck.

Hayashi, Tetsumaro, *A Study Guide to Steinbeck, Two Volumes.* Metuchen, NJ: Scarecrow Press, 1974. Hayashi edited a series of essays on many aspects of Steinbeck's work, as well as on individual Steinbeck books. Although the quality of these pieces proves somewhat uneven, overall they provide excellent beginnings for the consideration of many problems in Steinbeck's writing. The bibliographies will prove especially helpful for further study.

Levant, Howard, *The Novels of John Steinbeck: A Critical Study.* Columbia: University of Missouri Press, 1974. Levant's book provides a level-headed but complicated reading of Steinbeck's novels. His readings are ranged in chronological order, and they depend on each other for cumulative effect. His approach is difficult, but will repay the careful reader with excellent analyses of image and structure.

Lisca, Peter, *The Wide World of John Steinbeck.* New Brunswick, NJ: Rutgers University Press, 1958. Lisca's pioneering study was the first important book on Steinbeck, and it remains one of the best. The study combined careful consideration of Steinbeck's life with close critical reading of all the writer's works. Lisca's interpretations are both sympathetic and insightful, though he recognized the decline in Steinbeck's later works. He rather undervalues the non-fiction, but by and large his readings are still substantial and make excellent starting points for any reader.

Martin, Stoddard, *California Writers: Jack London, John Steinbeck, and the Tough Guys.* New York: St. Martin's Press, 1984. Martin's *California Writers* makes a substantial contribution to Steinbeck studies by placing the novelist within the context of a California tradition which includes Jack London and the "Tough Guys"—James M. Cain, Dashiell Hammett, and Raymond Chandler. In Martin's view, these two great novelists and one great school comprise a vital tradition because they combine fantasy and Naturalism in complex fictions. Certainly this balance prevails in Steinbeck's novels, and the causes Martin cites—the disparate geography, the Westering spirit, the clash of cultures and classes, the fantasy-land of Hollywood—all have important effects on Steinbeck.

McCarthy, John, *John Steinbeck.* New York: Frederick Ungar, 1980. The Modern Authors Series presents a short, competent introduction to Steinbeck and his works. Although there are some problems with biographical facts, McCarthy's overall reading of the writer's career is more than adequate.

Millichap, Joseph R. *Steinbeck and Film.* New York: Frederick Ungar, 1983. This book in the Ungar Film Series considers this neglected aspect of Steinbeck's career. It analyzes not only the many film and television adaptations of Steinbeck's books, but the influence of film on Steinbeck's writing. His later decline is explained here by his movement from 1930's documentary to Hollywood melodrama.

Joseph R. Millichap
Western Kentucky University

LAURENCE STERNE
1713–1767

Author's Chronology

Born November 24, 1713, in Ireland, the son of an itinerant soldier; *1733–1737* at Jesus College, Cambridge; first signs of pulmonary tuberculosis; *1737* awarded a B.A.; *1738* ordained and inducted into the vicarage at Sutton-on-the-Forest, Yorkshire; *1740* M.A. from Cambridge; named prebendary of Givendale; *1741* receives a prebendary stall in York Minster; marries Elizabeth Lumley, a clergyman's daughter; active in church politics in York; Sterne also frequents John Hall-Stevenson and the "Demoniacs" at Crazy Castle; *1744* secures the living of Stillington, near Sutton; *1745* birth of a daughter, Lydia, who lives less than a day; *1747* birth of his surviving daughter Lydia; *1750* quarrels with his uncle; his mother is imprisoned for penury; Sterne is named commissary of the Peculiar Courts of Alne and Tellerton, and later also of Pickering and Pocklington; *1759* publishes *A Political Romance,* most copies of which are burned; his wife suffers a mental breakdown; publishes *The Life and Opinions of Tristram Shandy, Gentleman,* which brings him instant fame; *1760* receives the curacy of Coxwold, his third living; *1762* travels with his family to Paris, Toulouse, and Montpellier; *1764* returns to London; *1765–1766* in France and Italy; *1766* in Coxwold; frequent hemorrhages; *1767* meets Eliza Draper; dies in London of pleurisy on March 18; his corpse is stolen by grave-diggers and carried to Cambridge for dissection.

Author's Bibliography (selected)

The Life and Opinions of Tristram Shandy, Gentleman, 1759–1767 (novel in five parts and nine volumes); *Sermons of Mr. Yorick,* 1760 (sermons); *A Sentimental Journey Through France and Italy,* 1768 (sentimental novel); *Letters from Yorick to Eliza,* 1773 (sentimental letters); *Complete Works,* 1904 (12 volumes, ed. Wilbur L. Cross); *Letters of Laurence Sterne,* 1935 (letters, ed. Lewis P. Curtis).

Overview of Biographical Sources

Sterne has always provoked strong reactions. In 1853 William Makepeace Thackeray famously denounced Sterne's moral vagaries, and the first full biography of Sterne, a sympathetic account by Percy Fitzgerald, *The Life of Laurence Sterne* (1864, 1906; rpt. Philadelphia: Century Bookbinding, 1983) may well have been written in an attempt to counteract the damage Thackeray's lecture had done to Sterne's reputation. *The Life and Times of Laurence Sterne,* by Wilbur L. Cross (1906; 3rd revised and expanded edition of 1929 rpt. New York: Russell & Russell, 1967) served as the standard biography of Sterne for decades until superseded by Arthur H. Cash's *Laurence Sterne: The*

Early & Middle Years (1975) for Sterne's life up to 1760. Most biographers agree that Sterne's corpse was indeed stolen by resurrectionists and recognized too late on a dissecting table at Cambridge; recent evidence tends only to confirm this grisly tale.

Good basic biographical and bibliographical information is amply provided in three excellent modern editions of *The Life and Opinions of Tristram Shandy, Gentleman,* by James Aiken Work (New York: Odyssey Press, 1940), by Ian Watt in the Riverside series (Boston: Houghton Mifflin, 1965), and by Howard Anderson in the series of Norton Critical Editions (New York: W. W. Norton, 1979).

Evaluation of Selected Biographies

Cash, Arthur H. *Laurence Sterne: The Early & Middle Years.* New York: Harper & Row, 1975. This is the most detailed and authoritative of the biographies, based on extensive and carefully presented documentary evidence, much of it previously unknown or unpublished. This is not a critical biography; indeed it stops at the very point when Sterne set out for London and literary fame in 1760. Cash appends a descriptive catalogue of all known "Portraits of Sterne," including some judged "unauthentic."

Fluchère, Henri, *Laurence Sterne: From Tristram Shandy to Yorick, An Interpretation of Tristram Shandy.* Translated and abridged by Barbara Bray. New York: Oxford University Press, 1965. A formidable work even in this abridged form which omits the "biographical" sections, this route should be taken only by those obsessed with Sterne. The translation is at the very least a remarkable attempt to convey a French vocabulary of humor and sentiment into English.

James, Overton Philip, *The Relation of Tristram Shandy to the Life of Sterne.* The Hague and Paris: Mouton, 1966. James reproaches biographers Cross and Work for their failure always to maintain a strict distinction between Sterne the man and Shandy his character, and undertakes to list and discuss discrepancies between the life and the work. This somewhat uneven but interesting dissertation was criticized in turn by Cash in *Modern Language Review,* 44 (1969), 649–650.

Autobiographical Sources

Late in his life Sterne wrote one brief autobiographical work for his daughter Lydia. Published under the title "Memoirs of the Life and Family of the Late Rev. Mr. Laurence Sterne," it is included in Curtis's edition of the *Letters of Laurence Sterne* (Oxford: Clarendon Press, 1935). Apart from this, Sterne's many sermons, letters, and assorted papers offer much evidence for autobiographical speculation; most of these materials are collected in Cross's *Complete Works and a Life of Laurence Sterne* (New York: J. F. Taylor, 1904), which also reprints Fitzgerald's biography.

Overview of Critical Sources

Sterne's early critical reception in England has been traced by Alan B. Howes in *Yorick and the Critics: Sterne's Reputation in England, 1760-1868* (New Haven: Yale University Press, 1948). Early American attitudes toward Sterne are sampled in a fine essay by bibliographer Lodwick Hartley in the *Southern Humanities Review*, 3 (1970), 69-80; rpt. *The Winged Skull: Papers from the Laurence Sterne Bicentenary Conference* (1971). Howes reprints excerpts from Sterne criticism from 1760 to 1830 in *Sterne: The Critical Heritage* (1974).

Although Sterne was unmentionable among eminent Victorians, his reputation in the twentieth century continues to increase. Modern criticism of Sterne is described by Lodwick Hartley in *Laurence Sterne in the Twentieth Century: An Essay and a Bibliography of Sternean Studies, 1900-1965* (Chapel Hill: University of North Carolina Press, 1966), later extended with *Laurence Sterne: An Annotated Bibliography, 1965-1977, with An Introductory Essay-Review of the Scholarship* (Boston: G. K. Hall, 1978).

Sternean studies are, like the objects of their interest, so diverse as to defy swift characterization. They range from Formalist studies of Sterne's techniques; to game theory and music; to philosophical attempts to trace Sterne's connections with his forerunner John Locke or the later tradition of Husserlian phenomenology; to the characters in *Tristram Shandy* as reflections of contemporaneous climate theory. Wayne Booth argued in an essay in *Modern Philology*, 48 (Feb. 1951), 172-183, that *Tristram Shandy* was in fact "finished" at the time of Sterne's death; but the issue Booth raised remains very much alive, as does the general issue of Sterne's treatment of fictional time.

Evaluation of Selected Criticism

Cash, Arthur H. and John M. Stedmond, eds. *The Winged Skull: Papers from the Laurence Sterne Bicentenary Conference.* Kent, OH: Kent State University Press, 1971. This is an important collection of essays on a wide range of topics, including a partial bibliography of Sterne's works in various editions and translations before 1800.

Howes, Alan B. ed. *Sterne: The Critical Heritage.* London: Routledge & Kegan Paul, 1974. This valuable work reprints Sterne criticism from 1760 to 1830, and includes a comprehensive introduction.

Traugott, John, ed. *Laurence Sterne: A Collection of Critical Essays.* (Twentieth Century Views Series.) Englewood Cliffs, NJ: Prentice-Hall, 1968. An important collection of essays, including an excerpt by A. A. Mendilow on Sterne's manipulation of time and Viktor Shklovsky's provocative study of Sterne's stylistic tricks. A different English version of Shklovsky's essay appears in Lee L. Lemon and Marion Reis, eds. *Russian Formalist Criticism: Four Essays.* Lincoln: University of Nebraska Press, 1965.

Other Sources

Curtis, Lewis P. ed. *Letters of Laurence Sterne.* Oxford: The Clarendon Press, 1935. This work marked a great milestone in Sterne criticism, and was the result of an exemplary effort in literary detective work. The letters are well annotated and indexed, so that this work may easily be read as a substitute autobiography.

Hartley, Lodwick, *Laurence Sterne in the Twentieth Century: An Essay and a Bibliography of Sternean Studies, 1900–1965.* Chapel Hill: University of North Carolina Press, 1966. An extensive review of early twentieth century scholarship, with detailed notes and comments.

————, *Laurence Sterne: An Annotated Bibliography, 1965–1977, with An Introductory Essay-Review of the Scholarship.* Boston: G. K. Hall, 1978. This extends the Sterne bibliography up to 1977, and Hartley offers a characteristically concise account of recent Sterne criticism in his introductory essay.

Selected Dictionaries and Encyclopedias

Dictionary of National Biography, Smith, Elder & Co., 1898. Vol. 14, 199–221. This is a sober encyclopaedic review of all the facts about Sterne known to the Victorians, including some material then new.

Gene M. Moore
Virginia Commonwealth University

WALLACE STEVENS
1879–1955

Author's Chronology

Born on October 2, 1879, Reading, Pennsylvania; *1897* enters Harvard; *1900* moves to New York, without formally graduating from Harvard; *1901–1903* attends New York Law School; *1904* admitted to New York State Bar; *1909* marries Elsie Kachel; *1916* joins Hartford Accident and Indemnity Company, his lifetime employer, and moves to Hartford, Connecticut, his lifetime home; *1923* publishes first poetry collection, *Harmonium;* *1924* Holly Bright Stevens, his only child, born; *1924–1930* abandons poetry writing almost completely; *1934* becomes a vice-president of Hartford Accident and Indemnity Company; *1946* elected to National Institute of Arts and Letters; *1950* wins Bollingen Prize in Poetry; *1951* wins National Book Award for *The Auroras of Autumn;* *1955* wins Pulitzer Prize for Poetry and National Book Award for *Collected Poems;* dies August 2.

Author's Bibliography (selected)

Harmonium, 1923 (poems); *Ideas of Order,* 1936 (poems); *The Man with the Blue Guitar,* 1937 (poems); *Parts of a World,* 1942 (poems); *Transport to Summer,* 1947 (poems); *The Auroras of Autumn,* 1950 (poems); *The Necessary Angel,* 1951 (essays); *The Collected Poems,* 1954; *Opus Posthumous,* 1957 (poems, essays, drama, selected and edited posthumously); *Letters of Wallace Stevens,* 1966 (selected and edited posthumously); *The Palm at the End of the Mind,* 1971 (poems and a play, selected and edited posthumously).

Overview of Biographical Sources

Stevens' reluctance to discuss himself and his work, his wife's reticence, and her reputed destruction of some of Stevens' journals and letters after his death combine to make it unlikely that there will ever be a definitive biography. In particular there is only very limited information on his boyhood. Nevertheless, a fairly detailed view of Stevens' adult life can be pieced together from three sources: Samuel French Morse's *Wallace Stevens: Poetry as Life* (1970); Holly Stevens' gathering of Stevens' early journals in *Souvenirs and Prophecies: The Young Wallace Stevens* (1977); and Peter Brazeau's *Parts of a World: Wallace Stevens Remembered* (1983). While a definitive biography would have the advantage of convenience, it would probably repeat much of the material available in the Holly Stevens and Brazeau texts and in Stevens' own *Letters.*

Evaluation of Biographical Sources

Brazeau, Peter, *Parts of a World: Wallace Stevens Remembered.* New York: Random House, 1983. Purely biographical, this book covers Stevens' life from

1916 on. Brazeau intersperses interviews with nearly one hundred people who knew Stevens with brief passages of his own biographical commentary. This unconventional approach yields a multifaceted but coherent portrait of Stevens. Brazeau divides the book into three parts, The Insurance Man, The Man of Letters, and The Family Man, with the texture of Stevens' daily life rendered fully in each area. Brazeau's own commentary is detailed and accurate but not pedantic. The book makes compelling reading for scholar and general reader alike.

Morse, Samuel French, *Wallace Stevens: Poetry as Life.* New York: Pegasus, 1970. Morse offers a general bio-critical introduction to Stevens, alternating chapters of biography and criticism. Even the biographical chapters are peppered with literary criticism, however, diffusing the focus of those chapters. Morse thinks earlier critics have over-analyzed Stevens. But his own efforts to avoid that trap only result in superficial criticism, while the biography confines itself to Stevens' intellectual life and does not go into sufficient detail either. Of limited use to the scholar, the book's clear, unpretentious style recommends it to the general reader.

Stevens, Holly, *Souvenirs and Prophecies: The Young Wallace Stevens.* New York: Alfred A. Knopf, 1977. Essentially an edition of Stevens' previously unpublished youthful journals with interpolated commentary by Ms. Stevens, the poet's daughter, this book covers the poet's life up to 1914, thus complementing Brazeau's account of his adult life. The journals form an early intellectual autobiography but contain few personal revelations. Ms. Stevens provides useful information on her father's childhood that is not available elsewhere. When she stays with verifiable evidence, her commentary, although less detailed than Brazeau's, is sound, and unbiased by her relationship to the poet. Her remarks connecting journal entries with later poems are openly speculative, however, and often unconvincing.

Autobiographical Sources

Since Stevens did not like to discuss himself or his work, it is not surprising that he never wrote an autobiography. The closest thing to an autobiography is the *Letters of Wallace Stevens,* selected and edited by Holly Stevens, (New York: Alfred A. Knopf, 1966). This selection prints 992 letters from over 3,000 that are extant, covering sixty years. Ms. Stevens selects letters in which Stevens comments on his own and others' poetry, or on poetry in general; letters notable for their style; and letters that contain biographical information. The editor's annotations add valuable information. Stevens' style in the letters is graceful, intelligent, witty, sometimes amusingly cranky, always delightfully readable. While the letters show only Stevens' public self, they do provide the main source outside of the actual poetry for observing the development of the poet's thinking about his art. They have proven an essential resource both for biographers and critics.

Overview of Critical Sources

As of early 1985, well over forty books of criticism have been written either wholly or partly on Stevens; thirty-four full-length studies are still in print. Until the mid-1970's most books concentrated on close readings of the poetry, frequently stressing its affinities with French Symbolism (Michel Benamou, *Wallace Stevens and the Symbolist Imagination* [Princeton: Princeton University Press, 1972]) and English Romanticism (George Bornstein, *Transformations of Romanticism in Yeats, Eliot, and Stevens* [Chicago: University of Chicago Press, 1976]; Helen Regueiro, *The Limits of Imagination: Wordsworth, Yeats, and Stevens* [Ithaca, NY: Cornell University Press, 1976]) and its philosophical bent (Frank Doggett, *Stevens' Poetry of Thought* [Baltimore: The Johns Hopkins Press, 1966]; Roy Harvey Pearce and J. Hillis Miller, eds., *The Act of the Mind: Essays on the Poetry of Wallace Stevens* [Baltimore: The Johns Hopkins Press, 1965]). Since the mid-1970s criticism on Stevens has grown more theoretical as more critics have begun to apply post-structuralist methods to his work. These critics tend to value Stevens' abstract later work more highly than it was valued before, and use that work as evidence that Stevens deconstructs or questions traditional humanist values, rather than affirming them as most earlier critics had argued. The American roots of Stevens' poetry have come to be stressed more frequently too, with a proportionate downplaying of its European roots.

Evaluation of Selected Criticism

Bloom, Harold, *Wallace Stevens: The Poems of our Climate.* Ithaca, NY: Cornell University Press, 1977. Bloom applies to Stevens his controversial theory of the anxiety of influence, representing Stevens as achieving his poetic identity by wrestling with the examples of Wordsworth, Keats, Shelley, Emerson, and Whitman. In the process Bloom offers provocative readings of most of Stevens' canon. While many readers question Bloom's speculative, Freudian theory of influence, and object to his sometimes complicated style, this immensely well-informed and humane study cannot be ignored.

Litz, A. Walton, *Introspective Voyager: The Poetic Development of Wallace Stevens.* New York: Oxford University Press, 1972. This chronologically organized study of Stevens' early work covers the period 1914–1937, up to and including *The Man with the Blue Guitar,* perceptively and in detail. Litz slights Stevens' later work, however, by covering it in one chapter, and this imbalance limits the value of the book. This remains one of the best studies of Stevens' early poetry, but few subsequent critics have abided by Litz's judgment that Stevens' later work is significantly weaker than his earlier.

Riddel, Joseph N. *The Clairvoyant Eye: The Poetry and Poetics of Wallace Stevens.* Baton Rouge, LA: Louisiana State University Press, 1965. Although

Riddel has repudiated this early New Critical reading of Stevens, his book remains one of the most useful chronologically ordered close readings of the entire Stevens canon. Two especially helpful features are detailed discussions of Stevens' longer poems and Riddel's attempt to define Stevens' theory of imagination, a topic that has occupied most of Stevens' critics.

Vendler, Helen Hennessy, *On Extended Wings: Wallace Stevens' Longer Poems*. Cambridge Harvard University Press, 1969. Vendler proposes that Stevens' best work lies in his longer poems, and provides painstaking, clearly written analyses of those poems. Her first chapter is a general discussion of the connection between Stevens' thought and his style, especially his syntax, and the following chapters discuss individual poems. She concentrates on Stevens' style, saying less than most critics of the period about his ideas. This book is still widely considered the best single critical book on Stevens.

Other Sources

Doggett, Frank and Robert Buttel, eds. *Wallace Stevens: A Celebration*. Princeton: Princeton University Press, 1980. This valuable collection contains previously unpublished poetry, prose, letters, and aphorisms; two biographical essays by Holly Stevens (on family holidays) and Peter Brazeau (on the poet's visits to New York); and essays from differing theoretical perspectives by a number of Stevens' best critics.

Miller, J. Hillis, *Poets of Reality: Six Twentieth-Century Writers*. Cambridge: Belknap Press of Harvard University Press, 1965. The chapter on Stevens is the best essay-length analysis of the poet's stylistic and thematic development that uses traditional critical methods.

————, "Stevens' Rock and Criticism as Cure, " *Georgia Review* 30 (1976): 330–348. A seminal article that applies deconstructive criticism effectively to Stevens' late poetry.

The Wallace Stevens Journal (before 1977 *The Wallace Stevens Newsletter*). Articles, reviews, bibliographies, news and comments, and poems about Stevens. Frequently publishes reminiscences about Stevens.

Willard, Abbie F. *Wallace Stevens: The Poet and his Critics*. Chicago: American Library Association, 1978. An invaluable research tool. Although it becomes dated with every passing year, this exhaustive book describes thoroughly and evaluates all the significant criticism on Stevens up to its date of publication.

Alan Golding
University of Mississippi

ROBERT LOUIS STEVENSON
1850–1894

Author's Chronology

Born November 13, 1850, at Edinburgh, Scotland; *1867* enters Edinburgh University; *1871* gives up engineering for law; *1873* begins stormy times with parents, meets Mrs. Sitwell and Sidney Colvin, goes to Menton in France for his health; *1875* admitted to Scottish Bar, goes to France with cousin Bob Stevenson where he meets Fanny Osbourne; *1877* in Paris with Fanny; *1878* makes walking tour with donkey in the Cevennes, France; *1879* sails for America, takes train across the country to join Fanny in Monterey, California; *1880* marries Fanny; August, returns to Scotland with Fanny and her children and is reconciled to parents; goes to Davos in Switzerland for his health; *1882* settles in France; *1883* publishes *Treasure Island;* *1884* returns to England and settles in Bournemouth; *1885* publishes *A Child's Garden of Verses;* *1886* publishes *The Strange Case of Dr. Jekyll and Mr. Hyde* and *Kidnapped;* *1887* leaves England for good, settles at Saranac in the Adirondack Mountains in New York for his and Fanny's health; *1888* quarrels with William Ernest Henley over Fanny's published story "The Nixie," leaves on first South Seas voyage; *1889* buys "Vailima," estate in Upolu, Samoa; *1890* cruises to islands, visits Australia; settles in Samoa; *1894* while working on *Weir of Hermiston* dies on December 3; buried on top of Mount Vaea in Samoa.

Author's Bibliography (selected)

Travels with a Donkey, 1879 (essays); *A Child's Garden of Verses,* 1885 (poems); *New Arabian Nights,* 1882 (collected stories); *Treasure Island,* 1883 (novel); *The Strange Case of Dr. Jekyll and Mr. Hyde,* 1886 (novel); *Kidnapped,* 1886 (novel); *The Master of Ballantrae,* 1889 (novel); *Weir of Hermiston,* 1896 (novel, unfinished, published posthumously).

Overview of Biographical Sources

Stevenson biography has gone through three stages. The first, immediately following his death and well into the twentieth century, was an outpouring of almost hagiographical personal memoirs of Stevenson: reminiscences of sea captain Morse and Lord Guthrie; books in a "Stevenson-was-here" mode— Stevenson in Edinburgh, Davos, Hawaii, Samoa, Saranak, California, France, New Jersey; even his nurse Cummy's diary. This trend toward idolatry was reversed by Frank Swinnerton in 1914 with a debunking biography; John A. Steuart added an unsympathetic portrait in 1924. After a fallow period, however, later biographers have attempted a balanced view. Malcolm Elwin, for example, in *The Strange Case of Robert Louis Stevenson* (New York: Russell and Russell, 1950) makes the case that Stevenson's art suffered from the limits of the popular taste of the day and from Fanny's restrictive influence. Stevenson has also been the subject of several juvenile biographies throughout the century, such as E. O. Grover's *Robert Louis Stevenson: Teller of Tales* (New York: Dodd, Mead, 1940: republished by Gale Research Co., Detroit, 1975), though these still tend to conceal Stevenson's faults. There is as yet no definitive biography, and favorite topics for speculation are Stevenson's relationship with Fanny, the influence of his health upon his art, and his quarrel with Henley.

Evaluation of Selected Biographies

Calder, Jennie, *Robert Louis Stevenson: A Life Study*. New York and Toronto: Oxford University Press, 1980. Calder comes closer than other biographers to a psychological examination of Stevenson. She conveys especially well his fragility and constant concern over his health which made Stevenson often difficult, and she explores more sympathetically than other biographers the effects of Stevenson's personality on Fanny, especially as Fanny grew older. The biography is gracefully written and presents on the whole a balanced portrait of both Stevenson and Fanny.

Furnas, J. C. *Voyage to Windward.* New York: William Sloan Associates, 1951. Though older than the other biographies summarized here, Furnas' study is still very complete and is regarded by many as the standard biography of Stevenson. Perhaps a bit self-conscious in its attempt to balance Stevenson's shifting reputation, Furnas' essay in his appendix, "Dialectics of a Reputation," clearly sets forth the problems for biographers and critics of such a reputation. Furnas is the first biographer to work from the full text of Stevenson's youthful letters to Mrs. Sitwell. The book is sensible and readable and includes a full and useful bibliography.

Hennessy, James Pope, *Robert Louis Stevenson.* London: Jonathan Cape, 1974. Hennessy's emphasis is on environment as a shaping factor. He includes many colorful details which other biographers do not, giving a sense of Stevenson's involvement in everyday life. His analysis of Stevenson's trip to California and meeting with Fanny is fuller and more interesting than that of most other biographers, and though his critical assessment at the end of the book is rather clumsy, he makes several telling points about Stevenson's effects on a reader. Hennessy's book is a balanced, professional biography, if at times somewhat wry and jaded in its tone.

Autobiographical Sources

Though Stevenson wrote no autobiography, he was a prolific letter-writer, and his letters constitute a relatively complete picture of his life, despite Sidney Colvin's repressive editing in 1925. Stevenson's collected essays move from precious subjects to, eventually, his personal life and view of his art, as in "Falling in Love," and "A Humble Remonstrance."

Overview of Critical Sources

Critical material on Stevenson is still relatively sparse compared to the biographical sources. Since Stevenson's two major genres, the essay and the adventure novel, differ so widely, critics have difficulty finding approaches to his work. Most acknowledge that his particular gifts were as story-teller and stylist and that he had not reached his full potential at his death. The influences on his work of his childhood, his health, and his travels also preoccupy most critics.

Evaluation of Selected Criticism

Daiches, David, *Robert Louis Stevenson*. Norfolk, CT: New Directions, 1947. Daiches approaches his fellow Scot with sympathy and intelligence, and this short book remains the best criticism of Stevenson's work. Daiches discusses romantic device and style in *Treasure Island* and *Kidnapped* and points out that with *The Master of Ballantrae* Stevenson moved into a more human, dramatic mode. He regards *Weir of Hermiston,* as do most critics, as a fulfillment of Stevenson's promise and includes a long summary of the book. Daiches' pithy analysis of style and content in Stevenson's essays and poems is very insightful. The bibliographical note appended to the book is now dated but Daiches' evaluations of Stevenson are still essential to an understanding of the author.

Eigner, Edwin M. *Robert Louis Stevenson and the Romantic Tradition.* Princeton: Princeton University Press, 1966. Eigner places Stevenson in the tradition of the "serious romance" as opposed to the "sensational romance" and acknowledges "thinness of characterization" as one of the marks of this genre. Eigner includes a long discussion of *Jekyll and Hyde,* especially its use of narrators and the *Doppelganger* theme. Eigner attempts to prove that certain themes run throughout and unify Stevenson's work, and frequently points out earlier works similar to Stevenson's from which the author borrowed. Eigner's is a thorough critical discussion and a competent piece of scholarship.

Kiely, Robert, *Robert Louis Stevenson and the Fiction of Adventure.* Cambridge: Harvard University Press, 1965. Kiely includes a useful summary of Stevenson's aesthetic theories and an analysis of the Victorian quest for adventure in faraway places, placing Stevenson's work in this tradition. There are full summaries and analyses of *Treasure Island, Kidnapped, The Ebb Tide, The Master of Ballantrae,* and *Weir of Hermiston.* Kiely keeps the emphasis on the works and only occasionally mentions biography as an informing element. He attempts to prove, finally, that for Stevenson, the adventure novel became a metaphor for the risks all men take in life. After Daiches, Kiely's study seems the most accurate assessment of Stevenson's lasting reputation among readers.

Other Sources
Chesterson, G. K. *Robert Louis Stevenson.* London: Hodder and Stoughton;
1927. In the old-fashioned critical tradition, attempts an early evaluation of
Stevenson's gifts and limitations.

Daiches, David, *Robert Louis Stevenson and his World.* London: Thames and
Hudson, 1973. Heavily illustrated with photographs and drawings, lively and
affectionate text.

Geduld, Harry, M. *The Definitive Dr. Jekyll and Mr. Hyde Companion.* New
York: Garland, 1983. Text, analogues, commentary and criticism, history of
the story in theatre and film.

Saposnik, Irving S. *Robert Louis Stevenson.* New York: Twayne, 1974. Brief,
readable, and well-selected overview of Stevenson.

Smith, Janet Adam, ed. *Robert Louis Stevenson: Collected Poems.* 2nd ed.:
New York: Viking, 1971. Most authoritative collection of the poems.

Smith, Janet Adam, *Henry James and Robert Louis Stevenson: A Record of
Friendship and Criticism.* London: Rupert Hart-Davis, 1948. Contains their
correspondence.

Swearingen, Roger G. *The Prose Writings of Robert Louis Stevenson.* Hamden, CT: Archon Books, 1980. Based primarily on the Beinecke Yale collection
of Stevenson's work, listing in chronological order and sometimes with extensive notes, all Stevenson's prose work from his childhood to his death.

Selected Dictionaries and Encyclopedias
Yesterdays Author's of Books for Children, Vol. 2, Gale Research, 1978. Long
entry with many quotes and illustrations, useful for entertaining overview.

Lucy E. W. Rollin
Clemson University

HARRIET BEECHER STOWE
1811-1896

Author's Chronology

Born June 14, 1811, Litchfield, Connecticut, daughter of a widely-known Congregationalist preacher, Lyman Beecher; *1820* barely survives scarlet fever; *1827* after studying in Litchfield Academy and Hartford Female Seminary begins teaching in latter; *1832* family moves to Cincinnati, where her father administers Lane Seminary; *1834* her sketch of "Uncle Lot" wins local literary contest; *1836* marries Calvin E. Stowe, professor of religion at Lane, bears seven children in the next twelve years; *1850* moves to Brunswick, Maine, where *Uncle Tom's Cabin* is written; *1852* moves to Andover, Massachusetts; *1853-1862* publishes four more novels, contributes to first issue of *The Atlantic;* visits Europe three times; *1862* visits President Lincoln, urges emancipation; *1864* settles in Hartford, Connecticut and winters thereafter in Florida; *1872* becomes neighbor of Mark Twain in Nook Farm area of Hartford; *1886* husband dies; *1896* dies at age eighty-five.

Author's Bibliography (selected)

The Mayflower, 1843 (stories); *Uncle Tom's Cabin,* 1852 (novel); *Dred,* 1856 (novel); *The Minister's Wooing,* 1859 (novel); *The Pearl of Orr's Island,* 1862 (novel); *Religious Poems,* 1867; *Oldtown Folks,* 1869 (novel); *Poganuc People,* 1878 (novel).

Overview of Biographical Sources

Of the many biographies of Harriet Beecher Stowe, few are worth the time of the serious student. No other American writer has been so popular and yet so controversial; reactions to her as both woman and writer have ranged from adulation to detestation. She is an almost legendary figure who continues to inspire biographies of the irresponsibly novelized sort. Two nineteenth-century lives remain valuable, Charles E. Stowe's *Life of Harriet Beecher Stowe* (1889) and Annie Fields' *Life and Letters of Harriet Beecher Stowe* (Detroit: Gale Research, 1970). Neither Charles, Harriet's youngest son, nor Fields, her close friend, faces up to the weaknesses of Stowe's complex character, but they do write from a personal knowledge impossible to all later biographers. They and subsequent biographers up to the time of Forrest Wilson's *Crusader in Crinoline: The Life of Harriet Beecher Stowe* (1941) refer guardedly if at all to the two scandals which touched her, one arising from her article and book "vindicating" Lady Byron in the matter of the poet's alleged sexual misconduct, the other being her brother Henry Ward Beecher's sensational adultery trial.

The most important of the Stowe controversies, of course, was that generated by *Uncle Tom's Cabin,* and if today she seems to be clearly on the side of the angels, biographers have not always been capable of recreating an 1850's perspective. By the time Wilson's book appeared, passions had receded to the point of permitting a full, evenhanded narrative of her life. Since the publication of *Crusader in Crinoline,* no one has even attempted a life on the same scale. Edward Wagenknecht's *Harriet Beecher Stowe: The Known and the Unknown* (1965) sensibly adopts a thematic, rather than narrative, approach. Milton Rugoff's *The Beechers: An American Family in the Nineteenth Century,* while useful for the purpose of placing Harriet within the context of Lyman Beecher's large and talented family, portrays its author's skepticism better than the Beechers' motives.

Evaluation of Selected Biographies

Stowe, Charles Edward, *Life of Harriet Beecher Stowe.* Boston: Houghton Mifflin, 1889. Authorized by the novelist, this life by her son quotes generously from her frequently chatty and expansive letters and from those of her correspondents. As might be expected, it is staunchly partisan. One of the most interesting chapters presents his mother's epistolary friendship with George Eliot, whose novel *Adam Bede* (1859) skyrocketed her to international prominence in the decade of *Uncle Tom's Cabin,* and whose approval of *Oldtown Folks* Harriet Beecher Stowe was particularly eager to elicit. Charles Stowe's own writing is pedestrian and his transitions awkwardly abrupt, but he furnishes a useful index.

Wagenknecht, Edward, *Harriet Beecher Stowe: The Known and the Unknown.* New York: Oxford University Press, 1965. Wagenknecht is interested in Stowe's roles, such as wife, mother, aesthete, and reformer, and he organizes each chapter around one of them. He begins and ends with that of daughter, first the daughter of the famed New England preacher and his second wife and finally the daughter of a heavenly Father. His notes on his sources constitute an excellent basic bibliography.

Wilson, Forrest, *Crusader in Crinoline: The Life of Harriet Beecher Stowe.* Philadelphia: J. B. Lippincott, 1941. Over seven hundred pages long and meticulously researched, this life remains the definitive one. Wilson evokes the persons and places of his subject's life deftly and narrates smoothly. It is possible to disagree with some of his interpretations but not to dispute the author's balance of sympathy and critical judgment. He is struck, for instance, by the absence of any mention of Cincinnati in any of her novels, but the more significant fact is surely that Cincinnati, an ideal place for this New Englander to observe the interaction of East and West and—even more significantly for her—North and South in the years leading to the passage of the Fugitive Slave Act, is tacitly present in both *Uncle Tom's Cabin* and *Dred.* Wilson's is the biography of a literary person rather than a literary biography, but it is an indispensable aid to anyone in pursuit of the essential Harriet Beecher Stowe.

Autobiographical Sources

Probably the only Stowe novel of distinctive autobiographical interest is her last, *Poganuc People,* which depicts the Litchfield of her childhood and a number of traits of the young Harriet Beecher in Dolly Cushing. *Sunny Memories in Foreign Lands* (1854) describes her first European trip, and *Palmetto Leaves* (1873) is a very early piece of Florida boosterism. Otherwise Stowe reveals herself in hundreds of letters, of which there are caches in the Stowe-Day Foundation in Hartford and in a number of university libraries. The biographies mentioned above must be consulted, for nothing like a satisfactory edition of her letters exists. According to Wilson, Stowe wrote several chapters of *The Autobiography of Lyman Beecher,* which has been edited by Barbara M. Cross (Cambridge: Harvard University Press, 1961).

Overview of Critical Sources

Of the books focusing on Stowe's most famous novel, Edwin Bruce Kirkham's *The Building of Uncle Tom's Cabin* (Knoxville: University of Tennessee Press, 1977) is one of the most judicious. In recent decades critics have paid increasing attention to her other fiction, especially the New England novels. After a long period of critical neglect, several essays by Edmund Wilson in the 1940's and 1950's signaled a change which has resulted in the works noted below and several others worth mentioning, including John R. Adams's *Harriet Beecher Stowe* (New York, Twayne, 1963), a somewhat harsh evaluation of her work that counterpoises a generally more respectful body of modern criticism; Ellen Moers' essay *Harriet Beecher Stowe and American Literature* (Hartford: Stowe-Day Foundation, 1978), worthwhile for its feminist insights; and *Critical Essays on Harriet Beecher Stowe,* edited by Elizabeth Ammons (Boston: G. K. Hall, 1980), which conveniently illustrates the ebb and flow of Stowe criticism from the publication of *Uncle Tom's Cabin* on.

Evaluation of Selected Criticism

Crozier, Alice, *The Novels of Harriet Beecher Stowe.* New York: Oxford University Press, 1969. Less unified than Foster's, Crozier's study is nonetheless particularly successful at demonstrating how Stowe's historical sense—including her sensitivity to history in the making as she wrote in the 1850's—nourished her fiction. Her two chapters on the "interesting failure" *Dred* contain some of the most enlightening comments yet made on Stowe's strengths and weaknesses as a novelist. Crozier is less convincing in her other chief purpose of applying techniques of modern psychological criticism to her subject, as in her attempt to explain the "fascination" with Lord Byron which Stowe shared with so many other nineteenth-century readers.

Foster, Charles H. *The Rungless Ladder: Harriet Beecher Stowe and New England Puritanism.* Durham, NC: Duke University Press, 1954. Foster considers Stowe second in importance only to Nathaniel Hawthorne among New England novelists. Although he overstates the case for Stowe's post-Civil War society novels, his assessment of *The Minister's Wooing* and *Oldtown Folks* has blazed a critical trail. Although some subsequent critics have questioned the thoroughness of Stowe's grasp of New England theologians such as Cotton Mather and Jonathan Edwards, Foster has shown that no other novelist has so successfully integrated the Puritan intellectual heritage and keen personal observation of New England culture.

Other Sources

Hildreth, M. H. *Harriet Beecher Stowe: A Bibliography.* Hamden, Connecticut: Shoe String Press, 1976. An extensive resource for advanced students.

Selected Dictionaries and Encyclopedias

Critical Survey of Long Fiction, Salem Press, 1983. A brief biography and analysis of her major novels.

Robert P. Ellis
Worcester State College

JESSE STUART
1907–1984

Author's Chronology

Born August 8, 1907 in Greenup County, Kentucky; *1926* enters Lincoln Memorial University, Harrogate, Tennessee and is graduated with B.A. degree three years later; *1931* spends academic year at Vanderbilt University; *1934* publishes *Man With a Bull-Tongue Plow,* a sequence of 703 sonnet-like poems; *1936* publishes first collection of short stories; *1937* receives Guggenheim Fellowship to work and study in Scotland; *1938* publishes *Beyond Dark Hills,* an autobiography whose first draft had been submitted as a term paper at Vanderbilt University; *1939* marries Naomi Deane Norris; *1940* publishes first novel; *1943* receives Thomas Jefferson Southern Award for *Taps For Private Tussie,* a comic novel; *1949* publishes *The Thread That Runs So True,* cited by the National Education Association as the year's most important book; *1954* designated poet laureate of Kentucky; suffers severe heart attack; *1961* receives $5000 Fellowship of the Academy of American Poets; *1962* travels and lectures for U.S. State Department; *1975* publishes *The World of Jesse Stuart: Selected Poems; 1982* suffers stroke which eventually brings death in February, 1984.

Author's Bibliography (selected)

Man With a Bull-Tongue Plow, 1934 (poems); *Head O' W-Hollow,* 1936 (short stories); *Beyond Dark Hills: A Personal Story,* 1938 (autobiography); *Men of the Mountains,* 1941 (short stories); *Taps For Private Tussie,* 1943 (novel); *Album of Destiny,* 1944 (poems); *The Thread That Runs So True,* 1949 (autobiographical fiction); *A Jesse Stuart Reader,* 1963 (selected poetry and prose); *The World of Jesse Stuart: Selected Poems,* 1975; *The Best-Loved Short Stories of Jesse Stuart.* Ed. and with commentaries by H. Edward Richardson. Introduced by Robert Penn Warren, 1982.

Overview of Biographical Sources

In a time when literary criticism favored difficult or obscure texts with extraterritorial themes, Jesse Stuart wrote accessible poetry and prose dealing almost exclusively with his own place and people, the hill folk of eastern Kentucky. Among more than sixty volumes Stuart produced over a long and prolific career are several memorable autobiographical accounts which blend fact and fiction, further complicating the problem for literary historians and biographers.

The autobiographical nature of Stuart's earliest work prompted immediate interest in his life. Brief bio-critical essays were appearing in literary journals by the mid-1930's. Beginning in the early forties a number of theses and dissertations combining biographical materials with critical assessments began to appear. Two of these contain biographical information available nowhere else. They are: Lee Oly Ramey's "An Inquiry into the Life of Jesse Stuart as Related to His Literary Development and a Critical Study of His Works" (Master's Thesis, Ohio University, 1941); and F. H. Leavell's "The Literary Career of Jesse Stuart" (Dissertation, Vanderbilt University, 1965).

Useful for general information on Stuart's literary career is Everetta L. Blair's *Jesse Stuart: His Life and Works* (Columbia: University of South Carolina Press, 1967). Particularly valuable is Hensley C. Woodbridge's *Jesse and Jane Stuart: A Bibliography,* 3rd ed. (Murray, KY.: Murray State University Press, 1979). This bibliography includes Woodbridge's earlier *Jesse Stuart: A Bibliography* (Harrogate, TN.: LMU Press, 1960) which contains prefatory essays concerning Stuart by undergraduate classmates, teachers and friends.

Evaluation of Selected Biographies

Foster, Ruel E. *Jesse Stuart.* New York: Twayne, 1968. Foster questionably allows an overview of Stuart's autobiographical writings to perform "the biographical function" of his opening chapter. However, subsequent chapters on Stuart's poetry, short stories and novels are informed and balanced assessments that place Stuart's life and work against a background of literary history, traditions and influences. In a conclusion mediating between academics who have deemed Stuart unworthy of their attention and the uncritical praise of journalistic reviewers, Foster maintains that Stuart's fictional place, W-Hollow, is a part of America's literary topography similar to William Faulkner's Yoknapatawpha County.

Richardson, H. Edward, *Jesse: The Biography of an American Writer, Jesse Hilton Stuart.* New York: McGraw Hill, 1984. While illuminating his subject from diverse perspectives, Richardson manages to convey a sense of Stuart's unique and forceful personality in a narrative informed by sensitivity and insight. He chronicles Stuart's childhood; college and university days; the influence of mentors such as Donald Davidson and Robert Penn Warren; Stuart's early publishing successes and critical reception; his ensuing success as a platform speaker; travels; introduction to the literary world and to other writers such as Thomas Wolfe and Edgar Lee Masters; his courtship, marriage and happy domestic life during energetic years of farming, lecturing, teaching and writing; a near-fatal heart attack in 1954; creative droughts and disappointments; the determined comebacks—until a stroke left him comatose in 1982.

Although he relies heavily upon Stuart's autobiographies and autobiographical fiction, Richardson does not allow Stuart's engagingly vivid personal narratives to substitute for genuine biography. With the cooperation of Stuart's widow, and with access to Stuart's unpublished manuscripts, Richardson draws on the recollections, observations and correspondence of Stuart's teachers, classmates, friends and other contemporaries to produce the definitive biography of Stuart. Richardson shows how Stuart's prose and poetry often follow "even the most subtle contours of reality." But he is also aware that imaginative writers "use facts for creative and dramatic purposes." Repeatedly he demonstrates how Stuart collapses times and places and blends events to shape his narratives. Aware that while Stuart's autobiographical accounts may be, in a profound sense, the best source of his biography, Richardson nevertheless distinguishes between the life of the poet and Stuart's story of a poetic life as it is told in hundreds of poems and in several books, prefaces and essays. Richardson's biography is useful in gaining a more discerning appreciation of the art in many of Stuart's seemingly artless narratives.

Autobiographical Sources

Stuart told his story many times, and with such sincerity that critics and literary historians were often persuaded he needed no biographer. *Beyond Dark Hills* (1938) chronicles Stuart's struggles as a child of the hills, student and aspiring writer. *The Thread That Runs So True* (1949) is a fictionalized account of his efforts as a teacher and school administrator. *The Year of My Rebirth* (1956) records his recovery from a serious heart attack. In *The Kingdom Within* (1979) Stuart attends his own funeral, along with many friends, family members, and the hundreds of characters he created in poems, stories and novels.

Overview of Critical Sources

While Stuart's personal narratives, novels, poems and short stories have gained a relatively wide and admiring popular readership, critical reception has been mixed. Admirers have often been critically superficial. Among academic critics, a general readiness to equate folk life with simplicity, combined with a predilection to stylistic and structural complexity have favored a critical relegation of Stuart's work. Allen Tate omitted Stuart from an influential anthology, admitting prejudice arising from Stuart's identification with southern Appalachia and the image of the hillbilly. Durable stereotypes associated with the southern highlands, together with uncertainty about the relation of the mountain South to lowland South, and to the nation generally, have abetted a view of Stuart as a gifted naif without precedent, a phenomenon apart from literary influences or traditions, difficult to categorize except as a regionalist. A more positive evaluation of Stuart, advanced by Foster, is that the difficulty some critics have in labeling Stuart may be the mark of an originality arising from primal sources.

Evaluation of Selected Criticism

Clarke, Mary Washington, *Jesse Stuart's Kentucky.* New York: McGraw-Hill, 1968. Clarke sees Stuart's work as an accurate reflection of life in a Kentucky hill community of his generation. Aspects of folklore and folklife dealt with are: housing; dress; folk medicine; folk forms of entertainment, including songs, ballads and tales; and folk religion. Clarke qualifies the designation of Stuart as a regionalist with a view of Stuart as both specialist and universalist who employs the life of his place and people as "a token of the world at large." The study concludes with a valuable bibliographical commentary.

LeMaster, J. R. and Mary Washington Clarke, eds. *Jesse Stuart: Essays on His Work.* Lexington: University Press of Kentucky, 1977. The editors and eight other writers contribute informed discussions focusing on aspects of Stuart's life and work. Three contributors assess Stuart's achievement as a poet, novelist and short story writer. Others address the relationship of Stuart's humor to native American traditions; his relationship to the Fugitive-Agrarian group centered at Vanderbilt University; the question of regionalism; the significance of Stuart's preoccupation with place; his use of folklore and folklife; and his views and influence as an educator.

LeMaster, J. R. *Jesse Stuart: Kentucky's Chronicler-Poet.* Memphis, TN: Memphis State University Press, 1980. This first full-length study of Stuart's poetry examines his development from the juvenilia to the work of his later years, with special attention to imagery, Stuart's shortcomings as a craftsman, and his relationship to the tenets of Agrarianism. Although Stuart was never a member of the Agrarian group at Vanderbilt University, he has proved to be, in LeMaster's estimation, "the most constant Agrarian of them all."

Other Sources

Fain, John Tyree, and Thomas Daniel Young, eds. *The Literary Correspondence of Donald Davidson and Allen Tate.* Athens: University of Georgia Press, 1974. Sheds light on Stuart's relation to the Fugitive-Agrarians.

LeMaster, J. R. *Jesse Stuart: A Reference Guide.* Boston: G. K. Hall, 1979. An essential guide to reviews, critical essays and book-length studies of Stuart's life and work appearing between 1934 and 1977.

Stewart, Randall, *Regionalism and Beyond: Essays of Randall Stewart.* ed. George Core. Nashville, TN: Vanderbilt University Press, 1968. These discussions of regionalism in the larger context of American literature are useful for any estimate of Stuart's achievement. The essay "Tidewater and Frontier" clarifies the relation of upland to lowland South, places Stuart in the Frontier, and most of the Agrarians in the Tidewater tradition of Southern literature, and helps to account for Stuart's having remained on the periphery of the Agrarian group.

Jim Wayne Miller
Western Kentucky University

SIR JOHN SUCKLING
1609–1641?

Author's Chronology

Born Twickenham, England, 1609; enters Cambridge; *1623* leaves without a degree; *1627* admitted to Gray's Inn to study law, but leaves one month later at his father's death; *1627* may have accompanied the expedition to Ile de Re'; *1629* military service in Holland; reputation for high living and dissipation; *1630* knighted; *1631* ambassador to Germany; *1632* returns to England and the prodigal life; *1633* with the King's backing begins the mercenary courtship of an heiress; *1634* gambling and legal problems; charged with assaulting another of his heiress' suitors; *1635* corresponds with "Aglaura," pseudonymous subject of his play and poems; *1637* matures as a writer, producing *Aglaura* and some of his best poems; *1638 Aglaura* staged; *1639–1640* Charles I's military expeditions to Scotland; *1640* member of Parliament; *1641* implicated in the First Army Plot against Parliament; flees to France; dies possibly by suicide in late 1641 or early 1642.

Author's Bibliography (selected)

Fragmenta Aurea. A Collection of All the Incomperable Peeces, Written by Sir John Suckling, 1646; *The Last Remains of Sir John Suckling, Being a Full Collection of All His Poems and Letters,* 1659; *Sir John Suckling's Poems and Letters from Manuscript,* 1960; *The Works of Sir John Suckling. The Non-Dramatic Works,* 1971; *The Works of Sir John Suckling. The Plays,* 1971.

Overview of Biographical Sources

Since Sir John Suckling was born into a well-to-do and powerful family and spent the majority of his adult life in or around the Stuart Court, most of the important events of his thirty-three plus years are well documented through church, county, family, government and military records. Furthermore, since Suckling was the epitome of the wild Cavalier gallant—"the greatest gallant of his time and the greatest gamester," Aubrey calls him—he was a constant source of gossip for the letters of his friends, relatives, superiors, and enemies. His name and the outrageous situations he found himself in are also frequently mentioned in period legal proceedings since he spent most of his adult years involved in any number of law suits. Just about the only time of Suckling's life which is not well documented is his last six months, the period after he was charged with involvement in the First Army Plot against Parliament, fled to the continent, and may or may not have been murdered or committed suicide. In spite of all this, there is no readily available, full-scale biography of Suckling. Readers may best be served by the detailed biographical introduction to Thomas Clayton's *The Works of Sir John Suckling. The Non-Dramatic Works*

(Oxford: Clarendon, 1971) or the brief biographical section which begins Charles L. Squier's *Sir John Suckling* (1978). An early, enjoyable, but not very accurate account of Suckling's life can be found in John Aubrey's gossipy *Brief Lives* (1669).

Evaluation of Selected Biographies

Berry, Herbert, "A Life of Sir John Suckling." Dissertation: University of Nebraska, 1953. This unpublished dissertation suffers from a number of minor problems of the sort common to such works, such as, occasionally awkward language and sometimes overwhelming annotation. It is, however, by far the most detailed biography and a solid and scholarly piece of work. Some of Berry's biographical information has seen print in the introduction and annotations to his edition of Suckling's letters.

Clayton, Thomas, *Times Literary Supplement* (29 January 1960). Containing some additional information on Suckling's life, the research for this article and Berry's dissertation form the primary basis for Clayton's biographical introduction in *The Works of Sir John Suckling. The Non-Dramatic Works*, 1971.

Autobiographical Sources

In his *Sir John Suckling's Poems and Letters from Manuscript* (London, Ontario: University of Western Ontario, 1960) Herbert Berry made available fourteen of Suckling's letters with heavy annotation. In his edition of *The Works of Sir John Suckling. The Non-Dramatic Works* (1971), Thomas Clayton published more than fifty such letters plus *An Account of Religion by Reason* and other miscellaneous writings by the poet. These letters, lively, outspoken, and full of anecdote as they are, give considerable insight into Suckling's personality and the facts of his life. Many of his early letters are addressed to his cousin, Mary Cranfield, whom he wooed in a rather off-handed manner throughout his early twenties, and a number are addressed to her father, Lionel Cranfield, Earl of Middlesex, the former Lord Treasurer of England. Other women receive a number of letters, most notably Anne Willoughby, Suckling's unsuccessfully attempted heiress, and Mary Bulkeley, the married lady he wrote of as the pseudonymous Aglaura. Finally there are letters to a number of important men, including the diplomat Sir Henry Vane, the writer/courtiers Sir Kenelm Digby and Henry Jerman, the scholar John Selden, and the Royalist military commander William Cavendish, Earl of Newcastle.

Overview of Critical Sources

For a poet whose works are regularly taught in universities, Sir John Suckling has received relatively little individual critical attention, in part because of the real or apparent simplicity of his lyrics, and in part because of the tendency to lump him with Richard Lovelace, Thomas Carew, Robert Herrick and others under the convenient label "Cavalier." There is only one published, full-length study of Suckling's poetry, Charles L. Squier's *Sir John Suckling* (1978). Thomas Clayton's edition of the poetry, however, has a brief but thorough essay on Suckling's reputation from his own day to the present, and there are a number of fine journal articles. Finally, Suckling's work does come under regular consideration in critical studies of seventeenth-century poetry, love poetry, and, of course, the work of the Cavaliers.

Evaluation of Selected Criticism

Anselment, Richard A. " 'Men Most of All Enjoy, When Least They Do': The Love Poetry of Sir John Suckling," in *University of Texas Studies in Literature and Language,* XIV (1972), 17–32. Discusses the role of cynicism in Suckling's love lyrics.

Beaurline, L. A. " 'Why So Pale and Wan': An Essay in Critical Method," in *University of Texas Studies in Literature and Language,* IV (1963), 553–63. A model essay on the subject of how the critic deals with the apparently transparent poem.

Squier, Charles L. *Sir John Suckling.* Boston: Twayne, 1978. This is a solid and fairly detailed introduction to Suckling's work. It includes discussion of his plays and prose as well as of his poems, concluding with a chapter on the poet's achievement and a good short bibliography.

Other Sources

Miner, Earl, *The Cavalier Mode from Jonson to Cotton.* Princeton: Princeton University Press, 1971. Perhaps the best attempt at a thematic approach to Cavalier poetry. Miner covers such important poetic themes as living the good life, escaping the troubles of the age, the value of friendship, and sexual love. Suckling comes into the discussion on a regular basis, and several of his poems are analyzed.

Skelton, Robin, *The Cavalier Poets.* "Writers and Their Work," No. 117. London: Longmans, Green, 1960. A fine, brief appreciation of Suckling and the other Cavalier poets by a major critic.

Summers, Joseph H. *The Heirs of Donne and Jonson.* New York: Oxford University Press, 1970. The title makes clear the author's purpose. The chapter on Suckling, Herrick, and Carew, entitled "Gentlemen of the Court and Art," emphasizes the conscious attempt by these poets to take the stance of what Summers calls "a gentleman in moral as well as stylistic *deshabille*," at once polished and off the cuff, elegant, but not learned. The book is particularly good on Suckling's debt to Donne and Jonson.

Wedgwood, C. V. *Poetry and Politics Under the Stuarts.* Ann Arbor: University of Michigan Press, 1964. This excellent cross-disciplinary study by one of the finest English historians barely mentions Suckling, but is perhaps the best possible introduction to his world, the Court of James and Charles Stuart.

Selected Dictionaries and Encyclopedias

Critical Survey of Poetry, Salem Press, 1983. Brief biography and analysis of Suckling's major poems.

Dictionary of National Biography, Oxford, 1968. Good brief biographical essay with some critical material.

Michael M. Levy
University of Wisconsin—Stout

JONATHAN SWIFT
1667-1745

Author's Chronology

Born November 30, 1667, in Dublin, Ireland; *1682* enters Trinity College, Dublin; undistinguished career as a student; *1686* graduates from Trinity with B.A.; *1689* joins household of Sir William Temple at Moor Park in Surrey, England; tutors young Esther Johnson (Stella); *1692* M.A. Oxford; *1694* ordained Anglican priest and granted prebend at Kilroot, near Belfast, Ireland; *1697-1698* at work on *A Tale of a Tub* while serving Temple again at Moor Park; *1699* death of Temple; *1702* D.D. from Trinity; *1704* anonymous publication of *A Tale of a Tub; 1710* active support of Tory ministry via newspaper essays and pamphlets; residence in England; involvement with Esther Vanhomrigh (Vanessa), which he tries to cool in subsequent years; *1713* appointed Dean of St. Patrick's, Dublin; *1714* death of Queen Anne and fall of Tories; returns to Ireland feeling exiled; *1715* impeachment of his formerly powerful friends and supporters Viscount Bolingbroke and the Earl of Oxford; *1723* death of Vanessa; *1724* publication of *The Drapier's Letters* makes Swift a celebrated Irish hero; *1726* returns to London to arrange for publication of *Gulliver's Travels; 1727* Stella dies; *1742* failing health; judged incapable of caring for himself; *1745* dies on October 19.

Author's Bibliography (selected)

A Tale of a Tub, 1704 (satiric prose); *The Bickerstaff Papers,* 1708 (essays); *An Argument against Abolishing Christianity,* 1708 (essay); *The Conduct of the Allies,* 1711 (political pamphlet); *A Proposal for the Universal Use of Irish Manufacture,* 1720 (essay); *The Drapier's Letters,* 1724-1725 (essays); *Gulliver's Travels,* 1726 (satiric fiction); *A Modest Proposal,* 1729 (essay); "Verses on the Death of Dr. Swift," 1731 (poem); *Collected Works,* 1734-1735 (published in 4 volumes, under Swift's supervision).

Overview of Biographical Sources

Jonathan Swift has been both blessed and cursed by constant biographical attention. The almost microscopic investigation of Swift, begun even before his death, has yielded a great deal of useful information about the many mysteries and puzzles of his life, including his shifting political allegiances, curiously ambivalent relationships to two young women he nicknamed Stella and Vanessa, and lifelong mental and physical complaints, ending in what has often been called the madness of his last few years. Though many of the roots of Swift's satiric greatness are uncovered by biographical research and psychoanalytical speculation, such approaches must be used carefully as they sometimes tend to hide Swift's genius behind what appear to be his many peculiarities.

John Middleton Murry offers some interesting but more than occasionally overstated interpretations of Swift's life and work in *Jonathan Swift: A Critical Biography* (London: Jonathan Cape, 1954). Phyllis Greenacre's tone is more moderate than Murry's, but her *Swift and Carroll: A Psychoanalytic Study of Two Lives* (New York: International Universities Press, 1955) is a somewhat rigid Freudian analysis. Far more radical, persuasive, and influential is Norman O. Brown's chapter on Swift and "The Excremental Vision" from *Life Against Death* (Middletown, CT: Wesleyan University Press, 1959). A useful place to begin reading about Swift is in Samuel Johnson's "Life of Swift" from *Lives of the Poets* (1779–1781), a classic essay worth consulting even though much has been discovered about Swift since Johnson's time. Of modern brief studies of Swift, two in particular stand out as easily accessible and yet authoritative: Ricardo Quintana's *Swift: An Introduction* (1955) and Nigel Dennis' *Jonathan Swift: A Short Character* (1964). The definitive biography, fully documented and indexed, is Irvin Ehrenpreis' magisterial *Swift: The Man, His Works, and the Age* (1962–1983), complete in three volumes. As exhaustive as Ehrenpreis' work is, it may be supplemented by two studies focused much more narrowly: J. A. Downie's *Jonathan Swift: Political Writer* (London: Routledge and Kegan Paul, 1984) covers Swift's entire life, with particular attention to the historical and political dimensions of his works; and A. C. Elias, Jr.'s *Swift at Moor Park* (Philadelphia: University of Pennsylvania Press, 1982) discusses in great detail Swift's pivotal years with Sir William Temple, the years of his first great satires.

Evaluation of Selected Biographies

Dennis, Nigel, *Jonathan Swift*. New York: Macmillan, 1964. Dennis' volume is an energetically written critical biography, clearly presented and forcefully argued but not particularly subtle in its approach to a very complicated subject. To Dennis, Swift appears as a rather melodramatic and peculiar character, and while these are indeed qualities that make him perpetually interesting to modern readers and perhaps even account for some of the strengths of his works. Dennis perpetuates some of the myths about the gloomy, unbalanced figure that Ehrenpreis tries to dispel in his more recent study. Dennis is particularly good, however, on the contrast between Swift and Defoe, and the personal background of Swift's characteristic satiric style.

Ehrenpreis, Irvin, *Swift: The Man, His Works, and the Age*. 3 vols. Cambridge: Harvard University Press, 1962–1983. In three full volumes totaling over 2000 pages Ehrenpreis has written a biography that is as comprehensive, authoritative, detailed, and balanced as one could ever expect. Volume I, *Mr. Swift and His Contemporaries* (1962), covers Swift's early years, emphasizing his relationship with Sir William Temple, in whose household and, to a great extent, in whose defense he composed his first great satires. Volume II, *Dr. Swift* (1967), begins with the death of Temple and traces in sometimes overwhelming detail Swift's immersion in political pamphleteering and his complicated friendships with Bolingbroke, Oxford, Stella, and Vanessa. Volume III, *Dean Swift* (1983), focuses on Swift's return to Ireland for the remainder of his life as a kind of exile that he always resented but nevertheless turned into a creative retreat. Throughout, Ehrenpreis sets out to correct what he feels are commonly repeated errors about Swift's life. Most importantly, he argues that Swift was not the gloomy, misanthropic, misogynistic, incipiently mad character he is often thought to be. Ehrenpreis aims his biography primarily at a scholarly reader, and those not well versed in eighteenth-century literature and history may find some sections difficult to follow. But these three volumes are essential to a full understanding of Swift's life and times.

Quintana, Ricardo, *Swift: An Introduction.* New York: Oxford University Press, 1955. Quintana outlines the major events of Swift's life in his first chapter and then uses the remaining chapters to sketch an intellectual biography, relating Swift's works to broad social, political, and literary contexts. For a short study, this book is remarkably comprehensive, commenting substantively on all the works by Swift likely to have continuing importance, including some of his poems. In discussing Swift's life, Quintana is far more interested in his ethical and political beliefs and sense of himself as a satirist than he is with such topics as his relationship to Stella and Vanessa and his physical and mental health. Supported by the knowledge but not the extensive documentation and formality of his earlier work *The Mind and Art of Jonathan Swift* (New York: Oxford University Press, 1936), Quintana's *Introduction* is extremely readable, reliable, and informative.

Autobiographical Sources

Swift wrote no autobiography, but much about his personality, habits, and day to day activities can be gleaned from his letters. *The Correspondence of Jonathan Swift* (Oxford: Clarendon Press, 1963–1965) fills five volumes, though the bulk of these materials covers Swift's later years. The *Journal to Stella* (Oxford: Clarendon Press, 1948) comprises sixty-five letters from Swift to Stella and her companion, Rebecca Dingley, often written in a kind of private code suggesting Swift's linguistic facility as well as his occasional childishness and playfulness. Many of Swift's poems are occasional, written to or for particular friends to communicate news or a joke, and therefore contain useful autobiographical information. Of special interest are such poems as "The Author upon Himself" (1714) and "Verses on the Death of Dr. Swift" (1731), which create a fictional "Swift" relevant to our knowledge of the real Swift.

Overview of Critical Sources

Swift is known primarily as one of the great satirists of the eighteenth century, and much of his fame rests on two commonly reprinted works, *Gulliver's*

Travels (1726) and the devastatingly ironic essay *A Modest Proposal* (1729). Swift's achievement, however, extends far beyond these texts: the modern edition of his writing runs to seventeen volumes and contains an astonishing variety of journalistic pieces, political pamphlets, satiric essays and allegories, and poems. An overwhelming number of books and articles have been written on Swift, focusing not only on the topics of his satire but also especially on his characteristic satiric techniques. Some of the best critical studies cover only one major work, say, *Gulliver's Travels* or *A Tale of a Tub,* but very often contain insights or background relevant to other texts as well.

Evaluation of Selected Criticism

Donoghue, Denis, *Jonathan Swift: A Critical Introduction.* Cambridge: Cambridge University Press, 1969. Donoghue's study is allusive and intellectually demanding, perhaps too much so for the first-time reader of Swift. When it is read through patiently, however, it is consistently rewarding, filled with shrewd comments on Swift's entire life and career. Donoghue is particularly good on the positive qualities of Swift's poetry, a topic often neglected by critics.

Ewald, Jr., William B. *The Masks of Jonathan Swift.* Oxford: Basil Blackwell, 1954. Ewald investigates Swift's use of personae or "masks" in the context of other seventeenth and eighteenth-century authors using the same device. His comments on the minor as well as major satires show how Swift used this technique repeatedly and for a variety of purposes. This topic has been studied by many critics since Ewald's book was published, but his study is still the most thorough.

Rosenheim, Jr., Edward W. *Swift and the Satirist's Art.* Chicago: University of Chicago Press, 1963. Rosenheim presents both a broad treatment of satire as a literary mode and a very sharply focused analysis of Swift's particular satiric devices, supported by detailed close readings of passages from the major works. He interprets these works not only as attacks on various abuses perceived by Swift but also as critical investigations of the fundamental ideas and beliefs of mankind. For all his focus on satire, Rosenheim also shows how such works as *A Tale of a Tub* and *Gulliver's Travels* are unique and successful because they draw on non-satiric as well as satiric traditions, such as comedy.

Williams, Kathleen, *Jonathan Swift and the Age of Compromise.* Lawrence: University of Kansas Press, 1958. Quite in contrast with those who emphasize the savagery and latent despair of Swift's satire, Williams argues that Swift is an energetic but eloquent spokesman for moderation and reason. In the major satires, the enemy is extremism, and Swift constantly battles to reinstate what he defines as the true Christian classical heritage.

Other Sources

Fussell, Paul, *The Rhetorical World of Augustan Humanism.* New York: Oxford University Press, 1965. An elegantly written and persuasive account of the values and images shared by the major eighteenth-century writers, including Swift.

Jones, Richard Foster, "The Background of *The Battle of the Books*," in *The Seventeenth Century: Studies in the History of English Thought and Literature from Bacon to Pope*. Stanford: Stanford University Press, 1951, pp. 10–40. A highly informative account of the Ancient vs. Modern controversy that animates many of Swift's works.

Leavis, F. R. "The Irony of Swift," in *The Common Pursuit*. London: Chatto and Windus, 1952, pp. 73–87. An unrelenting analysis of Swift as a savagely egotistical satirist delighting only in the destruction of his opponents.

Monk, Samuel Holt, "The Pride of Lemuel Gulliver," *Sewanee Review*, LXIII (1955), 48–71. Essential for a full understanding of Swift's use of personae and the distinction, often blurred, between Swift's temperament and beliefs and those of his satiric spokesmen.

Sidney Gottlieb
Sacred Heart University

ALGERNON CHARLES SWINBURNE
1837–1909

Author's Chronology

Born April 5, 1837, London, England to Admiral Charles and Lady Jane Swinburne; *1849* enters Eton College; *1851* writes "The Triumph of Gloriana" commemorating visit to Eton of Queen Victoria and Prince Albert; *1853* begins private tutoring for entering Oxford rather than return to Eton; *1854* wishes to join the army to fight in the Crimea but is prevented by his father; *1856* enters Balliol College, Oxford; *1857* meets Dante Gabriel Rossetti, William Morris, and Edward Burne-Jones; *1860* leaves Oxford without taking a degree; publishes *The Queen Mother and Rosamond; 1861* settles in London after visiting France and Italy; *1862* is rejected in love and writes "The Triumph of Time"; *1864* visits Walter Savage Landor in Florence; *1865* publishes *Atalanta in Calydon,* which brings wide recognition; publishes *Chastelard; 1866 Poems and Ballads* causes a public scandal; *1867* meets Guisseppi Mazzini; *1871* publishes *Songs before Sunrise; 1877* loses his health after his father's death; *1879* taken by Theodore Watts to live at The Pines in Putney; continues to publish in a variety of literary forms until his death; *1882* visits Paris and meets Victor Hugo, last visit to the Continent; *1909* dies on April 10 at The Pines.

Author's Bibliography (selected)

Laus Veneris, 1866 (poems); *A Song of Italy,* 1867 (poems); *William Blake: A Critical Study,* 1868; *Under the Microscope,* 1872 (criticism); *Bothwell,* 1874 (drama); *Erechtheus,* 1876 (drama); *A Year's Letters,* 1877 (novel); *A Study of Shakespeare,* 1880; *Mary Stuart,* 1881 (drama); *A Study of Victor Hugo,* 1886; *The Sisters,* 1892 (drama); *Studies in Prose and Poetry,* 1894; *A Channel Passage and Other Poems,* 1904; *Ballads of the English Border,* 1925; *Lesbia Brandon,* 1952 (novel).

Overview of Biographical Sources

Although Swinburne is regarded as the *enfant terrible* of the Victorian period by literary historians, he inspired great affection in many who knew him. The numerous reminiscences of Swinburne which appeared after his death present an idealized portrait of the man who was bedeviled by sexual perversions and alcoholism. Among these are Mary C. J. Leith's *The Boyhood of Algernon Charles Swinburne* (London: Chatto & Windus, 1917), Coulson Kernahan's *Swinburne as I Knew Him* (London: John Lane, 1919), and Clara Watts-Dunton's *The Home Life of Swinburne* (London: A. M. Philpot, 1922). Edmund Gosse's *The Life of Algernon Charles Swinburne* (1917) is the first book to communicate a sense of Swinburne's complexity, but Gosse was constrained by the family to withhold vital information. Later biographies have been more forthright in illuminating the darker reaches of the poet's character. Jean Overton Fuller's *Swinburne: A Critical Biography* (1968) stresses these darker aspects. Georges Lafourcade's *Swinburne: A Literary Biography* (1932) presents a balanced view of Swinburne and remains the most authoritative account. Philip Henderson's *Swinburne: Portrait of a Poet* (1974) makes use of much new material. It is a readable and scholarly book.

Evaluation of Selected Biographies

Fuller, Jean Overton, *Swinburne: A Critical Biography*. London: Chatto & Windus, 1968. This biography focuses on the seamier side of Swinburne's character and makes use of unpublished material to illuminate the poet's predilection for flagellation. It contains informative chapters on Swinburne's relationships with Adah Menkin and Simeon Soloman, but Fuller's argument that Swinburne's cousin, Mary Gordon was his mysterious lost love is unconvincing, and the book lacks the density of detail necessary for a compelling biography. Consideration of the literature takes the form of descriptive summary and lengthy quotation.

Gosse, Edmund, *The Life of Algernon Charles Swinburne*. New York: Macmillan, 1917. This is the first of the major biographies, and even today it is indispensable. Eight years in preparation, Gosse's biography remains the most detailed account of Swinburne's life. Events such as Swinburne's childhood meetings with Samuel Rogers and William Wordsworth and his later meeting with Walter Savage Landor are related with remarkable vividness. Of special value are Gosse's account of the publishing history, critical reception and popular appeal of *Poems and Ballads* (1866) and his treatment of Swinburne's life in the 1870's, especially the poet's relationship with James McNeill Whistler and Benjamin Jowett. Although Gosse does not address such matters as the influence of the Marquis de Sade and Swinburne's sexual depravities and alcoholism, he does convey a sense of the author's complex personality and prodigious creative energy. His treatment of Swinburne's poetry and plays is almost wholly laudatory and he makes only passing reference to *Lesbia Brandon,* but his evaluation of the criticism is more discriminating and hence more useful.

Gosse knew Swinburne personally and he had virtually unlimited access to the recollections of the poet's friends and acquaintances. The result is a mine of fascinating anecdotes about Swinburne, but because human memory is fallible this should be supplemented by other biographies, especially Georges Lafourcade's *Swinburne: A Literary Biography,* which repairs the major deficiencies of this one.

Henderson, Philip, *Swinburne: Portrait of a Poet.* New York: Macmillan, 1974. The best of the recent lives, this is a thoroughly researched book built on the previous biographies and making good use of Cecil Y. Lang's great edition of Swinburne's letters. Henderson sheds new light on the character of Mary

Gordon and provides a clearer understanding of the relationship with her cousin. This book is especially informative about the Pre-Raphaelite's influence on Swinburne both at Oxford and later in London and the terrible years after the death of Swinburne's father before Theodore Watts came to the poet's rescue. Although Henderson all but ignores Swinburne's voluminous critical writing, his discussion of the poetry at times has critical value and he provides a sensitive treatment of Swinburne's novels. Written in crystal clear prose and arranged chronologically by chapters covering short periods of time, usually two or three years, this biography is a pleasure to read.

Lafourcade, Georges, *Swinburne: A Literary Biography*. London: G. Bell and Sons, 1932. Although it has been superseded in some details by subsequent studies, Lafourcade's biography remains one of the most helpful of the full-length lives. At the time of publication it was a new biography utilizing previously unpublished letters and works of Swinburne and correcting various misconceptions and omissions of Edmund Gosse and other biographers. It has an interesting chapter on Swinburne's aristocratic lineage and is especially helpful in illuminating Swinburne's experiences at Oxford and his final years at The Pines. The great strength of Lafourcade's biography is its vivid re-creation of the milieu of Swinburne's world, done in a clear style and with a judicious use of detail. The focus throughout is on the man, with the result that one comes away from his book feeling one almost knows personally the author of *Atalanta in Calydon, Poems and Ballads* and the rest.

Watts-Dunton, Clara, *The Home Life of Swinburne*. London: A. M. Philpot, 1922. Although making no claims to scholarship or critical acumen, this memoir by the widow of Theodore Watts-Dunton offers intimate glimpses of Swinburne not to be found elsewhere. What emerges is an engaging boy-man with an impish sense of humor, a special love of the Hawthorne trees of his neighborhood, a fondness for the stories of Sherlock Holmes, and a childlike openness to those he was close to, counterbalanced by an almost pathological distaste for strangers. This is a loving portrait of "the Bard," as Swinburne was known at The Pines.

Autobiographical Sources

Swinburne wrote no formal autobiography but the bulk of his work strongly reflects his obsessive preoccupation with such matters as sex, religion, and political freedom, providing a clear measure of his aberrant attitudes and opinions. His two novels, *A Year's Letters* and *Lesbia Brandon* and his play, *The Sisters* contain pronounced autobiographical content, which has attracted the attention of numerous scholars; and "Thalassius" (1880) is often regarded as a spiritual autobiography. Swinburne was a prolific letter writer, many of which are intensely personal. Lang's monumental edition of *The Swinburne Letters*

(New Haven: Yale University Press, 1959–1962) is a rich source of autobiographical material.

Overview of Critical Sources

Because of his romantic sensibility and exuberance of imagery Swinburne was virtually ignored by the New Critics. Until recently the only useful criticism of Swinburne were the book-length studies that appeared in the earlier years of this century. But in 1971 the Spring-Summer issue of *Victorian Poetry* was devoted to Swinburne, an event hailed by Lang as the beginning of a new era in Swinburne studies. Several of the fifteen critical articles in this issue combine explication with historical research, which Lang sees as necessary for understanding Swinburne's poetry. T. Earle Welby's *A Study of Swinburne* (New York: Barnes & Noble, 1926), Samuel C. Chew's *Swinburne* (1929), Clyde Kenneth Hyder's *Swinburne's Literary Career and Fame* (Durham: Duke University Press, 1933), and Lafourcade's *Swinburne: A Literary Biography* (1932) have been reprinted in recent years, signalling a revitalized interest in Swinburne.

Evaluation of Selected Criticism

Chew, Samuel C. *Swinburne,* Boston: Little, Brown, 1929. Though first published over fifty years ago, this remains the best of the book-length studies of Swinburne. Chew's introductory chapter, which focuses on the personal and literary influences that shaped Swinburne's sensibility, is of great value. The chief strength of this book is Chew's discriminating and readable appraisal of Swinburne's *oeuvre* with special attention given to works usually ignored such as the Border ballads and the Arthurian poems. The one critical lapse is the dismissal of *A Year's Letters* and *The Sisters* as negligible. Chew clearly demonstrates Swinburne's cosmopolitanism by remarking affinities with various cultural phenomena as well as with other writers. The book has a fine chapter on Swinburne's criticism and it contains an excellent index.

Riede, David G. *Swinburne: A Study of Romantic Mythmaking.* Charlottesville: University Press of Virginia, 1978. In a striking departure from earlier criticism, Riede argues that Swinburne is essentially a mythopoeic poet in the tradition of the English romantics and he provides original and provocative readings of certain of Swinburne's works, notably *Poems and Ballads* (1866) and the Greek plays.

Welby, T. Earle, *A Study of Swinburne.* New York: Barnes & Noble, 1926. This general study gives a useful account of Swinburne's invective and contains a valuable discussion of *Songs before Sunrise,* which Welby regards as the pinnacle of Swinburne's poetry, with informative comments on the genesis and development of Swinburne's political sentiments. Welby awards high marks to the first series of *Poems and Ballads* for expanding the diction of English poetry, and he has a helpful chapter on the Poet as Critic. The approach is predominately biographical. The tone is uniformly appreciative and at times defensive.

Other Sources

Bush, Douglas, *Mythology and the Romantic Tradition in English Poetry.* Cambridge: Harvard University Press, 1937. The chapter on Swinburne is a rich exploration of classical influences on the poet's essentially un-Hellenic corpus. Marked by erudition and wit, Bush's criticism concludes that Swinburne remains "a mid-Victorian romantic."

Eliot, T. S. "Swinburne as Poet," in *Selected Essays.* London: Faber and Faber, 1932. Suggestive, though unsympathetic, comments about the language of Swinburne's poetry.

Praz, Mario, *The Romantic Agony.* London: Oxford University Press, 1933. The most extensive examination of the aberrant aspects of Swinburne's work.

Selected Dictionaries and Encyclopedias

British Writers, Charles Scribner's Sons, 1982. General introduction to Swinburne's life and work.

Critical Survey of Poetry, Salem Press, 1982. Critical overview of Swinburne and his writings.

Robert G. Blake
Elon College

ALLEN TATE
1899–1979

Author's Chronology

Born November 19, 1899, Winchester, Kentucky, of Scotch-Irish and English ancestry; *1918* enters Vanderbilt University, where he studies with John Crowe Ransom, rooms with Robert Penn Warren, participates in "Fugitive Group" discussions of literature and philosophy, and in publishing *The Fugitive*, magazine which marks inception of Southern Renascence; *1924* marries Caroline Gordon, novelist; *1924–1928* lives in New York; *1928–1929* in England and France on Guggenheim Fellowship; *1934–1942* teaches at Southwestern University, Woman's College of North Carolina, and Princeton; *1943–1944* holds the chair of poetry in the Library of Congress; *1944–1945* edits *Sewanee Review;* *1946* divorces Caroline Gordon; remarries her four months later; *1948–1951* lectures at New York University; joins Roman Catholic Church in 1950; *1951–1968* teaches at University of Minnesota; *1953* Fulbright Professor, University of Rome; *1956* receives Bollingen Prize; lectures in India for Fulbright program; *1958* receives honorary M.A., Oxford University; lectures at Oxford and Harvard; *1959* divorces Caroline Gordon; marries Isabella Gardner; *1962* receives the Gold Medal of the Dante Society in Florence, Italy; *1964* elected to American Academy of Arts and Letters; *1965* American Academy of Arts and Sciences; *1966* divorces Isabella Gardner; marries Helen Heinz; *1968* President of the National Institute of Arts and Letters; *1968* moves to Sewanee, Tennessee; *1979* dies February 9.

Author's Bibliography (selected)

Mr. Pope and Other Poems, 1928; *Stonewall Jackson: The Good Soldier*, 1928 (biography); *Jefferson Davis: His Rise and Fall*, 1930 (biography); *Poems: 1928–1931*, 1932; *The Mediterranean and Other Poems*, 1936; *Reactionary Essays on Poetry and Ideas*, 1936 (criticism); *Selected Poems*, 1937; *The Fathers*, 1938 (novel); *Reason and Madness: Critical Essays*, 1941; *Poems: 1922–1947*, 1948; *On the Limits of Poetry*, 1948 (criticism); *The Forlorn Demon*, 1953 (criticism); *The Man of Letters in the Modern World*, 1955 (criticism); *Collected Essays*, 1959; *Poems*, 1960; *Essays of Four Decades*, 1968; *The Swimmers and Other Selected Poems*, 1970; *Memoirs and Opinions 1926–1974*, 1975; *The Fathers and Other Fiction*, 1977; *Collected Poems, 1919–1976*, 1978; *The Poetry Reviews of Allen Tate, 1924–1944*, 1983.

Overview of Biographical Sources

Although a definitive biography of Tate has not yet been published, there have been several useful studies which combine biographical information with literary criticism of Tate's poetry, fiction and essays. George Hemphill's *Allen*

1153

Tate (Minneapolis: University of Minnesota Pamphlets on American Writers, 1964) is a reliable brief introduction. Ferman Bishop's *Allen Tate* (New York: Twayne, 1967) provides a biographical sketch. Radcliffe Squires', *Allen Tate: A Literary Biography* (1971) is the most inclusive study of Tate's life, though the emphasis is on Tate's literary career. Radcliffe Squires, editor, *Allen Tate and His Work* (Minneapolis: University of Minnesota Press, 1972) contains a number of portraits and reminiscences of Tate which evoke the man and fill in some biographical gaps. Two collections of correspondence serve as important biographical sources: John Tyree Fain and Thomas Daniel Young, editors, *The Literary Correspondence of Donald Davidson and Allen Tate* (Athens: University of Georgia Press, 1974); Thomas Daniel Young and John J. Hindle, editors, *The Republic of Letters in America: The Correspondence of John Peale Bishop & Allen Tate* (Lexington: University Press of Kentucky, 1981). As with all of the biographical materials on Tate, the emphasis in these two volumes is on the literary career; yet a rich sense of the man emerges from both volumes.

Evaluation of Selected Biography

Squires, Radcliffe, *Allen Tate: A Literary Biography.* New York: Pegasus, 1971. As the title of this volume suggests, the focus is more on the man of letters than the man, for Squires abides by what he calls in his preface the "gentlemanly contract" necessary when writing about a living contemporary. Thus the reader will learn here almost nothing about Tate's complex marital record, for example; the complicated (twice married, twice divorced) relationship with his first wife, Caroline Gordon the novelist, receives no direct attention, nor do other important matters such as Tate's conversion to Catholicism. As a biographical record, this volume is best on the early years, sketchiest on the later years. Written with the cooperation of Tate, the book is solid and reliable as far as it goes. As a critical biography, it is excellent, and the best overall study to date.

Autobiographical Sources

Tate's *Memoirs and Opinions, 1926–1974* is the only autobiographical source. Strictly speaking, it is not an autobiography, but a sequence of recollections, as Tate says, "of the literary life," of some five years in Europe as a "half-hearted expatriate," and of other phases of Tate's career. The freshest material is found in the brief chapter on Tate's boyhood and in the recollections of his time as a "literary tourist" in Europe. On the whole, Tate's letters, cited above, constitute the most significant body of autobiographical material.

Overview of Critical Sources

It is difficult to say whether Tate's primary reputation, now or during his lifetime, depends on his work as poet, or on his prolific career as essayist and literary critic. Perusal of the some two hundred and fifty works about Allen

Tate listed in the Squires bibliography *(Allen Tate and His Works)* reveals an almost equal interest in his criticism and in his poetry. Clearly, it was as poet-critic that he exerted a seminal influence in the years 1925-1960. Yet his only novel, *The Fathers,* continues to receive a good deal of attention and is correctly regarded as central in the fiction of the Southern Renascence. His work as biographer has received little attention. On the whole, his role as Southern Agrarian has been disproportionately emphasized at the expense of his primary identity: the engaged man of letters in the modern world.

Evaluation of Selected Criticism

Bishop, Ferman, *Allen Tate.* New York: Twayne, 1967. An introduction to Tate's work, this volume is a useful place to begin. It includes chapters on all phases of Tate's career, even the neglected category of Tate the biographer. There is a selected bibliography with annotations.

Meiners, R. K. *The Last Alternatives: A Study of the Works of Allen Tate.* Denver: Swallow Press, 1963. A detailed and perspicacious examination of Tate's criticism, fiction, and poetry, this volume successfully traces the continuity of Tate's ideas. Meiners illuminates Tate's style, and examines perceptively such major poems as "Seasons of the Soul" and "The Mediterranean."

Rubin, Louis D., Jr. *The Wary Fugitives: Four Poets and the South.* Baton Rouge: Louisiana State University Press, 1978. While this volume is not devoted entirely to Tate's work, Rubin—who has written extensively about Tate—provides here one of the best accounts of Tate as southerner and his role in the complex matter of the Fugitive-Agrarian group. Also included are perceptive readings of important Tate poems, the definitive discussion of "Ode to the Confederate Dead," and a solid treatment of *The Fathers.*

Squires, Radcliffe, ed. *Allen Tate and His Works.* Minneapolis: University of Minnesota Press, 1972. Along with the biographical portraits cited above, this volume contains extensive selections on Tate as essayist and as poet. Many of the best journal articles on Tate, including those by Cleanth Brooks, R. P. Blackmur, George Core, Arthur Mizener and Howard Nemerov, are conveniently gathered together here. For this reason, as well as for the extensive bibliography included, this volume, together with the literary biography by Squires cited above, is the most important work of Tate criticism to date.

Other Sources

Bradford, M. E. *Rumors of Mortality: An Introduction to Allen Tate.* Dallas: Argus Academic Press, 1969. A good introduction.

Cowan, Louise, *The Fugitive Group: A Literary History.* Baton Rouge: Louisiana State University Press, 1959. Of the number of books which deal with The Fugitives, this detailed, reliable, and well-written study is the best.

"Homage to Allen Tate" issue, *Sewanee Review,* 67 (Autumn 1959), 528–631. This contains tributes from Malcolm Cowley, Donald Davidson, T. S. Eliot, Robert Lowell, Andrew Lytle, Jacques Maritain, Katherine Anne Porter, John Crowe Ransom and others.

Selected Dictionaries and Encyclopedias

American Writers, Charles Scribner's Sons, 1974. Twenty-three page overview of Tate's life and work.

Contemporary Poets, St. Martin's Press, 1975. Biographical outline, sketch of career and bibliography.

Southern Writers: A Biographical Dictionary, Louisiana State University Press, 1979. Brief sketch of life and work.

H. R. Stoneback
State University of New York
New Paltz

EDWARD TAYLOR
1642?–1729

Author's Chronology

Born in or near Sketchley, Leicestershire, England, probably in the year *1642; 1662–1667* may have attended Cambridge University or one of the dissenting academies; eventually may have taught in Bagworth, Leicestershire; writes some early poems, largely occasional and satirical; forced by *1662* Act of Uniformity (requiring all clergy and schoolmasters to take an oath of allegiance to the Anglican Church) to immigrate to New England; *1668* sets sail for America and starts *Diary;* enters Harvard on July 23, given advanced standing; encourages Samuel Sewall, later to become author of his own famous *Diary,* to attend Harvard; rooms with Sewall and becomes acquainted with Chauncy, Mather, and other leading men of New England; *1671* receives B.A.; called by the congregation at Westfield, Massachusetts to preach; remains at Westfield where he serves as minister and as physician until his death; *1674* marries Elizabeth Fitch after courting her through verses and letters; *1682* begins *Preparatory Meditations,* his major poetic creations, which he continues at intervals (usually monthly) for the next forty-four years; *1689* after death of Elizabeth expresses his sorrow in the now famous "A Funeral Poem"; *1692* marries Ruth Wyllys; *1694* attacks Stoddard's "apostasy" in *Lord's Supper* sermons; *1701* writes *Christographia* sermons; *1720* becomes minister of a new and larger meetinghouse for the Westfield congregation and receives honorary M.A. from Harvard; *1729* dies on June 24, following his congregation's adoption of Stoddardeanism during the period of his illness and absence from his pulpit.

Author's Bibliography (selected)

The Poems of Edward Taylor, ed. Donald E. Stanford, 1960; *The Diary of Edward Taylor,* ed. Francis Murphy, 1964; *Edward Taylor's Christographia,* ed. Norman S. Grabo, 1962; *Edward Taylor's Treatise Concerning the Lord's Supper,* ed. Norman S. Grabo, 1966; *The Unpublished Writings of Edward Taylor,* 3 vols. eds. Thomas M. and Virginia L. Davis, 1981; *Harmony of the Gospels,* eds. Thomas M. and Virginia L. Davis, 1983 (prose).

Overview of Biographical Sources

Since details of Taylor's life remain sketchy, no "definitive" biography of this early American poet is yet available. Recent publications of manuscripts of sermons and church records (in *The Unpublished Writings of Edward Taylor*), however, continue to clarify Taylor's life and times. Some critics have attempted to reconstruct a life, which is usually couched within a volume of critical commentary. Among the most reliable "reconstructions" are those of Norman S. Grabo, distributed throughout the text of his *Edward Taylor* (1961) and of Donald E. Stanford in his fine 1960 edition of *The Poems of Edward Taylor* (New Haven: Yale University Press, 1960). John L. Sibley's treatment in *Biographical Sketches of Graduates of Harvard University,* II (Boston: Massachusetts Historical Society, 1881, pp. 397–412), continues to be worthwhile because of its numerous and provocative quotations from Taylor's *Diary,* from family, and from intimate associates.

Evaluation of a Selected Biography

Grabo, Norman S. *Edward Taylor.* Boston: Twayne, 1961. Although nearly twenty-five years have passed since this volume appeared, it still represents a reliable biography and an excellent critical introduction. Throughout, Grabo organizes the book about Taylor's vocation as Puritan minister. Emphasis is placed on the poetry, though it must be pointed out that Grabo is one of the first among Taylor's commentators to stress the importance by Loyola's *Spiritual Exercises* on the meditative tradition (the shaping force of the mental faculties of imagination, memory, understanding and will on the structure of a poetic meditation) out of which much of Taylor's poetry developed. This book also contains a still useful catalogue of primary sources (along with the locations of the major manuscripts) and of secondary sources (with brief annotations) through 1960.

Autobiographical Sources

Taylor's *Diary* is a charming record beginning with his departure from England's Execution Dock on April 26, 1668 and including details of his tenures and graduation from Harvard in 1671 along with additional information regarding his initial reticence to assume the ministry of the Congregational Church in Westfield. In this tract, Taylor reveals his capacity for close observation of nature and a tendency for getting himself into relatively innocuous difficulty with those in authority.

"The Pouring of the Sixth Vial: A Letter in a Taylor-Sewall Debate," dated September 29, 1696, edited by Mukhtar Ali Isani, and published in *Proceedings of the Massachusetts Historical Society,* 83 (1972), 123–129, explicates a controversy between Sewall, his former Harvard roomate, and the minister over the interpretation of Revelations 16:12.

Overview of Critical Sources

Despite the recent appearance of a great deal of prose from Taylor's pen, critical studies of Taylor's poems persist. Since the style of the prose is cast in the homelitic mode of the seventeenth century, it remains archaic and unattractive to today's readers, hardly matching the challenge of the metaphysical and vividly imagistic poetry. Investigations continue to appear which explicate single, enigmatic poems. Book-length treatments of the poetry are as yet rare with only two now in print. William J. Scheick in *The Will and the Word: The Poetry of Edward Taylor* (1974) explores the nature of Taylor's commitment to the quest for conversion or to his search for the human heart's revelation of God's love. Karl Keller in *The Example of Edward Taylor* (1975), provides in Taylor's poetry many elements identifiable as distinctly American characteristics. Keller is among the increasing number of critics who are investigating Taylor, and Puritan literature at large, for the aesthetic qualities of the verse. That is, analyses of how Taylor's poetry works as poetry, or does not work, or of how he constructs a theory of poetry are now coming to the forefront of Taylor criticism; this same pattern may be observed of treatments of Puritan literature in general.

Evaluation of Selected Criticism

Keller, Karl, *The Example of Edward Taylor.* Amherst: University of Massachusetts Press, 1975. Keller's penetrating analysis demonstrates admirably the profound necessity which the act of writing, especially of writing poetry, had for Taylor. Keller's work points its readers toward a revaluation of Taylor as poet and aesthetician. This daring and provocative work, which convincingly makes a case for viewing Taylor as a humanist, will continue to serve Taylor's readers as a reliable and substantial guide.

Martz, Louis L. "Forward" in *The Poems of Edward Taylor.* ed. Donald E. Stanford. New Haven: Yale University Press, 1960. Martz compares Taylor's meditative poetry to that of George Herbert, finding Herbert's superior to Taylor's "surface crudities." Martz is the first to treat Taylor's debt to Richard Baxter's *The Saints Everlasting Rest* (1650), particularly to Baxter's explication of the meditative process. As has Scheick, Martz also ignores Taylor's use of the fancy or imagination in the construction of his *Preparatory Meditations.* Nevertheless, he does analyze admirably the recurrence of memory, understanding and will as structural principles in Taylor's meditative poems.

Meserole, Harrison T. "Edward Taylor's Sources" in *Directions in Literary Criticism: Contemporary Approaches to Literature.* eds. Stanley Weintraub and Philip Young. University Park: Pennsylvania State University Press, 1973, pp. 121–126. Meserole issues important challenges to Taylor's readers to explore this poet's knowledge and use of folklore as well as the identification of sources for images taken from metallurgy, alchemy, music and gemology. Once again, this critic maintains such information will inevitably give Taylor's readers greater knowledge of how he constructs his poetics.

Scheick, William J. *The Will and the Word: The Poetry of Edward Taylor.* Athens: University of Georgia Press, 1974. Primarily concerned with analysis of the *Preparatory Meditations,* Scheick analyzes Taylor's search in his poems for spiritual conversion; the objective here is to explicate Taylor's poetic penetration into the human will, or heart, which the author maintains derives from

Taylor's grasp of St. Augustine's thought. Throughout the book, Scheick places emphasis on the importance faculty psychology plays on Taylor's quest for conversion in his poems.

Shields, John C. "Jerome in Colonial New England: Edward Taylor's Attitude Toward Classical Paganism" in *Studies in Philology.* 81 (Spring, 1984), 161–184. Shields maintains that, as has been demonstrated of St. Jerome, Taylor's attitude toward classical culture shifted from youthful enthusiasm to the fervent hostility of the young minister eager not to incur the accusation, *Ciceronianus non-Christianus,* and finally to the posture of mature scholar, confident in his religious commitment. Care is taken to establish a decisive difference between Taylor as public, orthodox minister and Taylor as tolerant poet-humanist.

Stanford, Donald E. *Edward Taylor.* Minneapolis: University of Minnesota Press, 1965. This brief monograph gives a solid introduction to the poetry, discusses Taylor's opposition to Stoddardeanism, and reveals its author's fondness for *God's Determinations,* Taylor's most substantial, dramatic attempt to justify the ways of God to man. Stanford adds to information about the background embracing Taylor's meditative technique when he discusses Lorenzo Scupoli's *The Spiritual Conflict,* written in Italian in 1589 and "Englished" first in 1598.

Selected Dictionaries and Encyclopedias

American Writers Before 1800: A Biographical and Critical Dictionary, James A. Levernier and Douglas R. Wilmes, eds. Greenwood Press, 1983. Succinct and comprehensive overview of Taylor's life and works.

Critical Survey of Poetry, Salem Press, 1983. Brief biography and analysis of selected poems, with special attention to Taylor's meditative technique and use of imagination.

Dictionary of Literary Biography: American Colonial Writers, 1606–1734, Gale Research, 1984. The best available brief introduction to Taylor's entire opus.

John C. Shields
Illinois State University

SARA TEASDALE
1884–1953

Author's Chronology

Born August 8, 1884, St. Louis to established Baptist family; experiences extremely sheltered early life punctuated with much illness; *1899* graduates from Hosmer Hall; *1905* first of many trips to Europe; *1907* publishes *Sonnets to Duse and Other Poems; 1910* invited to join Poetry Society of America; *1913* experiences severe emotional crisis; *1914* begins her life-long friendship with Vachel Lindsay; meets and marries Ernst Filsinger; *1919* severe personal and emotional problems; *1929* divorces Ernst Filsinger; *1933* dies of an overdose of sleeping tablets January 29.

Author's Bibliography (poetry)

Sonnets to Duse and Other Poems, 1907; *Helen of Troy and Other Poems,* 1911; *Rivers to the Sea,* 1915; *Love Songs,* 1917; *Flame and Shadow,* 1924; *Dark of the Moon,* 1926; *Strange Victory,* 1933; *Stars To-Night* 1930; *The Collected Poems of Sara Teasdale,* 1937.

Overview of Biographical Sources

There are only two major biographies of Sara Teasdale, both of which approach her life in very different ways. Margaret H. Carpenter's *Sara Teasdale: A Biography* (1960) is a conventional objective record of Teasdale's life, which draws heavily on all the major collections of letters and diaries available at the time it was published. The study is extremely thorough and provides an excellent picture of the period in which Teasdale lived, along with a great deal of insight into the activities of many of Teasdale's literary contempories. William Drake's *Sara Teasdale: Woman and Poet* (1979) takes a markedly feminist perspective, tracing in elaborate detail the inner tensions suffered by Teasdale. The author sees her as a classic nineteenth-century invalid in the Alice James tradition, whose sensual self came increasingly into conflict with her sexual inhibitions and Victorian repressions. The book traces the course of her increasingly severe bouts of mental and physical illness, and eventual suicide, through a close reading of both her letters and poetry.

Evaluation of Selected Biographies

Carpenter, Margaret H. *Sara Teasdale: A Biography.* New York: Schulte Publishing, 1960. Carpenter's biography is the first major work on Teasdale's life. It contains a wealth of resource material from diaries, letters, manuscripts and personal interviews conducted by Carpenter herself. Generous portions of the primary resource materials are printed in the book. What emerges is a very large compendium of information about the day-to-day activities of the poet from earliest childhood onward. This book is scholarly, unbiased and chronicle-like in its approach.

Drake, William, *Sara Teasdale: Woman and Poet*. San Francisco: Harper and Row, 1979. Drake is a feminist critic whose biography attempts to unravel the emotional dilemma of the poet through a close critical reading of the tensions expressed in her letters and poetry. He sees her as a tormented soul who on the one hand could not give up the romantic ideal of fulfillment through loss of self in another, and on the other a woman whose childhood repressions and Victorian social code rendered her unable to love men who were attainable. Drake, more than Carpenter, deals closely with the emerging style and themes of the poetry in light of these inner tensions. He also draws a vivid picture of the emergence of modern poetry in America and the dilemma of the early twentieth-century women writers.

Overview of Critical Sources

Major bibliographical listings as far back as 1920 contain no significant references to criticism of Sara Teasdale's verse, either in book-length studies or journal articles. This is in part because she is a minor poet, and in part because her verse belongs properly to the period immediately preceding modern American poetry. She was eclipsed by the "wastelanders" and their new poetic idioms. The above mentioned biographies are the best sources of what critical insight exists. All commentators agree that her verse is ultimately affirmative, full of personal ambivalences, natural in expression, dominated by the theme of love, full of a sense of anguish and isolation, highly connotative and reliant almost entirely upon nature imagery.

Other Sources

American Women Writers. "Sara Teasdale," Vol 4, S-Z. New York: Frederick Ungar, 1982.

Cohen, Edmund, "The Letters of Sara Teasdale to Jesse B. Rittenhouse," *Resources for American Literary Study*. 4 (1974): 225–227.

Perrine, Laurence, "The Untranslatable Language," *English Journal* 60 (1971), 61–63.

Perry, Ruth and Maurice Sagoff, "Sara Teasdale's Friendships," *New Letters*. 46 (1979), 101–107.

Saul, George Brandon, "A Delicate Fabric of Birdsong: The Verse of Sara Teasdale," *Arizona Quarterly*. X111 (1957), 62–66.

Sprague, Rosemary, *Imaginary Gardens: A Study of Five American Poets*. Philadelphia: Chilton, 1969.

Gloria L. Cronin
Brigham Young University

ALFRED, LORD TENNYSON
1809–1892

Author's Chronology

Born August 6, 1809, at Somersby, England, fourth son of Rev. George Tennyson; *1827* publishes his first volume of poetry; enters Trinity College, Cambridge; *1828* meets Arthur Henry Hallam; *1831* leaves Cambridge after the death of his father; *1832* publishes *Poems,* which receives harsh reviews; *1833* learns that Hallam has died in Vienna; *1836* meets Emily Sellwood, to whom he becomes engaged two years later; *1837* moves with his family from Somersby to Epping; *1840* moves again, to Tunbridge Wells, breaks engagement to Emily; *1842* publishes *Poems,* containing many revisions of earlier works; *1845* granted Civil List Pension; *1850* publishes *In Memoriam, A.H.H.;* marries Emily Sellwood in June; appointed Poet Laureate in November; *1852* a son, Hallam Tennyson, born; moves to Farringford on the Isle of Wight; *1854* a second son, Lionel Tennyson, born; *1868* begins construction of second home at Aldworth in Halesmere district; *1875* begins career as playwright; *1883* accepts offer of a baronetcy; *1886* learns of the death of his son Lionel; *1892* dies at Aldworth.

Author's Bibliography (selected)

Poems by Two Brothers, 1827; *Poems, Chiefly Lyrical,* 1830; *Poems,* 1832; *Poems,* 1842; *The Princess,* 1847 (long poem); *In Memoriam, A.H.H.,* 1850 (long poem); *Maud,* 1855 (long poem); *Idylls of the King,* 1859 (long poem [first four parts]); *Enoch Arden & Other Poems,* 1864; *The Holy Grail and Other Poems,* 1869; *Gareth & Lynette, Etc.,* 1872 (poems); *Queen Mary,* 1875 (drama); *Harold,* 1876 (drama); *Ballads & Other Poems,* 1880; *The Cup and the Falcon,* 1884 (drama); *Becket,* 1884 (drama); *Tiresias and Other Poems,* 1885; *Locksley Hall Sixty Years After,* 1886 (poems); *Demeter and Other Poems,* 1889; *The Foresters,* 1892 (drama); *The Death of Oenone, Akbar's Dream, and Other Poems,* 1892; *Works,* Eversley Edition, ed. Hallam Tennyson, 9 vols., 1907–1908.

Overview of Biographical Sources

Because he was an immensely popular poet in his own day, Tennyson was the subject of several biographies almost immediately after his death. Most of these combine biography with critical analysis. By far the most important early biography was Hallam Tennyson's *Alfred Tennyson: A Memoir* (1897). Most early biographies portray the poet in a favorable light. By contrast, Tennyson became an object of derision among literary critics during the first half of the twentieth century. Harold Nicolson's celebrated *Tennyson: Aspects of his Life, Character, and Poetry* (London: Constable & Co., 1923), focuses equally on the life and works, presenting the poet as a morbid, introspective individual, overly sensitive to the criticism of others. Since World War II, more balanced portraits of Tennyson have appeared. In addition to short sketches in encyclopedias, handbooks, textbooks, and introductions to studies of the poetry, significant interpretations of Tennyson's life have been published by Valerie Pitt (*Tennyson Laureate,* Toronto: University of Toronto Press, 1962); Christopher Ricks (*Tennyson,* London: Macmillan, 1972); R. B. Martin (*Tennyson: The Unquiet Heart,* New York: Oxford University Press, 1980).

Evaluation of Selected Biographies

Martin, R. B. *Tennyson: The Unquiet Heart.* New York: Oxford University Press, 1980. Those who suspect that there was something curious and quite disturbing beneath the facade of sanctimonious benevolence and wisdom that Tennyson presented to the public and that his son perpetuated in his authorized biography will find in Martin's work much to confirm their suspicions. Martin pieces together a portrait of the poet that makes sense of the "oddities" of his personality hinted at by contemporaries but ignored by Hallam Tennyson in his *Memoir.* By concentrating on the early years of the poet's life, Martin explains how family instability and a pattern of mental illness (which Tennyson did not inherit, but which worried him throughout his life) affected both his lifestyle and his poetry. The focus in this work is on the life, but Martin does offer some valuable insight into the biographical genesis of several works.

Tennyson, Sir Charles, *Alfred Tennyson.* London: Macmillan, 1949. In the half-century between the publication of Hallam Tennyson's *Memoir* and the end of World War II, much was written to smear the poet's reputation. Charles Tennyson, Alfred's grandson, writes a corrective account that explains the poet to a twentieth-century audience. He presents a careful study of the influence of family life and the development of Tennyson's poetic sensibilities as he moves from his position as a recluse to become a national figure. Paying considerable attention to friendships that helped shape Tennyson's outlook, Sir Charles draws a balanced portrait that recognizes faults as well as strengths in the poet's personality. While not particularly strong in literary analysis, this study does show how events in Tennyson's life helped shape his art. More importantly, it provides a sympathetic look at the poet's mind, detailing the breadth of his knowledge and interests.

Tennyson, Hallam, *Alfred, Lord Tennyson: A Memoir.* 2 vols. London: Macmillan, 1897. Hallam's *Memoir* of his father is one of the important literary documents of the Victorian age. Tennyson wanted no biography written about him, but he turned over all his personal papers to Hallam so that, if any "life" were done, Hallam could do it "correctly." Working with thousands of his father's and mother's letters, as well as written reminiscences sent to him from numerous friends of the poet, Hallam assembled a work that captures many of

Tennyson's thoughts about his work not recorded elsewhere. Since the poet wrote no literary criticism, the *Memoir* contains almost the only record of Tennyson's thoughts about his own and other writings. Hallam was careful to present his father in the best possible light, however, and subsequent investigations into the poet's life have revealed the shortcomings of this work.

Autobiographical Sources

Tennyson viewed with disdain and a bit of fear those who published unedited and unexpurgated volumes of letters and personal diaries of deceased literary figures. As a consequence, he entrusted his personal papers to his son Hallam, who destroyed many of them after compiling his *Memoir* of the poet. Scattered autobiographical fragments, mostly letters, can be found in diaries and reminiscences of Tennyson's contemporaries, and in Hallam Tennyson's *Tennyson and His Friends* (London: Macmillan, 1911). Edgar Shannon and Cecil Lang are editing the poet's letters; their first volume appeared in 1981, *The Letters of Alfred Tennyson, 1821-1850* (Cambridge, MA: Belknap Press, 1981). Many personal documents are also available at the Tennyson Center in Lincoln, England.

Critical Sources

Thousands of scholarly articles have been written about Tennyson's poetry. Full-length studies assessing the entire canon or individual works number close to one hundred. The earliest criticism was largely favorable. From the publication of *In Memoriam* in 1850 until World War I Tennyson was regarded by many as a great moral teacher. The first generations after the Victorian period reacted harshly against what they perceived as Tennyson's naive optimism; harsh criticism of his works characterizes many studies from the turn of the century until well after World War II. Nicolson's *Tennyson* and Paull F. Baum's *Tennyson Sixty Years After* (Chapel Hill: University of North Carolina Press, 1948) are especially critical in their judgment of the major long poems. Jerome Buckley's *Tennyson: The Growth of a Poet* (1960) restored a balance to critical observations of the poet's works. Since 1960, numerous studies of individual works have appeared, especially ones focusing on Tennyson's Arthurian poem, *Idylls of the King*. Studies of the poet's works as they illuminate particular themes or deal with literary or cultural problems have also proliferated. Among this category one finds works such as Gerhard Joseph, *Tennysonian Love* (Minneapolis: University of Minnesota Press, 1969); F. E. L. Priestley, *Language and Structure in Tennyson's Poetry* (Toronto: University of Toronto Press, 1973); and Robert Pattison, *Tennyson and Tradition* (Cambridge: Harvard University Press, 1979).

Evaluation of Selected Criticism

Buckley, Jerome H. *Tennyson: The Growth of a Poet.* Cambridge: Harvard University Press, 1960. Buckley's study marked a change in direction in Tennyson criticism, restoring the poet to a position of prominence among literary figures whose works are afforded serious scholarly study. Buckley presents the works of the poet in the context of Tennyson's life, but the criticism is far more important than the biography. Working with manuscripts not previously examined in detail, Buckley demonstrates that Tennyson was a master of his craft, a poet of exceptional sensibility and keen insight. His chapter on *Idylls of the King* is particularly significant; the first systematic explanation of the essential unity of the poem, it helped put to rest notions that Tennyson could not write narrative poetry, and spurred further debate among scholars about the merits of Tennyson's Arthurian poem.

Culler, A. Dwight, *The Poetry of Tennyson.* New Haven: Yale University Press, 1977. Culler's study of Tennyson's poetry focuses on Tennyson's poetics. An introductory chapter explaining Tennyson's belief in the magical power of words offers a framework for a revaluation of the poet's *oeuvre.* Culler devotes much attention to the early poems and *In Memorian,* suggesting that the English Idyls, long neglected because they display elements of Victorian sentimentality no longer considered fashionable, are actually works of significant merit. Underlying his study of the long narratives is his belief that Tennyson's method of creating these "composite" poems places him in the tradition of the classical Alexandrian poets.

Kincaid, James R. *Tennyson's Major Poems.* New Haven: Yale University Press. This study provides a wide-ranging survey of all of Tennyson's poetry, and blends the virtues of sound scholarship with informal prose style to present a sensible interpretation of the Tennyson canon. Kincaid adopts as his starting point Northrop Frye's distinctions of the major modes into which all literature may be grouped: tragedy, comedy, romance, and irony. Tennyson is seen as a poet constantly struggling to affirm the comic spirit, but driven to irony by the world he sees around him. The tension between the comic and ironic lies at the center of all of the poet's work, and almost all individual poems fall into one of these categories.

In the major poetry, Tennyson works consistently in one of these two modes. Either he views the world through the eyes of the ironist, seeing the grand designs of man destroyed by forces over which he has no control; or he adopts the mask of the comedian, attempting to maintain a vision of the world that offers happiness as an attainable goal. Tennyson begins as an ironist, achieves mastery of the comic form in the middle years of his life, and returns to the ironic mode in later years. Kincaid's analysis of *In Memoriam* as the poet's "Divine Comedy," and his assessment of *Idylls of the King* as the major ironic poem of the nineteenth century, are especially illuminating.

Other Sources

Hair, Donald S. *Domestic and Heroic in Tennyson's Poetry.* Toronto: University of Toronto Press, 1981. A study illustrating how domestic virtues are the source of the heroic in Tennyson's work.

Hellstrom, Ward, *On the Poems of Tennyson.* Gainesville: University Presses of Florida, 1972. A sound study of several poems, showing how they illustrate Tennyson's essential Victorian cast of mind.

Killham, John, ed. *Critical Essays on the Poetry of Tennyson.* London: Routledge & Kegan Paul, 1960. A valuable collection of essays providing a far-reaching assessment of many of the poet's works, examining them in the context of his own age and of various literary traditions.

Palmer, D. J., ed. *Tennyson.* Writers and Their Background Series. Athens: Ohio University Press, 1973. A collection of essays that offers a good introduction to the poet, his times, and his works.

Pitt, Valerie, *Tennyson Laureate.* London: Barrie & Rockliff, 1962. An important study of Tennyson as a public poet.

Ricks, Christopher, ed. *The Poems of Tennyson.* London and New York: Longmans/Norton, 1969. The standard modern edition of the poetry, containing bibliographical and critical materials about all of Tennyson's poems.

Selected Dictionaries and Encyclopedias

British Writers, Charles Scribner's Sons, 1981, IV: 323–339. A useful short account of Tennyson's life and an overview of his works and the major themes of his poetry.

Critical Survey of Poetry, Salem Press, 1983, Vol. 7: 2859–2870. Brief biography and short analysis of several of the poet's works.

Dictionary of National Biography, Oxford University Press, 1959, XIX: 546–555. An account of Tennyson's life, with some discussion of the major works.

Laurence W. Mazzeno
Annapolis, Maryland

WILLIAM MAKEPEACE THACKERAY
1811–1863

Author's Chronology

Born July 18, 1811, in Calcutta, India, of upper-class English parents; *1816* returns to England after the death of his father; *1829* enters Trinity College, Cambridge; *1830* tours Continent and visits Goethe; *1831–1835* law student at Middle Temple; settles in Paris and lives a Bohemian life as an art student; starts newspaper with stepfather which fails financially; loses most of his inheritance in a bank failure; *1836* marries Isabella Shaw; three daughters later born to the union; *1840* wife becomes insane but outlives Thackeray; *1844* publishes his first novel, *The Luck of Barry Lyndon; 1847–1848* publishes *Vanity Fair,* his first financially successful novel, and launches on a social career which involves friendships with many famous writers; *1852–1853* lectures on the English humorists of the eighteenth century in Britain and the United States; *1855–1856* lectures on the four King Georges in Britain and the United States; *1857* stands for Parliament from Oxford but is unsuccessful; *1860* becomes editor of *Cornhill Magazine;* December 24, 1863 dies suddenly in London.

Author's Bibliography (selected)

The Luck of Barry Lyndon, 1844 (novel); *Vanity Fair,* 1847–1848 (novel); *The Book of Snobs,* 1848 (sketches); *The History of Pendennis,* 1848–1850 (novel); *Rebecca and Rowena,* 1850 (satire); *The History of Henry Esmond,* 1852 (novel); *The English Humorists of the Eighteenth Century,* 1853 (lectures); *The Newcomes,* 1853–1855 (novel); *The Virginians,* 1857–1859 (novel); *The Four Georges,* 1860 (lectures); *Lovel the Widower,* 1860 (novel); *Roundabout Papers,* 1863 (essays, sketches); *The Adventures of Philip,* 1861–1862 (novel); *Denis Duval,* 1864 (unfinished novel).

Overview of Biographical Sources

Thackeray wished no biography written of him, and his family respected this desire. Thus, biographical materials are slight until well into the 1940's. The family provided no information until 1899 when Lady Ritchie (Thackeray's daughter) wrote a biography that was divided into introductions for the thirteen volume Biographical Edition of her father's work. Leslie Stephens, husband of Thackeray's now-deceased daughter, wrote a factual narrative for the *Dictionary of National Biography* which he also added to the Biographical Edition. Several studies followed after Lady Ritchie's death in 1924 which either dealt with Thackeray's psychological inconsistencies or his personal life but with very little hard evidence. In 1947, Lionel Stevenson published *The Showman of Vanity Fair* (New York: Charles Scribner's Sons) and based his study on fuller evidence than any biographer had earlier, and the biography remains an intelligent and concise treatment of Thackeray's life. Gordon Ray, however, is the supreme biographer of Thackeray. He started with publication of four volumes of the letters and papers, developed a biocritical study, *The Buried Life* (Cambridge: Harvard University Press, 1952), and finished with *Thackeray: The Uses of Adversity, 1811-1846* and *Thackeray: The Age of Wisdom, 1847-1864* (1955, 1958). These two volumes are an exhaustive study and will remain the definitive biography for generations. In 1983 Philip Collins published as part of a St. Martin's Press series *Thackeray: Interviews and Recollections* (New York: St. Martin's Press) in two volumes. This collection presents the contemporaries of Thackeray commenting on Thackeray and his works. The contemporaries are mostly friends, and thus the image of Thackeray is positive. Much of the material appeared earlier in Ray's definitive biography.

Evaluation of Selected Biographies

Ray, Gordon, *Thackeray: The Uses of Adversity, 1811-1846* and *Thackeray: The Age of Wisdom, 1847-1864*. New York: McGraw-Hill, 1955, 1958. This work is the culmination of years of work on Thackeray's career. Ray deals thoroughly with the life and provides thoughtful essays on the novels. He also deals with the era and background of Thackeray. Therefore, the books are valuable to the historian as well as the literary critic. Ray does not duplicate material from *The Buried Life* and the notes in *The Letters and Private Papers;* consequently, scholars must consult all these works for the fullest picture of Thackeray.

Stevenson, Lionel, *The Showman of Vanity Fair*. New York: Charles Scribner's Sons, 1947. Clearly, this is the biography for the beginning student of Thackeray. It is concise, balanced, readable and accurate. Like Ray, Stevenson had available to him sources not available earlier. Despite its conciseness, Stevenson does deal with whole life.

Autobiographical Sources

Thackeray's desire for privacy and his family's respect for his wishes leave the reader with few autobiographical sources. Gordon Ray's collection of the letters, *The Letters and Private Papers of William Makepeace Thackeray,* 4 volumes (Cambridge: Harvard University Press, 1945-1946), is the only autobiographical source of importance. Ray's policy on the editing is one of completeness so that the range of material is from the trivial to the important. Because Ray could not gain permission for the publishing of all known letters, the work is incomplete. In fact, Lionel Stevenson pointed out that there is enough material for yet another volume.

Overview of Critical Sources

Like many of the other great Victorian novelists, Thackeray evoked critical comment during his lifetime and for about a generation thereafter. He clearly fell into critical neglect from the turn of the century until the 1940's. Part of the renewed interest is contemporary with the pioneering work of Gordon Ray with the letters and the subsequent biography. Critics have been mixed in their approval of Thackeray's novels, and one noteworthy critic is quite hostile. Still, the work on Thackeray continues with new books focusing on various aspects of the novels: tone, characterization, style, but less so on theme. Most critics highlight Thackeray's differences from the other Victorian novelists.

Evaluation of Selected Criticism

Harden, Edgar F. *The Emergence of Thackeray's Serial Fiction.* Athens: University of Georgia Press, 1979. Harden deals with the serial structure of five novels: *Vanity Fair, The Newcomes, The Virginians, Lovel the Widower, The Adventures of Philip.* Harden focuses on the manuscripts and the process of composition, studying the novels as they evolve and showing how the serial installments shaped the forms of the novels.

Hardy, Barbara, *The Exposure of Luxury: Radical Themes in Thackeray.* Pittsburgh: University of Pittsburgh Press, 1972. Hardy concentrates on the major social themes of Thackeray which up to this point have received little attention. Hardy sees Thackeray as different from the other Victorian novelists, for he did not present a moral viewpoint. Hardy deals with such subjects as: rank, class, trade, commerce, money, insincerity, hospitality or lack of it, fellowship, and love.

Saintsbury, George, *A Consideration of Thackeray.* London: Oxford University Press, 1931. Saintsbury's introductions to the 1908 Oxford Edition are reprinted for this volume, and together make an enthusiastic case for Thackeray's style and humor. Because the material is reprinted from the introductions, Saintsbury gives equal time to both major and minor works.

Tillotson, Geoffrey, *Thackeray the Novelist,* Cambridge: Cambridge University Press, 1954. Tillotson breaks new ground, for he avoids the biocritical approach which had been the norm up to this period. He is consciously defending Thackeray against early detractors. In discussing major works, Tillotson focuses on Thackeray's realism, imagery, and philosophy.

Trollope, Anthony, *Thackeray,* New York: Harper, 1879. Trollope's book is a good beginning for a student because it deals clearly with the issues of satire and moral viewpoint. Trollope is laudatory and discusses the charm and the realism of the novels. The book is interesting also to the student of Trollope, for it reveals something of Trollope himself as he discusses another notable Victorian novelist.

Other Sources

Dodds, John Wendell, *Thackeray: A Critical Portrait.* New York: Oxford University Press, 1941. A mixture of biography and criticism and a quite reliable analysis of Thackeray's career.

Grieg, J. Y. T. *Thackeray: A Reconsideration,* London: Oxford University Press, 1950. A well-known and quite hostile book. Grieg uses both biography and criticism to dismiss both the man and his works.

Loofbourow, John, *Thackeray and the Form of Fiction.* Princeton: Princeton University Press, 1964. Loofbourow shows the interrelationship of form and content with *Vanity Fair, Pendennis, The Newcomes* and *Henry Esmond.*

Tillotson, Geoffrey and Donald Hawes, *Thackeray, the Critical Heritage.* New York: Barnes and Noble, 1968. Valuable reviews of Thackeray's work by his contemporaries.

Welsh, Alexander, ed. *Thackeray: A Collection of Critical Essays.* Englewood Cliffs: Prentice Hall, 1968. An excellent collection from the Twentieth Century Views Series of both excerpts from books and scholarly articles. Critics included are Mario Praz, Kathleen Tillotson, Georg Lukacs, et al.

Selected Dictionaries and Encyclopedias

The History of the English Novel, 10 volumes. Witherby, 1924–1939. The definitive history. Baker gives fifty pages to Thackeray and discusses both his life and most of his writings.

An Introduction to the English Novel, Kettle, Arnold, 2 volumes. Hutchinson Universal Library, 1951–1953. Kettle devotes one chapter to perceptive discussion of *Vanity Fair.*

A Thackeray Dictionary, E. P. Dutton, 1910. Provides synopses of the novels and full references to the characters, some of whom appear in various novels.

Dennis Goldsberry
College of Charleston

DYLAN THOMAS
1914–1953

Author's Chronology

Born Dylan Marlais Thomas on October 27, 1914, in Swansea, Wales; a sister, Nancy, eight years older; speaks no Welsh, though both parents had spoken it in their childhood homes; attends Swansea Grammar School, and at seventeen becomes an apprentice reporter; acts with an amateur company; *1934* moves to London; *1937* marries Caitlin Macnamara; after the outbreak of war, attempts to enlist but is rejected for military service; *1939* first child born, the second in 1943, the third in 1949; *1940–1946* the family lives in or near London; Thomas works on documentary films; *1945* becomes free-lance filmmaker for the BBC; *1948* begins making feature-length films; travels to Italy, Prague, and Persia (to write a film for the Anglo-Iranian Oil Company); *1950* makes his first trip to America to read his poetry at American colleges; *1952* second American visit, *1953* during third U.S. visit his play *Under Milk Wood* is performed in Cambridge, Massachusetts, and in New York City at the YM-YWHA; October, 1953 returns to the U.S. for a fourth time; November 9 dies in New York City; buried in Laugharne, Wales.

Author's Bibliography

18 Poems, 1934; *Twenty-five Poems,* 1936; *The Map of Love,* 1939 (stories and poems); *Portrait of the Artist as a Young Dog,* 1940 (stories); *Deaths and Entrances,* 1946 (poems); *Collected Poems,* 1952. The following volumes were published posthumously: *Under Milk Wood,* 1953 (play); *The Doctor and the Devils and Other Scripts,* 1953 (film scripts, radio script); *Quite Early One Morning,* 1954 (radio scripts); *A Prospect of the Sea,* 1955 (stories); *Letters To Vernon Watkins,* 1956; *The Beach at Falesa,* 1964 (film script); *Twenty Years A-Growing,* 1964 (film script); *Me and My Bike,* 1965 (film script); *Rebecca's Daughters,* 1965 (film script); *Selected Letters of Dylan Thomas,* 1966; *Poet in the Making: The Notebooks of Dylan Thomas,* 1968; *Dylan Thomas: Early Prose Writings,* 1971; and *The Collected Stories,* 1984.

Overview of Biographical Sources

All biographical material about Dylan Thomas should be read with great caution. Those who knew him well and were close to him are not necessarily the most objective sources. Thomas often said things about himself that were wildly untrue; many knew this, others did not. There are numerous reminiscences about Thomas. When he was alive and shortly after his death, the appeal of the "legend" of Dylan Thomas was as potent as the works themselves. Another problem is the tendency of those who have written about Thomas to be either very enthusiastic or stringently critical—for about ten or fifteen years after Thomas's death, few critics chose a middle approach. Most of the biographies are positive; those who disapproved of Thomas tended to write critical articles and books about his individual works rather than about his life. By the mid-1970's the either-or contentiousness about Thomas had begun to fade, and Paul Ferris's biography, written in 1977, struck a new note by successfully combining warmth with critical scepticism. Two biographies of Thomas stand out for their completeness and critical good sense: Constantine FitzGibbon's *The Life of Dylan Thomas* (1965) and Ferris' *Dylan Thomas* (1977).

Evaluation of Selected Biographies

Ackerman, John, *Dylan Thomas: His Life and Work.* Oxford: Oxford University Press, 1964. In this book Ackerman stresses Thomas's Welsh background and what the author calls the Welsh puritan tradition. Also, Ackerman's account of Thomas's "natural religion" is perceptive, and should be consulted by those who are interested in Thomas's use of religious themes or images. A second book by Ackerman, entitled *Welsh Dylan* (Cardiff: John Jones, 1979) further explores Thomas's Welsh roots.

Brinnin, John Malcolm, *Dylan Thomas in America: An Intimate Journal.* Boston: Little, Brown, 1955. This book covers Thomas's American period in detail. Brinnin was the one who first invited Thomas to America, and helped organize his tours. Himself a poet, he was an admirer of Thomas's poetry. The book is extremely readable. More than any other single person, Brinnin was instrumental in making the American reading public aware of Thomas.

Davies, Walford, *Dylan Thomas.* Cardiff: University of Wales Press, 1972. This is a good short treatment of Thomas's life; it also contains some perceptive remarks about his poetry.

Ferris, Paul, *Dylan Thomas.* New York: The Dial Press, 1977. This biography makes thorough use of the available documents, although there is no first-hand or "privileged" information. The book is clear, well-balanced, and always useful. It combines sympathy for its subject with a determined level-headedness.

FitzGibbon, Constantine, *The Life of Dylan Thomas.* Boston: Little, Brown, 1965. FitzGibbon knew Thomas well; much of the information imparted in this book is first-hand and of great intrinsic interest. The author is especially good on the period of war-time London, 1940–1946. The book is written with great skill—FitzGibbon was himself a writer and novelist. Most important, he had an acute critical faculty. Although he is always close to his subject, his attitude is never idolatrous, and many valuable critical insights can be culled from this book.

Jones, Glyn, *The Dragon Has Two Tongues.* London: Dent, 1968. Jones, also a writer, knew Thomas well, and he has written sensitive commentaries on Thomas the man and also on Thomas the poet.

Thomas, Caitlin, *Leftover Life To Kill.* London: P.G. Putnam's, 1957. This book by Thomas's wife contains many insights. Also, she understood her husband's poetry better than many professional critics. But this book should be consulted with care, as well as her second book, *Not Quite Posthumous Letters to My Daughter* (London: P.G. Putnam's, 1963). Like her husband she was a rhetorician, and had numerous animosities, among them John Malcolm Brinnin.

Autobiographical Sources

As with many other writers, it is often difficult to separate fact from fiction in Thomas's references to himself. Partly this is due to the legend about Thomas that grew up during his lifetime and was encouraged by Thomas himself. In addition, childhood was a major theme in Thomas's work, so was adolescence; references to them recur constantly, and they have a fluctuating autobiographical basis. The most clearly autobiographical of his writings are the ten stories in *Portrait of the Artist as a Young Dog.* These are relatively direct, uncomplicated evocations of the Swansea where Thomas had grown up. A number of his radio scripts are also autobiographical. For example, the well-known story "A Child's Christmas in Wales" began as a radio script, two versions of which can be found in *Quite Early One Morning.* The scripts "Quite Early One Morning" and "Return Journey"—that contributed to *Under Milk Wood*—can be found in the same collection of radio scripts; often Thomas "the reporter" is in the foreground, and these scripts might be called semi-autobiographical.

Overview of Critical Sources

Many critical books, articles, and collections of articles have been written about Thomas. It is extremely difficult to separate writings about Thomas's works from those about Thomas the man. The legend of Thomas the man constantly arises whether for better or for worse. During the 1950's and 1960's, critics of Thomas's work tended to fall into two different categories: those who related the poems to the author—and to a certain necessary extent, to the legend about the author—and those who attempted to explain the poems and other works only as texts, with as little reference to a biographical author as possible. The critics in the first category felt free to stress different aspects of Thomas's personality, and they used diverse approaches ranging from the uncritically enthusiastic to the entirely disenchanted. Critics in the second category tended to be associated with the "New Criticism" of I. A. Richards and William Empson. Yet, despite their efforts to ignore the life and legend, focusing exclusively on the text at hand, they were often influenced in an unavowed manner by the potent legend they tried to disregard. With the passage of time the two groups have become less mutually exclusive. Yet the longevity of this partisanship is remarkable—a good example is Donald Davie's review for the *New York Times* (Nov. 9, 1975) of Andrew Sinclair's *Dylan Thomas: No Man More Magical,* and subsequent letters to the editor, with Davie's rebuttal; "writing style" had become hopelessly confused with what was now called "life style."

With some writers it is possible to point to a single outstanding critical work and say that this has superseded most, if not all, previous critical works. This is not the case with Dylan Thomas. Some critical works still in print are remarkably bad. With Thomas the critics compete to a certain extent with equally critical biographers; often the critics do not show superior critical judgment. Although two collections of essays edited by C. B. Cox and J. M. Brinnin are useful, it should be stressed that each collection is very uneven.

Evaluation of Selected Criticism

Brinnin, John Malcolm, ed. *A Casebook on Dylan Thomas.* New York: Thomas Y. Crowell, 1960. This book is a grab-bag of poems, recollections, and critical studies. The appreciative essay by W. S. Merwin on "the religious poet" is excellent, as is Robert Graves' rejection of Thomas, taken from *These Be Your Gods, O Israel!*

Cox, C. B. ed. *Dylan Thomas. A Collection of Critical Essays.* Englewood Cliffs, NJ: Prentice-Hall, 1966. Especially noteworthy are the essays by John Bayley (taken from his seminal book *The Romantic Survival*), by Ackerman on the Welsh background, by Elder Olson on the early poems, and Ralph Maud on the late poems.

The following two books contain useful exegeses of individual poems:

Stanford, Derek, *Dylan Thomas.* London: Spearman, 1954. Stanford presents a very clear exposition of the evolution of Thomas's style; there is also a convenient list at the end of the book of poems discussed individually.

Maud, Ralph, *Entrances to Dylan Thomas's Poetry.* Pittsburgh: University of Pittsburgh Press, 1963. Maud's study is well researched, and he explicates the texture of many poems line by line. To this task he brings to bear a large amount of information of Thomas's own notes, comments, and occasional writings. Sometimes Maud is overly literal or, simply, wrong; but he is a good critic to consult. Those wanting further exegesis of individual images or lines may refer to William York Tindall's *A Reader's Guide to Dylan Thomas* (London: Thames + Hudson, 1962), and Clark Emery's *The World of Dylan Thomas* (London: Dent, 1971). A good concordance can cast much light on problems of texture: Gary Lane, *A Concordance to the Poems of Dylan Thomas* (Metuchen, NJ: Scarecrow Press, 1976).

Other Sources

Cleverdon, Douglas, *The Growth of Milk Wood.* New York: New Directions, 1969. This is an important book on a special subject, the growth of Thomas's manuscript for "The Town Was Mad" that evolved in the course of a decade into "Llareggub" and, finally, *Under Milk Wood.* Cleverdon was the BBC producer in charge of the radio feature version of the play.

Davies, Walford, ed. *Dylan Thomas. New Critical Essays.* London: Dent, 1972. Another essay by John Bayley stands out, "Chains and the Poet."

Maud, Ralph, *Dylan Thomas in Print. A Bibliographical History.* Pittsburgh: University of Pittsburgh Press, 1970. This book permits the reader to follow Thomas's career chronologically through his diverse magazine and newspaper publications. It contains more illustrative quotations than most bibliographies. For those interested in the development of Thomas's style, it should be consulted with another book edited by Maud, *Poet in the Making: The Notebooks of Dylan Thomas* (London: Dent, 1968), and with Walford Davies, ed., *Dylan Thomas: Early Prose Writings* (London: Dent, 1971).

Selected Dictionaries and Encylopedias

Critical Survey of Drama, Salem Press, 1985. A detailed account of the making of *Under Milk Wood,* of Thomas's intentions and the final structure of the play.

Critical Survey of Poetry, Vol. 7, Salem Press, 1982. Analysis of three poems, "And Death Shall Have No Dominion," "Altarwise by Owl-Light," and "Over Sir John's Hill."

Encyclopedia of World Literature in the 20th Century, Vol. III, Frederick Ungar, 1967. An excellent entry, both concise and perceptive, by Richard Hoggart.

A Reader's Guide to Fifty Modern British Poets, Barnes and Noble, 1979. A useful short consideration of Thomas's work.

John Carpenter
University of Michigan

HENRY DAVID THOREAU
1817–1862

Author's Chronology

Born July 12, 1817 in Concord, Massachusetts; *1826* earliest known essay, "The Seasons"; *1833* enters Harvard University; *1835* on leave from Harvard, teaches school in Canton, Massachusetts; *1837* graduates from Harvard; begins *Journal;* teaches for a few weeks in Concord public schools, dismissed for refusing to administer corporal punishment; *1838* opens private school with brother John; first of many lectures at Concord Lyceum; first trip to Maine; *1839* excursion on Concord and Merrimack rivers with brother John—the basis for *A Week; 1840* publishes first essay and poem in the *Dial;* proposes marriage to Ellen Sewall; *1841* begins two years residence in Emerson home; *1842* brother John dies; *1843* begins annual lectures before Concord Lyceum; assists Emerson editing the *Dial;* tutors William Emerson's children on Staten Island; *1844* returns home to work in family pencil factory; accidentally sets fire to Concord woods; *1845* builds and moves into Walden cabin; *1846* jailed for one night for refusing to pay taxes; *1846* makes first trip to Maine woods; *1847* leaves Walden Pond in September; second residence in Emerson's house; begins submitting nature specimens to Louis Agassiz at Harvard; *1849* returns to father's house; publishes *A Week on the Concord and Merrimack Rivers,* "Civil Disobedience"; first trip to Cape Cod; sister Helen dies; *1850* second visit to Cape Cod; visits Canada; *1853* second trip to Maine woods; *1854* publishes *Walden;* delivers "Slavery in Massachusetts"; *1855* third visit to Cape Cod; *1856* meets Walt Whitman in Brooklyn; *1857* fourth visit to Cape Cod; third visit to Maine woods; meets Captain John Brown; *1859* father dies; delivers "A Plea for John Brown"; *1861* visits Minnesota for health; revises many manuscripts; *1862* dies May 6 of tuberculosis; *Walden* and *A Week on the Concord and Merrimack Rivers* appear in second editions.

Author's Bibliography (selected)

A Week on the Concord and Merrimack Rivers, 1849 (journal); "Resistance to Civil Government" ("Civil Disobedience"), 1849 (essay); *Walden* (journal), 1854; *Journal,* (16 vols.), 1906; *The Correspondence of Henry David Thoreau,* 1958.

Overview of Biographical Sources

Since the first book-length biography of Thoreau appeared in 1873, he has been the focus of a veritable "industry." Among the first generation of biographers, several, still available, remain useful. F. B. Sanborn, author of *Henry D. Thoreau* (1882), boarded in Thoreau's house and knew all his Concord colleagues. The biography is a hodge-podge, but contains first-hand source material unavailable elsewhere. H. S. Salt's *Life of Henry David Thoreau* (1890) was written by a British vegetarian, socialist and pacifist who never visited the United States. Nonetheless, he was astute and sympathetic, and his biography is still regarded as eminent, as are his appraisals and analyses of Thoreau's works. Mark Van Doren's *Henry David Thoreau: A Critical Study* (1916) was the first complete study to appear after the publications of the *Journal.* However, Van Doren is often unsympathetic, stressing Thoreau's loneliness and eccentric personal life—a bias continued in some modern psychoanalytical biographies. Henry Seidel Canby's *Thoreau* (1939) was considered a standard work for some years; it contains much well-indexed factual information, and was the first to use the Ward family correspondence which yielded many intimate details of Thoreau's life. The book makes too much of the relationship between Thoreau and Lydian Emerson (Canby says Thoreau was in love with her), and the book contains numerous factual errors. Joseph Wood Krutch's *Henry David Thoreau* (1948), adds nothing factually new to the earlier works. However, Krutch, a fellow naturalist, brings much insight to the nature writings while slighting the social output. The book clearly distinguishes Thoreau's philosophical contributions from those of his early mentor, Emerson.

Evaluation of Selected Biographies

Harding, Walter, *The Days of Henry Thoreau: A Biography.* New York: Alfred A. Knopf, 1965. Reissued in a revised second edition: New York: Dover Publications, Inc., 1982. This work, by the leading American Thoreau scholar, remains the single best biography. It contains a detailed, virtually day-to-day account of Thoreau's life untainted by any *a priori* critical bias. The contradictions in Thoreau's life are objectively set forth, without attempting to "resolve" them according to some thesis which would ignore Thoreau's polarities. Differing from earlier biographers, Harding sees Thoreau as less a misanthropic loner and more integrated into Concord society, fundamentally "vibrant, creative, and happy to the very end." The book contains many illustrations and photographs that lend visual substance to the text. The work is ideal for undergraduates, but will challenge upper level students as well.

Lebeaux, Richard, *Young Man Thoreau.* Amherst: The University of Massachusetts Press, 1977. This is a controversial but brilliant psychobiography which deals with Thoreau's sexuality, and his ambivalent relationship to his parents and brother, John. Lebeaux, employing an Ericksonian focus, examines Thoreau's early Journals as "veiled autobiography," and discerns a prolonged adolescence and a protracted identity crisis. There are many expository endnotes that add clarity. The case is brilliantly argued, but hardly neutral or irrefutable, and thus is best suited to discriminating and somewhat sophisticated readers.

Wagenknecht, Edward, *Henry David Thoreau: What Manner of Man?* Amherst: The University of Massachusetts Press, 1981. This unique and superb work is essentially an intellectual biography. The "chronology" of Thoreau's life occupies only a small part of the book. The author then traces Thoreau's relationship to himself, others, "wider circles," and nature and phenomena through examination of the life and work. The book is lucid and especially insightful on Thoreau's social relationships and his attitudes on social and political institutions, nature, and religion. The extensive expository notes are superb in their own right; but, coming at the end of the book, one might overlook them. Wagenknecht's study is appropriate for upper level students and scholars, but his graceful prose makes the book approachable at all college levels.

Autobiographical Sources

While Thoreau wrote no autobiography *per se,* like Walt Whitman, all of his work was spun from the fabric of his life. Thoreau alters many of the experiences that formed the Walden experiment, for example, consciously molding life into art. However, the best sourcebook for Thoreau's own life is his *Journal,* started in 1837 and kept almost until his death. It began as a commonplace book, recording readings and thoughts that later were transformed into essays—much like Emerson's journal. From 1850 on, however, it became what Canby called "one of the most complete records extant of the inner life of an individual." It includes private thoughts, portraits of his acquaintances, and ideas on life, society, government, and religion. The publication of the *Journal* in 1906 in 16 volumes made much of this seminal material available, but it is incomplete. Some of the material was then unknown, some not extant. The Princeton University editions, a project of the Center for the Editions of American Authors, will form the definitive edition, and two volumes of the *Journals* have appeared to date, Volume I, 1837–1844, edited by John C. Broderick, 1980; and Volume II, 1842–1848, edited by Robert E. Sattelmeyer, 1984.

Overview of Critical Sources

Any student or scholar conducting research on Thoreau must know Walter Harding's *A Thoreau Handbook* (New York: New York University Press, 1959). A compendium of every piece of scholarship through 1958, Harding organizes the handbook into chapters covering Thoreau's life, works, sources, ideas, and fame, each chapter dealing with its topic in essay form, discussing relevant scholarship as it proceeds. Each chapter is followed by sources, again organized by topics discussed within each chapter. While this may make pinpointing a specific work more difficult than would an alphabetical or chronological format, the index at the end of the book can lead one to something already known; and wading through each chapter is an education in Thoreau scholarship. While the *Handbook* is exhaustive, *The New Thoreau Handbook,* edited by Harding and Michael Meyer (New York: New York University Press, 1980), is selective, choosing only that scholarship its authors feel is worthy of note, and which is likely to be available at a good college library. Even with those restrictions, the update contains an enormous trove of materials, organized this time by life, works, sources, ideas, art, and reputation. The discursive essay format is retained from the earlier work. Both editions are indispensable to Thoreau research.

Evaluation of Selected Criticism

Cavell, Stanley, *The Sense of Walden*. New York: Viking, 1972. Cavell's book is widely regarded as the best single study of *Walden* to date. It is difficult reading, but provocative and well worth the effort. Cavell suggests that Thoreau attempted to invest his language with scriptural meaning throughout *Walden,* and he analyzes the ways in which Thoreau enriched his language with layers of meaning so as to uplift both himself and his readers. Actions in *Walden* are seen as metaphors for the act of writing. Through detailed and often brilliant analysis, Cavell sheds new light on even the most familiar passages of Thoreau's most well-known work.

Garber, Frederick, *Thoreau's Redemptive Imagination*. New York: New York University Press, 1977. Building on the works of previous critics, including Sherman Paul (q.v.), Garber traces the relationship of Thoreau's ethos to his perceptions of external nature, and his attempt to assimilate nature and to make his piece with its "inadequacies." Garber's thesis is that Thoreau remained essentially separate from nature, transforming it into an emblem and extension of his consciousness. Garber is a scholar of comparative literature, and brings an original, if subjective focus to this study.

Paul, Sherman, *The Shores of America: Thoreau's Inward Exploration*. Urbana: University of Illinois Press, 1958. This exhaustively detailed and lengthy but lucidly written study is the best single book to date on Thoreau's intellectual development. Paul calls his work a "spiritual biography or a biography of vocation"; it is, in fact, a detailed study of all but the most minor works, analyzed in chronological order, against the backdrop of Thoreau's life and thought, especially his relationship to the Transcendental movement. Paul derives his conclusions largely through detailed and sensitive textual explication of not only Thoreau's well-known *oeuvre,* but of almost all of the unpublished writings as well. Paul reveals an exhaustive knowledge of preceding scholarship.

Other Sources

Matthiessen, F. O. *American Renaissance: Art and Expression in the Age of Emerson and Whitman*. New York: Oxford University Press, 1941. This classic of American literary criticism contains a superb study of Thoreau and his contemporaries which still forms one of the best evaluations of Thoreau's aesthetic. Matthiessen sees Thoreau "more of an Epicurean than a stoic," a judgment which might cause surprise, but which is well-defended. There is a particularly useful analysis of the structure of *Walden.*

Paul, Sherman, ed. *Thoreau: A Collection of Essays* (The Twentieth Century Views Series). Englewood Cliffs, NJ: Prentice-Hall, 1962. Typical of others in this well-known series in its collection of representative excerpts from criticism over the length and breadth of Thoreau scholarship, the book is notable for Paul's superb introduction which succinctly summarizes the trends in Thoreau scholarship, and contains an appreciation of Matthiessen's work (see above).

Selected Dictionaries and Encyclopedias

The Reader's Encyclopedia of American Literature, Thomas Y. Crowell, 1962. Brief biography with good succinct appraisal of Thoreau's major accomplishments.

The Literary History of The United States, 3rd edition. Macmillan, 1963. A substantial and thoughtful biography and appraisal by Townsand Scudder.

David Sadkin
Niagara University

JAMES THURBER
1894–1961

Author's Chronology

Born December 8, 1894, Columbus, Ohio to Mary Fisher Thurber and Charles L. Thurber; *1901* is blinded in left eye; *1913* enter Ohio State University; writes for campus paper, *The Ohio State Lantern; 1918* editor *The Sun-Dial,* the student monthly; leaves university in June without taking a degree; *1918–1920* serves as code clerk for U.S. State Department in Washington and Paris; *1920* returns to Columbus; works as reporter; *1921–1925* writes and directs musical comedies for Ohio State University; *1922* marries Althea Adams; *1924* resigns from the *Columbus Dispatch* to begin free-lance writing; *1925* becomes reporter for Paris and Riviera editions of the *Chicago Tribune; 1926* returns to the United States; reporter for the *New York Evening News; 1927* joins staff of *The New Yorker; 1929* publishes first book, *Is Sex Necessary?* in collaboration with E.B. White; *1929–1961* publishes twenty-four books; *1935* divorced from Althea Adams; marries Helen Wismer; *1940 The Male Animal* produced successfully in New York; *1940–1941* undergoes eye operations; begins to go blind; *1950–1951* becomes too blind to draw; *1953* is awarded honorary Litt.D. by Yale University; *1960 A Thurber Carnival* produced in New York; plays himself for eighty-eight performances; *1961* suffers blood clot on brain October 4; dies November 4.

Author's Bibliography (selected)

Is Sex Necessary? (with E.B. White), 1929 (satire of sex therapy books); *The Owl in the Attic and Other Perplexities,* 1931 (stories and satires); *The Seal in the Bedroom and Other Predicaments,* 1932 (cartoons and drawings); *My Life and Hard Times,* 1933 (burlesque autobiography); *The Middle-Aged Man on the Flying Trapeze,* 1935 (stories and essays); *Let Your Mind Alone!,* 1937 (stories and essays); *The Male Animal* (with Elliott Nugent), 1940 (play); *Fables for Our Time and Famous Poems Illustrated,* 1940 (fables and drawings); *My World—and Welcome to It,* 1942 (stories and essays); *Men, Women and Dogs,* 1942 (cartoons); *The Thurber Carnival,* 1945 (stories, essays, cartoons); *The White Deer,* 1945 (fantasy); *The Beast in Me and Other Animals,* (stories, essays, drawings); *The 13 Clocks,* 1950 (fantasy); *The Thurber Album,* 1952 (essays); *Thurber Country,* 1953 (stories, essays); *Further Fables for Our Time,* 1956 (fables); *The Wonderful O,* 1957 (fantasy); *Alarms and Diversions,* 1957 (stories, essays, cartoons); *The Years with Ross,* 1959 (biography); *Lanterns and Lances,* 1961 (stories and essays); *Credoes and Curios,* 1962 (stories and essays).

Overview of Biographical Sources

The first book on Thurber, Robert E. Morsberger's *James Thurber* (New York: Twayne, 1964) appeared three years after Thurber's death; though chiefly critical, it contains the overall details of Thurber's life. Charles S. Holmes, *The Clocks of Columbus* (1972) combines a biographical and critical study but is somewhat limited as a biography because the author was not given full access to Thurber's papers and correspondence. The only full biography is Burton Berstein's *Thurber, A Biography* (1975). Helen Thurber gave Berstein full access to all her husband's papers but was not satisfied with the result, which she found unbalanced and too dark in its portrait.

Evaluation of Biographies

Bernstein, Burton, *Thurber, A Biography.* New York: Dodd, Mead, 1975. Berstein, a staff writer on *The New Yorker,* had the permission denied Holmes to make full use of Thurber's papers and correspondence. Berstein's extensive quotes from this material provide statements by Thurber available nowhere else and give his biography a fullness of detail lacking in other studies. At times Berstein quotes too extensively and uncritically. Several early chapters consist almost entirely of Thurber's letters, quoted in full at tedious and unnecessary length. Bernstein also lacks critical detachment; repeatedly, he mocks Thurber's sex life, ridiculing him for keeping his virginity so long, claiming (with no evidence) that Thurber was sexually inadequate, and repeating scurrilous gossip from Truman Capote, a very unreliable source. Taking the official *New Yorker* point of view at a time when Thurber and the magazine were at odds, Bernstein attacks Thurber savagely for *The Years with Ross,* which he dismisses as a failure, though in fact it was one of Thurber's two best-selling books. Bernstein also puts so much stress on Thurber's drinking, fits of anger, and pessimism that he misses Thurber's charm, wit, friendships, hopefulness, and lucidity. In Bernstein's study the madness largely obliterates the magic.

Holmes, Charles S. *The Clocks of Columbus: The Literary Career of James Thurber.* New York: Atheneum, 1972. Because Burton Bernstein's work was in progress, Holmes was not allowed to quote freely and fully from Thurber's papers and correspondence. Accordingly, his biography lacks completeness of detail. Nevertheless, it gives a better-balanced portrait than that by Bernstein, who goes out of his way to stress the negative aspects of Thurber's life and career. Holmes' book is as much literary analysis as biography, but it is organized chronologically and biographically.

Autobiographical Sources

My Life and Hard Times (1933) is a burlesque autobiography which is for the most part not to be taken literally. *The Thurber Album* (1952) contains fifteen portraits of Thurber's family, friends, and favorite professors in Columbus during the early years of the twentieth century. A concluding chapter provides a few more brief sketches plus some autobiographical detail. *The Years with Ross* (1959), a portrait of the founding editor of *The New Yorker,* contains many autobiographical anecdotes, together with a vivid picture of life at the magazine with which Thurber was associated for most of his career. *Selected Letters of James Thurber* (1981) reprints slightly over 100 letters from Thurber's vast correspondence; the letters, many excerpted, were chosen not to provide a life in letters but for their innate interest. Though ranging from 1936 to 1961, they are not arranged in strict chronology but are grouped by recipients. Few deal with Thruber's own work. Showing Thurber's humor and courage under adversity, his generosity, his fiercely loyal friendships, they help dispel the negative portrait in Bernstein's unbalanced biography. Other autobiographical sources are fourteen interviews, cited in Morsberger's bibliography.

Overview of Critical Sources

Generally considered the greatest American humorist since Mark Twain, Thurber was not merely a funny man but a serious thinker and artist who used humor to examine the predicaments and perplexities of twentieth century man. In fables and fairy tales, Thurber presented the affirmative values of love, loyalty, and laughter. Criticism focuses on the affirmative and pessimistic elements of his thought; his comic romanticism; the targets of his satire; his war between men and women; the role of dogs, birds, and beasts in his art; the impact of blindness on his work; and the style of his prose and pictures.

Evaluation of Selected Criticism

Black, Stephen A. *James Thurber: His Masquerades.* The Hague: Mouton, 1970. Black's is a short, concise study that undertakes to establish Thurber's place as a significant American artist. Seeing Thurber's world as a comic nightmare, Black compares Thurber's comedy of the alienated and vulnerable individual to American humor from Washington Irving to Nathanael West.

Holmes, Charles S. *The Clocks of Columbus: The Literary Career of James Thurber.* New York: Atheneum, 1972. Blending criticism with biography, Holmes approaches Thurber's work chronologically, providing astute analyses of each book as it appears in Thurber's development and relating biographical details to the works created at the time. Holmes looks in some depth at Thurber's liberalism as reflected in his artistic reaction to the political developments during his career. For a combination of biography and criticism, *The Clocks of Columbus* is a uniquely valuable study.

————. ed. *Thurber: A Collection of Critical Essays.* Englewood Cliffs, NJ: Prentice Hall, 1974. Holmes has anthologized twenty-two of the best previously uncollected essays about Thurber, plus three chapters from the books by Morsberger, Richard C. Tobias, and himself.

Keeney, Catherine McGehee, *Thurber's Anatomy of Confusion.* Hamden, CT: Archon Books, 1984. McGehee covers no new ground but does a perceptive job of analyzing Thurber's melancholy humor, frustrated dreamers, aggressive women, and the "clash between chaos and order." She leaves out his political satire and offers almost no biographical background, but she is particularly good at analyzing Thurber's wordplay.

Morsberger, Robert E. *James Thurber.* New York: Twayne, 1964. Prior to Morsberger's work, criticism was limited almost entirely to articles in the popular magazines. Since the periodical indexes did not include *The New Yorker* until 1940, Thurber's uncollected articles, stories, and drawings for that magazine from 1927 to 1940 were not indexed anywhere. Morsberger discovered hundreds of them and compiled the first bibliography of both primary and secondary sources. Morsberger analyzes the predicaments and perplexities that confront Thurber's often bewildered protagonists; the thin dividing line between humor and tragedy; the precarious balance between pessimism and affirmation in Thurber's work; the romantic imagination that enables some Thurber characters to escape from or overcome the stresses of the modern world; the war between the sexes; the counterbalance provided by dogs and other creatures against the insane world; the contrast between his comedy of Ohio life and his portrait of sophisticated New Yorkers; the political satire in Thurber's attacks on both Communism and right-wing witch hunting; Thurber's works on stage and screen; his cartoons and drawings; his literary allusions, style, and word play.

————."James Thurber," in *American Writers: A Collection of Literary Biographies,* ed. Leonard Unger. New York: Charles Scribner's Sons, 1979. Morsberger's second study of Thurber is updated, shorter, and more concise.

Other Sources

Bowden, Edwin T. *James Thurber: A Bibliography.* Columbus: Ohio State University Press, 1968. Though comprehensive, Morsberger's bibliography is not definitive. Bowden gives all the alternative printings, reprintings in anthologies, and translations as well as a complete chronological list for all Thurber publications to that time. He does not include secondary bibliography; for that, the revised edition of Morsberger, though not entirely up to date, is still most complete.

Robert E. Morsberger
California State Polytechnic University,
Pomona

J. R. R. TOLKIEN
1892–1973

Author's Chronology

Born John Ronald Reuel Tolkien, January 3, 1892, Bloemfontein, South Africa, where his father, Arthur Tolkien, had moved his wife to take a position in a bank; *1895* Mabel Tolkien takes her two sons back to Birmingham, England with her; *1896* Arthur dies in South Africa; *1911* Tolkien enters Oxford; *1915* takes degree; *1917* begins to write "The Book of Lost Tales," which years later became *The Silmarillion; 1920* appointed Reader in English at Leeds University; *1925* publishes edition of *Sir Gawain and the Green Knight,* co-edited with E. V. Gordon, and becomes Rawlinson and Bosworth Professor of English at Oxford; *1930* begins to write *The Hobbit,* abandoning it later; *1936* presents his significant lecture, *Beowulf: The Monsters and the Critics; 1937* publishes *The Hobbit* and begins to work on its sequel; *1945* elected Merton Professor of English at Oxford; *1949* completes *The Lord of the Rings* (published 1954–55); *1959* retires from Oxford; *1965* paperback publication of *The Lord of the Rings* makes him a cult hero in the U.S.; *1973* September 2, dies in a nursing home, Bournemouth, England.

Author's Bibliography (selected)

Sir Gawain and the Green Knight, 1925 (edition with E. V. Gordon); "Beowulf: The Monsters and the Critics," 1936 (criticism); *The Hobbit,* 1937 (fiction); "Leaf by Niggle," 1945 (story); "On Fairy Stories," 1947 (criticism); *Farmer Giles of Ham,* 1949 (story); *The Fellowship of the Ring,* 1954 (Part I of *The Lord of the Rings*); *The Two Towers,* 1954 (Part II of *The Lord of the Rings*); *The Return of the King* (Part III of *The Lord of the Rings*), 1955; *The Adventures of Tom Bombadil and Other Verses from the Red Book,* 1962 (verse); *Tree and Leaf,* 1964 (collection including "On Fairy Stories" and "Leaf by Niggle"); *Smith of Wootton Major,* 1967 (story); publication of *The Silmarillion, Unfinished Tales,* and other posthumous works edited by his son, Christopher Tolkien, 1977-present.

Overview of Biographical Sources

Were it not for Tolkien's monumental, carefully crafted, and well-told Middle-earth narratives—*The Hobbit* and *The Lord of the Rings*—the life of this Oxford don would scarcely interest the general public. Certainly it was hardly extraordinary in nature; yet the acclaim generated by these four volumes has created the market for Tolkien biographies. Two book-length biographies have been published to date. One of them is virtually useless as a reliable source, while the other is not only reliable but quite illuminating and, above all, readable. These two works are Daniel Grotta-Kuska's *J. R. R. Tolkien: Architect of*

Middle Earth, A Biography (1976) and Humphrey Carpenter's *Tolkien: A Biography* (1977). Lacking in precision and accuracy, Grotta-Kurska's biography looks at Tolkien's life from the outside, without benefit of inside information. Carpenter's biography, however, is finely detailed, the result of Tolkien's cooperation and Carpenter's full access to the Tolkien papers after his death. Indeed, the book jacket announces this work as "the authorized biography." In addition to this biography, Carpenter has also published a biography of a "group," *The Inklings: C. S. Lewis, J. R. R. Tolkien, Charles Williams, and their Friends* (London: Allen & Unwin, 1978), which chronicles the rise and fall of the important club of Oxford writers who met periodically to read from early drafts of their works. This work, while of necessity devoting less space to Tolkien, nevertheless elaborates on aspects of relationships between and influences on individual group members. Carpenter's access to the *corpus* of Tolkien material has led to yet another biographical work—*The Letters of J. R. R. Tolkien* (1981), on which project Christopher Tolkien collaborated. This latter work functions as a kind of multifarious footnote to the Tolkien biography and as such is a complement to it.

Evaluation of Selected Biographies

Carpenter, Humphrey, *Tolkien: A Biography*. London: Allen & Unwin, 1977. Dubbed "the authorized biography" on the front cover, this work was undertaken with Tolkien's full cooperation and, after his death, with unrestricted access to the Tolkien papers. It is composed of eight sections—six of which are the text of the biography—plus four appendices and an index. Carpenter begins with an account of his first visit with Tolkien in 1967, recording first impressions. The six sections concern Tolkien's life during the periods 1892–1916 (the early years), 1917–1925 (the making of a mythology), 1925–1949 (the hobbit books), 1949–1966 (success), and 1959–1973 (last years). Carpenter treats his subject throughout with respect, care, and love, but he also treats him fairly, showing Tolkien's negative traits as well. Especially revealing are the references to Tolkien's relationship with C. S. Lewis and Charles Williams, the three of whom formed the core of the Oxford writer's group the Inklings. Readers will find interesting, too, the account of Tolkien's dealings with his publishers, the evolution of his Middle-earth stories, and his embarrassment at becoming a cult hero in his retirement years. The book is a must for any serious study of Tolkien's works.

Grotta-Kurska, Daniel, *J. R. R. Tolkien: Architect of Middle Earth*. Philadelphia: Running Press, 1976. Grotta-Kurska's biography suffers from a tragic flaw, which he relates honestly in the "Afterword," where he describes the reluctance of the Tolkien family to grant interviews and their request for the same of Tolkien's close friends and associates. Thus, Grotta-Kurska did not have access to the Tolkien literary papers, letters, or other materials necessary for a complete biography. The book is therefore a second-hand account drawn from published reviews, interviews, and other such sources. The text of the biography, occupying a scant 140 pages, is sandwiched between a prologue and the "Afterword." The eight chapters that compose the biography correspond with "periods" in Tolkien's life, headed by such titles as "The Young Lad (1892–1911)," "The Scholar (1919–1925)," "The Mythmaker (1937–1953)," and "The Recluse (1966–1973)." Explanatory footnotes make evident that Grotta-Kurska pictured his audience as young American casual readers, but errors of fact appear in some of the footnotes and errors in judgment appear in others, especially in his citation of unreliable "critical" sources such as Lin Carter and William Ready. A reader should therefore approach Mr. Gotta-Kurska's biography with caution.

Autobiographical Sources

Tolkien wrote no autobiography; however, what might pass for his autobiography emerges from the 354 letters selected for inclusion in Humphrey Carpenter's recent work, *The Letters of J. R. R. Tolkien* (London: Allen and Unwin, 1981). These letters have been edited carefully to cast light solely on his works and interests, though, and the editor avoids highly personal material such as the "very large body" of love letters which Tolkien wrote to Edith Bratt—first his fiancée and later his wife—from 1913 to 1918. These have been omitted as well as the majority of the small body of letters written between 1918 and 1937, which contain nothing about *The Hobbit* or *The Silmarillion*. The selection—some of which are portions—includes letters written to his children, such as the important war-era letters written to his son Christopher, now his literary executor. Other letters of interest are those to his publisher concerning arrangements for publishing his works, to other potential publishers when Allen & Unwin balked at *The Silmarillion*, to his readers on matters of interpreting *The Lord of the Rings*, and to friends and acquaintances. The volume is arranged in chronological order, from letter number one, written in 1914 to Edith Bratt, to letter number 354, written to his daughter Priscilla four days prior to his death. Each letter is preceded by a contextual note set in brackets, and following the last of the letters is a section of explanatory notes. The volume also has two indices—one of references to persons, places, and things in Tolkien's works and the other a general index.

Overview of Critical Sources

Tolkien's fiction appeals to two widely-differing reading audiences. The first group includes those who read solely for pleasure, whose study of his works usually focuses on learning more about the invented languages and about Tolkien's invented world. The second of these two groups includes scholars and literary critics, whose studies of his works focus on sources, influences, and critical interpretations. Students of Tolkien's works should read several issues of *Mythlore,* the journal of the Mythopoeic Society, for a sampling of both of these approaches to Tolkien's works. Although this journal is heavily oriented toward Tolkien's works, its range is the fantasy literature of Tolkien, Lewis, Williams, and their precursors and postcursors. Book-length studies of Tolkien also reflect this diverse interest. Lin Carter's *Tolkien: A Look Behind The Lord of the Rings* (New York: Ballantine, 1969) is an example of the first category: a chatty, somewhat superficial, wide-eyed appraisal of *The Lord of the Rings.* For the Tolkien trivia buff as well as for the scholar seeking a quick reference there is Robert Foster's *The Complete Guide to Middle-earth: from The Hobbit to The Silmarillion* (New York: Del Rey, 1978), an encyclopedia with page references. In the second category of publications one can find unevenness, yet there are several fine studies of backgrounds, themes, and meaning available, some of the best of which appear below.

Evaluation of Selected Criticism

Isaacs, Neil D. and Rose A. Zimbardo, *Tolkien: New Critical Perspectives.* Lexington: University Press of Kentucky, 1981. This collection of twelve essays is a revision of the editors' earlier *Tolkien and the Critics: Essays on J. R. R. Tolkien's Lord of the Rings* (Notre Dame: University of Notre Dame Press, 1968), an anthology of fifteen essays. Too numerous for mention here, the essays contained in these two volumes are well-reasoned, sensible, and, at times, quite illuminating studies of various aspects of Tolkien's art.

Kocher, Paul, *Master of Middle-earth: The Fiction of J. R. R. Tolkien.* Boston: Houghton-Mifflin, 1972. One of the best book-length critical studies of Tolkien's works, this book retains its importance even though written before the publication of *The Silmarillion* in 1977. Its seven chapters cover the cosmology of Middle-earth, the nature and meaning of *The Hobbit,* the cosmic order, the nature of evil, the free peoples of Middle-earth, the character of Aragorn, and the relationship of Tolkien's minor works to his *magnum opus.*

Noel, Ruth S. *The Mythology of Middle-earth.* Boston: Houghton-Mifflin, 1977. Noel makes comparisons between Tolkien's mythology and Norse and Celtic myths, and by so doing creates a complement to the earlier Christian readings of *The Lord of the Rings.*

Rogers, Deborah, and Ivor Rogers, *J. R. R. Tolkien.* Boston: Twayne, 1980. This study ranks as one of the best introductions to Tolkien, covering the minor works, *The Hobbit, The Lord of the Rings,* and *The Silmarillion* in readable discussions of sources and meaning.

West, Richard C. "The Interlace Structure of *The Lord of the Rings,*" in *A Tolkien Compass.* ed. Jared Lobdell. LaSalle, IL: Open Court, 1975. West cites the influence of the medieval narrative technique known as interlace structure on Tolkien's work and demonstrates the interweaving of the plot lines of the six books of *The Lord of the Rings* among three groups of main characters.

Other Sources

Crabbe, Katharyn F. *J. R. R. Tolkien.* New York: Frederick Ungar, 1981. A well-balanced, comprehensive introduction to Tolkien, beginning with a short biography and continuing with well-founded readings of the significant minor works as well as of the three major works. The chapter on *The Silmarillion* is especially illuminating.

Glover, Willis, "The Christian Character of Tolkien's Invented World," in *Mythlore,* 3, No. 2 (1975), 3–8. Glover probes the depths of the strong Christian coloring of *The Lord of the Rings* in this essay written and published before *The Silmarillion* clarified just how strong was that coloring. This is not the first of such studies, but it is among the best treatments of the religious background.

Lense, Edward, "Sauron is Watching *You:* The Role of the Great Eye in *The Lord of the Rings,*" in *Mythlore,* 4, No. 1 (September 1976), 3–6. This essay traces the image of the great eye of Sauron in *Lord of the Rings* to the Celtic myth of Balor of the Evil Eye and surveys the use of other evil eyes as well.

Selected Dictionaries and Encyclopedias

Current Biography Yearbook 1967, H. W. Wilson, 1967. A concise biography that is still useful.

Dale W. Simpson
Missouri Southern State College

JEAN TOOMER
1894–1967

Author's Chronology

Born December 26, 1894, Washington, D.C., of mixed-blood parents; *1914–1918* enrolls in six different institutions of higher learning but earns no degree; *1921* spends three months teaching in Sparta, Georgia, an experience that forms the basis for *Cane*; *1923* publishes *Cane*, his major work; *1924* begins studying spiritual philosophy of George Gurdjieff and spends next ten years spreading his teachings; *1931* marries Margery Latimer, who dies in childbirth 1932; *1935* marries Marjorie Content; *1936* moves with wife to Bucks County, Pennsylvania, where he lives until his death; dies March 30, 1967.

Author's Bibliography (selected)

Cane, 1923 (fiction, poems); *The Wayward and the Seeking*, 1980 (autobiography, fiction, poems, plays, selected and edited posthumously).

Overview of Biographical Sources

Despite the availability of ample unpublished information, no full-life biography of Toomer exists, and until 1984 there was no full-length biography of any part of Toomer's life. Before this date the most substantial biography to be found was part of a long chapter on Toomer in Darwin T. Turner's *In A Minor Chord: Three Afro-American Writers and Their Search for Identity* (1971). Nellie Y. McKay's *Jean Toomer, Artist: A Study of His Literary Life and Work, 1894–1936* (1984), written with the co-operation of Toomer's widow and with full access to unpublished materials, has the status of an authorized, definitive biography for the period it covers.

Evaluation of Selected Biographies

McKay, Nellie Y. *Jean Toomer, Artist: A Study of His Literary Life and Work, 1894–1936*. Chapel Hill: University of North Carolina Press, 1984. This critical biography covers Toomer's life from birth to his last literary publication, the long poem "Blue Meridian." Aware of the contradictions and idealizations in Toomer's autobiographical writings, McKay uses that work extensively without allowing it to distort her record of the artist's life. She gives accurate information on and thoughtful analysis of Toomer's literary and family relationships, his long-standing ambivalence about race, recurrent patterns in his behavior, and the interest in Gurdjieff's philosophy for which he forsook the literary world. She stresses Toomer's quest for personal harmony as the most powerful impulse behind his work and life. McKay's critical chapters are less informative and more ponderously written than her biographical chapters. Undistinguished as criticism, McKay's book is the central source for biographical information on Toomer.

Autobiographical Sources

Between 1928 and the 1940's, Toomer completed four unpublished autobiographies and drafted others. Darwin T. Turner makes substantial selections from most of these autobiographies in *The Wayward and the Seeking: A Collection of Writings by Jean Toomer* (Washington, D.C.: Howard University Press, 1980). He selects from "Earth-Being" (on Toomer's formative years and family relationships); from "Incredible Journey" (detailed descriptions of Toomer's family); from "Outline of an Autobiography" (Toomer's notes on his intellectual development, especially useful for understanding the years 1909–1922); and from "On Being an American," where Toomer, in trying to explain how his early life shaped his racial attitudes, also helps explain the genesis of *Cane*. Turner also selects stories, poems, and plays that contain strong autobiographical elements.

Toomer used the autobiographical mode to understand himself and to spread his philosophy. Since his self-understanding and the intensity of his didactic impulse constantly shifted, the accuracy and readability of the work varies. The liveliest sections are those in which Toomer narrates his early life; the more philosophical he grows, the more pedantic his prose becomes. Turner notes where Toomer's memory of events fails, or where his portraits of individuals (including himself) are inconsistent. Despite their occasional inaccuracies, the autobiographical writings have influenced significantly all biographical work on Toomer.

Overview of Critical Sources

Most book-length discussions of twentieth-century Afro-American writing and of the Harlem Renaissance contain some material on Toomer. Typically critics provide some biographical background and then a critical analysis of *Cane*, most of them agreeing that the book is a seminal text in Afro-American literature. The most recurrent single theme in Toomer criticism is the attempt to explain Toomer's espousal and subsequent denial of Afro-American heritage. Many articles have been written on Toomer, but only two full-length critical studies.

Evaluation of Selected Criticism

Benson, Brian Joseph, and Mabel Mayle Dillard, *Jean Toomer*. Boston: Twayne, 1980. This work begins with a generally solid biographical chapter that has one weakness: the authors deal superficially with the central conflict of Toomer's early life, his racial identity. The analysis of *Cane* is competent but contains nothing new, following the popular thesis that in denying his racial heritage Toomer lost the source of his creativity. The discussion of selected works outside *Cane* is useful, however, because so little criticism is available on this work.

Durham, Frank, comp. *The Merrill Studies in Cane*. Columbus, OH: Charles E. Merrill, 1971. In this collection, the only full-length study of *Cane* alone, the essays and reviews are grouped according to the writer's race, helping the reader to distinguish black and white perspectives on *Cane*. The reviews are useful for showing the response of Toomer's contemporaries to *Cane*, and the book also contains extracts from most of the important early *Cane* criticism. Despite its historical value, however, the book is outdated because the bulk of detailed Toomer criticism has been done since its publication.

Other Sources

Baker, Houston A., Jr. *Singers of Daybreak: Studies in Black American Literature*. Washington, DC: Howard University Press, 1974. Discusses *Cane's* importance for the development of Afro-American literature.

Perry, Margaret, *The Harlem Renaissance: An Annotated Bibliography and Commentary*. New York: Garland, 1982. Essential research tool, annotating sixty-nine critical pieces on Toomer.

Toomer, Jean, "Chapters From *Earth-Being*: An Unpublished Autobiography," *The Black Scholar* 2, 5 (January 1971), 3–13. Includes some paragraphs on Toomer's philosophy not reprinted in *The Wayward and the Seeking*.

Turner, Darwin J. *In a Minor Chord: Three Afro-American Writers and Their Search for Identity*. Carbondale: Southern Illinois University Press, 1971. Contains long bio-critical essay that remains one of the best-balanced overviews of Toomer's strengths and weaknesses.

Alan Golding
University of Mississippi

THOMAS TRAHERNE
1637–1674

Author's Chronology

Born Hereford, England, 1637 to shoemaker father; elder brother Philip twice mayor of Hereford; *1652* enters Brasenose College, Oxford; *1656* receives B.A. and begins journal entries; *1657* presented with living of Credenhill which position he holds until death; *1660* ordained deacon and priest; *1661* receives M.A. at Brasenose; continues at Credenhill becoming spiritual adviser to Mrs. Susanna Hopton, center of spiritual movement there (her niece later married to Philip Traherne) and working on *Centuries of Meditation* for her circle; *1667* becomes chaplain to Sir Orlando Bridgman, Keeper of the Seals in the Restoration; *1666–1668* reads Marsilio Ficino's commentary on Plato; *1669* receives B.D. from Brasenose; *1670* begins extensive literary activity, finishing *Centuries of Meditations, Church's Year-Book, Meditations on the Six Days of Creation, Thanksgivings,* early parts of *Christian Ethicks; 1673 Roman Forgeries* published anonymously (only work published during Traherne's lifetime); *1674* dies, buried beneath the reading desk in the church at Teddington.

Author's Bibliography

Roman Forgeries, 1673 (treatise); *Christian Ethicks,* 1675 (treatise); *Thanksgivings,* 1699 (treatise); *Meditations on the Six Days of the Creation,* 1717; *Centuries of Meditations* from the Dobell Folio, discovered 1895, published 1903, 1908; *Poems,* 1903; *Poems of Felicity,* 1910; *Select Meditations,* discovered 1964, as yet unpublished. Other unpublished manuscripts include "Early Notebooks," "Church's Year-Book," "Commonplace Book," all at Bodleian Library, Oxford; "Ficino Notebook," at British Museum, London.

Overview of Biographical Sources

Since Traherne's name and work were barely known before the 1903 publication of his *Poems* and the 1908 publication of *Centuries of Meditations* (both of which had been discovered only in 1895), the seeker of biographical information is basically limited to twentieth-century attempts to search out any extant materials. There are brief mentions in John Aubrey's *Miscellanies* (1696) and Anthony À Wood's *Athenae Oxoniensus* (1691–1692), but the bulk of the biographical material is collected in H. M. Margoliouth's *Thomas Traherne: Centuries, Poems, and Thanksgivings* (Oxford: Clarendon Press, 1958); Gladys Wade's *Thomas Traherne: A Critical Biography* (1944); as well as her *Poetical Works of Thomas Traherne* (Cooper Square, 1965, reprint of the 1932 edition of P. J. and A. E. Dobell); and K. W. Salter's *Thomas Traherne: Mystic and Poet* (1964). It is generally agreed that Margoliouth's 1958 edition is as close to definitive as possible; the biographical materials there are accepted as firm. It is highly possible that new works of Traherne remain to be discovered and that the continuing examination of the unpublished works will bring new biographical information to light.

Evaluation of Selected Biographies

Salter, K. W. *Thomas Traherne: Mystic and Poet.* London: Edward Arnold, 1964. Salter offers one of the best studies of the mystical tradition, its realization in Traherne, the poet's spiritual life, and relation of the poetry to the experiences of the poet. Especially helpful for anyone to whom terms like "mystic" need explanation and example.

Wade, Gladys, *Thomas Traherne: A Critical Biography.* Princeton: University Press, 1944. A pioneering study, important for its efforts to bring together as much material as possible. Wade perhaps over-reads in an attempt to explore Traherne's external and spiritual lives, but succeeds in making a believable picture of a writer whose work links him with the earlier seventeenth-century metaphysicals.

White, Helen C. *The Metaphysical Poets: A Study in Religious Experience.* New York: Macmillan, 1936. White's is an early major work, with two significant chapters on Traherne, particularly "The Pursuit of Felicity," in which White explores Traherne's intellectual background, probable reading in his course of study, and the relation of the poetry to the poet's own life. In contrast to later writers, who devote considerable source to Platonic and other currents in Traherne's thinking, White centers on the man; this approach, although not the only valid way to read the poet, is illuminating.

Autobiographical Sources

In a very real sense, all of Traherne's work can be taken as at least partially autobiographical; certainly the several unpublished journals and commonplace books contain vast amounts of autobiography.

Overview of Critical Sources

Critical material on Traherne tends to center on the religious and philosophical influences on the poet, the metaphysical and/or baroque traits of the poetry, and the mystical elements which run through both poetry and prose. Although the object of critical scrutiny is his poetry, Traherne himself devoted more energy to prose; the one work he published in his lifetime is in fact a prose treatise. All of Traherne's work is religious in nature and critics have focused on various aspects of his theology: Sharon Seelig Cadman's *The Shadow of Eternity* (Lexington: University of Kentucky Press, 1981) explores the dualities in the poetry of Herbert, Vaughan, and Traherne, noting Traherne's preoccupation with the present and eternity, time and the timeless, always simultaneously; Anthony Low's *Love's Architecture: Devotional Modes in Seventeenth-Century English Poetry* (New York: New York University Press, 1978) calls Traherne a "mystical hedonist" and analyzes elements of wonder, praise, and happiness in the poetry. Louis Martz's classic *The Paradise Within: Studies in Vaughan, Traherne, and Milton* (New Haven: Yale University Press, 1964) traces the structure of the *Centuries of Meditations* and notes a threefold pattern of finding God in the world, the self, and the attributes of God.

Evaluation of Selected Criticism

Day, Malcolm M. *Thomas Traherne.* Boston: Twayne, 1982. This is the most readable and comprehensive study of Traherne, with chapters on each of the major works of poetry and prose, an annotated bibliography, and other references. Using and acknowledging earlier works, Day gracefully compiles the various readings of Traherne's treatises and volumes. His treatment of the complex philosophical and theological background which influenced Traherne is lucid and enormously helpful.

Clements, A. L. *The Mystical Poetry of Thomas Traherne.* Cambridge: Harvard University Press, 1969. A sensitive study with primary focus on Traherne's poetry in its religious tradition, Clements divides the poems into three phases, "Innocence," "Fall," and "Redemption," and draws from the Dobell manuscript a rich meditation on the Christian life.

Stewart, Stanley, *The Expanded Voice: The Art of Thomas Traherne.* San Marino, CA: Huntington Library, 1970. Another major work, this one focuses on all of Traherne's works and highlights what Stewart terms Traherne's "rhetoric of erosion." Stewart also suggests alternative groupings for the poems in the Dobell manuscript.

Katherine Hanley, CSJ
The College of Saint Rose

ANTHONY TROLLOPE
1815–1882

Author's Chronology

Born April 24, 1815, Keppel Street, Bloomsbury, England, to Thomas Anthony and Frances Milton Trollope; *1827* enters Winchester College; *1830* returns to Harrow School; *1834* leaves Harrow due to family financial difficulties and lives with family in Bruges, Belgium; *1834* accepts junior clerkship in the London General Post Office; *1841* becomes Deputy Postal Surveyor in Ireland; *1843* begins first novel, *The Macdermots of Ballycloran* (published 1847); *1844* marries Rose Heseltine; *1855* publishes *The Warden*, first in the Barchester series; *1857* publishes *Barchester Towers* and confirms his popular recognition as a major novelist; *1858* travels on official postal mission to West Indies; *1859* publishes *West Indies and the Spanish Main; 1859* transfers from Ireland to England and settles at Waltham Cross; *1860* meets Kate Field in Florence; *1862* publishes *North America; 1863* Frances Milton Trollope, his mother and popular novelist, dies; *1864* publishes *Can You Forgive Her*, first of six Palliser or political novels; *1864* elected to the Atheneum; *1867* publishes *Last Chronicle of Barset* considered by Trollope to be his greatest novel; *1867* resigns from the Post Office; becomes editor of *St. Paul's Magazine; 1868* visits the U.S. again on official postal and copyright missions; November *1868* stands unsuccessfully in the General Election as Liberal candidate for Beverley; *1871* travels to Australia to visit son; *1872* settles in Montagu Square, London; *1873* publication of *The Eustace Diamonds* marks an upswing in declining sales; *1875* publishes *The Way We Live Now; 1876* finishes *Autobiography* (published posthumously); *1877* visits South Africa; *1880* leaves Montagu Square, settles at Harting Grange; *1882* visits Ireland for the last time; begins his last novel *The Landleaguers* (published incomplete in 1883); December 6, 1882 dies in London.

Author's Bibliography (selected)

The MacDermots of Ballycloran, 1847 (first Irish novel); *The Warden*, 1855 (novel); *Barchester Towers*, 1857 (novel); *The West Indies and the Spanish Main*, 1859 (travel book); *North America*, 1862 (travel book); *Can You Forgive Her?*, 1864 (novel); *Nina Balatka*, 1867 (novel, published anonymously); *The Last Chronicle of Barset*, 1867 (novel); *Phineas Finn, The Irish Member*, 1869 (novel); *He Knew He Was Right*, 1869 (novel); *The Eustace Diamonds*, 1873 (novel); *Phineas Redux*, 1974 (novel); *The Way We Live Now*, 1875 (novel); *The Prime Minister*, 1876 (novel); *The American Senator*, 1877 (novel); *Is He Popenjoy?*, 1878 (novel); *Thackeray*, 1879 (criticism); *The Duke's Children*, 1880 (novel); *The Life of Cicero*, 1880 (biography); *An Autobiography*, 1883 (published posthumously); *The Letters of Anthony Trollope*, 1851, 1871.

Overview of Biographical Sources

Anthony Trollope was the most popular and prolific member of a large literary family. His first biographer, T. H. S. Escott, was an intimate friend in Trollope's later years. Escott's *Anthony Trollope: His Work, Associates and Literary Originals* (London: John Lane, 1913) is written in a somewhat digressive style, but it contains many valuable personal anecdotes. The seminal bio-critical study, Michael Sadleir's *Trollope: A Commentary* (1927), was largely responsible for improved critical and popular reception given to Trollope's novels following World War I. A somewhat controversial biography of the entire Trollope family was written by Lucy Poate Stebbins, and her son, Richard Poate Stebbins: *The Trollopes: The Chronicle of a Writing Family* (1945). It includes important sections on Anthony's mother, Frances Milton Trollope, and on his older brother, Thomas Adolphus, but maintains a subtle bias against Anthony. There have been two excellent recent biographies. James Pope Hennessy's *Anthony Trollope* (1971) is by far the more detailed. C. P. Snow's *Anthony Trollope, His Life & Art* (1975) is a careful bio-critical study in sympathy with Sadleir's critical perspective; it is disarmingly casual in its style.

Evaluation of Selected Biographies

Hennessy, James Pope, *Anthony Trollope*. London and Boston: Jonathan Cape; Little, Brown, 1971. Pope Hennessy's personal affinity for his subject and thorough knowledge of the geographical areas to which Trollope traveled are evident in the descriptive detail of this work. Critical comments on the novels are of less interest than the focus on the author's life and personality. This is considered the most complete biographical study to date.

Sadleir, Michael, *Trollope, A Commentary*. London: Riverside Press 1927. Sadleir's famous study of Trollope's life and work presents Trollope as one of the few English authors who reflect the mind both of a period (mid-Victorian England) and of an individual psychology. It contains a chapter on Trollope's mother, Frances Milton Trollope, and is strong in the publication history of Trollope's novels. Sadleir defends Trollope's art on the strength of its characterization and effective dramatization of ordinary life.

Snow, C. P. *Trollope: His Life and Art*. New York: Charles Scribner's Sons, 1975. Snow's bio-critical study offers a good introduction to Trollope's work because of its informal style and its concise, yet insightful, treatment of Trollope's work. Snow agrees with Sadleir in his assessment of Trollope's basic gifts and dispels common criticisms of Trollope's style and subject matter.

Stebbins, Lucky Poate and Richard Poate, *The Trollopes, The Chronicle of a Writing Family*. New York: Columbia University Press, 1945. This is a very readable and apparently well researched biography on the entire Trollope family. The reader should be aware, however, that some of the authors' conclusions about Trollope's life and work have been challenged by many critics.

Autobiographical Sources

Trollope completed his autobiography in 1876, but according to his express wishes, *An Autobiography* (London: Blackwood & Sons, 1883) was published only posthumously, by his son, Henry. It is generally considered to be among the masterpeices of autobiography and is distinguished by the author's candor, integrity, his self-deprecatory tone, and by his lucid, simple style. Though the first three chapters contain a moving account of the author's unhappy childhood, subsequent chapters exclude references to his personal life. They focus rather on the financial rewards and publication history of Trollope's career, and on the author's critical assessment of his own work. In spite of its many excellent qualities, *The Autobiography* did much to harm Trollope's literary reputation in the late nineteenth century. Critics disliked the author's practical approach to his profession and dismissed Trollope's canon without considering its literary merits.

Trollope's letters, though few in comparison to those of other major Victorian authors, are an aid to appreciating Trollope's unembellished prose style, his cordial and efficient relationships with publishers, and the nature of his friendships. There are two excellent editions of his private letters: Bradford Allen Booth's *The Letters of Anthony Trollope* (London: Oxford University Press, 1951) and N. John Hall's *The Letters of Anthony Trollope* (Stanford: Stanford University Press, 1983). Hall includes over 1,800 letters in their entirety. *The Tireless Traveller,* Bradford A. Booth, ed. (Berkeley: University of California Press, 1941) includes twenty letters published in the *Liverpool Mercury* in 1875.

Overview of Critical Sources

An excellent history of the vicissitudes of Trollope criticism is found in Rafael Helling's *A Century of Trollope Criticism* (Port Washington, NY: Kennikat Press, 1956). Donald Smalley's *Trollope: The Critical Heritage* (London: Routledge & Kegan Paul, 1969) is a compilation of reviews of Trollope's novels by his contemporaries; David Skilton's *Anthony Trollope and His Contemporaries* (New York and London: St. Martin's Press; Longmans, 1972) discusses the same material in the context of the conventions of mid-Victorian fiction.

Recent criticism is marked by a wide range of critical views both of Trollope's novels and of his art in general. While few critics dispute Sadleir's positive assessment of Trollope's work, many have further explored various aspects of his distinctive 'genius'. *The Trollope Critics,* N. John Hall, ed. (Totowa, NJ: Barnes & Noble, 1981) offers a selection of important essays representing major twentieth century critical approaches to Trollope's work. General discussions of Trollope's work include Elizabeth Bowen's *Trollope, A New Judgement* (Oxford, 1946); Beatrice Curtis Brown's, *Anthony Trollope* (London: A. Barker Ltd., 1950); P. D. Edward's *Anthony Trollope, his Art and Scope* (New York: St. Martin's Press, 1977); Arthur Pollard's *Anthony Trollope* (London, Routledge &

Kegan Paul, 1978); R. C. Terry's *Anthony Trollope: The Artist in Hiding* (Totowa, NJ: Rowman & Littlefield, 1977); Robert Tracey's *Trollope's Later Novels* (Berkeley: University of California Press, 1978).

Two important discussions of Trollope's political concerns are John Halperin's *Trollope and Politics: A Study of the Pallisers and Others* (London: MacMillan, 1977); and Juliet McMaster's *Trollope's Palliser Novels: Theme and Pattern* (London: Macmillan, 1978). Trollope's theory of realistic fiction as articulated in *An Autobiography* is the focus of Walter M. Kenrick's *The Novel Machine: The Theory and Fiction of Anthony Trollope* (Baltimore: Johns Hopkins University Press, 1980). Finally, important treatments of the form of Trollope's fiction are found in J. Hillis Miller's, *The Form of Victorian Fiction: Thackeray, Dickens, Trollope, George Eliot, Meredith and Hardy* (Notre Dame: University of Notre Dame Press, 1968); and James R. Kincaid's *The Novels of Anthony Trollope* (Oxford: Clarendon Press, 1977).

Evaluation of Selected Criticism

apRoberts, Ruth, *The Moral Trollope*. Athens: Ohio University Press, 1971 (British title, *Trollope, Artist and Moralist*. London: Chatto & Windus, 1971). This well-known scholarly study examines Trollope's liberal humanitarianism and ironic perspective. Roberts discusses Trollope's style and technique, his religious inclinations, as well as his knowledge of the classical and English literary traditions which influenced his work.

Booth, Bradford Allen, *Anthony Trollope: Aspects of His Life & Art*. London: Edward Hulton, 1958. In this important and learned study, Booth examines Trollope's novelistic techniques according to the critical standards that the author himself established. Booth discusses Trollope's thematic concerns and assesses Trollope's debt to and place in the history of the English novel. Booth acknowledges a particular interest in the vagaries of Trollope's reputation and comments frequently on the merits or demerits of various critical positions.

Cockshut, A. O. J. *Anthony Trollope, A Critical Study*. London: Collins, 1955. Cockshut's thesis is that Trollope's vision became increasingly pessimistic as his art matured. Cockshut's first section is devoted to a discussion of Trollope's enduring attitudes toward religion, death, love, and politics. The second section, entitled "Progress Toward Pessimism," demonstrates the working out of these themes in selected novels. Cockshut's work has been described as the best English book length critical study, but readers should be aware that many critics do not entirely agree with his basic premise.

Polhemus, Robert M. *The Changing World of Anthony Trollope*. Berkeley: University of California Press, 1968. Polhemus is convinced that Trollope was obsessed by the idea of change. He traces this obsession to the experiences of Trollope's childhood, and examines his novels in light of religious, political, social, and historical developments that occurred in Victorian England. This is an important reading of Trollope.

Other Sources

Lansbury, Coral, *The Reasonable Man.* Princeton: Princeton University Press, 1981. Lansbury explores the conjunction of legal language and thought with creative imagination which shapes Trollope's fiction and travel literature.

Sadleir, Michael, *Trollope, A Bibliography,* London: Constable, 1928. Sadleir's famous bibliographical study analyzes the structure and history of Anthony Trollope's works and considers the factors which contribute to the rarity of a book's original publication.

The Trollopian, B. A. Booth, ed. (Los Angeles, 1945-1949) continued after 1949 as *Nineteenth Century Fiction.* This journal contains valuable articles on Trollope by John Hagan, Lionel Stevenson, Chauncey B. Tinker, and others.

Wijesinha, Rajviva, *The Androgynous Trollope: Attitudes to Women Among Early Victorian Novelists.* Washington DC: The University Press of America, 1982. Wijesinha documents prevailing attitudes toward women in mid-century England and compares Trollope's sympathetic attitudes toward women with those of other major Victorian novelists.

Selected Dictionaries and Encyclopedias

British Writers, Charles Scribner's Sons, 1982. Brief outline of Trollope's life and an assessment of his literary achievement. Excellent bibliography.

Dictionary of Literary Biography, Gale Research, 1983. Concise overview of Trollope's life and a discussion of his major works.

Marilyn D. Button
University of Delaware

MARK TWAIN
1835–1910

Author's Chronology

Born Samuel Clemens, November 30, 1835, Florida, Missouri; *1839* moves to Hannibal, Missouri; *1848–1853* apprenticed as printer; writes for local newspapers; *1857–1861* works as Mississippi river pilot until Civil War closes the river; *1861–1864* after a few weeks with Missouri militia, takes up prospecting and journalism in the Nevada territory; *1863* uses pen name "Mark Twain" for the first time; *1864* works as journalist in San Francisco; returns briefly to prospecting; *1865* gains fame with "The Celebrated Jumping Frog," widely reprinted from *The New York Evening Press*; *1866* begins forty year platform career with first lecture; travels to Hawaii as correspondent; *1867* visits Europe, Mediterranean, Palestine, as correspondent for *Alta California*; *1869* publishes his first travel book, *Innocents Abroad*; *1870* marries Olivia Langdon; becomes part owner of Buffalo, New York, newspaper; *1871* moves to Hartford, Connecticut; *1872* first child, Langdon, dies; *1878–1879* European travel; *1891* begins extended residence in Europe; *1894* bankruptcy of his publishing firm; *1895–1896* makes world lecture tour to recover losses; *1896* daughter Susy dies; *1897-1900* works on later writings in Europe; *1903* moves to Florence, Italy, for wife's health; *1904* Olivia dies; *1908* resides at "Stormfield," house in Redding, Connecticut; *1909* daughter Jean dies; *1910* April 21, dies at Stormfield.

Author's Bibliography (selected)

The Celebrated Jumping Frog of Calaveras County, 1867 (stories); *Innocents Abroad,* 1869 (travel); *Roughing It,* 1872 (travel); *The Gilded Age,* 1873 (fiction); *Adventures of Tom Sawyer,* 1876 (novel); *A Tramp Abroad,* 1880 (travel); *The Prince and the Pauper,* 1882 (novel); *Life on the Mississippi,* 1883 (local color); *Adventures of Huckleberry Finn,* 1885 (novel); *A Connecticut Yankee in King Arthur's Court,* 1889 (novel); *Pudd'nhead Wilson,* 1894 (novel); *Personal Recollections of Joan of Arc,* 1896 (fiction); *The Man That Corrupted Hadleyburg,* 1900 (stories).

Overview of Biographical Sources

Albert Bigelow Paine's monumental "official" life, *Mark Twain, a Biography: The Personal and Literary Life of Samuel Langhorne Clemens* (New York: Harper, 1912), still valuable in spite of idealizing the Clemens family, was followed by more provocative approaches to Twain's complex character. Van Wyck Brooks' *The Ordeal of Mark Twain* (New York: E.P. Dutton, 1920, rev. 1933) saw Twain betraying his gifts to the forces of gentility, such as his wife's censorship, and ending in impotent bitterness. Though now largely discounted, Brooks stimulated scholarship and directed debate by pointing out the splits between Twain's roles as satirist and establishment figure; his western origins and genteel aspirations; his private gloom and public image; and, finally, his popular success and true measure as an artist. Bernard DeVoto responded vigorously in *Mark Twain's America* (Boston: Little, Brown, 1932), diminishing eastern influences and demonstrating the vitality of a frontier Brooks found arid. Edward Wagenknecht's less combative *Mark Twain: The Man and His Work* (New Haven: Yale University Press, 1935) summarized biographical evidence in a topically arranged "psychograph" that went through two revisions (Norman: University of Oklahoma Press, 1961 and 1967). DeVoto again contributed by opening the Mark Twain Papers when he succeeded Paine as Twain's literary executor. These have provided invaluable information to later biographers and are scheduled to appear in a fifteen volume edition by the University of California Press. Delancey Ferguson's *Mark Twain: Man and Legend* (Indianapolis: Bobbs-Merrill, 1943) was a solid presentation, a standard for subsequent biographies. In the 1950's Kenneth Andrews' *Nook Farm: Mark Twain's Hartford Circle* filled in the eastern background, while Dixon Wecter's definitive *Sam Clemens of Hannibal* clarified the crucial early years. During the last thirty years virtually every aspect of the man, his writing, and his reputation has been dissected by a scholarly publishing industry, providing material for popular accounts such as Justin Kaplan's enormously successful *Mr. Clemens and Mark Twain: A Biography* 1966.

Evaluation of Selected Biographies

Andrews, Kenneth, *Nook Farm: Mark Twain's Hartford Circle.* Cambridge: Harvard University Press, 1950. Andrews surveys a lively cultural environment as it influenced Twain, 1871–1891, and discusses Joseph Twichell, a minister and close companion of Twain.

Budd, Louis J. *Our Mark Twain: The Making of His Public Personality.* Philadelphia: University of Pennsylvania Press, 1983. Budd shifts from private to public personality, demonstrating with a wealth of detail how Twain employed public relations, particularly the interview, to shape an enduring persona.

Emerson, Everett, *The Authentic Mark Twain: A Literary Biography of Samuel L. Clemens.* Philadelphia: University of Pennsylvania Press, 1984. Emerson investigates the disappearance of the "authentic" comic persona of *Innocents Abroad, Roughing It* and *Life on the Mississippi,* and discovers that Twain sacrificed himself to gentility, wealth, social philosophy, and a failure to master form. This is a balanced, cogent review of Twain's literary life, whose notes provide an excellent review of the criticism.

Hill, Hamlin, *Mark Twain: God's Fool.* New York: Harper, 1973. Hill used the unpublished diary of Isabel Lyon, Twain's secretary, to dim the halo with which Paine had surrounded the Clemens family. Hill presents Twain in his last ten years, a pitiable tyrant confronting his ruin, insecure and alienated from his family. Hill is unflinching in undermining Paine's hagiography, and some critics find him too unsympathetic.

Kaplan, Justin, *Mr. Clemens and Mark Twain: A Biography*. New York: Simon and Schuster, 1966. Winner of both a Pulitzer Prize and a National Book Award, this popular account looks at Twain as a divided personality whose public persona masked deep conflicts that shaped his career. While some scholars have found it too facile, this is a highly readable and lively book. Kaplan sought to remedy a chief flaw, its beginning with Twain at thirty, in *Mark Twain and His World* (New York: Simon and Schuster, 1975), a fine introduction for the general reader.

Wecter, Dixon, *Sam Clemens of Hannibal*. Boston: Houghton Mifflin, 1952. This richly detailed and well written study of Twain up to 1853, when he was eighteen, was to have been the first part of a definitive biography which was cut short by its author's death.

Autobiographical Sources

Twain's most important writings depend upon his memories; not surprisingly, he suggested a series of autobiographical dictations to direct Paine in the official life. Twain enjoyed these often rambling monologues from 1906 to 1909. Some were published in *The North American Review* while Twain still lived, and Paine employed sections in his biography. Devoto provided fragments in *Mark Twain in Eruption: Hitherto Unpublished Pages About Men and Events* (New York: Harper, 1940), and Charles Neider organized a chronological narrative, not really Twain's, from the dictations in *The Autobiography of Mark Twain, Including Chapters Now Published for the First Time* (New York: Harper, 1959). The dictations as a whole are unpublished, though according to scholars who have examined them, they contain no important revelations. Additional resources are to be found in published letters.

Overview of Critical Sources

Biography and criticism are never far apart in Twain studies; particularly significant are questions about Twain's use of his persona and his "failures" as an artist both in his later writings and in his major books. The later works were addressed by DeVoto in "The Symbols of Despair," an essay from *Mark Twain at Work* (Cambridge: Harvard University Press, 1942), employing works unknown to Brooks and ignored by Paine to assert that Twain's later writings served as means of regeneration by rehearsing the disasters of his life in art. Much critical labor has since gone into the establishment of the texts and dates of composition of later pieces. A famous example is *The Mysterious Stranger*, which John S. Tuckey in *Mark Twain and Little Satan: The Writing of "The*

Mysterious Stranger" (West Lafayette, IN: Purdue University Studies, 1963) showed to have a chronology other than DeVoto supposed, and a text different from that published by Paine in 1916. Such editorial work is also being applied to Twain's major writings in a new twenty-four volume collection begun in 1972 under the editorship of John C. Gerber. A few examples of criticism which see the works serving the psychological, philosophical or aesthetic needs of the man are Gladys Bellamy's *Mark Twain as a Literary Artist* (Norman: University of Oklahoma Press, 1950), which used four major themes to demonstrate how Twain gained a sense of distance and control through abstraction; James M. Cox's *Mark Twain: The Fate of Humor* (Princeton: Princeton University Press, 1966), which found Mark Twain effective only so long as he remained a humorist; and Albert Stone's *The Innocent Eye: Childhood in Mark Twain's Imagination* (New Haven: Yale University Press, 1961), which traced his fascination with immaturity.

Though Twain's other writings have been getting increasing attention, the center of critical discussion has been his *Adventures of Huckleberry Finn,* the artistic integrity of which occasioned a famous debate by such luminaries as Lionel Trilling and T.S. Eliot. This, along with other issues, may be conveniently reviewed in the "Norton Critical Edition" of the novel, edited by Sculley Bradley et al. (New York: W. W. Norton, 1977). A delightful companion is John Seelye's witty *The True Adventures of Huckleberry Finn* (Evanston, IL: Northwestern University Press, 1970), in which he responds to the critics' objections of the ending, and of the absence of profanity and sex.

Twain's work has been scoured by critics of every theoretical persuasion, and their production is vast, forming one of the largest critical canons of literary studies. A reader may gain a sense of historical perspective, however, from the late editor of the Mark Twain Papers, Frederick Anderson's collection *Mark Twain: The Critical Heritage* (New York: Barnes and Noble, 1971).

Evaluation of Selected Criticism

Blair, Walter, *Mark Twain and Huck Finn.* Berkeley: University of California Press, 1960. A definitive study of the genesis and reputation of Twain's central work, Blair's book is encyclopedic in its examination of *Huckleberry Finn's* composition and sources.

Carrington, George C., Jr. *The Dramatic Unity of 'Huckleberry Finn'.* Columbus: Ohio State University Press, 1976. Carrington's subtle and close analysis redeems the novel's controversial ending by examining its strategies for establishing dramatic situations. This criticism may be difficult going for general readers, but it offers new insights on old questions.

Gibson, William M. *The Art of Mark Twain.* Oxford: Oxford University Press, 1976. Gibson surveys Twain's works to pick out his best writing. He concludes that Twain ought to be viewed as a many faceted man of letters capable of writing in many genres. Gibson's assessments are clear and astute, and his discussion of Twain's style is especially effective.

Harris, Susan K. *Mark Twain's Escape from Time: A Study of Patterns and Images.* Columbia: University of Missouri Press, 1982. Harris provides a good example of a close reading of images—water, space, childhood, women—to show how Twain's narrators employ them to escape communal entanglements, and to deal with time.

Kahn, Sholom J. *Mark Twain's Mysterious Stranger: A Study of the Manuscript Texts.* Columbia: University of Missouri Press, 1978. Kahn uses William Gibson's edition of the texts to evaluate the unity and significance of the work. This is an example of evaluation through textual scholarship.

MacNaughton, William R. *Mark Twain's Last Years as a Writer.* Columbia: University of Missouri Press, 1979. MacNaughton finds no real decline in the quality of Twain's writing in his last years, and contests the picture offered by Hamlin Hill and DeVoto's characterization of the later writings as "symbols of despair."

Smith, Henry Nash, *Mark Twain: The Development of a Writer.* Cambridge: Harvard University Press 1962. Smith explores the relation of Twain's style to his ethical stances, revealing strategies for handling conflict between his origins as a vernacular writer and requirements of gentility.

Other Sources

Meltzer, Milton, *Mark Twain Himself: A Pictorial Biography.* New York: Thomas Y. Crowell, 1960. Over six hundred photographs and portraits make this a rich source of images of Twain.

Mark Twain-Howells Letters. ed. Henry Nash Smith and William Gibson. Cambridge: Harvard University Press, 1960. An important record of Mark Twain's most important literary friendship.

Tenney, Thomas A. *Mark Twain: A Reference Guide.* Boston: G.K. Hall, 1977. With more than five thousand annotated entries, this bibliography and its annual updates in the journal *American Literary Realism* are indispensable.

Henry J. Lindborg
Marian College of Fond du Lac
Wisconsin

JOHN UPDIKE
1932

Author's Chronology

Born March 18, 1932, Shillington, Pennsylvania, only child of Wesley and Linda Grace Hoyer Updike; lives with parents and maternal grandparents; *1937* enters public schools in Shillington, where his father teaches high-school mathematics; encouraged by his mother who has literary aspirations, becomes a writer and cartoonist for school papers; *1945* moves with parents and grandparents to his mother's birthplace, a farmhouse near Shillington; *1950* enters Harvard on full scholarship, majors in English, and writes for the *Harvard Lampoon*, eventually becoming editor; *1953* marries Mary E. Pennington, a Radcliffe student two years his senior; *1954* graduates from Harvard *summa cum laude* and enters Ruskin School of Drawing and Fine Arts in Oxford, England; sells first story to *The New Yorker; 1955* becomes staffwriter for *The New Yorker* and writes "Talk of the Town" columns; daughter Elizabeth is born; *1957* leaves *The New Yorker* to work full-time on fiction and poetry; moves to Ipswich, Massachusetts; son David is born; *1958–1959* publishes first poetry collection, first novel, and first collection of short stories; receives a Guggenheim Fellowship; son Michael born; *1960* receives Rosenthal Award for *The Poorhouse Fair;* daughter Miranda born; *1964* receives National Book Award for *The Centaur;* elected member of The National Institute of Arts and Letters, youngest person to receive this honor; travels to Russia, Romania, Bulgaria, and Czechoslovakia as part of the US-USSR Cultural Exchange Program; *1968* publishes best-selling *Couples* and sells the screen rights for a half-million dollars (no film was made); appears on the cover of *Time* magazine; *1973* travels as Fulbright lecturer in five African countries; *1974* separates from wife Mary and moves to Boston; *1976* divorces; *1977* marries Martha Bernhard and moves to Georgetown, Massachusetts; elected to the fifty-member American Academy of Arts and Letters; *1979* publishes *Too Far to Go,* story-cycle later produced as television drama; *1981* publishes *Rabbit is Rich* which receives the Pulitzer Prize, the American Book Award, and a commendation from the National Book Critics Circle; awarded Edward McDowell Medal for literature.

Author's Bibliography (selected)

The Carpentered Hen, 1958 (poems); *The Same Door,* 1959 (stories); *The Poorhouse Fair,* 1959 (novel); *Rabbit, Run,* 1960 (novel); *Pigeon Feathers and Other Stories,* 1962; *Telephone Poles and Other Poems,* 1963; *The Centaur,* 1963 (novel); *Olinger Stories,* 1964; *Of the Farm,* 1965 (novel); *Assorted Prose,* 1965 (non-fiction prose); *The Music School,* 1966 (stories); *Couples,* 1968 (novel); *Midpoint and Other Poems,* 1969; *Bech: A Book,* 1970 (story-cycle); *Rabbit*

Redux, 1971 (novel); *Museums and Women,* 1972 (stories); *Buchanan Dying,* 1974 (play); *A Month of Sundays,* 1975 (novel); *Picked-Up Pieces,* 1975 (non-fiction prose); *Marry Me,* 1976 (novel); *Tossing and Turning,* 1977 (poems); *The Coup,* 1978 (novel); *Problems,* 1979 (stories); *Too Far to Go,* 1979 (story-cycle); *Rabbit is Rich,* 1981 (novel); *Bech is Back,* 1982 (story-cycle); *Hugging the Shore,* 1983 (non-fiction prose); *The Witches of Eastwick,* 1984 (novel).

Overview of Biographical Sources

There is no book-length biography of this popular writer. The best critical biography to date is Robert Detweiler's revised edition of *John Updike* (1984). Other information can be found in three collections of his essays and interviews, many of which provide glimpses of his life and ideas. For example, in *Picked-Up Pieces* (1975) Updike includes a particularly informative interview by Jane Howard (published originally in *Life,* 4 Nov., 1966) in which he tells about his childhood and how he learned to "examine everything for God's footprints." He also includes in *Picked-Up Pieces* important interviews with Charles Samuels, Eric Rhode, and Frank Gado. Gado's interview is also available in *First Person* (Syracuse, NY: Syracuse University Press, 1973, pp. 80–109). The "First Person Singular" section of *Assorted Prose* (1965) and the lengthy appendix, "On One's Own Oeuvre" in *Hugging the Shore* (1983) are similarly rich in source material.

Evaluation of Selected Biographies

Detweiler, Robert, *John Updike.* rev. ed. Boston: Twayne, 1984. The first edition of Detweiler's book (1972) interprets Updike's early fiction (six novels and four short story collections). In the revision, Detweiler adds a biography (pp. 1–7) and discussion of eight more books (published 1972–1984) which show Updike to be a chronicler of American marital-sexual mores. Like many of the books in Twayne's United States Authors Series, Detweiler's book is a good starting place for study of its subject. Chronologically arranged, pithy, and illuminating, Detweiler's work frequently comments on the relationship between Updike's life and fiction, but the focus is clearly on the fiction. Detweiler does not deal with Updike's poetry, reviews, or essays.

Autobiographical Sources

Again and again in Updike's fiction, poetry, essays, and interviews, a reader sees the author's loving depiction of his boyhood in Shillington. One example of this is "The Dogwood Tree," the best of the six autobiographical essays in *Assorted Prose* (1965). In most of his early fiction, Shillington becomes Olinger (pronounced "O-linger" to suggest the writer's nostalgia). His memories of his parents and grandparents color characterizations in such popular stories as "Pigeon Feathers" where the protagonist's father is a teacher and the family lives in an old farmhouse without indoor plumbing. The high school teaching father becomes the central character in *The Centaur* (1963), which, like *Olinger Stories* (1964) and *Of the Farm* (1965), is set in the fictionalized, nostalgia-colored Shillington.

In *Rabbit, Run* (1960) and *Couples* (1968), Updike turns from his boyhood to write about a troubled middle-class marriage and a suburban society where sexual experimentation is rife. This emphasis on dissolving marriages continues in *Rabbit Redux* (1971), *Museums and Women* (1972), and *Too Far to Go* (1979), mirroring the increasing pressures on the Updikes' own union. In this period the nostalgia for youthful innocence becomes a nostalgia for happy marriages.

Even Updike's travels have found a way into his fiction. His impressions of his 1964–1965 trip to Eastern Europe were translated into the short stories collected in *Bech: A Book* (1970) and his 1973 trip to Africa provided material for some of the stories collected in *Bech Is Back* (1982) and his "African novel" *The Coup* (1978).

Overview of Critical Sources

Updike's distaste for critics is well known. He has spoken disparagingly in *Picked-Up Pieces* of the way in which "all the little congruences and arabesques you prepared with such anticipatory pleasure are gobbled up as if by pigs at a pastry cart" (p. 21). In spite of such caustic remarks, criticism of Updike's fiction is plentiful. Some critics have complained that his writing is all style and little content [e.g., Norman Podhoretz, *Doings and Undoings* (New York: Farrar, Straus, 1964) and John Aldridge, *Time to Murder and Create* (New York: David McKay 1966)]. Most critics, however, are more charitable. Alice and Kenneth Hamilton's pamphlet-length book *John Updike: A Critical Essay* (Grand Rapids: Eerdmans, 1967) and their later *The Elements of John Updike* (Grand Rapids: Eerdmans, 1970) stress Updike's Christian vision and point out religious allusions in both his poetry and fiction through *Couples.* Less stridently defending Updike, Charles Samuels' valuable monograph *John Updike* (Minneapolis: University of Minnesota Press, 1969) argues that although sometimes guilty of "bad" writing, Updike is an important and worthwhile author.

More recent criticism of Updike—that since 1970—has tended to focus on some particular theme or aspect of the writer's canon. Larry Taylor, for example, argues that early in his career Updike saw the pastoral as desirable but that he became progressively ironic in his treatment of pastoral assumptions [*Pastoral and Anti-Pastoral Patterns in John Updike's Fiction* (Carbondale: Southern Illinois University Press, 1971)]. George Hunt, Joyce Markle, and Edward Vargo also present particular theses rather than general discussions of the author's work (see below).

Two exceptions to this focus on a particular thesis should be mentioned. One is the excellent book by Detweiler already discussed. The other is Suzanne Henning Uphaus' *John Updike* (New York: Frederick Ungar, 1980). Uphaus' monograph is touted as "a lively introduction for the new Updike reader" and it is just that—short, readable, but in places superficial. However, it does contain some helpful comments and a rather thorough bibliography.

The student working with limited library resources will find two other books very helpful: *John Updike: A Collection of Critical Essays* by David Thorburn and Howard Eiland (Englewood Cliffs, NJ: Prentice-Hall, 1979) and *Critical Essays on John Updike* by William R. MacNaughton (Boston: G. K. Hall, 1982). Thorburn and Eiland have gathered together twenty-three essays on Updike's novels and short stories. MacNaughton's fine book contains reprints of sixteen reviews and eleven essays plus five original essays and a very thorough bibliographical essay.

Evaluation of Selected Criticism

Greiner, Donald J. *The Other John Updike: Poems, Short Stories, Prose, Play.* Athens: Ohio University Press, 1981. Over one-half of Updike's canon are poems, stories, essays, reviews, and one play, yet most critics have concentrated on the novels. Greiner's book is the first book-length analysis of this other part of Updike's work and is therefore a major contribution to Updike scholarship. Greiner analyzes individual poems, stories, and essays and in the process suggests the development of Updike's work away from early nostalgia to increasing irony.

Hunt, George W. *John Updike and the Three Great Secret Things: Sex, Religion, and Art.* Grand Rapids: Eerdmans, 1980. Hunt contends that Updike focuses on the three things mentioned in the title: first on religion; then, beginning with *The Music School* (1966), on sex; and finally, with *A Month of Sundays* (1975), on art and fictional creation. Hunt's difficult but provocative book discusses the novels through *The Coup* (1978), showing the influence of such thinkers as Karl Barth, Soren Kierkegaard, and Carl Jung.

Markle, Joyce B. *Fighters and Lovers: Theme in the Novels of John Updike.* New York: New York University Press, 1973. Markle suggests that each of Updike's protagonists fights against physical death and metaphoric death (dehumanization), but that each is opposed by well-intentioned but sterile people. She sees Updike's reservations about Christianity grow "increasingly obvious" while, as this happens, his characters lose their sense of self-worth. One way of fighting this decreasing sense of self-importance is through sexual activity. (Markle sees Denis de Rougemont's *Love in the Western World* as strongly influencing Updike's theories on religion and sex.) Thus Piet's tragedy in *Couples* "is the loss of tragedy" and Bech's self-deprecating humor shows his loss of religious faith. In *Rabbit Redux,* however, Markle sees a "reawakened sense of causality." Her thesis is a provocative one and in developing it she offers some sensitive interpretations of Updike's early fiction.

Vargo, Edward P. *Rainstorms and Fire: Ritual in the Novels of John Updike.* Port Washington, NY: Kennikat, 1973. Vargo emphasizes the Christian concerns in Updike's books which he says deal with the primitive God of rainstorms and fire. Updike's characters, says Vargo, keep trying to experience the transcendent by using the three elements of ritual—pattern, myth, and celebration.

Other Sources

Galloway, David, *The Absurd Hero in American Fiction.* 2nd rev. ed. Austin: University of Texas Press, 1981. Galloway's chapter on Updike, "The Absurd Man as Saint," is an existential discussion of Updike's fiction to *Marry Me* (1976).

Hendin, Josephine, *Vulnerable People: A View of American Fiction Since 1945.* New York: Oxford University Press, 1978. Her chapter "A Victim is a Hero" deals with Bellow, Heller, and Updike.

John Updike Newsletter. Published several times a year since 1977 by the Office of the Academic Vice President, Boston University.

Modern Fiction Studies 20 (Spring 1974). This number, devoted to John Updike, contains eight articles, reviews of Updike criticism, and a checklist of criticism.

Selected Dictionaries and Encyclopedias

Contemporary Authors, New Revision Series, Vol. 4, Gale Research, 1981. Good biography and bibliography.

Contemporary Writers of the English Language, St. Martin's Press, 1982. In this series, the volume *Contemporary Novelists* contains a concise overview of Updike's life and works.

Dictionary of Literary Biography, Gale Research, 1983. Three volumes in this series contain essays on Updike. All offer good overviews; however, Vol. 3 in the DLB Documentary Series provides the most thorough and readable essay.

Ann R. Morris
Stetson University

HENRY VAUGHAN
1621?–1695

Author's Chronology

Born 1621 or 1622, one of twin sons, Henry and Thomas, to Thomas and Denise Vaughan at Newton-upon-Usk, Breconshire, Wales; *1632–1638* twins study under Matthew Herbert, rector of Llangattock; *1638* Henry enters Jesus College along with Thomas; *1640* father removes Henry from Oxford to study Civil Law in London, where he comes under the influence of the group of poets known as the Tribe of Ben; *1642* returns to Wales at the outbreak of the Civil War; later becomes secretary to Sir Marmaduke Lloyd, Chief Justice of the Great Sessions of Brecon; c. *1645* probably sees military action on the Royalist side; *1646* publishes first volume of verse; marries Catherine Wise; *1648* death of his younger brother William is a possible factor in Vaughan's conversion to a deeper spiritual life that seemingly occurred before 1650, resulting in his dedication to writing religious poetry, and his reading of George Herbert, a major influence both spiritually and poetically; *1652* suffers a near-fatal illness; by 1655 death of first wife and marriage to her younger sister Elizabeth; possibly begins his successful practice of medicine about this time; *1695* dies on April 23; buried in Llansantffraed churchyard.

Author's Bibliography (selected)

Poems, with the Tenth Satyre of Juvenal Englished, 1646; first part of *Silex Scintillans*, 1650 (poems); *Olor Iscanus*, 1651 (poems and prose translations); *The Mount of Olives, or Solitary Devotions*, 1652 (prose, including one translation); *Flores Solitudinis*, 1654 (prose translations); enlarged edition of *Silex Scintillans*, 1655; *Hermetical Physick*, 1655, and *The Chymists Key*, 1657 (translations of works by Henry Nollius); *Thalia Rediviva*, 1678 (poems).

Overview of Biographical Sources

The biographical information about Henry Vaughan is relatively limited, and many details remain uncertain. A very brief biographical sketch of Vaughan appears in the 1674 and 1721 editions of Anthony À Wood's *Athenae Oxonienses*, based mostly on material that Henry had supplied in a letter of June 15, 1673, to his cousin, John Aubrey. Aubrey's own sketch of the brothers in his *Brief Lives of Eminent Men* (modern edition by Oliver Lawson Dick, 1949; rpt. Ann Arbor: University of Michigan Press, 1957) describes Henry as "ingeniose but prowd and humorous [whimsical]," but it is vague and inaccurate about the few biographical details he notes. Henry Vaughan's earliest modern editor, the Reverend H. F. Lyte, provided the first significant biocritical essay in *The Sacred Poems and Private Ejaculations of Henry Vaughan* (1847; rpt. Boston: Little, Brown, 1856). Lyte first set forth the theory that Vaughan underwent a deep and lasting religious conversion, owing chiefly to a nearly fatal illness, prior to his writing *Silex Scintillans* in 1650. Scholars have subsequently dated the illness after 1650 and removed that as a primary cause. However, Vaughan's spiritual and poetic conversion became generally accepted as a fundamental biographical and critical premise confirmed by Vaughan's own words in the 1654 Preface to the enlarged *Silex Scintillans*. E. C. Marilla is among the recent critics who have re-examined the question of Vaughan's conversion, in his article "The Religious Conversion of Henry Vaughan," *Review of English Studies* 21 (1945), 155–162. Helen C. White provides a useful and well-written biographical chapter in *The Metaphysical Poets: A Study in Religious Experience* (1936; rpt. New York: Collier Books, 1966). She considers the mystical element in his poetry, particularly his "nature mysticism," his underlying theological ideas, and his assimilation of Hermetic concepts. In *The Cultural Revolution of the Seventeenth Century* (London: Dennis Dobson, 1951), S. L. Bethell gives a biographical account based on Hutchinson; he provides a good discussion of the secular poetry, besides an analysis of the religious poetry, including a brief consideration of the philosophical background.

Evaluation of Selected Biographies

Friedenreich, Kenneth, *Henry Vaughan*. Boston: Twayne, 1978. This bio-critical study of Vaughan contains a short but comprehensive chapter on Vaughan's life, succinctly covering the principal events and the major biographical questions. Friedenreich views any "conversion" Vaughan experienced as a "turn of mind" involving an intensification of his religious and political convictions but not a radical change in his poetic development. The critical analysis considers both the secular and the sacred poetry, as well as the prose, focusing on Vaughan's use of the pastoral tradition. Freidenreich also provides a good annotated bibliography.

Hutchinson, F. E. *Henry Vaughan: A Life and Interpretation*. Oxford: Clarendon Press, 1947. In this standard biography of the poet, Hutchinson combined the results of his own research with the materials gathered by two earlier scholars who devoted many years to the study of Vaughan's life—Gwenllian E. F. Morgan and Louise I. Guiney. He meticulously examines the evidence in suggesting probable dates and analyzing biographical problems such as Vaughan's military service. The documentation is extensive. The book also contains helpful information about people, places, and events that were of interest to Vaughan. Hutchinson examines Vaughan's works as well as his life; his section on Vaughan's prose writings and translations provides a particularly good analysis. He takes a traditional view of Vaughan's conversion, finding in the religious poetry "heightened feeling and majestic utterance" not present in his earlier secular poetry.

Simmonds, James D. *Masques of God: Form and Theme in the Poetry of Henry Vaughan*. Pittsburgh: University of Pittsburgh Press, 1972. Although a major critical analysis rather than a biography, this work contains appendixes dealing with questions related to Vaughan's biography which Simmonds had discussed earlier in journal articles. He dates Vaughan's illness more precisely; re-examines the Amoret and Etesia poems and their connection with Vaughan's first wife; he also tackles the thorny question of the rejection of profane literature in the 1654 Preface to *Silex Scintillans*.

Autobiographical Sources

Vaughan's few extant letters provide some autobiographical material, especially the previously mentioned one to Aubrey (June 15, 1673). All the letters are printed in *The Works of Henry Vaughan*, ed. L.C. Martin, 2nd ed. (Oxford: Clarendon Press, 1957). The 1654 Preface to *Silex Scintillans* is a key document in the consideration of his conversion, and his rejection of secular poetry to dedicate himself to religious poetry. Hutchinson and others have commented on the autobiographical details reflected in his poetry.

Overview of Critical Sources

Much Vaughan criticism has focused upon the religious, philosophical, and literary influences—particularly the Bible, George Herbert, and the Hermetic philosophy. The place of Hermeticism in Vaughan's thought, a widely discussed issue, has been variously assessed, from being a major pervasive influence to playing a more limited, indirect role. Most critics have emphasized Vaughan's assimilation of Hermetic elements into an orthodox Christian framework of thought. Another major critical concern, Vaughan's mysticism, has evoked a similar range of response. Some find stages of the traditional mystical way expressed in Vaughan's work; others speak more generally of mystical elements or identify his mysticism with a fervent "living faith;" still others refuse to consider him a mystic at all. Vaughan's concern with Nature is another important critical focus, particularly his poetic interpretation of Nature as the Book of God's Works. He is no longer considered a pre-Romantic who influenced Wordsworth. Some recent critics have questioned the common judgment that Vaughan's secular verse is inferior to the religious verse. They find a continuity and a development between the two, instead of a radical transformation effected by his conversion.

Evaluation of Selected Criticism

Durr, R. A. *On the Mystical Poetry of Henry Vaughan*. Cambridge: Harvard University Press, 1962. Durr finds Christian mysticism the best context for understanding Vaughan's poems, which describe the soul's progress through "awakening, purgation, and illumination." The "major metaphors" analyzed all express the theme of regeneration, as he further demonstrates in detailed readings of "Regeneration," "The Proffer," and "The Night."

Garner, Ross, *Henry Vaughan: Experience and the Tradition*. Chicago: University of Chicago Press, 1951. Garner examines "the basic philosophical attitudes which underlie Vaughan's expression of experience." He covers the allegorical habit of mind, the Augustinian distrust of reason and the concept of the apostate will as the source of evil, and a religious awareness of both the divine immanence in the universe and the divine transcendence. Garner argues that Hermeticism exerted only a limited influence on Vaughan, serving merely as a source of analogues and metaphors for Christian truths.

Pettet, E. C. *Of Paradise and Light: A Study of Vaughan's "Silex Scintillans."* Cambridge: Cambridge University Press, 1959. Pettet provides a reading of four major poems, after background chapters on the Bible, Herbert, Hermetic philosophy, and Nature. He discusses Vaughan's prosody and has some good observations on Vaughan's imagery, particularly as a link between the two parts of *Silex Scintillans*.

Post, Jonathan F. S. *Henry Vaughan: The Unfolding Vision*. Princeton: Princeton University Press, 1982. Post views Vaughan's conversion as a literary rather than a religious event; the poet's reading of George Herbert, influenced by the chaotic developments of the Civil War, is the central experience in his religious development. Post presents an integrated view of Vaughan's literary career, considering both the sacred and secular poems, though giving principal consideration to *Silex Scintillans* and Herbert's catalytic effect upon Vaughan as he became a "self-styled pastor-poet" of a Church driven underground.

Simmonds, James D. *Masques of God: Form and Theme in the Poetry of Henry Vaughan*. Pittsburgh: University of Pittsburgh Press, 1972. Simmonds maintains that Vaughan is not an "artless poet" but has a strong sense of craft inherited from the Jonsonian tradition. His analysis postulates an organic continuity, not a radical change, between the sacred and the secular poetry. Particular topics covered include the love poetry, satire, and Vaughan's approach to Nature in his sacred poetry.

Other Sources

Holmes, Elizabeth, *Henry Vaughan and the Hermetic Philosophy*. 1932; rpt. New York: Haskell House, 1966. Analyzes the Hermetic elements in Vaughan's poetry, indicating sources and analogues in Thomas Vaughan, Agrippa, Paracelsus, and Boehme.

Kermode, Frank, "The Private Imagery of Henry Vaughan," in *Review of English Studies*, N. S. 1 (1950), 592–606. A seminal essay emphasizing that Vaughan's work must be judged as poetry, not prayer, and arguing that Vaughan's inspiration is literary rather than religious; he transforms his sources to produce his own distinctive imagery.

Lewalski, Barbara Kiefer, *Protestant Poetics and the Seventeenth-Century Religious Lyric*. Princeton: Princeton University Press, 1979. Important consideration of Vaughan among the devotional poets influenced by "Protestant assumptions about the poetry of the Bible and the nature of the spiritual life," including the Protestant meditative tradition.

Mahood, M. M. "Henry Vaughan: The Symphony of Nature," in *Poetry and Humanism*, 1950; rpt. New York: W.W. Norton, 1970, pp. 252–295. Analyzes selected symbols and image clusters; considers the various sources behind Vaughan's associations and the "complex undercurrents of meaning" suggested; explicates Vaughan's philosophy of Nature expressed through them.

Selected Dictionaries and Encyclopedias

British Writers, Vol. 2, Charles Scribner's Sons, 1979. Bio-critical account by Margaret Willy, providing excellent overview of Vaughan's life and poetry, particularly *Silex Scintillans*. Contains bibliography.

Gertrude K. Hamilton
St. John's University

KURT VONNEGUT, JR.
1922

Author's Chronology

Born November 11, 1922, Indianapolis, Indiana; *1940* graduates from high school and enrolls in Cornell University to study biology and chemistry; *1941* writes for the *Cornell Sun; 1942* joins the United States Army and is sent to Carnegie Tech and the University of Tennessee to study mechanical engineering; *1945* taken prisoner at the Battle of the Bulge and sent to Dresden; returns home after the war and is awarded the Purple Heart; marries Jane Marie Cox; moves to Chicago to attend the University of Chicago to study anthropology; *1947* moves to Schenectady, New York to write public-relations material for the General Electric Research laboratory; *1950* moves to Cape Cod to do freelance writing; *1952* publishes his first novel, *Player Piano; 1965* and *1966* teaches at the Writers' Workshop at the University of Iowa; *1967* receives a Guggenheim Fellowship; *1970* receives literature award from the National Institute of Arts and Letters; teaches writing at Harvard; *1973* appointed Distinguished Professor of English Prose by the City University of New York; *1974* awarded an honorary LHD by Indiana University; *1975* named a vice-president of the National Institute of Arts and Letters.

Author's Bibliography (selected)

Player Piano, 1952 (novel); *The Sirens of Titan,* 1959 (novel); *Mother Night,* 1961 (novel); *Canary in a Cat House,* 1961 (stories); *Cat's Cradle,* 1963 (novel); *God Bless You, Mr. Rosewater,* 1965 (novel); *Welcome to the Monkey House,* 1968 (stories); *Slaughterhouse-Five,* 1969 (novel); *Happy Birthday, Wanda June,* 1970 (play); *Breakfast of Champions,* 1973 (novel); *Wampeters, Foma and Granfalloons,* 1974 (reviews, addresses, and interviews); *Slapstick,* 1974 (novel), *Jailbird,* 1976 (novel); *Palm Sunday,* 1981 (autobiographical collage).

Overview of Biographical Sources

There are no book-length biographies of Kurt Vonnegut, Jr. *The Vonnegut Statement,* edited by Jerome Klinkowitz and John Somer (New York: Dell Publishing, 1973), a collection of essays on Vonnegut's career as a writer, includes biographical information as well, but only as it pertains to his literary career. The later work edited by Jerome Klinkowitz and Donald L. Lawler, *Vonnegut in America: An Introduction to the Life and Work of Kurt Vonnegut* (New York: Delacorte/Seymour Lawrence, 1977), provides both biographical material and critical analyses of Vonnegut's works. The main focus, however, is to show how Vonnegut, perhaps more than any other American writer, expresses the American culture and American milieu. The first section, which includes some biography, also includes photographs of Vonnegut from his childhood to the present. The introduction to Richard Giannone's book, *Vonnegut: A Preface to His Novels* (Port Washington, New York: Kennikat Press, 1977) also provides a worthwhile biographical-critical study.

Autobiographical Sources

In the Prologue to his novel *Slapstick,* Vonnegut says, "This is the closest I will ever come to writing an autobiography." Yet Vonnegut is a humorist and while this novel, as well as his other novels, has traces of biographical details, *Slapstick* as autobiography has "more psychological than literal veracity." Vonnegut himself qualifies his opening statement by saying, "It is what life *feels* like to me."

Two of Vonnegut's works are major sources of autobiography. *Wampeters, Foma and Granfalloons,* a collection of some of his reviews, essays, interviews, and speeches, says little about his life, but reveals the attitudes and ideas that he has fictionalized through the years in his many novels.

Palm Sunday: An Autobiographical Collage updates the first collection of essays and adds material biographical in nature but not necessarily written by Vonnegut. *Palm Sunday* is more humorous and more revealing than *Wampeters, Foma and Granfalloons.* The pieces that make up the later collage address almost all subjects, political, social, and even personal in nature. The work ends ironically with the sermon that he preached on Palm Sunday—hence the title— in 1980 in St. Clement's Episcopal Church in which he tells of his admiration of the Sermon on the Mount because of its unwavering "mercifulness." *Palm Sunday* is an important work as it aids the reader to peer behind the Vonnegut mask of his zany novels and to understand the significant message of his satire. Together, these works, *Wampeters, Foma and Granfalloons* and *Palm Sunday,* present a kaleidoscopic view of this marvelously funny—in a sardonic manner—sensitive, humanistic author. Throughout the seeming pessimism of his outlook, his love for mankind and his earnest and urgent concern for its future, is apparent.

Vonnegut has involved himself in numerous political-humanitarian causes. His attitude is reflected in the addresses and lectures which make up the two collections mentioned above. Another lecture, more recent and therefore not included in the collections is the short address delivered at the Episcopal Cathedral, St. John the Divine, in New York City on May 23, 1982, entitled "Fates Worse Than Death," published by the Bertrand Russell Peace Foundation, Ltd. The statement, sent by Vonnegut to be read to the European Conference for Nuclear Disarmament held in Brussels on July 2–4, 1982, declares that modern technology can serve to unite the peoples of the world instead of destroying mankind. Prophetically and Job-like, Vonnegut warns, "Humanity is running out of time."

Overview of Critical Sources

1977 was a banner year for lengthy criticism of Vonnegut. Of the nine book-length studies presently available, five were published in 1977. Four of the nine longer studies are monographs: one written for the Contemporary Writers Series in 1982; two published in 1977, one as part of The Milford Series, Popular Writers of Today and the other for the Modern Literature Monograph Series. The earliest was published in 1972 for the Popular Writers Series Number 2.

Evaluation of Selected Criticism

Giannone, Richard, *Vonnegut: A Preface to His Novels.* Giannone discusses both the "thematic affinities among the novels" and the individual texts themselves. He deals with the "evolution of Vonnegut's artistry," traces the "overarching changes," and establishes the "coherence of Vonnegut's thought." The work is limited to a discussion of Vonnegut's novels.

Klinkowitz, Jerome, *Vonnegut.* London: Methuen, 1982. This latest of Klinkowitz's studies on Vonnegut, the monograph for the Contemporary Writers Series, serves as an overview of Vonnegut's novels. Klinkowitz states that American fiction of the 1960's and 1970's has undergone "some fundamental transformation of style and value" and Vonnegut's fiction exemplifies this change by challenging the "familiar notions" of the American novel. This monograph is an intelligent study that adds much to the reader's understanding of Vonnegut in terms of what he has contributed to American fiction, how he fits into the American cultural scene, and what has made him so popular. Its fault lies in its crowding too much in too short a space: nine works are discussed in three brief chapters.

Klinkowitz, Jerome and John Somer, eds. *The Vonnegut Statement.* New York: Delacorte, 1973. This collection of essays seeks to answer the question why people like and read Vonnegut. The essays deal with Vonnegut as a "Public Figure," as a "Literary Figure," and his "Literary Art," and present both personal insights into the career of Vonnegut, as well as critiques of some works. They are written by people who have in some way had contact with him, either teaching his works, being part of his class at the University of Iowa, meeting with him personally and interviewing him, or simply coming to grips with his vision concerning the dilemma of contemporary man.

Lundquist, James, *Kurt Vonnegut.* New York: Frederick Ungar, 1977. In this Modern Literature Monograph, Lundquist argues that Vonnegut's emphasis indicates specifically "midwestern" characteristics: "the need for self-respect and his belief in the necessity of pacifism." He maintains also that although Vonnegut's works may appear simple, he deals with complex epistemological questions. Lundquist's approach to Vonnegut is to indicate how he poses and deals with these cosmic concerns.

Schatt, Stanley, *Kurt Vonnegut, Jr.* Boston: Twayne, 1976. Schatt's approach to the study of Vonnegut is to trace his simultaneous development of style and philosophy. Besides a careful discussion of the novels, Schatt devotes a chapter to Vonnegut's short stories, another one to his plays, and concludes with a discussion on Vonnegut as a public figure. Schatt's careful discussions of characters and themes for most of the works he deals with, makes this a useful study.

Selected Dictionaries and Encyclopedias

Dictionary of Literary Biography, Twentieth-Century American Science-Fiction Writers, Vol. 8, Gale Research, 1981. Brief article which includes biography and analysis of all Vonnegut's novels, a limited bibliography and a useful summary statement concerning Vonnegut's contribution and place in American literature.

Dictionary of Literary Biography, Documentary Series, Vol. 3, Gale Research, 1983. Includes biography, photographs, manuscript facsimiles, letters, interviews, critical assessments made by and about Vonnegut.

Science Fiction Writers, Charles Scribner's Sons, 1982. A lengthy, detailed, useful article, written by Charles L. Elkins, includes biography, a discussion of the category "science fiction writer" and Vonnegut's attitude toward it, as well as an analysis of three novels, *Player Piano, Sirens of Titan,* and *Cat's Cradle,* and a bibliography.

Liela H. Goldman
Michigan State University

EDMUND WALLER
1606–1687

Author's Chronology

Born March 6, 1606, Coleshill, England; *1624* member for Ilchester in the last parliament of James I; *1625* member for Chipping Wycombe in the first parliament of Charles I; *1628–1629* member for Amersham in the third parliament of Charles I; *1631* secretly marries Anne Banks, an heiress; *1634* first Mrs. Waller dies; *1635* meets Lady Dorothy Sidney, "Sacharissa"; *1640* member for Amersham in the Short Parliament; *1640* member for St. Ives in the Long Parliament; *1643* arrested for "Waller's Plot," defends himself before the House of Commons, is imprisoned in the Tower of London, and is exiled to France; *1643(?)* marries Mary Bresse; *1645 Poems* of Waller published in London in three editions; *1651* his banishment revoked by Commons, returns to Beaconsfield; *1655* writes *A Panegyric to My Lord Protector* and becomes Commissioner for Trade; *1660* writes *To the King, Upon His Majesty's Happy Return; 1661–1679* member for Hastings; *1677* second Mrs. Waller dies; October 21, 1687, dies.

Author's Bibliography (selected)

A Speech Made by Master Waller Esquire, in the Honorable House of Commons, Concerning Episcopacie, Whether It Should Be Committed or Rejected, 1641; *Mr. Wallers Speech in Parliament, at a Conference of Both Houses in the Painted Chamber, 6 July 1641,* 1641. *Mr. Wallers Speech in the House of Commons, on Tuesday the Fourth of July, 1643,* 1643; *Poems, Etc. Written by Mr. Ed. Waller of Beckonsfield, Esquire,* 1645; *The Works of Edmund Waller Esq. in Verse and Prose,* ed. Elijah Fenton, 1729; *The Works of Edmund Waller, Esq. in Verse and Prose. To Which Is Prefixed, The Life of the Author by Percival Stockdale,* 1772; *The Poems of Edmund Waller,* ed. G. Thorn-Drury, 1893.

Overview of Biographical Sources

There is no full-length biography of Waller. There are a number of short, chapter-length biographical essays dating back to the eighteenth century, but most of these cover the same material. Because Waller lived a long, prosperous life at a time of political upheaval, he is often criticized by biographers for being too much the opportunist. Particularly controversial is Waller's behavior when he was arrested for "Waller's Plot" in 1643. He readily confessed and gave evidence implicating a number of co-conspirators. Given the role he played in the worlds of letters and politics throughout the seventeenth century, a scholarly, full-length biography is long overdue.

Evaluation of Biography

Gilbert, Jack G. *Edmund Waller.* Boston: Twayne, 1979. Gilbert provides a biographical-critical introduction to the life and works of Waller. In the first chapter, Gilbert reviews Waller's life. The two middle chapters provide detailed discussions of songs, epigrams, and panegyrics. In the final chapter, Gilbert discusses Waller's views on art (the most original section of the book) and his place in English literature. The main strengths of Gilbert's study are its inclusiveness and its readability. If one wants a good introduction to what has already been said about Waller, this book will serve one's purpose. The main weakness is its lack of originality. In most of the book, Gilbert repeats what has been said before by others.

Overview of Critical Sources

Waller is seen by both detractors and admirers as an important transitional figure in seventeenth-century poetry. He made the poetic language of the Jacobeans easy and elegant, preparing the way for the poetry of the Augustan Age. His lyric poetry and the panegyrics have been discussed in detail, most modern critics pointing to *A Panegyric to My Lord Protector* as his greatest poem. Still needed are discussions of his religious poems and of contemporary musical settings of his lyrics as well as a critical edition of his poems.

Evaluation of Selected Criticism

Allison, Alexander Ward, *Toward an Augustan Poetic: Edmund Waller's "Reform" of English Poetry.* Lexington: University of Kentucky Press, 1962. Allison sees Waller as an important transitional figure in English poetry. He discusses Waller's departures from the dramatic and rational practices of Jacobean poetry, his refinement of the language of poetry, his use of wit, and his contribution to the neoclassic couplet. The main weaknesses in this study are its length and scope. Allison does not discuss in sufficient depth the poetic conventions of the seventeenth century, and he tends to oversimplify issues of great complexity. He does, however, provide a useful discussion of Waller's own poetic practices.

Chernaik, Warren L. *The Poetry of Limitation: A Study of Edmund Waller.* New Haven: Yale University Press, 1968. Chernaik's work is the only full-length general critical discussion of Waller. Chernaik discusses the different limitations found in Waller's poetry, mainly limitations of subject matter and poetic ambition. He also points to a significant poetic achievement given the specific goals Waller set himself. The heart of the book is a careful analysis of selected lyrics and panegyrics. Chernaik sees the panegyrics as Waller's major poetic efforts, and he offers original and insightful discussions of these poems. In addition to analyzing individual poems, Chernaik offers a brief life of Waller, giving particular attention to the different roles Waller played in seventeenth-century politics, and discusses Waller's influence on the poetry of Dryden and the Augustan Age.

Other Sources

Johnson, Samuel, "Waller," in *Lives of the English Poets.* Oxford: Clarendon Press, 1905. A discussion of Waller's life and work, containing a number of amusing anecdotes and an evaluation of Waller's contribution to English poetry.

Korshin, Paul J. "The Evolution of Neoclassical Poetics: Cleveland, Denham, and Waller as Poetic Theorists," in *Eighteenth-Century Studies,* II (December 1968), 102–137. An analytical essay that argues that elegance is Waller's main contribution to neoclassical poetics.

Richmond, H. M. "The Fate of Edmund Waller," in *South Atlantic Quarterly,* LX (Spring 1961), 230–238. A brief but highly readable defense of Waller's poetry.

Wikelund, Philip R. "Edmund Waller's Fitt of Versifying: Deductions from a Holograph Fragment, Folger MS. X. d. 309," in *Philological Quarterly,* XLIX (January 1970), 68–91. A discussion of Waller's trial-and-error method of composition.

Selected Reference Works

British Writers, Charles Scribner's Sons, 1979. A critical essay by Robin Skelton, emphasizing Waller's stylistic reforms of the Cavalier Poets.

The Dictionary of National Biography, Oxford, 1917. A life by George Thorn-Drury, editor of Waller's poems.

Edward V. Geist
Hofstra University

IZAAK WALTON
1593–1683

Author's Chronology

Born August 9, 1593, Strafford, England of middle class English parents; *1618* apprenticed as an ironmonger in London, also becomes involved in the drapery trade; *1626* marries Rachel Floud; lives in Fleet St. in London and befriends John Donne, John Hales, Henry King, and Henry Wotton; *1640* wife dies; publishes *Life of Donne* as a preface to a posthumous collection of Donne's sermons; *1646* marries Anne Ken; *1650–1661* travels in England and visits clergymen friends; *1651–1678* publishes lives of Sir Henry Wotton, Richard Hooker, George Herbert and Dr. Richard Sanderson; *1653* publishes first edition of *The Compleat Angler; 1655* publishes rewritten, expanded edition; *1662* wife dies; *1676* publishes final version of *The Compleat Angler,* with additions by Charles Cotton; *1683* dies and is buried in Winchester Cathedral, Winchester, England.

Author's Bibliography (selected)

The Compleat Angler, 1653 (pastoral); *The Compleat Angler,* 1676 (pastoral); *The Lives of Dr. John Donne, Sir Henry Wotton, Mr. Richard Hooker, Mr. George Herbert,* 1670 (biography); *The Life of Dr. Sanderson, Late Bishop of Lincoln,* 1678 (biography).

Overview of Biographical Sources

There is still no good, book-length twentieth century biography of Walton. Dr. A. M. Coon's unpublished Cornell University thesis "Life of Izaak Walton" (1938), remains the primary source for the articles and brief biographical notes that are available on the author. There are numerous nineteenth century biographies, but they inevitably emphasize the piousness of Walton to the point of being near useless for the literary student.

Evaluation of Selected Biographies

Bevan, Jonquil, ed. *The Compleat Angler.* Oxford: Clarendon Press, 1983. The best available biography of the author is in the preface to this, the standard edition of *The Compleat Angler.* Although short, it summarizes the state of Walton biography and dispells some of the illusions that have still held over from the nineteenth-century biographies.

Bottral, Margaret, *Izaak Walton.* London: Longmans, Green, 1955. This is a chatty pamphlet-length biography that contains some discussion of the author's work.

Cooper, John R. *The Art of The Compleat Angler.* Durham, NC: Duke University, 1968. Cooper presents a fairly long discussion of Walton's life, focusing on his education, possible literary influences, and relationship to various ecclesiastical figures.

Autobiographical Sources

As numerous critics have noted, *The Compleat Angler,* is largely autobiographical. It is hard not to associate the character of Piscator, the pious, garrulous fisherman, with Walton himself. Several of the other characters mentioned in the work, such as the poet John Chalkhill, were actually known to Walton. Walton's biographical writings also contain autobiographical information, as Walton was a friend of several of the figures he documents. This is especially apparent in the *Life of Donne.*

Overview of Critical Sources

The incredible popularity of *The Compleat Angler* in the nineteenth century has tended to cloud criticism of Walton's work with a focus on its pious sentimentality. Others have failed to take the book seriously as literature, dismissing it as a quaint "how-to" manual for would-be fishermen. Only recently has serious criticism on the work been forthcoming, and little of that has yet to appear in book form. Most of the critical writing on Walton has addressed *The Lives,* which have always been respected both as biographies and as elegant examples of seventeenth-century prose.

Evaluation of Selected Criticism

Butt, John, *Biography in the Hands of Walton, Johnson, and Boswell.* Los Angeles: University of California, 1966. The brief chapter on Walton analyzes the style and method of the biographical writings, and points out factual errors. Special emphasis is given to the *Life of Donne.*

Cooper, John R. *The Art of The Compleat Angler.* Durham, NC: Duke University Press, 1968. By far the best work done on the subject, Cooper relates *The Compleat Angler* to Vergil's *Georgics,* pastoral literature in general, and the dialogue narrative of such writers as Erasmus. The second half of the study explores Walton's prose style, literary borrowings, and the effects of the revisions between the 1653 and 1676 editions.

Nicolson, Harold, *The Development of English Biography.* London: Hogarth, 1927. Nicolson admits that Walton's biographies are literary masterpieces, but declares them to be failures as biographies because they reflect too strongly the author's own ethical biases. The argument might be better applied to Nicolson's own book, which is curiously biased against any form of biography that he considers non-scientific.

Novarr, David, *The Making of Walton's Lives.* Ithaca, NY: Cornell University Press, 1958. Primarily a bibliographical exploration of the biographical writings, Novarr does speculate on some of the literary merits of the work and on the composition of the biographies in relation to Walton's own life.

Stauffer, Donald A. *English Biography Before 1700.* Cambridge: Harvard University Press, 1930. Contains a large chapter on Walton in which Stauffer outlines the author's important contributions to the form of biography. Stauffer discusses Walton's theory and practice through a close reading of the *Life of Donne* and concludes that Walton was the last of the medieval hagiographers.

Other Sources

Greenslade, B. D. "*The Compleat Angler* and the Sequestered Clergy," *Review of English Studies,* 2nd ser. V (1954), 361–366. On the evidence of correspondence between clergymen in the 1650's, Greenslade suggests that Walton may have written *The Compleat Angler* for the practical instruction of the large number of sequestered clergy of the interregnum period.

Selected Dictionaries and Encyclopedias

Lives of the Stuart Age 1603–1714, Osprey Publishing Ltd., 1976. Concise overview of Walton's life and works that includes a short bibliography and a reproduction of the Huysmans portrait of the author.

Paul Budra
University of Toronto

ROBERT PENN WARREN
1905

Author's Chronology

Born April 24, 1905, Guthrie, Kentucky; *1925* graduates from Vanderbilt University; *1927* graduates from the University of California at Berkeley with an M.A.; *1927–1928* attends Yale University; *1929* publishes *John Brown: The Making of a Martyr,* a biography; *1930* graduates with B. Litt. from Oxford University, where he was a Rhodes Scholar; *1930* contributes to *I'll Take My Stand: The South and the Agrarian Tradition; 1930–1931* teaches at Southwestern College, Memphis, Tennessee; *1931–1934* teaches at Vanderbilt University; *1934–1942* teaches at Louisiana State University; *1935* publishes his first book of verse, *Thirty-six Poems; 1935–1942* co-founds and co-edits with Cleanth Brooks *The Southern Review; 1939* publishes first novel, *Night Rider; 1942–1950* teaches at the University of Minnesota; *1944–1945* Consultant in Poetry, Library of Congress; *1946* publishes *All the King's Men; 1947* wins Pulitzer Prize for Fiction; *1950–1956,* Professor of Playwriting, Yale University; *1958* wins Pulitzer Prize for Poetry; *1959* publishes *The Cave* and produces the play version of *All the King's Men; 1961* publishes the long essay, *The Legacy of the Civil War: Meditations on the Centennial* and *Wilderness: A Tale of the Civil War; 1962–1973,* Professor of English, Yale University; *1965* publishes *Who Speaks for the Negro?; 1967* wins Bollingen Prize for Poetry; *1970* awarded the National Medal of Literature; *1977* publishes *A Place to Come To,* his last novel; *1978*–present continues to write and publish collections of poetry.

Author's Bibliography (selected)

John Brown: The Making of a Martyr, 1929 (biography); *Thirty-Six Poems,* 1936 (poetry); *Understanding Poetry: An Anthology for College Students,* 1938 (textbook); *Night Rider,* 1939 (novel); *Eleven Poems on the Same Theme,* 1942 (poetry); *Understanding Fiction,* 1943 (textbook); *At Heaven's Gate,* 1943 (novel); *Selected Poems, 1923–1943,* 1944 (poetry); *All the King's Men,* 1946 (novel); *The Circus in the Attic and Other Stories,* 1947 (short stories); *World Enough and Time,* 1950 (novel); *Brother to Dragons: A Tale in Verse and Voices,* 1953 (poetry); *Band of Angels,* 1955 (novel); *Segregation: The Inner Conflict in the South,* 1956 (prose); *Promises: Poems, 1954–1956,* 1957 (poetry); *The Cave,* 1959 (novel); *You, Emperors and Others: Poems, 1957–1960,* 1960 (poetry); *The Legacy of the Civil War: Meditations on the Centennial,* 1961 (prose); *Wilderness: A Tale of the Civil War,* 1961 (novel); *Flood: A Romance of Our Time,* 1964 (novel); *Who Speaks for the Negro?,* 1965 (prose and interviews); *Selected Poems: New and Old, 1923–1966,* 1966 (poetry); *Incarnations: Poems, 1966–1968,* 1968 (poetry); *Audubon: A Vision,* 1969 (poetry); *Homage to Theo-*

dore Dreiser, 1971 (critical prose); *Meet Me in the Green Glen,* 1971 (novel); *John Greenleaf Whittier's Poetry: An Appraisal and a Selection,* 1971 (critical prose); *Or Else—: Poem/Poems, 1968–1973,* 1974 (poetry); *American Literature: The Makers and the Making,* 1974 (textbook); *Democracy and Poetry,* 1975 (prose); *Selected Poems: 1923–1975,* 1976 (poetry); *A Place to Come To,* 1977 (novel); *Now and Then: Poems 1976–1978,* 1978 (poetry); *Brother to Dragons: A Tale in Verse and Voices,* a new version, 1979 (poetry); *Being Here: Poetry 1979–1980,* 1980 (poetry); *Jefferson Davis Gets His Citizenship Back,* 1980 (prose); *Rumor Verified: Poems 1979–1980,* 1981 (poetry); *Chief Joseph of the Nez Perce, Who Called Themselves the Nimipu—"The Real People"—A Poem,* 1983 (poetry).

Overview of Biographical Sources

Compared to many other writers, Robert Penn Warren is relatively gregarious. He has been and continues to be willing to discuss history, literature, politics, or ideas. He perhaps has granted more interviews than any other major contemporary writer. However, until recently, biographical information on Warren has been limited generally to his days as a Fugitive poet or as a member of the Nashville Agrarians. Louise Cowan's *The Fugitive Group: A Literary History* (1959) and John L. Stewart's *The Burden of Time: The Fugitives and the Agrarians* (1965) help to trace Warren's early associations with the Fugitives and Agrarians. Charles H. Bohner, in *Robert Penn Warren* (1981), generally limits himself biographically to Warren's literary development and to his place in literary history. However, new biographical details relevant to Warren's poetry are now available in Floyd C. Watkins, *Then and Now: The Personal Past in the Poetry of Robert Penn Warren* (1982). Some of this information comes directly from Warren but most from citizens of Guthrie, Kentucky. Lewis P. Simpson's edition of *The Possibilities of Order: Cleanth Brooks and his Work* (Baton Rouge: Louisiana State University Press, 1976), opens with an informative conversation between Brooks and Warren.

Evaluation of Selected Biographies

Bohner, Charles H. *Robert Penn Warren.* Boston: Twayne, 1981. Bohner treats Warren's biography only generally as it pertains to his critical introduction to the major works. Bohner has revised his previous Twayne book on Warren (1964) to include more recent primary and secondary material.

Cowan, Louise, *The Fugitive Group: A Literary History.* Baton Rouge: Louisiana State University Press, 1959. Cowan's work continues to offer helpful and accurate details on the Fugitive Group, including Warren's roles in that group.

Stewart, John L. *The Burden of Time: The Fugitives and the Agrarians.* Princeton: Princeton University Press, 1965. While biography is not Stewart's primary aim, he does consider Warren's literary associations with the Fugitives and, later, with the Agrarians as formative influences.

Watkins, Floyd C. *Then and Now: The Personal Past in the Poetry of Robert Penn Warren.* Lexington: University Press of Kentucky, 1982. This study is an indispensable source for information on Warren's childhood and youth in Guthrie, Kentucky, although it, too, necessarily leaves gaps.

Autobiographical Sources

Warren has written no autobiography, but some of his various interviews are autobiographical in parts. In Floyd C. Watkins and John T. Hiers' edition of *Robert Penn Warren Talking: Interviews 1950-1978* (New York: Random House, 1981) Warren often discusses his life and artistic development.

Overview of Critical Sources

If Warren began his literary career as a poet and if he has always considered himself to be a poet first, much early criticism of Warren's art centered on his fiction. Undoubtedly the great popular success of *All the King's Men* did much to reinforce the public and critical view that Warren is primarily a novelist. Nevertheless, in the last decade Warren has attracted much critical attention as a major American poet. A renaissance in criticism on both Warren's poetry and prose begin in the 1970's. James H. Justus, *The Achievement of Robert Penn Warren* (1981), offers a comprehensive study of Warren as poet, novelist, critic, essayist—as a true man of letters. Continued interest in Warren's poetry has been kindled in such impressive studies as Watkins's *Then and Now: The Personal Past in the Poetry of Robert Penn Warren,* previously mentioned, and by Calvin Bedient's *In the Heart's Last Kingdom: Robert Penn Warren's Major Poetry* (1984).

Evaluation of Selected Criticism

Bedient, Calvin, *In the Heart's Last Kingdom: Robert Penn Warren's Major Poetry.* Cambridge: Harvard University Press, 1984. Bedient is a sensitive reader of Warren's verse. A study that is helpful to both novice and experienced readers of Warren's poetry, this book reflects the complexity of theme and structure of that poetry while remaining very readable. In many ways Bedient's work complements Justus' on Warren's major verse. One ideally should compare and contrast Bedient's analyses with those in the second section of Justus' *The Achievement of Robert Penn Warren,* "Making Peace with Mercutio: Warren the Poet," for a truly comprehensive and creative interpretation of Warren's poetic canon.

Clark, William Bedford, ed. *Critical Essays on Robert Penn Warren.* Boston: G. K. Hall, 1981. Although an uneven volume, this collection includes twenty contemporary reviews of various major works as well as a very provocative general essay by A. L. Clements, "Sacramental Visions: The Poetry of Robert Penn Warren."

Gray, Richard, ed. *Robert Penn Warren: A Collection of Critical Essays.* Englewood Cliffs: Prentice-Hall, 1980. This volume is perhaps the best of the several collections of essays on Warren. Presenting essays on all of Warren's major novels, it also devotes some space to his poetry and criticism. Some discussion of Warren's later fiction, such as *Meet Me in the Green Glen* and *A Place to Come To,* is included, but Frederick McDowell's essay on *Brother to Dragons,* a pivotal poem in Warren's career, is dated by Warren's later work on the poem. The final essay on Warren as historian is especially valuable.

Justus, James H. *The Achievement of Robert Penn Warren.* Baton Rouge: Louisiana State University Press, 1981. The single most important scholarly work on Warren to date, Justus' study unifies thematically Warren's approaches to reality in his fiction, poetry, and criticism. Arguing that Warren's themes are cyclical, Justus finds that Warren ultimately may be a moralist whose roots are bound in orthodox Christian thought—although Warren himself is agnostic. Justus cogently presents the relationships between Warren's poetry and criticism, and he offers convincing analyses of Warren's nonfiction prose as thematic extensions of his poetry and fiction. His interpretation of Warren's long poem, *Audubon: A Vision,* and *Who Speaks for the Negro?* are seminal. In section four, "The Lying Imagination: Warren the Novelist," Justus thoroughly analyzes all of Warren's novels in their order of publication. This work is the most comprehensive treatment of Warren as a true man of letters.

Longley, John Lewis, ed. *Robert Penn Warren: A Collection of Critical Essays.* New York: New York University Press, 1965. An early and in some cases a dated collection, this volume nevertheless remains helpful, especially with Warren's major themes.

Strandberg, Victor, *The Poetic Vision of Robert Penn Warren.* Lexington: University Press of Kentucky, 1977. In this study Strandberg updates and reconsiders much of his previous work on Warren's poetry, which had appeared earlier in *A Colder Fire: The Poetry of Robert Penn Warren* (Lexington: University Press of Kentucky, 1965). Strandberg argues that Warren writes three kinds of poetry: "poems of passage," poems which probe "the undiscovered self," and poems which are mystical.

Walker, Marshall, *Robert Penn Warren: A Vision Earned.* New York: Barnes and Noble, 1979. Although Walker assumes perhaps too much knowledge on behalf of his readers, his work here is useful in tracing the influence of Warren's early agrarianism on both his later poetry and criticism. He also argues well for Warren's last novel, *A Place to Come To,* as a work of dramatic power.

Watkins, Floyd C. *Then and Now: The Personal Past in the Poetry of Robert Penn Warren.* Lexington: University Press of Kentucky, 1982. Watkins finds that Warren's poems about Guthrie and Cerulean, Kentucky, "when assembled as a unit contained . . . [a] created village of the mind and art." Warren corresponded with Watkins, talked with him, and even read portions of his manuscript for this study, which presents some biographical details and analyses found nowhere else. It is an approach especially helpful with such later autobiographical poems as "American Portrait: Old Style" and "Red-Tail Hawk and Pyre of Youth."

Other Sources

Brooks, Cleanth, "Episode and Anecdote in the Poetry of Robert Penn Warren," *Yale Review,* LXX (Summer 1981), 551–567. Discusses Warren's major themes of "time, history, and human identity."

————, *The Hidden God: Studies in Hemingway, Faulkner, Yeats, Eliot, and Warren.* New Haven: Yale University Press, 1963. Discusses some Calvinistic traditions which underly Warren's art.

Modern Fiction Studies: Special Robert Penn Warren Number. VI (Spring 1960). A good source of the major earlier criticism on Warren, including seven articles and a checklist.

Nakadate, Neil, ed. *Robert Penn Warren: Critical Perspectives.* Lexington: University Press of Kentucky, 1981. Presents relatively recent essays on Warren's fiction and poetry and includes a useful checklist of secondary sources.

Selected Dictionaries and Encyclopedias

Contemporary Authors: A Bio-Bibliographical Guide to Current Authors and Their Works, Gale Research, 1975. Brief chronological sketches of Warren's life, including awards, honors, writings, and a listing of secondary help.

Contemporary Novelists, St. Martin's Press, 1976. Chronological sketch of Warren's life and works, with a general thematic introduction to his fiction.

Contemporary Poets, St. Martin's Press, 1975. Chronological sketch of Warren's life and works, with a general thematic introduction to his poetry.

Southern Writers: A Biographical Dictionary, Louisiana State University Press, 1979. Brief biographical sketch and chronology of Warren's life and works.

John T. Hiers
Valdosta State College

THOMAS WARTON
1728–1790

Author's Chronology

Born January 8, 1728 in Basingstoke, England; educated at home by his father, a clergyman-poet; *1744* enters Trinity College, Oxford University where he spends his career; *1747* receives B.A.; *1750* takes M.A.; *1751* gains fellowship at Trinity College; *1752–1753* first becomes acquainted with Samuel Johnson; *1754* assists Johnson in obtaining his M.A.; *1756* elected Professor of Poetry at Oxford serving two five-year terms; *1767* receives B.D.; *1771* assumes the living of Kiddington Parish and becomes a member in the London Society of Antiquaries; *1782* becomes involved in the Rowley controversy and joins Johnson's literary club; *1785* elected Camden Professor of History and becomes Poet Laureate; *1790* dies May 21.

Author's Bibliography (selected)

"The Pleasures of Melancholy," 1747, rev. 1755; "The Triumph of Isis," 1749 (poem); *The Union,* 1753 (edition of poetic miscellany); *Observations on the Fairy Queen of Spenser,* 1754, rev. 2 vols., 1762 (rpt. Haskell House, 1968); *The Oxford Sausage,* 1764 (collection of humorous verse); *History of English Poetry,* 3 vols. 1774–1781 (rpt. Gregg International, 1968); *Poems,* 1777; *Verses on Sir Joshua Reynolds's Painted Window* and *Enquiry into the Authenticity of the Poems Attributed to Thomas Rowley,* 1782; *Poems Upon Several Occasions, English, Italian, and Latin, with Translations,* 1785, rev. 1791 (poems by John Milton); *Poems by Thomas Warton Corrected and Enlarged,* 1789.

Overview of Biographical Sources

Warton's forty-six years as a student and fellow at Trinity College were largely undramatic, and early biographers depended on sometimes unreliable stories by those who knew him or knew of him. Scattered anecdotes from other literary figures of the time such as Johnson, James Boswell, and Fanny Burney have entered the Warton canon, added to by descendants of his brother Joseph. Johnson's remarks to Boswell in particular have created the image of an idler given to drinking ale. The story of the friendship between these two important figures and their rift has never been satisfactorily explained. No definitive biography exists, although Clarissa Rinaker's *Thomas Warton: A Biographical and Critical Study* (1916) is usually accepted as the standard. David Fairer is currently working on both a biography and an edition of the correspondence.

Evaluation of Selected Biographies

Mant, Richard, "Memoirs of the Life and Writings of Thomas Warton," in *The Poetical Works of the Late Thomas Warton B.D.* Oxford: University Press,

1802; rpt. Gregg International, 1969. Mant's treatment is based on brief contemporary biographical notes, on recollections by surviving relatives and friends, and on letters. He attempts to explain the disagreement between Johnson and Warton and he rightly tries to quell the stories about Warton's drinking and idleness. His discussion of the poems is largely appreciative, and he concludes by comparing the achievements of Warton to those of Thomas Gray. Mant's work has been considered the standard edition of the poems.

Vance, John A. *Joseph and Thomas Warton.* Boston: Twayne, 1983. Vance presents a general introduction to Warton's life and works using resources unavailable to earlier biographers. He makes passing reference to many of the poems, some not included by the poet in his last collected edition. Vance's assessment of Warton's critical works and his part in the controversy over Thomas Chatterton's "Rowley" poems is helpful.

Autobiographical Sources

Pending Fairer's completion of Warton's correspondence, the letters are scattered among several libraries or appear as relatively minor segments in the correspondence or biographies of others with two exceptions. Volume three of *The Percy Letters* (ed. David Nichol Smith and Cleanth Brook, 7 vols. Baton Rouge: Louisiana State University Press, 1944–1977) contains the Percy-Warton correspondence dealing with the writers' mutual interest in early English poetry. *Biographical Memoirs of the Late Joseph Warton, D.D.* by John Wooll (London, 1806; rpt. Gregg International, 1969) contains letters relative to Warton's seeking the history professorship and provides insight into academic maneuvering and the politics of literary dedications. "A Panegyric to Oxford Ale," written shortly after the poet's father's death, may reflect Warton's relative poverty at the time.

Overview of Critical Sources

Despite his importance in his own period as a scholar-poet, Warton has been generally known only to students of eighteenth-century literature, and even to most of them as a peripheral member of the Johnson circle. American scholars of the early twentieth century became interested in Warton's work to either place him in a movement or to assess his critical methods. After a period of neglect, Fairer, Joan Pittock, and John Vance have applied contemporary scholarly approaches to the man and his work. Most frequently Thomas Warton is being studied in tandem with his brother Joseph.

Evaluation of Selected Criticism

Pittock, Joan, *The Ascendancy of Taste.* London: Routledge & Kegan Paul, 1973. Pittock examines the Wartons in terms of their literary milieu and finds their work to be centrally important. She denies that they are either Augustans or Romantics, but major contributors to a period of sensibility and taste in which creative inspiration became increasingly internalized. Her study focuses largely on the background, however, and provides sparing discussion of the works.

Rinaker, Clarissa, *Thomas Warton: A Biographical and Critical Study.* Urbana: University of Illinois, 1916; rpt. 1967. Rinaker draws on Mant for her biographical materials but also uses later letters, notes, and manuscripts unavailable to Mant. Her critical treatment is the most thorough to date. She analyzes in some detail both the poetry and the criticism, but she sometimes becomes too enthusiastic in her claims for Warton as a Romantic. In detailing her thesis, Rinaker often avoids the issue of Warton's classical scholarship in favor of his antiquarianism. She does, however, make a strong case for Warton's influence on the younger poets of his day as well as show the high esteem in which Warton was held by such important nineteenth century literary figures as Robert Southey and William Hazlitt. Her study of Warton's sources for the *History of English Poetry* is still unsurpassed.

Vance, John A. *Joseph and Thomas Warton: An Annotated Bibliography.* New York: Garland, 1983. Also divided between the works of the Warton brothers, this work is indispensable to students. A brief introduction clarifies the past of Warton scholarship and its present status. Vance provides particularly valuable information in his comments on secondary sources.

Selected Dictionaries and Encyclopedias
Critical Survey of Poetry, Vol. 7, Salem Press, 1983. Appreciation of Warton's achievements, short biography, and explication of several poems.

James M. O'Neil
The Citadel

ISAAC WATTS
1674-1748

Author's Chronology

Born July 17, 1674, Southampton, England; mother of Huguenot descent; father, Isaac the elder, an Independent deacon, schoolmaster, and clothier; paternal grandfather, Thomas, a naval officer under Admiral Blake, died in the Dutch War; *1678* studies Latin with his father; *1680-1690* to King Edward VI School, Southampton, and taught by Rev. John Pinhorne, rector of All Saints Church; *1690-1694* at Newington Green Academy, London, under the principalship of Rev. Thomas Rowe, minister of an Independent congregation in Girdlers' Hall, Basinghall Street; *1694-1696* returns to Southampton, lives with parents; *1696-1702* in London as tutor to son of Sir John Hartopp, Stoke Newington; *1702* pastor of the Independent congregation at Mark Lane; *1703* prolonged illness; *1712* becomes the house guest of Sir Thomas Abney, where he resides the remainder of his life—at Stoke Newington and at the family's county seat in Hertfordshire; *1728* receives (unsolicited) Doctor of Divinity from the University of Edinburgh; dies November 25, 1748; buried at Bunhill Fields, London; commemorated by a monument in Westminster Abbey.

Author's Bibliography (selected)

The First Catechism, 1692 (for children); *Horae Lyricae. Poems Chiefly of the Lyric Kind,* 1706, 1709; *Hymns and Spiritual Songs,* 1707; *Divine and Moral Songs for the Use of Children,* 1715; *The Psalms of David Imitated,* 1719; *The Art of Reading and Writing English,* 1721; *Sermons on Various Subjects,* 1721-1727; *Logick, or the Right Use of Reason,* 1725; *An Essay toward the Encouragement of Charity Schools,* 1728; *A Caveat against Infidelity,* 1729; *Reliquiae Juveniles: Miscellaneous Thoughts in Prose and Verse,* 1734; *Useful and Important Questions concerning Jesus, the Son of God,* 1746.

Overview of Biographical Sources

Watts, a major hymnographer but a minor literary figure, has never generated a high degree of biographical interest. In terms of a "recent" effort, Arthur Paul Davis published his Columbia dissertation as *Isaac Watts* (1943), reissued as *Isaac Watts: His Life and Works* (London: Independent Press, 1948); it remains the standard work and the one most readily available. Equally accessible but more recent, Harry Escott's *Isaac Watts, Hymnographer* (1962) proves biographically less comprehensive than Davis; nonetheless, Escott provides more details of Watts' early and formative years than does Davis. The problem in both instances, however, concerns the lack of details surrounding Watts' life. Simply, the long illness forced the Nonconformist to activities of the heart and mind; interest generally emerges from the works, not the man. From Davis and

Escott, the path extends backward to Samuel Johnson's *Lives of the Poets* (1779), although his essay therein represents literary criticism. The first pure biography of Watts came from the Calvinist minister of the Independent congregation at Haberdasher's Hall, London (1743–1785), Thomas Gibbons (1720–1785); it appeared in 1780 as *Memoirs of the Rev. Isaac Watts, D.D.* (London: James Buckland and Thomas Gibbons). Although accurate in fact, the piece sags from the weight of Gibbons' homiletic style and reads as a lengthy sermon. Efforts by the Bostonian Congregationalist Jeremy Belknap (1744–1798)—*Memoirs of the Lives, Characters, and Writings of the Reverend Dr. Isaac Watts* (Boston, 1793); Thomas Milner *The Life, Times and Correspondence of the Rev. Isaac Watts, D.D.* (London: Simpkin and Marshall, 1834); Robert Southey—his prefatory essay to *Horae Lyricae* (London, 1834); the Congregationalist scholar Joshia Condor *The Poet of the Sanctuary.* (London, 1851); Edwin Paxton Hood *Isaac Watts: His Life and Writings, His Homes and Friends* (London: Religious Tract Society, 1875); Eric C. L. Shave, *Isaac Watts* (London: Independent Press, 1948)—all variations on the same sympathetic themes—serve to recount the same details of Watts' uneventful and restricted physical existence.

Evaluation of Selected Biographies

Davis, Arthur Paul, *Isaac Watts.* New York: The Dryden Press, 1943; rpt. *Isaac Watts, His Life and Works.* London: Independent Press, 1948. In publishing his Columbia University dissertation, Davis provided the first "modern" biography of Watts. Unfortunately, modernity and thoroughness do not always travel the same route. Davis's piece contains the necessary scholarly apparatus to prove his subject's discipline and emphasize his importance as a literary figure—as educator, theologian, philosopher, and poet. However, Davis also writes for the academy; he tends to understate, even ignore, details important to Watts' principal contribution to eighteenth-century letters—the English hymn and the Protestant psalm paraphrase. Unlike Escott, Davis downplays Watts' formative years at Southampton, while his discussion of the hymns echoes the observation of earlier hymnologists (principally Julian and Benson). Nonetheless, Davis should not be discarded. Indeed, he treads upon paths unknown to his predecessors, providing details on important concerns: Watts' relationships with Cotton Mather, Jonathan Edwards, George Whitefield, John and Charles Wesley. He offers a brief but clear view of Watts the person—the bachelor and chronic invalid, the dissenting minister dependent, throughout his adult life, upon others' beneficence.

Escott, Harry, *Isaac Watts, Hymnographer.* London: Independent Press, 1962. Escott establishes the image of Watts as originator and developer of the English hymn. The biographical details underscore the poet's divine odes rather than his life. Escott strives to uncover the inability of Watts' earlier biographers (from Gibbons to Davis) to highlight their subject's formative years—that period (1694–1696) when the poet returned to Southampton for meditation and study, when he began, in earnest, to contemplate the reform of English psalmody. Those twenty-seven months dominate Escott's biographical and critical commentary as he parades contributors to Watts' hymnodic development during the days of leisure and study with his father at Southampton. One may reasonably argue that Escott's biographical elements serve only as vehicles to approach the discussions of Watts' major poetic collections and the criticism of nineteenth-century hymnodic scholars and biographers. However, given the lack of interesting or even known details of Watts' life, Escott does identify relationships between literary criticism and pertinent biographical detail.

Johnson, Samuel, "Isaac Watts," in *Lives of the English Poets.* ed. George Birkbeck Hill, D.C.L. Oxford: Clarendon Press, 1905. Johnson's biographical-critical essay remains valid, although biography becomes secondary to criticism. Johnson respected Watts as poet, essayist, and preacher—even as hymnodist; thus, his essay reflects a balanced reaction. Biographically, he admitted to ignorance of Watts' life; "I would not willingly be reduced to tell of him only that he was born and died." The details, accurate enough, form a compendium of information from those familiar with Watts. Despite the appearance, later, of complete biographies, Johnson's essay, until the publication of Davis, became the source for generations of biographical discussions of Watts. Doubtless, Johnson's reputation carried considerable influence, overshadowing the superficiality of his details.

Overview of Critical Sources

Criticism of Watts focuses on (1) his reputation as a minor poet during the reign of Anne (particularly his translations and paraphrases from Latin poets) and his influence upon later poets (e.g. Blake, Christina Rossetti); (2) his reputation as a significant figure in the development of the English hymn. Tangentially, his popularity created associations with noted contemporaries, providing interesting reflections upon literary history.

Evaluation of Selected Criticism

Benson, Louis Fitzgerald, *The English Hymn. Its Development and Use in Worship.* 1915; rpt. Richmond, VA: John Knox Press, 1962, pp. 108–218. Benson presents (Chapter III, "Dr. Watts' 'Renovation of Psalmody' ") a thorough analysis of Watts' religious poetry within the context of a definitive survey of hymnody in English from its beginnings through the nineteenth century. For Benson, Watts proved an innovator of psalm paraphrase and divine ode, and the scholar develops the relationship between Watts' criteria for psalm paraphrase and hymnody and the actual poetry. Benson further discusses Watts' impact on eighteenth-century congregational song, including the editions and variants of his collections in England and America.

Manning, Bernard Lord, *The Hymns of Wesley and Watts. Five Informal Papers.* London: The Epworth Press, 1942, pp. 78–105. Manning (in Chapter IV, "The Hymns of Dr. Isaac Watts") examines Watts' methodology; he sees Watts "hewing his way through an almost unexplored territory, that his successors, not having his rough work to do again, will be able to polish and improve." Watts' hymnodic collections appear as "a laboratory of experiments," especially when one considers that the refined poet wrote largely for ignorant audiences. Since Manning likes comparisons, his essay stands as an anthology of examples—lines, verses, entire pieces substantiating Watts' Calvinism, his perception of Nature, the transitoriness of God's creatures, his simple language that "out-Wordsworths Wordsworth," his emotion, his meditative spirit, his repetition and parallelism. Manning provides a manual of hymnodic analysis, but the essayist always treats Watts as he really is—an original poet who "had it in him to do better . . . than he himself ever did."

Other Sources

Rogal, Samuel J. "A Checklist of Works by and about Isaac Watts (1674–1748)." *Bulletin of the New York Public Library,* 71 (April 1967), 207–215. Lists primary and secondary sources, dividing the latter into chronological sections.

Stone, Wilber Macey, *The Divine and Moral Songs of Isaac Watts.* New York: The Triptych, 1918. Bibliographical descriptions of 525 editions in Britain and America, 1715–1915; contains an essay on the history of the volume.

Watts, Isaac, *Hymns and Spiritual Songs.* ed. Selma L. Bishop. London: The Faith Press, 1962. Valuable for its textual variants and introductory essay on Watts' philological principles and on methods of hymnology.

Watts, Isaac, *Reliquiae Juveniles: Miscellaneous Thoughts in Prose and Verse.* ed. Samuel J. Rogal. Gainesville, FL: Scholars' Facsimiles and Reprints, 1968. The introductory essay establishes Watts' niche in literary history and his contributions to the "literature of power."

Samuel J. Rogal
Illinois Valley Community College

EVELYN WAUGH
1903–1966

Author's Chronology

Born October 28, 1903, Hampstead, England, to Arthur and Catherine Raban Waugh; *1917* enters Lancing College; *1921* wins scholarship to Hertford College, Oxford; *1924* enters Heatherley School of Fine Art; *1925* teaches at Arnold House in Wales; attempts suicide; *1926* teaches at Aston Clinton, Buckinghamshire; *1927* works short time for the *Daily Express* and the *Weekly Dispatch* and as school master in Nottinghill, London; *1928* marries Evelyn Gardner; *1930* divorces Evelyn Gardner; joins Roman Catholic Church; travels in Africa; *1932* travels to West Indies and British Guiana; begins book reviewing for the *Spectator; 1936* wins Hawthornden Prize for *Edmund Campion;* marriage to Evelyn Gardner annulled; *1937* marries Laura Herbert; settles in Piers Court, Gloucestershire; begins book reviewing for *Night and Day;* becomes a director of Chapman and Hall Publishing Company; *1939* commissioned as Commander in Royal Marines; *1940* with No. 8 Commando Forces in the Middle East; *1941* takes part in Battle of Crete; *1942* transfers to Royal Horse Guards; *1943* injured during parachute training; *1944* joins 37th British Military Mission to Yugoslavia; *1945* demobilized as Major; wins Gallery of Living Catholic Authors award for *Brideshead Revisited; 1946* attends Nuremberg Trials; *1947* receives honorary degree from Loyola College, Baltimore; *1948–1949* lecture tour of American Catholic universities; *1951* makes trip to Jerusalem for *Life Magazine; 1952* wins James Tait Black Memorial Prize for *Men at Arms; 1954* voyage to Ceylon; suffers hallucinations; *1956* moves to Combe Florey, Taunton, Somerset; *1963* elected Companion of Literature by the Royal Society of Literature; *1966* dies April 4, at Combe Florey after attending Easter Mass.

Author's Bibliography (selected)

Rossetti: His Life and Works, 1928 (biography); *Decline and Fall,* 1928 (novel); *Vile Bodies,* 1930 (novel); *Black Mischief,* 1932 (novel); *Ninety-Two Days: The Account of a Tropical Journey Through British Guiana and Part of Brazil,* 1934 (travel); *A Handful of Dust,* 1934 (novel); *Edmund Campion,* 1935 (biography); *Mr. Loveday's Little Outing and Other Sad Stories,* 1936 (stories); *Waugh in Abyssinia,* 1936 (travel); *Scoop,* 1938 (novel); *Put Out More Flags,* 1942 (novel); *Brideshead Revisited: The Sacred and Profane Memories of Captain Charles Ryder,* 1945 (novel); *The Loved One: An Anglo-American Tragedy,* 1948 (novel); *Helena,* 1950 (novel); *Men at Arms,* 1952 (novel); *Love Among the Ruins: A Romance of the Near Future,* 1953 (novella); *Tactical Exercise,* 1954 (stories); *Officers and Gentlemen,* 1955 (novel); *The Ordeal of Gilbert Pinfold: A Conversation Piece,* 1957 (novel); *The Life of the Right Reverend Ronald Knox,*

Fellow of Trinity College, Oxford, and Pronotary Apostolic to His Holiness Pope Pius XII, 1959 (biography); *Unconditional Surrender,* 1961 (novel); *Basil Seal Rides Again: or the Rake's Regress,* 1963 (stories); *A Little Learning: The First Volume of an Autobiography,* 1964 (autobiography); *Sword of Honor,* 1965 (trilogy consisting of *Men at Arms, Officers and Gentlemen,* and *Unconditional Surrender*).

Overview of Biographical Sources

Although Evelyn Waugh was well-known for his acerbic wit and satiric portraits of British life, only Frederick J. Stopp's *Evelyn Waugh: Portrait of an Artist* (London: Chapman and Hall, 1958) offered much in the way of biographical information during Waugh's lifetime. Even since Waugh's death, relatively little of strictly a biographical nature has been published. Most often referred to are Frances Donaldson's *Evelyn Waugh: Portrait of a Country Neighbor* (1968) and David Pryce-Jones's *Evelyn Waugh and His World* (1973). The only full-scale biography is Christopher Sykes's *Evelyn Waugh: A Biography* (1975) which must be regarded as an authorized biography since Waugh's family provided access to materials and encouraged the preparation of the book.

Three other studies discuss Waugh, although they do not deal with him exclusively: Alec Waugh's *The Early Years of Alec Waugh* (London: Cassell; New York: Farrar, Straus, 1962) and *My Brother Evelyn and Other Profiles* (London: Cassell; New York: Farrar, Straus and Giroux, 1967), and Harold Acton's *Memoirs of an Aesthete* (London: Methuen, 1948) which paints a vivid picture of Waugh at Oxford.

Since his death, selections from Waugh's letters, diaries, essays, reviews and journalism have appeared in book form: *The Diaries of Evelyn Waugh,* (ed. Michael Davie, Boston: Little, Brown, 1976); *A Little Order: A Selection from His Journalism* (ed. Donat Gallagher, London: Eyre Methuen, 1977); *The Letters of Evelyn Waugh* (ed. Mark Amory, New Haven and New York: Ticknor and Fields, 1980); and *The Essays, Articles and Reviews of Evelyn Waugh* (ed. Donat Gallagher, Boston: Little, Brown, 1984).

Evaluation of Selected Biographies

Donaldson, Frances, *Evelyn Waugh: Portrait of a Country Neighbor.* London: Weidenfeld and Nicholson; Philadelphia: Chilton Books, 1968. Donaldson's reminiscences of Waugh from 1948 until his death present him in a favorable light and limit themselves to Donaldson's personal interaction with the Waugh family.

Sykes, Christopher, *Evelyn Waugh: A Biography.* Boston: Little, Brown, 1975. This remains the only full-length biography of Waugh. A friend since 1930, Sykes's stance is a forgiving one. The book, therefore, tends to gloss over the less pleasant aspects of Waugh's personality: his often cruel wit, his depressions, his early homosexuality and his heavy drinking.

Several additional problems exist with this book. The narrative structure is fairly informal; Sykes continually interrupts himself, backtracks, and runs too rapidly through information. Furthermore, because he feels Waugh's autobiography dealt adequately with his early years, Sykes skims over that period, omitting much that an in-depth study of Waugh should include. Sykes's biases cloud the book's objectivity; yet, since this is the only complete biographical treatment of Waugh to date, readers must consult it.

Autobiographical Sources

Because Waugh wrote satirically about his times, much of his fiction is labeled as *roman a clef.* It is certainly true, for example, that Waugh drew on his own teaching experiences for *Decline and Fall* and on observations of his era to provide material for such novels as *Vile Bodies, Scoop,* and *Black Mischief.* Because Waugh was a social satirist, this crossover between fact and fiction is to be expected.

Waugh admitted that *The Ordeal of Gilbert Pinfold* (1957) was a thinly disguised treatment of the hallucinations he experienced on a voyage to Ceylon in 1954; it offers insights into Waugh's recurring attacks of paranoia and ill health. Most important, of course, is *A Little Learning: The First Volume of an Autobiography.* Waugh projected a three-volume work, but this is the only volume Waugh completed. It thoroughly covers his life through his years at Oxford.

Overview of Critical Sources

Criticism generally focuses on Waugh as a satirist or as a Roman Catholic author. Although he also wrote biographies and travel books, these rarely figure in the scholarship. Waugh frequently appears in studies of Aldous Huxley and other writers of black comedy and social satire. Critics have also analyzed his contribution to British fiction as it emerged after World War II.

Evaluation of Selected Criticism

Carens, James F. *The Satiric Art of Evelyn Waugh.* Seattle and London: University of Washington Press, 1966. Carens places Waugh in the context of British satire. This study is especially useful for Waugh's early novels.

Doyle, Paul A. Contemporary Writers in Christian Perspective Series. *Evelyn Waugh.* Grand Rapids: Eerdmans, 1969. Doyle discusses Waugh as both a Catholic author and a writer of tragi-comedy. Readers will find the study particularly useful for its treatment of *Brideshead Revisited.*

Greenblatt, Stephen Jay, *Three Modern Satirists: Waugh, Orwell, and Huxley.* Yale College Series, No. 3. New Haven: Yale University Press, 1965. This book establishes Waugh's place in the tradition of British satire.

Lane, Calvin W. *Evelyn Waugh.* Boston: Twayne, 1981. Lane provides readers with a sound basic introduction to Waugh, both as writer and as a personality. The book's bibliographies offer a well-rounded picture of Waugh scholarship.

Lodge, David, *Evelyn Waugh.* Columbia Essays on Modern Writers. New York: Columbia University Press, 1971. Lodge provides a concise overview for the student who is unfamiliar with Waugh.

Littlewood, Ian, *The Writings of Evelyn Waugh.* Totowa, NJ: Barnes & Noble, 1983. Littlewood explores basic aspects of Waugh's writing such as humor, nostalgia, and romanticism in order to demonstrate their interrelationships in his fiction.

Phillips, Gene D. *Evelyn Waugh's Officers, Gentlemen and Rogues: The Fact Behind His Fiction.* Chicago: Nelson-Hall, 1975. Phillips introduces Waugh's novels and illustrates the ways in which Waugh utilized his own experiences to provide material for his fiction.

Pryce-Jones, David, ed. *Evelyn Waugh and His World.* Boston: Little, Brown, 1973. Diverse recollections by people who knew Waugh at various stages in his life.

St. John, John, *To War With Waugh.* London: Whittington Press, 1973. St. John studies Waugh's own war years; the book can be read as a "preface" to *Men at Arms.*

Selected Dictionaries and Encyclopedias

Contemporary Authors, Vols. 85–88. Gale Research Company, 1980. Brief biography, bibliographic information and discussion of some of Waugh's important novels.

Dictionary of Literary Biography, Vol. 15. Gale Research, 1983. Well-presented treatment of Waugh's life and useful discussion of his major works.

Melissa E. Barth
Appalachian State University

H. G. WELLS
1866–1946

Author's Chronology

Born Herbert George Wells, September 21, 1866, Bromley, Kent, England to a shopkeeper and maid; *1874–1880* attends Thomas Morley's Commercial Academy; *1884–1887* attends London's Normal School of Science; *1887* severely ill; *1891* marries Isabell Mary Wells; begins literary career with publication of an essay in *Fortnightly Review; 1893* more illness prompts him to give up teaching career; *1895* divorces Isabell; marries Amy Catherine Robbins; *1903* joins Fabian Society; *1905* mother dies; *1908* resigns from Fabian Society; *1910* father dies; *1914* visits Russia; has son by Cicely Fairfield (Rebecca West); *1916* tours fronts of World War I; *1920* visits Russia again; *1927* wife Amy dies; *1934* meets with Stalin in Soviet Union; *1938* radio adaptation of *War of the Worlds* creates panic in the United States; *1940* tours United States; *1946* dies August 13, London, England.

Author's Bibliography (selected)

The Time Machine, 1895 (novel); *The Island of Dr. Moreau,* 1896 (novel); *The Invisible Man,* 1897 (novel); *The War of the Worlds,* 1898 (novel); *Love and Mr. Lewisham,* 1900 (novel); *The First Men in the Moon,* 1901 (novel); *The Food of the Gods,* 1904 (novel); *The War in the Air,* 1908 (novel); *The History of Mr. Polly,* 1910 (novel); *The Outline of History,* 1920 (nonfiction); *Men Like Gods,* 1923 (novel); *The Short Stories of H. G. Wells,* 1927; *The Shape of Things to Come,* 1933 (novel); *The Work, Wealth and Happiness of Mankind,* two volumes, 1931 (nonfiction); *Experiment in Autobiography: Discoveries and Conclusions of a Very Ordinary Brain (Since 1866),* 1934; *Things to Come,* 1935 (motion-picture script); *Mind at the End of Its Tether,* 1945 (nonfiction).

Overview of Biographical Sources

Although there are many biographies about Wells, no definitive biography has yet been published; nor can any of the available biographies be regarded as "standard." For many years, Wells's *Experiment in Autobiography* (1934) and his son's *H. G. Wells: A Sketch for a Portrait* (by Geoffrey West, pseudonym for Geoffrey H. Wells; New York: W. W. Norton, 1930) were the principal biographical resources. West's book misses the last years of Wells's life but provides an affectionate portrait of the man and an admiring one of the author.

Wells's personal life lends itself to sensationalized accounts and has attracted many biographical essays as well as books that attempt to capitalize on Wells's sexual peccadilloes. An example of these second-rate efforts is Antonina Vallentin's *H. G. Wells: Prophet of Our Day* (trans. Daphne Woodward; New York: John Day, 1950); the book is not even satisfactory as a scandal sheet.

Other efforts to write popular biographies are more palatable, although seldom more satisfactory as scholarly references. Vincent Brome's *H. G. Wells* (London: Longmans, Green, 1951), for instance, provides a pleasantly readable and sometimes insightful discussion of Wells's character, but its reconstructions of the events of Wells's life are unreliable. One admirable book that focuses on Wells's awkward sexual relationships is Gordon N. Ray's *H. G. Wells and Rebecca West* (New Haven: Yale University Press, 1974). Ray delves deeply into the character of Wells as he presents in vigorous prose the facts of the notorious love affair between Wells and West.

Another useful biographical resource from Ray is one he co-authored with Leon Edel—*Henry James and H. G. Wells* (Urbana: University of Illinois Press, 1958; London: Rupert Hart-Davis, 1958), which traces the friendship of Wells and James through their correspondence.

Evaluation of Selected Biographies

Dickson, Lovat, *H. G. Wells: His Turbulent Life and Times.* New York: Atheneum, 1969. Dickson openly admits that his biography is a sketch, rather than a full life. He has the advantage of having known Wells personally; the two first met in 1931. Most biographers emphasize the early years of Wells's life; Dickson's knowledge of Wells provides a fuller account of the author's last years than can be found elsewhere. Dickson admires Wells and recounts his subject's failings as well as strengths with sympathy. For Dickson, Wells represents an age, and in Wells's character he perceives the strengths and weaknesses of an era. Therefore, Wells comes off as larger than life, but Dickson's appraisals of his contributions to literature and society seem fair enough, although expressed in inflated language: ". . . for his bubbling humor, his outpouring of vitality, his stimulation of our insensate blindness, he surely deserves our thanks and our remembrance." This book is engagingly written and makes for a good introduction to Wells's life and work.

Mackenzie, Norman and Jeanne. *H. G. Wells: A Biography.* New York: Simon and Schuster, 1973. This is the most complete of the biographies of Wells. Like most similar studies, it emphasizes the life through World War I and is less detailed in its account of Wells's last twenty years. Although the Mackenzies provide a good account of Wells's childhood, this book is primarily an accounting of his career, without the insight into the author's personality provided by West, Ray, and Dickson. One advantage this book has over other biographies is that it does not over emphasize Wells's sex life at the expense of Wells's vigorous intellectual life. The conflict between earthiness and asceticism that characterizes much of Wells's intellectual life is not given its full due, but the wide range of Wells's interests and thought is well represented. Its factual detail makes *H. G. Wells: A Biography* the closest to a standard biography as yet published.

Autobiographical Sources

Wells is the author of an extraordinary autobiography, *Experiment in Autobiography: Discoveries and Conclusions of a Very Ordinary Brain (Since 1866).* (New York: Macmillan, 1934). The book is an account of Wells's internal life, focusing on psychological as well as external pressures that influence his personal life and his work. It was written, he asserts, in order to make his "discontents clear because I have a feeling that as they become clear they will either cease from troubling me or become manageable and controllable." The book is also an account of Wells's struggle against the social inhibitions placed on him by his lower-middle-class background. Written with the vigor of his novels and reflecting the major concerns of his fiction, Wells's *Experiment in Autobiography* has been a major reference for his biographers. For all of its exceptional literary merit, it is undervalued by critics.

Other autobiographical sources include *Arnold Bennett and H. G. Wells,* edited by Harris Wilson (Urbana: University of Illinois Press, 1960; London: Rupert Hart-Davis, 1960), a collection of letters. Another good resource for letters is Edel and Ray's *Henry James and H. G. Wells* (see above).

Overview of Critical Sources

Most criticism of Wells's work is mediocre; much of the rest is poor. Much of the early criticism of Wells, beginning with the publication in 1895 of *The Time Machine,* was eulogistic. During World War I, critics became unenamored of Wells's scientific fantasies and instead praised his novels of character, such as *The History of Mr. Polly* (1910). Wells and his friend Henry James broke off their friendship in part over a dispute about what made good fiction, with Wells preferring novels of ideas over novels of character. Wells's preference for writing about ideas cost him dearly with the critics after the 1920's. Although they found merit in his novels of social criticism, such as *Love and Mr. Lewisham* (1900), they tended to denigrate his nonfiction as too sketchy and his scientific fantasies, such as *The Invisible Man* (1897), and utopian novels, such as *The Shape of Things to Come* (1933), as being devoid of the characteristics that make novels great, especially well developed characterizations and depth of feeling. This critical point of view prevailed with few exceptions until the late 1960's; it was exacerbated by the rise in the 1950's of James in the estimation of critics; the divergent points of view of fiction of the two men were compared, to the disparagement of Wells.

In the late 1960's, a generation of scholars that had grown up reading science fiction began to come of age and began rehabilitating Wells's reputation, primarily for the sake of presenting him as a proto-science fiction writer. An early example of such criticism, still following the view that Wells's early writings are superior to his later one's, is Bernard Bergonzi's *The Early H. G. Wells: A Study of the Scientific Romances* (Toronto: University of Toronto Press, 1961), which uses psychoanalytical criticism to analyze Wells's qualities as a myth maker.

Frank McConnell, in *The Science Fiction of H. G. Wells* (New York: Oxford University Press, 1981), provides an uninspired overview of Wells's contributions to the development of the genre of science fiction. The influence of Wells is also emphasized in Mark R. Hillegas' *The Future as Nightmare: H. G. Wells and the Anti-utopians* (New York: Oxford University Press, 1967), which discusses Wells and dystopian fiction by Aldous Huxley, George Orwell and others. An anthology of generally commonplace studies devoted to Wells's place in recent science fiction is *H. G. Wells and Modern Science Fiction,* edited by Darko Suvin and Robert M. Philmus (Lewisburg, PA: Bucknell University Press, 1977; London: Associated University Presses, 1977).

Evaluation of Selected Criticism

Haynes, Rosalynn D. *H. G. Wells: Discoverer of the Future: The Influence of Science on His Thought.* New York: New York University Press, 1980. Haynes believes Wells to be an important interpreter of science for society. She examines in detail his scientific views and how he applied them to his art. This well written book has no equal in its analysis of Wells's application of science to his writing.

Huntington, John, *The Logic of Fantasy: H. G. Wells and Science Fiction.* New York: Columbia University Press, 1982. Huntington examines Wells's thought by discussing symbolism and the organization of individual writings. He devotes a chapter to *The Time Machine* (1895) and shows how the novel reflects Wells's deepest intellectual concerns, such as the "large questions of difference and domination" in a society. Huntington discusses many of Wells's lesser-known works.

Reed, John R. *The Natural History of H. G. Wells.* Athens: Ohio University Press, 1982. While covering some of the same ground as Haynes, Reed emphasizes Wells's world view, which he finds to be founded in Wells's understanding of natural history. Reed admires Wells as an innovator who anticipated the tastes and points of view of the twentieth century. Through his analysis of Wells's world view, Reed tries to determine the stature of the author in literature, concluding that if Wells is not one of the great writers, then he is at least among the near-great.

Williamson, Jack, *H. G. Wells: Critic of Progress.* Baltimore: Mirage, 1973. Williamson examines the style that makes Wells's writings enjoyable to read. He portrays Wells as a man of ideas who often did not think them out as carefully as he should have. This short book is an excellent introduction to Wells's literary merits and the major themes of his writings.

Other Sources

Borrello, Alfred, *H. G. Wells: Author in Agony.* Carbondale: Southern Illinois University Press, 1972. A summary of Wells's life and work that students will find helpful.

Costa, Richard Hauer, *H. G. Wells.* New York: Twayne, 1967. A general overview of the whole of Wells's corpus that points out the major critical issues of his writings.

Selected Dictionaries and Encyclopedias

The Science Fiction Encyclopedia, Dolphin Books, 1979. Brief summary of Wells's life and work.

Kirk H. Beetz
National University,
Sacramento

EUDORA WELTY
1909

Author's Chronology

Born April 13, 1909, Jackson, Mississippi; *1925–1927* attends Mississippi State College for Women in Columbus; *1927–1929* transfers to the University of Wisconsin in Madison and completes a B.A. in English; *1930–1931* studies advertising at the Columbia University School of Business in New York; *1931–1933* returns to Jackson and works part time for a local radio station and as a newspaper reporter; *1933–1936* is publicity agent for the State Office of the Works Project Administration in Mississippi; *1936* has first story, "Death of a Traveling Salesman," printed in *Manuscript; 1941* publishes first book, *A Curtain of Green and Other Stories; 1952* is elected to the National Institute of Arts and Letters; *1955* is awarded the William Dean Howells Medal of the Academy of Arts and Letters for *The Ponder Heart; 1971* becomes a member of the American Academy of Arts and Letters; *1972* receives the Gold Medal for Fiction of the National Institute of Arts and Letters; *1973* wins a Pulitzer Prize for *The Optimist's Daughter; 1985* resides in Jackson.

Author's Bibliography (selected)

A Curtain of Green and Other Stories, 1941; *The Robber Bridegroom,* 1942 (novella); *The Wide Net and Other Stories,* 1943; *Delta Wedding* 1946 (novel); *The Golden Apples,* 1949 (stories); *The Ponder Heart,* 1954 (novel); *The Bride of the Innisfallen and Other Stories,* 1955; *The Shoe Bird,* 1964 (juvenile); *Losing Battles,* 1970 (novel); *One Time, One Place: Mississippi in the Depression, a Snapshot Album,* 1971; *The Optimist's Daughter,* 1972 (novel); *The Eye of the Story: Selected Essays and Reviews,* 1978; *The Collected Stories of Eudora Welty,* 1980; *One Writer's Beginnings,* 1984 (autobiography).

Biographical Sources

No biography of Welty has been written but informative biographical summaries can be found in several of the general studies, most notably in Ruth M. Vande Kieft's *Eudora Welty* (Boston: Twayne, 1962) and Elizabeth Evans's *Eudora Welty* (New York: Frederick Ungar, 1981). Evans also explores Welty's interactions with her editors and publishers from the beginning of her career. A well-known early piece is Katherine Anne Porter's engaging biocritical introduction to *A Curtain of Green and Other Stories* (New York: Harcourt, Brace and Company, 1941) which evokes the texture of Welty's life up to 1941.

Autobiographical Sources

Although Welty has expressed her determination to protect her private life, she has shared some of her personal and artistic experiences in various writings of an autobiographical nature and in numerous interviews dating back to 1941.

One Writer's Beginnings (Cambridge, MA: Harvard University Press, 1984), Welty's autobiography of her childhood, adolescence, and first years as a writer, was originally delivered in lecture form at Harvard University in April 1983. Unmistakably the work of an accomplished storyteller, this slender volume is written in a simple yet poetic style and conveys its main ideas with convincing subtlety. The author sketches loving portraits of her parents, forebears, and most memorable mentors, narrates episodes that show her childhood self developing her powers of observation and imagination, and discusses in general terms how, as a budding writer, she came to locate her basic subject matter and literary method.

Further insight into Welty as an individual and as an artist is offered in a volume of her nonfiction and in a collection of her interviews. Along with essays of reminiscence about people and events that have touched her everyday life, *The Eye of the Story: Selected Essays and Reviews* (New York: Random House, 1978) contains her major statements on the art of fiction. These discussions of writers she admires and of the story-telling process as she has practiced it are mutually illuminating and suggest various useful approaches to her stories and novels. *Conversations with Eudora Welty,* edited by Peggy Whitman Prenshaw (Jackson: University Press of Mississippi, 1984), brings together the most notable interviews the author has given over the years to newspaper reporters, book reviewers, literary figures, and media personalities. As in the essays, recurring concerns of these conversations are Welty's thoughts and feelings about literature, the relationship of her life to her art, and her views on Southern culture.

Overview of Critical Sources

Scholarly commentary on Welty's writings has kept pace with the growth of her literary prominence. Six full-length studies and five shorter monographs provide various perspectives on her overall achievement while the offerings in three collections of essays, like most of the critical articles published in periodicals, treat individual novels and stories or examine specific aspects of her art. Generally thoughtful and illuminating, this scholarship has as its main concerns Welty's identity as a Southern writer; her techniques and style; her portrayal of women, marriage, and the family; and her use of myth, fantasy, and history. Other areas remain to be explored and critics also need to establish new vantage points from which this elusive and original writer can be viewed.

Evaluation of Selected Criticism

Evans, Elizabeth, *Eudora Welty.* New York: Frederick Ungar, 1981. Organized thematically, this balanced introduction to Welty and her works reads as a series of essays that are both critical and appreciative. Evans considers Welty's comedy and her explorations of such themes as isolation, violence, and the duality of experience, as well as her relationship to her cultural and literary background.

Kreyling, Michael, *Eudora Welty's Achievement of Order.* Baton Rouge: Louisiana State University Press, 1980. In this thoughtful general evaluation of Welty's fiction Kreyling adopts several complementary approaches. Besides tracing Welty's evolving artistry, emphasizing in particular the growth of her control over theme and point of view, he demonstrates how her short stories and novels reflect the concerns of modernism and move beyond the local and regional to embrace the world of larger experience.

Prenshaw, Peggy Whitman, ed. *Eudora Welty: Critical Essays.* Jackson: University Press of Mississippi, 1979. The twenty-seven previously unpublished essays in this collection touch on many aspects of Welty's literary versatility. Varied in their approach and ranging from general investigations of special topics to close readings of single works, they form a representative sampling of the current scope and direction of criticism on the author.

Vande Kieft, Ruth M. *Eudora Welty.* Boston: Twayne, 1962. This discriminating examination of the four volumes of short stories and three novels which Welty published prior to 1962 remains a profitable starting point for the study of her writings. Vande Kieft's analyses of the individual works reveal the flexibility of Welty's art but also highlight those themes, patterns, and stylistic qualities that give an overall coherence to her canon.

Other Sources

Devlin, Albert J. *Eudora Welty's Chronicle: A Story of Mississippi Life.* Jackson: University Press of Mississippi, 1983. Devlin emphasizes the social and historic dimensions of Welty's fiction.

Dollarhide, Louis and Ann J. Abadie, eds. *Eudora Welty: A Form of Thanks.* Jackson: University Press of Mississippi, 1979. This collection of seven papers presented at a symposium in honor of Welty at the University of Mississippi includes general appraisals in the form of appreciative tributes and a personal reminiscence by an intimate friend.

Isaacs, Neil, *Eudora Welty.* Austin, TX: Steck-Vaughan, 1969. In his helpful pamphlet-length study Isaacs focuses on mythic patterns in Welty's fiction.

Randisi, Jennifer Lynn, *A Tissue of Lies: Eudora Welty and the Southern Romance.* Washington, D.C.: University Press of America, 1982. In this study Welty's five novels are related to a tradition of Southern Romance as defined by Randisi.

Warren, Robert Penn, "The Love and Separateness of Eudora Welty," *Selected Essays of Robert Penn Warren.* New York: Random House, 1958. Originally published in *Kenyon Review* in 1944, this acute analysis of Welty's early fiction was influential in establishing the tone and direction of later commentary. Warren praises Welty's poetic style and identifies some of her essential themes and techniques.

Selected Dictionaries and Encyclopedias

American Women Writers: A Critical Reference Guide from Colonial Times to the Present, Frederick Ungar, 1982. Brief literary profile.

American Women Writers: Bibliographic Essays, Greenwood Press, 1983. A review of research and criticism on Welty up to 1981.

Dictionary of Literary Biography: American Novelists Since World War II, Gale Research, 1978. Concise biographical sketch and discussions of Welty's major works.

Southern Writers: A Biographical Dictionary, Louisiana State University Press, 1979. Brief biographical profile.

Winifred Farrant Bevilacqua
University of Turin, Italy

NATHANAEL WEST
1903–1940

Author's Chronology

Born October 17, 1903 in New York City as Nathan Weinstein, the first child of prosperous immigrants from Russian Lithuania; *1908–1917* attends public schools in Manhattan, with little distinction; *1917* enrolls at DeWitt Clinton High School, but fails to graduate; *1921* enters Tufts University on a forged transcript; *1922–1924* transfers to Brown University, graduates with degree in English; *1925* returns to New York to work in father's construction company; *1926* legally changes name to Nathanael West, enjoys three-month visit to Paris on allowance from father; *1927–1929* returns to New York to become night manager of a second-rate residential hotel, begins writing in earnest; *1930* meets and courts Alice Shepherd; *1932* engagement broken by Alice Shepherd; *1933* moves to Hollywood as contract writer with Columbia Pictures; *1934* returns briefly to New York; *1935* returns to Hollywood as contract writer with Republic; *1936–1939* works with increasing success as screenwriter, becomes involved in liberal causes; *1940* marries Eileen McKenney; is killed with wife in automobile accident on December 22.

Author's Bibliography

The Dream Life of Balso Snell, 1931 (novel); *Miss Lonelihearts,* 1933 (novel); *A Cool Million,* 1934 (novel); *The Day of the Locust,* 1939 (novel); *The Complete Works of Nathanael West,* 1957 (compendium).

Overview of Biographical Sources

Brief biographical sketches appear in three bio-critical studies of West: Stanley Edgar Hyman's *Nathanael West* (Minneapolis: University of Minnesota Press, 1962); James F. Light's *Nathanael West: An Interpretative Study 2nd ed.* (1971); and Kingsley Widmer's *Nathanael West* (Boston: Twayne, 1982). Each is flawed not only by its brevity: Hyman's is factually inaccurate; Light's contains little information on West's childhood; and Widmer's relies too heavily on secondary sources, and erroneously characterizes West as a devoted Stalinist in the 1930's. Far more sensible and thorough is Jay Martin's meticulously researched *Nathanael West: The Art of His Life* (1970). West left no explicitly autobiographical record, and his letters have not been collected or published as of this date.

Evaluation of Selected Biographies

Light, James F. *Nathanael West: An Interpretative Study 2nd ed.* Evanston, IL: Northwestern University Press, 1971. Light's was the first book-length study of West's life and writings. He presents his biographical information within the framework of critical discussions of West's novels. Light's readings of the novels are thoroughly grounded in Jungian psychological theory and pose the Quest motif as the central element in West's fiction. Light often suggests that West's immediate experience influenced his writings, as when he argues that West's brief trip to Paris in 1925, where he encountered Surrealists and Dadaists first-hand, shaped both the form and content of his first novel, *The Dream Life of Balso Snell*. Similarly, he comes to the unsurprising conclusion that West's screenwriting assignments in Hollywood greatly influenced *The Day of the Locust*. Light stresses West's college and later years at the expense of his childhood. This leads him to underestimate the importance of West's Jewishness in his life and art. Light's neglect of West's childhood appears to be the result of certain weaknesses in his research: he draws almost exclusively upon published materials about West and interviews with the writer's acquaintances; there are few references to West's correspondence, and those with rare exception are drawn from only two sources. Light apparently could not contact any of West's relations. Thus the life of West presented in this volume is incomplete, although generally accurate and clearly documented. The second (revised) edition contains token analyses of the significant scholarship on West which had appeared since Light's first edition in 1961, but it neither revises nor supplements the biographical material in the first edition.

Martin, Jay, *Nathanael West: The Art of His Life*. New York: Farrar, Straus and Giroux, 1970. Martin's exhaustively thorough life of West profited from his access to crucial correspondence, manuscripts and business records held by West's brother-in-law, S. J. Perelman. Martin also contacted scores of persons and brought to light many documents important to West's life, resulting in the best parts of this biography—Martin's meticulous reconstructions of the circumstances of and literary influences on the composition of West's four novels. Martin also provides fuller accounts than can be found elsewhere of West's other literary endeavors; for example, his editorial work with William Carlos Williams on *Contact* and his screenwriting career. Martin places West historically at the tale end of the Lost Generation of the 1920's, rather than with the more socially-conscious writers of the Depression. Martin works best as a critic when uncovering the sources and influences which inform West's novels, or when documenting their critical reception, or when providing their cultural and intellectual context; he does less well when trying to integrate West's life and art. Martin does not adequately explore West's admittedly guarded and complex personality, especially his unhappy sexual life, his deep conflicts over his Jewishness, or his ambivalent feelings about the role of the writer. Nor is Martin a graceful stylist. In spite of these weaknesses, Martin's life remains the key book on West.

Overview of Critical Sources

Critical interest in West peaked in the late 1960's and early 1970's, and at that time focused on West as a social satirist whose surrealistic and fragmented vision of contemporary existence anticipated the work of black comedians like Terry Southern and Kurt Vonnegut. West criticism basically divides into two camps: some critics search his work for Freudian themes and archetypal patterns, and esteem *Miss Lonelihearts* as his best work; others find West's ruthless exploration of the underside of the American dream to be his signal accomplishment, and single out *The Day of the Locust* for praise. To date, few critics have profitably used biographical insights to explore his work.

Evaluation of Selected Criticism

Comerchero, Victor, *Nathanael West: The Ironic Prophet.* Seattle: University of Washington Press, 1967. This first full-length, exclusively critical study of West focuses on Freudian and Jungian elements in West's novels. Comerchero's analysis divides into three parts: the first employs *gestalt* theory to trace how West unconsciously reveals his own psyche in his work; the second analyzes each novel individually in light of the first part; and the final section argues that a composite "Westian" man emerges from the novels read together. Comerchero carps excessively at other interpretations of West's work, and his narrow search for archetypes in West's novels leads him to misunderstand both West's intention and his achievement, as when he argues that Miss Loneliheart's religious conversion should be read as a shift from latent to overt homosexuality.

Reid, Randall, *The Fiction of Nathanael West: No Redeemer, No Promised Land.* Chicago: University of Chicago Press, 1967. Reid provides a thorough and methodical study of the literary sources and influences which inform West's novels, and presents West as an essential pessimist who believes there is "no redeemer, no promised land" for modern man. Reid's introduction focuses on the problems of parody as a literary form, and then separate chapters deal with each of the four novels as parodies of earlier literature. A final chapter takes issue with the Freudian interpretation of Miss Lonelihearts as a repressed homosexual. Reid writes cogently and sensibly, but offers no dramatic reevaluation of West's artistry.

Widmer, Kingsley, *Nathanael West.* Boston: Twayne, 1982. The most recent bio-critical study of West, Widmer finds in the concept of the hidden identity or "masquerade" a useful tool for examining West's life and art. Widmer conceives of West's novels as psychological dramatizations of the author's own identity crises. He deals swiftly and superficially with West's biography before analyzing each of the novels in turn, focusing on the ways in which his novels evidence West's essential attitude toward life, which Widmer defines as that of a prophet of modern role-playing. A final chapter surveys other critical approaches and attempts to place West in the American literary tradition. Widmer's prose is often florid, and his analyses speculative and thinly substantiated. His study offers few new insights into West and his work.

Other Sources

Hyman, Stanley Edgar, *Nathanael West.* Minneapolis: University of Minnesota Press, 1962. A short monograph on West which raises several of the critical issues discussed in more detail by later critics. Hyman emphasizes the presence of Freudian themes and archetypal patterns in West's fiction.

Madden, David, ed. *Nathanael West: The Cheaters and the Cheated.* Deland, FL: Everett/Edwards, 1973. A varied and informative collection of essays on West and his work, interspersed with series of short quotations on specific subjects from West himself, his acquaintances, and West scholars.

Malin, Irving, *Nathanael West's Novels.* Carbondale: Southern Illinois University Press, 1972. A New Critical approach to West, emphasizing his skill as a literary craftsman and posing ambivalence as the dominant theme in his work.

Schulberg, Budd, "Pep (Nathanael) West," in *Writers in America: The Four Seasons of Success.* New York: Stein & Day, 1983. A sympathetic portrait of West in Hollywood, emphasizing his thoughts on the life of the writer in America. Reissue of Schulberg's 1972 *The Four Seasons of Success.*

Selected Dictionaries and Encyclopedias

Dictionary of Literary Biography, Vol. 9. Detroit: Gale Research, 1981. An accurate summary of West's life, and brief discussions of his work.

Richard A. Fine
Virginia Commonwealth University

EDITH WHARTON
1862–1937

Author's Chronology

Born Edith Newbold Jones, January 24, 1862 to wealthy, socially prominent parents in New York City; *1866–1879* travels with family in Europe, spending winters in New York, summers in Newport; *1879* has debut on Fifth Avenue, New York; *1882* father dies; *1885* marries Edward Wharton, a wealthy Bostonian playboy; *1891* publishes two stories, beginning a writing career that will last until her death; *1903* husband suffers first of series of severe mental breakdowns, which will lead to their divorce in 1913; *1914* moves to Paris after selling her mansion in Lenox, Massachusetts in 1911; *1914* works with war relief effort in Paris; *1916* mourns the loss of her dear friend Henry James; *1918* buys her final residence, Pavillon Colombe, an eighteenth-century mansion near Paris; *1921* awarded the Pulitzer Prize for *The Age of Innocence; 1923* first woman awarded a Doctor of Letters by Yale University; *1927* mourns the death of her friend and companion for forty-three years, Walter Berry; *1937* dies following a stroke, leaving papers to Yale University with stipulation that they not be opened until 1968.

Author's Bibliography (selected)

The Decoration of Houses, 1897 (prose); *The Greater Inclination,* 1899 (stories); *The Valley of the Decision,* 1902 (novel); *The House of Mirth,* 1905 (novel); *The Fruit of the Tree,* 1907 (novel); *Ethan Frome,* 1911 (novella); *The Reef,* 1912 (novel); *The Custom of the Country,* 1913 (novel); *Xingu and Other Stories,* 1916; *Summer,* 1917 (novella); *The Age of Innocence,* 1920 (novel); *In Morocco,* 1920 (travel); *Old New York,* 1924 (novella); *The Mother's Recompense,* 1925 (novel); *The Writing of Fiction,* 1925 (prose); *A Backward Glance,* 1934 (autobiography); *The Buccaneers,* 1938 (novel).

Biographical Overview

Wharton's canon consists of seventeen novels, seven novelettes, eleven volumes of short stories, three volumes of poetry and miscellaneous writings on travel, architecture, war relief, and numerous other subjects. Because of her eclectic work, her acknowledged skill as a writer, her ironically critical look at the turn-of-the-century aristocrats of New York and her wide range of friendships, especially with Henry James, Edith Wharton has been the object of several biographical studies. However, because her papers were closed to scholars until 1968, the definitive biography was not written until R. W. B. Lewis published his fine study in 1975. Prior to Lewis' study were Katherine Gerould's *Edith Wharton: A Critical Study* (New York: D. Appleton, 1922), a short, eleven page pamphlet, and Robert Lovett's *Edith Wharton* (New York:

Robert M. McBride, 1925), focusing on Wharton's cultural milieu with helpful references to contemporary reviews. Percy Lubbock's *Portrait of Edith Wharton* (1947) was the next major full-length study of her life, followed by Louis Auchincloss' *Edith Wharton* (Minneapolis: University of Minnesota Press, 1961), a forty-three page introductory treatment. Olivia Coolidge's *Edith Wharton, 1862-1937* (New York: Charles Scribner's Sons, 1965) is deliberately juvenile, and focuses on the pain, loneliness and glamour of Wharton's life. Grace Kellogg's *The Two Lives of Edith Wharton: The Woman and her Work* (New York: Appleton-Century, 1965), is a popularized biography, best on her early years. Similarly, Louis Auchincloss' *Edith Wharton: A Woman in Her Time* (New York: Viking Press, 1971) is chatty and readable, with excellent pictures. Book-length studies of Wharton subsequent to Lewis' have all acknowledged their debt to his study, and have consequently turned their primary attention to biographical criticism of her works, as opposed to retelling her history. Margaret McDowell's *Edith Wharton* (Boston: G. K. Hall, 1976), a part of the Twayne Author's Series, is a comprehensive introductory survey of the biography and the major novels. Most important however, of the post-Lewis biographical criticism is Cynthia Griffin Wolff's *A Feast of Words: The Triumph of Edith Wharton* (1977) an excellent psychological analysis of Wharton and her work.

Evaluation of Selected Biographies

Lewis, R. W. B. *Edith Wharton.* New York: Harper and Row, 1975. Based on exclusive access to several collections of Wharton's letters and manuscripts, including the papers at Yale, Lewis' biography is definitive, invaluable. It is an objective retelling of her life, which, unlike previous biographies, does not shrink from discussing the more unorthodox aspects, including her passionate affair with Morton Fullerton and her brief attempt to write pornography. Lewis' biography is indispensable to any scholar of Wharton, and is to be admired for its thoroughness, its readability, and its careful attention to detail which does not diminish the drama of Wharton's life. It is acknowledged to have made a major contribution toward gaining Wharton recognition as a major American writer.

Lubbock, Percy, *Portrait of Edith Wharton.* New York: D. Appleton-Century, 1947. Lubbock presents a fine supplement to Wharton's autobiographical *A Backward Glance,* but is equally reticent to disclose Wharton's personal trials.

Wolff, Cynthia Griffin, *A Feast Words: The Triumph of Edith Wharton.* New York: Oxford University Press, 1977. Wolff acknowledges her debt to Lewis, who allowed her access to the Wharton Yale papers and other manuscripts in his possession. Wolff therefore builds on Lewis' work as she uses literary and psychological analysis of Wharton's life and work to explore the complex relationship between the two that compelled Wharton to write. Wolff is especially good at analyzing the interior life of a woman writer, though the entire biography is excellent for its insights, its critical analysis of Wharton's fiction, and its scholarly approach to her material.

Autobiographical Sources

Since many of Wharton's novels and stories are set in "Old New York" and its social environment, much of Wharton's fiction could be seen as autobiographical: most especially *Hudson River Bracketed* (New York: Appleton, 1929). She did, however, write one overtly autobiographical non-fiction work, *A Backward Glance* (New York: Appleton-Century, 1934). In *A Backward Glance* Wharton chronicles her own artistic growth, rather than attempting to give the story of her life. In fact, in her preface, she warns her audience that she will not be writing of sensational facts and scandalous occurrences: "I recall no sensational grievances. Everywhere on my path I have met with kindness and furtherance." The lack of candor here is emblematic, and Wharton deliberately avoids her own pain even to the point of ignoring her divorce. As a portrait of the artist, the book is valuable. Stately in tone, it begins: "Years ago I said to myself: There is no such thing as old age; there is only sorrow."; then the work traces the *writer's* growing understanding of herself. For a portrait of the woman, readers are advised to turn to more candid biographies.

Overview of Critical Sources

With the publication of Lewis' biography there has been a renewed interest in Wharton's work, though she has always been the object of major critical attention. Her literary reputation has been uneven. During her lifetime she was often measured against Henry James, her good friend, and found wanting. More recently, and especially since the increased critical focus on women writers, Wharton's reputation has gained in esteem. Once viewed primarily as an expert technician of fiction, critics now evaluate her much more favorably for the insight she has into the human condition, especially among the upper class in the Jamesean tradition. Wharton brings her ironic vision to the manner of her world, which valued manners and form above substance, and in so doing profoundly explores what she deemed to be the tragedy inherent in the dichotomy between what is and what ought to be.

Evaluation of Selected Criticism

Ammons, Elizabeth, *Edith Wharton's Argument with America*. Athens: University of Georgia Press, 1980. This book is the first to examine Wharton's work in an historical context. Ammons sees Wharton's argument on the issue of freedom for women as an evolving one. In the early novels, Wharton focused on economic obstacles, then moved to an exploration of the psychological claims of romantic love, then to a satiric study of marriage, and finally reverted to a reactionary endorsement of motherhood.

Bell, Millicent, *Edith Wharton and Henry James: The Study of Their Friendship.* New York: George Braziller, 1965. Bell provides a full account of the relationship between the two, drawing on the letters of both.

Lyde, Marilyn, *Edith Wharton: Convention and Morality in the Work of a Novelist.* Norman: University of Oklahoma Press, 1959. This is a thorough study of Wharton's views of changing social conventions, measured against her own moral philosophy. Lyde treats such themes as Wharton's concept of truth, the role of money, and her tragic view of life.

Nevius, Blake, *Edith Wharton: A Study of her Fiction.* University of California Press, 1953. This is an excellent critique of Wharton's major fiction. Nevius judges *The House of Mirth, The Custom of the Country,* and *The Reef* as her greatest novels, and argues that Wharton's fiction is one of literature's finest treatments of "the trapped sensibility."

Walton, Geoffrey, *Edith Wharton: A Critical Interpretation.* Rutherford, NJ: Fairleigh Dickinson University Press, 1970. Walton provides an important new interpretation of Wharton's works. Approaching her work thematically (dealing, for example, with the complex relationship between manners and morals), he corrects misunderstandings of earlier critics, without forcing Wharton into a new mold of his own.

Wershoven, Carol, *The Female Intruder in the Novels of Edith Wharton.* Rutherford, NJ: Fairleigh Dickinson University Press, 1982. Indicative of the new trends in Wharton scholarship, Wershoven's book takes a different approach to Wharton's social criticism. Arguing that Wharton was much less conventional than she is given credit for, Wershoven identifies the presence of a "female intruder" in many of Wharton's novels, a character who stands outside her society and forces other characters to reexamine their world, teaches protagonists alternative ways to live, reproaches false social mores, and in general embodies Wharton's own values.

Other Sources
Since the critical canon of Wharton is so large, readers are best advised to check bibliographies of Wharton criticism for further research. Standard bibliographies include:

Brenni, Vito J. *Edith Wharton: A Bibliography.* Morgantown: West Virginia University Library, 1966. An unannotated bibliography of primary works, translations, book reviews, and selected criticism.

Springer, Marlene, *Edith Wharton and Kate Chopin: A Reference Guide.* Boston: G. K. Hall, 1976. A comprehensive, annotated bibliography of scholarship, reviews, and miscellaneous commentary on Wharton. Covers criticism between 1897 and 1973, including dissertations. This is the definitive bibliography to date. It is updated to 1984 in *Resources for American Literary Studies,* to be published in Spring, 1985.

Selected Dictionaries and Encyclopedias

American Women Writers from Colonial Times to the Present, Vol. 4. Frederick Ungar, 1982. A brief biography and critical review of major fiction. Also includes commentary on Wharton's themes, style, and critical reception.

Concise Dictionary of American Biography, Charles Scribner's Sons, 1964. Short entry on Wharton outlining the essential facts of her life and brief commentary on major works.

Encyclopedia of World Literature in the Twentieth Century, Vol. 4, Frederick Ungar, 1984. A brief biography with overview of major works.

A Library of Literary Criticism: Modern American Literature, Vol. 3, Frederick Ungar, 1969. A selective list of short critical comments on Wharton's work.

Marlene Springer
University of Missouri-Kansas City

PHILLIS WHEATLEY
1753–1784

Author's Chronology

Born 1753, Senegal, W. Africa; abducted at eight and sold into slavery; becomes servant of wife of John Wheatley, Boston tailor; liberally educated by mistress; studies classic history, literature, English poets; *1767* first published poem, "On Messrs. Hussey and Coffin;" followed by elegy on the death of George Whitefield, famous minister, in *1770;* thereafter sought by Boston society for her intellect and conversation; freed in *1772; 1773* travels to England; first book, *Poems on Various Subjects, Religious and Moral,* published; *1778* marries John Peters, a free negro; bears three children; marriage declines along with her health; works domestic labor for meager support; *1784* dies in Boston, a few hours before her only surviving child dies too.

Author's Bibliography

Poems on Various Subjects, Religious and Moral, 1773, (American edition, 1784); *Letters of Phillis Wheatley, the Negro-Slave Poet of Boston,* 1864.

Overview of Biographical Sources

Early biographical treatments of Wheatley are limited. Eighteenth-century references most often appeared as part of letters published in literary magazines. Pieces citing Wheatley as an example of Negro ability also appeared then. The more extensive biographies which emerged were usually based on John Wheatley's sketch of Phillis which accompanied one version of her *Poems on Various Subjects, Religious and Moral,* or they resulted from personal contact such as the 1834 Odell memoir about Wheatley. Later in the nineteenth century some mainstream biographical publications such as *A Dictionary of American Authors* and the *Literary Digest of New York* included Wheatley. Early twentieth century biographies widened the biographical treatments of Wheatley, while more current efforts also approach her as part of the Black American experience.

Evaluation of Selected Biographies

Renfro, G. Herbert, *Life and Works of Phillis Wheatley.* Freeport: Books for Libraries Press, 1916, reprinted 1969. Renfro's work represents one of the earliest twentieth-century biographies of the poet. Contents include Wheatley's complete works, some letters to fellow slave Obour Tanner in Newport, and a complete biography. Although written in an awkward style by current standards, the biography offers good insights into the extraordinary treatment Phillis received from the Wheatley family and how she evolved out of the servant category and into her art. Her early enthusiasm for the classics is detailed here, as is her close relationship with Mrs. Wheatley. Throughout her ensuing years, Renfro emphasizes the isolation/loneliness Wheatley experienced. Both Mr. and Mrs. Wheatley had died by 1778, and their children had scattered. In that year Phillis married John Peters, but the marriage and three children who died in infancy seemed to underscore her loneliness. Renfro punctuates his biography with letters to or about Wheatley. The newspaper article announcing her funeral attests to the lingering strength of her acclaim at that time.

Richmond, M. A. *Bid The Vassal Soar*. Washington, D.C.: Howard University Press, 1972. Richmond devotes half of this study to Wheatley, half to George Moses Horton, nineteenth-century slave poet. He introduces Wheatley by recreating her meeting with Washington after she had sent a poem to him. This unorthodox opening highlights what a phenomenon she was for the time. Richmond posits that, because her poetry was so erudite and literate, many people actually did not know it was written by a Black slave. Richmond next moves back in time to the slave auction where Susannah Wheatley bought Phillis. Wheatley's life is presented in conjunction with political events of the times, including Washington's move to allow free Blacks in the army to counter a British move to do the same, and the fact that Wheatley's first volume of poetry, published in England, had trouble making its way to the colonies because Boston Harbour was blockaded by the British after the Tea Party. In relating the successes of her work, and her trip to London, Richmond also emphasizes the insular position Wheatley occupied. She could not associate with other Blacks on their level, nor could she associate with whites as an equal. She gained her freedom and married, but these changes only produced poverty and tragedy for her, epitomized by the unmarked grave she was buried in.

Autobiographical Sources

Since a majority of Wheatley's forty-six poems were elegies or occasional poems written for white society, they usually lack direct autobiographical information. However, some of her verses do offer insights into the poet's attitudes and feelings. Her 1772 "To the Right Honorable William, Earl of Dartmouth, His Majesty's Principal Secretary of State for North-America" refers to her removal from Africa and the sorrow she fears her parents suffered as a result. She also prays that no one else would ever have to endure similar tyranny and pain. "To the University of Cambridge" 1767, 1773 repeats allusions to the "dark" past Wheatley came from, while "On Being Brought from Africa to America" reflects her belief that she was removed from her pagan background to become an example of how people of her race could be made faithful Christians. The other aspect of Wheatley's life which her poetry reveals is the frustration she experienced as a poet. "To Maecenas" exemplifies this as she laments how Terence was the only poet of African descent whom the muses had aided; she wishes her song to rise just as gloriously as the classic poet's did.

Overview of Critical Sources

Early criticism of Wheatley's work is fragmented, often dealing more with the novelty of the Negro slave as poet than the poems themselves. Other than reprints of her poetry, virtually no book-length critical treatments of Wheatley appeared until well into the twentieth century. Even then some critics/writers seemed to feel that Wheatley's work was better suited for a youthful audience rather than being a subject for serious scholarship. Shirley Graham's *The Story of Phillis Wheatley* (New York: Messner, Inc., 1949) presents Wheatley's life and literature in a novel for younger readers. As late as 1968, Kathryn Borland and Helen Speicher published *Phillis Wheatley, Young Colonial Poet* (Indianapolis: Bobbs-Merrill), a children's version of the poet's life and works. The major critical works about Wheatley did not emerge until the late 1960's.

Evaluation of Selected Criticism

Mason, Julian D., Jr. *The Poems of Phillis Wheatley.* Chapel Hill: University of North Carolina Press, 1966. In addition to reprinting Wheatley's *Poems of Various Subjects, Religious and Moral,* along with seventeen miscellaneous poems, Mason includes a section of critical reaction to Wheatley's works from eighteenth and nineteenth-century sources, including both foreign and domestic journal articles, books and newspaper articles. Mason also concentrates on the responses of other poets to Wheatley's work, along with some of the responses which typically marvelled more at the fact that the verses were written by an African than at the poetry per se.

Robinson, William H. *Critical Essays on Phillis Wheatley.* Boston: G. K. Hall, 1982. This volume contains reprinted criticism of the poet, along with some original essays on Wheatley's work. The chronology is complete, ranging from Wheatley's contemporaries such as Washington and Jefferson, to the more modern critics. The fifty plus essays cover various aspects of the poet's work, including examination of the personal elements in Wheatley's poetry, discussion of her poetry as a reflection of pre- and post-revolutionary America, and a detailing of the influence of Pope in Wheatley's verses.

———. *Phillis Wheatley in the Black American Beginnings.* Detroit: Broadside Press, 1975. Robinson's purpose in this text is to show that Wheatley was both a poet of merit and a Black aware of the conditions and concerns of other members of her race. The text begins with a biographical sketch of Wheatley, together with some early "remarkable" verses. Robinson reiterates a theme found throughout his works on Wheatley, that she was treated more as a novelty by white society than as a significant poet. He contrasts this with criticism from nineteenth-century Black writers who approached Wheatley more seriously and saw her work as partial evidence that the assumed inferiority of the Black race was a fallacy. Emphasizing that Wheatley was certainly not a militant person, Robinson cites various verses and letters which show she did realize the conditions her people faced, and she was concerned about this. Her writings show her awareness as a Black and establish her as the originator of the Black American tradition in literature.

Other Sources

Mainiero, Lina, *American Women Writers.* Vol 4. New York: Ungar Publishing, 1982. A brief biography together with a one page analysis of the major elements in Wheatley's poetry.

Page, James, *Selected Black American Authors.* Boston: G. K. Hall, 1977. A brief biography and early bibliography on Wheatley.

Robinson, William H. *Phillis Wheatley: A Bio-Bibliography.* Boston: G. K. Hall, 1981. A year by year listing of the various sources which have dealt with Wheatley, 1761–1979.

Robinson, William H. *Phillis Wheatley and Her Writings.* New York: Garland Publishing, 1984. A combination of biography, criticism and reprinting of Wheatley's poems, to which Robinson adds some textual analysis of the poetic devices found in Wheatley's works.

Kenneth A. Howe
Michigan State University

WALT WHITMAN
1819-1892

Author's Chronology

Born May 31, 1819, West Hills, Huntington, Long Island, New York; *1838* founds and edits *The Long Islander,* Huntington; *1846-1848* edits *Brooklyn Daily Eagle; 1848* goes to New Orleans and edits the *Crescent; 1848-1849* edits Brooklyn *Freeman; 1855* publishes and helps set type for first edition of *Leaves of Grass; 1857-1859* edits Brooklyn *Daily Times; 1862* goes to Washington, D.C. to find brother George, wounded in Civil War; *1863-1865* serves as volunteer nurse for wounded soldiers; *1865* hired and later discharged from clerk position in the Bureau of Indian Affairs, Department of Interior; meets Peter Doyle; *1865-1873* works in Attorney General's office; *1873* suffers paralytic stroke; mother dies; moves to Camden, New Jersey, to live with his brother and sister-in-law; *1879-1880* travels to far West and Canada; *1884* buys house on Mickle Street, Camden, where he spends the rest of his life; dies March 26, 1892.

Author's Bibliography

Leaves of Grass, 1855 (poetry), revised 1856, 1860, 1867, 1871, 1876, 1881-1882, 1888, 1891-92, 1897; *Drum-Taps* and *Sequel to Drum-Taps* (poetry), 1865; *Democratic Vistas* (social-political criticism), 1871; *Memoranda During the War* (memoirs), 1875; *Specimen Days and Collect* (memoirs, nature writings, criticism), 1882; *November Boughs* (poetry and prose), 1888; *Good-Bye My Fancy* (poetry), 1891; *Complete Prose Works,* 1892; *Collected Writings,* 1961-present (continuing editions which includes early verse and fiction, journalism, correspondence, miscellaneous prose).

Overview of Biographical Sources

There may be as many biographies about Whitman as any other American writer, yet nothing in the passing decades has led to any significant revisionist look at his life. The major change has involved perspective, with a move toward increasing acknowledgment and examination of the homosexual content of Whitman's life and work. The earliest biographical material appeared during Whitman's lifetime and under his auspices, so these works—John Burroughs's *Notes on Walt Whitman, as Poet and Person* (New York: American News Co., 1867) and Richard M. Bucke's *Walt Whitman* (Philadelphia: David McKay, 1883)—emphasized him as the rugged, soil-formed, representative American his works so proudly sang. The first scholarly biography was Henry Bryan Binns's *A Life of Walt Whitman* (London: Methuen, 1905), but his extensive research did not prevent his conjecturing for Whitman a wholly imaginary heterosexual romance in New Orleans. Bliss Perry's *Walt Whitman* (Boston:

Houghton, Mifflin, 1906) performed further research but aroused the wrath of Whitman admirers for supposed slurs on his character and literary stature. George Carpenter's *Walt Whitman* (New York: Macmillan, 1909), based on Perry, stresses Whitman's personal development as related to his work. Leon Bazalgette's rather impressionistic and defensive *Walt Whitman: The Man and His Work* (translated from French, Garden City, N.Y.: Doubleday, Page, 1920) fictionalizes a bit. Later biographies—from Jean Catel's *Walt Whitman: La naissance du poéte* (Paris, 1929) and Frederik Schyberg's *Walt Whitman* (Copenhagen, 1933; translated 1951) to Edgar Lee Master's wide-ranging but somewhat inaccurate *Whitman* (New York: Charles Scribner's Sons, 1937) and Henry Seidel Canby's *Walt Whitman, an American* (Boston: Houghton-Mifflin, 1943)—benefited from the early journalism and other writings, including personal notebooks and manuscripts, that scholarship of the 1910's, 1920's, and 1930's had brought to light, especially through the work of Emory Holloway. By the centennial of the first *Leaves of Grass* in 1955, two major contributions to biography were available—by Roger Asselineau and Gay Wilson Allen. Barbara Marinacci's *O Wondrous Singer! An Introduction to Walt Whitman* (New York: Dodd, Mead, 1970) is far less detailed biographically, choosing rather to introduce both the man and his writings by reprinting and discussing selections in conjunction with the appropriate stages of Whitman's life (the homosexual aspects of which she clearly disapproves of). Two recent studies focus on the various influences leading to Whitman's creative outbursts: Floyd Stovall's more scholarly and methodical *The Foreground of Leaves of Grass* (University Press of Virginia, 1974) and Paul Zweig's impressionistic, chronological *Walt Whitman: The Making of the Poet* (New York: Basic Books, 1984).

Evaluation of Selected Biographies

Allen, Gay Wilson, *The Solitary Singer.* New York: New York University Press, 1955, 1967. Allen's monumental, extensively referenced work is the definitive biography, superbly detailed to give a complete picture of Whitman's surroundings and all facts significant to his life and the development of his work. A reader unfamiliar with Whitman's life, however, may find the amount detail excessive.

Asselineau, Roger, *The Evolution of Walt Whitman.* Cambridge: Harvard University Press, 1960–1962. As translated by the author and American assistants, Asselineau's study is divided into two volumes. *The Creation of a Personality* and *The Creation of a Book,* one focusing on the life, the other on the work, though both significantly interpenetrate each other. Asselineau presents Whitman's life as a whole, based on a struggle with his homosexual desires. This is the most comprehensive and sympathetic discussion of Whitman's homosexuality until Robert K. Martin in 1979. The two volumes read smoothly and quickly, with extensive notes at the back.

Holloway, Emory, *Whitman: An Interpretation in Narrative.* New York: Alfred A. Knopf, 1926. Holloway's scholarly thoroughness earned him a Pulitzer Prize, though the book lacks references. Holloway oddly insists on demonstrating Whitman's heterosexuality, even though he himself had already deflated the only possible evidence of a New Orleans romance when he showed in the *Dial* (November 1920) that the manuscript for Whitman's poem "Once I Pass'd through a Populous City" referred to a man rather than the woman of the published version.

Kaplan, Justin, *Walt Whitman: A Life.* New York: Simon and Schuster, 1980. Kaplan approaches his subject novelistically, with vivid descriptions and much concrete detail, presenting Whitman's life in a flashback from his old age. Quotations from the poetry and prose, Whitman's personal writings and letters, and others' correspondence and reminiscences give suitable authenticity. No note numbers appear in the text, but documentation is included at the back. Despite the more liberated era he is writing in, Kaplan follows earlier biographers in having difficulties with Whitman's homosexuality; while suggesting that Whitman never had sex with another man, he assumes probable sexual relations with female prostitutes.

Traubel, Horace, *With Walt Whitman in Camden,* Vols. 1-6. New York: Rowman and Littlefield; Carbondale: Southern Illinois University Press, 1906-1982. This is not a biography in any formal sense. Rather, Whitman's friend, Traubel, has transcribed their conversations and letters Whitman received from correspondents famous and not. The opinions and reminiscences offered give first-hand impressions of the man (though some friends like John Burroughs thought the flavor of the wording sometimes showed more of Traubel than of Whitman).

Autobiographical Sources
All that Whitman published as legitimate autobiography were the fragmentary jottings about his experiences in *Memoranda During the War, Specimen Days,* and other assorted prose. Actually, the biographical (and some critical) material published under John Burroughs's and Richard M. Bucke's names in their respective books of 1867 and 1883 was written largely by Whitman himself and can thus serve as autobiographical writings. Early biographers took this material at face value, but the research of later scholars has moved beyond the idealized image to the more mundane facts.

Overview of Critical Sources
The critical books on Whitman range from vague eulogizing about his spiritual values to detailed focus on specific aspects of or approaches to his work. Early analyses like John Burroughs's *Whitman: A Study* (Boston: Houghton Mifflin, 1896) and John Addington Symonds's *Walt Whitman: A Study* (Lon-

don: John C. Nimmo, 1893) were intended as explications, breaking down their subject by theme, with only occasional forays into style and form. The latter aspects began to be dealt with extensively only in the second half of the twentieth century, except for valuable chapters in the perceptive overviews of Basil De Selincourt and John Bailey—*Walt Whitman: A Critical Study* (New York: Mitchell Kennerley, 1914) and *Walt Whitman* (New York: Macmillan, 1926).

A writer like Whitman whose work went through so many stages—both before and after publication—is bound to provoke numerous textual studies. These have taken the form of both analyses of the accretions and changes in *Leaves of Grass* (as in Asselineau's *The Evolution of Walt Whitman*) and discussions of particular editions. Ivan Marki's *The Trial of the Poet* (New York: Columbia University Press, 1976) reads the first edition closely to show the creation of the poet through the writing of the Preface and the poem later titled "Song of Myself," seeing the book as structured according to themes of recurrence and change. Fredson Bowers edited *Whitman's Manuscripts: Leaves of Grass (1860), A Parallel Text* (Chicago: University of Chicago Press, 1955) to compare the manuscript versions of poems new to the 1860 edition with their published versions. Roy Harvey Pearce edited *Leaves of Grass: Facsimile Edition of the 1860 Text* (Ithaca: Cornell University Press, 1961), analyzing it as the most unified edition, having a pervasive argument. Arthur Golden edited *Walt Whitman's Blue Book* (New York Public Library, 1968), printing in facsimile and analyzing the changes Whitman made in his copy of the 1860 edition as he prepared the 1867 edition.

The changes in wording and arrangement have been ignored by many critics, who concentrate on analyzing the final versions and arrangement Whitman approved—that of the 1881–1882 edition. E. Fred Carlisle in *The Uncertain Self: Whitman's Drama of Identity* (East Lansing: Michigan State University Press, 1973), for example, though intelligently examining Whitman's poetry as a dialogue between Self and Other, chooses not to consider the dynamic dialogue that must have transpired as Whitman moved from edition to edition. The changes are generally relevant to most thematic approaches to Whitman, from the psychoanalytic—Stephen A. Black's *Whitman's Journeys into Chaos* (Princeton, NJ: Princeton University Press, 1975)—to the Marxist—Newton Arvin's *Whitman* (New York: Macmillan, 1938), which examines Whitman's political thought to discover to what extent he can be considered a socialist poet. Richard Chase's *Walt Whitman Reconsidered* (New York: William Sloane, 1955) looks at Whitman from a range of approaches, while Howard J. Waskow's *Whitman: Explorations in Form* (University of Chicago Press, 1966) has a thesis—Whitman's vision of reality as "bipolar unity"—applied concretely in helpful analyses of Whitman's major poems.

Evaluation of Selected Criticism

Allen, Gay Wilson, *The New Walt Whitman Handbook*. New York: New York University Press, 1946, 1975. Besides discussing the evolution of *Leaves of*

Grass and Whitman's ideas and poetic techniques, Allen offers overviews of Whitman studies, including biography and foreign reception, with bibliographies.

————, *A Reader's Guide to Walt Whitman.* New York: Farrar, Straus & Giroux, 1970. This helpful basic introduction covers Whitman's "foreground," the various editions in conjunction with Whitman's life, his mysticism, and matters of form and structure. Major poems are explicated ("Song of Myself" only minimally).

Crawley, Thomas Edward, *The Structure of* Leaves of Grass. Austin: University of Texas Press, 1970. Crawley analyzes the 1881 edition as the organic unity Whitman finally intended, examining the various poem-clusters in their relation to the whole, noting especially a careful balance and intermingling of personal and national themes.

Hollis, C. Carroll, *Language and Style in* Leaves of Grass. Baton Rouge: Louisiana State University Press, 1983. Appropriately and effectively, Hollis applies recent speech-act theory to Whitman's poetry, revealing much that is fresh and insightful without undue stretching to fit a thesis. In completely understandable fashion, he explains how Whitman presents himself as speaker in relation to his audience.

Martin, Robert K. *The Homosexual Tradition in American Poetry.* Austin: University of Texas Press, 1979. Martin offers a welcome antidote to the many Whitman commentators who see his homosexuality as a problem. He discusses Whitman as the inaugurator of the modern homosexual consciousness through a close reading of "Song of Myself" and the whole "Calamus" sequence, and then traces Whitman's influence on later significant gay poets.

Miller, Edwin Haviland, *Walt Whitman's Poetry: A Psychological Journey.* Boston: Houghton Mifflin, 1968. Miller reveals insightful interconnections among Whitman's works and life experiences, opening up new levels of understanding beneath the surface, although the shortcomings and inconsistencies of Freudian theory and application are in ample, occasionally humorous evidence.

Miller, James E., Jr. *A Critical Guide to Leaves of Grass.* University of Chicago Press, 1957. Instead of biographical, psychoanalytic, sociopolitical, and textual analyses, Miller discusses the structure of Whitman's poetry, both in individual major poems (especially "Song of Myself") and in the book, as a whole made up of many parts. He sees the poems as dramatic structures, with Whitman's various poses being appropriate for the genre.

Other Sources
Calamus. Journal published in Japan (in English) largely devoted to Whitman criticism; not widely available.

Giantvalley, Scott and Donald D. Kummings, *Walt Whitman, 1838–1939* and *1940–1975: A Reference Guide.* Boston: G. K. Hall, 1981 and 1982. Extensively indexed, annotated bibliographies of writings about Whitman.

Hyde, Lewis, *The Gift: Imagination and the Erotic Life of Property.* New York: Vintage Books, 1983, pp. 160–215. Analyzes Whitman's life and poetry (especially "Song of Myself") as gift.

Katz, Jonathan, *Gay American History.* New York: Thomas Y. Crowell, 1976. Prints and discusses significant documents relating to Whitman's sexuality.

Matthiessen, F. O. *American Renaissance.* New York: Oxford University Press, 1941, pp. 517–625. Extensive analysis of Whitman's innovation in poetry.

Mickle Street Review. Journal of Whitman commentary and poetry dedicated to Whitman.

Miller, Edwin Haviland, ed. *A Century of Whitman Criticism.* Bloomington: Indiana University Press, 1969. Assorted critical pieces from early reviews to contemporary close reading.

Walt Whitman Quarterly Review. Quarterly journal of Whitman criticism and scholarship, with a bibliography of current criticism in each issue. Continues *Walt Whitman Review.*

Selected Dictionaries and Encyclopedias

American Authors, 1600–1900. A Biographical Dictionary of American Literature, H. W. Wilson, pp. 807–810. Biographical analysis.

Critical Survey of Poetry, Salem Press, 1983. Brief biography, with analysis of Whitman's poetry.

Scott Giantvalley
California State University,
Dominguez Hills

THORNTON WILDER
1897–1975

Author's Chronology

Born Thorton Niven Wilder, April 17, 1897, Madison, Wisconsin, the second son—survivor of a pair of twins—of Amos Parker Wilder, Editor of the Wisconsin State Journal, and Isabella Thornton Niven Wilder; *1906* family lives six months in Hong Kong while father is American consul general; *1906–1915* attends schools in Shanghai and Berkeley, California, where he graduates from high school; *1915* family settles permanently in New Haven, Connecticut and Thornton enrolls at Oberlin College; *1917* transfers to Yale and graduates in *1920* after eight months interruption to serve in Coast Artillery during World War I; *1920–1921* scholar at American Academy in Rome; *1921–1925* teaches elementary French at Lawrenceville School, New Jersey; *1926* publishes first novel, *The Cabala; 1927* receives first of three Pulitzer Prizes for his second novel, *The Bridge of San Luis Rey; 1930–1936* teaches half each year at University of Chicago; *1935* meets Gertrude Stein in Chicago; *1938* wins second Pulitzer Prize for play *Our Town; 1942* wins third Pulitzer Prize for play *The Skin of Our Teeth; 1942–1945* serves as officer in United States Army Air Force during World War II; *1963* awarded United States Presidential Medal of Freedom; *1964* musical comedy *Hello, Dolly!* based on his play *The Matchmaker; 1965* awarded the first National Medal of Literature by President Lyndon Johnson on May 4; *1968* wins National Book Award for *The Eighth Day; 1975* dies in New Haven, December 7.

Author's Bibliography (selected)

The Cabala, 1926 (novel); *The Bridge of San Luis Rey,* 1927 (novel); *The Woman of Andros,* 1930 (novel); *Heaven's My Destination,* 1935 (novel); *Our Town,* 1938 (play); *The Merchant of Yonkers,* 1939 (play, revised as *The Matchmaker,* 1957); *The Skin of Our Teeth,* 1942 (play), *The Ides of March,* 1948 (novel); *The Eighth Day,* 1967 (novel); *Theophilus North,* 1973 (novel); *The Alcestiad,* 1977 (play).

Overview of Biographical Sources

Wilder was one of the most reserved of American celebrities and did not encourage biographers. The year before his death Wilder told Richard Goldstone that he wished Goldstone would put a torch to his work in progress. Goldstone persisted, however, because he had agreed with Wilder's sister Isabel that recollections of her brother's life should be preserved. When Goldstone's account appeared at last in 1975 just before Wilder's death, however, the family was not pleased and elder brother Amos took the extraordinary step in 1980 of describing the book as "in many respects highly informative," but to a member of the family, "to be skewed, apart from a good number of factual errors, and the portrait to be partial." This biography, like other less comprehensive ones, has gone out of print, to be replaced in 1983 by Gilbert A. Harrison's *The Enthusiast,* which was apparently written with the co-operation of the family. Reviewers have found Harrison's book much more detailed than earlier ones, but superficial in its treatment of Wilder's works and personality and sentimental in style. Readers need to consult both Goldstone's and Harrison's books to arrive at balanced accounts of episodes in Wilder's life, though much about his motives and intentions still remains enigmatic.

Evaluation of Selected Biographies

Goldstone, Richard H. *Thornton Wilder: An Intimate Portrait.* New York: E. P. Dutton, 1975. The work of a sophisticated College of the City of New York professor, who had known Wilder since they began officer training together in World War II, Goldstone's book provides what may be described as the exemplary Modernist account of Wilder's career, which was out of the mainstream of the literary Establishment. The account of Wilder's early life is speculative and particularly displeased the family, which thought that such "a main study" should be "more congenial" to Wilder's "own kind of Americanism," which Goldstone often finds "old fashioned."

Harrison, Gilbert A. *The Enthusiast: A Life of Thornton Wilder.* Boston: Ticknor and Fields, 1983. A meticulously detailed account by an editor of *The New Republic,* Harrison's book, as the title suggests, stresses the affirmative aspects of Wilder's art and his energetic response to life. Reviewers have generally found, however, that the study seems shackled to this approbatory message, so that the complexity of Wilder's thought is inadequately reflected.

Simon, Linda, *Thornton Wilder: His World.* Garden City, NY: Doubleday, 1979. Simon's is a short, cautious account, strong on names and dates, that stresses Wilder's humility and love of humanity, and seeks to minimize what small controversy he aroused.

Autobiographical Sources

Wilder had little use for confessional writing and rarely wished to talk about himself. Various novels, especially the first (*The Cabala*) and the last (*Theophilus North*) have been said to be autobiographical by some critics because events in the life of the first-person narrators (the only two in his fiction) correspond with some in his own; but it is difficult to derive much knowledge of the author's inner life from these genteel narratives. Wilder's closest *alter ego* may have been the stage manager in *Our Town,* a role that the playwright enjoyed performing on Broadway and elsewhere, for some chroniclers have reported that he was at times "meddlesome."

Overview of Critical Sources

Wilder's work has not received the amount of criticism that his popularity and reputation warrant. The principal Modernist critics have tended to avoid his work as lacking in the sense of alienation and the denunciation of bourgeois Philistinism that has characterized the mainstream of twentieth-century fiction and drama. Critics have vacillated between overpublicized attacks on *The Woman of Andros* and *The Skin of Our Teeth* to religiously oriented affirmations of the life-affirming qualities in his writings. His work has generally been far better received abroad, especially in post-World War II West Germany, than in his native country.

Evaluations of Selected Criticism

Burbank, Rex, *Thornton Wilder*. 2nd ed. Boston: Twayne, 1978 (originally published 1961). This comprehensive appreciation of Wilder's work stresses his optimistic attitude toward the possibilities of a democratic culture that distinguished his work from the disillusioned and rebellious writings of his contemporaries, but acknowledges also that in building his works on moral, religious and metaphysical ideas, Wilder often produced novels and plays that lacked social and psychological complexity.

Goldstein, Malcolm, *The Art of Thornton Wilder*. Lincoln: University of Nebraska Press, 1965. An early study that despite its title concerns mostly Wilder's ideas rather than his innovative artistic techniques.

Haberman, Donald, *The Plays of Thornton Wilder*. Middletown, CT: Wesleyan University Press, 1967. The first major consideration limited to Wilder's theatrical work, including *The Alcestiad,* that stresses his relationship with other dramatists.

Papajewski, Helmut, *Thornton Wilder* (translated from the German by John Conway). New York: Frederick Ungar, 1968. A series of very close readings of the individual novels and plays, without a critical framework evaluating Wilder's achievement as a whole, this introduction of his work to an appreciative German audience is the work of a critic especially sensitive to Wilder's formal experiments.

Williams, Mary Ellen, *A Vast Landscape: Time in the Novels of Thornton Wilder*. Pocatello: Idaho State University Press, 1979. A pioneering effort to scrutinize all of Wilder's work in terms of a single recurrent theme results in a provocative theory that "a primary purpose of his art is to transcend linear, historical time—more than that, to deny the validity of the concept," which leads to "a mystical acceptance of an unknowable but eternal ordering principle" that subsumes apparently transitory human time in "cosmic, eternal time."

Other Sources

Wilder is unique among recent American writers in the powerful support that he has received from his family. Two books by his siblings are especially valuable to an understanding of his life and art as it is rooted in the cultural traditions of New England.

Wilder, Amos Niven, *Thornton Wilder and His Public*. Philadelphia: Fortress Press, 1980. An extraordinary defense of Wilder's art by his elder brother, a distinguished theological scholar at Harvard, which argues that contemporary critics in dismissing Wilder's work as smacking of "Middle America and even a disguised religiosity" lack an ability to understand important aspects of American culture and, therefore, of Wilder's work, concerns and audience.

Wilder, Isabel, *Mother and Four*. New York: Coward-McCann, 1933. An autobiographical novel based on the early lives of the two Wilder brothers and their two sisters that provides valuable insight into the struggle of a widowed mother to provide a proper, genteel American family life for her growing children during the early decades of this century.

Selected Dictionaries and Encyclopedias

Dictionary of Literary Biography, Vol. 9, 146–152, Gale Research, 1981. Biographer Richard Goldstone's short account of Wilder's life and all of his major works.

Great Writers of the English Language, St. Martin's Press, 1979. Complete bibliography, with a short biography and critical account of the themes of Wilder's novels and plays (also in *20th-Century American Literature,* St. Martin's Press, 1980).

Warren French
Indiana University-Purdue
University at Indianapolis

TENNESSEE WILLIAMS
1911–1983

Author's Chronology

Born Thomas Lanier Williams on March 26, 1911, in Columbus, Mississippi; experiences unhappy childhood plagued by illnesses; *1919* moves with family to St. Louis, Missouri; begins to write as a lifelong means of escape and recognition; *1927* publishes first work, an essay entitled "Can a Good Wife Be a Good Sport?" in *Smart Set* magazine; *1928* publishes first story; *1929–1930* attends University of Missouri; withdraws due to parental pressure to work as a warehouseman for the International Shoe Company, St. Louis; *1935* suffers first nervous breakdown; spends a year recuperating at the home of grandparents in Memphis, Tennessee; first play is produced by Memphis Garden Players; *1936* enrolls at Washington University, St. Louis; *1937–1938* attends University of Iowa and receives bachelor's degree; *1939* begins to publish under the name Tennessee Williams; wins Group Theatre prize for playwriting; *1940–1944* wanders as an itinerant writer from Florida, to Louisiana, to California, to Mexico, and to New York; *1945* achieves first major success with *The Glass Menagerie;* wins New York Drama Critics Circle Award; *1947* wins the Pulitzer Prize for *A Streetcar Named Desire; 1952* elected to National Institute of Arts and Letters; *1955* wins second Pulitzer Prize for *Cat on a Hot Tin Roof; 1963* enters period of severe depression; *1969* converts to Roman Catholicism; continues to travel extensively; maintains residences in New York City, New Orleans, and Key West, Florida; dies February 25, 1983 in New York City.

Author's Bibliography (selected)

"The Summer Belvedere" in *Five Young American Poets,* 1944 (poems); *Battle of Angels,* 1945 (play); *The Glass Menagerie,* 1945 (play); *A Streetcar Named Desire,* 1947 (play); *One Arm and Other Stories,* 1948; *Summer and Smoke,* 1948 (play); *The Roman Spring of Mrs. Stone,* 1950 (novel); *Hard Candy: A Book of Stories,* 1954; *Cat on a Hot Tin Roof,* 1955 (play); *In the Winter of Cities,* 1956 (poems); *Suddenly Last Summer,* 1958 (play); *Sweet Bird of Youth,* 1959 (play); *The Night of the Iguana,* 1961 (play); *The Knightly Quest and Other Stories,* 1966; *Eight Mortal Ladies Possessed,* 1974 (stories); *Moise and the World of Reason,* 1975 (novel); *Memoirs,* 1975 (autobiography); *Androgyne, Mon Amour,* 1977 (poems); *Where I Live,* 1978 (essays); *A Lovely Sunday for Creve Coeur,* 1980 (play).

Overview of Biographical Sources

Deeply concerned with his public reputation, Tennessee Williams presents an intriguing and complex subject for biographers. Beginning his career as a poet and short story writer, Williams increasingly became more dependent on his plays as a vehicle to express his unique understanding and compassion of the strength and fragility of the human spirit. America's most prolific playwright since Eugene O'Neill and a major figure in contemporary theatre, Williams is also recognized by the reading public as an artist with celebrity status. This is presumably ensured by his admitted homosexuality adding a distinct dimension to his position in literary history.

Establishing an accurate picture of Williams' life has long presented a difficult and controversial task for nonacademic readers and scholars. Erroneous biographical information, often introduced by Williams himself, has been repeated to the point of acceptance as fact. This propensity to sacrifice detail for effect is openly acknowledged by Williams as an effort to further elaborate the events of his life. Often Williams' biography is distorted by commentators finding biographical information in his literary work. This is further complicated by Williams' lifelong habit of rewriting and retitling his material.

Early biographical treatments indicate an increasing demand for information but offer an incomplete perspective of Williams' life and work, intertwining biographical material with production detail surrounding the plays. A brief but insightful treatment is Gerald Weales' *Tennessee Williams* (Minneapolis: University of Minnesota, 1965), a pamphlet-length study combining biographical data with literary and thematic influences in Williams' work. Capitalizing on friendship with Williams, several authors produced semi-biographical treatments designed for a popular rather than scholarly audience. This includes Gilbert Maxwell's *Tennessee Williams and Friends* (Cleveland: World, 1965), Mike Steen's *A Look at Tennessee Williams* (New York: Hawthorn, 1969) and Richard Leavitt's *The World of Tennessee Williams* (New York: G. P. Putnam's Sons, 1978). During his lifetime Williams refused to authorize a biography, so consequently, the "definitive" biography, one documented from the Williams collection at the Humanities Research Center of the University of Texas at Austin, is yet to appear.

Evaluation of Selected Biographies

Tischler, Nancy M. *Tennessee Williams: Rebellious Puritan.* New York: Citadel, 1961. A well written and unified critical biography attempting to provide an understanding of the interrelationship between Williams' life and work. Referring to Williams as a "romantic nonconformist," Tischler investigates not only the plays but also the stories, poems, and prose as an autobiographical reflection of the author. Although limited in its scope, this is considered the most effective early summary of Williams' life and continues as an important resource.

Williams, Dakin and Shepherd Mead, *Tennessee Williams: An Intimate Biography.* New York: Arbor House, 1983. Published shortly after Williams' death, this is a partially successful account of Williams' life coauthored by his brother

Dakin, and Mead, a literary contemporary of Williams. Although respectful of Williams' achievements, this volume suggests a pretentious quality and an apparent need to set-the-record-straight concerning the relationship between brothers. Of significance, however, is the intimate knowledge of family background offering insight into Williams' homosexuality, his obsession with illness and death, and his tortured relationship with his sister Rose. The critical consensus is that this is not the "definitive" biography on Williams.

Williams, Edwina Dakin, as told to Lucy Freeman, *Remember Me to Tom.* New York: G. P. Putnam's Sons, 1963. An uneven, self-indulgent attempt at autobiography by Williams' mother, but of interest as a biography of Williams. This provides significant access into Williams' troubled world, while providing clues to the characters and themes of his later writing. Also included are some of Williams' early poems, journal entries and letters.

Autobiographical Sources

Published in 1975, Williams' long awaited autobiography entitled *Memoirs* was greeted with disappointment by the majority of critical response. Loosely structured, alternating from the past to the present and back again, this is a portrait of the artist as celebrity, providing an illuminating backdrop to the composition and production of his plays, while teasing rather than enlightening his audience concerning his controversial sexuality. Similar to his literary efforts, *Memoirs* unfolds as a confessional, radiating a sensitivity while exposing hidden elements of Williams' artistic and personal development. Although an imperfect, anecdotal account of Williams' life, this represents an immensely readable work and an important piece to the Williams puzzle.

Although Williams' collected letters have yet to be published, an important sampling has been provided by Donald Windham, novelist, early acquaintance, and collaborator with Williams on an early play entitled *You Touched Me,* produced in 1945. *Tennessee Williams' Letters to Donald Windham* 1940–1965, (New York: Holt, Rinehart and Winston, 1977), edited by Windham, is a collection of 159 letters, mostly received during the 1940's and several letters representing the period 1950–1965 when the exchange and friendship ceased. The letters are highly readable, providing information concerning early friendships, liaisons, and influences in Williams' career.

Overview of Critical Sources

Because of his renowned stature in contemporary theatre, the majority of existing criticism focuses on Williams as playwright. Most critical accounts agree on Williams' contributions as a dramatist, primarily his poetic use of language, his exploration of the boundaries of stage production, and experimentation with sensitive subject material. Negatively, critics argue that Williams was repetitious and lacked serious development as a writer, while glorifying a depraved world of violence, decadence, and sexual perversion. Welcoming his early original talent as daring and innovative, giving objective form to highly subjective experiences, Williams fell from grace with many critics who deplored his preoccupation with sensationalism and questioned whether he had sacrificed his talent to popular success.

Although Williams' poetry, like his fiction, has always been peripheral to his plays, comprehensive critical studies are increasingly more perceptive in investigating the nondramatic literature for its lyric qualities in language as well as its systematic progression of theme and character. Of special significance to scholars, due primarily to Williams' importance in literary history, several authors have attempted to organize the Williams' canon of published and unpublished materials, including both the dramatic and nondramatic literature. This includes Delma E. Presley's "Tennessee Williams: Twenty-Five Years of Criticism," *Bulletin of Bibliography* 30 (January-March 1973), 21–29, Drewey Wayne Gunn's *Tennessee Williams: A Bibliography* (Metuchen, New Jersey: Scarecrow, 1980), and most recently, John S. McCann's *The Critical Reputation of Tennessee Williams: A Reference Guide* (Boston, Massachusetts: Hall, 1983).

Evaluation of Selected Criticism

Falk, Signi Lenea, *Tennessee Williams.* New York: Twayne, 1962. Recognizing Williams' early writing as a primary source for his later work and suggesting its importance as a record of personal experience, Falk devotes a section of this critical study to a discussion of the poems, stories, and short plays. Connecting Williams with the rich and varied literature of a Southern Renaissance movement emerging in the middle decades of the twentieth century, Falk explores Williams' "principal of atonement through violence" in his fiction, while linking several stories to future plays.

Jackson, Esther Merle, *The Broken World of Tennessee Williams.* Madison: University of Wisconsin, 1965. Although concentrating her efforts on Williams' plays, this is generally regarded as an important piece of criticism for its discussion of the existential nature of Williams' work. Jackson reveals Williams' major characters as possessing "anti-heroic" qualities such as the potential for moral and spiritual disintegration, responsibility for their own suffering, sense of guilt, and quest for identity.

Tharpe, Jac, ed. *Tennessee Williams: A Tribute.* Jackson: University of Mississippi, 1977. A massive collection of fifty-three essays providing a wide range of criticism and opinion on Williams' work in all genres. Although the quality of essays vary, this is the most significant critical volume to date concerning Williams, and five essays are devoted to the nondramatic prose and poetry. Of exceptional value are Ren Draya's essay "The Fiction of Tennessee Williams," demonstrating aspects of Williams' nondramatic work serving as a "drawing board" for themes and characters later amplified in drama, and John Ower's essay "Erotic Mythology in the Poetry of Tennessee Williams" emphasizing a Freudian influence in the use of myth and symbolism in Williams' poetry.

Other Sources

Bowles, Paul, *Without Stopping: An Autobiography.* New York: G. P. Putnam's Sons, 1972. Distinguished American author and intimate of Williams provides a colorful glimpse into a literary friendship spanning a forty year period.

Buckley, Tom, "Tennessee Williams Survives," in *Atlantic Monthly* 226 (November 1970) 98–108; Interview-commentary highlighting Williams' concern over his public reputation and defending his present position as a productive writer.

Carr, Virginia Spencer, *The Lonely Hunter: A Biography of Carson McCullers.* Garden City, New York: Doubleday, 1975. Considered by Williams as a major writer sharing an affinity with the literary Southern Renaissance, this volume sheds light on the intricate social and professional relationship between McCullers and Williams.

Vidal, Gore, "Selected Memories of the Glorious Bird and The Golden Age," in *The New York Review of Books,* February 5, 1976, 13–18. Responding to the publication of Williams' *Memoirs,* Vidal presents a vivid portrait of Williams. Noteworthy is the much quoted reference to Williams as a writer "who does not develop; he simply continues."

Selected Dictionaries and Encyclopedias

American Writers: A Collection of Literary Biographies, Charles Scribner's Sons, 1974. Concise overview of Williams' life and works, including an informative section analyzing the nondramatic literature.

Dictionary of Literary Biography: Documentary Series, Gale Research, 1984. Incorporates materials from all periods of Williams' career as a writer of plays as well as of poetry and fiction, this volume serves as an important addition to the body of literature on the personal and professional life of a major American writer.

Steven Serafin
Long Island University

WILLIAM CARLOS WILLIAMS
1883-1963

Author's Chronology

Born September 17, 1883, in Rutherford, New Jersey of Puerto Rican mother and English father; attends schools in Rutherford, and New York City, with two years in Geneva and Paris; *1902* enrolls in medical school at the University of Pennsylvania; meets Ezra Pound and H. D. and the artist Charles Demuth; *1909* publishes *Poems; 1910* begins medical practice in Rutherford, where he lives and works the rest of his life; *1912* marries Florence Herman; *1915-1932* periodically edits *Contact* and *Pagany* magazines, *1926* wins Dial award for *Paterson; 1948* suffers first heart attack, and first stroke in 1951 but continues to write; *1950* wins National Book Award; *1953* Bollingen Award; *1952-53* Consultant in Poetry at the Library of Congress; never assumed the post due to controversy over his left-wing politics; *1955* reading tour of country; *1963* at work on sixth book of his epic *Paterson* at time of his death in Rutherford on March 4; awarded Pulitzer Prize and Gold Medal for Poetry posthumously.

Author's Bibliography (selected)

Poems, 1909; *The Tempers,* 1913 (poems); *Al Que Quiere!,* 1917 (poems); *Spring and All,* 1923 (poems); *The Great American Novel,* 1923 (novel); *In the American Grain,* 1925 (essays); *Collected Poems,* 1934; *The Broken Span,* 1941 (poems); *Paterson,* 1946-1958; *Collected Later Poems,* 1950; *The Autobiography of William Carlos Williams,* 1951; *The Desert Music and Other Poems,* 1954; *Selected Letters,* 1957; *The Farmers' Daughters: The Collected Stories,* 1961; *Many Loves and Other Plays,* 1961; *Pictures from Brueghel,* 1962 (poems); *Paterson,* 1963 (epic poem).

Overview of Biographical Sources

Always on the leading edge of literary exploration, Williams has become for many post-war American poets the most significant writer of his age, but until 1971 there was no extensive biography. Such works as Jerome Mazzaro, *Profile of William Carlos Williams* (Columbus, OH: Charles Merrill, 1971), a collection of short biographical and critical commentaries, helped establish the direction of biographical studies. Mike Weavers's *William Carlos Williams: The American Background* (1971) was the first full-length biography, followed in 1975 by Reed Whittemore's *William Carlos Williams: Poet from Jersey*. Even these biographies fail to deal with the richness and complexity of Williams's life. The definitive work appeared in 1981, *William Carlos Williams: A New World Naked,* by Paul Mariani. Briefer biographical-critical works have appeared since then, notably the collection by Carroll F. Terrell, *William Carlos Williams: Man and Poet* (Orono, ME: National Poetry Foundation, 1983), and

Neil Baldwin's portrait-biography of a poet-doctor deeply ruled by his emotions, *To All Gentleness: William Carlos Williams, the Doctor Poet.* (New York: Atheneum, 1984).

Evaluation of Selected Biographies

Mariani, Paul, *William Carlos Williams: A New World Naked.* New York: McGraw-Hill, 1981. Mariani, who has compiled an annotated overview of the critical reception of Williams, has written the most thorough, accurate and sympathetic account. Extensively and carefully researched, Mariani's work places Williams as the single most important figure in American poetry in the twentieth century. It is a fascinating and gracefully written, though perhaps over-meticulous study, running to over 700 pages.

Weaver, Mike, *William Carlos Williams: The American Background.* Cambridge: Cambridge University Press, 1971. A valuable literary biography discussing both the literary and non-literary worlds that serve as background to Williams's work, it presents a sympathetic portrait of the man.

Whittemore, Reed, *William Carlos Williams: Poet from Jersey.* Boston: Houghton Mifflin, 1975. Whittemore, writing in the tone of one of Williams's own tough, sentimental speakers, vividly depicts the turbulently creative times of the early years of Williams's career, and the struggles with depression, illness and handicaps of his last years. Although his style can be engaging, his underlying ambivalence towards Williams and his achievement discolors the work.

Autobiographical Sources

The Autobiography of William Carlos Williams, published in 1951, is a colloquial, unpretentious and affectionate backward look at Williams's life, his family and friends and his concerns as both a doctor and a poet in Rutherford, the "small world of the patch of ground" that was so important to him. It is, as he calls it, a "thin narrative" of selected hours that constitute his "particular treasure." He divides his book into three parts: 1) his early years, education, and beginning involvement in poetry; 2) his years of combining medical practice and poetry; and 3) another retrospective glance at the Rutherford where he grew up, with an account of his later life and his last work, *Paterson.* The autobiography makes for pleasurable though somewhat unreliable reading, very much an edited account of his life, leaving out the painful aspects of much of his experience and substituting milder episodes as illustration of certain events or relationships.

In *I Wanted to Write a Poem,* with Edith Heal (Boston: Beacon Press, 1958), Williams talks informally about the genesis of some of his poems. *Interviews with William Carlos Williams: Speaking Straight Ahead,* ed. Linda Welshimer Wagner (New York: New Directions, 1976), collects conversations and interviews, in addition to memoirs about him.

His letters, largely uncollected, and housed mainly in the libraries of the State University of New York at Buffalo, Yale University, and the University of Texas at Austin, show a more multidimensional man than does his autobiography. A selection of his letters appeared in 1957—*The Selected Letters of William Carlos Williams,* ed. J. Thirlwall (New York: McDowell, Obolensky, 1957); a complete edition is needed. Williams's memoir of his mother, *Yes, Mrs. Williams* (New York: McDowell, 1959), completes the autobiographical material.

Overview of Critical Sources

Until the last decade of his life, Williams felt inordinately neglected by the critics and the reading public. Indeed, until the 1970's, there was no real critical overview of his *oeuvre.* Now, criticism of his poetry is flourishing, with much recent scholarship focused on the relationship between his writing and his sense of place, and between his poetry—and his ideas of poetry—and the work of modernist painters. There is a serious lack of criticism devoted to his drama, fiction and essays, and to his sense of American history.

Evaluation of Selected Criticism

Breslin, James, *William Carlos Williams: An American Artist.* New York: Oxford University Press, 1970. An excellent overview of both the unity and range of Williams's writing, Breslin focuses his study on the relationship between Whitman and Williams. He concentrates on *Paterson,* the stories, and selected lyric poems, weaving biography into his criticism, and emphasizing the early poetry as the best.

Guimond, James, *The Art of William Carlos Williams: A Discovery and Possession of America.* Urbana: University of Illinois Press, 1968. Solid, competently researched, this study reviews Williams's entire opus as it seeks to explore the relationship of the poet to his immediate environment.

Ostrom, Alan, *The Poetic World of William Carlos Williams.* Carbondale: Southern Illinois University Press, 1966. Ostrom discusses Williams's Americanism in relation to language as well as to his sense of place. He quotes important poems, making the book an introduction to Williams as well as a commentary on his verse. As a whole, it lacks clear direction, but is useful in its close readings of different poems.

Miller, J. Hillis, ed. *William Carlos Williams: A Collection of Critical Essays.* Englewood Cliffs, NJ: Prentice-Hall, 1966. This seminal collection forms a brief history of critical opinion about Williams's work, moving from early essays by fellow poets Ezra Pound, Marianne Moore and Wallace Stevens, through a group of such critics as Hugh Kenner, Sister M. Bernetta Quinn and

Roy Harvey Pearce, concluding with essays by a younger generation of poets. Taken together, the collection testifies to the eminence of Williams as a poet.

Wagner, Linda Welshimer, *The Poems of William Carlos Williams: A Critical Study.* Middletown, CT: Wesleyan University Press, 1963. This work discusses Williams's theories in relation to his poetry, particularly his concept of the local. Concentrating on technical aspects of his poetry, it is a generally reliable, good general introduction.

Other Sources

Coles, Robert, *William Carlos Williams: The Knack of Survival in America.* New Brunswick, NJ: Rutgers University Press, 1975. A clear, intelligent book that treats Williams's stories and novels as examinations of his fascination with America.

Conarroe, Joel, *William Carlos Williams's Paterson: Language and Landscape.* Philadelphia: University of Pennsylvania Press, 1970. An unweaving of the central themes of the poem, Conarroe's approach is two-dimensional but useful.

Dijkstra, Bram, *The Hieroglyphics of a New Speech: Cubism, Stieglitz, and the Early Poetry of William Carlos Williams.* Princeton: Princeton University Press, 1969. One of the first serious examinations of the influence of modern art on Williams's poetry.

Mazzaro, Jerome, ed. *Profile of William Carlos Williams.* Columbus, OH: Charles Merrill, 1971. A chronological collection of essays including helpful readings of *Paterson* by Sister Bernetta Quinn.

Mazzaro, Jerome, *William Carlos Williams: The Later Poems.* Ithaca: Cornell University Press, 1973. A study of the poetics of Williams's last works, occasionally brilliant but written in a difficult style.

Wallace, Emily Mitchell, *A Bibliography of William Carlos Williams.* Middletown, CT: Wesleyan University Press, 1968. The authoritative bibliography.

Whitaker, Thomas R. *William Carlos Williams.* Twayne, 1968. A tightly focused and illuminating introduction examining Williams's major concerns in his poetry and prose.

Selected Dictionaries and Encyclopedias

Critical Survey of Poetry, Salem Press, 1982. A brief biography and concise analysis of Williams's major poetry, especially the early work, *Paterson,* and the late poems.

Nancy W. Prothro
United States Naval Academy

SIR ANGUS WILSON
1913

Author's Chronology

Born August 11, 1913, Bexhill, England, the youngest by thirteen years of six sons; *1921-1924* visits South Africa with parents; *1927* enters Westminster School; *1929* mother dies; *1932* enters Merton College, Oxford; *1935* B.A. in medieval history; *1936* begins work at British Museum, Department of Printed Books; *1938* father dies; *1942-1946* intelligence officer, Foreign Office; *1946* returns to British Museum and begins writing short stories while recovering from nervous condition; "Mother's Sense of Fun" published in *Horizon* (November 1947); *1951* studies notebooks of Émile Zola for commissioned biography; *1955* resigns as deputy superintendent of British Museum Reading Room to devote full time to writing, moves with Tony Garrett to cottage in Bradfield St. George, Suffolk; *1959* receives James Tait Black Memorial Prize for *The Middle Age of Mrs. Eliot; 1960* Bergen Lecture at Yale, Ewing Lectures at U.C.L.A.; *1961* Northcliffe Lectures, University of London, visits South Africa again; *1962-1963* Sir Leslie Stephens Lectures at Cambridge University; *1963-1978* Lecturer, then Professor, at new University of East Anglia; *1968* Commander, Order of the British Empire; *1971-1974* chairman of National Book League; *1977, 1979* honorary degrees from Universities of Leicester, Liverpool, East Anglia; *1980* knighted by Queen Elizabeth II.

Author's Bibliography (selected)

The Wrong Set, 1949 (short stories); *Such Darling Dodos*, 1950 (short stories) *Émile Zola*, 1952 (biography); *Hemlock and After*, 1952 (novel); *Anglo-Saxon Attitudes*, 1955 (novel); *The Wild Garden; or, Speaking of Writing*, 1963 (criticism); *No Laughing Matter*, 1967 (novel); *The World of Charles Dickens*, 1970 (biography); *As If by Magic*, 1973 (novel); *The Strange Ride of Rudyard Kipling*, 1977 (biography); *Setting the World on Fire*, 1980 (novel).

Overview and Evaluation of Biographical Sources

No book-length biography of Angus Wilson as yet exists. The introductory chapter in Jay L. Halio's *Angus Wilson* (Edinburgh: Oliver and Boyd, 1964), updated in *The Dictionary of Literary Biography: British Novelists, 1930-1959*, ed. Bernard Oldsey (Detroit: Gale, 1983), vol. 15, pp. 591-614, gives a good overview of Wilson's life. Both sources discuss Wilson's early years and his development as a writer; the *The Dictionary of Literary Biography* article provides particular information, based upon a personal interview, of Wilson's childhood. Jonathan Raban's profile in *The New Review*, I, #1 (April 1974), 16-24, contains additional information, especially about Wilson's career as a university professor. *Twentieth Century Literature*, XXIX, #2 (Summer 1983), a special "Angus Wilson Issue," contains several memoirs and personal reminiscences by Wilson's friends and colleagues, among them D. P. Walker (Wilson's oldest friend), Nicholas Brooke (a professor at East Anglia University), and Peter Conradi (a former student). A number of fellow novelists, such as Patrick White, James Purdy, and Nadine Gordimer, also contribute. Largely anecdotal, these short essays give insights into various aspects of Wilson's personality, such as his sense of humor and his tolerance of others. In the same issue, Averil Gardner writes on "The Early Years of Angus Wilson" and F. S. Schwarzbach on "A Portrait of the Artist as Householder," describing Wilson's cottage in Suffolk and his style of living.

Autobiographical Sources

Wilson has written several autobiographical pieces and has been characteristically generous in giving personal interviews, many of them published. *The Wild Garden,* which derives from his Ewing Lectures at U.C.L.A., is a detailed discussion of the experiences and influences that have affected his writing. A very personal and probing self-analysis, somewhat Freudian but free of jargon, it relates the pattern of his life to the themes of his work. "Bexhill and After" (*Spectator,* May 9, 1958) describes his childhood and early schooling at Seaford, where one of his brothers was headmaster, and then his life as a day boy at the Westminster School. His essay in *My Oxford* (ed. Ann Thwaite, 1977) gives a good account of his undergraduate years and the friends and interests he developed there. Among the many interviews that relate his experiences and ideas to his personal views on literature, ethics, politics, religion, etc., are those with Michael Millgate in *Writers at Work* (ed. Malcolm Cowley, 1959), F. P. W. McDowell in *Iowa Review,* III (Fall 1972), Jack Biles in *Critical Essays on Angus Wilson* (ed. Jay L. Halio, 1985), Betsy Draine in *Contemporary Literature,* XXI, #1 (1980), and C. W. E. Bigsby, *The Literary Review,* #28 (1980). In these interviews Wilson frequently refers to other writers and their work, usually very generously, as in his strong endorsement of William Golding's experiments in fiction. His views may also be found in *Diversity and Depth in Fiction: Selected Critical Writings of Angus Wilson* (ed. Kerry McSweeney, 1983).

Overview of Critical Sources

Most critics regard Wilson primarily as a novelist, as he does himself, although he first attracted attention as a short story writer and his stature as a literary critic has steadily increased. Critical essays on his fiction often focus on Wilson's humanism, comparing or contrasting it with E. M. Forster's. First viewed as a neo-traditionalist who upheld the virtues of the great nineteenth century novelists, like Dickens and Dostoevski, he has since been recognized more accurately as attempting to combine or consolidate the psychological probings of twentieth-century experimentalists with the social concerns of earlier writers. His own experiments in fiction are most evident in his later novels, but the seeds were planted in some of his earliest fiction, as critics have begun to recognize. His ear for dialogue and his mimicry have long been admired together with his moral earnestness, satire, and wit.

Evaluation of Selected Criticism

Faulkner, Peter, *Angus Wilson: Mimic and Moralist.* London: Secker and Warburg, 1980. The most comprehensive critical study of Wilson's work up to but not including *Setting the World on Fire.* Faulkner relates Wilson's criticism to his fiction, showing how his preoccupations with the theory of the novel are closely involved with his own practice, and includes assessments by other critics to demonstrate the growth of Wilson's reputation.

Halio, Jay L. *Angus Wilson.* Edinburgh: Oliver and Boyd, 1964. This, the first full length study of Wilson, treats both his short and long fiction, plays for the theater and television, and early criticism.

————. ed. *Critical Essays on Angus Wilson.* Boston: G. K. Hall, 1985. This volume contains an extended introduction by the editor, a selection of reviews of Wilson's early fiction, three interviews, and fourteen critical essays, including three not previously published. They support Wilson's position as a major novelist and give a fair assessment of his contributions to intellectual history and the novel as art.

Wogatzky, Karin, *Angus Wilson: "Hemlock and After." A Study in Ambiguity.* Berne: Francke Verlag, 1971. Wogatzky's monograph treats Wilson's first novel in great detail, focusing on such topics as Bernard Sands's humanism, the allusion to Socrates, and the novel's structure. It is the only book-length study of a single work by Wilson yet to appear.

Other Sources

Bradbury, Malcolm, "The Fiction of Pastiche: The Comic Mode of Angus Wilson," in *Possibilities: Essays on the State of the Novel.* London: Oxford University Press, 1973. Mainly on *No Laughing Matter,* the essay carefully explores Wilson's techniques.

Cox, C. B. "Angus Wilson: Studies in Depression," in *The Free Spirit: A Study of the Liberal Humanism in the Novels of George Eliot, Henry James, E. M. Forster, Virginia Woolf, and Angus Wilson.* London: Oxford University Press, 1963. A detailed discussion of Wilson's humanism as expressed in his fiction and as it relates to the humanism of other writers.

Gindin, James, "Angus Wilson," in *The Harvest of a Quiet Eye.* Bloomington: University of Indiana Press, 1971. Gindin links Wilson to nineteenth century writers like Hardy and James and to twentieth-century writers like Lawrence, Cary, and Bellow and regards him more as an ironist than a satirist.

Mander, John, "The Short Stories of Angus Wilson," in *The Writer and Commitment.* Philadelphia: Dufour, 1962. A detailed examination of Wilson's short fiction, which Manders finds "ahistorical" but psychologically interesting and significant.

McSweeney, Kerry, "Angus Wilson: Diversity, Depth, and Obsessive Energy," in *Four Contemporary Novelists.* Kingston and Montreal: McGill-Queen's University Press, 1983. Examines the interrelationship of Wilson's "social, moral, and expressive concerns" in each of the novels and their major technical devices.

Rabinovitz, Rubin, "Angus Wilson," in *The Reaction against Experiment in the English Novel, 1950–60.* New York: Columbia University Press, 1967. Rabinovitz associates Wilson with others like C. P. Snow and Kingsley Amis who have tried to restore traditional modes to twentieth-century fiction, a position subsequent critics have disputed.

Selected Dictionaries and Encyclopedias

Critical Survey of Long Fiction, Salem Press, 1983. Brief biographical sketch and analyses of Wilson's major fiction.

Contemporary Novelists, 3rd ed. St. Martin's Press, 1982. Outlines Wilson's career and analyzes Wilson's novels. Contains a 750-word statement by Wilson on his work.

Jay L. Halio
University of Delaware

THOMAS WOLFE
1900–1938

Author's Chronology

Born October 3, 1900, in Asheville, North Carolina of German-English-Scotch ancestry; *1906* his mother buys and runs a boarding house but his father remains a stone cutter; *1912* enters North State Fitting School; *1916–1920* attends the University of North Carolina and writes for newspaper and Carolina Playmakers; *1920–1923* studies playwriting at Harvard and earns M.A. degree; *1923 Welcome to Our City* produced at Harvard; *1924* begins teaching at New York University, makes first of seven European trips, rewrites *Mannerhouse,* and meets Aline Bernstein, who later becomes his mistress; *1926* playwriting hopes end, starts *Look Homeward, Angel; 1929* meets and works with Maxwell Perkins; *Look Homeward, Angel* published by Scribner's; *1930* wins Guggenheim Fellowship, argues with Aline; *1931* moves to Brooklyn; *1932* ends affair with Aline; *1934* Elizabeth Nowell becomes his literary agent; *1935 Of Time and the River* comes out; *1936* warns of Nazi power; *1937* visits Asheville, breaks with Scribner's, signs with Harper & Brothers; *1938* lectures at Purdue, tours western parks, falls ill in Vancouver, dies in Baltimore, and is buried in Asheville.

Author's Bibliography (selected)

Look Homeward, Angel, 1929 (novel); *Of Time and the River,* 1935 (novel); *From Death to Morning,* 1935 (stories and sketches); *The Story of a Novel,* 1936 (autobiography); *The Web and the Rock,* 1939 (novel); *The Face of a Nation: Poetical Passages from the Writing of Thomas Wolfe,* 1939; *You Can't Go Home Again,* 1940 (novel); *The Hills Beyond,* 1941 (stories and fragment of a novel); *A Stone, A Leaf, A Door: Poems by Thomas Wolfe,* 1945; *Mannerhouse,* 1948 (drama); *A Western Journal,* 1951 (travel writing); *The Correspondence of Thomas Wolfe and Homer Andrew Watt,* 1954; *The Letters of Thomas Wolfe,* 1956; *The Letters of Thomas Wolfe to His Mother,* 1968; *The Notebooks of Thomas Wolfe,* 1970; *Welcome to Our City,* 1983 (drama); *Beyond Love and Loyalty: The Letters of Thomas Wolfe to Elizabeth Nowell,* 1983; *My Other Loneliness: The Letters of Thomas Wolfe and Aline Bernstein,* 1983.

Overview of Biographical Sources

Despite an extraordinarily heavy autobiographical element in Wolfe's work, numerous biographies and memoirs (eighteen) have been written, and Pulitzer Prize winning historian David Donald is nearing completion of what will doubtless become the definitive biography, replacing the still readable, reliable biographies of Elizabeth Nowell and Andrew Turnbull. Since other biographies or memoirs treat specific periods of Wolfe's development, they should not be overlooked: Hayden Norwood's *The Marble Man's Wife: Thomas Wolfe's Mother* (New York: Charles Scribner's Sons, 1947); Mabel Wolfe Wheaton's and LeGette Blythe's *Thomas Wolfe and His Family* (Garden City, NY: Doubleday, 1961); Richard Walser's *Thomas Wolfe Undergraduate* (1977); Scott Berg's *Max Perkins: Editor of Genius* (New York: E. P. Dutton, 1978); Carole Klein's *Aline* (New York: Harper & Row, 1979). Turnbull's account and Berg's treatment of Wolfe's relations with Perkins reveal the importance of Perkins in Wolfe's personal and creative life, and Klein's exploration of Wolfe's liaison with Aline Bernstein highlights the joys and sorrows of their relationship. No significant discrepancies exist among the various biographies, though Wolfe comes off as caddish in Klein and Berg. The primary biographical sources are Wolfe's notebooks, letters, and novels and memoirs by his family, teaching associates, editors, and fellow novelists.

Evaluation of Selected Biographies

Nowell, Elizabeth, *Thomas Wolfe: A Biography*. Garden City, NY: Doubleday, 1960. Drawing skillfully upon her work as Wolfe's literary agent and editor of his letters, Nowell gives a balanced account of Wolfe's life and writings. She avoids jargon and steers clear of literary or psychological analysis but depends too heavily on autobiographical passages and letters for her largely sympathetic portrait.

Turnbull, Andrew, *Thomas Wolfe*. New York: Charles Scribner's Sons, 1967. An experienced biographer (author of *Scott Fitzgerald*) and trained literary critic, Turnbull focuses on Aline Bernstein and Maxwell Perkins as the central forces in Wolfe's career. Turnbull's book provides a traditional bio-critical approach but shuns the dreary piling up of facts found in the biographies of some of Wolfe's contemporaries.

Walser, Richard, *Thomas Wolfe Undergraduate*. Durham, NC: Duke University Press, 1977. Walser's brief, well-written book ably sets forth Wolfe's role as student, campus leader, and aspiring writer and shows clearly that the collegiate experiences and attitudes of Wolfe's surrogates, Eugene Gant and George Webber, cannot be blindly accepted as Wolfe's.

Autobiographical Sources

Upon deciding to forsake playwriting for fiction, Wolfe wrote an autobiographical outline, as yet unpublished, and used it as a way of starting *Look Homeward, Angel*, the first of his four autobiographical novels. Besides the outline, Wolfe left behind numerous pocket notebooks, portions of which have been published, a manuscript of experimental writing called "A Passage to England," still unpublished, and many sketches and stories left out of the posthumously issued novels. Hundreds of letters, most of them in print, and scores of cablegrams and postal cards, soon to be published, offer yet one more lode for biographers and critics. Almost an embarrassment of riches, these sources both help and hinder the reading of Wolfe's creative works, leading some readers to consider his novels as *romans à clef,* a good example being Floyd Watkins' *Thomas Wolfe's Characters* (Norman: University of Oklahoma Press, 1957). Like Coleridge and Joyce, his favorite authors, Wolfe sought to understand himself and humanity by knowing the surface and the depths of an absorbing and self-examining center of consciousness, believing with Matthew Arnold that the truest self is the buried one. It is a mistake, therefore, to count upon the novels as dependable autobiography, for Wolfe sometimes borrowed from the surface of other people's lives or invented episodes.

Overview of Critical Sources

Wolfe's critics have sought to understand his Southern Appalachia background, his study of Hegelian philosophy as an undergraduate, his efforts to become a playwright, his discovery of Joyce's fiction, his affair with an older woman, Aline Bernstein, his indebtedness to his editors in the shaping of his novels, his shift from a romantic aesthete, Eugene Gant, to a socially aware and concerned artist, George Webber, his hope of becoming a singer and mythic spokesman for America, and his wide range of styles, among them the lyrical, oratorical, satiric, dramatic, and epic. These concerns have led to more than a dozen book-length studies and a few pamphlets. Several critical books remain in print, including the cornerstone of Wolfe studies, Richard S. Kennedy's.

Evaluation of Selected Criticism

Gurko, Leo, *Thomas Wolfe: Beyond the Romantic Ego.* New York: Thomas Y. Crowell, 1975. Conceding Wolfe's failure to construct the well-made novel, Gurko finds success on several fronts: his mastery of a good many styles, his honesty about his purpose and limits, his capacity for growth both as a man and artist.

Holman, C. Hugh, *The Loneliness at the Core: Studies in Thomas Wolfe.* Baton Rouge: Louisiana State University Press, 1975. Capping a distinguished career as a Wolfe scholar, this collection of essential essays explores Wolfe's relation to the South and to Europe, comments on such themes as loneliness, hope, and despair, argues that Wolfe was at his best in the short novel, and expands wisely and insightfully upon Herbert J. Muller's thesis that Wolfe's grandest achievement lay in his celebration of America. Missing from this collection is Holman's pamphlet on Wolfe for Minnesota series on American writers, #6, 1960.

Johnson, Pamela Hansford, *The Art of Thomas Wolfe* (originally entitled *Hungry Gulliver*). New York: Charles Scribner's Sons, 1948, 1963. An early appreciation by the English novelist, this study examines Wolfe's style, philosophy, the buried life, and his four novels.

Kennedy, Richard S. *The Window of Memory: The Literary Career of Thomas Wolfe.* Chapel Hill: University of North Carolina Press, 1962. Kennedy closely follows the creation of each of Wolfe's works, identifying themes, tracing stages of development, and showing, wherever necessary, the role Wolfe's editors had in the form Wolfe's novels finally took.

Muller, Herbert J, *Thomas Wolfe,* Norfolk, CT: New Directions Book, 1947. A pioneering evaluation and still one of the best, this short book places Wolfe within the tradition of American literature, linking him with Whitman, Melville, and Emerson, and explains Wolfe's interest in myth and legend.

Rubin, Louis D., Jr. *Thomas Wolfe: The Weather of His Youth.* Baton Rouge: Louisiana State University Press, 1955. Rubin shows why Wolfe found autobiographical fiction a congenial form and reveals how a provincial Southern author dealt with his hometown and its people and how he reacted when he encountered the desired but alien culture of Boston and New York.

Other Sources
Evans, Elizabeth, *Thomas Wolfe.* New York: Frederick Ungar, 1984. Introduction to Wolfe's artistry and thought with good primary and secondary bibliographies.

Johnston, Carol, *Thomas Wolfe: A Descriptive Bibliography.* Pittsburgh: University of Pittsburgh Bibliography Series. Forthcoming. Will supersede all forerunners.

McElderry, Bruce E. *Thomas Wolfe:* New Haven, CT: College & University Press, 1964. A valuable brief assessment with annotated bibliography.

Phillipson, John S. *Thomas Wolfe: A Reference Guide.* Boston: G. K. Hall, 1977. Solid, dependable annotated bibliography of books and articles. Updated (to 1981) in *Resources for American Literary Study,* 11 (Spring 1981), 37–80.

Walser, Richard, *Thomas Wolfe: An Introduction and Interpretation.* New York: Barnes and Noble, 1961. A sound, crisp overview.

Selected Dictionaries and Encyclopedias
Critical Survey of Long Fiction, Vol. 7, Salem Press, 1983. Good, short analysis of the four novels and their relation to Wolfe's life.

Dictionary of Literary Biography. Gale Research, 1981, Volume 9, Part 3. Concise survey of Wolfe's life and work with selective bibliography.

John L. Idol, Jr.
Clemson University

MARY WOLLSTONECRAFT
1759–1797

Author's Chronology

Born of Edward John and Elizabeth Dickson Wollstonecraft, April 27, 1759, the second of six children; *1774* family moves to Hoxton; Mary meets Mr. and Mrs. Clare; *1775* meets intimate friend Fanny Blood; *1778* takes position as paid companion to Mrs. Dawson in Bath; *1780* nurses at mother's deathbed; *1782* lives with, and helps Fanny manage Blood family; *1784* helps sister Eliza separate from her husband; starts a day school for girls in Newington Green; *1785* nurses Fanny Blood in Lisbon, who dies in childbirth; *1786* closes day school because of debts to serve as governess in Ireland for Lord Kingsborough; publication of *Thoughts on the Education of Daughters; 1787* settles in London as writer for Joseph Johnson's *The Analytical Review; 1788* publishes *Mary, a Fiction, Original Stories from Real Life,* and other works; *1789 A Female Reader; 1790* publishes anonymously *A Vindication of the Rights of Men; 1792 A Vindication of the Rights of Woman; 1793* leaves for Paris, resigning a hopeless passion for artist Fuseli; *1793* falls in love with American businessman Gilbert Imlay in Paris; *1794* bears a daughter, Fanny, to Imlay out of wedlock; *1795* travels to Scandinavia from London as business representative of Imlay; attempts suicide twice over Imlay's inconstancy; *1797* publishes *Letters Written during a Short Residence in Sweden, Norway and Denmark,* and becomes intimate with William Godwin; *1797* marries Godwin; bears a daughter, Mary Wollstonecraft Godwin, on August 30: dies September 10 of septacaemia, infection incurred in an attempt to remove a retained placenta.

Author's Bibliography

Thoughts on the Education of Daughters: With Reflections on Female Conduct in the More Important Duties of Life, 1787 (essay); *Mary, a Fiction,* 1788 (short fiction); *The Female Reader: Or, Miscellaneous Pieces, in Prose and Verse: Selected From the Best Writers, and Disposed Under Proper Heads: For the Improvement of Young Women,* 1789 (a reader); *A Vindication of the Rights of Men, in a Letter to the Right Honourable Edmund Burke,* 1790 (political essay); *A Vindication of the Rights of Woman with Strictures on Political and Moral Subjects,* 1792 (political essay); *An Historical and Moral View of the Origin and Progress of the French Revolution; and the Effect it has Produced in Europe,* 1794 (political essay); *Letters Written during a Short Residence in Sweden, Norway, and Denmark,* 1796 (travel journal); *Posthumous Works of the Author of a Vindication of the Rights of Woman,* 1798 (includes the unfinished novel, *Maria, or The Wrongs of Woman*); various articles in *The Analytical Review.*

Overview of Biographical Sources

Four biographies written since 1950, each with original research, represent the sound state of biographical scholarship. Most recently, Claire Tomalin's *The Life and Death of Mary Wollstonecraft* (1974) presents a wealth of background detail for a sense of the author's times. Eleanor Flexner's *Mary Wollstonecraft: A Biography* (1972) includes letters to William Roscoe never before published, as well as documents related to Mary's father's inheritance, and a possible early love affair. Ellen Sustein's *A Different Face,* while more sympathetic towards its subject, is a less reliable source of information. Ralph Wardle's *Mary Wollstonecraft, A Critical Biography* (1951), provides the methodological base for these other more interpretive but interesting biographies. Wardle draws from a personal inspection of the Lord Abinger collection of Wollstonecraft's letters. Before Wardle, the collection had been inspected for scholarly purposes only by C. Kegan Paul, a biographer of Wollstonecraft's husband, William Godwin. Wardle has also inspected letters from Wollstonecraft to Amelia Opie and Mary Hays.

Several idiosyncratic biographies enliven the options available. Margaret George's very interesting *One Woman's "Situation": A Study of Mary Wollstonecraft* (Urbana: University of Illinois Press, 1970) presents a Marxist-Feminist analysis of Wollstonecraft's response to her social position. At the opposite extreme is Ferdinand Lundberg and Marynia Farnham's *Modern Woman, the Lost Sex* (New York: Harper and Brothers, 1947), an anti-feminist psychoanalytic discussion of Wollstonecraft's "penis-envy." Fictionalizations include *This Shining Woman* by George R. Preedy, pseud. Gabrielle Long (London: Collins, 1937) and *A Most Extraordinary Pair: Mary Wollstonecraft and William Godwin* by Jean Detre (New York: Doubleday, 1975), which includes selected letters transcribed from the Abinger collection.

William Godwin, Wollstonecraft's husband and noted philosopher, published *Memoirs of the Author of A Vindication of the Rights of Woman* (London: Joseph Johnson, 1778) shortly after her death. The account of their relationship is most authoritative; however, Godwin did not interview Wollstonecraft's sisters for details of her life before they met. Wollstonecraft's acquaintance with leading intellectuals of England in the 1790's and her daughters' association with Percy Bysshe Shelley also provide sources of biographical information.

Early biographical accounts include Elizabeth Pennell, *Life of Mary Wollstonecraft* (London: W. H. Allen, 1885) and C. Kegan Paul, *Letters to Imlay with a Prefatory Memoir* (London: C. Kegan Paul, 1879). Madeline Linford, in her brief biography, *Mary Wollstonecraft* (London: Leonard Parsons, 1924) states Wollstonecraft's significance to the feminist movement.

Evaluation of Selected Biographies

Flexner, Eleanor, *Mary Wollstonecraft: A Biography.* New York: Conard, McCann and Geoghegan, 1972. Seeing Wollstonecraft not as a philosopher but as an analyst of the realities of her own life, Flexner studies the irrational elements of her personality, noting her piety and her insensitivity to other women.

Tomalin, Claire, *The Life and Death of Mary Wollstonecraft.* New York: Harcourt Brace Jovanovich, 1974. Tomalin brings the darker colorations of Wollstonecraft's psychology to the fore, especially her moodiness and sensitivity to slights from her lovers. She criticizes Wollstonecraft's aid to her sister in escaping her marriage, presenting a different analysis of the events than Flexner (see below). She stresses the conflicts in Wollstonecraft's marriage with Godwin; however, the charm and warmth of the letters between them undercut Tomalin's argument.

Wardle, Ralph, *Wollstonecraft: A Critical Biography.* Lincoln: University of Nebraska Press, 1951. Wardle presents a factual description of Wollstonecraft's life and the growth of her intellectual convictions. He provides a philosophical context for the ideas expressed in Wollstonecraft's two most famous political pieces, and discusses the social standing and education of women in Wollstonecraft's time. Wardle's is an intelligent historical/critical assessment of the essays and fiction.

Autobiographical Sources

Autobiographical materials are plentiful and include the two novels, which are read as autobiographical by some scholars. Ralph Wardle's edition of the *Collected Letters of Mary Wollstonecraft* (Ithaca, NY: Cornell University Press, 1979) stands as the most recent and authoritative source of autobiographical material. His edition of *Godwin and Mary: Letters of William Godwin and Mary Wollstonecraft* (Lincoln: University of Nebraska Press, 1966) and Carol H. Poston's edition of *Letters Written During a Short Residence in Sweden, Norway, and Denmark* (Lincoln: University of Nebraska Press, 1976) are accessible volumes of selected letters. Benjamin P. Kurtz and Carrie C. Autrey have edited *Four New Letters of Mary Wollstonecraft and Helen Maria Williams* (Berkeley: University of California Press, 1937). William Godwin collected the *Posthumous Works of the Author of the Vindication of the Rights of Woman* (London: Joseph Johnson, 1798), which contains letters of Mary Wollstonecraft to Gilbert Imlay and several others. W. Clark Durant includes letters in his preface and supplement to *Memoirs of Mary Wollstonecraft by William Godwin* (London: Constable, 1927).

Overview of Critical Sources

Because of her political essay, *A Vindication of the Rights of Woman,* Wollstonecraft is recognized as the mother of feminism. This work, or excerpts of it, is included in the many collections of feminist theory published since the 1960's. Because of this reputation, Wollstonecraft's flawed and unfinished novels, *Mary, a Fiction* and *Maria, or The Wrongs of Woman,* are remarked in studies of women writers, and the political novel. The *Mary Wollstonecraft Newsletter,* now called *Women and Literature,* was first issued in 1973. Recent reprintings of Wollstonecraft's works, such as Carol H. Poston's edition of *A Vindication of the Rights of Women* and Moira Ferguson's edition of *Maria, or The Wrongs of Woman* (New York: W. W. Norton, 1975) contain useful critical introductions.

Discussion continues over the authorship of reviews in *The Analytical Review.* Ralph Wardle attributes 412 articles to Wollstonecraft in his "Mary Wollstonecraft, Analytical Reviewer" (*PMLA,* LXII, December 1947, 100–109). Derek Roper's "Mary Wollstonecraft Reviews" (in *Notes and Queries,* V, 37–38) and Eleanor Flexner, in her biography, continue the debate.

Earlier critical works include Emma Rauschenbusch Clough's *A Study of Mary Wollstonecraft* (London: Longmans, Green, 1898) and Dr. J. Bouten's *Mary Wollstonecraft and the beginnings of Female Emancipation in France and England* (Amsterdam: H. J. Paris, 1922).

Evaluation of Selected Criticism

Ferguson, Moira, and Janet Todd, *Mary Wollstonecraft.* Boston: Twayne, 1984. This study relates Wollstonecraft's radical ideas to the ideas of Burke, Rousseau and Locke, the ideals of the French Revolution and the status of women, and the literary tradition of sensibility. The authors address Wollstonecraft's major themes: education, class divisions within society, and the moral, political and social status of women. In *Maria, or The Wrongs of Woman,* Wollstonecraft was "the first woman to write a self-consciously political novel on behalf of women with the avowed intention of redressing their inequality" (p. 116). Often impugned by biographers, Wollstonecraft is here esteemed for daring to enact the radical political ideas of female emancipation that she advocates in her essays.

Charmaine Wellington
University of Illinois

VIRGINIA WOOLF
1882–1941

Author's Chronology

Born Adeline Virginia Stephen, January 25, 1882, London, daughter of eminent Victorian biographer Leslie Stephen; *1895* mother, Julia Stephen, dies; *1897* suffers first breakdown; *1904* Leslie Stephen dies; moves to 46 Gordon Square, Bloomsbury, with siblings Vanessa, Thoby, and Adrian Stephen; *1912* marries Leonard Woolf; *1913* completes first novel, *The Voyage Out; 1913–1915* suffers a severe breakdown; *1917* establishes Hogarth Press with Leonard Woolf, begins writing diary, writes reviews for the *Times Literary Supplement; 1919* establishes country residence at Monk's House in Rodmell, Sussex; *1924* the Woolfs take townhouse at 52 Tavistock Square; *1925* publishes *Mrs. Dalloway* and *The Common Reader; 1928* receives *Femina Vie Heureuse* prize; *1933* declines the Leslie Stephen lectureship at Cambridge; *1938* transfers ownership of Hogarth Press to John Lehmann; *1940* during the Battle of Britain, Mecklenburgh Square residence, Bloomsbury, is bombed; March 28, 1941 commits suicide by drowning in the Ouse River, near Monks House.

Author's Bibliography

The Voyage Out, 1915 (novel); *Night and Day,* 1919 (novel); *Jacob's Room,* 1922 (novel); *The Common Reader: First Series,* 1925 (criticism); *Mrs. Dalloway,* 1925 (novel); *To the Lighthouse,* 1927 (novel); *Orlando,* 1928 (novel); *A Room of One's Own,* 1929 (essay); *The Waves,* 1931 (novel); *The Second Common Reader,* 1932 (criticism); *The Years,* 1937 (novel); *Three Guineas,* 1938 (essay); *Roger Fry: A Biography,* 1940 (biography); *Between the Acts,* 1941 (novel).

Overview of Biographical Sources

As a member of the influential, compulsively literary Bloomsbury group, Virginia Woolf's life has received considerable attention; publication of Woolf's letters and diaries, along with her growing literary reputation, has contributed to a recent flood of biographical works. The earliest full-length biography is Aileen Pippett's *The Moth and the Star: A Biography of Virginia Woolf* (Boston: Little Brown, 1955), a somewhat ecstatic appreciation of Woolf's life and works that was superseded by Quentin Bell's authorized account, *Virginia Woolf: A Biography* (1972). Phyllis Rose's *Woman of Letters: A Life of Virginia Woolf* (1978) uses evidence from Woolf's own writings to revise previously-held assumptions about her mental illness. Beyond Woolf's own autobiographical works, the most intimate portrait of her private life is found in Leonard Woolf's *An Autobiography of the Years,* Vol. III: *Beginning Again, 1911–1918* (London: Hogarth Press, 1964); Vol. IV: *Downhill all the Way,*

1919–1939 (London: Hogarth Press, 1967); and Vol. V: *The Journey, Not the Arrival, Matters, 1939–1969* (London: Hogarth Press, 1969). Twenty-seven memoirs by Woolf's contemporaries are collected by Joan Russell Noble in *Recollections of Virginia Woolf* (London: William Morrow, 1972). Nigel Nicolson describes Woolf's relationship with his mother, Vita Sackville-West, in his *Portrait of a Marriage* (New York: Atheneum, 1973). John Lehmann's *Thrown to the Woolfs* (London: Weidenfeld and Nicholson, 1978) gives an account of his somewhat stormy years spent managing the Hogarth Press. Two composite biographies provide accounts of Woolf's life: *A Marriage of True Minds: An Intimate Portrait of Leonard and Virginia Woolf* (London: Harcourt, Brace, Jovanich, 1977), by George Spater and Ian Parsons, and Leon Edel's group biography, *Bloomsbury: A House of Lions* (London: Hogarth Press, 1979).

Evaluation of Selected Biographies

Bell, Quentin, *Virginia Woolf: A Biography*. New York: Harcourt, Brace, Jovanovich, 1972. Leonard Woolf asked Bell, Virginia Woolf's nephew, to write her official biography, giving him access to private letters and diaries not then published. Believing that biography and literary criticism should be kept separate, Bell limits his study to the events of Woolf's life, avoiding involved discussion of the literary works. His urbane, somewhat casual tone and his personal memories of his aunt balance the careful documenting of facts in this work, making pleasant reading. Although several more recent works challenge Bell's assumptions about Woolf's "madness," his is still the definitive biography.

Rose, Phyllis, *Woman of Letters: A Life of Virginia Woolf*. Oxford: Oxford University Press, 1978. Rose uses astutely culled evidence from Woolf's writings, from the novels to diaries and memoirs, to contradict Bell's emphasis on Woolf's illness, on her breakdowns, which he termed "madness," and on her eventual suicide. Discussing the novels in a biographical context, Rose uses feminist insights to present a more positive, happier view of Woolf's life than either Bell or Pippett does.

Spater, George, and Ian Parsons, *A Marriage of True Minds: An Intimate Portrait of Leonard and Virginia Woolf*. London: Harcourt, Brace, Jovanovich, 1977. Drawing on the huge Woolf archives and including more than one hundred previously unpublished photographs, this dual biography explores the Woolfs' lifetime collaboration thoroughly and sensitively. Instead of a strictly chronological account, this work focuses on the *themes* of the Woolfs' marriage, such as careers and friendships.

Autobiographical Sources

Only one volume of Woolf's memoirs is in print; this is *Moments of Being: Unpublished Autobiographical Writings*, edited by Jeanne Schulkind (New York; Harcourt, Brace, Jovanovich, 1976). Among these essays are accounts of

Woolf's childhood in London and at Talland House, St. Ives, Cornwall, where the Stephen family vacationed. Probably the most personally revealing of Woolf's writings, however, is her monumental diary, spanning the years 1915 to 1941, published in five volumes as *The Diary of Virginia Woolf,* edited by Anne Olivier Bell (New York: Harcourt, Brace, Jovanovich, 1977–1984). Leonard Woolf's earlier edition, *A Writer's Diary* (New York: Harcourt, Brace, Jovanovich, 1953), contains only Woolf's comments on her writing. Woolf also left hundreds of letters which appear in three collections: *The Letters of Virginia Woolf and Lytton Strachey,* edited by Leonard Woolf and James Strachey (London: Hogarth Press, 1956); *The Letters of Virginia Woolf,* edited in six volumes by Nigel Nicolson and Joanne Trautmann (London: Hogarth Press, 1975–1980); and *The Letters of Vita Sackville-West to Virginia Woolf,* edited by Louise DeSalvo and Mitchell A. Leaska (New York: William Morrow, 1984). Finally, Woolf's novel *To the Lighthouse,* by her own admission, provides a fictionalized version of the Stephen family's visits to St. Ives during Woolf's childhood.

Woolf's critical views are most easily discerned from her two major collections of wide-ranging critical essays: *The Common Reader* (New York: Harcourt, Brace & World, 1925), and *The Second Common Reader* (New York: Harcourt, Brace & World, 1932). She insists that subjective, though disciplined, reading, will create the most astute responses to literature; the reader himself must have "imagination, insight, and judgment." Two full-length essays, *A Room of One's Own* (London: Hogarth Press, 1929) and *Three Guineas* (London: Hogarth Press, 1938), maintain a feminist orientation.

Overview of Critical Sources

A huge amount of criticism about Woolf's writing is currently available, and the pace of its appearance is still accelerating. Her early reputation as a minor author, a mannerist and a bloodless aesthete, has been reversed; book-length studies recognize her as an innovator in fictional form, an expert prose stylist, a symbolist and a mythmaker. Structuralist and post-structuralist critics are investigating Woolf's experiments with the nature and limits of language itself, and feminist critics stress her implicit criticism of patriarchal society.

Evaluation of Selected Criticism

Fleishman, Avrom, *Virginia Woolf: A Critical Reading.* Baltimore: The Johns Hopkins Press, 1975. Taking an eclectic critical approach, Fleishman provides a perceptive explication for each of Woolf's nine novels, in chronological order. Generally "new critical" in approach, this work makes a good introduction to the novels. Fleishman's method combines insights from historical, mythic, biographical, and psychological literary approaches to demonstrate Woolf's learning. Woolf's method involves metaphorical motifs and illusions which, through their repetition, build up meaning in the novels.

Freedman, Ralph, ed. *Virginia Woolf: Revaluation and Continuity.* Berkeley: University of California Press, 1980. Designed to encompass a variety of interests in Woolf studies, Freedman's collection includes essays in diverse modes of criticism. Four initial essays provide a context for contemporary Woolf studies; each of the remaining nine discusses one of Woolf's major novels. Freedman's selections indicate that Woolf's recent appreciation in value springs from postmodern ideas about language, reading, and literary art. This collection is an essential source for the scholar who wants an overview of Woolf studies today. A bibliography of important critical works is included.

Guiguet, Jean, *Virginia Woolf and Her Works.* London: The Hogarth Press, 1965. trans. Jean Stewart. Although Guiguets's work is one of the earliest of the general studies of Woolf's work and life, it is still considered one of the most astute and thorough. Guiguet discusses two basic problems posed by Woolf's work: the apprehension of reality and the search for form. Guiguet's biographical segment has been superseded by the current outpouring of biographical materials, but his study of Woolf's fiction is still useful, emphasizing thematic connections among the novels. Guiguet sees Woolf's nine major novels as versions of the same novel; he sees Woolf as an artist in quest of reality, seeking herself.

McLaurin, Allen, *Virginia Woolf: The Echoes Enslaved.* Cambridge: Cambridge University Press, 1973. McLaurin explores rhythm and repetition as the essential aesthetic element of Woolf's novels. He locates a source for this formal characteristic in Roger Fry's art criticism. As Fry attacked photographic representation in visual art, so Woolf rejected the traditional "representative" form of the novel. Woolf's repetition of motifs creates a sense of circularity, of "refrain."

Marcus, Jane, *Virginia Woolf: A Feminist Slant.* Lincoln: University of Nebraska Press, 1983. Fourteen essays address aspects of Woolf's life, writings in general, and specific works from the perspective of feminist criticism. These articles, and feminist criticism in general, have shaped a revaluation of Woolf's work in recent years, recognizing her importance as a social critic as well as a novelist.

Marder, Herbert, *Feminism and Art: A Study of Virginia Woolf.* Chicago: University of Chicago Press, 1968. Examines the sociopolitical content of Virginia Woolf's novels and explores her androgynous ideal as embodied in her narrative style.

Naremore, James, *The World Without a Self: Virginia Woolf and the Novel.* New Haven: Yale University Press, 1973. Naremore's discussion of Woolf's unique style of interior monologue and stream of consciousness is invaluable. He argues that she adopts this voice in order to project her mystical vision of the mind's unity with the world. Naremore shows how Woolf's fiction demands a union between the narrative voice and an impersonal, though subjective, reality. He points out erotic and visionary characteristics of Woolf's prose style.

Novak, Jane, *The Razor Edge of Balance.* Coral Gables: University of Miami Press, 1975. Discusses balance among opposing forces as a central thematic, symbolic, and formal element of Woolf's nine major novels.

Other Sources

Bazin, Nancy Topping, *Virginia Woolf and the Androgynous Vision.* New Brunswick: Rutgers University Press, 1973. Pairs major novels to explore Woolf's attempts to construct models of androgynous equilibrium.

Love, Jean O. *Worlds of Consciousness: Mythopoetic Thought in the Novels of Virginia Woolf.* Berkeley: University of California Press, 1970. Explores Woolf's mode of perception as connected with a mythmaking consciousness.

Majumdar, Robin, *Virginia Woolf: An Annotated Bibliography of Criticism 1915-1974.* New York: Garland Publishing, 1976. Introduction chronicles Woolf's general critical history; thorough bibliography includes books, articles, memoirs, correspondence, and book reviews, briefly annotated.

Selected Dictionaries and Encyclopedias

British Writers, Vol. VII, Charles Scribner's Sons, 1984. Biographical article by Bernard Blackstone, including a brief account of her place as a modernist, her aesthetic principles, her achievements and influence. Includes a bibliography.

Pamela J. Clements
College of Charleston

WILLIAM WORDSWORTH
1770–1850

Author's Chronology

Born April 7, 1770, at Cockermouth in Cumberland, England, the second son of John Wordsworth and Anne Cookson: *1778* mother dies and family dispersed; *1778-1787* attends Hawkshead Grammar School and lives with Ann Tyson; schoolmaster William Taylor; *1783* father dies; *1787-1791* attends St. John's College, Cambridge; receives degree with no distinction; *1791* with no plans for the future, tours France, Switzerland, the Alps and Italy with Robert Jones; *1792* goes to France and at Orléans meets Annette Vallon; daughter Caroline born; comes under influence of French republicanism through Michel Dupuy at Blois; *1793-1795* unsettled years; *1795* settles with his sister Dorothy at Racedown (Dorsetshire), meets Samuel Taylor Coleridge; *1799* travels to Germany, then settles with sister Dorothy in Dove Cottage, Grasmere; *1802* year of many of best poems; travels with Dorothy to Calais to visit Annette Vallon and daughter Caroline; marries Mary Hutchinson on October 4; five children born of this union, of whom only two, John and William, survive their father; *1805* brother, John, drowns, causing Wordsworth's shift in attitude toward nature; *1810* becomes estranged from Coleridge; *1812* reconciled with Coleridge; *1813* moves to Rydal Mount, becomes a civil servant; *1831* has last meeting with Coleridge, who dies in *1834; 1843* succeeds Robert Southey as poet laureate; *1850* dies on April 23, at Rydal Mount, is buried in Grasmere churchyard.

Author's Bibliography (selected)

Poetry: *An Evening Walk, Descriptive Sketches,* 1793; *Margaret,* or *The Ruined Cottage,* 1796; *Lyrical Ballads* (with Coleridge), 1798, 1800; *The Recluse, Michael,* 1800; *Poems, in Two Volumes,* 1807; *The Excursion, Being a Portion of the Recluse;* 1814; *The White Doe of Rylstone, Collected Poems,* 1815; *Thanksgiving Ode, 18 January, 1816,* 1816; *Peter Bell, a Tale in Verse, The Waggoner,* 1819; *The River Duddon, a series of sonnets,* 1820; *Memorials of a Tour of the Continent,* 1822; *Ecclesiastical Sketches,* 1822; *Yarrow Revisited, and Other Poems,* 1835; *The Sonnets of William Wordsworth,* 1838; *Poems, Chiefly of Early and Late Years,* 1842; *The Prelude, or Growth of a Poet's Mind,* 1850.

Prose: *The Borderers* (play), 1796; *Preface to the Lyrical Ballads,* 1798, 1800; *The Convention of Cintra* (political tract); *Guide to the Lakes,* 1810, 1842; *Letter to Manthetes,* 1810; *Essay, Supplementary to the Preface,* 1815.

The standard edition of Wordsworth's poetry is the five-volume *Poetical Works of William Wordsworth,* edited by Ernest de Selincourt and Helen Darbishire (Oxford: Clarendon Press, 1940–1949). The standard prose edition is *The Prose Works of William Wordsworth,* edited by W. J. B. Owen and Jane

Worthington Smyser, in three volumes (Oxford: Clarendon Press, 1974). More recent editions are becoming available through the Cornell Wordsworth Series, under the editorship of Stephen Parrish and Mark L. Reed.

Overview of Biographical Sources

After William Shakespeare and John Milton, Wordsworth is the English author about whom the most works have been written. Compared to critical works, however, the biographical works are relatively limited. Wordsworth's first biographer was his nephew Christopher Wordsworth, who wrote a rather limited sketch in 1850–1851. William Knight's biography, as well as his edition of Dorothy Wordsworth's *Journals,* 1899, are considered faulty and incomplete. One of the earliest definitive biographies, which continues to be valuable today, is Emile Legouis, *La Jeunesse de Wordsworth,* 1895 (*The Early Life of William Wordsworth,* translated 1897; reprinted with new material in 1921 and 1932.

George M. Harper's *William Wordsworth: His Life, Works and Influence* (1916, 1929) was once considered the standard biography, but has since been replaced by Mary Moorman's two-volume work, *William Wordsworth* (1957, 1965). A very careful chronology has been established by Mark Reed in *William Wordsworth, the Chronology of the Early Years: 1770–1799* (Boston: Harvard University Press, 1967) and *The Chronology of the Middle Years, 1800–1815* (1975). In addition to listing daily events in the poet's life with minute precision, Reed also notes the progression of Wordsworth's literary work. Edith Batho's *The Late Wordsworth* (New York: Russel and Russel, 1933, 1963) devotes several chapters to politics and religion in Wordsworth without sacrificing events in his early life.

Since Wordsworth's sister Dorothy and his friend and fellow poet Coleridge are intimately connected with him, it is essential to consult their biographies also. The authoritative biography of Dorothy is Ernest de Selincourt's *Dorothy Wordsworth* (Oxford: Clarendon Press, 1933). H. M. Margoliuth's *Wordsworth and Coleridge 1795–1834* (London: Oxford, 1953) is a short but well-documented and very complete guide to the relationship between the two poets.

Evaluation of Selected Biographies

Harper, George McLean, *William Wordsworth: His Life, Works, and Influence.* London: John Murray, New York: Charles Scribner's Sons, 1916, 1923, 1929. The third edition, long time standard, contains Legouis and Harper's material on Annette Vallon and Caroline (see also Harper's *Wordsworth's French Daughter,* Princeton, 1921). Harper also makes extensive use of Ernest de Selincourt's 1926 edition of *The Prelude,* as well as letters and memoirs, especially of Dorothy Wordsworth and her *Journals.* Very few, if any footnotes, identify secondary sources, although primary sources are usually identified within the text. The work also contains literary criticism, especially of *Descriptive Sketches, Lyrical Ballads,* and *The Excursion.* Harper places great (and according to Moorman, undue) emphasis on Wordsworth's political activities and affiliations, especially in the 1790's.

Legouis, Emile, *The Early Life of William Wordsworth: 1770–1798.* London and Toronto: J. M. Dent, 1897. Subtitled "A Study of the *Prelude,*" Legouis' biography was one of the first books to use *The Prelude* as a basis for Wordsworth's early life. Written originally for French readers with little knowledge of Wordsworth, the book contains ample quotations from Wordsworth's poetical works. It is a poetic study of Wordsworth's inner life, with great emphasis on his early illuminations, and stresses the influence of Rousseau. There is a great deal of literary criticism contained in the work, which insists on the poet's mission as a writer. Of parallel importance is Legouis' *William Wordsworth and Annette Vallon,* 1922, one of the first studies of the poet's liaison and daughter Caroline.

Moorman, Mary, *William Wordsworth, A Biography. The Early Years 1770–1803.* Oxford: Clarendon Press, 1957. *The Later Years: 1803–1850.* Oxford: Clarendon Press, 1965. This now standard biography uses the 1941 edition of Dorothy's *Journals* and *Letters of William and Dorothy* from the Ernest de Selincourt and Helen Darbishire edition, to document Wordsworth's early years. New material is treated in Wordsworth's involvement with Godwin in 1795. The second part shows the high artistic quality of Wordsworth's later poetry and presents the author as a faithful friend and respected man of letters. The work has excellent and copious original sources, as well as critical references.

Autobiographical Sources
It is generally acknowledged that *The Prelude* is Wordsworth's literary autobiography in verse. Written during 1798–1799, 1803–1805, and revised many times thereafter, notably in 1826 and 1839, it was not published until 1850, after Wordsworth's death, and was named *The Prelude* by his wife Mary. Originally intended as a personal sharing with Coleridge, it was at first entitled *The Recluse, or Views on Man, Nature, and on Human Life.* The poem, in Wordsworth's mind, required ample revision and generalization in order to be accessible to the general public. It is generally considered that the revisions weaken the poem, although Wordsworth did add some genuine poetry through the years.

The Prelude is not autobiographical in the traditional sense, since the author pays little attention to dates, persons, and chronology. Like Proust, he chooses events that have meaning for his own inner life, and thus it is subtitled *The Growth of a Poet's Mind.* The 1850 edition consists of fourteen books, of unequal length, and treats basically the author's first twenty-seven years.

The first authoritative edition of *The Prelude* was made by Ernest de Selincourt, 1926, revised by Helen Darbishire in 1959 (Oxford: Clarendon Press).

The 1805 and 1850 texts are presented side by side, although de Selincourt considers the 1805 text as more reliable, since it is more spontaneous. The most recent text by Jonathan Wordsworth, M. H. Abrams, and Stephen Gill uses the three versions: 1798–1799, 1805, and 1850, and contains a number of other critical sources and recent scholarly essays by such authors as Jonathan Wordsworth, Geoffrey Hartman, and Herbert Lindenberger (New York, London: W. W. Norton, 1979).

Extensive autobiographical material is contained in Wordsworth's letters. Among the most important are *The Letters of William and Dorothy Wordsworth,* originally edited by Ernest de Selincourt. Revised editions are *The Early Years, 1787–1805,* by Chester L. Shaver (Oxford, 1967); *The Middle Years, 1806–1811,* by Mary Moorman (Oxford, 1969); *1812–1820,* by Mary Moorman and Alan G. Hill (Oxford, 1970); *The Later Years,* by Alan G. Hill (Oxford, 1978, 1979). *The Love Letters of William and Mary Wordsworth* have been edited by Beth Darlington (Ithaca: Cornell University Press, 1981).

Overview of Critical Sources

Wordsworth is known throughout the English-speaking world as a romantic poet and a mystic of nature. Hence most of the abundant criticism is directed to his poetry. His prose works are generally considered as inferior, and therefore receive less attention. A great deal of critical work is devoted to the *Prelude,* its sources, revisions, and its relationship to Wordsworth's poetry and poetic vision. Since Wordsworth revised most of his work, and did not publish many poems until years after their composition, the problem of chronology becomes critical, and had interested such scholars as John Alban Finch. Newer critics, such as John Beer, explore the question of time, consciousness, and vision in Wordsworth. Oxford is the British center for Wordsworth studies, and has published books on Wordsworth by such eminent critics as Ernest de Selincourt and Helen Darbishire. In the United States, the Cornell Wordsworth Series publishes critical texts and essays, the most important being the *Bicentenary Wordsworth Studies.* There is also a collection of essays by notable critics in the *Twentieth-Century Views* series, edited by M. H. Abrams (Prentice-Hall, 1972), containing studies of early and late poems, with special emphasis on *The Prelude.* The series contains a good bibliography and chronology.

For the numerous articles that continue to appear, the Wordsworth scholar should consult James V. Logan, *Wordsworthian Criticism: A Guide to Bibliography;* Elton Henley and David H. Stamm, *Wordsworthian Criticism: 1945–1964; Philological Quarterly; English Language Notes;* and *PMLA,* which print regular entries on recent scholarship.

Evaluation of Selected Criticism

Beatty, Arthur, *William Wordsworth: His Doctrine and Art in their Historical Relation.* Madison: University of Wisconsin, 1962. Beatty studies the mature theories and poetry of Wordsworth, from 1798 to the end of his active career. He shows how later poems developed from earlier ones, and examines some of Wordsworth's prose as well. He places special emphasis on Wordsworth's connection with English philosophers, especially Godwin.

Darbishire, Helen, *The Poet Wordsworth.* Clark Lectures, Trinity College, Cambridge. Oxford: Clarendon Press, 1950. This short book is an excellent appraisal of Wordsworth's poetic achievements written by an eminent specialist and editor. She pays special attention to *The Prelude,* examining its chronology and subject, which she considers as the central experience of a mystic.

Hartman, Geoffrey H. *Wordsworth's Poetry: 1787–1814.* New Haven and London: Yale University Press, 1964. This rather complex study examines the relationship of Wordsworth's poetry to his mind. Hartman aims to show that Wordsworth's central image is the halted traveler, and in his work, imagination is intrinsically opposed to nature. This leads him through what the mystics call a negative way, and prevents him from becoming a truly visionary poet, since he avoids apocalypse. The book contains a chronological study of Wordsworth's poetry up to *The Excursion,* and contains an excellent critical bibliography and notes.

Havens, Raymond Dexter, *The Mind of a Poet.* Baltimore: Johns Hopkins Press, 1941. This two-volume study addresses *The Prelude.* Volume I is a thematic study of Wordsworth's thought, based on the 1926 de Selincourt edition, considering however the 1850 edition as definitive. Havens sees animism and nature as important elements in Wordsworth's thought, and studies various passages to demonstrate the poet's mystic experience, arising from natural phenomena. Volume two is a line-by-line commentary on *The Prelude.*

Lindenberger, Herbert, *On Wordsworth's Prelude.* Princeton: Princeton University Press, 1963. Mainly a study of language, this work shows the relationship and debt of *The Prelude* to eighteenth-century rhetorical forms, as well as the relationship of the external world of nature and the inner world of the poet. Lindenberger sees Wordsworth as the ancestor of James Joyce, Marcel Proust, and Gertrude Stein, and a follower of Jean Jacques Rousseau. He also studies the social dimensions of the nonvisionary books, especially those referring to the city.

Noyes, Russell, *William Wordsworth.* New York: Twayne, 1971. This short book is a summary evaluation of Wordsworth the man and the writer. It is an excellent introductory text, following a chronological pattern, and using primary and secondary sources. Special consideration is given to *The Lyrical Ballads, The Prelude,* and *The Excursion,* but little attention to the later years. There is a good annotated bibliography at the end.

Wordsworth, Jonathan, *William Wordsworth: The Borders of Vision.* Oxford: Clarendon Press, 1982. This book by an eminent contemporary critic examines

Wordsworth's use of border imagery. His metaphors approach a boundary that is the entrance to another world. With this thesis, Jonathan Wordsworth examines the 1799 version of the *Prelude* and Wordsworth's poetry up to 1804. The study contains detailed notes and a very comprehensive, up-to-date bibliography.

Other Sources

Coleridge, S. T. *Biographia literaria.* ed. J. Shawcross. Oxford, 1907. Contains important criticism of Wordsworth's early works.

de Selincourt, Ernest, *The Journals of Dorothy Wordsworth.* New York: Macmillan, 1941. De Selincourt relies on William Knight's faulty edition of the Alfoxden Journal, but uses original sources for the Grasmere Journals (1800-1803), *Recollections of a Tour made in Scotland* (1803), and other important memoirs of Dorothy.

Griggs, Earl Leslie, ed. *Selected Letters of S. T. Coleridge.* 6 vols. Oxford: Clarendon Press, 1956-1971. Coleridge's letters reveal not only his personal life and problems, but treat in detail his relationship to Wordsworth the poet and the man.

Griggs, Earl Leslie, ed. *Wordsworth and Coleridge.* Studies in Honor of George McLean Harper. New York: Russell and Russell, 1962. Contains essays by distinguished scholars such as Legouis, Havens, and Ernest de Selincourt relating to the two poets.

(Sister) Irma M. Kashuba, S.S.J.
Chestnut Hill College

RICHARD WRIGHT
1908–1960

Author's Chronology

Born September 4, 1908 on a plantation near Natchez, Mississippi; *1915* placed in an orphanage with his brother; *1925* receives high school diploma and goes to Memphis, Tennessee to make first attempts at serious writing; *1927* moves to Chicago and works at succession of odd jobs; *1933* joins the Chicago John Reed Club and later the Communist Party; *1935* admitted to the Illinois Federal Writers' Project and attends first congress of the League of American Writers in New York as a delegate; *1936* works as a publicity agent for the Chicago Federal Negro Theater; *1937* editor for the Harlem Bureau of the *Daily Worker; 1939* marries Dhimah Meadman; later divorced; *1940* publishes *Native Son* which becomes a Book of the Month Club selection; *1941* marries Ellen Poplar; *1944* expelled from the Communist Party; *1946* sails to France as official guest of the French government; lives in the Latin Quarter in Paris; befriends Gertrude Stein; *1950* works on film of *Native Son; 1951* returns to Paris; *1952–1955* travels to London, Ghana, and Spain; *1956* helps organize the first Congress of Negro Writers and Artists; *1958* is refused permission to live in London by British officials; *1960* dies on December 5 in Paris.

Author's Bibliography (selected)

Uncle Tom's Children, 1938 (novella); *Native Son,* 1940 (novel); *Twelve Million Black Voices,* 1941 (nonfiction); *Black Boy,* 1945 (autobiography); *The Outsider,* 1953 (novel); *Savage Holiday,* 1954 (novel); *Black Power,* 1954 (nonfiction); *The Color Curtain,* 1956 (nonfiction); *Pagan Spain,* 1957 (nonfiction); *White Man, Listen!,* 1957 (essays); *The Long Dream,* 1958 (novel); *Eight Men,* 1961 (stories); *Lawd Today,* 1963 (novel); *American Hunger,* 1977 (autobiography).

Overview of Biographical Sources

The nature of Richard Wright's publications has resulted in critical work about him that combines literary criticism, biography, and historical context. Representative examples of this approach are Russell Carl Brignano's *Richard Wright: An Introduction to the Man and His Works* (Pittsburgh: University of Pittsburgh Press, 1970) and Robert Bone's *Richard Wright* (Minneapolis: University of Minnesota, 1969). Two lengthy studies, however, focus primarily on biography: Constance Webb's *Richard Wright: A Biography* (1968) and Michel Fabre's *The Unfinished Quest of Richard Wright* (1973). Fabre's biography is more accurate and scholarly than Webb's work.

Evaluation of Selected Biographies

Fabre, Michel, *The Unfinished Quest of Richard Wright.* New York: William Morrow, 1973. Fabre traces Wright's life in detail, showing the relationships between his work and his life. He concludes his biography with a controversial speculation and a provocative observation, suggesting that Wright died, not of a heart attack, but "from inner conflicts and pressure engendered by racism" and proposing Wright as an Emersonian "representative man" of the twentieth century. Extensive notes and a selected bibliography reinforce the careful, scholarly approach Fabre uses.

Webb, Constance, *Richard Wright: A Biography*. New York: G.P. Putnam's Sons, 1968. Webb wrote this biography with the help of Richard Wright, who gave her the galley sheets of the unpublished third of *Black Boy* which she had printed privately, as well as notes, letters, telegrams, and manuscripts. Webb also had conversations with Wright and his wife Ellen, who gave her access to Wright's files, including two diaries for the years 1945 and 1947. Despite these contributions by both Wright and his wife, this book reads more like a novel than a biography and does not reflect the precision or completeness character-istic of the best biographies.

Autobiographical Sources

Wright's autobiography, *Black Boy: A Record of Childhood and Youth,* is a portrait of this artist as a young man. The book relates Wright's pre-Northern, pre-Marxist experiences, emphasizing the autobiographer's dual awareness of racism and his own artistic drive. The narrative style makes this work appear to be a traditional autobiography, and *Black Boy* is definitely a classic example of a self-portrait; however, its combination of prose that is sometimes poetry and sometimes polemic makes it also a literary piece and a cultural document.

A later part of *Black Boy,* originally called *The Horror and the Glory* and eventually titled *American Hunger,* was published as a whole for the first time in 1977. It traces Wright's journey from Chicago to New York, from his enthu-siastic commitment to Communism to his disillusionment with the Party's methods. Like *Black Boy,* this book is social history as well as self-portrait.

Overview of Critical Sources

Richard Wright was the first black American novelist to write a "best seller" in the classic sense (*Native Son* almost immediately went into a second edition after its publication in 1940, became a Book of the Month Club selection, and subsequently has sold more than a million copies). His position as a novelist, however, is not the prime concern of most critical works. Instead, critics are interested in the complex interrelationship between literary and social criticism.

Evaluation of Selected Criticism

Hakutani, Yoshinobu, *Critical Essays on Richard Wright*. Boston: G.K. Hall, 1982. This book is an excellent collection of previously published and original articles on Richard Wright's life and works. The collection is divided into four parts: General Essays, Essays on Fiction, Essays on Nonfiction, and Essays on

Poetry. Hakutani's long introduction is also divided into these same four categories and offers an extensive overview of the scholarly reaction to Wright.

Kinnamon, Keneth, *The Emergence of Richard Wright: A Study in Literature and Society*. Urbana: University of Illinois Press, 1973. As the title indicates, this book is an effort to examine Richard Wright as both an imaginative writer and a social critic. Demonstrating how Wright converted his anger into creativity, Kinnamon asserts that Wright has "a threefold claim to enduring importance—as social critic, as articulator of the black agony, and as American writer."

Margolies, Edward, *The Art of Richard Wright*. Carbondale: Southern Illinois University Press, 1969. The earliest book-length study, Margolies' work shows how Wright is more than the proletarian writer some critics believe him to be. Wright's ability to weave his thematic concerns of human fear, alienation, guilt, and dread into the fabric of his work is, for Margolies, the reason Wright merits more than a sociological analysis.

Reilly, John M. *Richard Wright: The Critical Reception*. New York: Burt Franklin, 1978. Besides collecting all the major reviews of Wright's works, this book includes checklists of additional reviews at the end of each chapter.

Other Sources
Baldwin, James, "Everybody's Protest Novel," *Partisan Review,* 16 (June 1949), 578–585; rpt. in *Notes of a Native Sone* (1955). Having regarded Wright as his mentor, James Baldwin rebelled against him, as demonstrated in this essay which attacks the kind of fiction, from *Uncle Tom's Cabin* to *Native Son,* which he believes sensationalizes the ordeal of the American Negro. In 1951, Baldwin published "Many Thousands Gone," another article in *Partisan Review* and an even more explicit attack on Wright's naturalistic "protest" fiction.

Bone, Robert, *Richard Wright*. Minneapolis: University of Minnesota Press, 1969. Though a slim pamphlet, Bone's study is an excellent introduction to Wright and persuasive explanation of Wright's attraction to existentialism.

Ellison, Ralph, "The World and the Jug," *New Leader,* 46 (December 9, 1963), 22–26. Responding directly to Irving Howe's article, "Black Boys and Native Sons," Ellison argues that Howe's loyalty to Baldwin blinded him to a clear evaluation of both Baldwin's and his own writing. Ellison rejects Wright's Bigger Thomas, in *Native Son,* as a "final image of Negro personality."

Fabre, Michel, and Charles T. Davis, *Richard Wright: A Primary Bibliography*. Boston, G.K. Hall, 1982. This descriptive bibliography of the works of Richard Wright is the most comprehensive to date. It contains two main sections on Wright's published and unpublished works, two appendices on translations of Wright's published works and material by others related to his published works, and an index that contains all the titles of Wright's published and unpublished works.

Howe, Irving, "Black Boys and Native Sons," *Dissent,* 10 (Autumn 1963, 353–368); rpt. in *A World More Attractive.* New York, Horizon Press, 1963. An attack on Baldwin's criticism of Richard Wright, this article asserts that Baldwin's polemic avoided the complex question of the relationship between art and social protest. Additionally, Howe writes that Baldwin failed to register a major success in fiction and failed to get beyond protest.

Marjorie Smelstor
The University of Texas
San Antonio

SIR THOMAS WYATT
1503–1542

Author's Chronology

Born 1503, Kent, England, son of Sir Henry Wyatt, a loyalist to the new Tudor regime; may have attended Cambridge University; served in the Court of Henry VIII from *1516;* around *1520,* marries Elizabeth Brooke; leaves her six years later on grounds of adultery; *1525* or *1526* appears to have had an affair with Anne Boleyn, but he withdrew in *1527* on learning of King Henry VIII's interest in her; *1526* receives the first of several military and diplomatic missions that would take him to France, Italy, Flanders, and Spain; *1527* captured by the Spaniards but shortly escapes or was freed; *1533* attends the wedding of Henry VIII and Anne Boleyn; *1536* arrested in connection with Anne's downfall and put in the Tower; watches her beheaded through the iron grate of his cell; later released; *1537–1540* serves as Ambassador to Charles V, The Holy Roman Emperor; *1541* again imprisoned as a traitor; defends himself ably and is reinstated once more; *1542* dies of a fever contracted as he traveled to greet the Spanish Envoy. At the time of his death, Wyatt was a candidate for vice-admiral of the English fleet.

Author's Bibliography (selected)

Because Wyatt's poems appear differently in several manuscript collections and early printed sources, the text of his work is full of problems. Editors even differ on which poems are his. The most reliable editions are *Collected Poems of Sir Thomas Wyatt,* ed. Kenneth Muir and Patricia Thompson, 1969; *Sir Thomas Wyatt: Collected Poems,* ed. Joost Daalder, 1975; and *Sir Thomas Wyatt: The Complete Poems,* ed. R. A. Rebholz, 1981. Correspondence and other documents, including two statements concerning the 1541 treason charge, are available in *Life and Letters of Sir Thomas Wyatt,* 1963.

Overview of Biographical Sources

The facts of Wyatt's biography are open to dispute, but the best source is probably Kenneth Muir's *Life and Letters of Sir Thomas Wyatt* (1963). A revealing "psychobiographical," approach distinguishes Raymond Southall's *The Courtly Maker* (1964). Convenient tables of dates are included in the editions of the complete and collected poems.

Evaluation of Selected Biographies

Muir, Kenneth, *Life and Letters of Sir Thomas Wyatt.* Liverpool: Liverpool University Press, 1963. For most purposes this is the biography of choice. Muir has no special case to plead, so his account of Wyatt is both complete and reliable. Since Wyatt's known letters and other documents are included, this book can also be used as a primary text.

Southall, Raymond, *The Courtly Maker: An Essay on the Poetry of Wyatt and His Contemporaries.* Oxford: Blackwell, 1964. Covers Wyatt's life with reference to the social and psychological forces shaping his personality. Southall's facts are reliable, but some of his inferences, especially concerning Wyatt and Anne Boleyn, are necessarily conjectural.

Thompson, Patricia, *Sir Thomas Wyatt and His Background.* Stanford: Stanford University Press, 1964. Thompson is interested in Wyatt's relations to European writers and culture. Her book gives the most complete account of his travels and opportunities to meet leading Continental figures of his day.

Autobiographical Sources
A good deal of Wyatt's poetry reflects events in his life. Thus some poems, such as "The pillar perished is whereto I leant," have to do with his political career; while others—like "Whoso list to hunt," and "Who list his wealth and ease retain"—are associated with the Anne Boleyn affair. The three verse satires are full of personal details and comments. Finally, there are the letters and documents in Muir's *Life and Letters of Sir Thomas Wyatt.* Wyatt's letter to his son (Muir, 41–43) is particularly revealing.

Overview of Critical Sources
To an admirer of Wyatt, much early criticism of his work is objectionable. Often-cited commentators such as Sergio Baldi's *Sir Thomas Wyatt* (London: Longmans, 1961) and H. A. Mason's *Humanism and Poetry in the Early Tudor Period* (London: Routledge and Kegan Paul, 1959) stress Wyatt's limitations, which are considerable, but have little of use to say about his virtues, which are more important.

In the past twenty years, Wyatt's reputation has improved enormously, not only in recognition of his profound psychological insights, but because of a new appreciation of his handling of meter and sound. A monument in this reevaluation is Southall's *The Courtly Maker,* a brilliant but sometimes wayward book. Southall gives the most convincing picture yet of life in the Court of Henry VIII and its effect on Wyatt's work in an analysis that fully justifies his opening statement: "Wyatt is coming to be seen as the most important figure in English poetry from the death of Chaucer to the reign of Elizabeth." A continuing interest in what Wyatt made of his many sources is demonstrated by such studies as J. Glaser, "Wyatt, Petrarch, and the Uses of Mistranslation," *College Literature,* 11 (1984), 213–22; D. L. Guss, "Wyatt's Petrarchism: An Instance of Creative Imitation in the Renaissance," *Huntington Library Quarterly,* 29 (1965), 1–15; and Patricia Thompson, *Sir Thomas Wyatt and His Background,* (Stanford: Stanford University Press, 1964).

Evaluation of Selected Criticism

Friedman, D. M. Friedman has written a series of fine articles: "The 'Thing' in Wyatt's Mind," *Essays in Criticism,* 16 (1966), 375–381; "Wyatt's *'Amoris Personae,'* " *Modern Language Quarterly,* 27 (1966), 136–146; "The Mind in the Poem: Wyatt's 'They Fle From Me,' " *Studies in English Literature,* 7 (1967), 1–13; and "Wyatt and the Ambiguities of Fancy," *Journal of English and Germanic Philology,* 67 (1968), 32–48. Friedman is interested in the psychological and moral seriousness of Wyatt's work. His articles provide an excellent account of the way Wyatt's mind works in poetry, the themes with which he is preoccupied, and the psychological unity of his work, which Friedman attributes to an evolving sense of moral complexity and personal identity.

Greenblatt, Steven, *Renaissance Self-Fashioning: From More to Shakespeare.* Chicago and London: University of Chicago Press, 1980. Gives considerable attention to Wyatt and the world of ideas, assumptions, and language in which he lived—his "semiotic universe." Greenblatt stresses the violence Wyatt did in his poetry to the received theories and conventions of ideal love, but concludes that the changes Wyatt introduced were largely unconscious. Wyatt's poems are "charged with that will to power, that dialectic of domination and submission" that marked not just his work but the entire court culture of early Tudor England.

Southall, Raymond, *The Courtly Maker: An Essay on the Poetry of Wyatt and His Contemporaries.* Oxford: Blackwell, 1964. Southall's book is a corrective to earlier criticism, giving a chilling picture of court life under Henry VIII, and explaining the "characteristic inwardness" of Wyatt's poems, contrasting them with the glibness and artificiality of succeeding poets. Southall also has much to say about Wyatt's treatment of his sources. Unlike Greenblatt, he thinks Wyatt was in conscious control of the original elements he introduced into his translations and adaptations. A final interest of Southall's book is Wyatt's rhythms and meters, but here the criticism is too impressionistic and vaguely worded to be entirely useful.

Other Sources

Kökeritz, Helge, "Dialectal Traits in Sir Thomas Wyatt's Poetry," in *Franciplegius: Medieval and Linguistic Studies in Honor of Francis Peabody Magoun, Jr.* ed. J. B. Bessinger, Jr. and R. P. Creed (New York: New York University Press, 1965), pp. 294–303. Describes linguistic and dialect features of Wyatt's English.

Mason, H. A. *Editing Wyatt* (Cambridge: Cambridge University Press, 1972); and R. C. Harrier, *The Canon of Sir Thomas Wyatt's Poetry* (Cambridge, MA: Harvard University Press, 1975). Two technical books on editing Wyatt's poems and determining what he really wrote.

McCanles, Michael, "Love and Power in the Poetry of Sir Thomas Wyatt," in *Modern Language Quarterly,* 29 (1968), 145–160. The hostile tone of many Wyatt love poems is explained by his idea of love as an instrument of power, a notion already hinted at in Italian poets Wyatt knew.

Peterson, D. L. *The English Lyric from Wyatt to Donne* (Princeton: Princeton University Press, 1967). Assesses Wyatt's place in the English lyric tradition.

Stevens, John, *Music and Poetry in the Early Tudor Court* (Lincoln: University of Nebraska Press, 1961). Describes the role music played in Court life and in shaping the poetry of the period, much of which was intended to be sung.

Thompson, John, *The Founding of English Metre* (New York: Columbia University Press, 1961). An introduction to early English prosody, with special attention to Wyatt, whose metrical intentions are often difficult to decipher.

Twombly, R. G. "Thomas Wyatt's Paraphrase of the Penitential Psalms of David," in *Texas Studies in Literature and Language,* 12 (1970), 345–380. A special study of the psalm paraphrases.

Selected Dictionaries and Encyclopedias

British Writers, Charles Scribner's Sons, 1979. Discussion of Wyatt's life and works by Sergio Baldi.

Critical Survey of Poetry, Salem Press, 1983. Brief biography and appreciation of Wyatt's works.

The Critical Temper: A Survey of Modern Criticism on English and American Literature. Frederick Ungar, 1969. Contains several excerpts from critical commentaries on Wyatt.

Joe Glaser
Western Kentucky University

WILLIAM BUTLER YEATS
1865–1939

Author's Chronology

Born June 13, 1865, Dublin, Ireland; *1885* publishes first poems in *Dublin University Review;* founds Dublin Hermetic Society; *1887* joins London Lodge of Theosophists; *1889* meets Maud Gonne ("the troubling of my life began"); *1891* founds National Literary Society in Dublin; proposes to Maud Gonne (as he will again in 1899, 1900, 1901, and 1916); *1899* founds Irish Literary Theater (leads to the opening of the Abbey Theatre in 1904 of which Yeats was a director until his death); *1917* proposes to Maud Gonne's daughter Iseult; marries Georgie Hyde-Lees; *1918* begins restoration of tower at Coole (County Galway) and summers there in ensuing years; *1919* Anne Butler Yeats born in Dublin; *1921* Michael Butler Yeats born; *1922* becomes Senator of Irish Free State; *1923* awarded Nobel Prize for poetry; writes some of his strongest volumes of poetry thereafter; *1935* collaborates with Shri Purohit Swami in translation of *The Upanishads; 1939* dies on January 28; buried at Roquebrune, France; *1948* body reinterred at Drumcliff, Sligo, as foretold in "Under Ben Bulben."

Author's Bibliography (selected)

Mosada: A Dramatic Poem, 1886; *The Wandering of Oisin and Other Poems,* 1889; *The Countess Kathleen and Various Legends and Lyrics,* 1892; *The Celtic Twilight,* 1893 (tales); *In the Seven Woods,* 1903 (poems); *Ideas of Good and Evil,* 1903 (essays); *Stories of Red Hanrahan,* 1904; *Deirdre,* 1907 (play); *The Green Helmet and Other Poems,* 1910; *The Wild Swans at Coole,* 1917 (poems); *Michael Robartes and the Dancer,* 1920 (poems); *A Vision,* 1925 (philosophical essays); *The Tower,* 1928 (poems); *The Winding Stair and Other Poems,* 1933; *The Collected Poems of W. B. Yeats,* 1933; *The King of the Great Clock Tower,* 1934 (title play and poems); *Essays 1931–1936,* 1937; *Purgatory,* 1939 (play); *The Collected Poems of W. B. Yeats,* 1956. *Variorum Edition of the Plays of W. B. Yeats,* 1966.

The standard bibliography is Allan Wade's *A Bibliography of the Writings of W. B. Yeats* (3rd ed., rev. Russell K. Alspach, 1968). It is updated by K. P. S. Jochum's *W. B. Yeats: A Classified Bibliography of Criticism* (1978). Richard J. Finneran's *Anglo-Irish Literature: A Review of Research* (1976 and 1983 supplement) is a very useful guide.

Overview of Biographical Sources

It was an article of Yeatsian faith that lyric poetry "is no rootless flower but the speech of a man . . . ." More than for most poets, Yeats's poetry is an imaginative transformation of his personal life. Thus Yeatsian biography is a fruitful source of insight into the poetry. Currently in progress are Roy Foster's definitive biography and John Kelly's edition of the *Letters*. Meanwhile, Allan Wade's *Letters* (New York: Macmillan, 1955) is essential, as are two earlier authorized biographies, Joseph Hone's *W. B. Yeats* (1942) and A. Norman Jeffares' *W. B. Yeats: Man and Poet* (1949). Richard Ellmann's *Yeats: The Man and the Masks* (1948) remains an insightful critical biography. Augustine Martin's *W. B. Yeats* (1983) demonstrates that it is possible to write a short volume that is both accessible to the beginner and essential to the connoisseur. Frank Tuohy's *Yeats* (1976) summarizes the life and imparts a feeling for the texture with its evocative photographs and illustrations. Brenda Webster's *Yeats: A Psychoanalytic Study* (1973) is a flawed, and overly selective execution of an interesting idea. William Murphy's biography of the poet's father, *Prodigal Father* (Ithaca: Cornell University Press, 1978) is an informative backdrop for a study of the poet, an impressive achievement in the art of biography, and an account of an unforgettable life.

Evaluation of Selected Biographies

Ellmann, Richard, *Yeats: The Man and the Masks.* New York: Macmillan, 1948. It is a measure of Ellmann's achievement that no one has yet written the comprehensive study of Yeats's poetry in relation to his thought and age toward which Ellmann's early book points the way. This book is best on the earlier influences on Yeats's poetry, particularly magic and Irish nationalism. Throughout, it excites by showing how events and ideas illuminate the poetry.

Hone, Joseph, *W. B. Yeats.* London: Macmillan, 1942. Although marred by extensive paraphrase of various published and unpublished Yeats papers, this early work by Yeats's contemporary remains a basic source of facts about Yeats's life.

Jeffares, A. Norman, *W. B. Yeats: Man and Poet.* London: Routledge & Kegan Paul, 1949. Jeffares retraces some of the ground covered by Hone, but adds important information about Yeats's sources and library, as well as Jeffares' valuable insight into the poetry.

Martin, Augustine, *W. B. Yeats.* Dublin: Gill & Macmillan, 1983. Martin succeeds in letting the poetry, and his robust appreciation of it, dominate the stage, deftly supported by biographical fact and grounded in Yeats's intellectual and political *milieu.*

Tuohy, Frank, *Yeats.* London: Macmillan, 1976. The full page color plate of Orpen's Homage to Manet is but one of the photographs and illustrations in this artful portrait of an era which, as Eliot observed, cannot be understood apart from Yeats. The newest full-scale biography, it is probably the most accessible, currently available compendium of information about Yeats's personal life.

Webster, Brenda, *Yeats: A Psychoanalytic Study*. Stanford: Stanford University Press, 1973. A comprehensive psychoanalytic interpretation of Yeats's work is still to be written. Webster's book leaves the uneasy impression that she has not fully come to grips with the poetry.

Autobiographical Sources

If a less satisfactory text than the English *Autobiographies* (1926, 1955), *The Autobiography of W. B. Yeats* (1938, 1965) is the most easily obtainable for the American student. Its constituent autobiographical essays deal, among other things, with Yeats's life from childhood memories of Sligo to about 1902. *Memoirs* (1972) contains the draft of an autobiography covering 1887–1889 and the full text of the journal excerpted in *"The Autobiography."* While these materials fall far short of a comprehensive treatment of the poet's life, taken together, they provide a fascinating glimpse of Yeats's unremitting effort to transmute his life into art.

Overview of Critical Sources

Jochum and Finneran, in the works discussed in the bibliography section, cope manfully with the avalanche of Yeats criticism. (As of 1978, Jochum listed more than 7,000 items.) The selected evaluations presented below can do no more than highlight a few examples of the various forms, approaches, themes and subjects of Yeats criticism. Related works are discussed together. Two poem-by-poem "guides" to the poetry are useful: A. Norman Jeffares, *A New Commentary on the Poems of W. B. Yeats* (London: Macmillan, 1984), which updates his 1968 *Commentary*, and John Unterecker's *A Reader's Guide to W. B. Yeats* (London: Thames & Hudson, 1959). Both books provide a wealth of references to Yeats's life, sources, and critics. Unterecker tends more to give a reading of the poem; Jeffares to provide more detailed information.

Several studies of the extensive manuscript material preserved by Mrs. Yeats reveal something of what MacNeice called the "notorious labor pains" that preceded the birth of a Yeats poem. The manuscripts increase both an understanding of the poetry and admiration for the poet's craft. These studies include two by Jon Stallworthy, *Between The Lines* (Oxford: Clarendon, 1963) and *Vision and Revision in Yeats's Last Poems* (Oxford: Clarendon, 1969), and Curtis Bradford, *Yeats At Work* (Carbondale: Southern Illinois University Press, 1965). Cornell University Press has begun publication of an important series that will present a vast amount of manuscript material, including the extant manuscripts of the poems and plays. The wider availability of these materials is sure to stimulate further critical analysis. Probably the best example to date of the imaginative use of manuscript material as part of a broadly based criticism of the poetry is Thomas Parkinson's *W. B. Yeats: The Later Poetry* (Berkeley: University of California Press, 1966). Parkinson's discussion of "Among School Children" is a lesson in how a close reading can touch a wide range of bases.

Evaluation of Selected Criticism

Cullingford, Elizabeth, *Yeats: Poems, 1919–1935.* London: Macmillan, 1984. Cullingford offers a good sampling of some of the best Yeats criticism, and her lucid introductory essay permits the reader to view the selections in the context of the principal themes and approaches of Yeats criticism. Another good case book—one devoted to the frequently studied Byzantium poems—is Finneran's *The Byzantium Poems.* Columbus: Merrill, 1970.

————, *Yeats, Ireland and Fascism.* London: Macmillan, 1981. Cullingford demonstrates the flaws in O'Brien's case against Yeats (see below), but without coming to grips with the haunting question underlying his essay: how can it be that we are attracted to poems (like "Leda and the Swan") that seem to exult in violence.

Donoghue, Denis, *Yeats.* New York: Viking, 1971. Donoghue explores the Yeatsian sensibility, particularly in terms of the poet's pursuit of power, his role as great artificer of his own life. Energy, will and gesture are among the touchstones here, and thus the influence of Nietzsche is explored; ultimately, the dominant power is the transfiguring power of imagination. This volume is idiosyncratic but sometimes soars.

Eliot, T. S. "Yeats," in *Selected Prose of T. S. Eliot.* New York: Harcourt Brace Jovanovitch, 1975. One great poet's assessment of another cannot be ignored. Significantly, what Eliot finds most impressive is Yeats's "continual development" as a poet, his ability "to remain always a contemporary." In the same vein, Louis MacNeice, in *The Poetry of W. B. Yeats* (Oxford: Oxford University Press, 1941), singles out Yeats's vitality for praise in his insightful poet's analysis of the poetry.

Ellmann, Richard, *The Identity of Yeats.* New York: Oxford University Press, 1954, Ellmann elucidates the principal intellectual and aesthetic influences on Yeats and discerns the underlying continuity of poet and poetry. Ranging across such diverse influences as Blake, Blavatsky, Buddhism, Rosicrucianism, Irish nationalism, folklore and myth, Platonism, Nietzsche and Shelley, Ellmann's book remains the surest guide to thinking a la Yeats.

Frye, Northrup, "The Rising of the Moon," in *Spiritus Mundi.* Bloomington: Indiana University Press, 1983. Frye clears an illuminating path through the dense forest of *A Vision,* Yeats's "lunar philosophy" and an important source of what he called "metaphors for poetry", symbols and ideas that appear and reappear in the later poetry. Helen Vendler's *Yeats's Vision and the Later Plays*

(Cambridge: Harvard University Press, 1963) also contains a provocative explication of *A Vision,* complete with charts.

Melchiori, Giorgio, *The Whole Mystery of Art.* London: Routledge & Kegan Paul, 1962. Melchiori's is a stimulating study of visual influences on Yeats, a subject initially suggested in T. R. Henn's seminal *The Lonely Tower* (London: Methuen, 1950; 2nd ed. 1965). Melchiori is at his best in identifying the pictorial sources of "Leda and the Swan". David R. Clark's *Yeats At Songs & Choruses* (Gerrards Cross: Colin Smythe, 1983) shows just how much fun tracing visual sources can be.

Moore, Virginia, *The Unicorn.* New York: Octagon, 1973. Moore presents a wide range of useful information about Yeats's interests and reading in the esoteric tradition, but she fails to mix the ingredients into a significant whole. *Yeats and the Occult* (London: Macmillan, 1976), a collection edited by George Mills Harper, contains enough good essays to whet the reader's appetite for a more comprehensive work.

O'Brien, Conor Cruise, "Passion and Cunning: An Essay on the Politics of W. B. Yeats," *In Excited Reverie.* New York: Macmillan, 1965. This is perhaps the most famous—and most contentious—essay on Yeats. O'Brien's case for the assertion that Yeats, as politician, was a fascist is good polemics but, because overstated and ultimately unfair, bad poetics.

Olney, James, *The Rhizome and the Flower: The Perennial Philosophy—Yeats and Jung.* Berkeley: University of California Press, 1980. This is a fascinating, comprehensive study of the parallel use by Yeats and Jung of the exoteric aspects of the perennial tradition, the philosophy of Parmenides, Heraclitus, Empedocles and "world-famous golden-thighed Pythagoras".

Thuente, Mary Helen, *W. B. Yeats and Irish Folklore.* Dublin: Gill & Macmillan, 1980. A competent treatment of its subject.

Torchiana, Donald, *Yeats and Georgian Ireland.* Evanston: Northwestern University Press, 1966. An insight into the nation-building political thinker behind much of the poetry, and an important study of the relationship between Yeats and "the one Irish century that escaped from darkness and confusion." Torchiana paints a convincing picture of the "haunting kinship in isolation and hatred" between Yeats and Swift, and rounds out the scene with Goldsmith, Berkeley and "haughtier-headed Burke".

Joseph M. Hassett
Washington, D.C.

INDEX OF AUTHORS AND MAJOR SOURCES REVIEWED

1321